THE
NEW BOOK
OF
KNOWLEDGE

THE NEW BOOK OF KNOWLEDGE

Scholastic Library Publishing, Inc.
Danbury, Connecticut

VOLUME 2

B

ISBN 0-7172-0540-1 (set)

Trademark
THE BOOK OF KNOWLEDGE
registered in U.S. Patent Office

B, the second letter of the English alphabet, was also the second letter of the Phoenician, Hebrew, and Greek alphabets. The Phoenicians and Hebrews called it *beth*. The Greeks called it *beta*.

Many scholars believe that the Phoenician letters were pictures of objects. *Beth*, they say, was probably a simple picture of a house. It looked like this: **4**.

The Greeks borrowed this basic form for their *beta*, but they made a double-looped version. Since the Greeks wrote from left to right instead of from right to left like the Phoenicians, the *beta* was also reversed. By the 5th century B.C. it looked like this: **Β**.

In adapting the Greek alphabet, the Romans kept the form of the *beta* but changed its name to *be*—the name it still has today in most European alphabets.

The B is most frequently pronounced as in *baseball* or *bishop*, although in some English words, such as *comb* or *debt*, the letter is silent.

The English B stands for many things. It has even been used in punishment. In Europe during the Middle Ages, and in the United States at the time of the Puritans, anyone who spoke against God was called a blasphemer. Sometimes a B was branded on the foreheads of the guilty ones as a sign of their sinfulness.

In chemistry B stands for the element boron. In a list of things, it labels the second item. On a report card it means above-average work. In music B is the name of a note as well as an abbreviation for bass, the lowest part in a musical composition.

B occurs in abbreviations. The college degree bachelor of arts is shortened to B.A. When used in dates, B.C. means "before Christ," as in "48 B.C." Some B abbreviations employ the small b. "Born," for instance, is indicated before dates by a small b, as in "Queen Elizabeth I, b. 1533."

Reviewed by MARIO PEI
Author, *The Story of Language*

See also ALPHABET.

BABBITT, NATALIE. See CHILDREN'S LITERATURE (Profiles).

SOME WAYS TO REPRESENT B:

The **manuscript** or printed forms of the letter (left) are highly readable. The **cursive** letters (right) are formed from slanted flowing strokes joining one letter to the next.

The **Manual Alphabet** (left) enables a deaf person to communicate by forming letters with the fingers of one hand. **Braille** (right) is a system by which a blind person can use fingertips to "read" raised dots that stand for letters.

The **International Code of Signals** is a special group of flags used to send and receive messages at sea. Each letter is represented by a different flag.

International Morse Code is used to send messages by radio signals. Each letter is expressed as a combination of dots (•) and dashes (––).

Newborn babies can do very little by themselves, but by the age of a few months, they are alert and interested in what they see—and they learn to smile.

BABY

A baby cat is called a kitten, and a baby dog is called a puppy. A human baby is often referred to as an infant. All of these babies are mammals.

Mammals are animals whose young, or offspring, are born alive after a period of development inside the mother. (Only two primitive types lay eggs.) After birth the offspring depend on their mother's milk for survival. Mammals may be very large, like the elephant, or very small, like the mouse.

▶ BEFORE THE BABY IS BORN

By the time the human mammal, or baby, enters the world, it has spent 9 months in a complicated process of growth and development. This process begins when the **ovum,** or egg, of the mother unites with the **sperm,** or seed, of the father. The fertilized egg begins to grow inside the mother's **uterus,** or womb. In about 3 weeks various organs begin to form. The tiny fertilized egg is then known as an **embryo.** The embryo continues to develop. Later it is called a **fetus.** When the fetus is 3 months old, it is about 3 inches long (8 centimeters) long. By 4 months, it is about twice this length.

When the fetus is 4 or 5 months old, the fetal heartbeat may be heard through a stethoscope placed on the mother's abdomen. At about the same time, the mother may become aware of little movements within her body. These movements bring her great joy, for she knows she has begun to "feel life."

The fetus is developing and moving around in the bag, or sac, of fluid that surrounds and protects it. Inside the sac, the fetus is attached at the belly (abdomen) to the placenta by a cord containing blood vessels. The placenta is a pancake-shaped organ through which the mother's blood flows to give nourishment to the fetus until it is ready to be born.

After 9 months in the uterus of the mother, the fetus is ready to come into the world. More than 90 percent of all babies are born after 9 months, known as full term.

If the fetus is born too soon, or prematurely, it may be difficult for it to survive. Medical advances have made it possible for more than half of all babies born after 20 weeks in the uterus to survive. However, the risk of long-term defects increases as the fetus spends less time in the uterus before birth. The biggest problem faced by premature babies is breathing, because their lungs are immature, and they lack a crucial substance (surfactin) that helps them absorb oxygen into their lungs. That is why they are placed in incubators (special beds in which the environment can be controlled) that provide extra oxygen.

For many months, the baby's parents wonder what their infant will be like. Will it be a boy or girl? What color hair and eyes will it have? Will it inherit any diseases? These and other matters are determined long before the baby's birth. The father's sperm and mother's egg contain the ingredients (called chromosomes) that carry all the characteristics the baby will inherit from its parents. The sex of the baby is determined by chromosomes in the father's sperm. These chromosomes are present in the amniotic fluid that surrounds the fetus before it is born. An analysis of this fluid can identify certain medical disorders, and the sex of the baby, before birth.

▶ AFTER THE BABY IS BORN

At last the baby is born. If it is an average baby, it weighs about 7 or 8 pounds (3 or 3.5 kilograms), and it is about 20 inches (about 51 centimeters) long. Male babies are slightly larger than female babies.

The healthy baby's first action after birth is to utter a sharp cry. With a good loud cry the baby's lungs expand and adapt to the outside world. The lungs enable the baby to breathe the air that now surrounds it. The cry also indicates that the baby is off to a good start.

Most human mothers give birth to a single baby. In about 1 out of every 80 births twins are born. Some twins are **identical.** This means that they have developed from a single fertilized egg. Other twins are **fraternal,** which means that two eggs may have been fertilized at the same time. Identical twins are usually very much alike. Fraternal twins may be quite different from one another. Triplets are born about once in 6,400 births, quadruplets about once in 500,000. Quintuplets, five babies born at one time, are very rare indeed.

Healthy infants have a strong tendency to suck. For the first months of life, sucking enables babies to obtain the nourishment necessary for their growth.

During the months of pregnancy, the mother's breasts have been getting ready to make milk. If the mother chooses not to feed the baby with her own milk, the use of a "formula" is recommended. The formula is usually made of cow's milk mixed with a form of sugar and water. Sometimes vitamins are added. It is put into a bottle that has a nipple made to resemble the nipple of the mother's breast. When the baby's mouth is put to the nipple of the breast, or to the bottle, the strong sucking reflex makes it possible for the infant to suck and swallow this first important food.

Growth and Development

Although babies vary a great deal, there is a general timetable for their growth and development, especially during the first year.

The newborn period in a baby's life is the first month after birth. This is a period of great change not only for the baby, but also for the rest of the family who have awaited the arrival for 9 months.

Newborn babies can do some things by themselves. They can breathe, cry, sleep, and move their arms and legs. They can suck and swallow food, and their bodies can take care of eliminating waste products. But since human babies have little control over these simple actions, they are completely dependent on others for their care.

Very young babies sleep most of the time, about 16 hours per day. When they are awake they are usually eating or crying. Their hearing is good, especially for human voices, and they will react to loud noises. Newborns have trouble focusing but see best at a distance of about 7 to 9 inches (18 to 23 centimeters). They also are the most alert when they are held upright; in that position they can absorb the most information (smells, lights, sounds). When babies are about 2 weeks old, their eyes will follow light and fix on an object. At about the age of 2 months, babies can see colors and, to the delight of their parents, begin to smile.

Babies must be carefully guarded against illness. People with colds or other infections should not handle the baby or get close to it, especially if the baby is premature or delicate. If the baby is bottle-fed, the formula must be prepared carefully. The bottle and nipple should be sterile (free of germs).

Small babies, especially premature infants, have a very limited capacity to control their temperature. They are poorly insulated because they do not have much fat. So it is important to keep babies warm.

After the first few months the baby should be examined by a pediatrician (a doctor who specializes in treating babies and older children), who will discuss the baby's progress with the parents or other caretaker. The pediatrician may suggest the addition of vitamins

The development of babies is the object of extensive research. Doctors and psychologists are attempting to find out what infants know at birth and how they organize and use that knowledge during their early years.

and some foods, such as cereal, fruits, and vegetables, to the baby's diet. The pediatrician will also give the baby "shots," or oral vaccines that will protect the baby from certain diseases, such as measles, whooping cough, and polio.

Two- or three-month-old babies can hold their heads up. But babies cannot sit up alone until they are about 6 or 7 months old. By about 9 months, most learn to stand while holding on to something. By this time, babies are quite good at crawling around and exploring their world. The baby usually can take a few steps at about the time of its first birthday.

When do babies learn to talk? Well, if you listen carefully, you will notice that they begin to make sounds when they are still very young. We call these sounds "baby talk." Unfortunately, we do not understand baby talk very well, but we enjoy listening to it and talking back to the baby. Babies start to babble consistently, with some indication of meaning, around 6 to 9 months of age. They start to vocalize in response to others much earlier.

They learn the words of their own language by listening and copying. The process of using and understanding language depends on individual development.

Most babies have a few teeth by the time they are a year old. When babies are born, they have no teeth. But even at birth a baby's teeth are under the gums in the form of tooth buds. As the baby grows, the teeth begin to show through the gums.

▶ARE YOU A SIBLING?

Brothers and sisters in a family are called **siblings.** Siblings have an important role to play when a new baby arrives, just as parents do.

Parents sometimes worry that older siblings might be jealous of a new baby. Older children often feel that some of their parents' love and attention will have to be shared. Usually, however, siblings also welcome the arrival of a baby. They are proud of the newcomer and quickly discover the excitement of watching an infant grow.

Children who have the opportunity to live with a baby in the family gain valuable experience. If they are old enough, their parents will let them help take care of the new baby. They will learn to help feed the baby, change the diapers, and take the younger child for a walk in the carriage. All of this experience will help siblings to become good baby-sitters when they are old enough. It will also help them become good parents when they are adults.

In a family where love, tenderness, and respect for each member are important, babies and older siblings will thrive. Although no one really remembers what it was like to be a baby, what happened to all of us in our early years will probably have a great effect on us as we grow up.

JEAN PAKTER, M.D., M.P.H.
Director, Bureau of Maternity Services
and Family Planning
New York City Department of Health
Reviewed and updated by MICHAEL E. LAMB,
PH.D.
Professor of Psychology,
Psychiatry, and Pediatrics
University of Utah

BABYLONIA

Babylonia was a region in what is now southern Iraq where a talented people built a great civilization almost 4,000 years ago. Among their accomplishments, the Babylonians developed the exact sciences, especially mathematics and astronomy. Because the Babylonians sought to use their science to predict the future, their astronomy gave way to astrology, a belief that the motion of the heavenly bodies affects the course of human events. Thus, while the Babylonians laid a foundation for modern science, it remained for the later Greeks to separate science from superstition.

The Babylonians were a Semitic people whose language was related to Hebrew and Arabic. They were influenced by a people who lived earlier in the region, the Sumerians. Like the Sumerians, they used a style of writing called cuneiform (''wedge-shaped'') and developed a culture built around large cities.

The Tower of Babel. The most distinctive type of Babylonian building was the ziggurat, a towerlike temple, built in stages and topped by a religious shrine. Though the ziggurat was first developed by the Sumerians, the Babylonians carried on the tradition. The most famous ziggurat is the Tower of Babel mentioned in the Bible. The god of the Babylonians was Marduk, whose cult spread with the growth of the Babylonian Empire.

The capital of Babylonia was the city of Babylon, situated near the Euphrates River where it approaches the Tigris River, not far from present-day Baghdad, the capital of Iraq.

The Code of Hammurabi. Babylon became important after 1800 B.C. under a succession of kings known as the First Dynasty of Babylon. The most famous monarch in that line was Hammurabi (Hammurapi), who ruled from about 1792 to 1750 B.C. By the use of shrewd diplomacy and strong armies, he defeated his rivals, the kings of other city-states, and carved out the most powerful empire of his day. Hammurabi also established a code of laws that regulated society strictly, with justice but little mercy. For example, a builder was to be executed if the house he built collapsed and killed the homeowner. And an incompetent surgeon who cost a patient his or her eye or life was to have his operating hand cut off. Though harsh, Hammurabi's laws protected his subjects from injustice.

Hammurabi's Code, one of the world's oldest sets of laws, was inscribed about 4,000 years ago on this tablet. The seated figure is that of Hammurabi, king of Babylon.

Nebuchadnezzar II. The next great king of Babylon arose a thousand years later. Nebuchadnezzar II, who reigned from 605 to 562 B.C., made Babylon the greatest city on earth. He beautified his capital with structures such as the Hanging Gardens, famed as one of the Seven Wonders of the Ancient World. Nebuchadnezzar conquered many nations, including the Jews, whose Temple in Jerusalem he destroyed in 586 B.C.

The long rule of Babylon ended with its capture by the Persians under Cyrus the Great in 539 B.C. At least one great monument of the Babylonians survives, however. The development of modern Iraq is due in large measure to its restoration of the ancient irrigation canal system built by the Babylonians, which made the region between the Tigris and Euphrates rivers the most fertile in the world.

CYRUS H. GORDON
New York University
Author, *Hammurapi's Code*

A brilliant composer and organist, Bach wrote much of his music for the church. His work influenced such great musicians as Mozart, Haydn, and Beethoven.

BACH, JOHANN SEBASTIAN (1685–1750)

Johann Sebastian Bach was born on March 21, 1685, in Eisenach, Germany. He was the greatest member of a renowned musical family of more than 50 musicians who lived in central Germany between 1500 and the 1800's.

At the age of 10, Bach was left an orphan and went to live with his older brother, a church organist at Ohrdruf. When he was 15, Bach went to Lüneburg, where a scholarship allowed him to attend school. There he sang in the choir and learned much of the best music of the time. He also studied with the great organist George Böhm.

In 1703, Bach became church organist at Arnstadt and immediately began to compose for the organ, the harpsichord, and voices. He went to Mühlhausen in 1707, and while he was an organist in that city he married his cousin, Maria Barbara Bach. The following year they moved to Weimar, where Bach remained in the service of the Duke of Weimar for ten years.

Most of Bach's music at Weimar was composed for the organ and church choirs. When Bach wanted to change jobs again, the Duke put him in jail to try to make him stay. But Bach was determined to leave and journeyed to Cöthen, where he entered the service of Prince Leopold of Anhalt. During his six years at Cöthen, Bach composed many of his best-known instrumental works, such as the *Brandenburg* concertos, the English and the French suites for harpsichord, and much chamber music.

Bach's wife died in 1720. The following year he married Anna Magdalena Wilcken. Bach became the father of 20 children, and several of his talented sons became well-known composers.

Bach changed jobs for the last time in 1723 and became director of music at St. Thomas' Church and School in Leipzig. Though he was not happy with the post, he remained there for 27 years, until his death. Most of Bach's greatest religious works were composed during these years, including the *Magnificat*, the *St. John* Passion, the *St. Matthew* Passion, the B-minor Mass, and many cantatas. In Leipzig, Bach also completed *The Well-Tempered Clavier*, a collection of 48 preludes and fugues in all the keys. Like most of Bach's music, it was not published until long after his death. Bach was well known as an organist, but during his lifetime he never became a celebrated composer like his famous contemporary, George Frederick Handel.

In 1747, Bach journeyed to Potsdam to visit his son Karl Philipp Emanuel, who was a musician at the court of King Frederick II of Prussia. The King admired Bach and wanted to hear him play. To the King's delight Bach improvised on a melody that the King had given him. When Bach returned to Leipzig, he repaid the royal friendship by composing the *Musical Offering* based on the King's theme and dedicating it to the King.

Bach then turned to his last great work, *The Art of Fugue,* which remained unfinished at his death. It is the fruit of Bach's lifelong study of a musical technique called counterpoint. As Bach grew older his eyesight became increasingly poor, until toward the end of his life, he was totally blind. He died in Leipzig on July 28, 1750. It was not until almost 100 years later that the world recognized Bach as one of its greatest composers.

Reviewed by KARL GEIRINGER
Author, *The Bach Family*

BACKGAMMON

Backgammon is a game of luck and skill played with dice and checkers on a special board. The game was probably introduced into Europe by the Crusaders. In the eastern Mediterranean area, it has been played with such enthusiasm that for many years the better players of this region were the best in the world. But excellent players have developed elsewhere as the game's popularity has spread.

▶ EQUIPMENT

Each player has a set of 15 checkers. The checkers can be of any two different colors, but usually one set is dark and the other is light in color. Each player also has two dice and a cup in which to shake them.

The backgammon board is a rectangle. It is divided into two halves by a vertical line called the *bar*. One half of the board is called the *inner*, or home, *table*. The other half is called the *outer table*.

Twelve triangles, called *points,* stick out from each of the two long sides of the board. Six points are on each side of the inner table, and six points are on each side of the outer table. The players, usually identified as Black and White according to the color of their checkers, sit on opposite sides of the board.

▶ OBJECT OF THE GAME

At the start of the game, the checkers are arranged as shown in Diagram 1. Each player tries to move all his checkers to his own inner table by advancing according to the numbers rolled on the dice. The white checkers move clockwise and the black move counterclockwise. Each player is moving his checkers from the opponent's inner table around the board by way of the two outer tables and then to the inner table on his own side of the board. After all checkers are in a player's own inner table, the player *bears off* (removes the checkers from the board). The first player to bear off all of his checkers is the winner.

▶ NOTATION

Each point on the backgammon board has a number as shown on the outer rim of the board in the diagrams below. The numbers are used by writers of books and columns on backgammon to describe the moves that the players have made. These numbers do not appear on a real backgammon board, but a beginning player might find it helpful to lightly pencil them onto the board. This would enable the player to follow a written game or instructions move by move.

The points on both sides of the board are numbered from 1 through 12, going from the inner table to the outer. The initials B and W, referring to Black and White, indicate which side of the board the point is on. When a move is described, it indicates the point moved from, followed by the point moved to. For example, assume that White throws a 6 and a 1 as an opening move and chooses to move

Diagram 1. A board set up for play. White will move in direction of arrows, black the opposite direction.

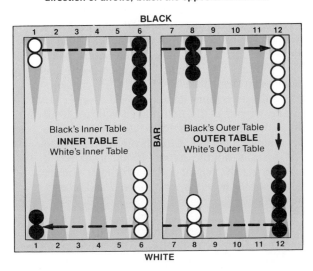

Diagram 2. White rolled a 6 and a 1 and has made an opening move. The notation is White: B12—W7, W8—W7.

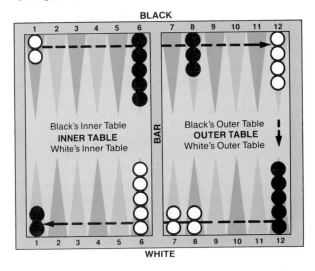

the checkers as indicated in Diagram 2. White has moved one checker from Black's 12 point to White's 7 point and another from White's 8 point to White's 7 point. The move would be notated as follows: White: B12–W7, W8–W7.

▶ START OF THE GAME

To begin a game, each player rolls one die. The player who throws the highest number plays first by using the numbers on both his and his opponent's dice. After this, the players take turns rolling their dice onto the board from their cups and moving their checkers.

▶ THE PLAY OF THE GAME

The numbers on the two dice, taken separately, show the number of points over which the player's checkers may be moved. When one checker has been moved the number of points indicated by one die, the number on the other die may be used to move the same checker further—or it may be used to move a different checker. For example, if a player throws a 5 and a 6, the player could choose to move one checker 5 points and a different checker 6 points, or he could opt to move one checker 11 points. No other combinations are possible—in other words, the total of 11 cannot be divided into moves of 7 and 4 or 8 and 3. The split can only be made according to the numbers on the individual dice.

If a player should happen to roll doubles (both dice the same), the player may move twice as many points as the total shown on the dice. For example, a roll of 3–3 counts as four 3's rather than the two 3's shown. The player can move a total of 12 points rather than 6. This move can be made in units of 3 using as many as four checkers. A possible opening move for White throwing double 3's might be: White: B1–B7 (2). The (2) shows that two separate checkers made the same move.

▶ MOVES

If a player has two or more checkers on a point, he has *made* that point. White has made point W7 in Diagram 2. His opponent can pass over that point but cannot land on it. A player can, however, land on a point on which the opponent has only a single checker. Such a point is called a *blot*. When a checker of the opposite color lands on a blot, the checker that was originally there has been *hit* and is re-

moved from the board and placed *on the bar*. A player who has a checker on the bar may re-enter the game by throwing a number that will place the hit checker on any open point on the opponent's inner table. All checkers on the bar must be entered before the player can move any of his other checkers.

Whenever possible, a player *must* move his checkers using both (or all four, in the case of doubles) numbers thrown. There will be cases, however, where the opponent's points prevent a player from moving any of his checkers. In this case, the play passes to the opponent. If only one number of a roll is usable, it must be the higher one.

▶ BEARING OFF

When a player has advanced all 15 of his checkers to his own inner table, he may begin to bear off.

A checker is borne off a point that matches the number rolled on one die. For example, on a 4–2 roll, a checker may be removed from the 4 point and another from the 2 point. When a number on one die is higher than the highest point on which a player has checkers, the player takes the checker off the highest occupied point. That is, if the player throws a 5, and the 5 point is empty but there is a checker on the 4 point, the player bears off the checker from the 4 point. It is not permitted to bear off a checker from a point higher than the number on the die.

If all the player's checkers are in his inner table, it is not required that they be borne off with each roll of the dice. Instead, they could be moved further into the inner table.

If a player's checker is hit during the bearing off, it is put on the bar. The checker must re-enter the game and move all the way around the board again to its inner table before bearing off can start again. In other words, a player can bear off *only* if all of his checkers are in his own inner table.

The winner is the first player to bear off all his or her checkers. If the loser has not borne off a single checker, this player is *gammoned* and loses a double game. If the loser has a checker on the bar or in the opponent's inner table, she or he is *backgammoned* and loses a triple game.

CHARLES H. GOREN
Author, *Goren's Modern Backgammon Complete*
BACKPACKING. See HIKING AND BACKPACKING.

BACON, FRANCIS (1561–1626)

Francis Bacon, an English statesman, philosopher, and essayist, was born in London on January 22, 1561. He showed great brilliance as a child and at the age of 12 entered Cambridge University. After two years at Cambridge, he began the study of law.

Bacon completed his law studies, and in 1584 was elected to Parliament. Ambitious as well as intelligent, he rose to political prominence under King James I. He was knighted and appointed attorney general. In 1618 he was made Baron Verulam and named lord chancellor, the highest legal post in England. He was created Viscount St. Albans in 1621.

Bacon was one of the King's closest advisers. But in 1621 he was charged with accepting gifts from persons whose cases were waiting to be tried in the courts. Since giving and receiving gifts was a common practice at the time, it was obvious that Bacon's political enemies were using the charge in order to rid the kingdom of his influence. He was convicted and imprisoned in the Tower of London. After a few days he was released, but his political career was over.

Bacon had begun to write his famous essays and other works during his busy years as a man of public affairs. Now he devoted the remainder of his life to philosophical and scientific writing. He had planned a long work that would reform philosophical and scientific study. "I have taken all knowledge as my province," he stated. But he was able to finish only two parts of the great work. Among his completed writings are *The Advancement of Learning, History of Henry VII*, and the collected *Essays*. Bacon made the essay a popular literary form in England.

Bacon's scientific curiosity led to his death. One winter day, it occurred to him that food could be preserved by cold. To demonstrate this, he bought a chicken and stuffed it with snow. While working in the snowy weather, he caught cold. The illness grew worse, and he died on April 9, 1626.

Reviewed by ELIZABETH S. WRIGLEY
Director, The Francis Bacon Library

BACON, ROGER (1214?–1292?)

Roger Bacon, an English scientist and philosopher, helped lay the foundations of modern scientific thinking. He recognized the need for research and accurate methods of scientific study at a time when many people still relied on myths and superstitions to explain events in the world around them.

Little is known for certain about Bacon's life. He was born sometime between 1214 and 1220, the son of a well-to-do family in Ilchester, England. He may have entered Oxford University as early as the age of 13. In the 1240's he taught at the University of Paris.

Europe during Bacon's lifetime was having a revival of learning, based on the discovery of great written works from ancient Greece and Rome. Most scholars simply accepted and taught this knowledge from the ancient world. But Bacon did something different. He learned from living people and from the world around him, as well as from ancient wisdom.

Bacon also conducted his own experiments. He spent years studying how the eye works. He sprayed water into the air to study the nature of rainbows. He tested superstitions by performing experiments with the actual materials.

About 1250, Bacon returned to England, entered the Franciscan order of monks, and began to teach science at Oxford. But his experiments made his superiors angry. In 1257 they sent Bacon back to Paris. He was told to write and teach only what they approved.

Nevertheless, Bacon secretly obtained a commission from Pope Clement IV to write a report on the importance of science. One part of it, the *Opus majus* ("Greater Work"), was an outline of scientific knowledge. The importance of this report lies in Bacon's emphasis on the need to observe, test, and measure.

In 1278, Bacon's religious superiors imprisoned him in Paris for his unusual ideas. He was freed in 1290, but he had become a weak old man. He returned to England and is thought to have died in Oxford in 1292. Today Bacon's ideas—unusual for their time—are considered an important part of modern science.

JOHN S. BOWMAN
Author and science editor

Few creatures other than bacteria can survive in such harsh environments as a hot spring (*left*) or a sea vent buried deep within an ocean trench (*right*).

BACTERIA

Although they are typically too small to be seen without a microscope, bacteria are the most common life-forms on Earth. They are everywhere in our world—even places where conditions are so extreme that plants and animals cannot survive. These small, simple creatures can be found in sea vents on the ocean floor, where the temperature climbs to 230°F (110°C)—higher than the boiling point of water! Others have been discovered in the frozen ice of the Antarctic and the dry, salty world of Death Valley. Some bacteria can even live in places without oxygen. Most bacteria live in the milder conditions found on the Earth's surface or on living or dead plants and animals. Large numbers of bacteria live on our skin and in our throat and intestine. In fact, there are more bacterial cells living on and in the human body than there are human cells making up the body.

▶ THE CHARACTERISTICS OF BACTERIA

Bacteria (plural of bacterium) are believed to have been the first life-forms on Earth. Fossils suggest that bacteria were present more than 3.5 billion years ago. While we are not sure what these first living organisms were like, they were probably small, simple creatures, much like the bacteria that now exist.

Size. A unique feature of bacteria is its size. Most bacteria can only be seen with a microscope that magnifies objects about 1,000 times their actual size. The internal parts of a bacterium are studied using an electron microscope, which magnifies objects several thousands of times. Bacteria are so very small—about 500 average bacteria could be placed side by side across the period at the end of this sentence—they are measured in units called micrometers (a micrometer is one-millionth of a meter). Typical bacteria are 0.3 to 2.0 micrometers in diameter. Because of its size, food, water, and waste products can pass quickly into and out of the bacterial cell.

Structure. Most bacteria have a thick, protective wall around their cell. This rigid layer, which is made of chemicals unique to bacteria, gives the bacterial cell its shape. A thin skinlike covering called a cell membrane lies just inside the cell wall. Within the cell membrane are all the essential molecules and fluid

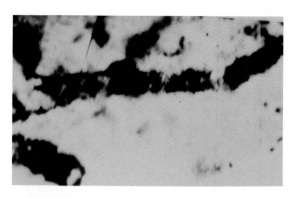

Fossil microbes found in ancient rock establish bacteria as the first—and for about 2 billion years the only—form of life on Earth.

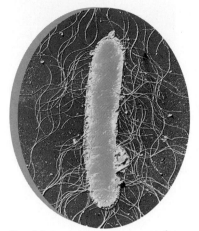

The Structure of a Bacterial Cell

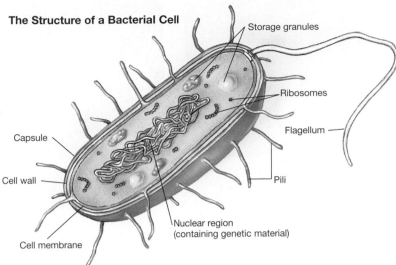

Storage granules

Ribosomes

Flagellum

Pili

Nuclear region
(containing genetic material)

Cell membrane

Cell wall

Capsule

Special structures, such as capsules, pili, or the flagella seen on *Proteus mirabilis* (*above*), appear on many types of bacteria.

that the cell needs to carry on its life processes. Unlike other living organisms, a bacteria does not have its cell substances contained in a nucleus or in other membrane-covered bodies. Instead, its essential materials are scattered throughout the cell. These materials include genes—the basic units of heredity that can transfer the traits of organisms to the next generation.

Special structures can be found on some bacteria. These structures allow the bacteria to survive in special environments. Some bacteria make a sticky slime layer, or capsule, around their cell walls. This layer allows the bacteria to attach to surfaces. Bacteria that cause tooth decay attach to the surface of teeth with this sticky capsule. The capsule also allows some bacteria to produce diseases, such as pneumonia.

Some bacteria have long, whiplike tails, called flagella, coming out of their cells. Flagella turn like motorboat propellers and help the bacteria move with a swimming motion. Other bacteria glide on surfaces or travel using a corkscrew motion. Bacteria move to

get to the food, air, or light that they need to grow.

Short, straight hollow tubes called pili or fimbriae are also seen on some bacteria. These hairlike structures form a border or fringe around the cell. Fimbriae help the bacteria attach to surfaces, such as the cells in our throats. Special types of pili can transfer genes from one bacterial cell to another.

Reproduction. Living cells, including bacteria, must be able to reproduce themselves. Bacteria do this by a simple process in which one cell increases in size and then divides into two equal cells. This form of asexual reproduction is called binary fission because one mother cell splits into two daughter cells. Instructions for copying itself are contained in the genes. The cell also contains the basic chemicals, cell machinery, and energy needed to complete the manufacturing process.

With abundant nutrients, bacteria will grow and reproduce very quickly. Some bacteria can divide every 20 minutes, if conditions are right. That means that a starting bacteria could multiply into a million bacteria in less than 7 hours. Fortunately, the Earth will not be overgrown by bacteria because inadequate food supplies and harmful conditions keep them in control.

Obtaining Food. Some bacteria can

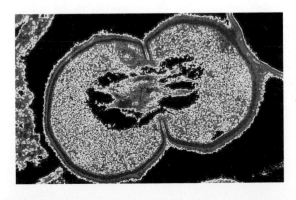

Each daughter cell that results from this dividing mother cell will be able to live independently, even though the cells may stay together, growing in chains or clusters.

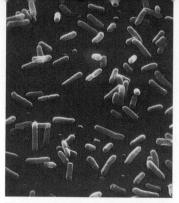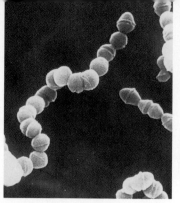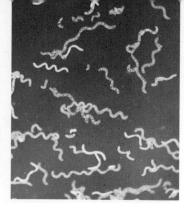

The many thousands of species of bacteria are typically classified according to whether they are rod shaped (*Salmonella*, *left*), round (*Streptococcus*, *center*), or spiral (*Rhodospirillum*, *right*).

make their own food and cell parts from basic materials such as carbon dioxide and water. These bacteria are called autotrophs, meaning "self-feeders." From sunlight or simple chemicals found in their environment, these independent creatures get the energy needed to synthesize organic nutrients. Other bacteria get nutrients and energy from foodstuffs originally made by other organisms. These heterotrophs, meaning "other-feeders," commonly break down plant and animal cells into simple organic nutrients. All animals and many bacteria are heterotrophs. For example, human beings, as well as bacteria that live in the intestinal tract, digest a meal of grains, vegetables, and meat to get nutrients and energy needed for growth.

▶ KINDS OF BACTERIA

The many different species, or kinds, of bacteria are grouped together in the Kingdom Monera. **Microbiologists**, the scientists who study bacteria and other microscopic organisms, have identified and described more than 10,000 species. There are several different ways to classify bacteria. They can be grouped based on how they reproduce, how they obtain food, or what kind of environment they inhabit. But the most common way to group bacteria is by how they are shaped. Although there are some unusual bacteria that are star shaped, triangular, or square, bacteria viewed under the microscope generally appear either rod shaped, round, or spiral.

The names of bacterial shapes come from Latin words. A rod-shaped bacterium is called a **bacillus**. A round bacterium is called a **coccus**. A spiral bacterium is called a **spirillum**. Some variations in bacterial shape and arrangement can occur. The rod-shaped bacteria can be cigar shaped or have pointed ends. Cocci can be oval or bean shaped. The spiral bacteria can be wavy or corkscrew shaped in pairs, chains, or clusters. For example, the organism *Streptococcus*, which can cause sore throats, is a type of round bacterium that is linked together in chains.

▶ THE IMPORTANCE OF BACTERIA

Although bacteria can be found everywhere, we notice them because of the infections they cause, like sore throats, or from the foods they spoil. While some bacteria can cause serious disease or threaten those people who have weakened immune defenses, most bacteria are harmless, and many are very helpful. Bacteria are the source of food for the many animals in our oceans, lakes, and rivers. They also recycle nutrients in the soil so plants can grow. These small creatures maintain the proper balance of chemicals in our world. Harmless bacteria living on us keep us healthy by competing with disease-producing bacteria. Some bacteria in our intestine even supply us with some vitamins. We enjoy the tasty foods that bacteria help to make, such as sourdough bread, cheese, yogurt, and pickles. In addition, bacteria can be modified in a process called genetic engineering to make substances that they normally do not produce. These modified bacteria can then help digest oil spills, recycle waste, make soil more fertile, or make drugs to treat disease.

CYNTHIA V. SOMMER
University of Wisconsin at Milwaukee

See also ANTIBIOTICS; DISEASES; FERMENTATION; FOOD PRESERVATION; GENETICS; MICROBIOLOGY.

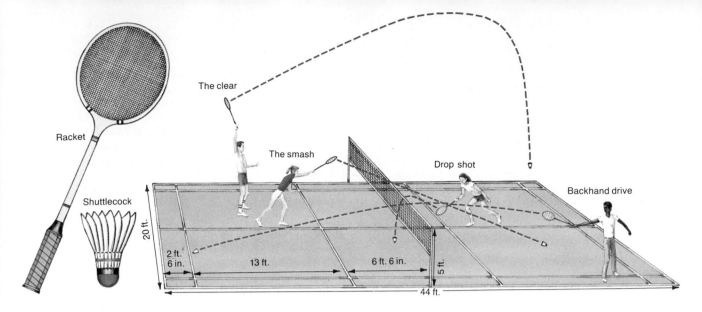

The clear
Racket
The smash
Drop shot
Backhand drive
Shuttlecock
20 ft.
2 ft. 6 in.
13 ft.
6 ft. 6 in.
5 ft.
44 ft.

BADMINTON

Badminton is a fast game played with rackets and a shuttlecock on a wood, dirt, or grass court. The court is somewhat like a tennis court, but smaller. The shuttlecock, often called simply the shuttle, or "bird," is hit back and forth over a net 5 feet (1.5 meters) high. It must be returned before it strikes the court. The game can be played by two persons (singles) or four persons (doubles). It can be played both indoors and outdoors. Official tournaments are played indoors.

Badminton developed from Battledore and Shuttlecock, an ancient game that was popular with children. There are several explanations of how the modern game began; one is that about the year 1870, English army officers brought a version of it to England from India, where it was called Poona. The new game took its name from the Duke of Beaufort's estate, Badminton, where the game was probably played indoors for the first time. Badminton became popular in England, and in the 1890's the Badminton Association was formed. In 1934 the International Badminton Federation was organized. The two international badminton championships are the Thomas Cup competition for men and the Uber Cup for women.

▶PLAYING BADMINTON

The game starts with the player in the right service court serving to an opponent in the diagonally opposite right service court. Allowed only one serve at the start of each point, the server continues serving to alternate courts until the rally is lost. If a rally is lost, a point is not lost, only the serve. This is called side out. An opponent then takes a hand at serving.

Any of the following is called a fault, and results in side out if committed by the serving side or loss of a point if committed by a receiver:

Server
(1) Serving outside the service court.
(2) Contact with the serve anyplace above the waist.

Server or receiver
(1) Hitting the shuttle out of bounds, or twice in succession on the same side of the net, or under or through the net, or before it crosses the net.
(2) Carrying the shuttle with the racket.
(3) Touching the net or its supports during play.
(4) Serving or receiving the serve with the feet on the line, or with both feet not in contact with the floor until the shuttle is hit.

A shuttle falling on a boundary line is good.

▶SCORING

Points can be scored only while serving. A game is won by the first player or side to score 15 points, except in women's singles, in which game is 11 points. If a tie score of 13 all is reached (9 all in women's singles), the side that reached the tie score first may, if it chooses, set the game at 5 (or 3 in women's singles). This means that game will not be reached until either side has scored 5 (or 3) more points. Similarly, if the score becomes tied at 14 all (or 10 all in women's singles), game may be set at 3 (or 2) more points.

The side that wins a game serves first in the next game. The opposing sides change ends of the court after each game.

THE BASIC STROKES

Overhead shots are played from above the head; underhand shots are those played from below waist level. Any stroke hit on the right-hand side of the body is a forehand; on the left-hand side of the body, a backhand. The descriptions and instructions in this article are for right-handed players. If you are left-handed, substitute "left" for "right" and "right" for "left."

The serve is the most important stroke because it puts the shuttle in play at the start of each point.

The smash, or kill shot, is the principal point-winning stroke in badminton. It is hit downward from an overhead position with as much speed as possible.

The clear is a shot that sends the shuttle high to the opponent's back boundary line.

The drop shot causes the shuttle to drop close to the net in the opponent's court. It may be hit either overhead or underhand.

The drive sends the shuttle skimming low over the net in a line parallel to the floor.

Several auxiliary shots are often useful in badminton. The hairpin and crosscourt net shots can be used to return a drop shot with a drop shot. They can be hit from one side of the court to the other (crosscourt), or directly back over the net (hairpin).

The round-the-head shot is an overhead backhand played as a forehand. It is protection against a weak backhand. The half smash is used to angle the shuttle downward sharply.

GRIPS AND FOOTWORK

There are different grips for holding the racket to make the various shots.

For the forehand and serve grip, hold the throat of the racket with your left hand. Keep the face of the racket perpendicular to the floor. Then place your right hand on the handle, as if shaking hands with it. Your fingers should be slightly spread.

For backhand shots the hand is turned slightly to the left, the thumb placed flat along the back of the handle, not around it.

Keep your wrist firm and yet flexible, not stiff and tense. The wrist must be cocked back at the beginning of the backswing. As the arm comes forward the wrist snaps or whips the racket head to meet the shuttle.

Good footwork enables you to move quickly in any direction and to have your feet properly placed while stroking. The weight must be on the balls of the feet, and the knees should be mobile. For forehand strokes the left foot is advanced toward the net and the left side faces the net. On the backhand the right foot is advanced and the right side faces the net. These same principles apply to overhead forehands and backhands.

TACTICS AND STRATEGY

The object of the game is to win the required number of points by forcing opponents to make errors. If opponents do not make outright errors they can be forced to make weak returns that can be put away—that is, placed beyond their reach.

Basic strategy in singles involves forcing your opponent to "set up" the shuttle high in the forecourt, where it can be put away with a smash. Use the clear and drop shots to run an opponent to the corners of the court. If an opponent is in the backcourt, try to drop shot. Use a clear shot against an opponent in the forecourt. Drive the shuttle to give an opponent less time.

Generally the singles serve is hit high and deep to the back boundary line. In doubles it should skim over the net and drop near the short service line. The value of a good low serve in doubles cannot be overestimated.

In doubles, attack by hitting the shuttle downward whenever possible. The shuttle is placed strategically to force the opponents to hit upward, or defensive, shots. In mixed doubles the woman usually plays the shots in the front half of the court. The man stands behind her and plays the shots coming to the backcourt.

WHAT MAKES A CHAMPION?

The outstanding characteristic of a champion at badminton is the ability to react in split-second time with eyes, mind, feet, and hands. Becoming a champion takes physical and mental effort at all times. Constant practice, physical fitness, reading instructional books, and observing expert players help make a winner. Habits of concentration, confidence, and self-determination are necessary. The great players of the game almost always have been good sports. This is apparent in their conduct on and off the court.

MARGARET VARNER
Former World Badminton Champion

BAGHDAD

Baghdad is the capital and largest city of Iraq. It is situated in a region of the Middle East called the Cradle of Civilization, a fertile area whose history dates back more than 4,000 years. Approximately 5 million people live in the city proper, which covers an area of 254 square miles (658 square kilometers).

The City. Baghdad spreads out on both sides of the historic Tigris River, which is spanned by twelve bridges. The main thoroughfares, notably Rashid and Sadun streets, come together in Tahir Square, the hub of the city.

Economic Activity. Baghdad is Iraq's main center of manufacturing. Chief industries include petroleum refining and the production of petrochemicals, textiles, and processed foods. The city is also noted for its handicrafts of gold, silver, brass, and copper.

History. Baghdad was founded in the A.D. 700's by Abdullah al-Mansur (ruled 754–75), a caliph of the Abbasid dynasty. Under the caliph Harun al-Rashid (ruled 786–809), the city saw the flowering of Arab culture. Grand palaces, imposing mosques (Muslim houses of worship), colleges and universities, well-paved streets, and public baths reflected the city's wealth and sophistication. For the next 500 years, Baghdad was one of the great cities of the world.

In 1258, Baghdad was almost destroyed by invading Mongols. For centuries thereafter it was largely a provincial town, first under the administration of the Persian and then the

The ancient city of Baghdad has been the capital of Iraq since the nation became a republic in 1958. It has suffered much war damage since the 1990's.

Ottoman empires. After the defeat of the Ottoman Empire in World War I (1914–18), Baghdad came under British rule. In 1921 it was designated the capital of the newly established kingdom of Iraq, which became an independent monarchy in 1932. When the monarchy was overthrown in 1958, Baghdad became the capital of the Republic of Iraq.

Baghdad's economy was strained by Iraq's long war with Iran (1980–88). The city also suffered severely from U.S. and allied bombings during the 1991 Persian Gulf war, which followed Iraq's invasion of Kuwait. Economic sanctions imposed on the country destroyed the city's prosperity. Baghdad sustained further damages when the United States targeted local military installations for Iraq's refusal to honor its postwar agreements with the United Nations.

In 2003, the United States and its allies invaded Iraq to bring down its dictator, Saddam Hussein. Air attacks on the capital damaged many government buildings, and some Baghdadis lost their lives in the assaults. On April 9, ground troops took control of the city, effectively ending Hussein's cruel regime. Baghdad then became the center of a transitional American-administered government.

BALKRISHNA G. GOKHALE
Director, Asian Studies Program
Wake Forest University

BAGPIPE. See WIND INSTRUMENTS.

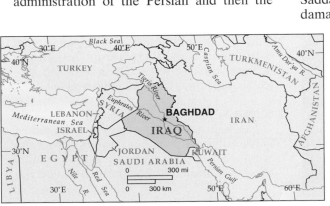

BAHAMAS

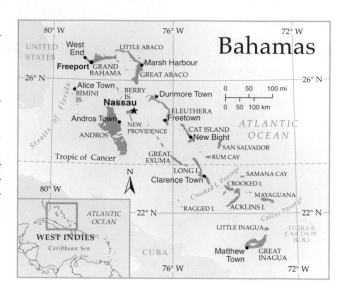

The Bahamas is a nation made up of many small islands in the Atlantic Ocean. The islands are bordered on the west by the Gulf Stream. They form an archipelago (a chain of islands) lying between the Florida coast of the United States and the Caribbean islands of Cuba and Hispaniola.

▶ PEOPLE

Most of the inhabitants of the Bahamas are people of African descent whose ancestors were brought to the islands as slaves. About 12 percent are people of European heritage, while Asians and Hispanics make up the remaining 3 percent. English is the official language, but Creole is spoken by Haitian immigrants. About 95 percent of the people are Christian; of that number, 32 percent are Baptist.

The country has an extensive primary and secondary school system, which contributes

The beautiful beaches of the Bahamas attract many tourists. San Salvador (*below*) is thought to have been visited by Columbus during his voyage to the Americas.

to its high literacy rate. School is compulsory for all children between the ages of 5 and 16. Students seeking higher education usually attend the College of the Bahamas; the University of the West Indies; or schools in the United States, Canada, or Britain.

▶ LAND

There are about 700 islands and more than 2,000 tiny sand cays (keys) and exposed bits of coral reef in the Bahamas. The islands extend in an arc for some 750 miles (1,200 kilometers) to the northern edge of the Caribbean Sea. They are formed largely of coral and are mostly low-lying. The highest elevation is almost 207 feet (63 meters). Only a relatively small number of the islands are permanently inhabited. More than half the people live on the island of New Providence, mostly in and around Nassau, the capital city. Grand Bahama is the second most populous island.

The climate of the Bahamas is tropical marine. Temperatures vary little with the seasons and are moderate in both winter and summer. Rainfall averages about 50 inches (1,300 millimeters) a year. On the smaller islands there is less rainfall, and there are often shortages of fresh drinking water. The islands are subject to hurricanes in the summer and fall.

▶ ECONOMY

The mainstay of the economy is the tourist industry. About 4 million visitors a year are attracted by the climate and beautiful beaches. Nassau and Freeport, on Grand Bahama, are the most popular tourist spots, but the waters near the Bimini islands off the Florida coast are famous for big-game fishing.

Nassau is also a finance center, as Bahamian tax laws have encouraged the growth of international banking there. Petroleum products rank among the country's leading exports. The islands are a transfer point for petroleum being shipped to the United States.

Manufacturing and agriculture play a relatively small role. There is light manufacturing on Grand Bahama, where a deepwater port has been dredged at Freeport. Specialty chemicals, cement, and rum are produced. Only about 1.5 percent of the land is cultivated. Main exports include citrus fruits. Crop production for export is concentrated on four islands: Great Abaco, Andros, Grand Bahama, and Eleuthera.

Crawfish (spiny lobster) is a main export. There are few mineral resources except for salt, which is produced on Great Inagua. Straw handicrafts provide additional income.

▶ MAJOR CITIES

Nassau is the capital and largest city. Founded in 1695, it has a population of about 172,000. Nassau's fine hotels, quaint houses, and shops selling goods from all over the world at low prices attract many tourists.

Freeport/Lucaya, on Grand Bahama, is the only other sizable Bahamian city. Founded in 1955, it boasts a diversified economy.

Marsh Harbour, established in 1784, is the third largest city in the Bahamas. It is the commercial center of Great Abaco Island, which, along with Little Abaco Island and its cays, is greatly cherished by yachtsmen.

▶ GOVERNMENT

The government of the Bahamas is headed by a prime minister, while a governor-general represents the British monarch, who is head of state. Parliament has two houses—the elected House of Assembly and the Senate, to which members are appointed.

▶ HISTORY

Christopher Columbus is believed to have first stepped ashore on one of the islands of the Bahamas during his voyage to the Americas in 1492. San Salvador (Watling Island) is long thought to have been the island, though other possible sites have been suggested.

FACTS and figures

COMMONWEALTH OF THE BAHAMAS is the official name of the country.

LOCATION: Archipelago in the Atlantic Ocean off the coast of Florida.

AREA: 3,888 sq mi (10,070 km^2).

POPULATION: 300,000 (estimate).

CAPITAL AND LARGEST CITY: Nassau.

MAJOR LANGUAGE: English, Creole (among Haitian immigrants).

MAJOR RELIGIOUS GROUP: Christian (Protestant, Roman Catholic).

GOVERNMENT: Constitutional parliamentary democracy. **Head of state**—British monarch, represented by governor-general. **Head of government**—prime minister. **International cooperation**—United Nations, Commonwealth of Nations, Organization of American States (OAS), Caribbean Community (CARICOM).

CHIEF PRODUCTS: Agricultural—citrus, vegetables, poultry products, crawfish. **Manufactured**—specialty chemicals, cement, rum, blended petroleum products, timber. **Mineral**—salt, aragonite.

MONETARY UNIT: Bahamian dollar (1 dollar = 100 cents).

The Spanish explored the islands in the 1500's but made no serious efforts to colonize them. The few Indians who lived there were shipped to the West Indies to work. In the 1600's the British gained control of the Bahamas and began to settle some of the larger islands. After the American Revolution, people loyal to the British Crown migrated to the Bahamas with their slaves. During the U.S. Civil War, Nassau was a meeting place for blockade runners from the Confederate states and ships from England. There cotton from the South was traded for English goods.

The Bahamas became self-governing in 1964, although Britain still handled foreign affairs, defense, and internal security. The Progressive Liberal Party (PLP) brought majority rule to the Bahamas with its victory in 1967 legislative elections. Complete independence was won in 1973. The PLP remained in power until 1992, when it was defeated by the Free National Movement. General elections in 2002 returned the PLP to power.

JOHN F. LOUNSBURY
Arizona State University
Reviewed by DR. KEVA M. BETHEL
Former President, College of the Bahamas

BAHRAIN

Bahrain, an independent kingdom once under British protection, consists of several islands off the coast of the Arabian Peninsula. It is one of the world's smallest countries. Bahrain's strategic location has made it important as a port and a center of trade for the Persian Gulf, and it has long been one of the region's wealthier states.

▶ PEOPLE

Bahrain's population is mostly Arab. Nearly 40 percent of the people are non-Bahraini and include many Pakistanis, Iranians, and Indians, as well as smaller numbers of Europeans and Americans. Arabic is the official language, although Persian and English are widely spoken. Islam is the official religion.

Traditional ways of life in the Persian Gulf began to change when oil was discovered—Bahrain was the first of the Gulf states in which oil was found, in the 1930's, so its impact there has long been evident. The government provides Bahrainis with many services, including free medical care and low-cost housing. Education is also free, and compulsory for children between ages 6 and 15. Schools of higher education include the Arabian Gulf University, the Bahrain Centre for Studies and Research, and the University of Bahrain. Bahrain's emphasis on education has resulted in a growing middle class and a skilled workforce.

▶ LAND

Bahrain is made up of more than 30 islands, islets, and sandbars, most of them uninhabited. The largest island, Bahrain (from which the country takes its name), is linked to Saudi Arabia by a 15½ mile (25 kilometer) causeway. Other important islands include Al Muharraq, Sitrah, Umm An Na'sān, and the Hawār Islands.

The land is mainly flat desert. The highest elevation, 440 feet (134 meters), is at Ad-Dukhān Hill on Bahrain Island. Most of this is barren except for a narrow strip of land in the north, watered by springs and wells. The waters of the Persian Gulf have abundant fish and are one of the world's richest sources of natural pearls.

Bahrain's climate is extremely hot and humid in summer. Winters are relatively cool. Rainfall is slight, averaging less than 4 inches (100 millimeters) a year.

▶ ECONOMY

For many years most of Bahrain's income came from oil. As oil reserves were depleted, efforts were made to develop other revenue sources. The economy is now based largely on petroleum production and refining. Bahrain also produces natural gas, iron, steel, chemicals, and aluminum and has many warehousing facilities and ship repair yards.

In addition, Bahrain has established itself as a major transportation, banking, and commercial center for the Persian Gulf and is home to many multinational firms with business in the region. Despite this, Bahrain faces several long-term economic problems, including unemployment and limited water resources. It receives economic aid from Saudi Arabia and other Gulf states.

Bahrain is one of the world's smallest nations. Its strategic location on the Persian Gulf has made it important as a port and trade center.

MAJOR CITIES

Nearly one-third of Bahrain's population is concentrated in the cities of Manama and Al Muharraq. These cities are on two separate islands and are connected by a causeway.

Manama, the nation's capital, is its largest city and chief port. A modern city with a population of 137,000, it is located on the north coast of Bahrain Island.

Al Muharraq, on Al Muharraq Island, is the country's second largest city. It has a traditional look, with old houses and narrow streets. The port of Al Muharraq is the center of Bahrain's boatbuilding industry.

HISTORY AND GOVERNMENT

Bahrain's history goes back to ancient times. Thousands of burial mounds indicate that people lived there perhaps as long ago as 3000 B.C. The Sumerians had contact with ancient Bahrain. Later the Greeks and Romans visited the islands.

Bahrain was colonized by the Portuguese in the 1500's, then fell under Persian control. In 1783 it came under the rule of the al-Khalifa family, which for a time controlled neighboring Qatar. The al-Khalifa descendants still rule Bahrain today.

In the early 1800's, Bahrain came under British influence. Several treaties were negotiated with Britain that were similar to those

it had signed with other Gulf states. In return for British protection, Bahrain agreed, among other things, not to engage in slavery or piracy. Bahrain remained a British protectorate until 1971, then became independent.

Bahrain was a member of the allied coalition against Iraq in the 1991 Persian Gulf War, participating in air and ground assaults. It remains a close ally of the United States and serves as home port for the U.S. Fifth Fleet. It aided the U.S. effort to combat international terrorism but did not participate militarily in the 2003 Iraq War.

In 1999, Sheik Hamad bin Isa al-Khalifa became Bahrain's ruler on his father's death. In 2001 he introduced a charter, overwhelmingly approved by voters, that established a two-house legislature. The lower house, which can make laws, is elected. Members of the upper house are appointed by the ruler.

Bahrain formally became a constitutional monarchy in 2002. That year, Bahrain held its first parliamentary elections in nearly 30 years. The elections marked the first time women in an Arab country in the Persian Gulf were permitted to vote and run for public office. Although no women were elected to Parliament's lower house, the sheik appointed six women to the upper house.

Reviewed by RUSTY CARTER ROOK
Center for Middle East Studies
The University of Chicago

BAKER, JOSEPHINE. See MISSOURI (Famous People).

BAKING. See BREAD AND BAKING.

FACTS and figures

KINGDOM OF BAHRAIN is the official name of the country.

LOCATION: Persian Gulf near Saudi Arabia.

AREA: 240 sq mi (622 km²).

POPULATION: 650,000 (estimate).

CAPITAL AND LARGEST CITY: Manama.

MAJOR LANGUAGE: Arabic.

MAJOR RELIGIOUS GROUP: Muslim.

GOVERNMENT: Constitutional monarchy. **Head of state**—king. **Head of government**—prime minister (appointed by the king). **Legislature**—Parliament (composed of an upper and lower house).

CHIEF PRODUCTS: Agricultural—fruits, vegetables, poultry, dairy products, shrimp, fish. **Manufactured**—petroleum, natural gas, iron, steel, chemicals, aluminum.

MONETARY UNIT: Dinar (1 dinar = 1,000 fils).

Balboa was the first European to sight the Pacific Ocean. Stepping into its waters, he claimed the great ocean and all the land it touched for Spain in 1513.

BALBOA, VASCO NÚÑEZ DE
(1475–1519)

Vasco Núñez de Balboa, a Spanish explorer and adventurer, was the first European to see the Pacific Ocean.

Balboa was born at Jerez de los Caballeros, Spain, in 1475. Little is known about his early life until about 1500, when he joined an expedition to seek his fortune in America. Finding no gold, he settled as a farmer on the island of Hispaniola (now Haiti and the Dominican Republic). Balboa soon found himself deeply in debt. To escape his creditors, he hid in a large barrel and was carried on board a ship bound for the settlement of San Sebastián, in Colombia.

When the ship was safely at sea, Balboa came out of hiding. The commander of the expedition, Martín Fernández de Enciso, was furious at the stowaway and threatened to abandon him on a desert island. However, Enciso allowed him to remain after Balboa convinced the crew that he would be valuable to them as a soldier.

This proved to be true, for when the expedition reached San Sebastián, they found it in ruins. Balboa took charge and led the survivors to Panama. There they started a new colony, which he called Darien.

But soon a quarrel broke out between Balboa and Enciso over who should be in command. Enciso was overthrown and sent back to Spain, and Balboa became governor of the new colony.

Balboa then set out to explore the surrounding country, hoping to find gold. His generosity won him the friendship of the Indians. The Indians had little use for gold. But seeing that Balboa prized it so highly, they told him of a marvelous land to the south where people ate from golden plates and drank from golden cups. They also said that just beyond the mountains lay a great sea. Balboa did not know that only a narrow strip of land (the Isthmus of Panama) lay between the Atlantic and Pacific oceans. He thought that this sea might be the route to Cathay (China), which Columbus had sought in vain.

Meanwhile, Enciso had returned to Spain and angrily complained about Balboa to King Ferdinand. Anxious to regain the King's favor, Balboa set out to discover the great sea the Indians had described. With 190 Spanish troops and 1,000 Indians he cut his way across the jungle-covered mountains of Panama. On September 25, 1513, Balboa left his companions and climbed the last mountain peak by himself. From its summit he saw the gleaming Pacific Ocean stretching as far as the eye could see. He named it the South Sea and on September 29 claimed it and all the land it touched for the King of Spain.

Balboa then planned to explore Peru—the land of gold. Before he could carry out his plans, a new governor, Pedrarias Dávila, arrived from Spain. Pedrarias, jealous of Balboa, had him arrested on a false charge of treason. And in 1519, not far from the colony he had founded and the ocean he had discovered, Balboa was executed.

Reviewed by KENNETH S. COOPER
Author, *World Ways*

BALDR. See NORSE MYTHOLOGY (Profiles).

BALDWIN, JAMES (1924–1987)

James Baldwin was a black American novelist, playwright, and essayist. He was a leading literary voice in the civil rights movement of the 1950's and 1960's.

Baldwin was born in New York City on August 2, 1924, the oldest of nine children. His father, a Baptist preacher, was a violent man who died when James was a teenager. A gifted student, James read widely and displayed a talent for writing. By his early twenties, he was writing essays and reviews for *The Nation* and other respected periodicals.

Baldwin's first novel, *Go Tell It on the Mountain* (1953), is perhaps his best. The partly autobiographical work tells of a black teenager and his struggles with a tyrannical stepfather at home and with racial injustice in the outside world. Baldwin continued to explore racial conflict in his later works, including the novels *Another Country* (1962), *Tell Me How Long the Train's Been Gone* (1968), and *Just Above My Head* (1979), and the play *Blues for Mister Charlie* (1964).

Baldwin's essays, which reached a wide audience, were highly acclaimed for their insights into black experience in a white-dominated society. His most important essay collections were *Notes of a Native Son* (1955), *Nobody Knows My Name* (1961), and *The Fire Next Time* (1963). *The Evidence of Things Not Seen* (1985) is an essay on the murders of 28 black children in Atlanta in 1980 and 1981.

Noted writer James Baldwin explored the experiences of black Americans.

After 1948, Baldwin lived mainly in France, returning to the United States to teach and lecture. He died in St. Paul de Vence on December 1, 1987.

Reviewed by PETER CONN
Author, *Literature in America:
An Illustrated History*

BALDWIN, MATTHIAS WILLIAM. See RAILROADS (Profiles).

BALFOUR, ARTHUR JAMES (1848–1930)

Arthur James Balfour is considered one of the most brilliant and intellectual of all the British prime ministers. A member of Parliament (MP) for 48 years, he served as Conservative prime minister from 1902 to 1905.

Born on July 25, 1848, at Whittingehame in the Scottish border country, Balfour was 6 when his father died. He was greatly influenced by his mother, whose brother, the Marquess of Salisbury, would later serve four terms as prime minister.

At Cambridge University it was thought that Balfour would become a philosopher. In 1874, however, he chose to enter politics. At first he seemed to be little more than a lightweight, witty conversationalist, whose career advanced in his uncle's shadow. But he rapidly won a reputation for firmness and fairness in his political dealings.

As government leader in the House of Commons (1891–92 and 1895–1902), Balfour became especially skillful in debate. He was the natural choice to succeed Salisbury as Conservative prime minister in July 1902.

Balfour's government achieved school reforms brought about by the Education Act of 1902, but little else. Disputes over tariff reform caused the Conservatives to lose the 1906 general election to the Liberals. Despite criticism, Balfour continued to lead his party in opposition until 1911.

The Balfour Declaration

During World War I, Balfour returned to government office as foreign secretary (1916–19). His most famous achievement was to issue the Balfour Declaration (1917), a statement pledging British support for the establishment of a Jewish homeland in Palestine following the war (providing the non-Jewish communities already living there would be safeguarded). Balfour also helped draw up the Treaty of Versailles (1919) and other postwar settlements. Later, as Earl Balfour, he served in Stanley Baldwin's cabinet (1925–29).

ALAN PALMER
Author, *The Penguin Dictionary of
Modern History*

BALKANS

The Balkans are a region of southeastern Europe of great strategic and historical importance. Physically, the region consists of a peninsula that juts southward into the Mediterranean Sea. It is bounded on the west and southeast by the Adriatic, Ionian, and Aegean seas (arms of the Mediterranean) and on the east by the Black Sea. Politically, the Balkans usually include the countries of Albania, Bulgaria, Greece, Romania, Serbia and Montenegro, Bosnia and Herzegovina, Croatia, Macedonia, and Slovenia.

THE BALKANS

▶ PEOPLE

The Balkan Peninsula is home to varied peoples. The majority are Slavs, the descendants of South Slavic peoples who arrived in the region in the A.D. 500's and 600's. Greeks, Romanians, Albanians, and Magyars (Hungarians) are the main non-Slavic groups, and there are Turkish, German, Macedonian, and other minorities.

The six major languages of the region are Serbo-Croatian, Slovenian, Albanian, Bulgarian, Greek, and Romanian. Serbo-Croatian, Slovenian, and Bulgarian are Slavic languages. Romanian is a Romance language, derived from Latin. It is a legacy of the time when Romania was a Roman colony.

Most Balkan peoples traditionally have belonged to the Roman Catholic or Eastern Orthodox churches. There is a considerable Muslim population as well, a reminder that the region was long ruled by the Ottoman Turks.

▶ LAND

The word *balkan* is of Turkish origin and means "wooded mountain range." The name is apt, for rugged mountains are the dominant feature of the Balkan landscape. The Carpathians in Romania extend, as the Balkan Mountains, into Bulgaria. The Dinaric Alps run parallel to the Adriatic coast in Montenegro and Albania and continue, as the Pindus Mountains, into Greece. The Rhodope range forms the boundary between Bulgaria and Greece.

The mountains isolated the different peoples of the region and tended to create a number of small states, which were often in conflict with one another. At the same time, certain

valleys and rivers, particularly the Danube, the region's chief river, provided access for foreign invaders. The mountainous terrain also limited the amount of land that could be used for farming, although the valleys can be fertile.

The climate ranges from the continental, with long, cold winters and relatively short summers, to the Mediterranean, with mild winters and long, hot summers.

▶ HISTORY

The first great civilization in the region was that of ancient Greece, followed, in the 300's B.C., by the short-lived empire of Alexander the Great. The Balkans became part of the Roman Empire in the A.D. 100's and 200's. With the division of the Roman world in 395, the region came under the rule of the Eastern Roman, or Byzantine, Empire.

The arrival of the Slavs and the decline of Byzantine power permitted the development of distinct Balkan nationalities. There were, at different periods, large Bulgarian and Serb empires. Between the late 1300's and the mid-1500's, the region was conquered by the Ottoman Turks. As Ottoman power itself began to wane in the late 1600's, parts of the Balkans fell to an expanding Austria.

The Struggle for Independence. The struggle for Balkan independence began in earnest in the early 1800's, with the rise of Serbia and the liberation of Greece from Turkish rule. Over the next century, Montenegro, Bulgaria, and Romania won independence. In 1912 an alliance of Serbia, Bulgaria, Greece, and Montenegro defeated Turkey in the First Balkan War. As a result, Albania gained its independence and Turkey was forced to give up almost all of its remaining European lands. Disputes over territorial claims, however, led to the Second Balkan War in 1913, in which Bulgaria was defeated by its former allies, joined by Turkey.

The Modern Balkans. Meanwhile, the great European powers, particularly Britain, France, Austria-Hungary, and Russia, had also become entangled in Balkan affairs. World War I (1914–18) arose out of a Balkan issue—the ambition of Serbia to take Bosnia and Herzegovina from Austria-Hungary. The war brought about the destruction of the Austro-Hungarian empire. As a result a new nation, Yugoslavia, was formed from Serbia, Bosnia and Herzegovina, Montenegro, and other states, and the present-day Balkan states came into being. The war also led to the final collapse of the old Ottoman Empire.

The Balkans fell under Nazi German domination between 1941 and 1945, during World War II. After the war, a Communist political system was imposed on the Balkan countries, except for Greece. As Communism crumbled in the late 1980's and early 1990's, the regimes were replaced by popularly elected governments. In Yugoslavia the changeover led to the breakup of the country and to civil war. The fighting was most severe among Serbs, Croats, and Muslims in Bosnia and Herzegovina and between Serbs and ethnic Albanians in the Serbian province of Kosovo and later Macedonia.

ARTHUR CAMPBELL TURNER
University of California, Riverside

See also articles on individual countries.

BALL

All over the world, people play ball and have done so since prehistoric times. Some early people wove reeds into rounded shapes. Others used leather stuffed with feathers for ball playing. Later, Greeks and Romans used an air-filled leather ball called a *follis* in games of catch. They also inflated balls of larger sizes, with which they played a kind of soccer and other kicking games.

Balls have been made from many materials. Native Americans used balls made of deer hide, while across the world from them, Japanese children played with balls of tightly wadded tissue paper wrapped with string. It is said that Columbus found the Indians of Central America playing with solid, black balls made of vegetable gum and took some of these rubber balls back to Europe.

We learn from the history of people and their folklore that some of our modern ball games started as religious and magical ceremonies. The Egyptians seem to have been among the first people to have ceremonial ball games. Each spring two large groups of people, each representing one of their gods, acted out a contest that used a round, wooden ball and crooked sticks. The object was to drive the ball through the opposing goal. The side that knocked the ball past the defenders won.

Today a ball and stick are used in playing such games as polo, field hockey, and lacrosse. Each team tries to score while keeping the other side from scoring goals.

At first, ball games were played mainly to develop skill in tossing and catching. Over time, many different sticks, bats, and rackets were added to strike or otherwise control the motion of the ball, and many special games were invented. Today there are more than thirty major sports in which a ball is the key object used in the game. These range from the oval football to the tiny table-tennis ball.

The ball has played a part in many other customs unrelated to sports. The ballot, used in voting, is named after the Italian *ballotta* ("little ball"), from the ancient Greek custom of casting votes with small balls. Often, white and black balls were used—white to vote yes and black to vote no. The word "blackball," meaning to exclude someone from membership by casting a negative vote, goes back to this practice.

The ball belongs to everyone, so it is difficult to find out who invented it or from what country it first started to roll to the four corners of the world.

JACQUE HETRICK
Spalding

BALL, LUCILLE. See NEW YORK (Famous People).

BALLADS

The ballad is a type of folk song that tells a story using simple words and a simple melody. The words are often in the form of a dialogue between two people.

The ballad developed in Europe during the Middle Ages. The name comes from the Latin word *ballare* ("to dance"). Originally ballads were dancing songs, but by the 1200's they had become solo songs. Today they may or may not be danced or performed with an instrumental accompaniment, but they always emphasize the story and are sung in a way that stresses the words over the melody. Ballad melodies are, nevertheless, beautiful and varied. They range from those based on Gregorian chants in western Europe to Slavic types in eastern Europe.

Scholars once believed that the ballad dated back to primitive times and was composed by groups of people. Since then, experts have decided that it has far more recent and sophisticated beginnings. Ballads were composed by individuals with some artistic background and training. As the songs were passed from singer to singer and from generation to generation, they were varied, shaped, and recreated to reflect the concerns, beliefs, and tastes of the time.

The ballads sung in America can be divided into three groups: traditional British ballads, later products of British city presses, and native American narrative songs.

Traditional ballads were first created in Great Britain six or seven centuries ago. Passed on by word of mouth, they usually rhyme and are divided into stanzas. The best ones are strikingly beautiful and moving. The traditional ballads are sometimes called Child ballads, named after Professor Francis James Child, who collected 305 of them in his classic five-volume book, *The English and Scottish Popular Ballads* (1882–98). "Lord Randal," "Sir Patrick Spens," "Barbara Allen," and "The Twa Corbies" are some well-known Child ballads.

Ballads from the British presses of the 1600's to the 1800's are known as broadside ballads. Many were printed on large sheets of paper called broadsides and were sold for a penny. Others were printed in small books called chapbooks. These songs usually recounted tales of mistaken identity, disguised lovers, or cruel crimes. Often the broadsides were based on traditional ballads. They were performed and sold by professional singers on city streets and at country fairs.

Using these British songs as models, Americans composed ballads about outlaws like Jesse James and Billy the Kid, folk heroes like John Henry, and tragic young women like Young Charlotte and Naomi Wise. Sometimes these songs are American versions of British stories.

English-speaking countries are not the only ones with highly developed ballad traditions. Scandinavia has a large stock of ballads, many of which are variants of well-known British and American songs. In most of the Balkan countries of eastern Europe, the ballad is an important form of literature, preserving many legends. Ukrainian ballads are also outstanding.

French and Italian ballads often stress emotion and melody instead of story. Ballads are less common in Germany and the Low Countries; Germany, however, has many ballad-like pieces based on political and religious themes.

Spain's ballads, called *romances*, are frequently semihistorical, focusing more on personality than on factual details. Many of them consist of groups of songs on a single theme.

Russian *byliny* are narrative songs, like British ballads. They usually deal with the exploits of fabulous heroes. *Byliny* do not rhyme and are not divided into stanzas.

Traditional ballads continue to survive from ages past. The old songs are reshaped and new songs are created from the older models. These songs spread to more distant areas, where they continue to undergo change. Thus the ballads that people sing are a good indication of their present concerns, beliefs, and musical tastes.

TRISTRAM P. COFFIN
American Folklore Society
Revised by MELVIN BERGER
Author, *The Story of Folk Music*

See also FOLK MUSIC.

Rudolf Nureyev and Margot Fonteyn in *Romeo and Juliet,* based on the play by Shakespeare.

BALLET

A ballet is theatrical entertainment combining dance with other art forms, usually stage design and music. It may tell a story or merely depict an idea or mood. Ballet is a French word that comes from the Italian *ballo,* "a dance."

The exercises, or techniques, of ballet are designed to display the human body in the most elegant and harmonious way possible. Ballet technique is strict, and the training is strenuous. But the result on stage is natural and beautiful.

Ballet is nearly 500 years old. Yet it is very young compared with dance itself, which began with primitive people. Ballet began in Italy about the time of Columbus' voyages to America. It was quite different then from what it is today. At that time ballet was a court entertainment for the amusement of the nobility at lavish balls and banquets. Dancing, music, pantomime (acting without words), poetry, and drama were combined. The first ballet dancers were the royalty and nobles of the court, since there were no professional dancers. The steps were modeled on the elegant but rather simple social dances of the day.

Ballet as we know it is the product of many countries. The French organized the technique and gave it liveliness. The Russians added strength and passion. The English gave it delicacy and tenderness. The Americans gave it speed and variety.

▶ BALLET IN FRANCE

Queen Catherine de Médicis of France was familiar with the elaborate dance productions of Italy, her native land. In 1581, she ordered a grand entertainment—a ballet—to celebrate a royal wedding. The result was most spectacular. Thousands of people witnessed its lavish blending of dance, dramatic scenes, music, and complex scenery. Hundreds of dancers, singers, and actors took part, portraying the goddess Circe and all of her friends and enemies. Huge machines and stage effects were moved about the room so that the audience, seated on three sides, could see them.

All this was the work of an Italian musician best known by his French name, Balthasar de Beaujoyeulx. He was probably the first choreographer, or maker of dances, as we know the word today. He called his work *Le Ballet Comique de la Reine* ("The Queen's Comic Ballet"). Ever since then, performances of this kind have been called ballets.

Catherine's grandson, Louis XIV, loved to dance. He received lessons daily. At the age of 13, he danced in the *Ballet de Cassandre.*

1st position

2nd position

3rd position

The ballets in King Louis' time were formal and quite solemn. Usually they dealt with mythology or history. For a while only members of the court danced in them, but the King soon tired of their lack of skill. He had already brought together professional writers like Molière, Philippe Quinault, and Isaac de Benserade; the composer Jean-Baptiste Lully; and the choreographer Pierre Beauchamp. To improve the dancing, King Louis organized the Royal Academy of Dance in 1661. This academy was the beginning of the Paris Opera Ballet and today's Paris Opera Ballet School.

By 1681, France had its first prima ballerina, the leading female dancer in a ballet company. She was Mademoiselle Lafontaine. Pictures of the time show her to be lovely and very dignified in her long, stiff gown, her high-heeled slippers, and her plumed headdress. She danced that year in *Le Triomphe de l'Amour* (''The Triumph of Love''), with choreography by Beauchamp and music by Lully. Mademoiselle Lafontaine was the first of a series of professional ballet dancers. Each of these experts brought something new to the art of ballet.

In a children's ballet class, a teacher helps a young student position his body correctly. The long wooden railing, called a barre, helps dancers keep their balance while practicing.

4th position   5th position

The five basic positions are learned by all ballet dancers. Every classical ballet step or movement begins and ends with the feet in one of these positions.

Several names stand out in the history of ballet in the 1700's. Marie Camargo boldly shortened the ballet costume to mid-calf. She also removed the heels from her slippers. Thus she could move more quickly and perform small, intricate steps like the *entrechat-quatre,* a double crossing of the feet in midair. Gaetan Vestris was the first male dancer to show in his *jetés* (leaps) and *tours en l'air* (turns in the air) that men could develop a ballet style very different from that of women. Danish and Russian dancers later stressed this difference even more.

But no matter how versatile they are, dancers depend on the imagination of choreographers. The great choreographer Jean Georges Noverre looked at the productions around him and saw that ballet was deteriorating into a mere display of technique. He believed that ballet should express strong emotions. After his reforms, ballet became more like drama. Noverre's ballets are not danced today. But his book, *Letters on Dancing and Ballets,* is still widely read by choreographers.

Marie Taglioni (1804—84)

All of us have at some time wished to fly. The female dancers of the early 1800's felt that way, too. As imaginary creatures like ondines (water sprites) or sylphides (tree sprites), they were actually attached to wires so that they could soar above the stage. More often they gave the illusion of lightness by rising to the very tips of their toes. Pictures of Marie Taglioni, one of the foremost dancers of the time, show her this way.

In 1832, Taglioni's father, Filippo Taglioni, created a ballet especially for her. Called *La Sylphide,* it was about a mysterious forest creature so playful and so touching that she lured a young Scot, James, away from his fiancée on his wedding day. Poets and composers of this period, known as the romantic age, loved sadness. In *La Sylphide,* as in most romantic ballets, the end was tragic. The sylphide died, leaving James alone in the forest to mourn her.

Carlotta Grisi (1819—99)

While Taglioni was touring in Russia, an Italian dancer, Carlotta Grisi, arrived at the Paris Opera. Jules Perrot, a celebrated dancer, fell in love with her, as did the poet Théophile Gautier. Gautier wrote a ballet story for her. It was *Giselle* (1841), the tragedy of a gentle peasant girl who loved to dance. Jean Coralli was the choreographer, but *Giselle's* variations (special solos) were made by Perrot.

A scene from *La Sylphide,* a romantic 19th-century ballet, is performed by members of the American Ballet Theatre.

A scene from *The Nutcracker*, which is often danced during the Christmas season.

Giselle is even more tragic than *La Sylphide* because Giselle is a real girl and not a sprite. She is wooed by the handsome Albrecht. She falls deeply in love with him, not knowing that he is a count in disguise and can never marry her. To make matters worse, he is already engaged to the Countess Bathilde. When Giselle learns of the betrayal, she goes insane and dies. Later, she rises from her tomb to dance with the remorseful Albrecht and to protect him from being destroyed by the Wilis, spirits of young girls who died before marriage.

▶ RUSSIAN BALLET

If you were to ask a friend to name two favorite ballets, the answers might be *Swan Lake* and *The Sleeping Beauty* or *Scheherazade* and *Petrouchka*. These—and many more— came from Marius Petipa and Michel Fokine, two Russian choreographers whose ballets are now performed all over the world.

Marius Petipa (1819–1910)

Petipa, born in France, won fame as a choreographer in St. Petersburg. In 1862 he devised a three-act spectacle called *The Pha-*raoh's *Daughter*. Like his later ballets, it took all evening to perform and had a complicated plot. This gave plenty of opportunity for a stilted kind of mime that described what was going on but told the audience very little about the person doing the mime. There were also interludes of beautiful pure dance, usually solos, called variations. They had little or nothing to do with the story. But they were beautifully made and were perfectly suited to the music.

For his most celebrated ballets, Petipa was fortunate to have the composer Peter Ilyich Tchaikovsky. His music was so inspired and so perfectly made that it could stand on its own when played separately from the ballets. The grandest collaborations of Petipa and Tchaikovsky were *The Sleeping Beauty* (1890) and *Swan Lake* (1895). In *Swan Lake,* Petipa shared the choreography with his assistant, Lev Ivanov. This ballet returned to a theme very popular during the romantic period—that of a young prince falling in love with a bewitched creature. And like the romantic ballets, *Swan Lake* ends in death. Two of its variations, the *White Swan Pas de Deux* and the *Black Swan Pas de Deux,* are very often danced separately from the ballet. (A pas de deux is a dance for two people.)

Petipa planned the action of *The Nutcracker* (1892) and gave complete musical instructions to Tchaikovsky. But the choreographer fell ill, and Ivanov actually staged the ballet. It has become a favorite for the Christmas season, and children often have starring roles.

When Petipa planned a new ballet, he did not care whether the costumes and sets were suited to the period and place of the story. They were done according to a formula. This bothered Michel Fokine, who was a student at the Imperial School of Ballet when Petipa was director of its company.

Michel Fokine (1880–1942)

Many of the students at the Imperial School of Ballet were satisfied merely to learn technique and dance in Petipa's ballets. But Fokine had a lively, curious mind. He studied history and painting and spent hours in museums.

One day Fokine wrote a letter to the director of the school and said that he would like to make a new kind of ballet. The mime and the variations would not be separate. They would be part of the action. The style of movement and the style of the costumes and sets would be suited to the period of the ballet. And the stories of the ballets would be simple and believable.

Fokine was not allowed to go ahead, so he began to work on his own. His smallest dance, a five-minute solo called *The Dying Swan* (1905), became his best known. It was made for his classmate Anna Pavlova to dance at a charity ball. To this day it is associated with her.

Then, to show that he knew his craft and that he knew the styles of different periods, Fokine created a ballet in the romantic style, *Les Sylphides.* He borrowed the atmosphere but not the story of *La Sylphide.* The music was a series of piano pieces by Frédéric Chopin. The delicacy of this ballet and the ease with which the movement flows along with the music have made it Fokine's best-known and most performed ballet.

Fokine was staging ballets outside of the Imperial Ballet in Russia. But his first important opportunities came when Sergei Diaghilev formed his Ballets Russes in Paris.

Sergei Diaghilev (1872–1929)

In St. Petersburg, the home of the Imperial Ballet, a group of young authors, painters, and composers often met in the evenings to talk about their work. They started a magazine called *The World of Art,* with Sergei Diaghilev as its editor.

Diaghilev could not write or paint or compose. But he had exquisite taste, and he knew how to bring the right people together to make interesting things happen. He arranged an exhibit of Russian painting in Paris in 1906, and he produced the opera *Boris Godunov* in Paris in 1908. In 1909 he put together his own ballet company. He turned to Fokine as his chief choreographer, and he gave Fokine four of the world's greatest dancers as the principals for his ballets. They were Anna Pavlova, Tamara Karsavina, Vaslav Nijinsky, and Adolph Bolm.

Given this freedom, Fokine's imagination began to soar. In quick succession he turned out the wild *Polovtsian Dances* from the opera *Prince Igor;* the playful *Carnaval;* the lush *Scheherazade,* with its brilliant leaping dance for Nijinsky as the Golden Slave; the myste-

Anna Pavlova in a 1910 production of *The Dying Swan,* the role she made famous.

Marina Kondratieva and Maris Lieta in the Bolshoi Ballet's production of _Spring Water_.

rious Russian fairy tale _Firebird;_ and _Pe-trouchka,_ a touching story of puppets brought to life. The last two ballets introduced a new ballet composer, Igor Stravinsky.

Diaghilev was restless. One choreographer was not enough for him. He was constantly searching for new talents in the different arts, and he combined them imaginatively. For example, the choreographer Léonide Massine worked with the painter Pablo Picasso and the composer Manuel de Falla for _The Three-Cornered Hat._ The choreographer George Balanchine worked with the painter Georges Rouault and the composer Sergei Prokofiev for _The Prodigal Son._ Nijinsky, as chore-ographer, came together with the painter Nich-olas Roerich and the composer Igor Stravinsky for _The Rite of Spring._

Other ballets that were made famous by the Ballets Russes include Massine's _La Boutique Fantastique_ and Balanchine's _Rossignol,_ in which 12-year-old Alicia Markova danced the nightingale.

Diaghilev's company was disbanded after his death, but the ballets he produced are still presented. Russian dancers have continued to play an important part in ballet. Some, such as Vladimir Vasiliev, Yekaterina Maximova, Galina Ulanova, and Maya Plisetskaya, danced with the Bolshoi Ballet, Russia's leading company. Others, such as Rudolf Nureyev, Natalia Makarova, Aleksandr Godunov, and Mikhail Baryshnikov, left to live and work in other countries.

▶ **BALLET IN ENGLAND**

When the Diaghilev company was dis-banded, several of its dancers settled in Lon-don, where the company had often toured. Two of them, the Irish-born Dame Ninette de Valois and the Polish-born Dame Marie Rambert, became the pillars of British ballet.

Like Diaghilev, Marie Rambert liked to take chances on young and unknown artists. Thus she gave a first start to two of England's finest 20th-century choreographers, Sir Frederick

Ashton and Antony Tudor. Their first ballets appeared in Rambert's tiny Mercury Theatre.

Ninette de Valois was an organizer. She wanted a national ballet company and would settle for nothing less. In 1933 she became head of the Vic-Wells Ballet. Alicia Markova was its ballerina. The company grew in size and support to become the Sadler's Wells Ballet. For this company, De Valois gambled on an unknown 16-year-old dancer, who made her debut as the Swan Queen in *Swan Lake.* She was Margot Fonteyn, who later became one of the world's best-loved dancers. Finally, in 1957, De Valois saw her dream come true. As Dame Ninette, she was artistic director of Britain's Royal Ballet.

In the meantime, she had engaged Frederick Ashton as choreographer for the company. His ballets—whether witty, as in *A Wedding Bouquet,* or serious, as in *Ondine*–showed a refined, poetic style and respect for the classical tradition. They provided Fonteyn with some of her finest roles. Ashton's style is shown at its best in two works produced after his retirement as the company's artistic director in 1970. They were *Enigma Variations,* created to music by Edward Elgar, and *A Month in the Country.* In these ballets, every detail of movement was not only precisely made but seemed perfectly suited to the person performing it.

▶ DANISH BALLET

In the 1950's, the Royal Danish Ballet began to travel outside Denmark. It had a tremendous impact. The Danes gave special attention to the acting parts of ballets. In the hands of artists such as Niels Bjorn Larssen and Gerda Karstens, standard roles came alive in a new way.

The Danes had an interesting tradition from the 1800's. It came from the teaching and choreography of August Bournonville, which the Danes had lovingly preserved. The Bournonville style stressed the differences between men and women dancers. It featured strong movements and brilliant leaps for the men and intricate *terre-à-terre* (close to the ground) steps for the women. Because he traveled much during his career, Bournonville created ballets in a variety of styles. Many are performed today, among them *Napoli, Far from Denmark, Flower Festival at Genzano,* and *La Ventana.*

La Fille Mal Gardée (The Unchaperoned Girl) is a comic ballet with a happy ending.

George Balanchine's ballet *Jewels* is in three parts: *Emeralds*, *Rubies*, and *Diamonds*.

Some present-day Danish dancers combine the Bournonville style with the stronger Russian style. They have made their mark on companies in other parts of the world where they have gone to live and work. Among them are Toni Lander, Erik Bruhn, Peter Martins, Helgi Tomasson, and Peter Schaufuss.

▶ BALLET IN CANADA

The Royal Winnipeg Ballet is Canada's oldest company. It began as the Winnipeg Ballet Club in 1938 and became a fully professional company in 1949. Today it is famous for performing the works of 20th century choreographers such as Gweneth Lloyd, Arnold Spohr, Brian MacDonald, and Michel Conte.

The National Ballet of Canada, based in Toronto, was established in 1951. The company is noted for its performances of original works by Grant Strate and David Adams. Les Grands Ballets Canadiens began in Montreal in 1952 as a television troupe. The company performs classics and original works.

▶ BALLET IN THE UNITED STATES

In the 1800's, the United States produced such fine ballet dancers as George Washington Smith, Mary Ann Lee, and Augusta Maywood. But it was not until the 1900's that ballet began to find a wide and enthusiastic public. It all began with the tours of Anna Pavlova between 1910 and 1930. Pavlova was tireless. She went to every community that would have her. She did not encourage daring choreography. The members of her company were often modestly trained young dancers acquired along the way. But to many people of the United States, Pavlova was ballet.

Two years after Pavlova's death in 1931, the Ballet Russe de Monte Carlo arrived in the United States. Some of its dancers were from Diaghilev's company. Others were new. Audiences fell in love with stars such as Alexandra Danilova, Natalie Krassovska, Mia Slavenska, Irina Baronova, Tatiana Riabouchinska, Tamara Toumanova, and Igor Youskevitch.

At first the Ballet Russe depended on Russian choreographers such as Léonide Massine, David Lichine, and Michel Fokine. Gradually it turned to Americans such as Agnes de Mille, whose *Rodeo* (1942) gave an image of cowboys and ranchers that audiences still enjoy when it is performed today.

Dancers and choreographers of the United States soon began to found their own companies. Lincoln Kirstein, a wealthy young Harvard graduate with a strong writing talent, lured former Diaghilev choreographer George Balanchine to New York. The promises were a company of his own with a school behind it to train the dancers. It took time. Their modest company first performed in 1933. The company grew and in 1948 became the New York City Ballet.

The repertory of the New York City Ballet is extremely varied. Yet it is dominated by Balanchine and by the United States choreographer Jerome Robbins, who has blended jazz and modern dance with more traditional elements in ballets such as *Fancy Free*. Outstanding artists such as Maria Tallchief, Melissa Hayden, Suzanne Farrell, Jacques D'Amboise, Edward Villella, and Mikhail Baryshnikov have danced with the company.

In 1940 another major company, Ballet Theatre (later called the American Ballet Theatre), was created. It has developed the careers of many choreographers, among them Agnes de Mille, Jerome Robbins, and Eliot Feld. While developing new talents, it has kept the classics alive. Antony Tudor, the British choreographer who began his career with Marie

Two great stars of ballet, Mikhail Baryshnikov and Natalia Makarova, in *The Sleeping Beauty*.

Karen Brown and Keith Saunders of the Dance Theater of Harlem, in *Allegro Brillante* by George Balanchine.

Rambert in London, was associated with the company from its earliest days.

In the United States, the American Ballet Theatre and the New York City Ballet are the equivalent of the great national companies of Europe and the former Soviet Union. But smaller companies contribute to dance in the United States. Among them are the Dance Theater of Harlem, a classically oriented company of black dancers, and the Joffrey Ballet. The Joffrey Ballet has presented the works of its resident choreographer, Gerald Arpino. It has also staged 20th-century classics such as Kurt Jooss's *Green Table* and modern works such as José Limón's *The Moor's Pavane*.

While these companies have made New York City a world center of dance, the entire country has come alive with companies such as the Boston Ballet, the Pennsylvania Ballet, the Houston Ballet, and the Minnesota Dance Theatre. These and many more hold the key to the future of ballet in the United States.

DORIS HERING
Critic-at-large, *Dance Magazine*

See also DANCE.

BALLOONS, RESEARCH. See BALLOONS AND BALLOONING.

BALLOONS AND BALLOONING

Have you ever wondered what it would be like to float on the wind, drifting silently above your town? You could find out—if you were a balloonist. Every flight would be an adventure because in ballooning, you must travel where the wind takes you.

Balloons are aerostats, or lighter-than-air craft. A modern balloon is a bag made of a light material such as nylon or plastic. Air is blown into the bag and is then heated by a burner. Or the bag may be filled with a gas such as helium or hydrogen. The gas or hot air causes the balloon to rise. The pilot and passengers ride in a basket or gondola suspended underneath the balloon.

Not all balloons carry passengers. Scientists launch balloons carrying instruments to study the upper atmosphere and to gather information about the weather. And balloon satellites orbit the earth. Today balloons have two main uses—as tools in research and as a means of recreation in the sport of ballooning.

▶ HISTORY

Early in the 18th century Bartholomeu de Gusmão, a Portuguese priest, developed a small hot-air balloon. But the first big balloon was built by two French brothers, Joseph Michel and Jacques Étienne Montgolfier, in 1783. They made a huge bag of paper and cloth, which they held over a fire. When they released the smoke-filled balloon, it soared into the sky.

Encouraged by their success, the Montgolfier brothers built a balloon with a basket underneath to carry passengers. In the basket they put a rooster, a duck, and a young sheep. The balloon was filled with hot air from a fire and was released. The basket, with its animal passengers, floated upward. High above the earth the warm air inside the balloon cooled off, and the balloon slowly floated to earth. Live passengers had been carried into the air and returned safely for the first time in history.

This feat inspired two men to become the first human beings to fly above the earth. They were Jean François Pilâtre de Rozier, a French physician, and François Laurent, the Marquis d'Arlandes. A huge blue and gold hot-air balloon carried them aloft over Paris on November 21, 1783.

Colorful balloons rise into the air at the beginning of a race in Iowa. Ballooning is best in open country, far from tall buildings, traffic, and high-tension wires.

Fire was always a danger at these early balloon launchings. One spark could send a balloon up in flames. But in the same year that the hot-air balloon was developed, Jacques A. C. Charles, a French scientist, invented the gas balloon. Charles built a sphere of rubberized silk and filled it with hydrogen, a gas that is lighter than air without being heated. The balloon soared into the air and landed in a field near Paris, where it was destroyed by frightened farm workers.

With the help of others, Charles later developed a balloon that could carry passengers. To rise higher, the balloonist released sand from bags tied to the side of the basket. To come down, the balloonist pulled a rope that opened a valve located at the top of the balloon. The open valve allowed hydrogen to escape, so that the balloon would slowly deflate and return to earth.

The Age of Ballooning

The popularity of the safer gas balloons soon surpassed that of the hot-air type, and a ballooning craze swept Europe. Balloonists of this period were daring souls whose exploits were memorable.

In 1785, Jean Pierre Blanchard, a French balloonist, and John Jeffries, an American, crossed the English Channel in a gas balloon. Blanchard later made the first free flight in the United States, in Philadelphia, on January 9, 1793. President George Washington was among those who watched his ascension. On this occasion, Blanchard carried the first airmail letter and made scientific observations of the effects of altitude on the human body. For example, he discovered that his heart beat more rapidly at high altitudes. And he brought bottles filled with air back to earth. When the air was studied, it was found to contain less oxygen than air near the ground.

Blanchard's wife, Madeline-Sophie, was famous for spectacular ascensions at night. In 1819 she was killed when fireworks she had carried aloft ignited her balloon.

Ballooning was furthered by several inventions. In 1797 a French balloonist, André Garnerin, astonished spectators by leaping from a balloon and floating safely to the earth. In secret, he had invented the first practical parachute. In 1839, John Wise, an American, invented the rip line. By pulling this line, a

Above: The balloon that carried two French balloonists on the first piloted flight in 1783. Below: Preparing for the first successful piloted balloon flight in the United States—in Philadelphia, 1793.

balloonist near the ground could open a large panel in the balloon and deflate it quickly in an emergency.

The jet streams—long currents of air moving at high altitudes—had not been discovered in Wise's time. But he was convinced that a balloon could cross the Atlantic Ocean by traveling on rivers of wind.

Balloons in War

Balloons became important in military operations during the U.S. Civil War (1861–65) and the Franco-Prussian War (1870–71). Balloonists were sent up in tethered balloons—balloons anchored to the ground by long lines—to observe the enemy troops and even to report descriptions of battles from an aerial position. From their high positions, they could direct cannon fire more accurately. Balloons were also used to carry messages.

During World War I (1914–18), balloons were again used for observation. In both world wars, barrage balloons were anchored by long cables along Britain's coast to block enemy aircraft. During World War II (1939–45), Japan sent balloons carrying bombs across the Pacific Ocean toward the northwestern coast of North America. But few of the balloons completed the trip, and most of those that did landed in remote areas.

Reaching for Height and Distance

Balloonists have ventured to the limits of their endurance to learn about the upper atmosphere and to discover how high and how far balloons can travel.

In 1862, James Glaisher, an English scientist, and Henry Coxwell, his balloon pilot, rose to a height of 30,000 feet (more than 9,000 meters) without oxygen. But early high-altitude research could be dangerous. At high altitudes, the air contains so little oxygen that a person can suffocate. In 1875, three French balloonists floated up in a balloon called the *Zenith,* carrying bottles of oxygen with them. But they lost consciousness at about 25,000 feet (7,500 meters), before they could use their equipment. When the *Zenith* returned to the earth, only one was alive.

In 1927, an American military balloonist, Captain Hawthorne Gray, also died during a high-altitude ascension. He lost consciousness at about 44,000 feet (13,400 meters), although he was wearing an oxygen mask. Notes made

by Gray gave valuable information about the atmosphere at high altitudes.

Auguste Piccard, a Swiss scientist and inventor, developed a way to explore the upper atmosphere safely in a balloon. He invented an airtight aluminum gondola that was round, like a ball. Inside it he put oxygen and pressure tanks. In 1931 he ascended to more than 51,000 feet (15,500 meters) and became the first person to look without a telescope into the black depths of outer space. Piccard made many other ascents into the upper atmosphere, as did his brother, Jean Piccard. They brought back information about cosmic rays and high-altitude electricity. Since then, balloons have risen higher and higher. In 1961, Malcolm Ross and Victor A. Prather, Jr., of the U.S. Navy, reached a height of over 113,500 feet (34,500 meters).

Balloonists have attempted to set records in distance as well. But the dream of crossing the Atlantic was not realized until 1978. Three U.S. balloonists—Ben Abruzzo, Maxie Anderson, and Larry Newman—made the crossing. Their helium balloon, *Double Eagle II,* traveled from Maine to France. In 1981, four balloonists crossed the Pacific. Ben Abruzzo, Larry Newman, Ron Clark, and Rocky Aoki flew the *Double Eagle V* from Japan to California, a distance of 6,000 miles (9,500 kilometers).

The first nonstop balloon flight around the world was achieved in 1999. Bertrand Piccard and Brian Jones piloted the *Breitling Orbiter 3* westward from Switzerland, landing 19 days later in the Egyptian desert.

What makes a balloon rise?

A big balloon soars up into the sky because it is filled with a gas that is lighter than air.

Air itself is made up of gases, the chief ones being oxygen and nitrogen. Certain other gases are lighter than air. One of these is helium, and that is why a balloon filled with helium rises.

Hot air will also make a balloon rise because hot air is lighter than cold air. It is lighter because as air is heated, its gas particles spread out and become less dense.

You can demonstrate with this simple experiment that air expands as it is warmed. Snap the open end of a small balloon over the top of an empty soda bottle. The balloon hangs limp. Now set the bottle in a pan of hot water. The hot water heats the bottle and warms the cold air inside it. Gradually the warm air in the bottle pushes its way into the balloon. The balloon slowly fills with air and begins to inflate.

▶ BALLOONS IN SCIENTIFIC RESEARCH

Balloons are of value in scientific research because they can go very high and stay up a relatively long time. Rockets can go higher, but they stay up only briefly and so cannot collect as much information as balloons can.

Three types of gas balloons are most commonly used in scientific research today—extensible balloons, zero-pressure balloons, and superpressure balloons. They are made of various kinds of plastic. Tethered hot-air balloons are sometimes used as observation platforms— to study the skies, for example, or to locate archeological sites.

Extensible balloons are small. As a balloon of this type rises, the gas inside it expands because the pressure of the surrounding air is less at high altitudes. When the balloon reaches a certain height, the pressure inside it causes it to burst. A parachute opens and carries the instruments back to the earth.

Zero-pressure balloons are among the largest balloons. They can carry heavy loads to high altitudes. They are only partly filled with gas when they are launched. But as they rise, the gas expands to fill the balloon. Excess gas escapes through a vent. Zero pressure balloons usually stay aloft for several days.

Superpressure balloons can remain aloft for months. Like zero-pressure balloons, they are launched partly filled with gas. But then they are sealed, so that the expanding gas will not escape. The excess pressure that builds up as the balloon rises keeps it aloft at a constant altitude.

The instruments sent up in these balloons include devices that measure the temperature, pressure, humidity, and chemical composition of the air. The information they provide is used in studying the atmosphere and the weather. Communications equipment is also sent aloft in balloons.

Radiation—in the form of visible light, X rays, gamma rays, cosmic rays, or infrared or ultraviolet radiation—gives us information about space. But the earth's atmosphere blocks much of the radiation from space. From the edge of the atmosphere, instruments in a balloon can gather more information about the sun, the planets, and distant stars—their temperatures, speed and direction of motion, chemical composition, and so on—than can be gathered on the earth. The instruments in-

Research balloons help scientists gather information not easily obtained on earth. This balloon, shown during launching, carries an infrared telescope.

clude telescopes, spectroscopes, photometers, and cosmic ray counters.

During the 1950's, balloons paved the way for people to enter outer space. Balloons as tall as 50-story buildings rose to gather information about cosmic rays and other radiations from outer space. Monkeys were sent aloft in balloons as a test of what happens to the body at high altitudes. Guided missiles were carried aloft by balloons and then fired from the edge of space out into space. Since then, several balloon satellites have been launched into orbit by rocket. New equipment is often tested in balloons before being sent up in rockets or space probes.

In 1978, *Double Eagle II* carried three United States balloonists on the first flight across the Atlantic Ocean.

▶ **THE SPORT OF BALLOONING**

Ballooning has become popular as a sport that offers competition and the enjoyment of floating freely above the earth. Many rallies and events are held each year. In one of the best-known events, balloonists from all over the world travel over the Alps from Switzerland to Italy.

Competition takes various forms. There are long-distance races, in which the winner is the balloonist who travels farthest. There are cross-country and spot-landing contests, in which the pilot must take off and land within a specified time. In the cross-country event, the balloonist who travels farthest is the winner. In spot-landing contests, balloonists attempt to land at a designated point. In a hare-and-hounds chase, a single "hare" balloon flies off, followed minutes later by the other balloons, or "hounds." The hound balloon that lands closest to the hare wins.

Both gas and hot-air balloons are used in competition. Modern hot-air balloons that carry propane burners to heat the air have been widely used since the early 1960's. Several hot-air balloons that rely on the heat of the sun have also been developed.

Sport balloons vary in size. The smallest are flown by a pilot dangling in a harness beneath the balloon. The average sport balloon can carry three people.

To inflate a typical hot-air balloon, the ground crew assembles the gondola, lays the balloon (a huge nylon bag) flat on the ground, and attaches the gondola to it. A fan is directed into the mouth of the balloon until the balloon is almost half filled with cold air. Then a propane burner is lighted, and the flame is directed into the mouth of the balloon to heat the cold air. As the air in the balloon is heated, the balloon begins to drift upward. The ground crew lets the balloon rise slowly until it has reached the necessary height. The gondola is held on the ground until the pilot has finished a preflight inspection and is ready for takeoff.

The propane burners are carried at the mouth of the balloon, above the gondola. They enable the pilot to regulate the air temperature. In this way the pilot can control the altitude of the balloon—but nothing else. Balloons travel where the wind takes them. The pilot can do nothing except change the altitude of the balloon to take advantage of air currents blowing in different directions.

In the United States, both the balloon and the pilot must be licensed by the Federal Aviation Agency. You may obtain a student balloon license when you are 14 years old. A student balloonist may fly alone but may not carry passengers. When you are 16 years old, you may become a private balloon pilot. To earn the license, you must have ten hours of instruction in balloons, including one ascent to 3,000 feet (915 meters) and a solo flight. You must also pass a flight test and an examination on weather conditions and on federal aviation rules.

Balloon Federation of America

BALLOT. See ELECTIONS.
BALTIC SEA. See OCEANS AND SEAS OF THE WORLD.

BALTIMORE

Baltimore is the largest city in Maryland and one of the major ports of the United States. It lies on the banks of the Patapsco River near Chesapeake Bay, about 40 miles (65 kilometers) northeast of Washington, D.C. Baltimore is a center of industry, culture, education, and transportation. To visitors, it has the flavor of both an old southern city and a modern industrial community.

Through the years, manufacturing industries grew along with shipping and other port activities. Today the chief industries turn out steel and other metal products, chemicals, electronic equipment, and processed foods. Approximately 650,000 people live in the city.

Baltimore was chartered in 1729 and was named after the Lords Baltimore who founded the Maryland colony. The Continental Congress met in Baltimore during the Revolutionary War. The Cumberland Road brought prosperity to the city in the early 1800's. But when the Erie Canal opened in 1825, Baltimore was threatened with a loss of trade. The city met this threat by building the first railroad in the United States—the Baltimore and Ohio (B&O).

Many monuments and landmarks reflect the city's long and colorful history. The oldest U.S. warship still afloat, the wooden frigate *Constellation*, is anchored not far from where it was launched in 1797. During the War of 1812, Fort McHenry in the Baltimore harbor was heavily bombarded by the British fleet. This event inspired Francis Scott Key to write "The Star-Spangled Banner" (1814). Baltimore also contains such landmarks as the nation's first Roman Catholic cathedral and the home and burial place of writer Edgar Allan Poe.

For many years the city has been a leader in urban renewal. One of the most ambitious projects was the redevelopment of the Inner Harbor. A popular attraction of the Inner Harbor is the National Aquarium in Baltimore, where visitors can view many kinds of exotic plant and animal life.

Among the city's many universities is Johns Hopkins University, which has a world-famous school of medicine. Residents and visitors enjoy the city's symphony orchestra and opera company and the outstanding art collections at the Walters Art Gallery and the Baltimore Museum of Art. Sports fans cheer baseball's Orioles at Oriole Park at Camden Yards and watch horses run in the Preakness each spring at Pimlico Racetrack.

GEORGE BEISHLAG
Towson State University

Shops, restaurants, and commercial buildings line Baltimore's Inner Harbor, where many boats are anchored. At the far right is the National Aquarium in Baltimore.

BALZAC, HONORÉ DE (1799–1850)

The French writer Honoré de Balzac is known around the world for the novels and shorter works of fiction that he collected under the general title *La Comédie humaine (The Human Comedy)*. His ambition in this great work was to describe all of French society.

Balzac was born on May 20, 1799, in Tours, where his father was a civil servant. At the age of 8, he was sent to boarding school. He was an undisciplined child, and he was often sent to detention, or "kept in." He looked on this punishment as a blessing in disguise because it gave him all the time he wanted for reading. When his family moved to Paris in 1814, he went to school there.

For a while Balzac studied law, but he had no taste for legal work. He wanted to write plays, but his first play, *Cromwell* (1819), was a failure. He turned to writing sensational novels under various pen names. Realizing that he would never make his fortune this way, he went into business as a publisher and later as a printer. But he earned only debts.

In 1829, Balzac started the novels that made him famous. Some were fantastic, like *The Wild Ass's Skin* (1831). This novel tells how a young man acquires a magic piece of leather that grants his every wish but shrinks a little every time he uses it. He knows he will die when the leather has shrunk to nothing. Others were realistic, like *Eugénie Grandet* (1833), the story of a miser who loves his gold more than his daughter.

Balzac lived extravagantly, and he was always in debt. His many women friends inspired the sensitive portraits of women in his novels. Just before his death, he married a Polish countess, Eveline Hanska.

Balzac worked as intensely as he lived. By writing as much as 16 hours a day, he published over 80 titles between 1829 and 1847. This great labor brought on a serious illness before he was able to complete *The Human Comedy*. But when he died in Paris on August 18, 1850, he left a vivid record of his time.

F. W. J. HEMMINGS
Author, *Balzac: An Interpretation of La Comédie humaine*

BAMBOO. See GRASSES.

BANANA

The banana is a tropical fruit. People used it as a food even before history began to be written. The armies of Alexander the Great found bananas growing in India in 327 B.C. No doubt they grew there long before that time. Because of an old story that the sages of India rested in the shade of the plant and ate its fruit, the banana is often called the "fruit of the wise men."

Plant scientists believe that roots of banana plants were carried to the east coast of Africa by a people who moved there in ancient times. From there the banana plant was carried across the African continent to the Guinea Coast by early Arab traders.

When Portuguese explorers discovered the Guinea Coast of Africa in 1482, they found bananas growing there. These explorers took roots of the plant, and its African name, banana, to the Portuguese colonies in the Canary Islands. The next step in the journey of the banana plant was across the Atlantic Ocean to the New World. In 1516, only a few years after Columbus' famous voyages of discovery, a Spanish missionary brought this useful plant to the Caribbean island of Hispaniola. Other missionaries followed his example and planted bananas on the other islands of the Caribbean and on the tropical mainland. Thus, the banana plant had to go more than halfway around the world to reach Central America, where so many of the world's bananas are grown today.

It was not until the latter part of the 19th century that bananas were brought into the United States in quantities for sale in stores. Before that time, very few Americans other than those who had traveled in tropical countries had ever seen or tasted a banana. Even after banana schooners began entering New Orleans, Boston, and other ports, only people who lived in or near the port cities were able to eat bananas. The banana is perishable. Unlike some other fruits, it cannot be stored. Within a period of ten to twenty days, bananas must be harvested, shipped several thousand kilometers, ripened, and sent to the stores where they are sold. Today's modern transportation —fast, refrigerated ships, trains, and trucks— makes it possible for families in Chicago, in the United States, or Calgary, in Canada, to eat bananas every day of the year.

▶ THE BANANA PLANT AND ITS GROWTH

The banana plant is often called a tree. But it is not a real tree because there is no wood in the stem that rises above the ground. The stem is made up of leaves growing very close together, one inside the other. The leaves that spread out at the top of the stem usually are from 2.5 to 3.5 meters (8 to 12 feet) long and more than 0.5 meters (about 2 feet) wide. These leaves spread out and rise in the air, making the banana plant look like a palm tree. When the plant is old enough to bear fruit, it is from 4.5 to 9 meters (15 to 30 feet) tall.

Bananas grow in bunches. Each bunch consists of 9 to 16 clusters of fruit, called "hands," and each hand contains from 12 to 20 separate bananas, called "fingers." A bunch of bananas usually weighs from 25 to 45 kilograms (55 to 100 pounds).

The size of the plant and the size of the bunch of fruit depend on the climate and the kind of soil in which the plant grows. Bananas grow best where the soil is deep and rich and the climate is warm and moist. They cannot be grown satisfactorily in any place where temperatures fall below 13°C (55°F). For good fruit, the temperature should not go below 21°C (70°F) for any length of time.

Bananas grow in all the moist, tropical areas of the world. Most of the bananas sold in North America and Europe are grown in Central America, northern South America, tropical Africa, and the Caribbean islands. Bananas are grown in Taiwan and the Philippines for sale in Japan. In other tropical areas, bananas are grown mainly for local use.

To grow new banana plants, pieces of rootstock (bits cut from the base of growing plants) are planted in holes about 3 meters (10 feet) apart. Each piece of rootstock must have one or more sprouts, or "eyes," like the eyes of a potato. Green shoots appear above the ground three or four weeks later. Only the strongest shoot is allowed to become a plant. This plant forms its own rootstock, from which other plants continue to grow. Careful pruning

Bananas grow well in tropical Costa Rica. This bunch will be cut while still green and sent to far-off markets.

ensures that one strong, fruit-producing plant follows another.

Banana plants need care and attention to produce fruit of good quality. They must be provided with water by irrigation if the normal rainfall does not supply at least 250 centimeters (100 inches) per year. The leaves must be sprayed to prevent damage by insects and diseases. The area around the plants must be kept free of weeds and grass. The plants must be fertilized with nitrogen and potash. On a large plantation, many workers are required to care for the plants and harvest the fruit.

About eight to ten months after planting, a flower appears on the banana plant. This flower is at the end of a long stalk, which grows from the base up through the center of the stem and turns downward when it emerges from the top. Small bananas form on this flower stalk as it grows downward. Bananas really grow upside down. As the small bananas form on the stalk, they point downward, but as they grow they turn and point upward. In three months they are plump and ready to harvest. Bananas are harvested while they are still green. Even when they are to be eaten where they are grown, they are not allowed to ripen on the plant. A banana that turns yellow on the plant loses its flavor. Also, the peel bursts open and insects get into the fruit. The finest flavor develops only when the fruit is cut while green and ripened afterward. The bananas sold in stores in the United States, Canada, and Europe are shipped there under refrigeration while still green. They are then ripened in special rooms where cool tempera-tures of 16 to 21°C (60 to 70°F) and moist air combine to allow the best-tasting fruit to be developed.

Each banana plant bears only one bunch of fruit. When the bunch is harvested, the plant is cut down. But as the plant has been growing to maturity and producing fruit, another plant has been growing beside it from the same rootstock. Soon this plant's fruit will be ready to harvest. This cycle of production will continue for years, if the plants are not destroyed by diseases, high winds, or floods.

NORWOOD C. THORNTON
Formerly, United Fruit Company

BANDS AND BAND MUSIC

Everyone loves a band. No football game, parade, circus, or Fourth of July celebration would be quite complete without a rousing march. Not only does everyone love to hear a band, but almost everyone loves to play in one. In the United States alone there are millions of people who play in bands now or who have played in school, college, or town bands.

The word **band** is a broad term that describes a group of musicians performing on wind and percussion instruments. One thinks immediately of a brightly uniformed marching band, perhaps part of an army or navy unit or the band of a college or high school.

Aside from marching bands and bands that entertain at fairs, public ceremonies, and informal social gatherings, there are other bands that exist only to perform music in a concert, just as an orchestra does. Such bands are known as concert or symphonic bands, or wind ensembles. What all bands have in common is that they are composed of wind and percussion instruments in various combinations. Bands usually have at least 50 players.

Since bands often perform out-of-doors, they require instruments whose sounds carry easily. Trumpets, trombones, tubas, horns, drums—all are instruments capable of making plenty of noise with little effort on the part of the player. The large family of woodwinds, including clarinets, oboes, bassoons, and flutes (and their relatives, bass clarinets, English horns, saxophones, and piccolos), also has this advantage.

A second requirement is that the instruments be easy to carry. It is impossible to march while playing a cello or a double bass; even the violin is not easy to play while one is walking. But one can easily play brass and woodwind instruments while marching. And of course the band has always required instruments that create the proper military excitement. For this the brass and percussion instruments are perfect.

There is a special type of band called a brass band. As its name implies, it uses only brass instruments and no woodwinds. Many excellent Salvation Army bands are of this type. They usually have 24 players and produce a good, well-blended sound despite their limits of tone quality and range.

A fife and drum band from Newport, Rhode Island.

Bands of some sort have existed almost from biblical times. Armies have always marched to the beat of drums, and soldiers have always taken their signals from the sounds of a trumpet or bugle of some sort. Little groups of wind-instrument players have sounded the hours of the day. (In 16th-century Germany the players assembled on the tower of the town's tallest building for this.) Bands have added to the beauty and impressiveness of church services and accompanied all kinds of outdoor public ceremonies.

Until the middle of the 18th century, however, there were practically no regularly organized bands. The combination of instruments used for any occasion was determined by whatever instruments were available in the town and whatever players were free at the moment and could be assembled for the occasion. New instruments were being invented (the clarinet, for instance, appeared around 1700) and old ones improved. Great excitement was created in Europe when, around 1750, a whole family of new percussion instruments was introduced by traveling bands from Turkey. Composers were soon busy writing "Turkish music," with parts for tambourines, cymbals, triangles, bass drums, and other clanging and beating instruments.

In 1763 King Frederick the Great of Prussia was the first to regulate the kinds and number of instruments used in his bands. He ordered that all of his military bands have at least two oboes, two clarinets, two horns, and two bassoons. To this basic group other instruments, including flute, trumpet, and drum, were gradually added. By the end of the 18th century, the bands were playing regularly not only for military parades but also for special court functions and popular outdoor concerts.

► BEGINNINGS OF THE MODERN BAND

The modern band was born in the year 1789 as a result of the French Revolution. In that year Bernard Sarrette (1765–1858) founded the Band of the National Guard in Paris. This group of 45 players was immediately in demand for the popular demonstrations and numerous public ceremonies of the new government. By 1790 this band had 70 players and led to the formation of many military and town bands throughout Europe.

Many of the leading composers of the time served as bandmasters and wrote pieces for their bands. François Joseph Gossec (1734–1829) served for a time as bandmaster of the National Guard Band, with Charles Simon Catel (1773–1830) as his assistant. Their symphonies and overtures are still played by bands today. Others who composed for band included Luigi Cherubini (1760–1842), Ferdinando Paër (1771–1839), Etienne Mehul (1763–1817), and even the great composer Ludwig van Beethoven (1770–1827). The French band tradition reached its highest point in the great *Funeral and Triumphal Symphony* of Hector Berlioz (1803–69). It was written for a band of 208 players for the dedication of the Bastille Column in 1840.

► WILHELM WIEPRECHT (1802–72)

Wilhelm Wieprecht was chiefly responsible for organizing the band as we know it today. A forward-looking musician, he experimented with mechanical improvements for the instruments. It was through his example that the use of horns and trumpets with valves, or keys, became universally accepted. It was then possible to play these instruments in more difficult kinds of music, and a greater variety of sound in band music resulted. This and the work of Adolphe Sax (inventor of the saxophone) and Theobald Boehm (who developed the modern flute) contributed to the development of the modern band and its music.

Wieprecht was responsible for the first of the massed-band festivals and band contests, forerunners of today's school and college band festivals. In 1838 he organized a grand festival in which over 1,000 players plus 200 extra side drummers performed. The occasion was the visit of the Russian Emperor Nicholas to the King of Prussia. What a royal welcome it must have been!

By the middle of the 19th century, bands in Europe had become an important part of every country's musical as well as military life. Among the most famous bands in England were the band of the Royal Horse Guards and the band of the Grenadier Guards led by Sir Daniel Godfrey (1831–1903). Godfrey was probably the best-known bandmaster of his time. His many arrangements for band are still performed in England and America.

BANDS IN THE UNITED STATES

The development of bands and band music in the United States is one of the most colorful stories in American history. The earliest American bands were based on British models, and even before the American Revolution there is record of a band led by Josiah Flagg, of Boston. He was one of the first organizers of concerts in the American colonies. It is an interesting fact that Flagg's *Collection of the Best Psalm Tunes* was engraved by Paul Revere.

Although there is little historical record of bands in America before 1800, we know there was a wealth of band music composed in Revolutionary times and shortly thereafter. People, then, must have enjoyed band concerts and employed small bands for military purposes and public celebrations. Every American schoolchild knows the famous painting *The Spirit of '76.*

Marches were composed to celebrate patriotic occasions. The *Federal March* of Alexander Reinagle, performed in 1788, was written for the Fourth of July procession in Philadelphia celebrating the ratification of the United States Constitution. There were also many marches written in honor of the country's leading citizens and military heroes, such as *General Washington's Grand March* and *Jefferson's March.* During this period almost every town had its local band, attached to the town's militia.

PATRICK SARSFIELD GILMORE (1829–92)

Patrick S. Gilmore, born in County Galway, Ireland, in 1829, arrived in the United States at the age of 19. He was a man of enormous energy and vivid imagination and a born showman. In 1859 he took over the Boston Brigade Band, clad the players in bright new uniforms, rehearsed them over and over, and began an enormous schedule of performances. His band played for concerts, parades, and public ceremonies of all kinds. Also, as was the custom then, he provided dance music for balls and other events.

During the Civil War Gilmore conceived the idea of a huge band festival. With the help of the Army, he organized a Grand National Band consisting of 500 Army bandsmen plus a number of additional drum and bugle players. They were accompanied by a chorus of 5,000 schoolchildren. As a crowning touch Gilmore added 36 cannons, firing them by pushing hidden electric buttons. The great event took place in New Orleans on March 4, 1864.

Spectacular as this event was, it was only a hint of greater things to come. Returning to Boston after the war, Gilmore began to work on his next celebration, the National Peace Jubilee, given in 1869. This time he used an orchestra of 500, a band of 1,000, a chorus of 10,000, two batteries of cannons, and 100 firemen with hammers and anvils. The Jubilee lasted 5 days.

But Gilmore had even grander ideas. For 10 days, in 1872, he presented a World Peace Jubilee. His performers included an orchestra of 1,000, a band of 2,000, a chorus of 20,000, cannons, anvils, organ, and bells.

In 1873 Gilmore moved to New York, where he became leader of the 22nd Regiment Band. This became known as Gilmore's Band. He made several tours with the band in the United States, Canada, and Europe. He died in 1892.

JOHN PHILIP SOUSA (1854–1932)

John Philip Sousa was perhaps the greatest bandsman who ever lived. Trained as a violinist, he was only 24 years old when he was asked to take over the United States Marine Band. During Sousa's 12 years as director of the Marine Band, it achieved a national reputation for brilliance of performance that it retains to this day.

In 1892 Sousa left the Marine Band and formed a band of his own. He then toured extensively throughout the United States, Canada, and Europe. Sousa's band was probably the greatest band in the history of America. Its members included the leading virtuoso players of the day. His band had something that no band before him had and that every band since his has depended upon: Sousa's own marches. Brilliant in sound, rousing in spirit, and absolutely perfect for a band, they still form the backbone of band music everywhere. In fact, when most people think of band music, it is the sound of a Sousa march that they usually have in mind. Sousa wrote about 140 marches, including the famous *Stars and Stripes Forever, The Washington Post,* and *El Capitan.*

The United States Marine Band at Washington, D.C.

▶ EDWIN FRANKO GOLDMAN (1878–1956)

In the 20th century the nature of the band changed. The great touring bands of Sousa's time disappeared. Movies, television, and radio took the place of the old-time touring band that gave concerts wherever it went.

There is, however, no lack of popularity for the concert band, the kind that does not go on tours. The leading band of this type in the United States is the Goldman Band, founded in 1911 by Edwin Franko Goldman. Trained as a trumpet player, Goldman was for 10 years a member of the Metropolitan Opera Orchestra, in New York City. While he was playing there, he conceived the idea of forming a permanent concert band. By 1918 he was giving a regular series of outdoor summer band concerts; his players were among the leading musicians of the day. The summer concerts he started have become a tradition in the musical life of New York. They are now given under the direction of his son, Richard Franko Goldman.

Edwin Franko Goldman was the first bandmaster to encourage leading composers of the day to compose original works for band. It is through his efforts that today we are able to hear a large variety of music composed especially for bands.

RICHARD FRANKO GOLDMAN

See also PERCUSSION INSTRUMENTS; WIND INSTRUMENTS.

The Band of the Canadian Guards at Ottawa, Ontario.

Left: Tourists take in a view of the Bow River and the surrounding area from atop Sulphur Mountain in Banff National Park in Alberta. Banff is Canada's oldest national park.

Below: Banff National Park features spectacular mountains, emerald green forests, and glacial lakes. Boating on Moraine Lake is just one of the many ways to enjoy the scenery.

BANFF NATIONAL PARK

Banff National Park in Alberta is the oldest and one of the largest of Canada's national parks. Engineers were surveying a route for the Canadian Pacific Railway in 1883 when they discovered hot springs on the eastern slopes of the Rocky Mountains, at the spot where the town of Banff now stands. When the discovery of these springs amid the beautiful snowcapped peaks became known, the Canadian government decided to preserve the mountain scenery and wildlife of the area as a public park. In 1887 an area around Banff was set aside as Rocky Mountains National Park. Later it was renamed Banff National Park. The area has been expanded over the years; it now covers more than 2,500 square miles (6,500 square kilometers).

Through the deep valleys of Banff National Park, between such famous mountains as Castle, Rundle, and Temple, glacier-fed streams flow into crystal-clear lakes. The main river is the Bow, which runs southeastward through most of the park. The most famous lake is Louise, renowned for its magnificent natural setting. The towns of Banff and Lake Louise are two world-famous resorts located in this park. People come long distances to enjoy such sports as skiing and tobogganing in winter and hiking, golf, and mountain climbing in summer. Banff's popular swimming pool uses water from the hot springs at the foot of Sulphur Mountain. Because wild animals are protected from hunters, tourists may get to see moose, elk, mountain sheep, and bears close by the highways.

Lake Louise is on the main Canadian Pacific Railway line at the east end of Kicking Horse Pass. Banff is also on the Canadian Pacific Railway and on the Trans-Canada Highway as well.

The Banff Center, now a part of the University of Calgary, was established at Banff in 1933 as a summer school to teach subjects connected with the theater. Since then it has grown tremendously. It offers courses in drama, ballet, opera, creative writing, and fine arts. Every summer students come from many countries to attend this unusual school.

JOHN S. MOIR
University of Toronto

BANGKOK (KRUNG THEP)

Bangkok is the capital, largest city, and cultural center of Thailand and a leading city of Southeast Asia. It lies on the Chao Phraya River, near the Gulf of Thailand.

The Thais call their capital Krung Thep ("city of angels"), a short form of the name Rama I, the first Chakri king, gave his new capital. The Chakri dynasty is Thailand's royal family.

Bangkok is famous for its beautiful Buddhist temples. Today the glittering spires of hundreds of temples rise on the skyline beside modern skyscrapers. The population of Bangkok's metropolitan area, which includes Thon Buri, is approximately 5.9 million.

The City. Bangkok is an exciting place to live in or visit. The city has not one but many centers that developed as the city grew. In the oldest part of the city is the walled Grand Palace. It contains the famous Temple of the Emerald Buddha, which houses a statue of the Buddha that is sacred to the Buddhists of Thailand. Across the river is another landmark, the Temple of the Dawn.

Near the Grand Palace are many large government buildings, theaters, museums, and Silpakorn and Thammasat universities. To the north is the palace where the present king

Buddhists light incense and pray among the glittering spires at Bangkok's Grand Palace, a complex of buildings that is almost a small city itself.

lives. To the south, Thai merchants and artisans of Chinese ancestry own small shops.

People once moved about Bangkok mainly by boat. As the city spread outward from the riverbanks, canals—many of which have since been filled in and paved—were built to provide transportation links to the river. These canals caused Bangkok to be called the Venice of the East. Streets on land were often only narrow lanes for walking.

Economic Activity. Bangkok is Thailand's center of industry and banking, its busiest port, and a hub of international air and railroad transportation. Factories turn out a variety of goods, including processed foods, lumber, and metal and electrical goods. Tourism is also important to the economy.

History. The modern city of Bangkok was founded in 1782 when Rama I, who reigned from 1782 to 1809, moved the capital from Thon Buri (now part of Greater Bangkok) across the river to the east bank. Much modernization occurred during Rama IV's reign, from 1851 to 1868, as experts helped him modernize the government and opened Bangkok to foreign trade. Increased trade relations and treaties with foreign countries continued with his son, Rama V.

The city has grown rapidly, especially since World War II. In 1998 Thailand hosted the 13th Asian Games in Bangkok, for which many new roads and sports facilities were constructed. An elevated electric railway in the city center began service in 1999.

In 2000, experts warned that the city was rapidly sinking a few inches per year. During monsoon season, the Chao Phraya River rises as the ocean levels rise. Unregulated construction and the paving over of most canals have caused many blocked drainage systems.

JAMES BASCHE
Author, *Thailand: Land of the Free*

BANGLADESH

Bangladesh is a small nation in South Asia that is largely surrounded by its giant neighbor, India. It is one of the world's poorest and most heavily populated countries, with a population of 129 million within 55,598 square miles (143,999 square kilometers). Formerly known as East Pakistan, Bangladesh declared its independence from Pakistan following a civil war in 1971.

▶ PEOPLE

Bangladesh means "Land of Bengalis," and most of the people are Bengalis who are related to the Bengalis of neighboring India. The largest minority groups are the Biharis, who emigrated from India, and the tribal people of the Chittagong Hills.

Language. Bengali (or Bangla) is the official language. It has two main dialects: Sadhubhasa, a more traditional and literary style, and Chaltibhasa, which is more conversational. English is also spoken among the educated.

Religion. Most of the people in Bangladesh are Muslims. There are also many Hindus and a smaller percentage of Buddhists and Christians.

Education. Every village has one or more local schools. Although attendance is not mandatory, the government provides free ed-

Most people in Bangladesh live in elevated thatched huts or prefabricated buildings that are located along roads, rivers, or canals. Rivers and canals are the chief means of transportation.

The long, colorful garments worn by many women in Bangladesh are called saris.

ucation for the first five years. Bangladesh has three major universities: Chittagong University, the University of Rajshahi, and the University of Dhaka.

Way of Life. Most people in Bangladesh live in elevated thatched huts or prefabricated buildings in villages located along rivers, canals, or roads. Their diet usually consists of rice and fish with some vegetables. Because clean drinking water is not always available, many people become ill from waterborne diseases.

Men traditionally wear the lungi, an ankle-length piece of cloth that is wrapped around the waist and often tucked up to the knees. More educated men often wear European-style clothing. Women frequently wear saris— long, colorful garments draped around the body from the shoulder to the ankles. Traditionally, Muslim women cover their faces, especially around strangers.

▶ LAND

Bangladesh, a land of low plains criss-crossed by rivers, is slightly smaller than Wisconsin. To the southeast is a higher region called the Chittagong Hills. Here, the highest point is Keokradong, with an elevation of 4,035 feet (1,230 meters). This hill country, the home of the tribal people, is covered with dense tropical forest.

Rivers. The most important rivers are the Brahmaputra (or Jamuna) and the Ganges (or Padma). These rivers enter from the north and, with their tributaries, flow into the Bay of Bengal.

Climate. Bangladesh is a tropical country. The average temperatures range from over 60°F (16°C) to over 90°F (32°C). It is also a land of torrential monsoon rains, which fall from June to October. In addition, violent storms called cyclones (or typhoons) regularly bring heavy flooding to the region, causing many deaths and widespread devastation. Since Bangladesh's independence, cyclones have killed hundreds of thousands of people and left many millions more homeless.

Natural Resources. Aside from natural gas, Bangladesh has few useful mineral resources. It has deposits of coal, but they are difficult to mine. Other resources include its vast tracts of timber and fertile land.

Rice, a staple of the diet in Bangladesh, is usually grown in flooded fields.

▶ ECONOMY

Since the 1980's the government has gradually liberalized the economy by making some public businesses private, lowering tariffs, and attracting foreign investment. Although economic growth was strong during the 1990's, Bangladesh is still a very poor nation. Its economy remains primarily agricultural.

Manufacturing. Until recently, the export of jute (a plant fiber used for burlap, sacking, and twine) was the country's chief source of income. Since the 1990's, clothing has replaced jute as the leading export. The garment industry has grown rapidly because there are many people willing to work long hours for very low wages. Other manufactures include textiles, paper, cement, fertilizer, and sugar.

Agriculture. The main food crop is rice. In 2000, its production finally exceeded population increases, and Bangladesh achieved self-sufficiency in that area. Tea is the second most important cash crop. Other crops include sugarcane, wheat, mangoes, coconuts, pineapples, potatoes, spices, and oilseeds, from which cooking oil is derived. Livestock is also raised.

Transportation. Rivers and canals are the chief means of transportation, although there are paved highways and a rail system. In addition, there is an international airport in

Pedicabs and other vehicles crowd the busy streets of Dhaka, the capital of Bangladesh and an educational and cultural center.

Dhaka and many smaller airports in other locations. Major ports are located in Chittagong, Dhaka, and Mongla (Chalna) Port.

▶ **MAJOR CITIES**

There are fewer than a dozen major urban centers in Bangladesh. The most important of these is Dhaka, the capital and largest city, with a population of 3.6 million. Formerly the capital of East Pakistan, the city has many historic buildings and is an educational and cultural center. It is also the nation's chief industrial area. Chittagong is a major industrial and rail center as well.

▶ **GOVERNMENT**

The constitution of Bangladesh, adopted in 1972 and revised several times, provides for a 330–member parliament. Its executive branch includes a president; prime minister, who is head of government; and cabinet of ministers. There are two main political parties, the Awami League and the Bangladesh Nationalist Party (BNP), and a number of others. A civil court system is based on the British model.

▶ **HISTORY**

Bangladesh was once part of the larger Bengal region of eastern India. Over many centuries, this area was ruled by successive groups of invaders—the Turks, the Moguls, and, finally, the British. In 1947, India gained its independence from Britain, and East Bengal (now Bangladesh) became part of Pakistan. This new nation was created because the Muslim League demanded an independent and separate nation for the parts of the former British Indian Empire where the Muslims were a majority.

Pakistan was born with built-in flaws. It originally consisted of two parts, East Pakistan and West Pakistan, which were separated by India and were about 1,000 miles (1,600 kilometers) apart. The people and cultures of these two parts were quite different, and problems began when groups from West Pakistan took control of East Pakistan. East Pakistanis claimed they were not receiving their share of political and economic power. Also, the government at first refused to accept Bengali as one of the national languages. Popularly elected local governments in the East were dismissed on charges of wanting to secede from Pakistan. Bengali leaders were imprisoned as traitors. There were frequent riots, and a long period of military rule (from 1958 to 1971) created dangerous tensions in the East.

The Birth of Bangladesh. The climax came with the elections of 1970. The Awami League, led by Sheikh Mujibur Rahman (Mujib), won most of the seats in the East Pakistani provincial legislature and a majority in the national legislature. The victory would have given him a decisive role in Pakistani politics. This situation was unacceptable to General Yahya Khan, the leader of the national government, and Zulfikar Ali Bhutto, the leader of the Pakistan People's Party, West Pakistan's majority party. They particularly objected to the Awami League's proposal for self-government in the eastern region. West Pakistani leaders believed this would lead to the breakup of Pakistan.

The two parts of Pakistan tried to form a plan to restore civilian rule and draft a new constitution. Their failure to do so set off riots in the East, which were brutally suppressed by the West Pakistani army. It is charged that millions of people lost their lives and hundreds of villages were destroyed. Some 10 million Bengalis fled to India. This placed a great economic burden on India. Incidents mounted until, in December 1971, India and Pakistan went to war. The war was swift. In less than two weeks, the Indian army, with the aid of the Bengali guerrillas from East Pakistan, compelled the Pakistani forces to surrender.

Sheikh Mujibur Rahman, who had been imprisoned in West Pakistan, was released. On January 10, 1972, he arrived in Bangladesh and became prime minister of the new nation. He later became its president.

Political Unrest. Bangladesh faced enormous problems. Millions of people had become refugees. The economy had been disrupted, and the country was torn by political quarrels. In 1975 the government was overthrown by army officers, and President Mujib was killed.

Bangladesh was governed under martial, or military, law by General Ziaur Rahman (known as Zia). In 1978, Zia was elected president. Martial law was lifted in 1979, and elections were held for the legislature. In 1981, Zia was killed in an attempted coup.

FACTS and figures

PEOPLE'S REPUBLIC OF BANGLADESH is the official name of the country.
LOCATION: South Asia.
AREA: 55,598 sq mi (143,999 km²).
POPULATION: 129,194,224 (estimate).
CAPITAL AND LARGEST CITY: Dhaka.
MAJOR LANGUAGES: Bengali, or Bangla (official), English.
MAJOR RELIGIOUS GROUP: Muslim.
GOVERNMENT: Republic. **Head of state**—president. **Head of government**—prime minister. **Legislature**—Jatiya Sangsad (National Assembly).
CHIEF PRODUCTS: Agricultural—jute, rice, tea, sugarcane, spices, potatoes, fruits, oilseeds, wheat, livestock. **Manufactured**—clothing, jute products, textiles, refined sugar, leather goods, cement, ceramics, fertilizer, paper. **Mineral**—natural gas.
MONETARY UNIT: Taka (1 taka = 100 poisha).

Recent History. In 1982, General Hussain Mohammed Ershad seized power and reimposed martial law until 1986, when he was elected president. His opponents, charging widespread fraud, had refused to take part in the elections. Elections held in 1988 were also boycotted by the opposition. Political protests forced Ershad to resign in 1990. In elections held in 1991, the Bangladesh Nationalist Party won the largest number of seats, and Khaleda Zia, party leader and widow of the former president, became prime minister.

In 1994, continuing political unrest forced Zia to step down until new elections were held in 1996. Her party won because the opposing Awami League refused to take part, charging fraud. Widespread demonstrations forced new elections that same year, which the Awami League won. Hasina Wazed, daughter of the late President Mujib, was named prime minister. But in the 2001 election, Zia was returned to power by an impressive majority of votes, having campaigned against corruption and lawlessness.

JOHN ECHEVERRI-GENT
Department of Government and Foreign Affairs
University of Virginia

See also INDIA; PAKISTAN.

BANGOR. See MAINE (Cities).

BANJO. See STRINGED INSTRUMENTS.

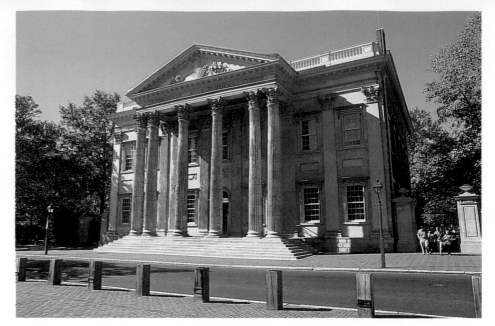

The Bank of the United States, which received its charter in 1791, was the country's first federal bank. In 1797 it moved into this building, which is considered to be the oldest U.S. bank building. The bank stayed in business only until 1811 when its charter expired, but the building still stands on South Third Street in Philadelphia.

BANKS AND BANKING

What can you do when you have money that you do not want to spend, or carry around, or keep at home? You could deposit the money at a bank in a checking or savings account. On the other hand, if you didn't have enough money to meet your needs, you could ask a bank to lend you money. By providing these two functions—holding money and lending money—banks play a very important role in the United States economy. They make the money in bank accounts available to people who need to borrow money.

When you deposit money in a bank as savings, you also earn interest. The interest is a fee paid to you for the use of your money. Suppose, for example, that you deposit $100 in a bank offering an interest rate of 5 percent on savings. At the end of one year the amount of money in your account would be $100 plus the additional interest.

Money deposited in a bank as savings is loaned to borrowers at a higher interest rate than is paid to savers. For example, a bank that pays 5 percent interest on savings may charge 10 percent interest on the money when it is loaned to borrowers. The interest the bank receives is income for the bank. It is used to pay interest to depositors, as well as to pay for the salaries of bank employees, and for equipment, supplies, and other costs of operating the bank.

Banks are owned by stockholders who have invested money in the bank. Part of a bank's total assets are the funds invested by these stockholders. But most of a bank's assets come from money that people have deposited and from interest paid on loans.

▶ HISTORY OF BANKING

Banking activities are almost as old as the earliest civilizations. The earliest bankers were moneychangers or moneylenders. These people had strongboxes in which to keep money, and people left money with them for safekeeping or borrowed money from them in exchange for a fee. As early as A.D. 534 the ancient Romans had laws and regulations concerning moneylending and banking activities.

Today most banks have safe-deposit boxes in their vaults, which customers may rent and use to store important papers and other valuable items.

Modern banking is generally thought to have begun in Italy during the late 1500's. In fact, the word "bank" comes from the Italian word *banco*, which means bench. The term became associated with banking because many early Italian bankers conducted their business from benches in the street.

In England during the 1600's it became common practice for people to give their gold and silver to local goldsmiths for safekeeping. These goldsmiths, who made jewelry and other items, had strong vaults in which they kept precious metals. It was only natural that people who did not have safe places for their valuables would want to keep their gold and silver in these vaults. The goldsmiths issued paper receipts, or notes, to the people who left precious metals with them. Eventually, people began to use these paper notes as money; the goldsmiths became bankers.

As trade flourished in Europe in the 1600's and 1700's banking became so important that commercial banks were set up. These commercial banks were privately owned, and their chief business was to help merchants finance trading activities. They accepted deposits of money, made loans, collected bills, and acted as places of exchange in which money from one country could be converted into the money of another country.

Banking in the United States

The first banks established in the United States were state banks. In 1781, the Bank of North America, the first bank to receive a charter, or license to operate, was organized in Philadelphia. Other states soon issued charters to banks of their own. The first national bank, the Bank of the United States, was established in 1791 and had branches in several cities.

During the late 1700's and early 1800's many state banks in the United States followed unsound banking practices. They issued far too many loans in the form of paper bank notes (paper money). The Bank of the United States had the authority to control the amount of paper money issued by the state banks, but in 1811 its charter expired and the Bank of the United States no longer had any control.

Increasing numbers of people became concerned about the value of their paper notes and asked state banks to exchange the notes for gold and silver coin (called **specie**). Many

banks, however, did not have enough precious metals to back the notes and they stopped exchanging gold and silver for paper notes. As a result, the notes quickly lost their value. This dangerous financial situation led to the failure of many banks. When the banks failed, depositors lost their life savings.

The National Bank Act of 1863, which was amended in 1864, created a national banking system in the United States. Under the provisions of this system, the state banks were driven out of the business of issuing paper notes. The national banks were allowed to continue issuing bank notes until 1935. Federal laws then gave the power to issue paper notes solely to a centralized banking system called the Federal Reserve.

Bank tellers help customers with many different transactions, including making deposits to and withdrawals from their accounts and taking care of bills such as loan payments.

▶ THE AMERICAN BANKING SYSTEM

The banking system in the United States today is made up of many banks operating at different levels. All these banks, however, must operate under the jurisdiction and rules of the Federal Reserve System, the centerpiece of American banking.

The Federal Reserve System

The Federal Reserve System was established by Congress in 1913 in an effort to correct some serious problems that existed in American banking. Prior to the establishment of the Federal Reserve System, the United States experienced several severe financial panics during which many businesses failed and many banks were forced to close. The national banking system at the time was unable to deal with these crises. It was decided that major reforms were needed, and the Federal Reserve System was the result.

The Federal Reserve System—or the Fed, as it is commonly called—is made up of three levels of organization. The top level consists of the Board of Governors, the Federal Open-Market Committee, and the Federal Advisory Council. The Board of Governors is the most important of these three groups. It is the central policy-making body of the Federal Reserve System. It consists of seven members appointed by the president and confirmed by the Senate. Each member is appointed for a 14-year term and is ineligible for reappointment. The Board of Governors remains relatively independent of politics. Board decisions do not have to be approved by the president or Congress, and board members do not have to fear losing their jobs when a new president is elected.

The second level of the Federal Reserve System consists of the Federal Reserve Banks. The United States is divided into twelve districts, and there is a separate Federal Reserve Bank for each district. The twelve Federal Reserve Banks are located in Boston, New York, Philadelphia, Cleveland, Richmond, Atlanta, Chicago, St. Louis, Minneapolis, Kansas City, Dallas, and San Francisco. The activities of these Federal Reserve Banks are coordinated by the Board of Governors. The Federal Reserve Banks do not deal directly with the public. They are "bankers' banks" that deal only with other financial institutions and the government.

The third level of the Federal Reserve System consists of other financial institutions, including commercial banks, savings and loan associations, credit unions, and savings banks. These financial institutions utilize the services of the Federal Reserve System and are subject to reserve requirements established by the Fed. They perform the regular day-to-day business of banking in the nation.

The Federal Reserve System performs many important functions, the most important of which is controlling the nation's money supply. It also plays a major role in clearing checks. The Fed supervises member banks and serves as a depository for the money that banks are required to keep as reserves. The Fed is also responsible for supplying the nation's paper money in the form of Federal Reserve Notes.

Types of Banks

There are several different types of financial institutions in the United States that are commonly thought of as banks.

Commercial Banks. Commercial banks make up the largest banking group in the United States. At one time, commercial banks could easily be distinguished from other financial institutions by the fact that only they could

The Savings and Loan Crisis of the 1980's

Before the 1980's, savings and loan institutions were allowed to make loans only to individuals to buy houses. This changed in 1982 with the enactment of a deregulation act that changed the way the savings and loan industry operated. The deregulation of the industry led to one of the worst financial disasters since the Great Depression and was one of the worst scandals in American history.

As a result of deregulation, an estimated $250 billion of depositors' money was lost through poor management practices or, in some cases, fraud. Questionable construction projects — shopping centers in the desert, suburban developments with almost nobody to live in them, and unneeded high-rise office buildings

— were financed by the savings and loan industry. A massive building binge occurred, and buildings of all types were built, often on pure speculation; that is, on the chance that buyers would be found.

When developers could not sell these properties, they defaulted on (could not repay) their loans. Since the savings and loan institutions could not sell these properties either, many went bankrupt. The government took over these bankrupt institutions and the unneeded real estate became the property of the American taxpayers. Most of the property will probably be sold eventually at a fraction of its cost, and taxpayers will have to absorb an estimated loss of at least $250 billion.

Savings and loan associations, which have always offered loans to their customers for building or buying houses or for buying real estate, now provide many other types of loans and services, including checking accounts.

offer checking accounts. However, changes in the banking laws now allow other financial institutions to offer checking accounts as well.

Commercial banks can be established and operated only after being granted a charter by either the federal government or a state government. Commercial banks chartered by the federal government are called national banks. Those chartered by one of the states are called state banks. The primary functions of commercial banks are to receive deposits, make loans, and provide checking and other services to customers. Commercial banks primarily make short-term commercial loans to businesses and personal loans to individuals.

Savings and Loan Associations. Savings and loan associations are owned and operated by individuals who, as shareholders, elect a board of directors to manage the organization. Historically, savings and loan associations primarily made long-term loans—twenty years or longer—to individuals for the purpose of building homes or buying existing homes and other real estate. Today, however, savings and loan associations make many other types of loans as well. They also make checking account services available to depositors.

Savings Banks. Savings banks specialize in individual savings accounts. These banks may be owned by stockholders, although most function as **cooperatives**, or **mutuals**, and are owned by their depositors. Mutual savings banks originated in the United States in the early 1800's when commercial banks were not interested in handling the small savings deposits of wage earners. By pooling their savings in a mutual savings bank, wage earners with individual savings could find profitable investment opportunities for their money.

Credit Unions. Credit unions are cooperative nonprofit associations owned and operated by their members. They are often organized by the employees of large companies or the members of labor unions for the benefit of their membership. The primary purpose of credit unions is to offer high-interest savings accounts and low-interest loans to members.

Investment Banks. Investment banks specialize in distributing the **securities**, or stocks and bonds, of corporations to the public. Investment banks purchase newly issued stocks and bonds from companies and then resell these securities to individual investors in smaller quantities. Investment banks buy securities from a company at a particular price with the intention of reselling them at a higher price. The difference between the purchase price and the sale price is the investment bank's profit. Investment banks provide companies with the money they need without the companies having to wait for the general public to buy stock.

The World Bank. While some of the nation's major banks do business with foreign countries, there are a few specialized banks that deal exclusively in international finance. One of these, the International Bank for Reconstruction and Development (IBRD), more commonly known as the World Bank, officially began operating in 1944. The original purpose of the World Bank was to help finance the reconstruction of areas of the world damaged during World War II. Since that time, the World Bank has also assisted in the economic growth of underdeveloped countries by providing them with long-term loans. In 1956, the World Bank established the International

Bank customers often find themselves in long lines during their lunch hours or just before bank closings on Fridays. This is when many people deposit or cash paychecks, or make withdrawals for weekend trips.

Finance Corporation (IFC), the purpose of which is to stimulate private investments in developing countries. While the World Bank lends money only for public, or publicly sponsored, projects, the IFC helps to finance private enterprise.

Banking Services

Banks provide many services to the public and the government. But most of the regular business of a bank involves accepting deposits from savers and making money available to borrowers in the form of loans.

Time Deposits. In time deposits, money usually stays in an account for an extended period of time. Savings accounts are a type of time deposit. Most people who put money in a savings account plan to leave it there until it is needed—perhaps to buy a house, to pay for a child's education, or to use during retirement. Banks pay interest on the money deposited in a savings account, so the amount of money left in an account will gradually increase.

A person who deposits money in a savings account often receives a savings passbook. This passbook shows the amount of money in the deposit. When money is deposited or withdrawn from the account, the balance in the passbook will be updated. Periodically, the bank will add the interest that has been earned on the account to the balance.

People who have large amounts of money to deposit as savings often put the money in a special account called a **certificate of deposit (CD)**. An advantage of certificates of deposit is that they usually pay higher interest rates than passbook savings accounts. However, certificates of deposit are only payable at a definite date in the future, called the maturity date. This maturity date might range from 30 days to several years. If a person withdraws money from a certificate of deposit before the maturity date, he or she will have to pay a penalty in the form of lost interest.

Demand Deposits. Demand deposits are checking accounts, which allow individuals to deposit, withdraw, and transfer their money whenever they want. Checking accounts pro-

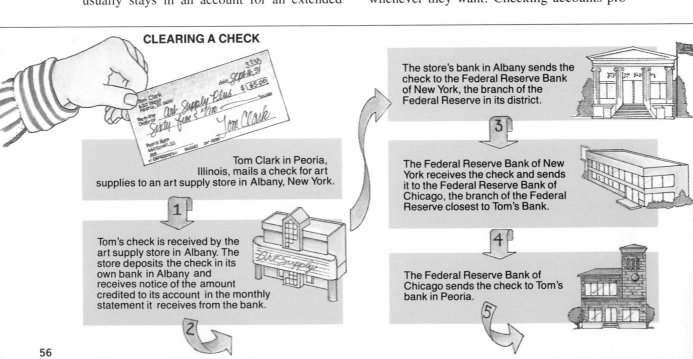

CLEARING A CHECK

Tom Clark in Peoria, Illinois, mails a check for art supplies to an art supply store in Albany, New York.

1 Tom's check is received by the art supply store in Albany. The store deposits the check in its own bank in Albany and receives notice of the amount credited to its account in the monthly statement it receives from the bank.

2 The store's bank in Albany sends the check to the Federal Reserve Bank of New York, the branch of the Federal Reserve in its district.

3 The Federal Reserve Bank of New York receives the check and sends it to the Federal Reserve Bank of Chicago, the branch of the Federal Reserve closest to Tom's Bank.

4 The Federal Reserve Bank of Chicago sends the check to Tom's bank in Peoria.

vide a convenient way for people to have access to their money without having to carry it around as cash. A person can write checks against a checking account at any time. These checks can be made payable to oneself to withdraw money, or they can be made payable to someone else to transfer money to that person. Banks sometimes pay interest on checking accounts, usually with the provision that a minimum amount of money be kept in the account at all times.

Each month banks send detailed statements to customers with checking accounts. These statements show how much money was deposited during the month, the number of checks written and the amount of each, and the current balance of the account. Enclosed with the statement will be the checks that were written, cashed, and returned to the bank during the month. These checks, for which money has been withdrawn from the checking account, are called cancelled checks. They can serve as receipts for any bills paid by check.

Loans. Banks make many types of loans to individuals or businesses. One major type of loan is a home mortgage loan, which is provided to people who want to buy or build a home. Home mortgage loans usually require repayment over a loan term, perhaps as long as twenty to thirty years. After the buyer pays a down payment on the home, the bank finances the balance of the cost. The buyer then pays off this amount, plus interest, in periodic (usually monthly) installments. On a large

Many banks post the rates they offer for making loans to customers for different items. Customers may compare the rates of different banks to find which one offers the best rate for their needs.

loan repaid over many years, the buyer will pay a large amount of interest as a part of each payment.

Banks make many short-term loans to both individuals and businesses. For example, a person might borrow $1,000 from a bank for a period of six months. The person signs a note promising to repay the money borrowed in addition to interest charged by the bank for the use of its money. Usually, the person must also offer something of value, such as an automobile, as security, or collateral. If the person fails to repay the loan, the bank can take possession of this collateral.

The rate of interest that banks charge depends on the type and length of the loan. The **prime rate** is the rate of interest that large city banks charge their best customers (large businesses that have excellent credit ratings). The rate of interest paid by the average borrower is usually higher than the prime rate.

Other Services. Banks also provide many other services to their customers. Most banks have safe-deposit boxes in their vaults, which they rent to customers for safekeeping of valuable possessions. Banks also provide financial advice to their customers, sell traveler's checks, and issue credit cards.

Financial experts in a bank's trust department provide a variety of services. They manage real estate and collect rents, invest money in stocks and bonds, sell securities, give advice on drawing up wills, and manage company pension and health-insurance plans. Money left to charities is often handled by the

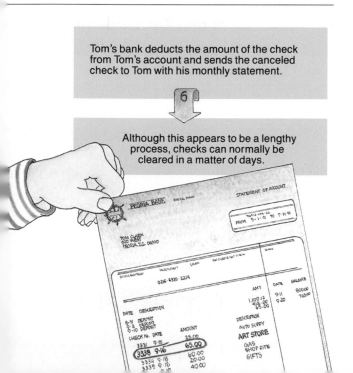

Tom's bank deducts the amount of the check from Tom's account and sends the canceled check to Tom with his monthly statement.

6

Although this appears to be a lengthy process, checks can normally be cleared in a matter of days.

trust departments of banks as well. Of course, the bank charges a fee for all of these services.

Many banks also offer bank credit cards to their customers. These credit cards enable people to buy items on credit by charging the items on their cards. The banks pay the merchants for the purchases and then bill the credit card holders, who make payments to their banks. The banks charge interest only on the amounts of the monthly bills that are not paid on time. Bank cards can also be used by customers to get cash advances from banks.

Many banks today have automatic teller machines (ATM's) that let customers have access to their accounts 24 hours a day. The bank customer inserts a special card into the machine and then enters a secret identification number. Once this is done, the customer has access to his or her bank account and can deposit, withdraw, and transfer money without the assistance of a bank employee.

Another service offered by many banks is electronic funds transfer (EFT). An electronic funds transfer system moves money into or out of a customer's account electronically. For example, some employees have their salaries electronically credited to their accounts, eliminating the need to cash or deposit paychecks. Electronic funds transfer speeds service to customers and also eliminates much of the paperwork involved in various banking services.

Safety of Bank Deposits

During the Great Depression of the 1930's many people lost their life savings when banks failed. In order to prevent that from happening again, government insurance funds were created. These insurance funds guaranteed that depositors would be paid the full amount of their deposits if a bank failed.

Prior to 1989, accounts in savings and loan associations were insured by the federal Savings and Loan Insurance Corporation (FSLIC), and accounts in commercial banks were insured by the Federal Deposit Insurance Corporation (FDIC). In the late 1980's, however, the failure of many savings and loan associations caused the bankruptcy of the FSLIC insurance fund. As a result, beginning in 1989, the FDIC became responsible for insuring accounts in both commercial banks and savings and loan associations.

To handle all these accounts, two separate insurance funds were established within the FDIC—the Banking Insurance Fund (BIF) and the Savings Association Insurance Fund (SAIF). The BIF insures deposits in commercial banks up to $100,000 per deposit. The

Above: By using automatic teller machines (ATM's), customers have quick and easy access to their accounts day or night. *Right:* Banks provide statements to their customers every month that show opening and closing balances, cancelled checks, and transactions such as deposits, withdrawals, and service charges.

SAIF insures deposits in savings and loan associations up to a total of $100,000. If a bank or savings and loan association has financial troubles and is unable to repay depositors, repayment will be made out of the insurance funds. Credit union deposits are also insured up to $100,000 by insurance funds.

▶ BANKING IN CANADA

Attempts to establish a Canadian bank go back to the late 1700's. But it was not until 1817 that the first bank in Canada was successfully launched. Early banks in Canada were established as private partnerships, by provincial law, or by royal charters obtained in England. However, by 1867 the federal government had assumed sole responsibility for the country's banking system.

Canada's central bank, the Bank of Canada, is the centerpiece of Canadian banking. It was founded in 1934 and nationalized in 1938. In addition, there are five large banks chartered under Canadian law, each of which has a nationwide network of branch banks.

The Bank of Canada is directed by law to regulate credit and currency in such a way as to promote the best interests of the Canadian economy. It carries out banking policies by changing rates of interest on loans, altering the amount of reserves that must be held by chartered banks to back up deposits, buying and selling securities, and responding to changes in foreign exchange rates. Canadian banks provide basically the same services as American banks. There are differences, however, in policy and in the services provided.

▶ CAREERS IN BANKING

Most of the people working in banks are either bank officers or clerical workers. Bank officers, depending on their rank, usually have some authority to make business decisions involving the bank. Bank officers might include positions such as president, vice president, and comptroller. Some, such as loan and trust officers, head specific departments.

Clerical workers in banks include secretaries, bank tellers, bookkeepers, and various other employees who do clerical work. These positions generally outnumber bank officers by a ratio of about six to one.

ALLEN SMITH
Professor of Economics
Eastern Illinois University

See also CREDIT CARDS; ECONOMICS; INFLATION AND DEFLATION; MONEY.

BANNEKER, BENJAMIN.   See WASHINGTON, D.C. (Famous People).
BANSHEES.   See FAIRIES.

BANTING, SIR FREDERICK GRANT (1891–1941)

Frederick Grant Banting, a Canadian doctor and scientist, was born on November 14, 1891, in Alliston, Ontario. He is remembered for his contribution to the control of diabetes, a serious disease in which the pancreas, a large gland near the stomach, produces too little insulin. Insulin is a chemical needed by the body to use and store sugar. Scientists knew that insulin from a healthy animal could help human patients, but no one—until Frederick Banting—knew how to obtain it.

Banting earned a medical degree at the University of Toronto and served with the Canadian Army Medical Corps in World War I (1914–18). After the war Banting returned to his medical practice and to teaching in London, Ontario. While preparing a lecture on the pancreas, he suddenly realized how he might obtain insulin. Working in the laboratory of Professor John J. R. Macleod at the University of Toronto, Banting set to work in May 1921. He was assisted by Charles H. Best, a young graduate student.

Within weeks Banting and Best obtained the first insulin from a dog pancreas. By January 1922, after many tests, they gave insulin to a diabetic, who immediately improved. Other patients also improved when given insulin. Another researcher, James B. Collip, perfected the method of preparing insulin.

In 1923, Banting and Macleod were awarded the Nobel Prize, which they shared with Best and Collip. The University of Toronto set up a new medical research institute named after Banting, and he was knighted in 1934. Banting was killed in an airplane crash in Newfoundland on February 21, 1941.

JOHN S. BOWMAN
Author and Science Editor

BARBADOS

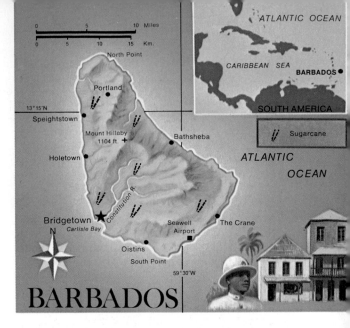

BARBADOS

Barbados is an island nation in the West Indies. Although it has been independent of Britain since 1966, there are many reminders of over 300 years of British rule. People play cricket, a British game, and take afternoon tea. Drivers use the left-hand side of the road, as the British do, and the hills are dotted with tiny cottages that remind one of Britain.

The People and Economy. Most of the people are descendants of slaves brought from Africa centuries ago. The rest are mainly of British origin. English is the official language but is spoken in a distinctive, lilting way. The people are known as Barbadians, though they often call themselves Bajans.

Barbados has a high standard of living compared to other developing countries; still, overpopulation is a major problem. The island's economy was once dominated by sugar and related industries, such as the production of rum and molasses. But Barbados' fine beaches and pleasant climate have made tourism the chief source of the country's income.

The Land. Barbados lies in the Atlantic Ocean but it is considered the easternmost of the islands of the Caribbean Sea. From its highest point—Mount Hillaby, 1,104 feet (336 meters)—the island slopes gently down to the sea. The Atlantic coast is rugged, with a high surf. The Caribbean coast has smooth, wide beaches and calm, blue waters. Bridgetown, the capital, is located on the Caribbean side of the island. The climate is warm, but the trade winds have a cooling effect on the temperature. Rainfall is abundant, especially in the north.

History and Government. Barbados was uninhabited when the Portuguese Pedro a Campos landed there in the early 1500's. He named the island Barbados, meaning "bearded," probably for the beardlike vines or moss that hung from the trees.

The British established the first permanent settlement in 1627. Slaves were imported to work on the tobacco, cotton, and sugarcane plantations, until slavery was abolished in the 1800's. Barbados gained self-government in 1961 and full independence in 1966.

Barbados recognizes the British monarch, represented by a governor-general, as the head of state. Real political authority, however, rests with the Barbadian Parliament. It is made up of the House of Assembly, elected by popular vote, and the Senate, whose members are appointed by the governor-general. The prime minister is chosen from the majority party in the House of Assembly.

BRANFORD M. TAITT
Former Consul General of Barbados

BARBAROSSA. See FREDERICK (Holy Roman Emperors: Frederick I).

FACTS and figures

BARBADOS is the official name of the country.

LOCATION: West Indies.

AREA: 166 sq mi (430 km²).

POPULATION: 259,000 (estimate).

CAPITAL AND LARGEST CITY: Bridgetown.

MAJOR LANGUAGE: English (official).

MAJOR RELIGIOUS GROUP: Christian (Protestant).

GOVERNMENT: Constitutional monarchy. **Head of state**—British monarch, represented by a governor-general. **Head of government**—prime minister. **Legislature**—Parliament (consisting of the House of Assembly and the Senate).

CHIEF PRODUCTS: Agricultural—sugarcane, sweet potatoes, corn, cassava, beans. **Manufactured**—sugar, rum, molasses, cotton clothing, pharmaceuticals.

MONETARY UNIT: Barbados dollar (1 dollar = 100 cents).

BARCELONA

Barcelona, situated on the Mediterranean Sea, is Spain's second largest city and chief port. With about 1.6 million people (nearly 5 million in the metropolitan area), it is exceeded in population only by Madrid, the national capital.

The City. As the capital and largest city of the autonomous region of Catalonia, Barcelona has long been at the center of Catalan history and culture. The older part of the city, which lies just above the harbor, dates from the 1100's. Its main thoroughfare is La Rambla, a handsome promenade lined with trees, flower stands, cafés, and bookstores. La Rambla leads past the Gothic Quarter, site of the medieval cathedral, and ends at the Plaza Catalonia, a hub of commercial activity. Barcelona's busy streets are filled with people traveling on mopeds (motorized bicycles). But the fastest way to travel around the inner city is by subway.

Northwest of the Plaza Catalonia is the famous church of the Sagrada Familia (Holy Family), designed by Antonio Gaudí in the late 1880's. Two other major modern artists, Pablo Picasso, who came to Barcelona as a

The Plaza Catalonia is a hub of commercial activity in Barcelona, Spain's second largest city and the capital of the autonomous region of Catalonia.

boy, and Joan Miró, who was born here, are celebrated with museums devoted to their works. The city is also a center of literary life. Among its institutions of higher education is the University of Barcelona, founded in 1450.

Economic Activity. Barcelona is Spain's chief shipping center and an important industrial city. It produces about 25 percent of Spain's manufactured goods, including motor vehicles and high-technology equipment. The city is also a major tourist destination.

History. Barcelona traces its origins to the Phoenicians and their successors, the Carthaginians, who founded the settlement of Barcino in the 200's B.C. The city was later ruled by Romans, Visigoths, Muslim Moors, and Franks, before an independent Catalan state was established under the counts of Barcelona in the A.D. 1000's.

In 1137, Catalonia was absorbed by the kingdom of Aragon, and Barcelona became a leading center of commerce on the Mediterranean. But its power declined when Aragon was incorporated into a united Spain in 1517.

Catalonia rebelled against Spain in 1640 and again in 1705. From 1808 to 1813, during the Napoleonic Wars, it was ruled by France. By the mid-1800's, the Catalan language and culture had almost disappeared, but an improved economy helped bring about a cultural rebirth and the dream of independence. A center of resistance to the Nationalists during the Spanish Civil War (1936–39), Barcelona suffered under the postwar government of General Francisco Franco. Catalonia's cultural aspirations revived when Franco died in 1975. Barcelona's selection as the site of the 1992 Summer Olympics was a symbol of the city's renewal.

ROBERT W. KERN
Editor, *Historical Dictionary of Modern Spain*

BARKLEY, ALBEN. See VICE PRESIDENCY OF THE UNITED STATES.

BARLEY

Barley is a cereal grain belonging to the grass family, which includes wheat, oats, rye, and rice. It is an important cereal grain because it is able to thrive in a variety of climates. From the Arctic to the Andes, from the Himalayas to Ethiopia, in climates that are too cold or too dry for other cereal grains, barley grows.

Barley was the first grain cultivated by people. Although wild barley was probably domesticated by several early civilizations, some of the earliest archeological evidence indicates that it was cultivated 10,000 years ago along the Euphrates River in what is now Syria. Cultivated barley seeds were carried from place to place and bred with other wild barley of the area to make the barley more suitable for growing in a specific region. By 5,000 years ago, barley was a staple crop in Ethiopia, Tibet, China, and India. Columbus introduced barley to the Americas on his first voyage there. Today, leading producers of barley are Russia, Canada, and the United States.

The Barley Plant. Barley is similar in appearance to other members of the grass family. Like all grasses, it flowers and produces seeds. Grain heads form at the top of stems. The plant usually reaches a height of about 30 inches (76 centimeters). Size, color, length, and stiffness of the head are just a few of the characteristics that vary among the many hundreds of varieties of cultivated barley that exist worldwide. But no matter what their special characteristics, all types of barley can be classified by the arrangement of the grains in the head. The most important commercial barleys are the two- and six-row types.

Growing and Harvesting Barley. Barley grows best in the world's temperate regions. It is well suited to a climate where the ripening period is long and cool, the soil is well drained, and the growing period has moderate rainfall and humidity. Different types of barley are grown depending on the altitude, climate, and whether the barley will be used for food, ground as grain, or to produce malt for brewing beer. Planting takes place in the spring and fall. Spring barley is usually planted in early spring and harvested in summer. Winter barley, which is planted in the fall, grows throughout the winter and is harvested the following spring.

Barley, originally a plant of arid lowlands in the Near and Middle East, is grown throughout the world in a wide variety of climates, often in places where other crops refuse to grow.

Diseases and pests can attack and damage barley as it grows, causing serious losses in crop production. A variety of methods are used to prevent damage. The main methods for controlling diseases are the planting of disease-resistant varieties and the use of fungicide seed treatment. Insect damage can be avoided by planting those varieties that are resistant to insects, varying the time of planting, introducing predators and parasites that feed on the insects, and using insecticides.

While some countries continue to harvest barley by hand, the fastest and most common method in the developed world is to harvest the dry, fully ripe grain with machines called combines. Sometimes barley is cut when it is less ripe, while the straw is still slightly green. Then the barley is cut and tied into bundles (shocks) or left in cut rows (windrows). The grain is allowed to dry and is threshed out later. This method is preferred when it is important to have undamaged kernels.

Uses of Barley. Most of the barley produced is used for animal feed. The barley is processed and mixed with other ingredients to produce different kinds of feeds. Barley is also important in the production of food. It is made into the malt that is used in brewing beer. Other foodstuffs, such as soups and bread, are also made with barley.

ETHEL M. DUTKY
University of Maryland

See also BEER AND BREWING; PLANTS.

BARNARD, CHRISTIAAN (1922–2001)

Christiaan Barnard was the South African surgeon who performed the first human heart transplant. This historic operation took place on December 3, 1967. Barnard removed the healthy heart of a young woman who had been fatally wounded in an automobile accident. He transplanted her heart into the chest of Louis Washkansky, a 55-year-old man whose heart was failing. Washkansky lived for 18 days with the transplanted heart.

Although Washkansky died of pneumonia soon after the transplant, the operation was considered a success—Washkansky's new heart beat strongly until the end. Barnard performed his second heart transplant operation a month after the first one. This time, the recipient of the transplanted heart lived for 18 months. Barnard continued doing transplant operations with critically ill patients. His innovative surgical procedures included another first. In 1974, he transplanted a second heart in a human being. The hearts were linked together, forming a kind of double pump to circulate blood throughout the body.

Christiaan Barnard was born on November 8, 1922, in a small town called Beaufort West, South Africa. His father was a minister and the family was quite poor. Barnard's mother had high expectations of her children and urged them to work hard and strive to be the best in their classes. Barnard studied hard and was admitted to medical school in Cape Town, South Africa. He received advanced training in heart surgery at the University of Minnesota in the United States. It was in 1958 that Barnard returned to South Africa and introduced the revolutionary new technique of operating directly on the heart—the procedure called open-heart surgery.

Barnard retired as a surgeon in 1983. The effects of chronic arthritis eventually made it difficult for him to operate. After retiring, Barnard continued doing research related to transplant operations and authored several books on health and medical topics. His writings also include his autobiography, *Christiaan Barnard: One Life* (1970).

ELIZABETH KAPLAN
Science Writer

See also HEART.

BARNUM, PHINEAS TAYLOR (1810–1891)

Phineas T. Barnum was an American showman with a genius for staging and promoting unusual events. His claims about his shows were often exaggerated or false, and he considered himself a master of the art of "humbug," or fooling the people. Yet he was one of the first entrepreneurs to recognize the importance of publicity, using techniques such as brass bands and sensational advertisements to draw attention to his shows.

P. T. Barnum was born on July 5, 1810, in Bethel, Connecticut. He began his show business career at age 25 in New York City, where he exhibited an aged woman named Joice Heth, claiming she had been George Washington's nurse. Hundreds of people paid to see Heth, said to be 161 years old.

In 1841, Barnum acquired the American Museum in New York City, where he displayed amusing and astonishing oddities—both genuine and fake—including sword swallowers, giants, bearded ladies, and the midget known as General Tom Thumb. In 1850 he promoted and managed a highly successful American concert tour by the famous Swedish singer Jenny Lind.

In 1871, Barnum launched a traveling circus that he billed as the "Greatest Show on Earth." Ten years later he joined his circus with that of a competitor, James A. Bailey. Under Barnum and Bailey the spectacular three-ring circus became an American institution. The Barnum and Bailey Circus was purchased by the Ringling Brothers in 1907.

Barnum published an autobiography in 1855. He also was a member of the Connecticut state legislature and served one term as mayor of Bridgeport, Connecticut. He died in Bridgeport on April 7, 1891.

Reviewed by ROBERT S. PELTON
Curator, The Barnum Museum

BAROMETER

The air around you is made up of tiny molecules of gas that are constantly in motion. Pulled by the Earth's gravity, these air molecules also press down on the Earth and everything on it. In fact, about 1 ton of air presses down on each square foot (about 10 metric tons on each square meter) of the Earth's surface. The force of the air pressing down on the surface of the Earth is called **air pressure**. A barometer is an instrument that measures air pressure.

You may have seen a barometer hanging on a wall. Inside it there is a small box, or chamber, with thin metal walls. Most of the air has been drawn out of this chamber so its thin walls will move in or out slightly when there is an increase or decrease in the air pressure outside of it. A pointer on the front of the barometer, which is connected by a series of levers to the chamber walls, indicates these small changes. The pointer moves in front of a dial that is marked off in units of air pressure. These units are usually measured in inches or centimeters.

An Aneroid Barometer

Air pressure is important in weather forecasting. A change in air pressure usually means a change in weather. A drop in pressure often means that bad weather is coming. A rise in pressure usually means that clear weather is on the way.

Air pressure also changes when you move from sea level to higher altitudes. It is usually greater at the surface of the Earth near sea level than it is at mountaintops or above as you move through the upper levels of our atmosphere. When you climb a mountain, for example, you will find that because the air presses down less strongly it feels "thinner." Airplane pilots often use barometers called **altimeters** to tell them how high they are above the ground.

The barometers you have read about so far are called aneroid barometers. Aneroid means "without liquid." There are other barometers that do use liquids. The very first barometer was of this type. An Italian scientist named Evangelista Torricelli (1608–47) designed it in 1643. He took a long glass tube that was closed at one end and filled it with mercury. He turned this tube upside down in a pan that contained more mercury. The mercury in the tube started running out, of course. Soon the mercury stopped running out because the weight of the mercury in the tube was balanced by the pressure of air on the mercury outside the tube.

Mercury barometers are still used today. Scientists read a mercury barometer by seeing how high the column of mercury in the tube is. When air pressure increases, the mercury column goes up. When the pressure decreases, the column goes down.

Mercury barometers are very accurate. But they are clumsy to move around, and they have to be kept upright so that the liquid stays level. That is why ordinary barometers used in homes or the barometers used on ships and airplanes are aneroid barometers. Mercury barometers are used mainly in weather stations and scientific laboratories.

Reviewed by SERGE A. KORFF
New York University

See also WEATHER.

A Fortin Mercury Barometer ►
Mercury level
Reading scales
Thermometer
Mercury cup

Cross Section of an Aneroid Barometer ▼
Hollow metal box
Springs
Levers
Pointer

The Triumph of Divine Providence, a ceiling fresco by the Italian artist Pietro da Cortona, has the swirling shapes and rich detail characteristic of some baroque art.

BAROQUE ART AND ARCHITECTURE

The term baroque is used by art historians to describe European painting, sculpture, and architecture created in the period from about 1600 to 1750. When first applied to the visual arts, at the very end of this period, the term conveyed a rather negative attitude toward its subject, suggesting bizarre or simply bad taste. Only in modern times was the term baroque freed from such unflattering associations and used to describe art produced in the period between the end of the Renaissance in the 1500's and the beginnings of modernism in the later 1700's. The baroque period is so rich and so diverse, however, that no single term can accurately describe all of the art produced in these years.

▶CHARACTERISTICS

The diversity of baroque art is the result of several factors. The first is geographical. While Renaissance culture originated in Italy about 1400 and gradually spread from Flor-

ence throughout much of Europe, baroque art appeared almost at the same time in nearly every European capital. In the early 1600's, artists of several nationalities working in several different countries—Spain, France, and the Netherlands as well as Italy—created works of great originality.

Although there were shared preferences among artists from different nations with respect to subject matter and style, there were also significant differences. In each country there was a considerable variety of styles from which to choose. An earthy realism that copied life was one choice; a more refined manner that revived the classical styles of ancient Greece and Rome and of the Renaissance was another; and a dramatic, emotionally charged style that sought to represent the supernatural was yet a third. Choices of subject matter frequently went hand in hand with such choices of style.

Religious beliefs and practices played perhaps the greatest role in the various expressions of baroque art. The Reformation of the mid-1500's divided Europe into Catholic

In *The Calling of St. Matthew*, the Italian artist Caravaggio set a biblical story in his own day. Christ, at the far right of the painting, calls on Matthew, who points at himself questioningly, to follow him. The costumes and setting are those of Caravaggio's Rome, not of the time of Christ. Only the dramatic lighting suggests the sacred subject matter.

countries and Protestant countries. In most Protestant countries, including Germany and England, art was considered an unnecessary luxury and was suppressed. But in one Protestant country, Holland, an entirely new kind of art was created. It was based on the routines of everyday life, while still following the Calvinist doctrine of banning images that depicted religious subjects. In Catholic countries such as Italy, Spain, and France, on the other hand, painters and sculptors continued the longstanding practice of using biblical stories as their primary subject matter.

▶ ITALY

The first painter who might be called baroque was Michelangelo Merisi da Caravaggio. Caravaggio, as he was known, worked mostly in Rome, where he painted a number of large canvases that depicted religious subjects from the New Testament. But if his subject matter remained traditional, his realistic treatment of the human figure and the setting was radically new. In such paintings as *The Calling of St. Matthew* (1599–1602), Caravaggio set the story not at the time of Christ but in his own time. The costumes of the fig-

ures as well as the architecture and furnishings of the interior setting are based on contemporary Roman fashions. Sometimes the figures in his paintings can be identified as his friends. The only element in Caravaggio's religious paintings that suggests a divine presence is his use of **tenebrist** light, a sharply contrasting spotlighting that resembles stage lighting.

Caravaggio's realistic depiction of biblical stories was very different from the approach taken by his contemporary Annibale Carracci. Carracci's paintings return to the clarity of design and balanced composition of such High Renaissance artists as Raphael. Most of Carracci's paintings were of religious subjects, but his most famous works, the frescoes on the ceiling of the Farnese Gallery in Rome (1597–1605), illustrate mythological scenes from the writings of the Roman poet Ovid. Many of the figures are based on classical statues or the paintings of Raphael and Michelangelo. Although they appear lifelike, they are so idealized that they could never be confused with real figures in real settings.

A third approach to art was taken by Pietro da Cortona, who excelled as both an architect and a painter. His large ceiling fresco *The*

Triumph of Divine Providence (1633–39) in the Palazzo Barberini, Rome, is a dazzling composition of loosely arranged, colorful figures that swirl freely overhead. In style as well as in subject, this is far removed from the realism of Caravaggio or the timelessness of Carracci. Cortona's *Triumph* is, in fact, a representation of the supernatural, an imaginary vision of the ascent to immortality of a living person, Pope Urban VIII Barberini.

One artist who seemed to capture the spirit of his time in all its diversity and vitality was the sculptor Giovanni Lorenzo Bernini. His statue *David* (1623), done when he was still a young man, expresses most of the characteristic features of baroque art. While its pose imitates sculpture from the ancient past, it is also very realistically rendered. Like many works of art

In works such as *David*, the Italian sculptor Giovanni Lorenzo Bernini captured the vitality of the baroque age. The sculpture, based on a biblical story, depicts the young David in the act of hurling a stone at the giant Goliath. The figure imparts a sense of movement and drama that draws the viewer into the action of the story.

from this period, it represents one moment in a continuous action, in this case David hurling a stone from his sling at Goliath. Finally, it draws the spectator into the action, making him or her an active participant in the story being told.

Although he preferred sculpture, Bernini also designed a number of architectural projects that contribute to the magnificence of Rome. Chief among these was his completion of the rebuilding of St. Peter's Basilica, the most important church in the Catholic world. In addition to sculpting a number of works for the interior of the great church, in the 1650's he designed and built the enormous open square that stands in front of it. This square, or piazza, consists of two curving colonnades that are shaped like arms that reach out to gather in the faithful, a symbolic gesture that Bernini noted in writings that accompanied his plans. Walking through St. Peter's Square today, one still experiences the majesty, the authority, and the self-confidence of the baroque popes.

▶SPAIN

Spain also experienced a Golden Age during the 1600's. In art as in literature, a simple and humble realism emerged just after the turn of the century. In Seville and Madrid, painters and sculptors created works so lifelike that at times one cannot tell the difference between art and reality. Sculpture in particular frequently blended the two—statues were made of carved and painted wood, rather than the white marble used in Italy, and often were clothed in actual garments.

The greatest Spanish artist of the period was Diego Velázquez. Velázquez began his career in Seville as a painter of scenes of everyday

Spanish artist Francisco de Zurbarán specialized in realistic portrayals of saints. His painting *St. Serapion* depicts a monk who died for his beliefs.

life and while still a young man moved to Madrid, where he was appointed court painter to King Philip IV. His masterpiece, *The Maids of Honor* (1656), depicts the artist himself at work in his studio on what seems to be a portrait of the Infanta Margarita Teresa, daughter of the king and queen. Servants attend the little girl, the family dog rests by her side, and the furnishings of the studio are precisely detailed. Among the framed paintings that hang on a dark rear wall is a mirror in which the likenesses of Philip IV and his queen are recognizable. When a viewer stands in front of the painting, he or she occupies the same space as the king and queen. Art and reality are so perfectly blended that the experience of looking at this picture is positively magical. A reproduction of *The Maids of Honor* appears in the article SPAIN, ART AND ARCHITECTURE OF in Volume S.

Catholicism was a powerful influence in Spanish life of this period, and paintings of religious subjects became ever more popular. Velázquez' contemporary Francisco de Zurbarán specialized in painting realistic portrayals of Christ and the saints. The figures are highlighted with sharply contrasted tenebrist light that gives them intense spiritual power.

▶ **FRANCE**

Baroque art in France was for the most part an expression of the values of the French crown, especially of King Louis XIV. The great palace of Versailles (1669–85) was built by Louis a few miles outside of Paris as a symbol of his absolute authority. The design of the palace and of the surrounding parkland is the product of a rational and rigidly disciplined approach that echoes the king's control of government. The architecture and the painting and sculpture that decorate the palace are purely classical in style, conveying to all a sense of the orderly and timeless truths of the king's political policies.

Not every artist in France was content to work for the government. Many painters chose to leave the country rather than place their creativity in the service of politics. Indeed, the two greatest French painters of the baroque period, Nicholas Poussin and Claude Lorrain, spent their entire careers in Italy. Both artists turned to the gentle Roman landscape for inspiration. Claude, as he is known, painted the poetry of the lovely countryside, populated with grazing flocks of sheep and picturesque ruins of ancient monuments. Poussin depicted some of the same features of the Roman countryside, but his paintings were intended to do more than delight the viewer. He used the classical setting as a stage for presenting the drama of human history. His paintings instruct as well as delight. The purpose of his art was to elevate the mind to its highest and most moral state.

▶ **THE NETHERLANDS**

In the northwestern part of Europe, political and religious differences led to the division of the region then known as the Netherlands into two independent states. The southern provinces, called Flanders (comprising present-day Belgium and part of northern France), were in the 1600's part of the Spanish Empire. The northern provinces, known as Holland (the present-day Netherlands), broke away from Spain at the end of the 1500's, establishing an independent democracy that was one of the first of its kind.

Flemish Art. The art of Flanders in the baroque period continued to reflect the religious beliefs of Catholicism and the rigid class distinctions of Spanish society. Peter Paul Rubens expressed the values of this culture better than anyone. His painting *The Adoration of the Magi* (1624) depicts the birth of Christ as an aristocratic pageant, with none of the simplicity usually found in Nativity scenes. Instead of humble shepherds in a rustic stable, there are splendidly costumed Magi in a grand setting offering expensive gifts.

The palace of Versailles was built for France's King Louis XIV. The design of the palace and its gardens conveys the power and grandeur of the French crown.

Left: The Adoration of the Magi, by Flemish artist Peter Paul Rubens, portrays the birth of Christ as an elegant pageant, with richly costumed Magi bearing expensive gifts. *Above:* Dutch baroque artists often depicted scenes from daily life rather than religious subjects. *Woman Pouring Milk*, by Jan Vermeer, finds a simple beauty in the routines and surroundings of everyday life.

Rubens' younger contemporary Anthony Van Dyck specialized in painting portraits of members of the same upper class that would have appreciated the material finery of *The Adoration*. Van Dyck was so successful at flattering the aristocracy that his works were in demand in all the courts of Europe, especially England. The ladies and gentlemen in his pictures are always taller, slimmer, more elegant, and more graceful than they were in life. Some of the artist's methods are still used in fashion advertisements today, while the pointed beard and mustache worn by many of his male sitters remain known as a Vandyke.

Dutch Art. Life was very different in the northern Netherlands during this period. Along with political and economic freedom, the Dutch insisted on religious freedom. Catholicism was abolished as the official religion, and most of the population followed the Protestant teachings of John Calvin. Although Calvinism left no place for art in religious practice, the art of painting did not disappear

in Holland. Instead the arts flourished, with an increasing number of painters turning to Dutch life itself for their subject matter.

Jan Vermeer specialized in painting the interiors of simple middle-class households in his native town of Delft. There are no biblical or mythological subjects in Vermeer's paintings to distract us from their plain compositions and pure colors. A work such as *Woman Pouring Milk* (about 1660) is surprisingly modern in its simple design and its reflection of the mood of the artist's own daily life.

Other Dutch painters specialized in outdoor scenes, in landscape, in still lifes of flowers, fish, or fruit, or in portraiture. Frans Hals painted only portraits, and a comparison of his informal likenesses with the society portraits of Anthony Van Dyck reveals the deep cultural differences between Holland and neighboring Flanders in this period.

The greatest Dutch artist of the baroque period was Rembrandt van Rijn. Rembrandt spent most of his life in Amsterdam, where his

Left: The Syndics of the Cloth Merchants' Guild, by the Dutch artist Rembrandt van Rijn, captures the individuality of each of the prosperous Dutch businessmen it portrays. This emphasis on the individual is typical of baroque art.

Below: St. Paul's Cathedral, in London, was built by the architect Christopher Wren in an English version of the baroque style. Its massive dome is modeled on the dome of St. Peter's Basilica in Rome.

imagination and curiosity led him to explore a far wider range of subjects than did most of his contemporaries. He painted many biblical scenes, not for churches and not as aids to religious worship, but as imaginary records of significant moments in human history. Human feeling in all its mystery and complexity is the true subject of his work. Many of his most moving paintings are portraits—most of individuals, some of groups, and many of himself. His *Syndics of the Cloth Merchants' Guild* (1662), a group portrait of five Amsterdam businessmen, is typical in the way it creates unity out of informality, preserving the indi-

viduality of each member of the group while knitting their personalities together into a coherent whole. The soft coloring, mellow light, and sketchy brushwork of Rembrandt's paintings contribute to the sense of unity found in his work. While these are personal elements that distinguish him from other artists of his time, Rembrandt's interest in capturing a fleeting moment and his emphasis on the inner life of individuals who share their thoughts and moods with the viewer are characteristics found throughout baroque art.

▶ENGLAND

In geography and culture, England has always remained apart from the rest of Europe. Like many Protestant countries, England was suspicious of the power of visual images. Painting all but died out during the 1600's. Architecture, on the other hand, flourished in London after the Great Fire of 1666. St. Paul's Cathedral was rebuilt by Christopher Wren not in the Gothic style of the old cathedral but in the up-to-date baroque manner. If its plan and interior remain recognizably English, its impressive facade and stately dome are based on the architectural styles of Paris and Rome. Like so many works of art from the period around 1700, St. Paul's speaks a truly international language, pronounced, however, with a distinct regional accent.

JOHN VARRIANO
Mount Holyoke College
Author, *Italian Baroque and Rococo Architecture*

A performance of an opera at the palace of Versailles, France, in the 1600's. Opera was one of many important musical forms developed during the baroque period.

BAROQUE MUSIC

Baroque is the term used to describe the music of the period extending roughly from 1600 to 1750. The baroque era includes all the music from the time of Italian composer Claudio Monteverdi in the late 1500's to German composers Johann Sebastian Bach and George Frederick Handel in the 1700's. Many of the most important musical forms were developed during this period, including the sonata, symphony, concerto, suite, opera, oratorio, and many others.

The composers of the baroque era tried to use their music to express intense emotions. As a result, music became much more dramatic than it had ever been before. Further, secular (nonreligious) music was considered to be as important as sacred music in the baroque era. While most of the best music of earlier times was composed for the church, much baroque music was written for other purposes.

In baroque music we can see the beginnings and early development of modern harmony. Before the beginning of the baroque period, the most common type of music was **polyphonic music**, in which two or more melodies are sounded together. Baroque composers developed a style of vocal music, called **monody**, with only one melody and a supporting harmony. This innovation encouraged composers to invent new and interesting harmonies.

The importance of harmony led to a new kind of musical notation called the **figured bass**. It was used so widely during the baroque era that the period is sometimes called the figured-bass period. Only the melody line and a simple bass part were written out in the musical score. The composer indicated the harmony by writing figures—numbers and symbols—under the bass part below the staff. The performer playing accompaniment (usually the keyboardist) filled in the harmony according to the figures. The figures suggested a general harmonic outline but allowed room for improvisation by the performer. Figured bass was used first in vocal music and later spread to instrumental music.

▶VOCAL MUSIC

Opera was developed in Florence, Italy, near the end of the 1500's. A group of amateur poets, musicians, and painters, known as the Florentine Camerata, wanted to revive ancient classical Greek drama, which they knew had been accompanied by music. They decided to write plays based on classical subjects and to set the plays to music. But instead of reproducing the drama of ancient Greece, they invented something new—the opera.

New vocal forms were invented for this new kind of music. **Recitative** imitates the inflections of speech. It consists of a single melodic line for solo voice with a simple instrumental accompaniment. With recitative, words could be clearly expressed and the story could be easily followed. The **aria** is a more lyrical form for solo voice, used to show the emotional state of a character rather than to move the story along. Arias are usually in A-B-A form; that is, the first part is repeated after the end of the contrasting second, or middle, part. These are called *da capo* arias, a form that became very popular in baroque vocal music. *Da capo* means to repeat from the beginning of a piece. In the *da capo* aria, singers often have an opportunity to show off their vocal skills.

The world's first opera was *Dafne*, which had its premiere performance in 1598. It was the work of two members of the Florentine Camerata, the poet Ottavio Rinuccini and the composer Jacopo Peri. Most of the music for *Dafne* has been lost, but all of Peri's second opera, *Euridice* (1600), still exists. Both operas were popular successes.

In 1607, ten years after the first performance of *Dafne*, Italian composer Claudio Monteverdi wrote *Orfeo*, an opera that is still performed today. Monteverdi was the first to write ensemble numbers such as duets and trios, and to give an important role to the orchestra. He made expressive use of colorful orchestral effects. He enlarged the orchestra and developed new performance techniques. For this reason many people consider Monteverdi the father of the symphony orchestra.

The opera developed rapidly. In Naples, Italy, Alessandro Scarlatti established many of the traditions of Italian opera that later composers followed. In France, Jean-Baptiste Lully laid the foundations of French opera. Lully emphasized the drama in his operas and gave the orchestra a more important role. He also established the ballet in French opera. In England, Henry Purcell composed *Dido and Aeneas* (1689), which has remained one of the most important English operas.

The Oratorio and the Passion. Baroque musicians also enriched church music with new vocal forms such as the oratorio and the Passion. These required choruses, recitatives, solo and ensemble numbers, and orchestral interludes and accompaniment. Both the orato-

rio and the Passion were dramatizations of Bible stories. They were usually meant to be performed without scenery or costumes.

The first composer to write a fully developed oratorio was Italy's Giacomo Carissimi. His oratorio *Jephte* (before 1649) established some of the traditions that later oratorio composers followed: It was one of the first to leave out scenery and costumes; it had a narrator, who kept the story moving; and it had dramatic and expressive choruses. For these reasons, Carissimi's *Jephte* is considered the first modern oratorio.

The Passion was a musical setting of the suffering and death of Christ. It had been used occasionally by Renaissance composers as a piece for unaccompanied chorus, but it underwent great change in the baroque era. The baroque Passion added solo voices and orchestra. It also added a chorale, a four-part setting of a hymn tune, which the church congregation joined in singing. Germany's Heinrich Schütz was the first important composer of Passions. Schütz studied in Italy, and he was strongly influenced by the Italian composers, especially Monteverdi.

The Cantata. The cantata was another major musical form that developed in the ba-

A painting by Dutch artist Jan Vermeer shows a woman playing a virginal (an early type of harpsichord). Much baroque music was written for keyboard instruments.

roque era. It began as a secular form of music and later was introduced into the church. The cantata was a small composition that required fewer musicians than large works like the oratorio. Cantatas were composed for one or two solo voices accompanied by a small instrumental group. They usually began with an introduction for instruments alone, followed by contrasting sections of recitatives and arias.

Church cantatas were based on biblical texts and became very popular in the 1600's and 1700's. The form was perfected by German composer Dietrich Buxtehude. Many of Buxtehude's cantatas use chorale melodies of the Lutheran Church. The most famous Italian composer of cantatas was Alessandro Scarlatti, who is better known for his operas. Scarlatti wrote some 600 cantatas in addition to more than 100 operas and about 35 oratorios.

▶INSTRUMENTAL MUSIC

Probably nothing else in the baroque period has had more far-reaching effects than the development of instrumental music. For the first time, instrumental music was regarded as equal in importance to vocal music. As in vocal music, many baroque instrumental forms began in Italy.

Renaissance composers had written many pieces for the organ. But they wrote them in the polyphonic vocal style, as though the organ were a combination of human voices rather than an instrument. Baroque composers of organ music, on the other hand, began to develop a distinctly instrumental style of writing. They emphasized the tonal qualities for which the organ was best suited. Italian composer Girolamo Frescobaldi perfected some of the chief forms of organ music. These included the organ toccata, fugue, and partita. Dietrich Buxtehude was another important composer of organ music. With Buxtehude, organ music reached a stage of development that remained unsurpassed until Johann Sebastian Bach.

Music for instruments other than the organ also had to develop a nonvocal style before it became independent from vocal music. Instrumental music developed rapidly because brilliant new stringed instruments were being made by the famous violin-making families of Cremona, Italy. First the Amati family and later the Guarneri and Stradivari families made wonderful new violins, violas, and cellos.

These instruments have never been surpassed for their beautiful rich tone and finely crafted construction.

The Sonata and the Concerto. Early in the baroque era, a new musical idea emerged for which a new term was invented—sonata. A sonata was a composition that could be performed only on an instrument, just as the cantata was a piece of music that was meant only to be sung. Once composers started making this distinction, they began to develop a strictly instrumental style that was completely different from vocal music.

Italian violinist and composer Arcangelo Corelli was influential in the development of the sonata and the concerto, two leading instrumental forms.

The first master to do so was Italy's Arcangelo Corelli. Corelli was the foremost violin virtuoso of his time and the first important composer of violin music. He produced two landmark works. One of these consisted of twelve sonatas for violin and keyboard accompaniment. In these sonatas a new style of violin performance was demonstrated fully for the first time. His second great contribution was a set of twelve *concerti grossi* (grand concertos) for a combination of instruments. Corelli's violin sonatas and concertos were the ancestors of the later solo sonata and the classical concerto.

The practice of contrasting the tone color, or timbre, of instruments with each other was a baroque invention. For the first time on a large scale, the special tone quality of individual instruments was fully used. This formed the basis on which modern orchestral writing was built. Baroque composers wrote many concertos for violin, flute, cello, and keyboard. Later in the period, concertos for other instruments such as the horn and the oboe also became popular.

The sonata and the concerto developed rapidly. The leading composers were Italy's

An engraving (*left*) portrays the baroque composer George Frederick Handel presenting his *Water Music* to King George I of England. The set of orchestral suites was first performed on a barge during a royal procession down the River Thames. Handel and Johann Sebastian Bach (*below*) were two giants of the baroque age. Their works, which represent the pinnacle of baroque music, paved the way for the achievements of the classical period that followed.

Antonio Vivaldi, Giuseppe Tartini, and Domenico Scarlatti, the son of Alessandro. Scarlatti was the first important composer in Italy to write sonatas for a keyboard instrument. He also created a brilliant new style of keyboard writing and perfected a new technique of performing on the harpsichord.

The Dance Suite. Outside Italy, too, great advances were being made in instrumental music. Composers were creating a treasury of smaller pieces for keyboard instruments. These pieces often were based on dances. Composers began to arrange them in groups called suites. The dance suite consisted of several dance move-

ments contrasting in mood, tempo, and rhythm. The basic arrangement consisted of four dances: an allemande in moderate tempo; a courante, or running dance; a slow and stately sarabande; and a quick and lively gigue, or jig. Composers often added dances between the sarabande and gigue, such as the minuet or gavotte. Outstanding com-

posers of dance suites and other beautiful keyboard pieces were Germany's Johann Froberger, England's Henry Purcell, and France's François Couperin and Jean-Philippe Rameau.

▶**HANDEL AND BACH**

Baroque music reached a climax with two of the greatest composers who ever lived: George Frederick Handel and Johann Sebastian Bach. With these creative giants, baroque music came to its final fulfillment. With Handel, opera in the old Italian tradition reached its highest development. Henceforth opera would develop in completely new directions. With Handel, too, the oratorio—and with Bach, the Passion—reached a stage of near perfection. See the biographies of Bach and Handel in volumes B and H.

Few composers before Bach and Handel wrote instrumental music with such expressiveness, emotion, and beauty. Both of these masters composed sonatas, concertos, suites, and solo instrumental music that fully achieved all the possibilities of the baroque style. They also pointed the way for the future. The works of Bach and Handel not only represent the end of the baroque era, they look forward to the beginnings of the classical period that followed.

DAVID EWEN
Music Historian
Reviewed by KENNETH NOTT
Hartt School, University of Hartford

BARRIE, SIR JAMES MATTHEW
(1860–1937)

James Matthew Barrie, the creator of Peter Pan, was born in the Scottish town of Kirriemuir on May 9, 1860, the son of a local weaver. When James was 6, his older brother David was drowned in a skating accident. Their mother was heartbroken but consoled herself with the idea that in dying so young, David would remain a boy forever. It was this idea that Barrie later turned into his most famous play, *Peter Pan*.

Barrie knew from an early age that he wanted to be a writer. He graduated from Edinburgh University in 1882, and in 1885 he moved to London and began writing novels. The most famous was *The Little Minister* (1891). But Barrie is best known as a writer for the stage. His first successful play, *Walker, London* (1892), was followed by *The Admirable Crichton* (1902), *What Every Woman Knows* (1908), and *Dear Brutus* (1917).

Barrie married the actress Mary Ansell in 1894, but they had no children of their own. One day in the summer of 1898, while walking his dog in Kensington Gardens, Barrie met three young brothers, George, Jack, and Peter. Their parents, Arthur and Sylvia Llewelyn Davies, and the Barries soon became friends. The story of Peter Pan had been in Barrie's mind since childhood, and now he started writing it as a play to entertain the Davies boys. But instead of making Peter a tragic boy who *could* not grow up, Barrie changed him into the carefree boy who *would* not grow up. *Peter Pan* was first performed in London on December 27, 1904, and it has been a favorite of children ever since. The story has been retold in books and as an animated cartoon.

Barrie was made a baronet in 1913. In 1929 he donated the entire copyright in *Peter Pan* to a London children's hospital. He died on June 19, 1937.

ANDREW BIRKIN
Author, *J. M. Barrie and the Lost Boys*

Peter, Tinker Bell, and the three Darling children fly over the rooftops of London in this illustration from an early edition of James M. Barrie's *Peter Pan*.

▶PETER PAN

Peter Pan and the fairy Tinker Bell flew from Never-Never Land, where Peter was leader of the Lost Boys, right into the Darling children's nursery. Peter told Wendy, John, and Michael Darling about Never-Never Land and about the mermaids, pirates, and Indians who lived there. He said he would teach the Darlings to fly if they would go back with him.

Just then Liza, the Darlings' maid, and Nana, the Newfoundland dog who was the children's nursemaid, came into the nursery. The children hid until they left. This excerpt picks up the story from there.

"It's all right," John announced, emerging from his hiding-place. "I say, Peter, can you really fly?"

Instead of troubling to answer him Peter flew around the room, taking the mantelpiece on the way.

"How topping!" said John and Michael.

"How sweet!" cried Wendy.

"Yes, I'm sweet, oh, I am sweet!" said Peter, forgetting his manners again.

It looked delightfully easy, and they tried it first from the floor and then from the beds, but they always went down instead of up.

"I say, how do you do it?" asked John, rubbing his knee. He was quite a practical boy.

"You just think lovely wonderful thoughts," Peter explained, "and they lift you up in the air."

He showed them again.

"You're so nippy at it," John said "couldn't you do it very slowly once?"

Peter did it both slowly and quickly. "I've got it now, Wendy!" cried John, but soon he found he had not. Not one of them could fly an inch, though even Michael was in words of two syllables, and Peter did not know A from Z.

Of course Peter had been trifling with them, for no one can fly unless the fairy dust has been blown on him. Fortunately, as we have mentioned, one of his hands was messy with it, and he blew some on each of them, with the most superb results.

"Now just wriggle your shoulders this way," he said, "and let go."

They were all on their beds, and gallant Michael let go first. He did not quite mean to let go, but he did it, and immediately he was borne across the room.

"I flewed!" he screamed while still in mid-air.

John let go and met Wendy near the bathroom.

"Oh, lovely!"

"Oh, ripping!"

"Look at me!"

"Look at me!"

"Look at me!"

They were not nearly so elegant as Peter, they could not help kicking a little, but their heads were bobbing against the ceiling, and there is almost nothing so delicious as that. Peter gave Wendy a hand at first, but had to desist, Tink was so indignant.

Up and down they went, and round and round. Heavenly was Wendy's word.

"I say," cried John. "why shouldn't we all go out?"

Of course it was to this that Peter had been luring them.

Michael was ready: he wanted to see how long it took him to do a billion miles. But Wendy hesitated.

"Mermaids!" said Peter again.

"Oo!"

"And there are pirates."

"Pirates," cried John, seizing his Sunday hat, "let us go at once."

BARROW, CLYDE. See OUTLAWS (Profiles).

BARRY, RICK. See BASKETBALL (Great Players).

BARRYMORE FAMILY

Ethel Barrymore said of herself and brothers Lionel and John: "We became actors not because we wanted to go on the stage, but because it was the thing we could do best."

The Barrymores were a noted family of actors who traced their connection with the stage back to Shakespeare's day. Ethel, Lionel, and John appeared together on film only once—in *Rasputin and the Empress* (1932). Separately, they displayed the acting talent that made the name Barrymore a synonym for actor.

Ethel Barrymore (1879–1959) became a star at the age of 21 in *Captain Jinks of the*

From Left: Actors Lionel, Ethel, and John Barrymore in costume for *Rasputin and the Empress*, the only film in which all three siblings appeared together.

Horse Marines. She appeared in a series of comedies and later in plays by Ibsen and Shakespeare. She crowned her stage career in 1940 in Emlyn Williams' *The Corn is Green*. She also acted in films, winning an Academy Award for *None But the Lonely Heart* (1944).

Lionel Barrymore (1878–1954) was a skillful character actor. In 1918 he made a great hit in *The Copperhead*, followed by *The Jest* in 1919 (with his brother), *Macbeth* (1921), and *The Claw* (1921). After that he devoted most of his time to motion pictures. Troubled in his later years by a hip injury, he remained active in films, performing from a wheelchair.

Stunning portrayals of Richard III and Hamlet established **John Barrymore** (1882–1942) as one of the greatest actors of the English-speaking stage. He later starred in a variety of films, including *Grand Hotel* (1932) and *Twentieth Century* (1934). His charm, his classic profile, and his headline romances added a new chapter to the Barrymore legend—a legend that lives on in younger generations of Barrymores, including the actress **Drew Barrymore** (1975–).

JAMES KOTSILIBAS-DAVIS
Author, *The Barrymores*

BARTLETT, JOSIAH. See NEW HAMPSHIRE (Famous People).

BARTÓK, BÉLA (1881–1945)

Béla Bartók, the great modern composer, was born in Nagyszentmiklós, Hungary (now in Romania), on March 25, 1881. At age 5 he was given his first piano lessons by his mother. Four years later he began to compose.

In 1899, Bartók was admitted to the Academy of Music in Budapest as an advanced student in piano and composition. During 1903, his last year at the academy, he won much praise for his brilliant piano recitals. His symphonic poem *Kossuth*, written in the same year, brought him international recognition.

As a young man, Bartók was greatly influenced by the spirit of Hungarian nationalism. In 1905 he began making field trips to the Hungarian countryside to learn about the folk music of his land. There he discovered that the villagers had often taken the music of neighboring areas of Eastern Europe and mixed it with their own. He began to use the melodies and rhythms of these mixed styles in his compositions, combining them with a new approach to harmony for which he would become famous. Later he collected folk songs from other countries and wrote books on the special features of folk music. His work encouraged other composers to make use of folk music in their own compositions.

In 1907, Bartók was appointed professor of piano at the Academy of Music. Shortly afterward he began to compose the first of his six string quartets, which were completed between 1909 and 1939. They are thought to be among the finest string quartets ever written.

During the 1920's, after studying old Italian keyboard music, Bartók achieved a completely original style of composing. He combined the sounds and rhythms of folk music with the techniques of composers such as Frescobaldi, Beethoven, and Debussy, as in the First Piano Concerto. He also began his *Mikrokosmos*, pieces for piano students.

Political unrest in Hungary caused Bartók to settle in the United States in 1940. For a time he was associated with Columbia University, where he was able to continue his study of folk music. Bartók was also a successful pianist until ill health forced him to stop performing in public. But he made recordings and continued to compose. His popular Concerto for Orchestra was written in 1943. Bartók died in New York City on September 26, 1945.

BENJAMIN SUCHOFF
Author, *Guide to the Mikrokosmos of Béla Bartók*

BARTON, CLARA (1821–1912)

Clara Barton devoted most of her life to helping people. Her greatest accomplishment was the founding of the American Red Cross.

Clarissa Harlowe Barton was born on Christmas Day, 1821, on a farm near Oxford, Massachusetts. The youngest of five children, she received her early education from her brothers and sisters. At the age of 15, Clara became a teacher.

After 18 years of teaching, Clara Barton moved to Washington, D.C., where she worked in the Patent Office. When the Civil War broke out, reports on the suffering of wounded soldiers troubled her. She urged people to contribute medicines and bandages. She often took these supplies to the battlefield herself, caring for the wounded during action.

When the war was over, Clara Barton headed a group that searched for missing soldiers. She also gave lectures on her war experiences. After four years of this work, she became ill and went to Switzerland to recuperate. There she first learned of the international Red Cross, an organization for the relief of suffering caused by war. When the Franco-Prussian War began in 1870, she remained in Europe to work with the Red Cross.

In 1873, Clara Barton returned to the United States. Although she was not well, she devoted all her energy to establishing an American branch of the Red Cross. In 1881 she succeeded, becoming its first president. As a result of her efforts, the work of the Red Cross was enlarged to aid victims of peacetime disasters such as earthquakes and floods. In 1904, at the age of 83, Clara Barton retired. She died eight years later, on April 12, 1912, at Glen Echo, Maryland.

Reviewed by ALLEN F. DAVIS
Temple University

See also RED CROSS.

BASALT. See ROCKS (Igneous Rocks).

BASEBALL

Baseball is called the American national pastime. Every spring and summer, millions of fans watch professional major-league games in ballparks or on television. There are also professional minor leagues, which serve as a training ground for the majors, as well as thousands of college, high school, Little League, and other amateur teams. In addition to organized competition for every age group, the game is played on an informal basis in parks, school yards, and sandlots. Hardly a child in the United States has grown up without playing baseball in one form or another, and hardly an adult is not familiar with at least some of the rules, terms, and stars of "the great American game."

Baseball began in the United States during the mid-1800's. Through the years, baseball has developed a rich and colorful history. The popularity of the game today owes much to its tradition and folklore. Many fans spend hours recalling dramatic moments and great achievements of the past, reciting statistics, and comparing old-time and present-day stars. Some fans root for the same team for their whole lives, watching games or reading about them in the newspaper every day.

Baseball is so much a part of American life that its terms have been adopted into the everyday speech of the people. "Pinch-hit," "going to bat," "three strikes you're out," and scores of other baseball terms and sayings are used even by people who are not well acquainted with the game.

As baseball became the national pastime of the United States, it also spread to other countries. Today the sport is popular in Latin America, Canada, Japan, and elsewhere.

Colorful, exciting, and rich in tradition, baseball is often called the American national pastime. During the spring and summer, millions of fans flock to major league stadiums to root for their favorite teams. Before the game starts, some youngsters are lucky enough to get the autograph of a star player. When the action begins, attention focuses on the batter (*top right*), the pitcher (*bottom right*), and the fielders and base runners (*bottom left*).

▶HOW BASEBALL IS PLAYED

The basic rules of baseball have undergone little change in more than 100 years. Two teams, consisting of nine or ten players each, play the game on a large field. During the course of the game, the two teams alternate between **batting** (offensive play) and **fielding** (defensive play). The equipment needed to play baseball includes a bat, a ball, and padded gloves worn by players in the field. The object of the game is to score more **runs** than the opposing team. Generally, a run is scored when a batter hits the ball with the bat and runs safely around four bases, starting from home plate. The fielders try to catch the batted ball and halt the runner's progress to prevent the runner from reaching a base safely.

Field and Equipment

A baseball field has two main sections—the **infield** and the **outfield**. The infield is often called the diamond because it contains four bases—called **home plate**, **first base**, **second base**, and **third base**—that are arranged in the shape of a diamond. The outfield extends to a fence or a grandstand that encloses the entire playing area.

The infield and outfield are contained within two straight lines extending diagonally from home plate. One line goes past first base, and the other line goes past third base; they each extend all the way to the outfield fence or grandstand. These two lines are called foul lines. The area between them is **fair territory**; the area outside them is **foul territory**.

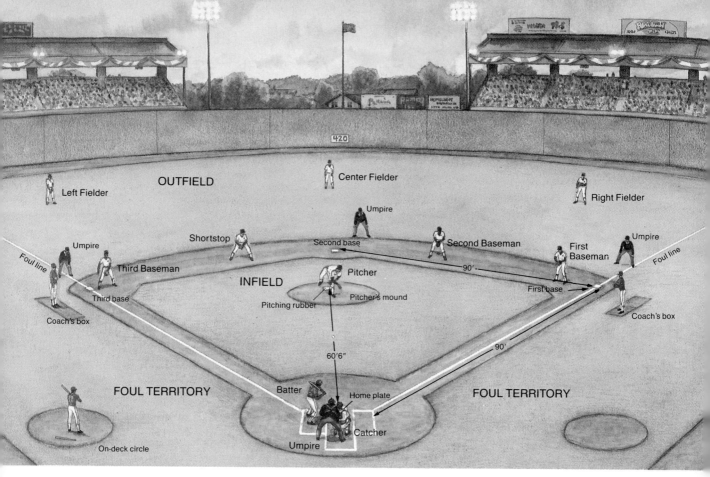

In a standard baseball diamond, each base is 90 feet (27.4 meters) apart. The size of the outfield varies from field to field. In major league stadiums, the outfield fence or grandstand is generally between 300 and 450 feet (91 and 137 meters) from home plate. Except for dirt areas around each base, most of the infield and all of the outfield is grass. (Some major league stadiums use artificial grass.)

An official baseball has a cork center, surrounded by layers of rubber and tightly wound yarn. The outer cover, made of bleached white cowhide, is stitched on with thick red thread. The ball weighs between 5 and 5¼ ounces (142 and 149 grams) and is 9 to 9¼ inches (23 to 24 centimeters) in circumference.

Until recently, all bats had to be made of wood (usually ash but sometimes hackberry or hickory). Today aluminum bats are permitted at every level of competition up to the minor and major leagues, where wood is still required. A bat must be no more than 2¾ inches (7 centimeters) in diameter at the thickest part and no more than 42 inches (107 centimeters) long.

The nine defensive players all wear padded leather gloves, or mitts, when they go out in the field. The gloves allow them to catch the ball without hurting their hands. Different fielders use different kinds of gloves.

Baseball uniforms usually include a cap, jersey, knicker-style pants, socks, and shoes. The shoes have metal spikes or rubber cleats on the soles to give the player a solid footing. Batters are required to wear a hard plastic helmet to prevent injury if the ball hits them in the head.

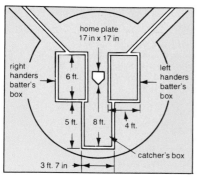

Defensive players occupy nine positions on the field: pitcher, catcher, first base, second base, shortstop, third base, left field, center field, and right field. The batter (offensive team) stands in the batter's box (*left*) at home plate and tries to hit the ball beyond the reach of the fielders. Base runners try to advance to home plate, thereby scoring a run.

BASIC BASEBALL EQUIPMENT

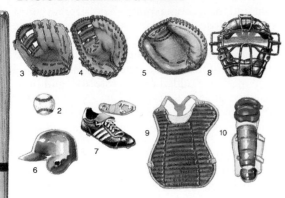

The basic equipment used in baseball includes a wooden or metal bat (1), a ball (2), and leather gloves for fielding. Most fielders use a standard five-fingered glove (3); a first baseman's mitt (4) has a larger "pocket"; a catcher's mitt (5) is round and heavily padded. Other gear includes a batting helmet (6); spiked or cleated shoes (7); and a mask (8), chest protector (9), and leg guards (10) for the catcher.

Players and Positions

Each of the nine players in the field occupies a specific position and performs a specific defensive role. Together they try to keep the team at bat from getting on base and scoring runs.

The main defensive player is the **pitcher**. From a dirt mound in the middle of the diamond, the pitcher throws the ball to the batter. In an effort to keep the batter from hitting it, the pitcher may use a variety of overarm or sidearm pitches—fastballs, curveballs, knuckleballs, and others. The pitcher also fields batted balls (catches and throws them to a teammate), keeps a watchful eye on base runners so they will not advance, and covers first base or home plate when necessary. The pitcher has the most responsibility for seeing that the team at bat does not score. If the pitcher loses control of the game and lets too many opposing players get on base and score

Throwing different kinds of pitches at different speeds, the pitcher tries to keep the batter from hitting the ball. With one foot on the rubber, the pitcher winds up, takes a long stride toward home plate, and hurls the ball with full force. The motion should be smooth and easy, with a strong follow-through. It is important to end up in a balanced position, ready to field a batted ball.

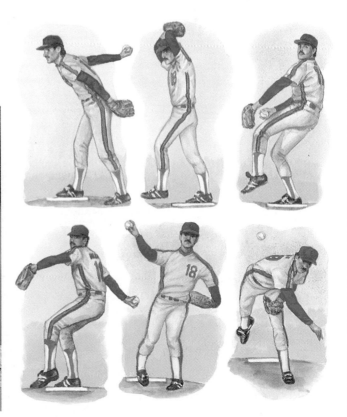

Teamwork in the field is an essential ingredient of winning baseball. *Above:* With the infielder in perfect position, a throw arrives at third base just ahead of the sliding runner. *Below:* An outfielder catches a fly ball as his teammate tries to avoid a collision.

ners who try to score, and to field batted balls that fall near home plate. The catcher must play in close harmony with the pitcher. The catcher studies opposing batters and gives signals to the pitcher indicating what type of pitches to throw. The catcher wears a metal face mask, a padded chest protector, and plastic shin guards to prevent injury from balls tipped by the bat. The catcher's mitt is very thickly padded because pitches are thrown very fast.

Four other members of the defensive team are called infielders. These players try to catch any balls hit by the batter within the infield. The **first baseman** guards first base and the area around it. The **second baseman** plays on the side of second base toward first, while the **shortstop** plays on the other side of second base; together they defend the middle of the infield. The **third baseman** covers third base and the area around it.

Finally, three players called outfielders try to catch any balls hit over or past the infielders. These players are the **left fielder** (on the third-base side), the **center fielder**, and the **right fielder**.

For the offensive team, players take their turns at bat in an order listed before the game starts. This batting order, or **lineup**, normally consists of nine players who also have positions in the field. But because pitchers are not usually good hitters, the American League in 1973 decided to allow another player—the designated hitter—to bat instead of the pitcher. This created a ten-player team. The designated hitter does not play a fielding position.

If substitute batters, called **pinch hitters**, come into the game, they normally bat in the same places in the lineup as the players they replace. But if two or more substitutes (other than pinch hitters) enter at the same time, they can be inserted in any vacant spots in the lineup.

The person in charge of the players and strategies for each team is the **manager**, often a former player. The manager sets the team's lineup, makes substitutions, and directs many plays on the field. The manager also has several coaches, who help train members of the team in skills and strategies. During a game, coaches stand just outside first base and third base, where they make hand signals to base runners and batters.

runs, the starting pitcher may be replaced by a relief pitcher.

The next most important defensive player is the **catcher**, who crouches in a boxed area behind home plate. The catcher's job is to catch all the pitcher's throws that are not hit by the batter, to guard home plate against run-

Every batter has his or her own way of standing at the plate, gripping the bat, and swinging. All good batters assume a balanced position and concentrate fully on the pitch. In the split second it takes the ball to reach home plate, the batter must decide whether or not to swing. If the batter decides to swing, the bat begins to level out as the ball approaches. When contact is made, the batter's head should be down, eyes still focused on the ball. A quick snap of the wrists and a full follow-through add power and distance to the hit. Once contact has been made and the swing is completed, the hitter drops the bat and runs toward first base.

Conduct of Play and Basic Rules

The visiting team takes the first turn at bat. It remains at bat until the home team, fielding, has gotten three **outs**, or put out three visiting players. The home team then bats until three of its players have been put out. When each team has had a turn at bat and a turn in the field, one **inning** is over.

A complete baseball game normally consists of nine innings. However, if the home team is ahead after eight and a half innings or takes the lead in the last half (or bottom) of the ninth inning, then the home team is automatically the winner, and the game is over. Also, if play is stopped because of rain or any other reason after five innings (four and a half innings if the home team is ahead), the game is considered complete; if play is stopped before five innings of play, the game is continued at a later date. Finally, if the score is tied at the end of nine innings, the game goes on until the tie is broken and both teams have had an equal number of times at bat.

The focus of action in any baseball game is the confrontation between pitcher and batter. The batter stands in a boxed area on either side of home plate, depending on whether he or she bats right-handed or left-handed. The

The strike zone is the area directly over home plate between the top of the shoulders and the top of the uniform pants to the top of the knees. If the batter does not swing at a pitch in this zone, the umpire calls a strike. If the pitch is outside the strike zone, the umpire calls a ball.

pitcher throws the ball toward the batter, and the batter tries to hit it. The pitcher aims the ball at an area called the **strike zone**. To be in the strike zone, the ball must pass over home plate within an area extending from the midpoint between the top of the batter's shoulders and the top of the uniform pants to the top of the knees. If the pitch passes through the strike zone and the batter does not swing, a **strike** is called on the batter. A strike is also called if the batter swings at the ball and misses, or if the batter hits the ball into foul territory. The batter is out when three strikes have been made. (A foul ball is not counted as the third strike unless it is a foul bunt or a foul tip caught by the catcher before it touches the ground.)

There are other ways in which a batter can be put out. If the batter hits a ball in the air (fair or foul) that is caught before it touches the ground, the batter is said to have flied out. If the batter hits a fair ground ball that is caught by a fielder and then thrown or carried to first base before the batter gets there, the batter is said to have grounded out.

There are also a number of ways in which a batter can get on base. If a batted ball lands in fair territory and the batter reaches first base before the fielder gets the ball there, the batter has made a **single**. If the batter can reach second base safely on the same hit, it is a **double**. If the batter can reach third base, it is a **triple**. A fair ball hit over the fence or into the stands is a **home run**. The batter can also make a home run by hitting a fair ball onto the playing field and running around all the bases before the fielders get the ball back to home plate. This exciting (and rare) play is called an inside-the-park home run. Any single, double, triple, or home run is called a **hit**.

A batter sometimes can proceed to first base without getting a hit. Each pitch to the batter that passes outside the strike zone is called a **ball**. After four balls, the batter is credited with a **walk** and advances freely to first base. The batter also is awarded first base if hit by a pitched ball; if interfered with by the catcher; or if the catcher drops the ball on a third strike and fails to throw it to first base before the batter arrives there.

In addition to pitching, fielding, and batting, **base running** is an important part of the game of baseball. Once a batter gets on base, the object is to advance to each of the next bases and finally to score a run by reaching home plate. Base runners may advance to the next base any time they think they can do so safely. Usually they wait until the batter hits the ball and then decide whether or not to try to advance. On a fly ball, however, they must wait, or **tag up** at the last base they held until the ball is caught; after tagging up, they may run to the next base. If a runner advances to the next base without the aid of a batted ball or a fielder's error, the runner is said to **steal** a base.

But base runners must always be alert because the fielding team can put them out in several ways. Base runners are out if they are tagged with the ball by a fielder when they are off base or if they go outside the base lines to avoid being tagged. Base runners also can be forced out. For example, if the runner is on first base and the batter hits a ground ball, the runner must advance to second base so that

A play at the plate is one of the most thrilling in baseball. As a base runner slides into home, the catcher receives a throw from another fielder and tries to tag the runner before his foot touches the plate. The two players collide in a cloud of dust, and the umpire signals "safe" (*as left*) or "out."

BASEBALL TERMS

Assist: A play by one fielder that makes it possible for another to make a put-out.

Balk: An illegal motion by the pitcher, entitling base runners to advance one base each.

Bases loaded: When there is a runner at each base.

Battery: A team's pitcher and catcher.

Batting average: Number of hits divided by times at bat (as: 18/60 = .300). If a batter reaches base safely on an error or fielder's choice, the batter does not get credit for a hit. If the batter hits a sacrifice or gets a base on balls or is hit by a pitched ball, the batter is not charged with a time at bat.

Bullpen: A special area where relief pitchers warm up.

Bunt: A batted ball tapped with the bat rather than hit with force.

Doubleheader: Two games played consecutively on a single day.

Double play (DP): A play in which the batter and a runner, or two runners, are put out.

Dugout: The seating area, often below the level of the playing field, reserved for players, managers, and coaches.

Earned run: Any run scored except one that results from a fielding misplay.

Earned run average (ERA): Number of earned runs charged against a pitcher divided by total innings pitched times 9 (as: $10/50 \times 9 = 1.80$).

Error: Any play on which a fielder misses a reasonable opportunity to put out a batter or runner, or a misplay that allows a runner to advance.

Fielder's choice: An attempt by the fielder of a fair ground ball to put out a runner instead of the batter who hit the ball.

Fielding average: Total put-outs and assists divided by total chances (put-outs, assists, and errors) (as: $\frac{66 + 33}{66 + 33 + 1} = \frac{99}{100} = .990$).

Force play: A play in which a runner is put out when forced to advance to the next base to make room for the next runner.

Full count: When there are three balls and two strikes on the batter.

Grand slam: A home run with the bases loaded.

Infield fly: A fair fly ball hit above the infield when there are runners on first and second or on all three bases and there is not more than one out. The umpire declares "infield fly," and the batter is automatically out.

Line drive: A ball hit in the air but on a straight line, usually not far off the ground.

No-hitter: A game in which the pitcher does not give up a single hit.

Passed ball: A failure of the catcher to hold a pitched ball (other than a wild pitch), permitting a runner to advance; not scored as an error.

Percentage (team or pitcher): Number of games won divided by total games won and lost (as: $\frac{15}{15 + 9} = \frac{15}{24} = .625$).

Pickoff: A throw by a pitcher or catcher to another fielder, catching a runner off base.

Rookie: A player in his first year in the major leagues, or a young player trying out for a big-league team.

Runs batted in (RBI): A run that scores and is credited to a batter as a result of the batter's safe hit, sacrifice, or infield out; or the batter's reaching first base on a fielder's choice; or the batter's getting a base on balls or being hit by a pitched ball with the bases full, forcing in a run.

Sacrifice: A successful attempt by the batter (before two are out) to advance a runner or runners by means of a bunt or a long fly out.

Shutout: A game in which a team fails to score.

Spring training: The period before the start of the regular season when major league teams train and play exhibition games to prepare for the season. Many teams hold their spring training camps in Florida or Arizona.

Squeeze play: An attempt to bring home a runner from third base by means of a bunt.

Stolen base: The act of a runner in advancing one base without the aid of the batter or any misplay by the defending team.

Switch-hitter: A player who can bat right-handed or left-handed.

Wild pitch: A pitch too high, low, or wide for the catcher to handle, allowing a base runner to advance.

---

first base will be left open for the batter. If the ground ball is caught and thrown to a fielder at second base before the runner arrives, the runner is forced out.

On the same play, if the fielder at second base then throws the ball to a fielder at first base and the ball arrives there before the batter, then the batter is out as well. This is called a **double play**, because two outs were made on one batted ball. A double play also can occur if a fielder catches a fly ball and throws the ball to a base before the runner gets back to it. Sometimes the fielding team can even get three outs on one batted ball—a rare **triple play**.

A Game of Inches

Baseball is often called a game of inches. For example, a speedy ground ball may pass within an inch or two of a infielder's reach, making the difference between a hit or an out. Sometimes even a fraction of an inch can determine whether a pitch is a ball or a strike, whether a batted ball is fair or foul, or whether a base runner is safe or out. Even one close play can decide the outcome of a whole game.

The job of making these decisions and enforcing the rules of the game falls on a group of **umpires** stationed around the field. Major league games usually have four umpires—one each at home plate, first base, second base, and third base. The home plate umpire decides whether pitches are balls or strikes and whether runners attempting to reach home plate are safe or out. The other umpires rule on plays at or near their designated bases.

While some rules of baseball may seem complicated, a good player should know every detail, understand many strategies, and react quickly to every situation. Almost every play is different, presenting batters, fielders, and base runners with a variety of choices and opportunities. To play well requires speed, power, pinpoint accuracy, split-second timing, and a special instinct for the game.

▶ LEAGUES AND COMPETITION

Millions of Americans play organized baseball, participating on teams that usually compete in groups called leagues. All the teams in a league play each other at least once during the course of a season. The team that has won the most games in a league at the end of the season becomes the champion. Sometimes the top several teams in a league compete in a special post-season tournament to determine the champion. There are baseball leagues for nearly every age group. Adult players who are paid to play on a team are called professionals. The top professionals play in the major leagues. Most people who play baseball, however, are unpaid amateurs who play for enjoyment and competition. Amateur programs range from Little League for youngsters to high school, college, and adult leagues.

Major Leagues

There are 30 teams in major league baseball today—29 based in U.S. cities and one in a Canadian city. These teams are divided into two leagues: 14 in the **American League** and 16 in the **National League**. Each league consists of an Eastern Division, a Central Division, and a Western Division.

A major league season starts in April and lasts until October. Every team plays a total of 162 games during the **regular season**. Most games are played between teams in the same league, but some interleague play was begun during the 1997 season. Each team plays half of its games at its home ballpark and half of them away at the ballparks of other teams. There are day and night games, and occasion-

ally teams play two games in one day—a **doubleheader**. At the end of the regular season, the three top teams in each division and a fourth team, a wild-card team—the team in the league with the next best record—compete for the league title, or **pennant**. The two pennant winners then play in the **World Series**, which is sometimes called the Fall Classic because it usually takes place in October. The winner of the World Series is then recognized as the world champion.

Another highlight of the major league season is the all-star game, a special game between the best players in the American and the National leagues. The game has no effect on the standings, but fans enjoy seeing the top stars compete against each other.

Minor Leagues

Major league teams get many of their players from the minor leagues. Each major league club provides financial support to minor league teams. Promising players receive training and experience on these teams. When a minor league player performs well, the parent team usually brings the player up to its major league team.

The minor leagues are generally classified into three groups according to the level of play—Class A, Class AA, and the highest level, Class AAA. There are also winter leagues and leagues for rookies, or first-year players, some of which are in Mexico and other Latin American countries.

MAJOR LEAGUE TEAMS

National League

Eastern Division	Central Division	Western Division
Atlanta Braves	Chicago Cubs	Arizona
Florida Marlins	Cincinnati Reds	Diamondbacks
New York Mets	Houston Astros	Colorado Rockies
Philadelphia Phillies	Milwaukee Brewers	Los Angeles Dodgers
Washington Nationals	Pittsburgh Pirates	San Diego Padres
	St. Louis Cardinals	San Francisco Giants

American League

Eastern Division	Central Division	Western Division
Baltimore Orioles	Chicago White Sox	Los Angeles Angels
Boston Red Sox	Cleveland Indians	of Anaheim
New York Yankees	Detroit Tigers	Oakland Athletics
Tampa Bay Devil Rays	Kansas City Royals	Seattle Mariners
Toronto Blue Jays	Minnesota Twins	Texas Rangers

Amateur Competition

Organized amateur baseball begins with Little League, with divisions for several age groups. The Little League rules are similar to those of the major leagues. The biggest difference is that, for the younger players, the diamond is smaller and the pitcher's mound is closer to home plate. Also, Little League games last six innings instead of nine. (See LITTLE LEAGUE BASEBALL in Volume L.)

American Legion and Babe Ruth leagues also offer youngsters the opportunity to continue playing competitive baseball. Most high schools and colleges also have baseball teams and leagues. In addition, local groups such as park and recreation boards, boys' clubs, and others frequently offer baseball programs for people of all ages.

▶ AN INTERNATIONAL GAME

Although baseball is regarded as the American national pastime, the game is popular in other countries. Minor leagues in Canada and Mexico have been sending players to U.S. professional teams for many years. In 1969 the Montreal Expos became the first major league team based outside the United States. Another Canadian team, the Toronto Blue Jays, was added in 1977. In 1992 the Blue Jays became the first team outside the United States to win the World Series.

Baseball is also widely played and followed enthusiastically in Puerto Rico, the Virgin Islands, and many Latin American countries such as the Dominican Republic, Cuba, Venezuela, Panama, and Nicaragua. These countries have, in fact, developed a number of great players who became stars in the major leagues in the United States—Roberto Clemente, Juan Marichal, Tony Oliva, Orlando Cepeda, Moises Alou, and a host of others. Because competition at all levels is held year-round in these countries, during the winter months many U.S. professionals go to them to take part in competitive league play.

Baseball was introduced to Japan by an American teacher, Horace Wilson, in 1873. The level of play in Japanese baseball is very high, and it has produced its own stars. Among the most famous was Sadaharu Oh of the Yomiuri Giants, who hit 868 career home runs. A number of American players also have played professionally in Japan.

The game is also popular, especially with youngsters, in Asian countries such as Taiwan and South Korea. Since the 1960's, Asian teams have won many Little League World Series championships.

Because of its worldwide popularity, baseball became a demonstration sport at the 1984 Summer Olympics and an official medal sport in 1992.

SELECTED MAJOR LEAGUE RECORDS

Highest batting average, lifetime: .367, Ty Cobb; .358, Rogers Hornsby; .346, Ed Delahanty.

Highest batting average, season: .440, Hugh Duffy (1894); .435, Tip O'Neill (1887); .432, Ross Barnes (1872).

Most hits, lifetime: 4,256, Pete Rose; 4,191, Ty Cobb; 3,771, Hank Aaron; 3,630, Stan Musial.

Most hits, season: 262, Ichiro Suzuki (2004); 257, George Sisler (1920).

Longest consecutive-game hitting streak: 56 games, Joe DiMaggio (1941); 41 games, George Sisler (1922).

Most runs batted in, lifetime: 2,297, Hank Aaron; 2,213, Babe Ruth; 2,076, Cap Anson; 1,995, Lou Gehrig; 1,951, Stan Musial.

Most runs batted in, season: 191, Hack Wilson (1930); 184, Lou Gehrig (1931); 183, Hank Greenberg (1937).

Most home runs, lifetime: 755, Hank Aaron; 714, Babe Ruth; 708, Barry Bonds (end of 2005); 660, Willie Mays.

Most home runs, season: 73, Barry Bonds (2001); 70, Mark McGwire (1998); 66, Sammy Sosa (1998).

Most stolen bases, lifetime: 1,406, Rickey Henderson; 938, Lou Brock; 912, Billy Hamilton.

Most stolen bases, season: 138, Hugh Nicol (1887); 130, Rickey Henderson (1982); 129, Arlie Latham (1887); 118, Lou Brock (1974).

Most runs scored, lifetime: 2,295, Rickey Henderson; 2,245, Ty Cobb.

Most runs scored, season: 192, Billy Hamilton (1894); 177, Babe Ruth (1921); 167, Tip O'Neill (1887) and Lou Gehrig (1936).

Most consecutive games played: 2,632, Cal Ripken, Jr. (1982–98); 2,130, Lou Gehrig (1925–39).

Most games won by a pitcher, lifetime: 511, Cy Young; 417, Walter Johnson.

Most games won by a pitcher, season: 54, Al Spalding (1875); 53, John Clarkson (1885); 52, Al Spalding (1874); 49, John Clarkson (1889).

Most strikeouts, lifetime: 5,714, Nolan Ryan; 4,502, Roger Clemens (end of 2005).

Most strikeouts, season: 417, Charlie Buffinton (1884); 383, Nolan Ryan (1973).

PENNANT AND WORLD SERIES WINNERS—YEAR-BY-YEAR RECORD

The winner of the World Series is indicated by an asterisk (*).

Year	American League	National League	Games Won	Games Lost	Year	American League	National League	Games Won	Games Lost
1903	*Boston	Pittsburgh	5	3	1954	Cleveland	*New York	4	0
1905	Philadelphia	*New York	4	1	1955	New York	*Brooklyn	4	3
1906	*Chicago	Chicago	4	2	1956	*New York	Brooklyn	4	3
1907	Detroit	*Chicago	4	0	1957	New York	*Milwaukee	4	3
1908	Detroit	*Chicago	4	1	1958	*New York	Milwaukee	4	3
1909	Detroit	*Pittsburgh	4	3	1959	Chicago	*Los Angeles	4	2
1910	*Philadelphia	Chicago	4	1	1960	New York	*Pittsburgh	4	3
1911	*Philadelphia	New York	4	2	1961	*New York	Cincinnati	4	1
1912	*Boston	New York	4	3	1962	*New York	San Francisco	4	3
1913	*Philadelphia	New York	4	1	1963	New York	*Los Angeles	4	0
1914	Philadelphia	*Boston	4	0	1964	New York	*St. Louis	4	3
1915	*Boston	Philadelphia	4	1	1965	Minnesota	*Los Angeles	4	3
1916	*Boston	Brooklyn	4	1	1966	*Baltimore	Los Angeles	4	0
1917	*Chicago	New York	4	2	1967	Boston	*St. Louis	4	3
1918	*Boston	Chicago	4	2	1968	*Detroit	St. Louis	4	3
1919	Chicago	*Cincinnati	5	3	1969	Baltimore	*New York	4	1
1920	*Cleveland	Brooklyn	5	2	1970	*Baltimore	Cincinnati	4	1
1921	New York	*New York	5	3	1971	Baltimore	*Pittsburgh	4	3
1922	New York	*New York	4	0	1972	*Oakland	Cincinnati	4	3
1923	*New York	New York	4	2	1973	*Oakland	New York	4	3
1924	*Washington	New York	4	3	1974	*Oakland	Los Angeles	4	1
1925	Washington	*Pittsburgh	4	3	1975	Boston	*Cincinnati	4	3
1926	New York	*St. Louis	4	3	1976	New York	*Cincinnati	4	0
1927	*New York	Pittsburgh	4	0	1977	*New York	Los Angeles	4	2
1928	*New York	St. Louis	4	0	1978	*New York	Los Angeles	4	2
1929	*Philadelphia	Chicago	4	1	1979	Baltimore	*Pittsburgh	4	3
1930	*Philadelphia	St. Louis	4	2	1980	Kansas City	*Philadelphia	4	2
1931	Philadelphia	*St. Louis	4	3	1981	New York	*Los Angeles	4	2
1932	*New York	Chicago	4	0	1982	Milwaukee	*St. Louis	4	3
1933	Washington	*New York	4	1	1983	*Baltimore	Philadelphia	4	1
1934	Detroit	*St. Louis	4	3	1984	*Detroit	San Diego	4	1
1935	*Detroit	Chicago	4	2	1985	*Kansas City	St. Louis	4	3
1936	*New York	New York	4	2	1986	Boston	*New York	4	3
1937	*New York	New York	4	1	1987	*Minnesota	St. Louis	4	3
1938	*New York	Chicago	4	0	1988	Oakland	*Los Angeles	4	1
1939	*New York	Cincinnati	4	0	1989	*Oakland	San Francisco	4	0
1940	Detroit	*Cincinnati	4	3	1990	Oakland	*Cincinnati	4	0
1941	*New York	Brooklyn	4	1	1991	Minnesota	Atlanta	4	3
1942	New York	*St. Louis	4	1	1992	*Toronto	Atlanta	4	2
1943	*New York	St. Louis	4	1	1993	*Toronto	Philadelphia	4	2
1944	St. Louis	*St. Louis	4	2	1994	World Series canceled by a strike.			
1945	*Detroit	Chicago	4	3	1995	Cleveland	*Atlanta	4	2
1946	Boston	*St. Louis	4	3	1996	*New York	Atlanta	4	2
1947	*New York	Brooklyn	4	3	1997	Cleveland	*Florida	4	3
1948	*Cleveland	Boston	4	2	1998	*New York	San Diego	4	0
1949	*New York	Brooklyn	4	1	1999	*New York	Atlanta	4	0
1950	*New York	Philadelphia	4	0	2000	*New York	New York	4	1
1951	*New York	New York	4	2	2001	New York	*Arizona	4	3
1952	*New York	Brooklyn	4	3	2002	*Anaheim	San Francisco	4	3
1953	*New York	Brooklyn	4	2	2003	New York	*Florida	4	2
					2004	*Boston	St. Louis	4	0
					2005	*Chicago	Houston	4	0

▶ **HISTORY OF BASEBALL**

Games with a stick and ball were played as early as 5,000 years ago as part of religious rites in ancient Egypt. Later, the Christian church in France popularized a game in which a ball was swatted with two sticks by two teams of worshipers. This custom spread throughout Europe, giving rise in England to a children's game called rounders. Rounders was surprisingly similar to modern baseball. A batter hit a thrown ball and ran around one or more bases, which were in the form of rocks, sticks, milk stools, or wooden posts. In rounders, fielders threw the ball at base runners. A runner struck by a thrown ball while off base was out. In the 1880's, Americans called the game town ball. When there were not enough players for two entire teams, they played one old cat, two old cat, or three old cat, depending on the number of bases used.

Origins and Early Growth

According to a popular legend, baseball was invented in 1839 by a young West Point cadet named Abner Doubleday at Cooperstown, New York. Most baseball historians now dispute that story, emphasizing the evolution of the sport from such earlier bat-and-ball games as rounders and town ball. The person generally given credit for the biggest role in the evolution of modern baseball is Alexander J. Cartwright. In 1845, Cartwright drew up some rules that are very much like those followed today. Cartwright's rules set four bases 90 feet apart. They also established the foul lines, the strikeout, three-out innings, and nine-player teams. But the ball had to be pitched underhand, runs were called aces, and 21 or more aces made a game.

Cartwright also helped organize the first regular baseball team, the New York Knickerbockers. On June 19, 1846, the Knickerbockers lost the first recorded game to the rival New York Nine, 23–1, in four innings, at Hoboken, New Jersey. After that, amateur baseball spread to other eastern cities. Baseball attracted wide interest during the Civil War (1861–65), when soldiers took up the game.

The Rise of Professional Baseball

By the 1860's, baseball teams were paying some of their players a share of the money paid by fans to watch games. But the first professional team to pay a regular salary to all its players was the Cincinnati Red Stockings of 1869.

Modern professional baseball got its true start in 1876, when the eight-team National League was founded. A rival American Association was formed in 1881 but it disbanded after ten years. The American League, also originally founded with eight teams, had its first season in 1901.

The rivalry that developed between the National League and the American League greatly increased popular interest in baseball. In 1903 the championship teams of the two leagues met in the first World Series, which was won by the Boston Red Sox.

Baseball today is played much as it was in the late 1800's (*above*), when the first professional leagues were organized. One major difference is the vast stadiums, some with plastic domes and artificial grass. Houston's Astrodome (*right*) was the first indoor ballpark.

GREAT PLAYERS IN THE HISTORY OF BASEBALL

The National Baseball Hall of Fame was established in 1936 and dedicated in 1939. It is located in Cooperstown, New York, which is regarded as the home of baseball. Many of the best players in baseball history are honored in the Hall of Fame. They are chosen by an annual secret ballot of the Baseball Writers' Association of America (BBWAA) or by the Committee on Baseball Veterans. All players profiled here have been elected to the Hall of Fame. Biographies of three important members, Lou Gehrig, Jackie Robinson, and Babe Ruth, can be found in the appropriate volumes. Consult the Index to find more information on other important players and managers, including Yogi Berra, *Roy Campanella, *Roberto Clemente, Dizzy Dean, *Bob Gibson, *Josh Gibson, *Roger Maris, *Pete Rose, and *Tom Seaver. (An asterisk indicates players whose pictures appear later in this article.)

HANK AARON (1934–) broke Babe Ruth's home run record in 1974 when he hit his 715th home run. By the end of his career, he had set a new lifetime record of 755 home runs. Aaron played for the NL's Milwaukee Braves, later the Atlanta Braves, and the AL's Milwaukee Brewers. He was the NL batting champion for two years and was named MVP in 1957. Aaron was elected to the Hall of Fame in 1982.

HANK AARON

GROVER CLEVELAND ALEXANDER (1887–1950) was one of baseball's greatest pitchers. During his 20-year career with NL teams (Philadelphia, Chicago, and St. Louis), he won 373 games and lost only 208, winning 30 or more games in three consecutive seasons, a league record he shares with Christy Mathewson. In 1916 he pitched 16 shutouts, a major league record. He was elected to the Hall of Fame in 1938.

GROVER CLEVELAND ALEXANDER

GEORGE BRETT (1953–) spent his entire major league career with the Kansas City Royals, where he established himself as one of the best hitters in the history of the game. Brett was named the Royals' Player of the Year eight times, was an All-Star 13 times, won three batting titles, and was named the AL's MVP in 1980 when he batted .390. He retired after the 1993 season with a lifetime batting average of .305 and was elected to the Hall of Fame in 1999.

GEORGE BRETT

ROD CAREW

STEVE CARLTON

TY COBB

JOE DIMAGGIO

BOB FELLER

ROD CAREW (1945–), a left-handed hitting infielder, played for the Minnesota Twins and the California Angels. In 1977, his best season, Carew had a .388 batting average and won the AL's MVP award. By the end of his career he had 3,053 hits and a .328 batting average. He won seven batting titles. He was elected to the Hall of Fame in 1991.

STEVE CARLTON (1944–), known as Lefty for his excellence as a left-handed pitcher, was the first pitcher to win four Cy Young Awards. He is among the leaders in career strikeouts (4,136) and wins for left-handers (329). Playing for the Philadelphia Phillies, Cleveland Indians, St. Louis Cardinals, San Francisco Giants, Chicago White Sox, and Minnesota Twins, Carlton had six 20-win seasons and won 27 games in 1972. He was elected to the Hall of Fame in 1994.

TY COBB (1886–1961), nicknamed the Georgia Peach, holds the highest lifetime batting average (.367) in baseball history and is one of the leaders in hits (4,191), runs (2,245), runs batted in (1,938), and stolen bases (892). Cobb played outfield for 24 seasons. He played most of his career with the Detroit Tigers but played the last two years with the Philadelphia Athletics. In 1936, Cobb was the first player elected to the Hall of Fame.

JOE DIMAGGIO (1914–99) played outfield for the New York Yankees from 1935 to 1943 and again from 1946 to 1951. He was named the AL's MVP three times and set a major league record for hitting safely in 56 consecutive games. DiMaggio compiled a lifetime batting average of .325 and a slugging percentage of .579. He was elected to the Hall of Fame in 1955.

BOB FELLER (1918–) was known for his strikeouts while pitching for the Cleveland Indians (1936–41 and 1945–56). During his career he won 266 games and lost 162. Feller was nicknamed Rapid Robert because of his fastball, which was clocked at 98.6 miles (158.7 kilometers) per hour. He was elected to the Hall of Fame in 1962.

HANK GREENBERG (1911–86) was a first baseman and

outfielder for the Detroit Tigers (1933–46) and first baseman for the Pittsburgh Pirates (1947). Twice named the AL's MVP, Greenberg hit 331 career home runs, including 58 in 1938. His slugging percentage of .605 is among the best in the history of major league baseball. Greenberg was elected to the Hall of Fame in 1956.

HANK GREENBERG

ROBERT MOSES "LEFTY" GROVE (1900–75) was primarily a fastball pitcher. During his career with the Philadelphia Athletics (1925–33) and the Boston Red Sox (1934–41), Grove won 300 games and lost 141, and he struck out more than 2,000 batters. He was elected to the Hall of Fame in 1947.

ROGERS HORNSBY (1896–1963) was a right-handed hitter whose .358 career batting average is second only to that of Ty Cobb. Hornsby, usually a second baseman, played for the St. Louis Cardinals, New York Giants, Boston Braves, Chicago Cubs, and St. Louis Browns. During his career he won seven NL batting titles (six in a row), including a single-season record .424 in 1924. His slugging percentage was .577. Hornsby was elected to the Hall of Fame in 1942.

LEFTY GROVE

ROGERS HORNSBY

REGGIE JACKSON (1946–   ) was a left-handed slugger who was an outfielder and a designated hitter. Jackson played for the Oakland A's, Baltimore Orioles, New York Yankees, and California Angels. During his career he hit 563 home runs, and during the 1977 World Series he set a record by hitting five home runs. Jackson was elected to the Hall of Fame in 1993.

WALTER JOHNSON (1887–1946) was nicknamed the Big Train because of his size and overpowering fastball. During his career as a right-handed pitcher for the Washington Senators, Johnson won 417 games, struck out 3,508 batters, and pitched 110 shutouts (the most in major league baseball history). His record of 417 lifetime wins is second only to that of Cy Young. In 1936 Johnson was elected as one of the five original members of the Hall of Fame.

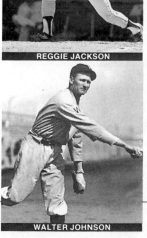

REGGIE JACKSON

WALTER JOHNSON

SANDY KOUFAX

CHRISTY MATHEWSON

MICKEY MANTLE

WILLIE MAYS

SANDY KOUFAX (1935–   ) was a left-handed pitcher for the Brooklyn (and later Los Angeles) Dodgers from 1955 to 1966. During his career he hurled four no-hit games and won the Cy Young award as the NL's best pitcher in 1963, 1965, and 1966. Koufax retired after the 1966 season because of arthritis in his pitching arm. His lifetime record is 165 wins and 87 losses. Koufax was elected to the Hall of Fame in 1972.

MICKEY MANTLE (1931–95) was an outstanding centerfielder and switch-hitter for the New York Yankees from 1951 to 1968. He was voted the AL's MVP three times (1956, 1957, and 1962) and won the Triple Crown in 1956 for leading the league in batting average, home runs, and runs batted in. Mantle hit 536 career home runs. He was elected to the Hall of Fame in 1974.

CHRISTY MATHEWSON (1880–1925), a right-handed pitcher, played most of his career for the New York Giants. Mathewson set an NL record with 373 lifetime wins, among the most in major league history. He helped the Giants win four pennants and the 1905 World Series. Known for his fastball and "fadeaway," or screwball, Mathewson won 37 games in 1908. His three World Series shutouts in 1905 are still a record. In 1936, Mathewson became one of the original five players elected to the Hall of Fame.

WILLIE MAYS (1931–   ) was a great batter, outfielder, and base runner. His 660 career home runs are among the most in Major League Baseball history. After joining the New York Giants, later the San Francisco Giants, in 1951, he was named Rookie of the Year. He was the NL's MVP in 1954 and 1965. In 1972 Mays joined the New York Mets and retired at the end of the 1973 season with a .302 career batting average. He was elected to the Hall of Fame in 1979.

STAN MUSIAL (1920–   ), an outfielder and first baseman for the St. Louis Cardinals, was voted the NL's MVP three times (1943, 1946, and 1948). He won seven league batting titles. Nicknamed Stan the Man, Musial ended his 22-year career with a .331 lifetime batting

AL	American League
MVP	Most Valuable Player
NL	National League

average, compiling 3,630 career hits. He is one of baseball's all-time career leaders in total bases (6,134), runs (1,949), runs batted in (1,951), games played (3,026), and consecutive games (895). Musial was elected to the Hall of Fame in 1969.

MEL OTT (1909–58) was one of the NL's most feared batters. In 22 years with the New York Giants, he hit 511 home runs and had a career batting average of .304. Ott is also an all-time career leader in runs (1,859) and runs batted in (1,860). He was chosen for the All-Star team eleven times. After retiring as a player, Ott managed the Giants from 1942 to 1948. He was elected to the Hall of Fame in 1951.

SATCHEL PAIGE (1906?–1982), a right-handed pitcher, spent 20 years in the Negro Leagues at a time when blacks were not allowed in major league baseball. In 1948, at the age of 42, he joined the Cleveland Indians and became the first black pitcher in the AL. Although past his prime, he won six of seven games for Cleveland, helping them win the pennant. Paige was elected to the Hall of Fame in 1971.

FRANK ROBINSON (1935–   ) was a star outfielder and right-handed slugger who became the first black manager in the major leagues. Robinson's 586 lifetime home runs rank among the best in baseball. He is the only player in history to be named MVP in both the NL and the AL. Most of his playing career was with the Cincinnati Reds (NL) and Baltimore Orioles (AL). Among the teams he managed were the Cleveland Indians, Baltimore Orioles, and Washington Nationals. Robinson was elected to the Hall of Fame in 1982.

NOLAN RYAN (1947–   ) was a right-handed pitcher best known for his blazing fastball. In 1973 Ryan set a modern record for the most strikeouts in a season (383), and in 1989 he became the first pitcher to strike out 5,000 batters. His 5,714 career strikeouts are a major league record. Ryan played for the New York Mets,

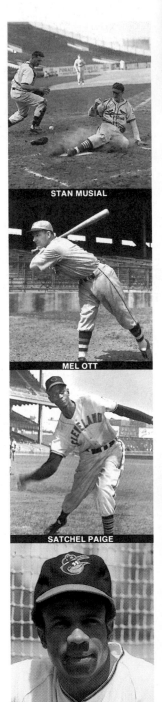

STAN MUSIAL

MEL OTT

SATCHEL PAIGE

FRANK ROBINSON

NOLAN RYAN

WARREN SPAHN

HONUS WAGNER

TED WILLIAMS

CY YOUNG

California Angels, Houston Astros, and Texas Rangers. He was inducted into the Hall of Fame in 1999.

WARREN SPAHN (1921–2003) was an outstanding pitcher for the Boston Braves, later the Milwaukee Braves, New York Mets, and San Francisco Giants. Spahn won a total of 20 games in 13 different seasons and threw two no-hitters. His 363 career wins are a record for left-handed pitchers and the all-time sixth best among all pitchers. Spahn also ranks among the top ten best in innings pitched (5,243). He was elected to the Hall of Fame in 1973.

HONUS WAGNER (1874–1955), nicknamed the Flying Dutchman because of his deceptive speed, is considered by many to be the greatest shortstop and one of the greatest all-around players in baseball history. His career batting average of .327 includes 3,415 hits, 640 doubles, and 252 triples. Wagner was one of the original five players named to the Hall of Fame in 1936.

TED WILLIAMS (1918–2002) was a natural-born hitter. Williams played with the Boston Red Sox from 1939 to 1960 (except when he was in the Armed Forces during World War II and the Korean War). He won six batting championships, batted .406 in 1941, and was twice voted the AL's MVP. His career batting average (.344), slugging percentage (.634), and home runs (521) are among the best in baseball history. His slugging percentage is surpassed only by that of Babe Ruth. Williams was elected to the Hall of Fame in 1966.

CY YOUNG (1867–1965) was the first person in modern baseball to pitch a perfect game. During his 22-year career, he pitched in 906 games, winning a major league record 511. He also holds the record for innings pitched (7,356) and is fourth best in shutouts (76). Young played for NL teams in Cleveland, St. Louis, and Boston, and AL teams in Boston and Cleveland. He was elected to the Hall of Fame in 1937. Baseball's annual pitching awards are named for him.

The Modern Era

Baseball became the "great American game" during the early 1900's. Stadiums were built that could seat thousands of spectators, and soon games were broadcast on radio. Record-setting performances, dramatic World Series games, memorable plays, and colorful personalities became part of a history and folklore that continue to grow.

The period from 1900 to 1919 is sometimes called the dead ball era in baseball history. The balls used during that time were used until they were battered out of shape. Very few home runs were hit, and games usually ended with low scores. Nevertheless, these early years produced some of the greatest players in the history of the game—Cy Young, Walter Johnson, Grover Cleveland Alexander, Christy Mathewson, Ty Cobb, Honus Wagner, Tris Speaker, Nap Lajoie, and others.

The leading teams during this period were the Chicago Cubs and New York Giants in the National League, and the Philadelphia Athletics and the Boston Red Sox in the American League. The Cubs, featuring the fabled double-play combination of "Tinker to Evers to Chance," played in four World Series in five years, winning in 1907 and 1908. The Athletics, managed by the legendary Connie Mack, appeared in four of five World Series from 1910 through 1914, winning three.

Baseball's darkest moment came in 1919, when the Cincinnati Reds defeated the heavily favored Chicago White Sox in the World Series. It was later discovered that eight White Sox players had accepted bribes from gamblers to lose the series. In what became known as the Black Sox Scandal, the eight players were banned from baseball for life.

The next two decades, from 1920 to 1939, have been called the golden era of major league baseball. In 1920 the New York Yankees purchased a hard-hitting player named Babe Ruth from the Boston Red Sox. Many still regard "The Babe" as the greatest baseball player ever. In 1920, Ruth hit an amazing 54 home runs. In 1921 he hit 59 home runs, and in 1927 he hit 60—a record that lasted 34 years. The era of the dead ball was over. Fans flocked to games to see The Babe play.

In addition to the great feats of Babe Ruth, several off-the-field developments boosted the image and popularity of professional baseball. In 1921, Judge Kenesaw Mountain Landis be-

The exploits of Babe Ruth (*above*), including his 714 home runs in 22 seasons (1914–35), increased baseball's popularity. His record of 60 home runs in a year, set in 1927, lasted until 1961, when Roger Maris (*right*) hit 61.

came the major league's first commissioner. Landis helped restore honesty and integrity to the game in the aftermath of the Black Sox Scandal. Meanwhile, many radio stations began broadcasting play-by-play accounts of games, bringing baseball to vast new audiences during the Roaring Twenties.

In the 1930's, more milestones were reached. The first all-star game was played in 1933 at Comiskey Park in Chicago. The first night game was played in 1935 in Cincinnati. The Hall of Fame was dedicated in 1939, and the first television broadcast of a baseball game was made in 1939 from Ebbets Field in Brooklyn.

Besides Babe Ruth, other stars such as Lou Gehrig, Rogers Hornsby, Lefty Grove, Dizzy Dean, and Mel Ott attracted thousands of fans to ballparks. Ruth, Gehrig, and others led the New York Yankees in one of the greatest suc-

sional baseball, black players had been barred from competing in the major leagues. They competed in what were called the Negro Leagues, which produced some of the game's best players, including Satchel Paige, Josh Gibson, and "Cool Papa" Bell. The breaking of the color line by Robinson in 1947 opened the door to the major leagues for other black players. (Admission rules to the Hall of Fame were changed in 1971 so that great players from the Negro Leagues could be admitted.)

The 25 years after World War II gave fans the treat of watching a galaxy of stars. Among the many top hitters of the era were Hank Greenberg, Joe DiMaggio, Ted Williams, Stan Musial, Ralph Kiner, Duke Snider, Hank

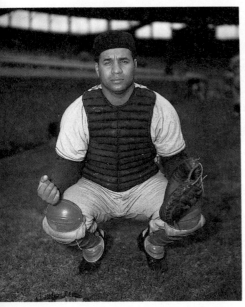

Among the great Hall of Fame catchers are Josh Gibson (*top*), considered the greatest hitter in the black baseball leagues of the 1930's and 1940's; Roy Campanella (*far left*), named Most Valuable Player in the NL three times during the 1950's; and Johnny Bench (*left*), a fine slugger and fielder who won ten consecutive Gold Glove awards from 1968—77 as the NL's best defensive catcher.

cess stories in professional sports history. From 1921 through 1939, the "Bronx Bombers," as they were called, won eleven American League pennants and eight World Series. Another strong team of this era was the New York Giants, who won seven pennants and three World Series.

Over the next three decades, major league baseball continued to grow and change. An important breakthrough occurred in 1947, when 28-year-old Jackie Robinson signed a contract with the Brooklyn Dodgers and became the first black player in the major leagues. From the very beginning of profes-

Aaron, Mickey Mantle, Willie Mays, Ernie Banks, Eddie Mathews, Roberto Clemente, and Frank Robinson. Great pitchers included Whitey Ford, Warren Spahn, Bob Feller, Robin Roberts, Bob Lemon, Early Wynn, Sandy Koufax, Don Drysdale, Juan Marichal, and Bob Gibson.

Another important change after World War II was the movement of existing franchises, or teams, to different cities and the addition of new ones. Among the teams that changed cities during the 1950's were the Brooklyn Dodgers, who moved to Los Angeles, and the New York Giants, who went to San Francisco.

In 1961 the American League expanded to ten teams with the addition of the Washington Senators. In 1962 the National League added the New York Mets and Houston Colt .45's (now called the Houston Astros). In 1977, the Seattle Mariners and Toronto Blue Jays joined the American League.

Meanwhile, new stars were born and new records were set. In 1951, Bobby Thomson clinched the pennant for the Giants with a dramatic ninth-inning home run in a playoff game against the Dodgers. In 1956, Don Larsen pitched the only perfect game (no batters reach first base) in World Series history. Between 1941 and 1964, the Yankees won an amazing 18 pennants and 12 World Series.

The mid-1960's also marked the end of the old Yankee dynasty. From that time until the early 1990's, only a few teams managed to repeat as World Series champions: the Oakland Athletics (1972-74), the Cincinnati Reds (1975-76), the Yankees (1977-78), and the Toronto Blue Jays (1992-93). In the late 1990's, however, the Yankees again dominated, winning four out of five World Series, including three consecutively (1996, 1998-2000).

Some of baseball's most cherished records have fallen. In 1974, Hank Aaron hit his 715th home run, surpassing Babe Ruth's all-time mark. Pete Rose reached and then passed Ty Cobb's record of 4,191 lifetime base hits. Sev-

No list of the game's Cy Young award winners for outstanding pitching would be complete without Roger Clemens (*left*), who won the award a record five times (1986–87, 1991, 1997–98). Tom Seaver (*right*) won three Cy Young awards (1969, 1973, 1975), and Bob Gibson (*below*), who led the Cardinals to two World Series titles in 1964 and 1967, won two (1968, 1970).

The late 1960's signaled another new era in baseball as attendance climbed yearly and baseball became big business. With the expansion of the two leagues in 1969, the present post-season play-off format, called the League Championship Series, was introduced. In 1973 the American League adopted the designated-hitter rule, and in 1993 two new teams, the Colorado Rockies and the Florida Marlins, were added to the National League. Two more teams joined the major leagues in 1998, the Arizona Diamondbacks in the National League and the Tampa Bay Devil Rays in the American League.

Baseball's outstanding hitters include Pete Rose *(far left)*, who had a record-setting 4,256-hit career, and Roberto Clemente *(left)*, who won 4 NL batting titles (1961, 1964–66). Rose was the only player to get 200 or more hits in ten different years, while Clemente won twelve Gold Glove awards as the NL's best right fielder.

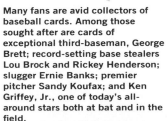

Many fans are avid collectors of baseball cards. Among those sought after are cards of exceptional third-baseman, George Brett; record-setting base stealers Lou Brock and Rickey Henderson; slugger Ernie Banks; premier pitcher Sandy Koufax; and Ken Griffey, Jr., one of today's all-around stars both at bat and in the field.

eral pitchers have exceeded Walter Johnson's career total of 3,508 strikeouts, with the record now held by Nolan Ryan, the strikeout king of baseball. Cal Ripken, Jr., surpassed Lou Gehrig's record of most consecutive games played, 2,130, during the 1995 season. And in 1998, Roger Maris' single-season home run record was broken by two players: Mark McGwire, who hit 70, and Sammy Sosa, who hit 66.

A key change came in 1976. For the first time, players with at least six years of experience in the majors could become **free agents**. Players who once had to stay with the same team until traded, sold, or released now could offer their services to any team. With franchise owners bidding against each other, veteran stars can often sign multimillion-dollar contracts to move from team to team.

The 1994 baseball season ended when a dispute between players and club owners over salary issues led to a players' strike on August 12, 1994. It lasted for 34 days, until the club owners canceled the rest of the regular season and all post-season play. The dispute was still not resolved by the spring of 1995, and the 1995 season did not begin until April 26, 23 days late and shortened by 18 games. A new wild-card playoff format was introduced in 1995 to stimulate fan interest by keeping more teams involved in the pennant race. The dispute was finally resolved in late November 1996.

Reviewed by PETER V. UEBERROTH
Former Commissioner of Baseball

See also LITTLE LEAGUE BASEBALL; ROBINSON, JACK ROOSEVELT (JACKIE); RUTH, GEORGE HERMAN (BABE).

Basketball is an exciting, fast-paced sport in which success often depends on the ability of five strong individuals with special athletic skills to work together as a team.

BASKETBALL

Basketball is the most popular indoor sport in the world. It is also one of the few sports whose year of birth and originator can be traced accurately. The game was invented in 1891 by Dr. James A. Naismith. Although basketball grew and developed in the United States, the game today is played and watched in more than 150 countries.

Two teams, of five players each, play the game on a court. At each end of the basketball court is a round metal rim, or hoop, placed 10 feet (3 meters) above the floor. The rim is attached to a backboard made of wood or fiberglass. Hanging from the rim is a white cord net. The rim and net together are called the basket, or goal.

The object of the game is to score points by shooting a large ball through the basket while preventing the other team from scoring points. The winning team is the team that has scored the most points during the course of the game.

Basketball is a fast-paced, exciting game. Much of its appeal lies in its unique blend of teamwork and individual athletic skills. Speed, strength, stamina, quick reflexes, leaping ability, and shooting accuracy are just some of the important skills for a basketball player to possess. Taller players generally have an advantage over shorter players because taller players can reach closer to the bas-

ket. Shorter players, however, can be valuable for their quickness, ball-handling ability, and other contributions. For any player, the most important asset is the ability and willingness to play in close harmony with the other players on the team. Above all, basketball is a team sport, not an individual sport. At any level of competition—from playground to professional—the most successful teams are the teams that work together as a unit.

When Dr. Naismith invented the game of basketball, he was a physical education instructor at the International Training School of the Young Men's Christian Association (YMCA) in Springfield, Massachusetts. It was winter, and his students needed a fast-action game that could be played indoors. He decided on a game in which the players would have to throw a ball into baskets. So he attached a couple of old wooden peach baskets to the ends of the gym balcony and established some basic rules.

Although the rules laid down by Dr. Naismith are still basic to the game, basketball has come a long way since it was first played in the Springfield YMCA. Every four years, amateur players from all over the world compete in an Olympic basketball tournament. In the United States, millions of fans attend games in sports arenas and gyms. Many millions more watch on television. The top male players compete as professionals. Colleges and high schools sponsor teams for both male and female players. Recreational centers and youth organizations run leagues for younger players.

Part of basketball's popularity stems from the fact that it can be played in many ways. Although organized competition calls for five-player teams, the game can be played for practice or recreation with any number down to "one-on-one." It can even be played alone. In addition, basketball does not cost much money to play, as little equipment is required —only a ball and a hoop.

▶ THE COURT AND EQUIPMENT

A full-size, regulation basketball court is 94 feet (28.7 meters) long and 50 feet (15.2 meters) wide. However, a smaller court is generally used for competition up through the high school level. Indoor courts have a hardwood surface, while outdoor courts are made of asphalt or some other weather-resistant material. The boundaries of a basketball court are marked by two pairs of parallel lines called the side lines and end lines (or baselines). The court is divided in half by a midcourt line parallel to the end lines. Other lines on the court mark off special areas, such as the free-throw lanes, free-throw circle, and center circle.

The basket at each end of the court is attached to a backboard suspended above the floor. The backboard is set midway between the side lines and parallel to the end line. The backboard is usually rectangular in shape, but a fan-shaped backboard also can be used. Painted on the backboard, directly above the rim, is a large rectangle. This helps a player aim when trying to bounce the ball off the backboard and into the basket.

The metal rim should be exactly 10 feet (3 meters) above the floor. It is 18 inches (45.7 centimeters) in diameter, nearly wide enough to fit two basketballs at the same time. The net hanging from the rim is open at the bottom so the ball can fall through.

A regulation basketball is 30 inches (76.2 centimeters) in circumference and weighs from 20 to 22 ounces (567 to 624 grams). (The ball used in the women's game is slightly smaller.) The surface of the ball is made of leather or rubber, usually orange or brown in color. It has a pebble grain for easy gripping. The ball is inflated with air so that it bounces easily.

The only other equipment really needed to play basketball are a pair of athletic socks and sneakers with rubber soles. In formal competition, the two teams also wear uniforms. Each team wears a different color uniform. The standard basketball uniform includes shorts and a sleeveless jersey or T-shirt. On the back of each jersey is a number to identify the player.

Basketball Court

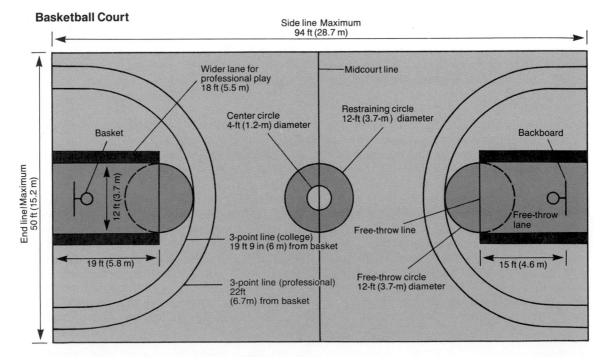

Side line Maximum
94 ft (28.7 m)

Wider lane for professional play
18 ft (5.5 m)

Midcourt line

Center circle
4-ft (1.2-m) diameter

Restraining circle
12-ft (3.7-m) diameter

Basket

Backboard

End line Maximum
50 ft (15.2 m)

12 ft (3.7 m)

Free-throw lane

3-point line (college)
19 ft 9 in (6 m) from basket

Free-throw line

19 ft (5.8 m)

15 ft (4.6 m)

3-point line (professional)
22ft
(6.7m) from basket

Free-throw circle
12-ft (3.7-m) diameter

▶HOW THE GAME IS PLAYED

Each team defends the basket at its own end of the court (backcourt) and tries to shoot the ball into the basket at the other end (frontcourt). The team in possession of the ball, and trying to score, is said to be on **offense**. The team without the ball, and trying to prevent the other team from scoring, is said to be on **defense**. Players can advance the ball up and down the court only by passing (throwing) it or dribbling (bouncing) it.

The Team

The five players on the court for each team normally are a **center**, two **forwards**, and two **guards**. The center is usually the tallest player and takes a position close to the basket. A good center can dominate a game by scoring baskets, rebounding (grabbing missed shots), and blocking the opponents' attempts at the basket. The two forwards are stationed to the sides of the center, along the end lines or farther out on the wings. They are strong players who try to maneuver for close shots at the basket; they should also be good rebounders. The two guards are usually smaller and quicker than the center and forwards. They also play farther away from the basket. The main responsibilities of the guards are to guide the offense and set up the plays. The guards should be good dribblers, passers, and outside shooters.

Although the center, forwards, and guards have somewhat different roles, their positions are not fixed or stationary. They can move anywhere on the court and perform any role in the offense or defense. In fact, a team can change the positions at any time. For example, it might use three forwards and two guards, or two centers and three guards.

In addition to the five players on the court, a basketball team has several substitute players. The substitutes are brought into the game to give the other players a rest or to take advantage of their own special abilities. For example, a substitute who is especially good at defense may be brought into the game to guard the other team's best shooter. Or the team's best shooter may be brought into the game when scoring is especially needed.

Coaches

The coach organizes the basketball team, instructs the players in important skills, and

Professional basketball coaches such as Paul Westphal (*above*) must prepare their teams well for league competition and be ready to outline new strategies during a close game to strengthen a team's defenses or increase its scoring opportunities.

holds regular sessions to drill the team and to prepare for each game. The coach also designs plays and strategies to use against opposing teams. During a game the coach determines which players to use, tells them what to do, and decides when to call time outs. The coach of a college or professional team often has at least one assistant coach.

Over the years, there have been a number of well known college and professional coaches in the sport. Adolph Rupp won a record 879 games as coach at the University of Kentucky from 1930–72 and led the team to four national championships. He also coached the 1948 Olympic gold-medal team. "Red" Auerbach led the Boston Celtics to nine league championships. The 767 career wins of Hank Iba, coach of Oklahoma A&M from 1934–70, is the second best record after the record of Adolph Rupp. Other memorable coaches are Frank McGuire, Pete Newell, Joseph Lapchick, Dean Smith, Lenny Wilkens, and Bobby Knight.

Officials

The conduct of play is controlled by two officials on the court. (Sometimes three are used.) They ensure that the game is played

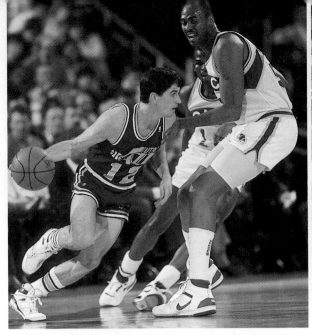

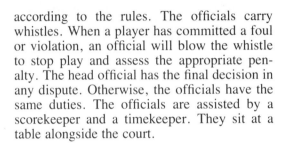

Good ball handlers like John Stockton (*above left*) find ways to dribble around formidable defenders. Two strong centers, Patrick Ewing and Hakeem Olajuwon (*above*), vie for a jump ball to tip to a teammate who could help the team score early during a game in the 1994 NBA championship series.

according to the rules. The officials carry whistles. When a player has committed a foul or violation, an official will blow the whistle to stop play and assess the appropriate penalty. The head official has the final decision in any dispute. Otherwise, the officials have the same duties. The officials are assisted by a scorekeeper and a timekeeper. They sit at a table alongside the court.

Time

The team that scores more points in the specified amount of time wins the game. A high school basketball game is played in four 8-minute quarters, while younger teams play 6-minute quarters. College games are divided into 20-minute halves, professional games into 12-minute quarters. There is a rest period at halftime. (In the second half of the game, the teams "trade" ends of the floor, and each now shoots for the basket that it had defended during the first half.) In case of a tie score at the end of the last period, overtime periods are played—3 minutes in high school games, 5 minutes in college and professional games.

During the course of a game, the clock is stopped when the buzzer sounds to end a quarter or half or when an official blows the whistle for any reason. For example, an official will blow the whistle when the ball goes out of bounds, or to signal that a foul or violation has been committed, or when a team calls a time-out. Each team is allowed only a limited number of time-outs during the game.

The Action

The game begins with a "jump ball" at the center of the court. Two opposing players, usually the centers, face each other at the mid-court line. Their teammates get in position around the center circle. The referee tosses the ball in the air between the two facing players. Each one jumps up and tries to tap the ball to a teammate.

As soon as one team gains possession of the ball, it goes on the offense and advances toward the other team's basket. A shot for the basket may be made from anywhere on the court. It is best, however, to move the ball as close to the basket as possible before shooting.

Players may pass the ball back and forth or from side to side in order to confuse the defensive players. If this happens, one member of the offensive team can get under the basket for a clear, easy shot. Passes do not have to stay in the air—the bounce pass is commonly used. But the ball must stay on the playing court. Should it go out-of-bounds, the official decides which player touched it last. The ball is then awarded to the opposing team.

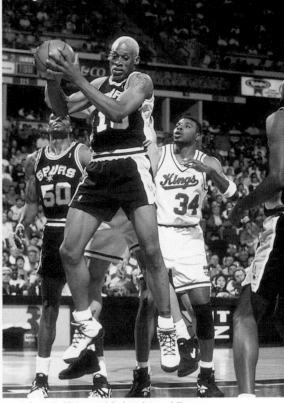

Kenny Anderson (*above left*) keeps his head up while dribbling, searching for a teammate closer to the basket to whom he can pass the ball. Important points can also be scored at the free throw line. Mahmond Abdul-Rauf (*above center*), a good shooter, gets ready to put one up. Grabbing rebounds, as Dennis Rodman does here (*above right*), is essential to a winning effort.

The only other legal way a player can move the ball is by bouncing it along the floor with one hand. This is called **dribbling**. Once a player stops dribbling and holds the ball with both hands, it must be either passed or shot for a basket. If the player dribbles again, before another player touches the ball, or walks or runs while holding the ball (**traveling**), the ball is turned over to the other team.

When a basket is scored, the opposing team gains possession of the ball and passes it inbounds from behind the end line. That team goes on offense and tries for a basket at the other end of the court. The team that just scored now becomes the defensive team. Defensive players try to guard their opponents very closely. They will attempt to steal the ball, intercept a pass, block a shot, or force the team on offense to take only a difficult shot.

A very important part of the game of basketball is **rebounding**. Every missed shot results in a rebound (unless the missed shot goes out-of-bounds). Whichever team can catch the rebound keeps possession of the ball and goes on the offense. Tall players generally get the most rebounds because they are positioned close to the basket and they can reach very high. But smaller players can also grab rebounds if they get in a good position and can legally block their opponents.

Rules and Scoring

Players may not interfere with the progress of an opponent by holding, pushing, slapping, or tripping. Such violations are called **personal fouls**. If a player commits five personal fouls (six in professional competition), that player is disqualified from the game and replaced by a substitute. Another kind of foul is called the **technical foul**. A technical foul is assessed for unsportsmanlike conduct or such other violations as delaying the game, calling too many time-outs, or having too many players on the court.

In basketball, points are scored on either a **field goal** or a **free throw** (also called a "foul shot"). A field goal is a basket made from the court during normal play. A field goal counts 2 points. In professional basketball, 3 points are counted for a field goal shot from beyond a line marked in an arc 22 feet (6.7 meters) from the basket. In men's college basketball,

3 points are counted for a field goal shot from beyond a line 19 feet 9 inches (6.0 meters) from the basket.

A free throw is awarded to a player after certain fouls. The player who is fouled takes a free (unguarded) shot from the free-throw line, which is 15 feet (4.6 meters) from the basket. The other players line up along the free-throw lane to await a rebound. A successful free throw counts 1 point. Two free throws are allowed for a personal foul against a player in the act of attempting a field goal. (If the field goal is made, it counts 2 points, and the fouled player gets one free throw.) In some situations, a **one-and-one** free throw is allowed. That is, if the first free throw is made, the shooter is awarded a second free throw. (The one-and-one free throw is not used in professional basketball.) In professional basketball, three foul shots are awarded to a player fouled while attempting a three-point field goal. Free throws are also awarded to a team if the opposing team commits a technical foul.

Several rules in basketball concern time limitations. From out-of-bounds, a player has 5 seconds to pass the ball inbounds to a teammate. If a team gains possession of the ball in the backcourt, that team has 10 seconds to advance the ball across the midcourt line. Once the ball is across the midcourt line, it may not be passed or dribbled back behind the midcourt line. In high school and college games, no guarded player may hold the ball for more than 5 seconds without dribbling or passing. In any game, no offensive player may stay inside the free-throw lane for more than 3 seconds. In professional basketball, the offensive team has 24 seconds, from the moment of gaining possession of the ball, to attempt a field goal; in a men's college game, the limit is 45 seconds; in a women's college game, the limit is 30 seconds. (There is usually no such restriction in high school basketball.) If time-limit violations occur, the official stops play and gives the ball to the opposing team.

A defensive player may block a shot that is on its way up. But the defensive player may not block a shot that is on its way down; knock the ball off the rim or away from the area above the basket; pin the ball against the backboard; or block a shot that has already hit the backboard. Any of these illegal blocks, called **goaltending**, results in the shooting team being awarded a field goal.

▶ASPECTS OF OFFENSE

In trying to score a basket, the offensive team works together to free one player for a good shot. The guards, forwards, and center move around constantly, trying to get free of the defense. They pass the ball among themselves and dribble when necessary while trying to create an opening for someone to shoot. Breaking through an opponent's defense is sometimes very difficult, and usually requires skillful passing, clever fakes, and acrobatic shooting.

There are two basic styles of offensive play. One is called the **set-pattern** offense. This is a deliberate, pre-arranged series of movements and passes. Each player begins from an assigned spot on the court and follows a specified route through or around the area in front of the basket. Such a pattern can be very complicated. Sometimes the pattern has to be altered or rerun several times, with many passes, before any player gets free for a shot. In a set-pattern offense, **picks** and **screens** are very effective in getting someone free. In a pick or screen, an offensive player takes a firm, stationary position to block the path of one or more defensive players. Another offensive player can then get away for a clear shot. Set-pattern offenses are designed to include many picks and screens.

The other basic style of offense is called the **fast break**, or **running game**. In a fast break, the offensive team tries to score as quickly as possible after gaining possession of the ball. A fast break begins with a rebound at the defensive basket. Then the offense moves the ball downcourt as fast as it can, trying to beat the defensive players to the basket.

▶ASPECTS OF DEFENSE

Good defense is as important as good offense to the success of a basketball team. When the other team has the ball, all five players must work hard on defense to keep the opponents from scoring.

There are two basic types of basketball defense. One is **man-to-man**, in which each defensive player is assigned a certain offensive player to guard. Sometimes a defender will have to help a teammate guard a particular offensive player. This is called "double teaming." The other basic defensive system is called **zone defense**. In this type, each defensive player is assigned a certain area of the

The physical strength required of basketball players on both offense and defense can be seen in this moment when Magic Johnson is trying to power by Michael Jordan on his way to the basket.

court to protect. The player guards any opponent who enters that area. In a zone defense, the players can be arranged in several different ways. The various arrangements have such names as "2-1-2," "1-3-1," "2-3," and "3-2." For example, in a "2-1-2" zone defense, two defensive players are positioned between the free-throw line and midcourt, one is positioned near the free-throw line, and two are positioned close to the basket.

Zone defenses are used in high school and college basketball along with man-to-man defense. Teams often will switch their defense during a game, perhaps changing from one zone to another or from a zone to a man-to-man, trying to confuse their opponents. In professional basketball, however, zone defenses are illegal, and only the man-to-man defense is allowed.

▶ HINTS ON PLAYING BASKETBALL

For the individual player, success in basketball depends on the ability to perform certain basic skills. Coaches call these the **fundamentals** of the game. Young players should concentrate on learning the fundamentals. Even experienced players should practice them often. The most important areas are footwork, dribbling, passing, shooting, and defense.

Exceptional playmaker Scottie Pippin always executes the fundamentals of basketball well. Here he snaps a chest-high pass up court to a teammate who could be headed for a score.

Footwork. Good footwork is important in every aspect of the game. Balance, speed, quick changes of direction, and the ability to stop and go suddenly give any player a big advantage. To be in a position to move fast, stand with one foot slightly forward. Your knees should be bent slightly, your shoulders a bit forward. Hold your arms out a little, with the fingers spread. When you start to run, use your rear foot as a spring. Take short steps. To move to the side or rear, pivot on the back foot. Use the front foot to guide you in whatever direction you want to go.

Dribbling. Dribbling must be done with one hand. Any player should be able to dribble with the right hand or the left hand. Always keep your head up while dribbling so you can be alert for a teammate to whom you can pass.

When you are unguarded and dribbling the ball down court, use the high, or normal, type of dribble. Lean forward a little and bend your knees slightly. The hand that controls the ball should have the fingers spread wide. Your other hand should be at your side for balance. The ball should be bounced about waist high.

If a defender is near, use a low dribble and protect the ball with your body. The stance is the same as for the high dribble except that you bend your knees more. When you are crouching, keep the ball closer to the floor, bouncing it easily as you move around.

Passing. The fastest way to get the ball down court is by passing it. Passing is the key ingredient in offensive play. There are several different kinds of passes, but it is always best

to use the simplest pass you can to complete the play.

The **chest pass** is the most widely used for short, quick throws. Hold the ball chest high with both hands, fingers forward, thumbs behind the ball. As you get ready to pass, bring the ball back toward your chest, turning it so that your thumbs are now under the ball. Then step out with your forward foot while pushing your arms straight ahead. With your wrists snap the ball to the receiver.

The **bounce pass** is effective when your defender keeps his or her hands in the air. With your knees bent, hold the ball waist high with both hands. When you see that your receiver is clear, bend your back knee almost to a kneeling position. Straighten your arms and flip the ball downward on a single bounce toward your receiver.

To throw high to a teammate, you can use the **two-hand overhead pass**. Hold the ball as you would for a chest pass, but with your fingers a little more behind the ball. Keep your feet just apart, and bend your knees slightly. Lift your hands above and a little in front of your head. Take a step forward and bend your wrists back. Then push the ball forward with a quick snap of the wrists.

For getting the ball to a teammate on the run, the best choice might be a **shovel pass**. This is a two-handed underhand pass. It should be short and soft, with no spin on the ball.

To make a long pass, especially on a fast break, you may use the **football pass**. It is made with one hand, the ball cocked behind your head. As you begin to throw, step forward with the opposite leg—just as if you were throwing a football. (Interestingly, this pass is also called the baseball pass, because a baseball is thrown the same way.)

It is also important to learn how to fake. Look high, pass low. Look low, pass high. Fake a pass one way and then pass another. When you have mastered the basic passing techniques, you can try more difficult passes. Just make sure the ball gets to your teammate.

Shooting. No basketball skill is more important than shooting for the basket. In trying to make a basket, a player can choose any of several different kinds of shots. Always choose the easiest shot for the situation. Whatever the shot, maintain good balance, concentrate on the rim, and do not rush. To become a good shooter, practice, practice, and practice some more.

The easiest shot in basketball is the **lay-up**. Dribbling the ball, stride hard toward the basket and jump off one foot. In the air, lay the ball gently off the backboard and into the hoop. When you take a lay-up, push off the floor with the foot opposite your shooting hand. Practice taking lay-ups with either hand, from either side of the basket.

The **dunk** is the most spectacular shot in basketball. The player leaps high in the air,

Reggie Miller (*below*), known for his accurate shooting, prepares to put a good spin on his outside jump shot. Shaquille O'Neill (*right*) completes another of his spectacular slam dunks.

bringing the ball well above the rim. Then the player simply slams it down through the hoop. Usually, only very tall players can reach high enough to perform a dunk. But shorter players who are extremely good leapers can often perform dunks, too.

Another shot for tall players is the **hook shot**. Use the hook only when you are near the basket. After getting the ball, turn so that you are sideways to the basket. With the hand farther from the basket, raise the ball in a circular motion above your head. At the highest point, release the ball with a quick snap of the wrist.

Shots taken farther away from the basket are called "outside" shots. There are two basic ways of shooting from the outside. One is the **set shot**. The two-hand set is best for younger players. Keep your feet slightly apart, knees bent. Hold the ball on each side, with the seams running horizontally. Keep your fingers spread and thumbs back. As you raise the ball near your chin, bend your knees a bit more. Bring your wrists back so that the ball is cupped in your hands. Then straighten your knees and arms, pushing the ball toward the basket with a snap of the wrists. For a one-hand set shot, put the weight of the ball on one hand and use the other hand to guide the ball as you raise it toward the basket.

For more experienced players, the **jump shot** is the most commonly used outside shot.

It is taken like a one-hand set shot, except that the player jumps before shooting. Bend your knees and jump slightly off the floor with both feet. At the peak of your jump, release the ball toward the basket with the same wrist-snapping action.

Always try to take an outside shot the exact same way. Maintain good balance and rhythm. Feel comfortable. It is very important to concentrate on the basket. Snap your wrists, putting backward spin on the ball. Follow through on the release, as if guiding the ball after it has left your hands.

Defense. Guarding an opponent well requires as much concentration as shooting does. Always know where the ball is. Always know where your opponent is. Also know your opponent's abilities and playing habits. Can this player make long shots? Can this player dribble well with either hand? Also be alert for a teammate who needs defensive help. Most of all, work hard and hustle.

When on defense, always keep your knees bent. In guarding, spread your feet with one slightly in front. If your left foot is forward, hold your left arm head-high with fingers spread. Hold out your right arm to the side, between knee and hip. When your opponent has the ball, stand in front and move your arms constantly. Your object is to block any pass and keep a shot from being taken. The

A well-executed hook shot, like this one of Dikembe Mutombo's (*below left*), is an effective scoring tool near the basket. Mark Price (*below right*) gets ready to release a classic one-handed set shot.

GREAT PLAYERS IN THE HISTORY OF BASKETBALL

The Naismith Memorial Basketball Hall of Fame elected its first members In 1959. However, it was not opened to the public until 1968. The Hall of Fame is located in Springfield, Massachusetts, the birthplace of the sport. Most of the players profiled here have been elected to the Basketball Hall of Fame.

KAREEM ABDUL-JABBAR (LEW ALCINDOR) (1947–) began his NBA career in 1969 after playing college ball at UCLA. He played for the Milwaukee Bucks (1969–75) and the Los Angeles Lakers (1975–89). The leading scorer in NBA history (38,387 points), he was named the league's MVP six times. He also scored 10 or more points in more than 600 consecutive games. He retired in 1989 and was elected to the Hall of Fame in 1995.

RICK BARRY (1944–) was named Rookie of the Year when he joined the San Francisco Warriors, later the Golden State Warriors, in 1965. During Barry's 14-year career in the ABA and NBA, he became the only player to lead both leagues in scoring (the NBA in 1967 and the ABA in 1969). In 1975 he led the Golden State Warriors to the NBA championship and was named MVP in the Finals. Barry was elected to the Hall of Fame in 1986.

ELGIN BAYLOR (1934–) was one of the leading scorers in NBA history. He joined the Minneapolis Lakers in 1958 and was named Rookie of the Year in 1959. Baylor remained with the Lakers when they moved to Los Angeles in 1960 and retired from the team in 1972. In the 1962 NBA Finals, Baylor scored 284 points, the most ever by one player in a playoff series. An All-Star ten times, he was elected to the Hall of Fame in 1976.

LARRY BIRD (1956–), an All-American at Indiana State University, played professionally for the Boston Celtics. Considered by some to be the greatest all-around basketball player in history, Bird was named the NBA's MVP for three

KAREEM ABDUL-JABBAR

RICK BARRY

ELGIN BAYLOR

LARRY BIRD

WILT CHAMBERLAIN

BOB COUSY

DAVE COWENS

JULIUS ERVING

consecutive years (1984–86). He led the Celtics to three league championships (1981, 1984, 1986) and played on the 1992 U.S. Olympic championship team. He retired in 1992. Bird was the head coach for the Indiana Pacers from 1997 to 2000. He was elected to the Hall of Fame in 1998.

WILT CHAMBERLAIN (1936–99) played with the Philadelphia Warriors, the Philadelphia 76ers, and the Los Angeles Lakers. Chamberlain was the NBA's leading scorer for seven consecutive seasons (1959–65). He holds the NBA record for career rebounds and was named MVP four times. He holds the NBA record for the most points (100) scored in one game. Chamberlain retired in 1973 and was elected to the Hall of Fame in 1979.

BOB COUSY (1928–), a guard with the Boston Celtics, was one of the NBA's finest players. A brilliant playmaker, he led the league in assists for eight consecutive seasons. His Celtics won six NBA championships, and he was chosen for the NBA All-Pro team ten years in a row. After retiring in 1963, Cousy coached at Boston College and for the NBA's Cincinnati Royals. In 1969 he was a player and coach for seven of the Royals' games. Cousy was elected to the Hall of Fame in 1971.

DAVE COWENS (1948–) played with the Boston Celtics for ten seasons. He was chosen for the NBA All-Stars seven consecutive times (1972–78) and was named MVP in the NBA in 1973. Cowens was the Celtics' player and coach for 68 games during the 1978–79 season. After his retirement in 1980, Cowens played one season (1982–83) with the Milwaukee Bucks. He was elected to the Hall of Fame in 1991.

JULIUS ERVING (1950–), nicknamed Dr. J, became known for his spectacular leaping ability and acrobatic moves. Erving played for the Virginia Squires and New York Nets in the ABA and the Philadelphia 76ers in the NBA. He led the ABA in scoring in 1973 and 1974 and the NBA in 1976. Erving was named MVP in the ABA three times and once in the NBA. He retired in 1987 and was elected to the Hall of Fame in 1993.

JOHN HAVLICEK (1940–) spent his entire career with the Boston Celtics. He was one of the top scorers in NBA history with 26,395 career points. For four consecutive years he was named to the first team NBA All-Pro. He also helped the Celtics win eight NBA titles and was named MVP in the playoffs in 1974. Havlicek was elected to the Hall of Fame in 1984.

ELVIN HAYES (1945–) was named College Player of the Year in 1968 while at the University of Houston. During a 16-year NBA career, Hayes averaged 21.0 points per game. He is the sixth leading scorer in league history with 27,313 career points and the fourth leading rebounder with 16,279 rebounds. A twelve-time All-Star, Hayes was elected to the Hall of Fame in 1990.

EARVIN "MAGIC" JOHNSON (1959–) joined the Los Angeles Lakers in 1979. He was named league MVP three times (1987, 1989, 1990) and won five NBA championships with the Lakers (1980, 1982, 1985, 1987, and 1988). He is third in NBA career assists (10,141). In 1992 Johnson retired from basketball after testing positive for the HIV virus. Since then he has promoted AIDS awareness. He played on the 1992 U.S. Olympic gold medal team, and he was elected to the Hall of Fame in 2002.

MICHAEL JORDAN (1963–) spent most of his career with the Chicago Bulls and has been hailed as one of the greatest players of all time. His career began with Rookie of the Year honors in 1985. He was MVP five times and an All-Star eleven times; set an NBA record by leading the league in scoring for ten seasons (seven of which were consecutive seasons); and holds the Bulls' record for total points scored (29,277). Jordan retired briefly from basketball in 1993 to play professional baseball, spending just over a season in the minor leagues. He returned to the NBA in 1995, helping the Bulls to win three more championships before retiring again in 1999. Jordan returned in 2001 to play with the Washington Wizards. He retired a final time in 2003.

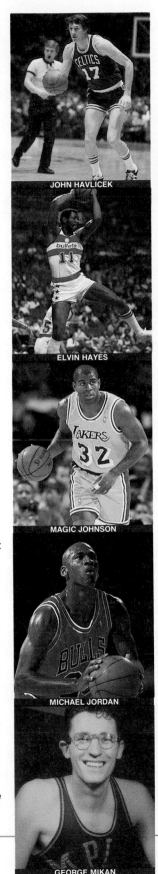
JOHN HAVLICEK

ELVIN HAYES

MAGIC JOHNSON

MICHAEL JORDAN

GEORGE MIKAN

BOB PETTIT

OSCAR ROBERTSON

BILL RUSSELL

JERRY WEST

GEORGE MIKAN (1924–2005) was considered the first outstanding tall center in professional basketball. In 1950, sports writers voted him the greatest basketball player of the first half of the 20th century. As a center for the Minneapolis Lakers, he was a three-time NBA scoring leader and helped lead his team to four league championships. In 1959 Mikan became one of the first players elected to the Basketball Hall of Fame.

BOB PETTIT (1932–) was the first player in NBA history to score 20,000 points. When Pettit retired from the Milwaukee Hawks, later the St. Louis Hawks, in 1965, he had amassed 20,880 points. At 6 feet 9 inches, Pettit was also a leading rebounder. He was elected to the Hall of Fame in 1970.

OSCAR ROBERTSON (1938–), an All-American at the University of Cincinnati, was named Rookie of the Year when he joined the Cincinnati Royals in 1960. He went on to become one of the leading scorers in NBA history with a career total of 26,710 points. With a total of 9,887 assists, he ranks fourth on the NBA's all-time list. Robertson retired in 1974 and was elected to the Hall of Fame in 1980.

BILL RUSSELL (1934–), played on the gold-medal–winning U.S. basketball team at the 1956 Olympics. He then joined the Boston Celtics and led them to eleven NBA championships. Named MVP five times, Russell became a player and coach for the Celtics in 1966, the first black to coach a major professional sports team. Russell became a TV sportscaster in 1969. Then he coached the Seattle SuperSonics and later the Sacramento Kings. He was elected to the Hall of Fame in 1975.

JERRY WEST (1938–) was one of the leading scorers in NBA history, with 25,192 points during his career. He played guard with the Los Angeles Lakers during his entire professional career, and was selected to play in 14 consecutive NBA All-Star games. After retiring as a player, West coached the Lakers from 1976 to 1979 and became their general manager in 1982. He was elected to the Hall of Fame in 1980.

ABA	American Basketball Association
MVP	Most Valuable Player
NBA	National Basketball Association
NCAA	National Collegiate Athletic Association

hand on the side is for blocking a pass. The raised hand is for blocking a shot or high pass. If your opponent tries to get away from you by dribbling to the side, move in the same direction with a shuffle, or side step.

When your opponent is in scoring territory, guard as closely as possible. But be careful not to foul. When your opponent is out in the middle of the court or beyond, you can stay a few feet away. If your opponent is awaiting a pass near the basket, stand a bit behind in a straddle position and keep one hand in front to knock away the ball.

In guarding an opponent, try never to leave your feet. Work hard with your legs, not your hands. If your opponent shoots, put both arms straight in the air. Try not to jump—if you do, you will probably foul your opponent. If you must jump, make sure to jump straight up, not toward your opponent.

▶ **EARLY HISTORY**

When Dr. Naismith invented basketball in 1891, the game was played with peach baskets and a soccer ball. Every time a goal was made, someone had to climb a ladder to retrieve the ball. Over the next several years, changes were made to improve the game. In 1893, hoops with net bags began to be used. In 1894, backboards and a slightly larger ball were introduced. The standard metal rim and bottomless netting first appeared in the early 1900's. The modern seamed ball was developed by the 1930's.

When the game was first played, nine people formed a team. Later it was changed to permit nine, seven, or five to play. Standard rectangular courts were established in 1903. As the game spread and formal competition was organized, other regulations gradually were introduced. By the mid-1930's, most of the modern rules had been set.

▶ **MODERN COMPETITION**

Basketball today is still played most widely in the United States. There is organized league competition for boys and girls, men and women, amateurs and professionals. And the popularity of the game continues to grow, both in America and throughout the world.

High School

Most high schools in the United States today, whether public or private, sponsor bas-

ketball teams for both boys and girls. A school's top team is called the varsity. For freshmen and sophomores, many high schools also field a junior varsity squad. Schools within the same general area are organized into a league, with a full schedule of games among all the teams. In some states, high schools are divided into groups based on the number of students enrolled. After the regular season, a statewide tournament is held to determine the champion in each group. Large cities such as New York and Chicago also hold championship tournaments.

In the United States, the National Federation of State High School Associations is the governing body of organized basketball for high school players. The federation is made up of 50 state high school athletic associations, plus one for the District of Columbia, and determines the rules for high school competition.

College

The game of basketball began to catch on in American colleges and universities within only a few years after its invention. By the beginning of the 1900's, the game was being played by more than 50 U.S. colleges. By the 1930's, some intercollegiate games were attracting thousands of fans. Still, it was not until after World War II (1939–45) that college ball became extremely popular. Competition improved and rivalries developed. Some colleges began building big arenas and giving scholarships to good players. Then television brought the excitement into everybody's living room. Since the 1970's, women's college basketball has boomed along with men's.

The National Collegiate Athletic Association (NCAA) governs major college basketball competition. The largest schools compete in Division I; those with smaller enrollments compete in Division II and Division III. Certain other small colleges belong to the National Association of Intercollegiate Athletics (NAIA).

Most colleges also belong to conferences of 8 to 13 teams each. The schools in each conference are located in the same part of the country. Each team plays the other teams in the conference at least twice each year. Then there might be a tournament to determine the conference champion. Some of the

Some Common Basketball Terms

Assist — A pass to a teammate that leads directly to a field goal.

Backboard — The surface of wood or fiberglass to which the basket is attached.

Backcourt — The half of the court away from the basket under attack.

Basket — (1) The iron rim (or hoop) and the attached net through which goals are scored; (2) a field goal.

Blocking — A foul by a defensive player who blocks the legal path of an offensive player.

Charging — A foul by an offensive player who runs into a defensive player having legal position.

Dribbling — Continuous bouncing of the ball with one hand, the only legal way a player may move with the ball.

Fast break — A style of offense in which a team attempts to race to the offensive basket before the defense can get set.

Field goal — A basket made from the court during normal play. A field goal is worth 2 or 3 points, depending on the part of the court from which it is attempted.

Free throw — A free (unguarded) shot from the free-throw line, awarded to players after certain fouls by the opposing team.

Free-throw lane — The area on the floor bounded by the free-throw line, the end line under the basket, and connecting lines forming a 12-foot lane (high school and college) or 16-foot lane (professional). The free-throw lane is also called the "foul lane."

Free-throw line — A line, 15 feet from the basket, behind which the shooter must stand in attempting a free throw. The free-throw line is also called the "foul line."

Frontcourt — The half of the court in which the basket is under attack.

Goaltending — An illegal block of an attempted field goal.

Held ball — Possession of the ball by opposing players at the same time. In professional basketball, a jump ball determines which team will get possession of the ball; in college basketball, possession is determined on an alternating basis.

Jump ball — A means of putting the ball into play in which an official tosses it upward between two opposing players. Each player jumps and tries to tap the ball to a teammate.

Man-to-man defense — A style of team defense in which each player is assigned one specific opponent to guard anywhere on the court.

Offensive foul — A personal foul committed by a member of the offensive team, usually not involving a free throw as part of the penalty. Also called "player control foul."

Palming — An illegal means of carrying the ball while dribbling.

Personal foul — Any of a variety of body-contact fouls. A player who has committed five personal fouls (six in professional basketball) is disqualified from the game.

Pick — A legal method of providing shooting room for a teammate by taking a stationary position that "picks off" or blocks a defensive player.

Pivot — A position taken by a player with his or her back to the basket, at the head of or alongside the free-throw lane, from which the player can spin or shoot or pass the ball to teammates moving toward the basket.

Post — A synonym for pivot. "High post" means farther from the basket, "low post" means closer to the basket.

Press — A style of defense in which defensive players closely guard the offensive players. (A "full-court press" is applied all over the court; a "half-court press" is applied only after the ball is brought across the midcourt line.)

Rebound — The recovery of a missed field goal attempt.

Shot clock — A timer that indicates how much time remains for the offensive team to attempt a field goal. In professional basketball, for example, a team has 24 seconds to attempt a field goal after gaining possession of the ball.

Steal — The capture of the ball from the hands of a player by the defender; also, an intercepted pass.

Technical foul — foul imposed for misbehavior or some technical rule infraction. The penalty is a free throw (sometimes two free throws). In high school and college games, the team shooting the free throw also receives possession of the ball.

Ten-second rule — The rule that a team must bring the ball across the midcourt line within 10 seconds after gaining possession in the backcourt.

Three-point shot — A field goal made from behind a line marked in an arc a certain distance from the basket; such field goals are credited with 3 points.

Three-second rule — The rule that offensive players may not take set positions within the free-throw lane for more than 3 seconds.

Traveling — Running or walking with the ball without dribbling it. Also called "steps" or "walking."

Turnover — Loss of possession of the ball without attempting a field goal.

Violation — Any infraction of the rules that is not classified as a foul. The penalty is loss of possession of the ball.

Zone defense — A style of team defense in which each player is assigned to guard a designated floor area rather than a specific opponent.

Some signals used frequently by officials

| Jump ball | Personal foul | Points scored (1, 2, or 3 fingers) | Traveling | Illegal dribble | Offensive foul |

best-known basketball conferences are the Big Ten, Atlantic Coast Conference, Big East, Big South, Southeastern Conference, and Pacific 10. During the regular season, a team also plays several schools from outside its own conference.

The highlight of the college basketball season is the NCAA championship, a tournament held after the regular season and conference championships. Tournaments are held in three divisions for both men and women.

The men's NCAA tournament has been held every year since 1939. The most successful team has been the University of California at Los Angeles (UCLA), which won ten NCAA titles in the 1960's and 1970's. The first women's NCAA tournament was held in 1982.

International

Outside the United States, most formal competition is either amateur or semiprofessional. The rules used in international basketball are established by the International Basketball Federation (FIBA). The game is played basically as it is in the United States, though with certain minor differences.

The first official basketball competition in the Olympic Games was held in 1936, for men only. Women's basketball became an official Olympic sport in 1976.

Men's Professional Basketball

The first professional basketball teams also date from the early days of the game. The most famous early pro team was the Buffalo Germans. They were created in 1895 and lasted 30 years. During one stretch, the Germans won 111 straight games.

The greatest professional team of the 1920's was the Original Celtics of New York City. The Celtics were the first basketball team to sign players to exclusive contracts. In the 1930's the Renaissance Big Five, or Rens, a team of black players, dominated the game.

Probably the best-known professional team of all time is the Harlem Globetrotters, formed in 1927 by Abe Saperstein. This team of black players is not part of any league. Instead, they tour the world playing exhibition games in which they use their skill and clowning routines to entertain spectators.

The National Basketball League was formed in 1937. It was composed of professional and industrial teams from small midwestern cities. Another pro league, the Basketball Association of America, was established in 1946.

NATIONAL BASKETBALL ASSOCIATION

EASTERN CONFERENCE

Atlantic Division	Central Division	Southeast Division
Boston Celtics	Chicago Bulls	Atlanta Hawks
New Jersey Nets	Cleveland Cavaliers	Charlotte Bobcats
New York Knicks	Detroit Pistons	Miami Heat
Philadelphia 76ers	Indiana Pacers	Orlando Magic
Toronto Raptors	Milwaukee Bucks	Washington Wizards

WESTERN CONFERENCE

Southwest Division	Northwest Division	Pacific Division
Dallas Mavericks	Denver Nuggets	Golden State Warriors
Houston Rockets	Minnesota Timberwolves	Los Angeles Clippers
Memphis Grizzlies	Portland Trail Blazers	Los Angeles Lakers
New Orleans Hornets	Seattle SuperSonics	Phoenix Suns
San Antonio Spurs	Utah Jazz	Sacramento Kings

NATIONAL BASKETBALL ASSOCIATION CHAMPIONS

Year	Champion	Year	Champion
1951	Rochester Royals	1979	Seattle SuperSonics
1952–54	Minneapolis Lakers	1980	Los Angeles Lakers
1955	Syracuse Nationals	1981	Boston Celtics
1956	Philadelphia Warriors	1982	Los Angeles Lakers
1957	Boston Celtics	1983	Philadelphia 76ers
1958	St. Louis Hawks	1984	Boston Celtics
1959–66	Boston Celtics	1985	Los Angeles Lakers
1967	Philadelphia 76ers	1986	Boston Celtics
1968–69	Boston Celtics	1987–88	Los Angeles Lakers
1970	New York Knicks	1989–90	Detroit Pistons
1971	Milwaukee Bucks	1991–93	Chicago Bulls
1972	Los Angeles Lakers	1994–95	Houston Rockets
1973	New York Knicks	1996–98	Chicago Bulls
1974	Boston Celtics	1999	San Antonio Spurs
1975	Golden State Warriors	2000–02	Los Angeles Lakers
1976	Boston Celtics	2003	San Antonio Spurs
1977	Portland Trail Blazers	2004	Detroit Pistons
1978	Washington Bullets	2005	San Antonio Spurs

In 1949, owners of Eastern hockey arenas wanted to sell seats when hockey was not being played. With these large arenas available, the National Basketball League merged with the Basketball Association of America to form the modern National Basketball Association (NBA). The American Basketball Association (ABA) began in 1967 as a league for cities without NBA teams. It was dissolved in 1976, and some of its teams and best players were absorbed into the NBA.

The NBA now has 30 teams divided into two conferences. The Eastern Conference consists of the Atlantic, the Central, and the Southeast divisions; the Western Conference has the Southwest, the Northwest, and the Pacific divisions. Each team plays a regular-season schedule of 82 games, many against teams in the same division. But all the teams play each other a few times every year.

At the end of the regular season, the top teams compete in a series of playoffs to determine the NBA champion. The Boston Celtics, with 16 championships, have been the most successful team in NBA history. From 1959 to 1966 they took the crown eight years in a row. During the 1980's the Los Angeles Lakers won the championship five times (1980, 1982, 1985, 1987–88). In the 1990's, the Chicago Bulls won the championship six times (1991–93, 1996–98).

In 1998, a labor dispute between NBA owners and players resulted in the postponement of the 1998–99 season. However, an agreement was reached between the two sides in January 1999, just before the entire season was about to be canceled.

With talented players such as Chamique Holdsclaw (right), the WNBA has become as exciting and popular as the NBA.

Women's Professional Basketball

The first women's pro league was organized in 1978. This league, the Women's Professional Basketball League (WBL), did not prove to be popular and it ceased operating in 1981. A surge of interest in women's basketball led to the formation of a new women's pro league, the eight-team American Basketball League (ABL), in September 1995. This league also lasted only three years, declaring bankruptcy in 1998.

The Women's National Basketball Association (WNBA) is sponsored by the NBA and began play in June 1997. The WNBA has expanded from its original 8 teams to a total of 13, which are divided into an Eastern and Western Conference. Players who have risen to stardom in the WNBA's short history include Sheryl Swoopes and Tina Thompson of the Houston Comets, Chamique Holdsclaw of the Los Angeles Sparks, and Lauren Jackson of the Seattle Storm. The Houston Comets have been the WNBA's most dominant team, winning the League's first four championships.

Reviewed by DAVE DEBUSSCHERE
Member, Basketball Hall of Fame

BASTILLE. See FRENCH REVOLUTION.

BASUTOLAND. See LESOTHO.

BATES, DAISY LEE GATSON. See CIVIL RIGHTS MOVEMENT (Profiles).

BATON ROUGE. See LOUISIANA (Cities).

WOMEN'S NATIONAL BASKETBALL ASSOCIATION

EASTERN CONFERENCE	WESTERN CONFERENCE
Charlotte Sting	Houston Comets
Connecticut Sun	Los Angeles Sparks
Detroit Shock	Minnesota Lynx
Indiana Fever	Phoenix Mercury
New York Liberty	Sacramento Monarchs
Washington Mystics	San Antonio Silver Stars
	Seattle Storm

WOMEN'S NATIONAL BASKETBALL ASSOCIATION CHAMPIONS

1997–2000	Houston Comets
2001–02	Los Angeles Sparks
2003	Detroit Shock
2004	Seattle Storm
2005	Sacramento Monarchs

Bats are the only mammals that fly. They are also among the most social of mammals. Some species have been known to live in colonies of more than a million members.

BATS

In the animal kingdom, bats are classed as mammals. Like all mammals, bats nurse their young on milk. Like most mammals, they have hair and bear living young. But in one way, bats are different from all other mammals: Bats can fly.

There are mammals known as flying squirrels and flying lemurs, but they do not truly fly. Rather they glide from tree to tree. Bats are the only mammals that move through the air with wings.

A bat's wing is not like a bird's wing. While the bird's wing is formed chiefly of feathers, the bat's wing is a double layer of skin stretched over the thin bones of its arm and fingers. A bat's skeleton is the framework for these wings. The arm extends from a shoulder socket, bends at the elbow, and ends with long, slender fingers. The fingers are almost as long as the rest of the body. They support the main part of the wing and are covered with skin.

The wing covers all fingers except a short thumb, which is left free. A sharp claw on the end of the thumb forms a hook at the top of the wing. When its wings are folded, the bat uses its hooks to climb tree trunks, rocky walls, and other rough surfaces.

The skin connecting the webbed fingers is also attached to the bat's clawed feet. This makes the back part of the wings. Most bats have an extra flap of skin connecting their feet. While flying, many can fold this flap into a pocket for catching insects.

Since its leg bones and leg muscles are included in its wings, a bat can fly more easily than it can walk. But the feet are far from useless. Like human hands, a bat's feet can turn inward, which enables them to grasp objects like twigs and branches. Sharp claws hook securely into cracks or around bumps in the wall or ceiling of a cave. These claws are so strong that they support the bat's whole weight, even during sleep.

When resting, a bat can use its claws to cling to a wall or tree trunk—or it may hang upside down, suspended by its feet. Bats hang upside down because it is easier for them than perching upright.

Bats may be less than 1 inch (2.5 centimeters) in length or as long as 15 inches (38 centimeters). Their wing spread can be as wide as 5 feet (1.5 meters). Bats have fur that may be white, red, brown, gray, or black.

▶HOW BATS LIVE

There are nearly a thousand different species, or kinds, of bats. They live in almost every part of the world except the polar regions. Each kind of bat has different habits, though the various species also have many things in common.

Bat Colonies

Bats are usually social animals. That is, they live in groups. Often they can be found living in caves. If you see one bat flying into a cave, you can be reasonably sure there are other bats inside. In some caves thousands of bats crowd together on walls or ceilings. Smaller bat colonies numbering only ten or twelve bats may live in a hollow tree.

Caves and hollow trees are not the only places where bats live. Some bats simply roost in trees, hanging like leaves from twigs and branches. Two kinds of tropical bats make tents from palm leaves. Such a bat slits the leaf with its teeth, then hangs inside the folds.

Bats live in the pyramids of Egypt and in the fruit trees of Australia. In North America and Europe people sometimes share a house with bats and never know they are there. A bat can squeeze through narrow cracks and roost between layers of wall and ceiling.

Night Creatures

Most bats are nocturnal. This means that they are active only at night. They sleep in the daytime and come out at night to find food. Only a few kinds of bats venture out in bright sunlight. Bats are probably night creatures for the same reasons that most small mammals are. A small animal is in less danger at night. In the daytime it is in constant danger of being eaten by larger animals that sleep at night. Also, at night bats can catch insects with less competition from birds.

The Search for Food

Most bats live on insects alone. Some eat only fruit. Some eat both insects and fruit. A few kinds of bats eat other things—meat, fish, and even flower nectar.

In Canada and the United States, the most familiar bats are insect eaters, though there are nectar-feeding bats in Arizona and California. Probably the best-known fruit bats are the huge flying foxes. In Australia these giant bats have become a serious nuisance to fruit growers. They swarm over the orchards, devouring fruit at night and roosting in the trees by day.

In India one kind of bat has been seen eating mice, birds, and lizards. When captured, the large spear-nosed bats of tropical America will eat almost anything. They have been fed bananas, horsemeat, liver, and hamburger. They will even eat smaller bats.

The bats with the most unusual diets are found in the tropics. *Noctilio* bats of South and Middle America eat fish. They skim over a pond or lake, dragging their sharp claws

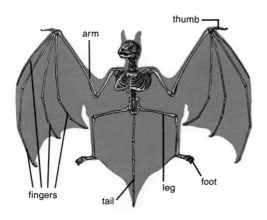

The bat's anatomy is specially adapted for flying. The hands and arms form the wings. The highly developed arm bones hold out flaps of skin from the bat's back and belly. A double layer of thin, flexible skin covers the elongated bones of the fingers.

Bats eat a wide variety of food, some species consuming up to half their weight each night. At left, a bat uses its long tongue to obtain nectar. At right, a mother and baby bat rest. Bats roost by hanging upside down with their wings folded over their bodies.

through the water to catch small fish swimming near the surface. Another group of jungle bats, the tiny hummingbird bats, eat chiefly the pollen and nectar of flowers.

Probably the most famous tropical bats are the vampires, found only in South and Middle America. The vampire bat has inspired legends, superstitions, and horror tales—all of them false. A vampire bat does bite other animals and drinks their blood. But a vampire bat may bite a sleeping horse, cow, or goat—or even a person—without being noticed. Its sharp teeth make a shallow cut. Then the bat simply laps up a small amount of blood and flies away. The chief danger to the victim is not loss of blood but rather infection. Vampire bats—as well as several other species—are known carriers of rabies.

Migration and Hibernation

Bats cannot survive in extremely cold weather. So some fly to warmer climates for the winter. When spring comes, these bats return to a favorite roost. They may make long flights, flying as far as 800 miles (1,287 kilometers) during a migration.

Instead of migrating, other bats avoid winter conditions by hibernating deep in caves, where the temperature changes very little from season to season. For many weeks hibernating bats hang head downward, sometimes packed together in thick clusters. They each have an extra layer of body fat that provides the fuel they need to keep alive until spring.

Birth of Young

Bats mate in the fall, before hibernating or flying away for the winter. When the weather begins to warm up, female bats gather in the roosts that will become nurseries. In late spring or early summer, the baby bats are born. Most mother bats have just one baby at a time. (Some have up to four, but this is as rare as twins in human families.)

When a baby bat is born, the mother forms a living cradle by hanging belly-up from the ceiling or a branch. She may hang by the hooks at the top of her wings as well as by her feet. The newborn bat rests in this cradle. The baby bat is able to hang on to its mother's fur, using its own sharp teeth and claws.

Young bats grow so rapidly that a 10-day-old bat can be too heavy for its mother to carry. Within a month after birth, the baby bat has grown to its full size. A bat born in June is flying on nightly hunting trips by August. It may live as long as 10 to 14 years, a remarkably long lifetime for a small mammal.

▶ ANCESTORS

Ancestors of today's bats were flying about the Earth at least 50 million years ago. Since that time some bats have changed very little. One 40-million-year-old bat fossil found in Europe looks very much like the skeleton of a modern bat.

Some scientists think that the first bats may have evolved from a tree-climbing mammal that could leap and glide after insects. Over millions of years the limbs of some gliding animals may have developed into wings. These winged animals would have been the first bats. Scientists are still looking for fossils that would prove this theory.

▶ FINDING THEIR WAY

For centuries, people who studied bats wondered how they find their way in the dark. Many people thought that bats had unusually keen eyesight and could see by light too faint for human eyes to detect. Scientists now know that a bat's ability to navigate depends not on its eyes but on its ears and vocal organs.

The first steps toward understanding how bats navigate were taken in the 1780's. An Italian zoologist named Lazzaro Spallanzani suspected that bats could not see in the dark. To find out, he blinded some bats and released them into a room crisscrossed with silk threads. The bats flew through the maze without touching the threads. Then he tried plugging their ears with wax. The animals blundered about, flapping their wings helplessly and becoming entangled in the threads.

In 1920, Cambridge University professor H. Hartridge suggested that bats sent out signals that were beyond the range of human hearing. (Such sounds are called **ultrasonic**.) He thought bats might use the echoes of these signals to navigate in the dark. But Hartridge could not prove his theory because he had no way of listening to ultrasonic sounds.

In 1941 two scientists in the United States proved that Spallanzani and Hartridge had been on the right track. Donald R. Griffin and Robert Galambos of Harvard University placed bats in front of a new electronic instrument that could detect ultrasonic sounds. The men could hear no sounds, but patterns on a screen showed that the bats were uttering high-pitched cries.

Griffin and Galambos strung a room with a network of wire and repeated some of Spallanzani's experiments. They added their own modern equipment—microphones and recording devices. Patterns on the electronic screen showed that the bats were constantly squeaking as they flew successfully through the maze of wires.

A bat sends out signals—high-pitched squeaks—that bounce off anything in its path. A sound that is bounced back, or reflected, is called an echo. The bat uses echoes to locate things in the dark. So scientists call this system **echolocation**. It is often compared to the radar and sonar systems used by people, which also use reflected signals to locate objects. But radar and sonar are newcomers. Bats have been using echolocation for millions of years.

BARBARA LAND
Columbia Graduate School of Journalism
Reviewed by KARL F. KOOPMAN
The American Museum of Natural History

See also ECHO; RADAR AND SONAR; SOUND AND ULTRASONICS.

A bat locates and judges distance to its prey by bouncing ultrasonic signals off it. The same technique, called echolocation, helps a bat navigate in the dark.

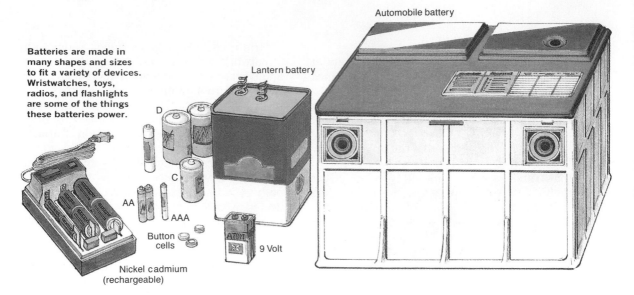

Automobile battery

Lantern battery

Batteries are made in many shapes and sizes to fit a variety of devices. Wristwatches, toys, radios, and flashlights are some of the things these batteries power.

D

C

AA

AAA

Button cells

9 Volt

Nickel cadmium (rechargeable)

BATTERIES

When you enjoy music from a portable radio or find your way in the dark with a flashlight, you are using the most common portable power source known—the battery.

Batteries are very much a part of our lives. Without them many toys would not work, automobiles would not start, and digital wristwatches would not tell time. Even satellites in orbit would stop relaying their signals to Earth.

▶ WHAT IS A BATTERY?

A battery is a device that produces electrical energy, usually by means of a chemical reaction. This chemical reaction takes place in the part of the battery known as the **cell**. Cells are the battery's building blocks. Each battery contains one or more cells. The common transistor radio battery is made up of six cells. The common "D" battery is just a single cell.

Batteries can be either **primary** or **secondary** devices. Primary batteries are those that can be used only as long as the supply of chemicals inside them lasts. (The process of producing electricity uses up the chemicals.) When a primary battery stops producing power, it must be replaced. The "dead" battery should be taken to a recycling or waste-disposal center.

Secondary batteries, on the other hand, can be recharged. When these batteries are exhausted, an electrical current can be applied to the battery to reverse the chemical reaction that took place inside the cells. The result is a battery with a new supply of energy; it can be used until it runs down again.

▶ HOW PRIMARY BATTERIES WORK

One of the most common primary batteries is the "D" battery, also known as the flashlight battery or the dry cell. The dry cell is not really dry. It contains a central carbon rod surrounded by a damp paste of chemicals. These are enclosed in a container made of zinc. When the battery is being used, the carbon, chemicals, and zinc react with each other to produce electricity.

To start the chemical reaction, the battery must be in an electrical circuit. Only when there is a demand for power will the battery produce electricity. When the "on" switch is moved—on a flashlight, for example—a complete path, or electrical circuit, is formed that includes the battery, switch, connecting wires, and bulb. Electricity can now flow through the circuit, and the flashlight bulb lights.

Often more than one battery is needed to provide sufficient power to run a device. Several batteries can be used together if they are lined up in a certain way. In a **series connection**, the positive end of one battery is in contact with the negative end of another battery. This arrangement multiplies the force that pushes the electricity (like a pump pushing water) through the device being powered.

Sometimes cells can be wired in a **parallel connection**, that is, positive end to positive end and negative end to negative end. When this is done, the "push" available is the same as from a single battery, but the amount of electricity is multiplied. This type of connection is used where heavy loads, such as electrical motors, must be powered.

Types of Primary Batteries

The flashlight battery is just one of many kinds of primary batteries. Another common type of dry cell is the 9-volt battery, also known as the transistor radio battery. This device is made up of six flat, 1.5-volt cells stacked one upon the other in a package that will easily fit the small spaces in pocket-size transistor radios and calculators. (These devices do not all use 9-volt batteries. Some take "A" or "AA" cells.) The battery's connecting posts, called **terminals**, are made into clips, and both are located on the top of the package. This helps avoid the problem of putting the battery into a device upside down.

Another type of primary battery is the alkaline battery, which is popular because of its longer life. Its operation is similar to that of the carbon-zinc dry cell, except for the chemicals used. Since the early 1980's, manufacturers have reduced the amount of mercury used in alkaline batteries because of concerns of mercury poisoning in the environment.

Other types of primary batteries are the silver-oxide battery used in electronic wristwatches and the very long-life lithium battery. These batteries are named for the chemicals they contain.

Because all primary batteries in time will run down and have to be replaced, they are most widely used in products or applications where low cost is important or where recharging is not practical, such as in a wristwatch.

▶ HOW SECONDARY BATTERIES WORK

Secondary batteries are often referred to as "wet cells" since many do contain liquids (unlike the dry or damp chemicals in primary batteries). Secondary batteries are also often called storage batteries because when they are being recharged, they are storing energy.

The most common secondary battery is the lead-acid automobile battery. This device is made up of six cells, each of which contains metal plates made of lead and lead dioxide. The plates are immersed in a weak solution of sulfuric acid and water. On the outside of the battery, positive and negative terminals are used to make the electrical connection to the metal plates and acid solution inside.

The automobile battery is turned on by the ignition switch in the car. This action forms a completed electrical circuit. As the battery is being used, or discharged, the lead plates chemically change into different compounds of lead. This process can provide electricity as long as enough lead is present on the plates.

When the battery runs low, however, it can be recharged by forcing electricity to flow into it in the reverse direction. This is the process called charging. It is carried out in a car by a device called an alternator, which is a small electrical generator run by the automobile engine. During charging, the chemical compounds change back into the original lead and lead dioxide. The life of such a battery is measured in years, because it can be charged thousands of times as it runs down.

Types of Secondary Batteries

Other types of secondary batteries are the nickel cadmium and nickel-metal hydride batteries, which are named for the chemicals they contain. Like lead-acid automobile batteries,

A Primary Battery

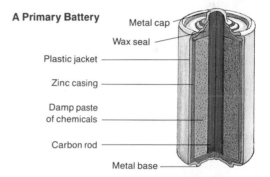

The carbon-zinc dry cell, or flashlight battery, is a common type of primary battery. A chemical reaction between the carbon, zinc, and damp chemical paste causes an electrical current to be produced.

A Secondary Battery

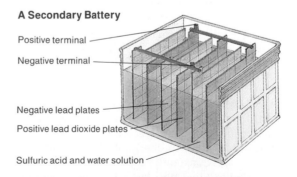

The lead-acid automobile battery, a type of secondary battery, contains lead and lead-dioxide plates set in a solution of sulfuric acid and water. This kind of battery can be charged and used over and over again.

they can be charged many times. This is done with a charging device that plugs into an electrical outlet. These batteries can be used in the same applications as primary batteries. They also are used to power rechargeable flashlights, cellular phones, and a variety of battery-operated household appliances that are supplied with their own chargers.

In general, secondary batteries are used where large amounts of power are needed or where charging is practical to carry out. Though they initially cost more than primary batteries, secondary batteries can be very economical because they are not discarded and replaced every time they run down.

▶ HOW POWERFUL ARE BATTERIES?

The amount of power that a battery can deliver is directly related to the amount and type of chemicals it contains. This power depends on two measurements, amperes and volts. An ampere is the amount of electricity the battery can produce in 1 second. Volts are a measure of the "push" the battery can give to electricity flowing through a wire.

The amount of chemicals in a battery also influences the battery's size, so a large battery is more powerful than a small one. Small "AAA" penlight batteries (1.5 volts and $^1\!/_8$ ampere) will run a penlight for an hour or so. An automobile battery (12 volts and 50 amperes) will provide enough power to start a car or run an electric golf cart.

The life of a battery also depends on the amount of power it must deliver to the device it is running. An automobile battery can start a car and keep it running for a short while, but it will very quickly run down if the car's alternator (turned by the engine) does not begin to charge it. On the other hand, tiny button-size batteries will operate a digital wristwatch for a year or more. This is because the power requirements of a wristwatch are very small.

▶ NEW TYPES OF BATTERIES

All of the batteries described ultimately will run down and have to be replaced. Even rechargeable units will reach a point where they will not respond to charging. As a result, scientists are constantly trying to develop the ideal battery that will last for years (when not in use) and will deliver maximum power for long periods of time when needed. Two candidates are the solar cell and the fuel cell.

Solar Cells

Solar cells are unique because no chemical reaction occurs to use up material. Electricity is produced when light, particularly sunlight, strikes the surface of the cell. This surface is a thin wafer of specially treated, pure silicon.

The power produced by such cells is directly related to the amount of light present. With enough light, a 3-inch (8-centimeter) solar cell will produce about one-third the amount of electrical energy of a "AAA" penlight battery. It will do so, however, as long as light falls on the cell—even for years.

Individual solar cells are almost always connected together to form solar batteries. They are used in applications where it is impractical or even impossible to replace worn-out batteries. The power source for most artificial satellites circling Earth consists of large solar batteries that are made up of hundreds of individual cells. Solar batteries are also being used as inexpensive power sources for hand-held electronic calculators.

Fuel Cells

Another candidate for the ideal battery is the fuel cell. This device produces electricity from the interaction of two gases—typically hydrogen and oxygen. This battery works by passing hydrogen and oxygen gas over a heated substance in a specially constructed chamber. A complex chemical process combines the two gases and produces electricity as a result.

An interesting by-product of fuel cells is pure water. Because the gases are obtained inexpensively and the by-product is useful, fuel cells are suitable for space travel and may become a major source of power for our cities.

Nuclear Batteries

A third type of battery that exhibits extremely long life is the nuclear battery, which powers some space probes. It produces electricity as the result of the decay of radioactive material. A nuclear battery has a lifetime that is measured in hundreds or even thousands of years. However, the problem with this device is the danger of radioactive contamination. For this reason the widespread use of these batteries probably will not occur in the near future.

IRWIN MATH
Author, *Wires and Watts: Understanding and Using Electricity*

See also ELECTRICITY.

BATTLES

A battle is an organized conflict between two or more competing armies, navies, or air forces that is fought to achieve victory at a particular location in the shortest possible amount of time.

The first armies were organized about 3000 B.C. to protect the civilizations that developed in the fertile river valleys of Mesopotamia (modern Iraq). Such armies fought back raiders with stone weapons, but they did not have armor to shield their bodies. Then about 2000 B.C., humans discovered how to make the copper and tin alloy called bronze, which could be sharpened and hammered to make long swords, axes, spearheads, and armor in the form of helmets and breastplates. Conflicts between bronze-equipped soldiers led to the first organized battles, in which they had to choose suitable ground, stand in line, and use their weapons in a disciplined way.

Cavalry soldiers on horseback were the dominant power in battle from about 500 B.C. to A.D. 1500. The most important cavalry armies were those of Attila the Hun, who attacked western Europe in the A.D. 400's; the Mongols under Genghis Khan, who created an empire from China to western Russia in the 1200's; and the Turks, who conquered the eastern Roman Empire (Byzantium) in the 1400's. Foot soldiers in China, India, the Middle East, Russia, and eastern Europe were easily defeated by the superior mobility of these horse soldiers.

While Asians were adapting the horse as an instrument of warfare, Europeans were perfecting iron weapons and armor, which made them equally fearsome on the battlefield. Iron, which had come into general use about 1000 B.C., was superior to bronze because it was cheap, plentiful, and easily worked into blades, helmets, and breastplates. The Greeks of the city-states, about 400 B.C., were the first to organize armies equipped with iron weapons, but it was the Romans who created the first large armies based on iron technology. By the first century A.D. the Roman Empire extended across the whole of western Europe, North Africa, and much of the Middle East.

The secret of Roman success was discipline on the battlefield. Legions of soldiers were drilled to fight in close formation. They were trained not to yield, no matter how terrifying

Superior weaponry enabled Alexander the Great to defeat Darius III at the Battle of Gaugamela (331 B.C.) and conquer the Persian Empire in the Middle East.

the attack. Occasionally Roman armies were overwhelmed, but for five hundred years, they proved generally invincible. It was only when the empire was pressed by huge numbers of German warriors in the 400's that the power of legions was broken and the Roman Empire destroyed.

Europeans nevertheless maintained the tradition of close-order combat with iron weapons. They also managed to adapt their style of warfare to fighting on horseback, which made them formidable opponents of the Mongols and Turks in battle. During the Crusades, from about 1095 to 1291, in which Christians tried to recapture the Holy Land from the Muslims, small armies of European knights on horseback frequently defeated much larger numbers of Muslim cavalry.

The principal contribution to fighting on the battlefield, however, came from the perfection of gunpowder weapons by the Europeans in the 1500's. Equipped with firearms and

The Scots Greys, a British cavalry regiment, charged the French infantry at the Battle of Waterloo in 1815.

25 of the World's Most Important Battles *(in historical sequence)*

Megiddo, 1469 B.C. The first recorded battle of history, fought between the Pharaoh Thutmose III of Egypt and rebel chieftains, took place near Mount Carmel in modern-day Israel.

In 1588, the English fleet defeated the Spanish Armada in the English Channel.

In 1863, Union forces (right) defeated the Confederates (left) on the third and final day of the Battle of Gettysburg. This battle turned the Civil War in the Union's favor.

Marathon, 490 B.C. The victory of the Greeks over the invading forces of the Persian emperor Darius I near Athens rescued Greek democracy from the threat of foreign tyranny.

Salamis, 480 B.C. In this first important naval battle of history, the Greek navy defeated the Persian fleet near Athens.

Gaugamela, 331 B.C. Alexander the Great's victory over the Persian Empire on the Tigris River in modern-day Iraq led to the establishment of Greek rule in the Middle East.

Cannae, 216 B.C. In the Second Punic War, Hannibal of Carthage invaded southern Italy, where he was badly outnumbered by Roman forces. Nevertheless, by using a deceptive battle strategy, he was able to encircle and defeat the Romans.

Alesia, 52 B.C. Roman general Julius Caesar established the Roman Empire by completing the conquest of Gaul (modern France) and capturing the Gaulish chief Vercingetorix.

Adrianople, A.D. 378 The Roman emperor Valens was killed and his army destroyed by German invaders. The western half of the Roman Empire then fell under German rule.

Châlons, 451 Attila the Hun's army of Central Asian horse soldiers was defeated in western Europe by the allied forces of Roman general Flavius Aëtius and Theodoric I, King of the Visigoths. The victory saved Europe from non-Christian domination.

Tours, 732 Charles Martel, the Christian king of France, defeated an Arab invasion coming northward from Spain, saving France from Muslim rule.

Talas, 751 The Chinese empire was defeated by Arabs in Central Asia, blocking the advance of Chinese rule toward the Middle East.

Hastings, 1066 William, Duke of Normandy, defeated the Anglo-Saxon king Harold. Normans then became the rulers of England.

Manzikert, 1071 The Turks of Central Asia defeated the army of Byzantium (the eastern Roman Empire) and captured modern Turkey.

Ain Jalut, 1260 The advance of the Mongol Empire into the Middle East was at last halted by the Turks.

Constantinople, 1453 The Turks captured the capital of the eastern Roman Empire, killed the last Christian emperor, and established Muslim rule in southeastern Europe.

Spanish Armada, 1588 The English fleet defeated the Spanish in the English Channel, saving England from invasion and preventing the conquest of Protestant northern Europe by the Catholics.

Vienna, 1683 An alliance of Christian kings halted the advance of Muslim Turks into central Europe.

Yorktown, 1781 British forces, under the command of General Charles Cornwallis, were forced to surrender to the Americans, led by General George Washington. This action guaranteed the independence of the American colonies.

Valmy, 1792 The armies of the French Revolution defeated an alliance of European monarchs, paving the way for the rise of Napoleon.

Waterloo, 1815 The combined forces of Britain and Prussia defeated Napoleon and brought down the French Empire.

Gettysburg, 1863 In this decisive battle of the U.S. Civil War, the Union army defeated the Confederacy and began the conquest of the South.

The Marne, 1914 At the outset of World War I, the Allies halted the advance of the invading German army outside Paris. A line of trenches was established, along which most of the rest of the war was fought.

The Meuse, 1940 In the first full year of World War II, German tanks broke the French line of defense and captured France in six weeks. The British army escaped to England from Dunkirk.

Midway, 1942 The American aircraft carrier fleet in the Pacific defeated the Japanese carrier fleet, avenging the attack on Pearl Harbor and beginning the defeat of Japan in World War II.

Stalingrad, 1943 A German army, which had invaded the Soviet Union in 1941, was surrounded on the Volga River and was forced to surrender. This victory led to the defeat of the Germans on the eastern front in World War II.

D-Day, 1944 An Allied force of American, British, and Canadian troops landed on the coast of France in Normandy. They drove back the Germans and began the advance which led to Hitler's defeat on the western front in World War II.

Allied troops invaded Normandy on D-Day, June 6, 1944.

horses, Europeans easily conquered the native peoples of the Americas in the New World, beat back the Turks in southeastern Europe, and extended their power into the Middle East, India, and Africa.

As the use of firearms spread, armies continually sought out new technologies and more sophisticated weaponry. Following the Napoleonic Wars in the early 1800's, steam power increased the efficiency of naval forces, and steam-powered railroads rapidly moved armies between battlefields. Heavy artillery, such as cannons, became larger and more powerful.

During World War I (1914–18), the introduction of the machine gun forced infantry units to dig and live in trenches to shield themselves from the constant barrage of bullets. In World War II (1939–45), one of the key weapons was the armored tank, which had been developed to withstand machine-gun fire. Aircraft also were adapted for armed combat against the tanks and became the dominant weapon at sea. Ordnance dropped from the air could cause crippling damage to surface ships and also could destroy submarines below the surface. The most terrifying weapon of all, the atomic bomb, threatened the survival of entire civilizations. Today battlefield technology is so highly developed that traditional battle styles have become increasingly obsolete.

JOHN KEEGAN
Author, *A History of Warfare*

A brown, or grizzly, bear displaying aggression. Bears generally avoid people and can be very dangerous when startled or defending their young.

BEARS

A shaggy giant wades into a stream. Ducking its head, it lunges forward with a huge splash. Then it comes up, a big salmon flopping between its jaws. The huge beast clambers ashore to eat its meal in comfort. This expert catcher of fish is a grizzly bear.

Bears are large mammals belonging to the family Ursidae. They are found on every continent except Australia, Antarctica, and Africa, in habitats ranging from dense forest to icy tundra.

▶ CHARACTERISTICS OF BEARS

All bears have bulky bodies, small ears, and stubby tails. Their legs are thick and powerful, and each foot has five toes tipped with strong, curved claws used for digging and climbing. The claws cannot be drawn in, as a cat's claws can. When bears walk, their heels touch the ground, just as people's do. The prints of their hind feet are remarkably like those of a huge, flat-footed human being. In fact, Native Americans called grizzly bears "the beasts that walk like people."

Bears ordinarily move at a lumbering walk, but they can run very fast when necessary. They have an excellent sense of smell, and their eyesight and hearing are about the same as humans'. Although bears are scientifically classified as carnivores (meat eaters), many species also eat roots, berries, fruits, eggs, and insects. Bears live from 15 to 40 years in the wild.

The largest bear is the polar bear; a few males have been recorded at over 1,700 pounds (765 kilograms). The smallest bear is the sun bear of Southeast Asia, which generally weighs less than 150 pounds (68 kilograms). Only bears that live in northern regions hibernate during the winter, but some polar bears may not hibernate at all. Females of all species are smaller than males of the same age, and most become dormant and sleep a lot when giving birth to their cubs (from one to four). Bears are not very social; they form pairs only during mating season. Females generally try to avoid males the rest of the year.

▶ KINDS OF BEARS

All species of bears evolved from a common ancestor that lived about 40 million years ago. Today there are eight species of bears: the American black bear; the brown, or grizzly, bear; the polar bear; the spectacled bear; the sloth bear; the sun bear; the Asiatic black bear; and the giant panda. Until recently, the giant panda was believed to be a

The polar bear of the Arctic is the largest bear. Cubs stay with their mother for a year or more while learning to survive in their harsh environment.

member of the raccoon family, like the red panda. But genetic evidence has proven that they are much more closely related to bears than to raccoons.

American Black Bear

The American black bear, which averages about 300 pounds (135 kilograms), is found from Alaska and northern Canada to central Mexico. In spite of its name, the black bear appears in a variety of colors. Brown cubs are often born in the same litter with black ones. A subspecies with grayish fur—the glacier, or blue, bear—lives in southern Alaska. About one in ten Kermode bears, which are found on the coast and islands of British Columbia, are a creamy white color; the others are black.

Like bears everywhere, the American black bear fills up on many different kinds of food during the summer and fall. By the time cold weather comes, the bear is very fat and ready for a long winter's nap. It curls up in a den, which it digs in the ground, and goes to sleep. Eating nothing and living off its fat, the bear usually stays in this snug retreat until spring. On mild days it may awake and leave its den for short walks.

Scientists used to disagree over whether the bear's winter sleep is true hibernation. A bear's body temperature does not drop close to freezing like most hibernators. However, during its inactive state the bear's heart rate decreases to only eight to ten beats a minute. Therefore, most scientists now consider bears to be hibernators.

Cubs are born in mid-winter while the mother is in her den. Usually she has two cubs. Their eyes are closed, and they are almost naked. They are tiny and weigh less than a pound. They remain in the den with the mother until late March or early April. By then they are covered with warm fur. They come out and follow their mother, who watches over them and teaches them how to hunt for food. The cubs usu-

Many species of bears, such as this American black bear, give birth to their young while hibernating in a den during the cold winter months.

ally stay with the mother until they are over a year old.

Brown, or Grizzly, Bear

Brown bears live in North America, Europe, and Asia. Brown bears living in the interior of North America are called grizzlies, a name derived from the fact that some brown bears have light-tipped hair that gives them a grizzled appearance. The largest subspecies of brown bears, Kodiak bears, have been estimated at over 1,300 pounds (585 kilograms). Coastal brown bears feed almost entirely on salmon during spawning season. They often have a visible shoulder hump and very long, straight claws. Their claws are used for digging. These bears range in color from blonde to black.

Brown bears hibernate during the winter; in warmer climates they sleep for about five months, but in the Arctic they sleep for seven months or longer. Cubs in the Arctic grow slowly and may stay with their mothers for up to five years, while elsewhere they may leave her after a year and a half.

WONDER QUESTION

How dangerous are bears?

Bears are adapted to catch prey and eat meat. Even species that now eat mainly plants still have sharp teeth, claws, and powerful muscles. They do not normally prey on humans, and they try to avoid people as much as possible. But when cornered, or surprised at close range, bears can attack and even kill people. Mothers with cubs and bears defending a meal can be the most dangerous.

If you choose to camp or hike in an area where bears are known to live, there are several basic steps you can take to minimize the chances of a dangerous encounter. If you are hiking, travel in a group and talk, sing, or make other noises so any bears nearby will hear you coming and have time to move away. Keep to open areas where bears could see you from a distance. Stay away from sources of bear food, such as berries or carrion (dead animals). If you happen to see a bear in the distance, do not approach it; keep as much space between you and the bear as possible. When camping, store all food and toilet articles in sealed plastic bags and hang them 15 feet (4.5 meters) above the ground.

To learn all the rules you should follow to ensure both your safety and the safety of bears, consult a park ranger or enroll in a bear safety education program.

Brown bear populations have been greatly reduced worldwide. In the United States only about 1,000 animals still remain in wild parts of Wyoming, Montana, and Idaho; but over 30,000 live in Alaska.

Polar Bear

The polar bear roams the ice packs and coasts of the Arctic Ocean, which surrounds the North Pole. They are powerful swimmers and are sometimes found far out at sea. Polar bears have keen eyes and an extra-sharp sense of smell. They are true carnivores, eating only meat. They are expert hunters, waiting motionless near breathing holes in the ice, where they catch seals and sometimes even beluga whales that come up to breathe.

The only polar bear that stays in a den during the Arctic winter is a female that is expecting cubs. Before winter comes, she digs a den in deep snow. There her tiny cubs are born. Like cubs of all bear species, they are born with their eyes closed and have little hair. They cling to their mother and nurse while she sleeps. They begin moving around the den after several weeks, and they stay with their mother for at least a year and often longer.

Spectacled Bear

Spectacled bears are found only in South America. They can reach 340 pounds (153 kilograms). They get their name from the dark fur that encircles their eyes like spectacles, or glasses. They live along the western slopes of the Andes mountains, where they are found from the edge of the coastal deserts up to the snowline. Spectacled bears can occupy a wide variety of habitats, but they are most commonly found in dense forests. Spectacled bears feed on plants, small mammals, and even birds, but their preferred foods are fruits and plants of the bromeliad family. Spectacled bears spend much of their time in the treetops, where they often build nest platforms from branches they break off.

Sloth Bear

Sloth bears live primarily in tropical forests and grasslands in Southeast Asia and India. They can grow to 310 pounds (140 kilograms). During the heavy rains of the monsoon period, between April and June, they move to higher, drier forest areas. Their pri-

Above left: The spectacled bear is found only in South America. **Above:** Southeast Asia's sun bear is the smallest bear. **Left:** The sloth bear of Asia eats ants and termites.

mary food consists of ants and termites, which they dig out of the ground with their long front claws. After exposing an insect nest, they use their large mobile lips to "vacuum" up the scurrying insects and their eggs. They also feed on seeds, honey, and flowers.

Sun Bear

Sun bears have short, fine, mostly black fur. They have lighter faces and a light crescent-shaped patch on their chests. They inhabit lowland tropical rain forests in Southeast Asia. Sun bears feed primarily on plants, especially fruits, and are particularly fond of honey. They have very long tongues that are useful for extracting honey and insects from deep crevices in trees. They climb high into the trees but also travel on the ground.

Asiatic Black Bear

Asiatic black bears live in two groups. One group extends from Southeast Asia through the Himalayas as far as the Middle East. The other group is found along the western coast of Asia and includes Japan, Korea, and the Russian Far East. Asiatic black bears are about the same size as their American black bear cousins, reaching about 440 pounds (200 kilograms). They prefer to live in forests at high elevations, where they feed on fruits, leaves, flowers, honey, and insects. At the east-

ern edge of their distribution, in Iran, they eat olives, figs, and insects.

Giant Panda

Giant pandas are not really giant when compared with other bears; they can weigh up to 275 pounds (125 kilograms). Pandas have striking black and white coats, and they are found only in southern China. Their diet consists primarily of bamboo plants. Pandas are the most endangered of all the bear species and are on the brink of extinction; only about 1,000 still live in the wild. For more information, see the article PANDAS in Volume P.

▶ BEARS AND THEIR ENVIRONMENT

Bears have coexisted with people for hundreds of thousands of years. All cultures that have lived with bears include them in their stories, myths, legends, and art. But as human civilization has developed and spread, bear populations have declined worldwide. Today, most bear species are endangered, either from over-hunting or destruction of their habitats.

ROBERT M. McCLUNG
Author, science books for children

Revised by LANCE CRAIGHEAD
Author, *Bears of the World*

The Beatles in 1966. *Clockwise from left:* John Lennon, Paul McCartney, George Harrison, and Ringo Starr.

BEATLES, THE

During most of the 1960's, the Western world seemed to move to the beat of four young rock musicians from Liverpool, England. They called themselves the Beatles.

John Lennon (1940–80), a guitarist and singer, was the original leader of the group. He explained the name Beatles in this way: "When you said it, it was crawly things [beetles]; when you read it, it was beat music." The other members were Paul McCartney (1942–) and George Harrison (1943–2001), also guitarists and singers, and the drummer and singer Ringo Starr (1940–), whose real name was Richard Starkey.

Before the Beatles, many people thought rock was American music that was not to be taken seriously. The Beatles proved them wrong.

Each Beatle brought different strengths to the group. John had a strong personality and a sharp wit. Paul was a showman, who charmed audiences with his melodic voice. George was known as a gifted and serious musician. Ringo was adored for his "goofy," down-to-earth personality.

Brian Epstein, a young record dealer, became their manager. He was a major force in their success. With great difficulty, he found a record company willing to sign the Beatles. Their first single recording, "Love Me Do" (1962), quickly became popular. Their second record, "Please Please Me" (1963), was a big hit. Teenagers—in a frenzy known as "Beatlemania"—struggled to get close to their new heroes.

The Beatles appeared in New York for the first time in 1964. Their engaging personalities and energetic sound turned Britain's most popular rock group into an overnight success in the United States. Within weeks, the top five best-selling records there were all by the Beatles.

Before long, adults found it hard to ignore the Beatles' talents. John Lennon's first book, *In His Own Write,* and the group's first movie, *A Hard Day's Night,* won enthusiastic reviews. Beatles tunes like "Yesterday" were recorded by hundreds of other artists in many musical styles. In 1965, Queen Elizabeth II honored the Beatles by making them members of the Order of the British Empire.

As time went on, the words of their songs, written mainly by Lennon and McCartney, became more poetic. The subjects ranged from the haunting loneliness of "Eleanor Rigby" to the fantasy of "Yellow Submarine" (the theme song for the full-length cartoon of the same name). Their music changed, too. The Beatles began experimenting with electronic effects and instruments from around the world. And they invited jazz and classical musicians to perform on their recordings.

The Beatles produced their masterpiece, the album *Sergeant Pepper's Lonely Hearts Club Band*, in 1967. Later that year, the four wrote and directed a film, *Magical Mystery Tour*, in which they toured the English countryside in search of wonder and fun.

The group made several more recordings during the late 1960's, including the hit songs "Hey Jude," "Get Back," "Something," and "Let It Be," but the members had begun to pursue separate interests. In 1970, the Beatles disbanded.

All of the former Beatles enjoyed some success as solo artists, but fans' hopes for a reunion were ended in 1980 when John Lennon was assassinated in New York City. Paul McCartney was knighted in 1997. In 2001 George Harrison died of cancer in Los Angeles.

NICHOLAS SCHAFFNER
Author, *The Boys from Liverpool*

See also ROCK MUSIC.

BEAUMONT, WILLIAM (1785–1853)

William Beaumont was a frontier surgeon who discovered how the human stomach works. He made his discoveries in a remarkable way: by acquiring a patient with a hole in his stomach. His work ranks as a landmark in medicine. Yet compared with modern doctors, Beaumont had almost no training.

Born on November 21, 1785, in Lebanon, Connecticut, he was one of nine children. His father was a veteran of the Revolutionary War. Young William received some schooling, but no one knows how much. In 1806 he moved to upstate New York, where he taught school. Here he began to read many books about medicine. Four years later he became an apprentice to a doctor and did everything from sweeping floors to assisting in surgery. That was his first medical training. In 1812 he entered the army as a surgeon's assistant.

When the War of 1812 ended, Beaumont practiced medicine in Vermont for a few years. Then he re-enlisted in the army and was assigned to Fort Mackinac, an outpost in northern Michigan. Before going west in 1821, he married. In time he and his wife had three children.

Beaumont was post surgeon at the fort. One day in 1822 he was called to treat a wounded French-Canadian Indian named Alexis St. Martin. St. Martin, who was 18, had been accidentally shot. The bullet had both exposed his stomach and made a hole in it the size of a man's finger.

Beaumont placed him in the post hospital. There, for almost a year, Beaumont treated the wound and kept St. Martin alive. Later Beaumont took St. Martin into his own home and fed and clothed him.

By 1825 St. Martin was well enough to chop wood, but he still had a hole in his stomach. A small flap had grown over the hole, but it could be easily pushed aside. This meant Beaumont could study a human stomach at work and see how it digested food —if St. Martin would let him. Beaumont made an offer. If St. Martin would serve as a human laboratory, Beaumont would give him food, drink, and lodging.

St. Martin agreed, and Beaumont began ten years of experiments that were to make him famous. He tied bits of food to string

William Beaumont, as he appeared about 1821.

and held them in the opening. In this way, he discovered that the stomach produces gastric juice, which dissolves food. He collected the juice in bottles and noted that it continued to dissolve food there. He saw how the movements of the stomach muscles helped to shred the food. Beaumont also found that some meats were digested more easily than others and that small pieces were digested more easily than large ones. His studies still stand as the greatest single contribution to understanding digestion.

The army assigned Beaumont to various posts, and he always took St. Martin with him. But St. Martin often tired of being a human laboratory. He twice left and returned to his native Canada.

Beaumont received some help from other scientists and some support from the U.S. government. But for the most part he carried on the work on his own. He paid St. Martin's expenses even after St. Martin married and had children. When Beaumont finished writing his classic book about his work, he had to pay for publishing it.

In 1834 St. Martin left for the third time, and Beaumont could not persuade him to return. Still, the important discoveries had been made. Beaumont retired from the army in 1840 and settled in St. Louis as a private doctor. He died on April 25, 1853.

JOHN S. BOWMAN
Author and Science Editor

BEAUREGARD, PIERRE G. T. See CIVIL WAR, UNITED STATES (Profiles: Confederate).

The beaver is a talented lumberjack that uses giant chisel-like front teeth and well-developed chewing muscles to fell trees.

BEAVERS

Beavers inhabit ponds and streams in wooded areas from Alaska to northern Mexico. Their bodies are ideally constructed for their varied activities on land and in the water. A beaver's large hind feet are webbed for swimming. Its broad, flat tail is scaly and naked, except for a few bristles. The tail serves as a prop when the beaver stands up to gnaw on trees; it becomes an alarm signal when slapped against the water; it also is a rudder and an oar to aid in swimming.

Although they are air breathers, beavers are thoroughly at home in the water. They can remain submerged for 15 minutes at a time. When a beaver dives, flaplike valves in its ears and nostrils close, shutting out the water. Except for its tail, the beaver is clothed in a shiny coat of soft, thick underfur; this is overlaid with longer, coarser guard hairs. Glands on either side of the tail supply oil, which keeps the coat waterproofed and glistening. The two inner claws of the beaver's hind feet are grooved; they make efficient combs for grooming the coat and spreading the oil through it.

▶CHAMPION HEWERS OF WOOD

Beavers live in family groups, or colonies. The family usually consists of the parents and their young of the past two years. Together they cut trees, build and repair their dams and lodges, and store branches for the winter food supply. This work makes them the most remarkable engineers among the Rodentia, the order of gnawing mammals to which they belong. And among mammals, only human beings are better engineers than beavers.

For felling trees, a beaver uses its four front teeth—the orange-colored, chisel-edged gnawing teeth (incisors). With these sharp tools it takes only a few minutes to cut down a small willow tree. Occasionally beavers fell trees as big as 2 feet (0.6 meter) in diameter. Favorite beaver trees are softwoods like aspen, poplar, and willow. But the beaver also cuts birch, sugar maple, wild cherry, alder, hemlock, and pine.

Building dam

After selecting a tree to cut, the beaver gouges out first one chip and then another a few inches below. Next it tears out the middle chip of wood. Working in this way, the beaver girdles the tree, then cuts deeper and deeper until the tree falls. The beaver cannot control the direction in which the tree will fall. As it begins to totter the beaver dashes for safety.

When all is quiet, the work begins again. But first the beaver may make a meal of tender green bark, buds, and twigs. Holding a section of wood in its front paws, the beaver nibbles away like a person eating corn on the cob. Stomach full, it starts cutting the tree into convenient lengths for moving to the pond.

▶ **BUILDING DAMS AND LODGES**

In deep streams with high banks, beavers sometimes make underground dens in the bank instead of building lodges. Digging the entrance underwater, they tunnel upward beyond the water level. There they hollow out a living chamber in the bank. In such a den the beaver family is safe from most enemies. Even in shallow streams beavers often build bank dens when they first settle in an area. Then they start to dam the stream.

The dam blocks the flow of water and creates a pond where the beavers will live. The dam keeps the pond level constant during spring rains and summer droughts. It is deep enough not to freeze solid in winter.

To build a dam, the beavers drag branches to the place they have selected in the stream. The branches are laid side by side, parallel to the current. Their ends are often thrust into the bottom mud to anchor them. Mud and debris are piled on top. Layer upon layer, the dam is built up. To prevent leaks, the beavers plaster the upstream face with mud, leaves, and stones scooped up from the stream bottom.

Beaver dams vary considerably in size. They can be from 3 feet (1 meter) in length to more than 100 feet (31 meters). Exceptionally large dams may be as much as 10 feet (3 meters) in height.

In the pond that forms behind their dam the beavers usually build an island lodge. Pulling boughs and branches into the water, they build up a broad foundation of sticks and wood—sometimes more than 30 feet (9 meters) across. Making the huge pile slope inward, they construct mounds that may stand up to 8 feet (2.4 meters) above the pond's surface. When the outer structure is complete, the beavers plaster the chinks and holes with mud and debris. A section of the roof is left unchinked, as an air hole. Underwater entrances lead to

Beavers are industrious builders. They use wood, mud, and rocks to construct lodges and dams. Inside the lodge, beaver parents shelter their young. A beaver colony builds a dam to make sure the entrances to the lodge are safely hidden under the water's surface. Beavers also forge canals to make transporting supplies easier.

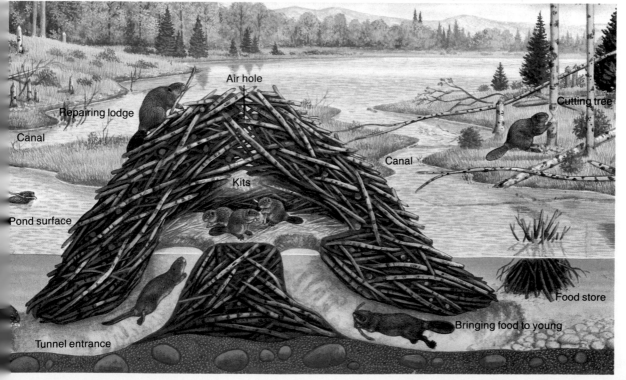

Woody plants are important to the colony's way of life. Gnawing on a tender shoot (*left*) helps satisfy the beaver's nutritional needs. A beaver uses a tree branch (*above*) to make underwater repairs to the lodge.

the main living space. This chamber may be as big as 8 feet (2.4 meters) across and 5 feet (1.5 meters) high.

As time goes by, the beavers have to travel farther and farther from the pond to find suitable trees. Dragging branches and logs, they wear smooth paths, or "tote roads," through the woods. To make the going even easier, they dig canals from the pond to connect with the tote roads. Whenever the job of bringing wood in from increasing distances becomes too difficult, the beavers leave the area. Then in a new location, they start all over again.

▶ FAMILY LIFE OF THE COLONY

From early spring until late fall, all the members of the beaver colony are busy. They repair their dams after the spring floods. They build or enlarge their lodge. They stock food for winter eating. By the time ice and snow arrive, the beavers have a huge quantity of branches stored in the bottom of the pond, close to the lodge. These are thrust into the pond bottom, where they stay fresh.

When the surface of the pond freezes over, the beavers retire to their lodge. Whenever they are hungry, they simply swim out under the ice, cut a fresh branch from the food supply, and carry it into the lodge. Stripped of its tender bark, the branch is finally thrown out.

It may be used the next spring for repairing the dam or lodge.

As spring approaches, the expectant mother beaver prepares a soft nest of wood and bark shavings on the floor of the lodge. Here her young, usually three or four in number, are born during April or May, nearly four months after mating. When the female is expecting, the father beaver moves out for the time being. The year-old youngsters may move out with him. The 2-year-olds leave home for good at this time; they search for mates with whom they will live for the rest of their lives.

The baby beavers, called kits, weigh about 1 pound (0.5 kilogram) at birth. They are born with their eyes open, and they can move about. They grow rapidly and may reach 25 pounds (11 kilograms) in a year's time.

▶ THE BEAVER AND CONSERVATION

In a few areas beavers may become nuisances when their dams flood roads, croplands, or timber areas. But the beaver's good points far offset such problems. Beaver ponds act as fire guards in the forests. They provide homes and breeding places for fish, water birds, and other wildlife. Beaver dams help to control floods and conserve water. They keep soil from washing away. Rich silt backs up behind the dams year after year. When the beavers finally move on, the ponds gradually fill in. They become part of wide, gentle valleys covered with fertile soil.

ROBERT M. McCLUNG
Author, science books for children

BECKET, SAINT THOMAS À
(1118?–1170)

Thomas à Becket was archbishop of Canterbury during the reign of Henry II of England. As archbishop, he clashed with the king over the rights of the church against the rights of the crown. The conflict led to Thomas' death. It has become one of the most famous episodes in English history and literature.

Thomas was born in London, probably on December 21, 1118. His father, a merchant, came from Normandy, in France. Thomas was educated in London and Paris. While in his 20's, he entered the service of Theobald, archbishop of Canterbury. In 1154, he was appointed archdeacon of Canterbury. That same year, 21-year-old Henry of Anjou came to the English throne as King Henry II. He made Thomas his chancellor, or chief official. Thomas served the king faithfully, and a warm friendship grew up between them. After Theobald died in 1161, Henry offered Thomas the office of archbishop. Thomas accepted reluctantly. He feared that the policies of the strong-willed king would conflict with his own views of his duty as head of the church.

In 1164, the king had a document prepared known as the Constitutions of Clarendon. Its purpose was to restore some of the power of the crown, which had been weakened during the period before Henry became king. Among other things, it provided that members of the clergy who were convicted of crimes by church courts were to be punished by civil courts. Previously, the church had both tried and punished its own members. Thomas refused to sign the document. This infuriated the king, who had expected his friend's support.

Thomas fled to France, where he continued to speak out on the rights of the church. In 1170, Thomas and the king were partly reconciled, and Thomas returned to England. But his refusal to lift the ban against two excommunicated bishops angered the king again. On December 29, 1170, four of Henry's knights murdered Thomas in the cathedral of Canterbury. Henry denied that he had ordered Thomas' death. But he did penance at Thomas' tomb in the cathedral, which at once became a shrine for pilgrims. In 1173, Thomas was made a saint.

Reviewed by ROBERT LACEY
Author, *Majesty*

BECQUEREL, ANTOINE HENRI
(1852–1908)

Antoine Henri Becquerel is known as the man who discovered radioactivity—a discovery that influenced the development of atomic weapons, nuclear energy, and radioactive medical treatments.

Becquerel was born on December 15, 1852, in Paris, France. Both his father, Alexandre Edmond Becquerel, and his grandfather, Antoine Cesár Becquerel, one of the founders of electrochemistry, were physicists.

Becquerel worked as an engineer as well as a professor of physics. His discovery of radiation occurred in February 1896. A few months before, Wilhelm Roentgen had discovered X rays—invisible penetrating forms of radiation. Becquerel wanted to find out whether or not phosphorescent materials—materials that glow in the dark after being stimulated by sunlight—would also give off X rays. What he discovered was that certain substances, such as uranium, would give off X rays even when they had not been stimulated by light.

Soon scientists discovered that other elements give off energy in this way. These are the radioactive elements, whose atoms are decaying. Particles from the atoms break away and release the energy that held the atoms together. When harnessed, this produces the enormous energy needed to produce nuclear power.

In 1901, while experimenting with radium, Becquerel developed what looked like a reddish-brown sunburn on his skin. He reasoned that the burn was caused by the radium—that the rays emitted were able to penetrate and cause changes to living things. His discovery led to the controlled use of radioactivity in the treatment of some diseases. For his discoveries he was awarded, along with Marie and Pierre Curie, the Nobel prize in physics in 1903.

Becquerel died on August 25, 1908, in Le Croisic, France.

RACHEL KRANZ
Editor, Biographies
The Young Adult Reader's Adviser

See also CHEMISTRY, HISTORY OF; URANIUM.

BEECHER, HENRY WARD (1813–1887)

Henry Ward Beecher was the most famous American preacher of his time. He was born on June 24, 1813, in Litchfield, Connecticut. His father, Lyman Beecher, was a distinguished Presbyterian minister, and four of Henry's brothers also became clergymen. Among his sisters, Catharine Beecher was a notable educator, and Harriet Beecher Stowe won fame for her novel *Uncle Tom's Cabin*.

Beecher graduated from Amherst College, in Massachusetts, in 1834. He was not a disciplined student, but he loved literature and read widely. He was athletic, fun-loving and friendly, and a fine storyteller. After Amherst, he studied at Lane Theological Seminary, in Cincinnati, Ohio. In 1837, he married Eunice White Bullard and began his ministry. Soon he became pastor of a church in Indianapolis, Indiana. He developed his skill as a preacher and in 1847 moved to Brooklyn, New York,

as minister of Plymouth Church of the Pilgrims (Congregational). He remained there until his death, on March 8, 1887.

Beecher's sermons were informal, impulsive, witty, emotional, and dramatic. They mirrored his warm personality and attracted between 2,000 and 3,000 people each week. He had a fine voice and a poetic command of language. His physical appearance helped make him a striking figure in the pulpit. He had a strong build and a lionlike head with hair that reached his coat collar. Beecher aimed for the hearts of his listeners and stressed God's love for sinners. He was tolerant of other views. For example, he defended the theory of evolution when most of the clergy attacked it. And he spoke out on the social and political issues of the day, opposing slavery and championing the right of women to vote.

ARI HOOGENBOOM
City University of New York,
Brooklyn College

BEER AND BREWING

Beer is an alcoholic beverage that has been drunk for thousands of years. The making, or brewing, of beer appears to have begun very early in many parts of the world. A beerlike beverage was made in Mesopotamia as early as 6000 B.C. Beer was also brewed in ancient Egypt, Greece, and Rome.

During the Middle Ages most beer was brewed by monks, and almost every monastery had a brew house. Eventually others took over this task and brewing grew into an industry with organizations, or guilds, of brewers. Beer in the Middle Ages was a thick, heavy beverage with a much higher alcohol content than today's beer. This thick, nourishing beer, almost as much a food as a drink, was an important item in people's daily diet.

In medieval England, beer, or ale, was often the chief drink at festivals and celebrations. It was such an important part of these revels that the word "ale" was sometimes used to mean a festival. Lamb-ales were celebrations held at lamb-shearing time. College-ales were parties at which students drank the ale they had brewed. The word "bridal" comes from "bride-ale," which was a wedding feast.

The knowledge of brewing beer was brought to the New World by the early colonists. At first, beer was made in small home breweries. However, as the colonies grew, brewing was established as an industry. One of the first breweries was built in 1683 at Pennsbury, Pennsylvania. Within a hundred years, the brewing industry had become an important part of the nation's economic life.

▶ HOW BEER IS MADE

The brewing of beer starts with grain, primarily barley, although corn or rice is sometimes used as well. The grain is mixed with water and is kept warm until it begins to germinate, or sprout. After a week, the grain is roasted and the germination stops. This partly sprouted grain is known as **malt**.

The malt is mixed with water and boiled to form a sweet liquid called **wort**. The dried seed cones of a plant called the hop vine are added to the wort and the mixture is boiled again. These seed cones, called **hops**, have a slightly bitter taste and give beer its characteristic tangy flavor. All solid matter is then filtered out of the mixture and **yeast** is added. Yeast contains microscopic organisms that

The copper brew kettle at left is located at the Boston Beer Company brewery. Here an employee carefully monitors the simmering of malt and water, which forms the liquid called wort.

feed on sugars and starches. As these organisms feed on the sugars of the wort they release alcohol as a waste product. The change from sugar to alcohol is called **fermentation**, the most important step in the brewing process. Fermentation also produces carbon dioxide gas, which gives beer its bubbles.

After fermentation, the beer is pumped into closed storage tanks where it ages. Then it is filtered again before it is put into barrels, bottles, or cans. From start to finish, the brewing process may take several months.

There are several common types of beer. **Lager beer** originated in Germany. Its name comes from the German word for "storage" (*lager*) because the beer is stored or aged before it is packaged. Lager is usually pale yellow in color, and it has an alcoholic content of about 3 or 4 percent. Special kinds of lager beer include **bock beer**, a darker and heavier type of lager, and **Pilsner**. **Light beer** is a type of lager with reduced carbohydrate contents and fewer calories. **Dry beer** is a lager that is specially brewed to be less sweet than other lagers. **Ale** has a paler color and sharper taste

than lager beer and has an alcoholic content of about 4 or 5 percent. **Porter** is a dark brown beer with a slightly sweet taste. **Stout** is one of the darkest, heaviest, and strongest beers. Its alcoholic content is about 5 to 6.5 percent.

In many parts of the world, people prefer to drink beer chilled. In some places, however, beer is served either at room temperature or slightly warmed. Differences in climate and culture may have something to do with this.

Despite their skill at brewing, old-time brewers could never be certain that each batch would be the same. Today, however, brewing is a highly scientific process—all ingredients are carefully tested and each step is closely controlled. As a result, today's beer is as uniform in quality as any other manufactured product. The amount of beer produced has also changed over the years. In the past, beer was usually brewed for personal use or in small quantities by professionals. Today, most beer is mass-produced in large quantities, although in some places home-brewing or small breweries have become quite popular.

UNITED STATES BREWERS ASSOCIATION

A honeybee (*left*) laden with pollen, which it has stored in special "pollen baskets" on its hind legs, burrows within dandelion petals to suck up the flower's sweet nectar. A beekeeper (*above*) collects the honey produced in a hive from the gathered nectar.

BEES

In a field of blooming flowers, bees are a familiar sight buzzing about seeking the rich stores of nectar and pollen held within the flower blossoms. Bees gather the nectar and pollen for food. They turn the nectar into delicious, sweet honey, which people eat. They also produce beeswax, which is used to make candles, crayons, and cosmetics. Many plants would not grow without their help. As bees fly about searching for food, they fertilize plants by spreading pollen from one plant to another. This allows the plants to reproduce.

There are about 20,000 different kinds, or species, of bees. They are found on every continent except Antarctica. There are two general groups of bees: **solitary bees**, which live alone, and **social bees**, which live together in large groups called **colonies**. A colony of bees can contain hundreds, sometimes thousands, of members.

▶THE BODY OF A BEE

Like all insects, the bee has three body parts: head, thorax, and abdomen. Its body looks fuzzy because it is covered with many fine hairs. Even its antennae, or feelers, are covered with tiny hairs. In addition to a pair of antennae on its head, the bee has five eyes and has chewing and sucking mouthparts. The bee uses its eyes—one pair of large compound eyes and three small eyes—to distinguish colors and different flower shapes. The antennae, or feelers, have sense organs that provide the bee with the senses of touch and smell. Along with the **mandibles** (jaws) that it uses to cut

and chew, the bee has a long tubelike tongue that it uses for sucking.

The thorax of the bee is composed of three segments. The bee has two pairs of wings on its thorax—a large front set and a smaller hind set. The wings, which move up and down and forward and backward, allow the bee to fly forward, backwards, and sideways, and even hover in midair. A pair of legs is attached to each of the thorax segments.

The abdomen of the bee has two very important features. One is a special sac called the **honey stomach**. In it, the bee carries the nectar it collects. The other is its sting. The sting is attached to the abdomen and is found only on female bees. Some species of bees have better developed stings than others. Within one species, there is also a difference between the sting of the female worker bee and that of the queen bee. The worker bee has a straight sting with hooks. The queen bee has a smooth, curved sting. The worker bee defends its life and home with its sting, while the queen bee only uses its sting to kill other queens.

▶ SOCIAL BEES

The honeybee is the most social bee of all. An average honeybee colony has about 30,000 bees, but there may be up to 80,000. The bees live together in their home, called a **hive**, dividing the labor of the colony. Within the hive, the bees produce wax, which they use to build **honeycombs**. A honeycomb is made up of a mass of six-sided compartments, or **cells**.

The colony contains three different kinds of bees: the queen, the drones, and the worker bees. The **queen bee** is a large female who lays all the eggs in the colony. Although the queen lays eggs from January to November, the majority of eggs are laid between the first warm days of spring and the end of the summer.

At the height of the season, the queen may lay as many as 1,000 to 2,000 eggs a day. Since she lives about five years, she may lay up to 1 million eggs in her lifetime. The queen is the mother of the entire colony, and the whole hive is one big family of bees.

The **drones** are the males of the colony. They take no part in the work of the hive. They have only one function—to fertilize the eggs of a queen. A typical colony has several hundred drones.

The **worker bees** are all females. They are smaller in size than the queen. They are able to lay eggs, however, they usually do not lay eggs when the colony has a queen. Worker bees do all the labor in the hive necessary for

Within the bee colony, there are three different kinds of bees: (a) the female worker bee, (b) the male bee, called a drone, and (c) the queen bee.

The External Body Structures of a Honeybee

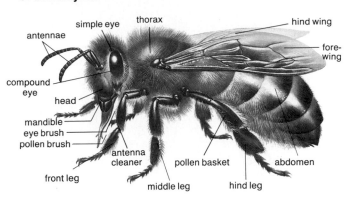

the maintenance and growth of the colony. Tens of thousands of worker bees live in a typical hive.

Inside the Hive. The beehive is a smoothly run, organized society. Each bee has a job to do. If you watch the entrance of a beehive, you will see the busy traffic of bees coming and going. One after another, bees fly out of the hive. Other bees, heavily loaded with the food needed to supply the colony, land and enter the hive.

Workers called **foragers** fly out to flowers and collect pollen and nectar. Pollen, necessary for the formation of seeds in plants, is a source of protein, vitamins, and minerals for bees. When the bees who collect pollen groom themselves, they put the pollen grains that cling to the fine hairs of their bodies into special "pollen baskets." These baskets are flattened areas on their hind legs surrounded by long hairs. Nectar is a sweet, sugary liquid. It is 40 to 80 percent water. The bee sucks it into its mouth with its flexible tongue and stores it in its honey stomach.

When a bee returns to the hive, it spits up its load of nectar through its mouth. The nectar is handed over to other worker bees that place it in empty cells. Special chemicals called **enzymes** are added to the stored nectar. As the nectar dries out, it changes into honey and is a great source of energy for the bees. The nectar gathered by one bee during its entire lifetime is enough to produce about 1.5 ounces (45 grams) of honey.

Duties of a Worker Bee. Some worker bees build the honeycomb. Some clean out empty cells and prepare them for the eggs that the

**From An Egg
to An Adult Bee**

The queen bee (1) deposits one egg in the cell, and a wormlike larva (2) hatches from the egg. The larva grows as it is fed royal jelly or bee-bread. When the larva finishes spinning its cocoon, workers seal the cell with wax (3); the larva starts to pupate, its wormlike body changing into the form of an adult bee. With its growth complete, the young adult bee breaks through the wax cap and (4) emerges from its cell.

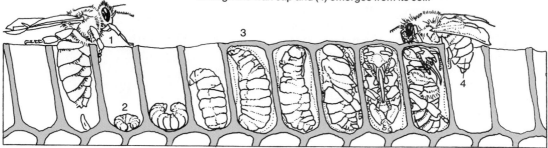

queen will deposit there. Some feed and nurse the growing young. Guard bees stand at the entrance to the hive and protect the hive against enemies, such as wasps, wax moths, and bees from other colonies. Fanning bees ventilate the hive. Still other worker bees take care of the nectar and pollen.

The task of a worker bee depends on its age. For the first three days of its life, the worker cleans a section of the hive called the **brood nest**, which is the part of the hive where the eggs are laid and the young bees are raised.

During the time the worker bee is preparing the brood nest for new eggs, special glands in its head are developing. Once the glands fully develop, they will secrete a creamy substance called **royal jelly**. Then the worker becomes a **nurse bee**, tending the developing larvae (wormlike grubs that hatch from the eggs) and feeding them royal jelly. After several days, the worker stops producing royal jelly and be-

gins to produce wax from glands in its abdomen. At about 12 days, the same bee is a builder of wax cells.

At about 16 days, some workers stop building and start standing guard at the entrance to the hive. There they defend the hive against intruders. Other workers this age receive the nectar and pollen brought by foragers. From the age of 3 weeks until the end of its life, the worker bee shifts to its last and longest job—the collecting of nectar and pollen.

Every bee gathers its own information about the needs of the hive. In any one day it spends part of its time patrolling the hive, inspecting cells and larvae, interacting with other workers, and looking over the building areas and the stores of food. From such inspection tours, new forms of activity start—nursing, building, or cleaning, as each need arises.

In summer when there is a lot of work in the hive, a worker bee may live to only 5 or 6

This page, left: The queen bee checks the brood nest for empty cells in which to lay her eggs. *Right:* Wormlike larvae hatch from the eggs the queen has deposited in the cells. *Opposite page, left:* After the larvae have spun cocoons, the worker bees crawl over the cells in the brood nest, sealing the cells with wax. *Right:* Breaking through the wax cap of its cell, a full-grown bee emerges.

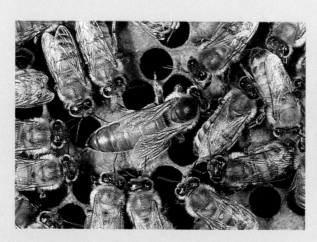

weeks. During the fall and winter there is less work, so a worker may live several months.

The Mating Flight of the Queen. Each time the hive has a new queen, there is a mating flight. A new queen is needed when the old queen dies, leaves to establish a new hive, or becomes feeble. Special cells in the brood nest house developing queen bees. The first queen to emerge destroys those developing in other cells. If two queens emerge at the same time, they fight until one is killed. An old queen may fight the new queen or leave the hive. Only one queen will emerge from the battles.

When the new queen is about a week old, she leaves the hive for her mating flight. During the flight, she will mate with one or more drones. When they mate, the drone transfers sperm (male sex cells) into the queen's body. The queen stores the sperm until she is ready to lay eggs.

The drones die after mating and the queen returns to the hive. A few days later, the queen starts to move over the honeycombs, looking for empty cells in which to lay her eggs.

From Egg to Adult Bee. If the queen exposes her eggs to the sperm she is storing just before they are laid, the eggs will be fertilized. If she does not, the eggs will be unfertilized. All the unfertilized eggs become males (drones). All the fertilized eggs become females (either egg-laying queens or workers).

The eggs develop into larvae after three days. All the larvae receive the same food, royal jelly, for the first three days. Then some of the larvae receive a mixture of honey and pollen called **beebread**. The larvae that are fed beebread will become worker bees. Some lar-

WONDER QUESTION

Are there really "killer" bees?

The so-called "killer" bees are just very good at protecting themselves when bothered. They are the descendants of bees brought from Africa to South America as part of an effort to develop a stronger breed of honeybee. But before a breed could be developed, 26 queen bees escaped from the research hives.

The sting of the Africanized "killer" bee is no different from that of any other honeybee. However, the Africanized bees are quicker to attack and more of them will join in an attack. For the bees to actually kill anything, a mass stinging involving hundreds of bees would have to take place.

vae are selected to be fed only royal jelly. These larvae will develop into queen bees.

The nurse bees carefully tend the larvae, visiting each larva with food nearly 1,300 times a day. At 6 days, the larva starts to spin a cocoon, a shell of silk, inside its wax cell. When the cocoon is completed, the cell is sealed with wax by the worker bees. The larva changes into a pupa within the cocoon. During the pupa stage, the wormlike body of the larva changes into the form of an adult bee. A full-size queen bee emerges from the cell after 16 days. A full-size worker bee makes its way out of its wax cell in 21 days.

Unfertilized eggs go through the same

stages as fertilized eggs. They change into larvae and then become pupae. Full-size drones emerge from the cells in 24 days.

With a queen laying 1,500 eggs a day, a new bee emerges almost every minute to take its place in bee society.

How Bees Communicate. Some foragers, acting as "scouts," return from a food hunt and tell other bees from their hive about the food source they have found. The scouts pass on their information by performing a "dance." There are two basic dances that are used to tell the direction and distance from the hive to a source of nectar and pollen: a **round dance** and a **waggle** dance. If the returning scouts do a **round dance**, it means that food is near the hive. The scouts use the **waggle dance** to describe the exact distance to the food and the direction of the food in relation to the sun. The faster the dances, the closer the food.

In the darkness of the hive, the other worker bees surround the dancing scouts. Using the sense organs on their antennae, the worker bees pick up the flowers' nectar scent clinging to the dancers. The worker bees become excited and start to follow the dancers.

After following the dance, the workers leave the hive and—without the dancing bees to lead them—fly directly to the area of the food source. Once there, the workers search the area for the flowers with the particular scent that clung to the dancing scouts.

The bees form groups just large enough to collect the available food. When the source of the food is plentiful and rich, the worker bees recruited by the scouts also dance on returning

While scouts search for a new location for the colony, the queen and her group of workers cluster in a swarm around a fence post.

to the hive. When the amount of food is reduced, the incoming bees simply deliver the nectar and pollen and do not dance. In this way many bees appear at a good source of food and as the supply wanes, fewer and fewer bees visit those flowers.

Bees also communicate information by the secretions in their bodies. Bees that attend the queen constantly lick a substance from her body and share it with other members of the colony. If the hive loses its queen, the other bees of the colony become aware of her absence in a few hours. They look for her, and if she cannot be found, they immediately set about replacing her with a new queen.

Swarming. When a hive gets overcrowded, the queen lays fewer and fewer eggs. The worker bees build a new type of cell in the

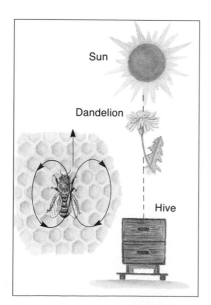

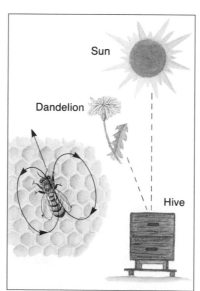

During the waggle dance (which has a figure-eight pattern), the scout tells others about the food source. Here the scout shows the relationship of the food source, dandelion, to the sun by starting the dance facing toward the sun (*left*) or away from the sun (*right*).

hive. These are much bigger than the other wax cells and are shaped somewhat like peanuts. Inside these special cells, the queen deposits the eggs from which a new queen will emerge. After the larvae develop from the eggs, the cells are covered with wax.

Soon after the cells are covered with wax, the old queen gathers many of the workers and leaves the hive to start a new colony. The departing queen and her group of workers is called a **swarm**. Their journey from the hive to find a new home is called a **swarming**. Left behind in the hive are workers that will tend the new queen and developing larvae.

Many scouts search for a new location for the colony. While the scouts search, the swarm gathers around a tree branch or other support. The scouts report back to the swarm using their "dance" language to describe the various locations they have found. The scouts then check out each site. Once one is chosen, the entire swarm travels to the new site.

Bumblebees are another familiar kind of social bee. Their colonies are not as large or complex as those of honeybees, and they do not produce as much honey. Also, the duties of the bumblebee queen are quite different from those of the honeybee queen.

Each spring the bumblebee queen must start a new colony because all of her workers die each year when winter comes. At first, the queen performs the work for the entire hive. She gathers pollen and nectar, builds wax cells, and feeds the young. Not until the larvae become adult workers does the queen have any help with her duties.

The hive thrives for a short time. In the fall, cold weather kills all but the new queens that hatched, and then mated, late in the season. The new queens hibernate and start new hives when the warm weather returns.

▶SOLITARY BEES

Many of the solitary bees have curious habits. **Carpenter bees** bite tunnels through solid wood. In the tunnels they make a series of cells, one on top of the other and separated by walls of tiny wood chips. **Mason bees** cement pieces of stone together, forming groups of cells that are attached to cliffs or stone walls. **Leaf-cutter bees** use their jaws like scissors and snip out pieces of leaves or flowers. They use this plant material to line their nests and make partitions between the cells. **Burrowing bees** tunnel into the ground.

Most solitary bees live alone. The female solitary bee puts pollen and nectar in the cells of the nest. She lays an egg on each lump of food, seals the cells, and flies away. She usually dies at the end of the summer. When the eggs hatch, the developing young feed on the food left for them. They are completely on their own, having no contact with the mother. When they are adults, male and female mate.

MILLICENT E. SELSAM
Author, science books for children
Reviewed by GENE E. ROBINSON
Department of Entomology
University of Illinois

See also FLOWERS; HONEY; INSECTS.

Nests of Solitary Bees

Mason bee

American carpenter bee

Leaf-cutter bee

BEETHOVEN, LUDWIG VAN (1770–1827)

The great composer Ludwig van Beethoven was born in Bonn, Germany, on December 16 or 17, 1770, and was baptized on December 17. His father, Johann, and his grandfather Ludwig van Beethoven were both musicians.

Beethoven revealed his own musical talents when he was very young. His father, an irresponsible drunkard, hoped the boy would be a profitable child prodigy like Mozart. Beethoven was often dragged out of bed in the middle of the night and forced to practice the piano. At the age of 7 he was playing in public. When Beethoven was 13, the elector of Cologne made him assistant organist at his chapel in Bonn.

In 1787 Beethoven traveled to Vienna and met his idol, Mozart. When Beethoven improvised on a melody that Mozart had given him, the great master was astounded.

But Beethoven could not stay in Vienna. His mother fell ill, and he rushed back to Bonn. The death of his mother left Beethoven and his brothers at the mercy of their drunken father. At the age of 18 Beethoven assumed full responsibility for the family.

In 1792 Beethoven returned to Vienna, where he spent the rest of his life. He became a pupil of Haydn. But he was dissatisfied with Haydn's method of teaching, which he considered not thorough enough. To avoid offending the famous master, he took lessons in secret from another composer, Johann Schenk.

Beethoven presented a strange appearance to the people of Vienna. He was a short, stocky man, untidily dressed, with dark, piercing eyes and a wild shock of black hair. Knowing himself to be a genius, he lived by his own rules. The German poet Goethe called him an "utterly untamed personality."

Nevertheless, he quickly became famous. Several princes became his patrons, and for a few years he was happy. Then, about 1800, tragedy struck. He discovered that he was slowly becoming deaf. This was the great crisis of his life.

After this, Beethoven's music became more profound. He developed a completely original style of composing. It reflected his violent emotions, his sufferings and joys. At this time Beethoven composed the most popular of all symphonies, his fifth. Other famous works of

Beethoven with the score of his great *Missa solemnis.*

this period are the *Eroica* and *Pastoral* symphonies, the *Appassionata* Sonata, the *Emperor* Concerto, his only opera, *Fidelio*, and the *Rasumovsky* string quartets.

In 1815 Beethoven became the guardian of his nephew Karl. Beethoven adored the boy, who gave his uncle nothing but trouble. Beethoven's hearing problems steadily increased; by 1820 he was almost totally deaf and had to carry on all conversation in writing.

Despite his deafness Beethoven now composed his greatest works. These include the last five piano sonatas, the *Missa solemnis*, the Ninth Symphony, with its choral finale, and the last five string quartets, which many people consider the finest of all his works.

In 1826 Beethoven became seriously ill. It is said that as he lay unconscious on his deathbed, on March 26, 1827, there was a loud clap of thunder. In response Beethoven sat straight up, shook his fist at the heavens, and fell back dead.

Beethoven is perhaps the most popular and revered of composers. He was a man of profound vision and his music has deeply moved its listeners for generations.

Reviewed by KARL GEIRINGER
University of California—Santa Barbara

Beetles vary greatly, not only in appearance but also in lifestyle. While the dung beetle (*left*) busily forms a dung ball to use as a nest for its eggs, the locust borer beetle (*above*) lays its eggs on plentiful goldenrod.

BEETLES

Wherever you look, on the ground, in the air, or in lakes and ponds, they can be found. They go busily about their daily tasks—whether it is nibbling on plant leaves, chewing wood from rotting logs, or cleaning the bones of dead animals. They are beetles, the most common of all the insects. In North America alone, there are more than 30,000 different kinds, or species, of beetles. Throughout the world, about 300,000 species of beetles can be found; and every year, new species are being discovered.

Beetles make up the insect order, or group, called Coleoptera. It is the largest order of the animal kingdom. The name Coleoptera, which means "sheath wing" in Greek, refers to the beetle's pair of hard, inflexible outer wings. The wings, called **elytra**, lock together down the beetle's back to provide a protective shell for the beetle.

Sometimes called the armored tank of the insect world, the beetle owes much of its ability to survive to the leathery elytra. With this tough outer shell, the beetle can live under stones and in other sheltered areas that insects with soft bodies cannot use, because they would be crushed. The beetle's shell also makes it resistant to dryness. This allows the beetle to live in places that are drier than the habitats of many other insects.

▶ THE CHARACTERISTICS OF BEETLES

There is a great variety in the appearance of beetles. Some beetles are dark brown so that they blend in with the soil. Other beetles have bright colors or complex patterns on their elytra. Still others are iridescent, changing color in the sunlight. Although beetles vary greatly in size, shape, and color, they all share the same body plan. Like that of other insects, the beetle's body is divided into three main parts: the head, the thorax, and the abdomen.

Body Parts. The **head**, at the front of the body, holds the main sense organs (eyes and antennae), chewing mouthparts, and a primitive brain. Projecting from the head, the beetle's two antennae are covered with tiny hairs. The hairs are special sense organs that help the beetle detect sounds and odors. A pair of compound eyes, one on each side of the head, gives the beetle a well-developed sense of sight.

The chewing mouthparts of most beetles are designed to crush or break food into small pieces before the food actually enters the

The External Body Structures of a Beetle

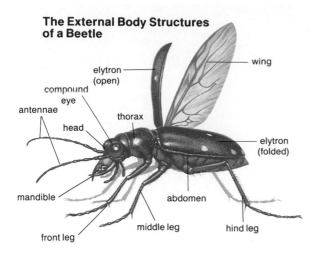

- elytron (open)
- wing
- compound eye
- antennae
- head
- thorax
- elytron (folded)
- mandible
- abdomen
- front leg
- middle leg
- hind leg

mouth. Plant-eating beetles have mouthparts that allow them to slice leaves, cut stems, bore under bark, or crush seeds. Beetles that eat other insects or animals have mouthparts that allow them to pierce, stab, or crush their prey. Some of these beetles can cause painful bites to an inexperienced insect collector.

The **thorax** forms the middle part of the body and holds the beetle's three pairs of legs as well as the elytra and a pair of hind wings. Different kinds of beetles have different kinds of legs. Many predatory beetles have long, slender legs that enable them to pursue their prey swiftly. Beetles that dig through the soil have legs that are flattened with toothed edges,

allowing the beetles to sweep large amounts of soil behind them.

The **abdomen** houses the organs that help the beetle digest food, get rid of waste, and produce offspring. The beetle does not have special organs, like our lungs, to help it breathe. Instead, holes called **spiracles** pierce the abdomen. Air enters the beetle's body through the spiracles and passes through tubes into open spaces in the abdomen and the rest of the body.

Locomotion. If the beetle needs to fly, it unlocks the elytra and the hind wings unfold. Only the hind wings are used for flight. When the beetle is not flying, the elytra cover and protect the thin, delicate hind wings.

Some beetles spend most of their life in water. An aquatic beetle has flattened legs that are used for paddles as it pushes through the water. A built-in air tank helps the beetle swim and dive underwater. The space between the elytra and the soft body underneath fills up with air. While the beetle is under water, it breathes using the stored air.

Behavior. Most beetles, unlike many types of bees, ants, wasps, and termites, are solitary insects. They live alone rather than in large nests or hives. Different types of beetles have

Two behaviors that are important to a beetle's survival are its ability to defend itself and its ability to reproduce. The bombardier beetle (*below*) effectively repels its enemies with a hot pulsing jet of chemicals. The mating blister beetle (*right*) provides for its offspring by laying its eggs near a larval food source.

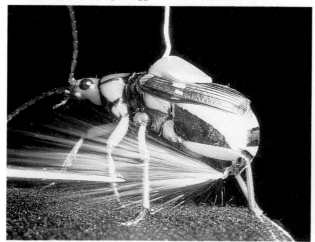

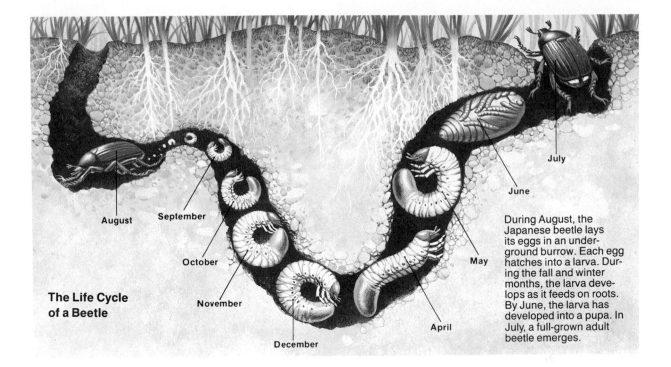

The Life Cycle of a Beetle

August

September

October

November

December

April

May

June

July

During August, the Japanese beetle lays its eggs in an underground burrow. Each egg hatches into a larva. During the fall and winter months, the larva develops as it feeds on roots. By June, the larva has developed into a pupa. In July, a full-grown adult beetle emerges.

different types of behavior that allow them to adapt to their environment, feed, defend themselves from predators, and breed.

People have been interested in some of the more unusual beetles for hundreds, even thousands, of years. In ancient Egypt, people were fascinated by the scarab, or dung beetle. This insect makes a ball of dung to lay its eggs in. Often the ball is as large or larger than the scarab itself. Some beetles make dung balls as big as softballs.

The Egyptians considered the ball of dung and the life of the scarab to be symbols for the world and the cycles of nature. So important was the scarab that it was used as a seal on many important Egyptian documents.

Another beetle with unusual behavior is the tortoise beetle. As it grows, it is protected by a collection of its own waste and shed skins. Stuck to its body, this material helps camouflage, or hide, the young beetle from predators. It also serves as a defense, because the foul odor of the pile of wastes discourages other insects and animals from coming close for an attack. Nicknamed the trash peddler, the young tortoise beetle develops into a brilliant, shiny metallic adult.

The bombardier beetle has an even more dramatic defense against predators. When an attacking animal approaches, the bombardier beetle raises its rear end into the air and shoots out a hot spray of burning liquid at the attacker. The spray is released with an explosion that is quite loud. The combination of the surprising sound and harmful spray wards off most animals that would prey upon this beetle.

▶**THE LIFE CYCLE OF THE BEETLE**

Beetles, like many other insects, have a life cycle during which they pass through several different stages before becoming an adult. This process of growth and change is called **metamorphosis**.

The Egg. Most beetles begin the first stage of life as an egg. Beetle eggs are generally oval in shape with a tough but flexible outer shell. Inside the egg, the growing beetle feeds on the large yolk. The first stage ends when the developing beetle cuts its way through the shell, hatching into a beetle larva.

The Larva. The larval stage is the only one in which the beetle grows in size. Because beetles lay eggs on or in a food source, a newly emerged larva does not have to hunt for food. The larva, also called a grub, spends most of its time eating. When the larva grows too large for the hard shell (called an exoskeleton) that covers its body, the shell splits. The soft grub that emerges will quickly grow a new, larger exoskeleton. The new covering

Some Common Beetle Families

Firefly
Family: Lampyridae
Common name:
lightning bug or firefly
   The name *Lampyridae* means "shining fire" in Latin. In some species, the eggs, larvae, pupae (plural of pupa), and adult fireflies all emit a glowing light.

Two-spotted Ladybug
Family: Coccinellidae
Common name: ladybird beetle or ladybug
   The name *ladybug* originated in the Middle Ages. Named the beetle of Our Lady, this insect was dedicated to the Virgin Mary.

Colorado Potato Beetle
Family: Chrysomelidae
Common name: leaf beetle
   There are more than 25,000 species of leaf beetles in the world. Both the larvae (plural of larva) and the adult leaf beetles feed on leaves. This makes many leaf beetles serious crop pests.

Dung Beetle
Family: Scarabaeidae
Common name: scarab
   The scarab beetles are one of the largest families of beetles, with almost 1,300 North American species and 20,000 species in the world.

Striped Blister Beetle
Family: Meloidae
Common name: blister beetle
   When a predator attacks a blister beetle, the beetle discharges a drop of blood containing an oily chemical. This chemical causes severe blistering of the skin.

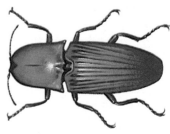

Fiery Searcher Ground Beetle
Family: Carabidae
Common name: ground beetle
   Almost all ground beetles are nocturnal, so they hide during the day and search for food at night. They are very aggressive predators, even climbing trees to get their prey.

Boll Weevil
Family: Curculionidae
Common name: snout beetle or weevil
   With 40,000 species of snout beetles, this is the largest family of beetles in the world. These beetles get their name because they have a long snout, with their mouthparts attached at the farthest end.

Click Beetle
Family: Elateridae
Common name: click beetle or snapping beetle
   When attacked, the click beetle falls backward and plays dead. To right itself, the beetle bends at the thorax and hooks a long spine into an abdominal groove. It unhooks the spine with a click, throwing itself in the air and flipping end over end.

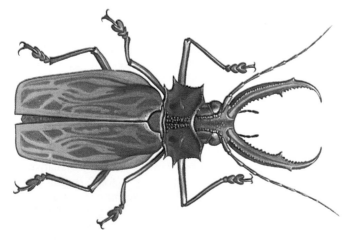

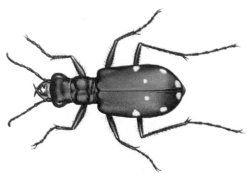

Giant Longhorn Beetle
Family: Cerambycidae
Common name: long-horned or wood-boring beetle
   Larvae of this family are wood borers. They are easy to capture because they can be picked out of the wood with hooked sticks. Partly for this reason, the larvae are used as food in many parts of the world.

Tiger Beetle
Family: Cicindelidae
Common name: tiger beetle
   Tiger beetle larvae wait for prey at the entrance of their vertical burrows. They attach themselves to the burrow wall with a hooklike spine on the abdomen that prevents them from being pulled out of the burrow when capturing large prey.

will also be shed as the larva continues to eat and grow. This process of growing and shedding the outer layer is called **molting**. A larva may molt three to seven times before it enters the next stage.

The Pupa. As it enters the pupal stage, the beetle buries itself underground or in a tree trunk or a plant so that it will not be attacked by predators. It usually forms a hard casing around itself for protection. Then it stops all movement for several days or weeks. On the outside it looks as if nothing is happening. But inside its case, the insect is transforming itself. The pupa forms legs, wings, and elytra. Its digestive system changes, and its reproductive system develops. When its development is complete, an adult beetle emerges and crawls or flies away.

The Adult. Although long-lived compared with most other insects, adult beetles live for less than a month. During this time they must mate, and the females must find a suitable place to lay their eggs. These ends accomplished, the adult beetle dies.

▶ BEETLES AND THEIR ENVIRONMENT

Many plant-eating beetles are considered serious pests because they feed on farm crops, trees, bushes, and other plants. One of the most destructive of these beetles is the boll weevil. Until 1843 the boll weevil lived only in Mexico, where it fed on a wild relative of the cotton plant. By 1892 the boll weevil had reached the southern tip of Texas, where there were vast fields of domesticated cotton. The boll weevil was able to spread quickly through the acres and acres of cropland, spreading northward into the southern United States at a rate of about 60 miles per year. Nothing the farmers could do prevented the expansion of this beetle's range.

One reason the boll weevil was able to spread so quickly is that a female boll weevil can lay as many as 300 eggs in her lifetime. The entire life cycle of the boll weevil takes only two or three weeks. Therefore, several generations of boll weevils can hatch in one summer, quickly increasing the population. Today, cotton farmers use a variety of methods to control the spread of the boll weevil, from insecticides and fertilizers to the introduction of sterile boll weevils that prevent the beetle from breeding sucessfully. But the boll weevil is a very adaptable insect. No

As a larva and an adult, the plant-eating Mexican bean beetle (*top*) is considered a pest. Carrion beetles (*above*) provide a beneficial service by feeding on animal wastes and dead animals.

method has enabled farmers to get rid of the boll weevil completely.

Other beetles are considered important in controlling insect pests on farm crops and in gardens. Ladybugs, or ladybird beetles, attack and eat aphids, scale insects, mites, and other pests. They have been used commercially since 1888 to control these insects in greenhouses and orchards. Many gardeners use ladybugs today to try to get rid of unwanted insects without using pesticides.

GAIL M. TERZI
Forest Biologist
Contributor, *Insect Biochemistry* journal

See also INSECTS; PLANT PESTS.

BEGIN, MENACHEM (1913-1992)

Menachem Begin, prime minister of Israel from 1977 to 1983, was the first Israeli leader to make a peace settlement with an Arab country. In a varied career, he was successively a law student, political agitator, terrorist, politician, and prime minister.

Begin was born on August 16, 1913, in Brest-Litovsk (now Brest, in Belarus). He grew up a Polish citizen and received a law degree from the University of Warsaw, but never practiced law. While in his teens, he joined (and later became head of) Betar, a militant youth organization that sought to create a modern Jewish state in Palestine, then governed by Britain. In 1941, during World War II, he enlisted in the Polish forces under British command in the Middle East.

There, Begin used his military training against the British as leader of the Irgun Zvai Leumi, an extremist wing of the Jewish Underground, which he founded in 1943. Its most notorious terrorist act was the bombing of the King David Hotel in Jerusalem, site of British headquarters, in 1946. When the British departed and the state of Israel was established in 1948, Begin founded the Herut Party and won a seat in the Knesset, the Israeli parliament. Herut merged with other conservative groups to form the Likud bloc, which Begin led to victory over Israel's long-ruling Labor Party in 1977 elections.

As prime minister, his greatest, and most surprising, achievement was a peace treaty with Egypt. In 1977 he invited a former enemy, Egyptian president Anwar el-Sadat, to come to Israel. This first meeting resulted in a treaty signed two years later. He and Sadat shared the Nobel Peace Prize for 1978. Begin's later years were less successful, culminating in the much-criticized Israeli military incursion into Lebanon, in an effort to destroy bases of the Palestine Liberation Organization (PLO), in 1982. He retired in 1983, after the death of his wife of 43 years, Aliza. He died in Tel Aviv on March 9, 1992.

ARTHUR CAMPBELL TURNER
University of California, Riverside
Coauthor, *Ideology and Power in the
Middle East*

See also ISRAEL (History); SADAT, ANWAR EL-.

BEHRING, EMIL VON (1854–1917)

Emil Adolf von Behring was a pioneer in immunology, the science that explores how the human body protects itself from disease. For his innovative work, especially in the treatment of the diseases diphtheria and tetanus, he received the first Nobel Prize awarded for physiology or medicine in 1901.

Born in Hansdorf, Germany, on March 15, 1854, Behring spent the major part of his career engaged in intensive, and mostly solitary, research of his original ideas on serum therapy. He was particularly interested in combating diseases through the use of antitoxins, the substances that neutralize disease toxins.

In experiments, Behring injected the blood serum from an animal that had recovered from tetanus into an uninfected animal. He discovered that the unaffected animal reacted by producing an antitoxin that made the animal immune to the disease. Behring was convinced that immunity could be passed on to other animals by using this antitoxin. Behring and his associate Shibasaburo Kitasato worked to isolate and define the antitoxin that provided the protection. Their success supported Behring's theories, theories that led to the development of preventative vaccinations against the dread diseases diphtheria and tetanus.

Behring's works, which are all published in German, include *The Practical Goals of Blood Serum Therapy* (1892) and *The History of Diphtheria* (1893). Behring died in Marburg, Germany, on March 31, 1917.

GAIL KAY HAINES
Author, *Micromysteries: Stories of
Scientific Detection*

BEIJERINCK, MARTINUS. See VIRUSES (The Discovery of Viruses).

BEIJING

Beijing (also spelled Peking) is the capital and cultural heart of the People's Republic of China. It is the country's second largest city, after Shanghai. Although known by various names, a city has existed on the site since ancient times. Its present name means "northern capital." Modern Beijing has the status of a municipality, which includes much of the surrounding area, and is administered directly by the national government. The population of the city proper is about 7 million; the metropolitan area has some 9.5 million people.

Location and Climate. Beijing is located at the northeastern edge of the North China Plain, the region where Chinese civilization began. Situated between the Pai and Yungting rivers, it lies about 100 miles (161 kilometers) inland from the Bo Hai, a gulf that forms part of the Yellow Sea. Some 35 miles (56 kilometers) to the north is the Great Wall, built centuries ago to protect China against nomadic invaders. Most of the landscape is mountainous, except for a lowland area on the southeast that merges into the plain.

Beijing has a variable climate. Autumns are pleasant, but summers can be quite hot, while in winter, temperatures average only 23°F (-5°C) and the city is frequently whipped by winds and sandstorms. The relatively little snow usually falls in early spring. Rainfall is moderate and occurs mainly in summer.

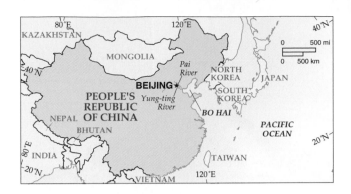

Layout of the City. The core of Beijing consists of two old sections, traditionally known as the Inner City and the Outer City. The Inner City, which is actually situated in the north, contains the former Imperial City, which was the seat of the government during the time of the emperors. Within the Imperial City stands the Forbidden City, with the palaces and shrines once used by the emperors and their families. Entry was forbidden to all but members of the imperial household. The buildings are now part of a museum, open to the public. The Legation Quarter, located in the southeastern corner of the Imperial City, was at one time the site of foreign embassies and other diplomatic residences.

Historically, the Inner and Outer Cities were fortified by massive stone walls. The walls of the Inner City, in particular, were pierced by nine great gates and surmounted by lofty guard towers. Most of the city walls have been torn down, but a few parts remain as

The Forbidden City (foreground) stands in the heart of Beijing, China's capital and second largest city. Surrounded by high walls, the Forbidden City was for centuries the seat of China's emperors, closed to all but the imperial household. It is now part of a museum, open to the public.

Tourists visit the Temple of Heaven (*left*), where emperors once prayed for a good harvest. Bicycles (*below*) are Beijing's most common form of transportation.

thoroughfares cross the two sections of the city, branching out into narrow lanes where the great majority of the people live. At most hours of the day, the streets are thronged by bicyclists, the bicycle being the most common form of transportation.

Beyond the city proper lie the suburbs, industrial districts, and farmlands that form part of the Beijing municipality. In all, the municipality encompasses an area of about 6,500 square miles (16,835 square kilometers).

Some Places of Interest. Near the southern edge of the Forbidden City is the vast Tiananmen (Gate of Heavenly Peace) Square. Situated in what is now the center of Beijing, it is frequently used for parades and other formal state occasions. The Great Hall of the People, where the country's legislature meets, stands on the western side of the square. On the eastern side are the Museum of the Revolution and the Chinese Historical Museum.

The most imposing of the palace buildings of the Forbidden City is the Hall of Great Harmony, which served as the imperial throne room. There are two places of particular interest in the southern part of the Outer City: the Temple of Heaven, where the emperors prayed at the time of the summer solstice to ensure a bountiful harvest, and the Temple of

monuments of the past. The walls and moat (a protective, water-filled trench) of the Forbidden City have been preserved.

The Outer City, in the south, is rectangular in shape. A colorful and lively district, it is largely commercial and residential. Its main entrance to the Inner City is by way of a broad, straight boulevard that passes through the enormous Qianmen (Front Gate). Other wide

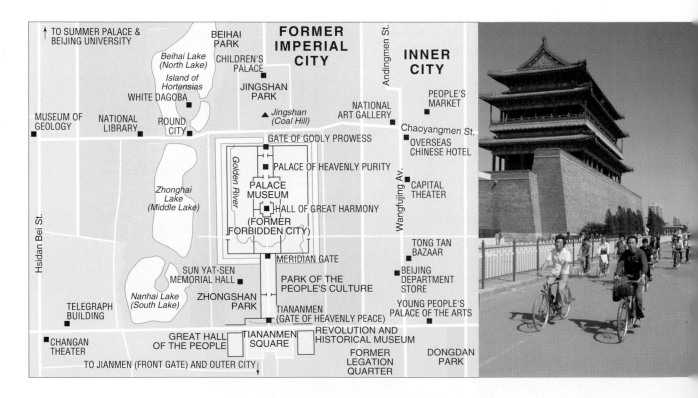

↑ TO SUMMER PALACE & BEIJING UNIVERSITY

FORMER IMPERIAL CITY

INNER CITY

BEIHAI PARK

Beihai Lake (North Lake)

CHILDREN'S PALACE

Island of Hortensias

JINGSHAN PARK

WHITE DAGOBA

▲ Jingshan (Coal Hill)

NATIONAL ART GALLERY

PEOPLE'S MARKET

MUSEUM OF GEOLOGY

NATIONAL LIBRARY

ROUND CITY

Chaoyangmen St.

OVERSEAS CHINESE HOTEL

GATE OF GODLY PROWESS

PALACE OF HEAVENLY PURITY

Golden River

Zhonghai Lake (Middle Lake)

PALACE MUSEUM

HALL OF GREAT HARMONY

CAPITAL THEATER

(FORMER FORBIDDEN CITY)

Hsidan Bei St.

MERIDIAN GATE

SUN YAT-SEN MEMORIAL HALL

PARK OF THE PEOPLE'S CULTURE

TONG TAN BAZAAR

BEIJING DEPARTMENT STORE

Nanhai Lake (South Lake)

ZHONGSHAN PARK

YOUNG PEOPLE'S PALACE OF THE ARTS

TELEGRAPH BUILDING

TIANANMEN (GATE OF HEAVENLY PEACE)

CHANGAN THEATER

GREAT HALL OF THE PEOPLE

TIANANMEN SQUARE

REVOLUTION AND HISTORICAL MUSEUM

FORMER LEGATION QUARTER

DONGDAN PARK

TO JIANMEN (FRONT GATE) AND OUTER CITY ↓

Andingmen St.

Wangfujing Av.

Tiananmen Square (*left*) lies at the southern edge of the Forbidden City, which can be seen in the background. The vast square was the scene, in 1989, of massive protests by university students demanding democratic reforms. The emperor Kublai Khan (*below*), founder of the Yuan dynasty, made Beijing, then called Cambaluc, his capital in the 1260's.

Agriculture. The Summer Palace of the Qing emperors and Beijing University (one of the many educational institutions) are located in the northwestern suburbs. The Summer Palace is an especially popular tourist site, famed for its palaces, gardens, and lakes. The Beijing Zoo is noted for its pandas, animals native only to China. The numerous parks and artificial lakes add to the city's attractiveness.

Economic Activity. Beijing is not only the center of China's political and cultural life but one of its most important industrial regions as well. Among its chief manufactured products are iron and steel, machinery, chemicals, textiles, motor vehicles, and processed foods. Printing and publishing are other major industries. Beijing is also the hub of the nation's communications and transportation network. The city's own transportation system includes a subway, which was expanded in 1988.

History. Beijing has been a site of human settlement since before recorded history. Under the name of Chi, it was first established as a capital of the small kingdom of Yen in the 700's B.C. Destroyed and rebuilt a number of times as a result of war and conquest, it emerged as an important city under the Khitan Tatars in the A.D. 900's. As Cambaluc (Khanbalik), it became the capital of the emperor Kublai Khan, founder of the Yuan (Mongol) dynasty of Chinese rulers, in the 1260's. It was this city that the Venetian traveler and merchant Marco Polo visited and whose wealth and splendor he recounted on his return home. See the article on MARCO POLO in Volume P.

The architectural beauty of the city was greatly enhanced by succeeding dynasties, the Ming and the Qing (or Manchu), the last imperial dynasty. After the overthrow of the Qing and the founding of the Chinese republic in 1912, Beijing remained the capital until 1928, when the seat of government was moved to Nanjing (formerly Nanking), meaning "southern capital." Beijing was renamed Beiping (Peiping), or "northern peace."

Beijing's name and status as the national capital were restored in 1949, when the Communists gained control of the mainland and proclaimed the People's Republic in Tiananmen Square. The great square was also the scene of massive protests in 1989, when thousands of university students gathered to demand democratic reforms in China. The demonstrations, which lasted for more than six weeks, captured the attention of much of the world before they were crushed by the military.

HYMAN KUBLIN
City University of New York, Brooklyn College
Author, *The Rim of Asia*

BELARUS

Belarus, once known as Belorussia (also spelled Byelorussia), is a new nation of Eastern Europe. Formerly a part of the Soviet Union, it won its independence as a result of the breakup of the Soviet Union in 1991. Belarus is surrounded by five other nations—Poland on the west; Lithuania and Latvia on the northwest; Russia on the north and east; and Ukraine on the south. This location, at the crossroads of Eastern Europe, has played an important role in Belarus' history.

The People. The Belarusians trace their origins to Eastern Slavic tribes that settled in the region between the A.D. 500's and 600's. The name *Belarus* means "White Russia," but the origins of the name are lost in time. The Belarusian language belongs to the Eastern slavic language group, which also includes Russian and Ukrainian. Both Belarusian and Russian are official state languages.

Native Belarusians make up about 80 percent of the population. Russians are the largest minority, with about 13 percent. Poles and Ukrainians are the other major ethnic groups. Most of the people adhere to the Eastern (or Greek) Orthodox faith. There are smaller numbers of Roman Catholics and members of the Greek Catholic, or Uniate, Church, which recognizes the supremacy of the pope but observes the Orthodox rite. There is also a significant Jewish community.

At one time, the majority of Belarusians were engaged in agriculture and lived in small rural farming communities. Intensive development of the country's resources led to greater economic diversity. It also brought about great changes in where the people lived. The population today is concentrated mainly in the industrial central and northern parts of the country, especially around the cities of Minsk, the capital and largest city, Gomel, and Mogilyov.

The Land. Most of Belarus consists of flat or rolling plain. A small area of uplands near the city of Minsk reaches a height of about 1,135 feet (436 meters). The Pripet Marshes occupy most of the southern part of the country. A region of rivers, lakes, bogs, and woodlands, it is inhabited by a wide variety of wild animal life. Large parts of the marshes have been drained to create new farm land.

FACTS and figures

REPUBLIC OF BELARUS is the official name of the country.

LOCATION: Eastern Europe.

AREA: 80,154 sq mi (207,600 km²).

POPULATION: 10,300,000 (estimate).

CAPITAL AND LARGEST CITY: Minsk.

MAJOR LANGUAGE(S): Belarusian, Russian (both official).

MAJOR RELIGIOUS GROUP(S): Eastern Orthodox, Greek Catholic (Uniate), Jewish.

GOVERNMENT: Republic. **Head of state and government**—president. **Legislature**—Supreme Council.

CHIEF PRODUCTS: Agricultural—wheat, rye, and other grains, potatoes, sugar beets, and other vegetables, fodder, flax, hemp. **Manufactured**—processed agricultural products, textiles, machine tools heavy farm equipment, fertilizers. **Mineral**—oil, coal, potash.

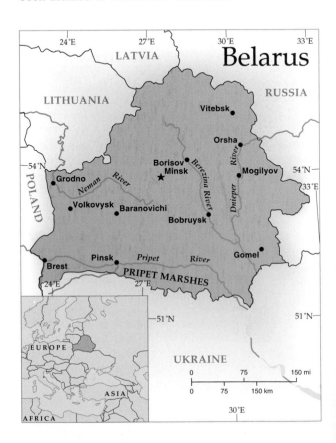

Galloping horses enjoy a moment of freedom on a farm in western Belarus. The grassy plains that make up most of Belarus' landscape are especially suited to the raising of livestock, an important part of the country's agriculture.

About one-third of Belarus is covered with forests, one of its most important natural resources. Its mineral deposits include oil, coal, and potash. Peat, obtained from the southern bogs, is used as fuel.

The climate is moderately continental, with hot summers and cool winters.

The Economy. Before the collapse of the Soviet Union, Belarus had a Communist economic system, centrally planned and controlled by the state. Economic reforms now taking place are based on a market, or free-enterprise, system.

About two-thirds of the country's income comes from manufacturing, but agriculture is also important to the economy. Major crops include wheat, rye, and other grains; potatoes, sugar beets, and other vegetables; fodder, or feed for livestock; flax (from which linen is made); and hemp (used to make rope). The raising of cattle and other livestock is an important part of Belarusian agriculture. The chief manufactures include processed agricultural products, textiles, machine tools, heavy farm equipment, fertilizers, and other goods.

Early History: Polish Rule. By the A.D. 800's, Belarus was ruled by various princes who were linked to the ancient state of Kievan Rus (whose center was located in what is now Ukraine). The Kievan state was eventually destroyed by invading Mongols, and in the 1300's Belarus fell to Lithuania. For more than 400 years, Belarus was dominated first by Lithuania and then by Poland, which united with Lithuania in the 1500's. During this period the Belarusians, separated from the Eastern Slavs of Russia and Ukraine, developed their own language and culture, and emerged as a distinct people.

From Russian to Soviet Rule. When Poland was partitioned (divided) among its neighbors in the late 1700's, Belarus became a part of the Russian Empire. The Russian imperial government discouraged Belarusian cultural activities and prohibited the use of the Belarusian language in schools. This policy, however, did not succeed in destroying the idea that Belarus was a distinct nation with a history and tradition worth preserving.

During the social and political confusion caused by World War I and the Russian revolutions of 1917, Belarusian leaders issued a declaration of independence, but the infant state was crushed by political and military events. Under the Treaty of Riga (1921), Belarus was partitioned between newly independent Poland and Soviet Russia, the state that succeeded the Russian Empire. When the Union of Soviet Socialist Republics (or Soviet Union) was founded in 1922, Belarus—then called Belorussia—was one of its founding republics. In 1939, the Polish part of Belarus was taken over by the Soviet Union.

Independence. On July 27, 1990, as the Soviet Union began to break apart, the Belorussian parliament approved a declaration of sovereignty. The name Republic of Belarus was adopted in August 1991. In December 1991, with the complete collapse of the Soviet Union, Belarus and other former Soviet republics formed the Commonwealth of Independent States, with its administrative headquarters in Minsk.

Belarus adopted a new constitution in 1996. It extended the term of elected president Aleksandr Lukashenko, who sought to restore a Soviet-style system, and greatly increased his powers. In 1997, Belarus and Russia signed a treaty in which they agreed to coordinate military, foreign, and economic policies. Lukashenko's landslide re-election in 2001 raised questions of voting irregularities.

PETER CZAP, JR.
Amherst College

BELFAST. See UNITED KINGDOM (Major Cities).
BELGIAN ART. See DUTCH AND FLEMISH ART.

BELGIUM

Since the Middle Ages, canals linked to the North Sea have brought trade and industry to the charming city of Bruges (*left*). Belgians are a mix of French-, Dutch-, and German-speaking peoples.

Belgium is a small nation located in northwestern Europe. Although not much larger than the state of Maryland in the United States, Belgium has always been more important than its small size suggests. This is due in part to its strategic location. Belgium shares borders with the Netherlands, Germany, Luxembourg, and France and is separated from Great Britain by just a narrow strip of the North Sea. Because of its location, Belgium historically has been caught up in the struggles and quarrels of its more powerful neighbors.

Belgium is a relatively young nation, having won its independence in 1830. But the region that is now Belgium has a long history. During the Middle Ages, it was one of the most prosperous parts of Europe, famous for its woolen textiles, lace, and great culture. Today Belgium is a highly industrialized country, sometimes known as the Workshop of Europe. The nation also plays an important role in the affairs of modern Europe.

▶ PEOPLE

Belgium is inhabited by approximately 10 million people, who are known as Belgians. They are divided into three groups.

The Flemings, who make up close to 60 percent of the population, live in the northern region called Flanders. The Flemings, descended from ancient Germanic peoples, speak Dutch.

The Walloons, who make up more than 30 percent of the population, speak French. Most Walloons live in Wallonia, a region in southern Belgium. They are descended from the Belgae, an ancient people whom the Romans conquered in the 1st century B.C.

German-speaking Belgians live in the eastern portion of the country, near the German border. They are a small minority, numbering about 60,000.

Language. Belgium is divided into distinct linguistic (language) regions. In Flanders, Dutch is the official language. French is the official language of Wallonia. Brussels, the capital, is officially bilingual; that is, both French and Dutch are used. Through the years disputes over the status and use of French and Dutch have caused considerable friction among Belgians. Some German is spoken in eastern Belgium.

Religion. Although Belgians are divided in language, they are united in their religion. Most of the people are Roman Catholics. Religious freedom, however, is guaranteed by the constitution.

Education and Libraries. All Belgian children between the ages of 6 and 18 are required to attend school. Private as well as public schools may receive financial support from the government.

Higher education is provided by several excellent universities. The Catholic University at Louvain, just east of Brussels, was founded in the 1420's and is the country's oldest university. The University of Antwerp and the Free University of Brussels place a high priority on scientific research.

Belgium's national library is the Royal Albert I Library in Brussels. Other important libraries include the Antwerp City Library and the University Library of Ghent.

Food and Drink. The Belgians are expert cooks and enjoy good food and pleasant dining. Every region of Belgium has its own specialties, but certain dishes are popular all over the country. A typical Belgian meal might begin with mussels (*moules*) or a chicken stew called *waterzooï de poulet*. The main course might be *carbonnade à la flamande*, a beef stew made with beer. Belgium is noted for its wide variety of superior beers.

▶ **LAND**

Belgium is shaped somewhat like a triangle. There is also a tiny 7-square-mile (18-square-kilometer) fragment of northern Belgium, called Baarle-Hertog, that is entirely surrounded by the Netherlands.

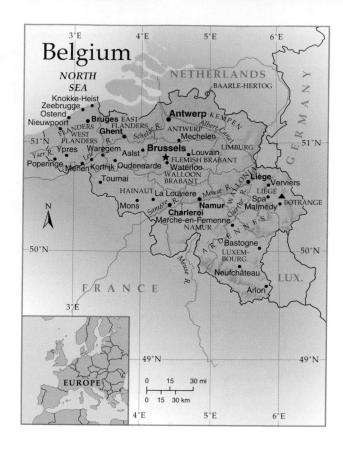

Land Regions. Belgium can be divided into three equal sections—the Lowlands, the Central Low Plateaus, and the Ardennes. The Lowlands in the north and west are practically flat. Parts of the northwestern lowlands were reclaimed from the sea and marshes during the Middle Ages. The northeastern lowlands are known as the Kempen.

The southern two-thirds of Belgium is more elevated. Central Belgium is part of the European Low Plateau. The hillier southern region belongs to the Rhine Massif.

In contrast to the almost flat coastal region, the Ardennes in the southeast feature plateaus, large forests, and picturesque rivers. Belgium's highest point, the Botrange, is located in this region.

Rivers. From northwest to southeast the principal Belgian rivers are the Leie, Schelde, Sambre, Meuse, Yser, and Ourthe.

Hiking is a popular activity in the Ardennes, a forested region in southeastern Belgium that borders Luxembourg and Germany.

A merchant displays a variety of local seafood delicacies on a bustling side street in one of the oldest sections of downtown Brussels.

Most Belgian rivers are tributaries of the Schelde or Meuse. Northern and central Belgium are crisscrossed by many waterways, including artificial ones used for drainage and navigation.

Climate. Belgium's climate is known as marine west coast, which is typical of northwestern Europe. It has changeable and cloudy weather with frequent rains and moderate temperatures. Winters are generally mild except in the interior uplands. Summers are usually cool rather than warm. Daytime temperatures rarely rise above 80°F (27°C).

About 30 inches (760 millimeters) of precipitation—mostly in the form of rain—falls on northern Belgium in an average year. The Ardennes receive an even greater amount.

Natural Resources. Belgium is quite poor in natural resources. Coal was once plentiful, but today only phosphates, used in fertilizers, are found in large quantities. Sand and clay, used to make glass, brick, and cement, are also found.

▶ ECONOMY

Belgium is a highly industrialized nation with a generally high standard of living. The capital, Brussels, is the center of manufacture and commerce.

Services. Tourism throughout Belgium supports a wide range of service establishments, such as hotels, restaurants, and cultural institutions. The seashore, Brussels, and the Ardennes are among the most popular tourist destinations.

Manufacturing. Belgian industries depend to a large extent on imported raw materials.

For example, Belgian steel is made from iron ores imported from France and Luxembourg. Belgium produces more than 12 million tons of steel a year, making it one of the world's important steel-producing countries. Other leading industries include the manufacture of railroad equipment and armaments and the processing of such metals as zinc, copper, and lead.

The manufacture of woolens, lace, cloth, and other textiles has been important in Belgium since the Middle Ages. "Made in Belgium" is also found stamped on such products as glassware, foods, tobacco goods, timber, and paper products.

Agriculture. The major crops produced by Belgian farmers are wheat, oats, barley, potatoes, sugar beets, and rye. Flax, used for linen making, and tobacco are also grown. Belgium is also one of the biggest exporters of decorative flowers and plants.

Belgium's climate is good for grass growth, and as a result the country has a flourishing livestock industry. Dairy cattle, beef cattle,

FACTS and figures

KINGDOM OF BELGIUM (Royaume de Belgique in French and Koninkrijk België in Dutch) is the official name of the country.

LOCATION: Northwestern Europe.

AREA: 11,781 sq mi (30,513 km²).

POPULATION: 10,300,000 (estimate).

CAPITAL AND LARGEST CITY: Brussels.

MAJOR LANGUAGES: Dutch, French, German.

MAJOR RELIGIOUS GROUP: Roman Catholic.

GOVERNMENT: Constitutional Monarchy. **Head of state**—king. **Head of government**—prime minister. **Legislature**—parliament, consisting of the Senate and the Chamber of Representatives.

CHIEF PRODUCTS: Agricultural—wheat, oats, barley, potatoes, sugar beets, rye, flax, fruits, flowers, tobacco, livestock. **Manufactured**—iron and steel, textiles, machinery, railroad equipment, armaments, processed metals, processed food, lace, cut diamonds, glassware, chemicals, cement, tobacco products. **Mineral**—phosphates, coal.

MONETARY UNIT: Euro (1 euro = 100 cents).

and hogs are the most important. Livestock feed crops are widely grown and occupy about one-half of the cultivated acreage.

Trade. Belgian products are sold all over the world. Foreign trade is very important to the Belgian economy, which has widespread commercial interests, particularly in Europe. Belgium is a member of the European Union (EU). It also has trading connections with the United States. The Belgium Luxembourg Economic Union (BLEU), established in July 1921, maintains a system of monetary association between Belgium and Luxembourg.

Transportation. Belgium's farms and industries are served by an excellent transportation system. Roads reach every corner of the country. Belgium has one of the world's densest networks of railroad facilities and an extensive system of navigable rivers and canals.

Belgium has a small navy used for commercial purposes. Its national airline, Sabena, is partly owned by the government. Antwerp, Belgium's most important port, competes with Rotterdam in the Netherlands and Hamburg in Germany as northwestern Europe's leading port.

Communication. Belgium has six television broadcasting corporations—four public and two commercial. Three broadcast in Dutch and three in French. The number of regional television stations is growing. There are twelve public radio broadcasting companies—seven broadcasting in Dutch, four in French, and one in German—in addition to hundreds of local, private radio stations.

More than 30 newspapers are published daily. Those with the largest circulations include *De Standaard* and *Le Soir*.

▶ **CULTURAL HERITAGE**

Belgium has long been a rich center of cultural activities.

Music. Belgium's musical heritage began in the Middle Ages. In the 1800's, Flemish music was revived by Peter Benoit, a composer and teacher,

Flax, a fibrous plant used to make linen, is stacked to dry in the fields near Kortrijk. Flax has been grown in Flanders for more than a thousand years.

who founded the Flemish School of Music in Antwerp. Adolphe Sax, another Belgian, invented the saxophone in 1846. The best-known modern Belgian composer, César Franck, is remembered for such beautiful works as *Symphony in D Minor* (1889) and *Symphonic Variations* (1886). Jacques Brel, born in Brussels, was one of the most famous cabaret singers of the 1900's. For more information on Belgian music, see the article DUTCH AND FLEMISH MUSIC in Volume D.

Art and Architecture. Belgian artists have been world famous for many centuries. Many great Flemish artists lived between the 1400's and 1700's, including Jan van Eyck, Rogier van der Weyden, Hans Memling, Hieronymus Bosch, Pieter Brueghel the Elder and his son Jan, Peter Paul Rubens, Sir Anthony Van Dyck, and David Teniers the Younger. In modern times, the most acclaimed artists have been the expressionist James Ensor and the surrealists Paul Delvaux and René Magritte.

Surrealist painter René Magritte (1898–1967) was one of Belgium's most acclaimed artists. His paintings often include dreamlike images of men in bowler hats.

The architect Victor Horta was a pioneer of the Art Nouveau style. Among his most notable structures are Tassel House (1893) and his personal residence, now the Horta Museum. Other art museums include the Cinquantenaire Museum of Art and History and the Mu-

Brussels is the headquarters of the European Union (EU), a political and economic association of European nations. The city also serves as headquarters of the North Atlantic Treaty Organization (NATO).

seum of Modern Art, both in Brussels. For more information on Belgian art, see the article DUTCH AND FLEMISH ART in Volume D.

Literature. Belgians have also made important contributions to world literature. Among the most outstanding Belgian authors of the 1800's and 1900's were Charles de Coster, who wrote about the legendary prankster Till Eulenspiegel; Count Maurice Maeterlinck, winner of the Nobel Prize for literature in 1911; and Camille Lemonnier (1844–1913), the founder of the Belgian literary renaissance. Modern writers include Georges Simenon, the popular mystery story writer and creator of Inspector Maigret.

Cartoons. Many famous cartoonists have originated in Belgium. Hergé (Georges Remi) created *The Adventures of Tintin*, a series of stories featuring a world-famous boy reporter and his dog, Snowy. Peyo (Pierrot Culliford) created the little blue cartoon characters known as the Smurfs, which are popular in the United States and around the world.

▶ MAJOR CITIES

Brussels is the capital of Belgium and the nation's most populous city. Because it is headquarters of the European Union (EU) and the North Atlantic Treaty Organization (NATO), Brussels is also known as the capital of Europe. Many of the city's 1 million people are bilingual in Dutch and French.

Founded in the Middle Ages, Brussels was once the center of the cloth industry. In the 1500's it became the capital of the Spanish Netherlands. It has been Belgium's seat of government since the country became independent in 1830.

Brussels has many interesting sites. The Grand' Place, a square in the center of the oldest part of the city, is lined with exquisite guildhalls built in the baroque style of the 1600's. Another landmark is the Atomium. This enormous iron structure, built in the shape of a molecule, was the centerpiece of the 1958 World's Fair.

Antwerp, one of Europe's busiest seaports, is located on the Schelde River, which leads to the North Sea. Antwerp is also linked by canal to the Meuse River.

Founded in the early Middle Ages, Antwerp became the chief port of Flanders in the 1400's and later the financial capital of northern Europe. As trade grew, the city became the center of the diamond trade, and it remains so to this day.

▶ GOVERNMENT

Belgium is a hereditary, constitutional monarchy. The king is the head of the state and commander of the army. The king must approve all laws passed by Parliament.

Although the Belgian king would appear to have great powers, the actual government is headed by a prime minister, who is helped by other ministers. The Belgian Parliament is divided into two houses—the Senate and the Chamber of Representatives. The minimum voting age is 18. All qualified voters are required by law to vote.

▶ HISTORY

Julius Caesar wrote, "Of all the tribes of Gaul, the Belgae are the bravest." These words of the man who conquered the Belgic tribes in the 1st century B.C. have been echoed by others who tried to conquer Belgium during its long history.

Roman rule over Gallia Belgica lasted about 500 years. During the early Middle Ages, Belgium's history was closely interwoven with that of its neighbors. By the end of the Middle Ages, northern Belgium, under the rule of the counts of Flanders, had grown strong and prosperous. Commerce, manufacture, and the arts grew. Guilds and other trade organizations were established and run by a powerful and well-educated middle class.

Spanish, Austrian, French, and Dutch Rule. After being tied to the Austrian Empire for more than 200 years, Belgium passed to Spanish control in 1519. Then, in 1598, Belgium began a brief period of independence. This ended in 1621, when the Spanish once again took over the area they called the Spanish Netherlands. In 1713 Belgium was made a part of the Austrian kingdom, but in 1797 France annexed the country. After the final defeat of the French under the emperor Napoleon I at Waterloo (near Brussels) in 1815, Belgium and the Netherlands were set up as a united kingdom. The Belgians were unhappy about this union and on October 4, 1830, declared their independence.

Independence to World War I. The first king of independent Belgium was a German prince, Leopold of Saxe-Coburg-Gotha, an uncle of Britain's Queen Victoria. During his reign, Belgium began its industrial development. The late 1800's were also a period of active European colonization. Though at first Belgium did not participate directly, King Leopold II, acting more or less as a private individual, claimed a huge expanse of land in Africa's Congo River basin. In 1908 the Belgian Congo colony was placed under the direct control of the Belgian Parliament.

In 1909, Albert I became king. The early years of his reign were prosperous and happy ones for Belgium. But at the outbreak of World War I in 1914, German armies invaded and quickly occupied most of Belgium. Some of the bloodiest battles of the war were fought there, particularly at Ypres, Antwerp, Namur, and Mons. For more information, see the article ALBERT in Volume A.

World War II. In May 1940, during World War II, Belgium again became a European battleground. Belgian soldiers, aided by British and French allies, were unable to resist a German invasion.

Allied armies succeeded in driving the Germans out of Belgium in September 1944,

but in December of that year, German armies re-entered the country. The savage Battle of the Bulge was fought in the Ardennes region during the winter of 1944–45. At last, in February 1945, Belgium regained its freedom. In 1951, King Leopold III, who had come to the throne in 1934, was forced to abdicate because many Belgians disapproved of his wartime behavior. He was succeeded by his son Baudouin. In 1957, Belgium became a founding member of the European Community (now the European Union).

The magnificent guildhalls surrounding the Grand' Place in the heart of Brussels were built in the 1600's. They served as meeting places for merchants and craftsmen.

Recent History. During the early 1960's, Belgium granted independence to the Belgian Congo and to Rwanda-Urundi (now the Democratic Republic of the Congo, Rwanda, and Burundi). At home, Parliament tried to settle a long-standing language dispute between the Flemings and the Walloons. Limited self-rule was granted to Dutch-speaking Flanders and to French-speaking Wallonia in 1980. Brussels, officially bilingual, was made a third federal region in 1989.

King Baudouin, after a reign of some 42 years, died in 1993. He was succeeded by his brother, Albert II.

KENNETH THOMPSON
University of California, Davis
Reviewed by CAROLINE LACOCQUE
Belgian-American Chamber of Commerce

See also DUTCH AND FLEMISH ART; DUTCH AND FLEMISH MUSIC.

BELGRADE

Belgrade is the capital and largest city of Serbia and Montenegro. Called Beograd by the Serbs, its name means "white fortress" or "white city." With a population of more than 1.6 million in its metropolitan area, Belgrade is the major city of the central Balkans. It owes its existence and its importance to its strategic location on the high cliffs at the junction of two rivers, the Sava and the Danube, the main travel routes between Central Europe and the lower Balkans.

The City. One of Belgrade's most historic landmarks is the Kalemegdan fortress, which dates from the Middle Ages. Other important public buildings are the Eastern Orthodox cathedral, the former royal palace, a folklore museum, and the university, founded in 1863. Handsome broad boulevards link the various parts of the city.

A rapidly developing suburb, Novi Beograd (New Belgrade), has grown up on the west bank of the Sava River. Many government buildings and the newer residential areas are located here.

Economic Activity. Belgrade is an important river port and railway hub. It is also one of the largest commercial centers in the Balkans. Goods produced there include motors, tractors, machine tools, chemicals, electrical equipment, and textiles.

History. Belgrade has had a long and tumultuous history. A fortified Roman settlement existed on the site until its destruction by invading Huns in the A.D. 400's. Subject to repeated invasion and conquest, the city had various rulers, including the Byzantine emperors, in the centuries that followed.

Belgrade became the Serbian capital in the 1400's, but in 1521 it fell to the Ottoman Turks. Except for a few brief periods, when it was controlled by the Austrians, the city remained under Turkish rule until 1867, when it was restored as the capital of an independent Serbia.

With the creation of a unified Yugoslav kingdom in 1918, Belgrade was made the national capital. It remained the capital of a smaller Yugoslavia when the country broke apart in 1991–92 and of the new nation of Serbia and Montenegro in 2003.

In 1999, NATO air strikes destroyed parts of Belgrade during the war against Serbian aggression in the province of Kosovo. Following the overthrow of the Serbian dictator Slobodan Milošević in 2000, the new democratic government sought to attract foreign investment and create new industries.

Reviewed by JANUSZ BUGAJSKI
Director, Eastern European Project
Center for Strategic and International Studies

Belgrade, the capital of Serbia and Montenegro, is a major city on the Balkan Peninsula in southeastern Europe. Its location at the junction of the Danube and Sava rivers ensures its importance as a center of transportation and industry.

BELIZE

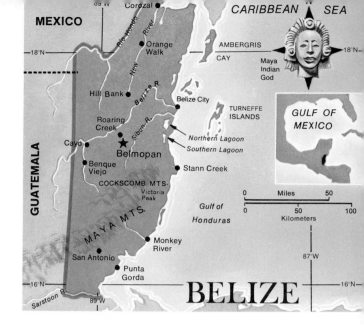

Belize is a small nation located on the eastern, or Caribbean, coast of Central America. Formerly a British colony known as British Honduras, it gained its independence in 1981. Belize is distinctive in being officially an English-speaking country in a region where Spanish is the common language.

▶THE PEOPLE

Belize is the home of many different peoples. The Creoles form the largest ethnic group. They are chiefly descended from black Africans, who were originally brought to the region as slaves. Mestizos, or people of mixed Indian and European ancestry, make up the next largest group. There are smaller numbers of Maya and Carib Indians, East Indians, Europeans, Syrians, and Chinese.

While English is the official language, Spanish is also widely spoken. The Indians speak their own languages. Many Creoles speak an English dialect that contains numerous African words and is often difficult for other English-speaking people to understand. Over half the people are Roman Catholics. The remainder are Protestants.

Most of the people live along the Caribbean coast. About one-third of the population lives in Belize City, the largest city, chief port, and former capital.

▶THE LAND AND THE ECONOMY

Belize has a long, swampy, and irregular coastline, fringed by small islands known as

Belize's long coastline on the Caribbean Sea (*left*) is fringed by numerous small islands called cays. Most are uninhabited. Parts of the interior (*below*) are mountainous and covered with dense rain forests.

Most of Belize's rivers are shallow and not very long. But they provide transportation for small craft, such as dugout canoes, carrying village produce to market.

cays. The low coastal plain rises gradually toward the interior. In the south are the Maya Mountains and the Cockscomb Mountains. Victoria Peak, in the Cockscombs, rises to 3,681 feet (1,122 meters).

The hot and humid climate is cooled along the coast by northeast trade winds. In the south more than 170 inches (4,300 millimeters) of rain may fall each year. Belize lies within the Caribbean hurricane belt, and storms have caused great damage in the past. Belize City was nearly destroyed twice by hurricanes. For this reason a new capital, Belmopan, was built inland about 50 miles (80 kilometers) from Belize City. Belmopan has been the official capital since 1972.

Belize has many rivers, but most are shallow, and none is very long. The most important is the Belize River. A considerable part of the land is still covered with dense tropical forests. For much of Belize's history, lumbering was its most important economic activity. African slaves were brought to the territory to fell the valuable hardwood trees. Sugar is now the leading export.

▶HISTORY AND GOVERNMENT

Belize was once a part of the vast Maya Indian Empire. The first known European settlers were British sailors who had been shipwrecked off the coast in 1638. Other British settlers followed. For many years, Spain, which ruled the surrounding region, disputed Britain's possession of the territory. When Guatemala won independence from Spain in 1821, it assumed the Spanish claims.

British Honduras became a British crown colony in 1862. It was granted internal self-government in 1964, and in 1973 its name was changed to Belize, which came from an older name for the territory. Belize's movement toward independence was complicated by Guatemala's continued claims to the territory. Even after Belize won its independence in 1981, the territorial dispute was still not resolved. Relations between Belize and Guatemala have improved considerably in the years since, however. In 1991 diplomatic relations were established between the two countries.

The government of Belize is based on the British model. The British monarch, represented by a governor-general, is the head of state. Real political power, however, lies with the National Assembly, which is composed of an elected House of Representatives and an appointed Senate. The leader of the majority party in the House of Representatives becomes prime minister, or head of government.

Belize is a member of the Caribbean Community and Common Market (CARICOM).

Reviewed by SIR PETER STALLARD
Former Governor, Belize

FACTS and figures

BELIZE is the official name of the country.

LOCATION: Central America.

AREA: 8,867 sq mi (22,965 km²).

POPULATION: 170,000 (estimate).

CAPITAL: Belmopan.

LARGEST CITY: Belize City.

MAJOR LANGUAGE(S): English (official), Spanish.

MAJOR RELIGIOUS GROUP(S): Christian (Roman Catholic, Protestant).

GOVERNMENT: Constitutional monarchy. **Head of state**—British monarch, represented by a governor-general. **Head of government**—prime minister. **Legislature**—National Assembly (composed of a House of Representatives and a Senate).

CHIEF PRODUCTS: Agricultural—sugarcane, citrus fruits, bananas, rice, corn, beans. **Manufactured**—refined sugar, processed citrus fruits, lumber, clothing.

MONETARY UNIT: Belize dollar (1 dollar = 100 cents).

BELL, ALEXANDER GRAHAM
(1847–1922)

The date was March 10, 1876. The place was a small laboratory in a Boston boarding-house. A young man was working with an electrical instrument that was wired to one in another room. Suddenly the instrument spoke: "Mr. Watson, come here. I want you." Watson rushed into the other room, where his employer, Mr. Bell, had spilled some acid. Both men forgot the acid in their excitement over Watson's report: Bell's words, spoken near one instrument, had issued clearly from the other. These words had become the first spoken telephone message.

Alexander Graham Bell was born on March 3, 1847, in Edinburgh, Scotland. He was born into a family with an interest in speech and hearing. Both his grandfather and his father were teachers of correct speech. His father had developed "visible speech," a method of helping the deaf and hearing impaired to learn how to speak. From his mother, who was a portrait painter and an accomplished musician, he inherited a talent for music.

Bell's schooling was far from regular. In his early years he was taught at home along with his two brothers. At the age of 13 he spent a year in London with his grandfather. In his grandfather's library he read all he could about sound and speech—about the vibrations set up by the voice. He later recalled this year as the turning point of his life. By the age of 16, Graham, as he was called by his family and close friends, was teaching music and speech at a boys' school. Within a few years he was teaching his father's visible speech to deaf and hearing-impaired children.

While studying how the human voice works, Bell came upon the writings of Hermann von Helmholtz. Helmholtz was a German scientist who had used electric vibrations to make vowel sounds. Interested, Bell at once began to study electricity so that he could repeat Helmholtz's experiments.

Bell's family had moved to London, and he joined them there in 1868. But by 1870 both of Bell's brothers had died of tuberculosis, and his own life was in danger. Seeking a more healthful climate, the Bells left Britain and moved to Brantford, Ontario.

With his health improved, Bell went to Boston, Massachusetts, in 1871. There he again

Although Bell invented the telephone and made important contributions in many fields of science, he described his occupation as "teacher of the deaf."

took up his life's work of teaching the deaf and hearing impaired. Bell also continued his experiments. By now his work with electricity had led him to think about inventing a harmonic telegraph. This was a system that could carry several messages over one wire at the same time.

Bell needed money to carry on his experiments. It was given to him by two wealthy men, Gardiner Hubbard and Thomas Sanders. Hubbard had a deaf daughter, and Sanders a deaf son, both of whom were receiving instruction from Bell. It was arranged that the two fathers would share in any profits from Bell's work. Bell was now able to hire a skilled assistant, Thomas A. Watson.

It was during the summer of 1874 that Bell's thinking first went beyond his plan for a harmonic telegraph. What if an electric current could be made to vary, just as the air varies with sound waves? Then any sound— including human speech—could be carried by electricity. This was the idea of the telephone.

The next year was a busy one for Bell. Now that he had the idea of a telephone, he wanted to develop it. On June 2, 1875, Bell and Watson were experimenting with their telegraph, which made use of thin steel reeds. One of the reeds was stuck, and Watson plucked it with his finger. In another room Bell heard a reed in his instrument vibrate as if he himself had plucked it. The electric current had reproduced in this second reed the vibrations of the first.

If the current had done this, then surely it should also reproduce vibrations caused by the human voice. Bell now knew that the telephone was a practical idea. It was only a matter of time before he could perfect an instrument that would send words clearly. Success came on March 10, 1876, with the famous words, "Mr. Watson, come here. I want you."

By the end of 1877 the Bell Telephone Company had been formed, and many phones were in use. Bell himself did not take part in the telephone business that developed. Rather, he leased the right to build a company around his invention.

In the meantime Bell had married Mabel Hubbard, the deaf girl whom he had taught. They had two daughters. In 1882 Bell became a citizen of the United States. He divided his time between Washington, D.C., and his summer home, Beinn Bhreagh, on Cape Breton Island, Nova Scotia.

Bell had invented the telephone before he was 30. In the remaining 45 years of his life he applied his talents to many questions. He experimented with sending sound by light waves. He was interested in heredity and carried on breeding experiments with sheep. As early as the 1890's, Bell was experimenting with the problems of airplane flight. Throughout his life Bell continued working for the deaf and hearing impaired. His work in all these fields won him many honors. Bell died on August 2, 1922. He was so greatly admired that during the funeral the telephones of North America were silent in his honor.

JOHN S. BOWMAN
Author and Science Editor

See also ELECTRICITY; TELEPHONE.

BELLINI FAMILY

During the 1400's, Jacopo Bellini, a Venetian painter, owned one of the busiest workshops in Italy. He painted portraits for rich people and altars for the Church and taught

Madonna of the Trees (1487), by Giovanni Bellini.

young artists who came to study under him. Among his students were his sons, Gentile and Giovanni. Gentile was the elder.

Jacopo was born about 1400, and his sons were born about 1429 and 1430. The three artists worked in the shop for years, experimenting with a new medium, oil paint. The brothers continued to paint after Jacopo died (about 1470). In 1474, they began a series of historical paintings for the palace of the chief magistrate of Venice.

The sultan of Turkey asked the rulers of Venice to lend him one of their best painters. Gentile was chosen and was sent to Constantinople in 1479. Giovanni remained in Venice, working at the palace, teaching, and painting. He was the first of the great Venetian painters to capture a sense of open space and light. Today, he is regarded as the greatest of the Bellinis. When Gentile returned to Venice in 1480, the brothers worked together again.

Gentile died in 1507, and Giovanni in 1516. In 1577, a fire burned through the palace. It destroyed countless Bellini canvases—among the first masterpieces of oil painting.

Reviewed by ADRIANE RUSKIN BATTERBERRY
Author, *The Pantheon Story of Art for Young People*

BELLOW, SAUL (1915–2005)

Saul Bellow was one of the foremost American writers of the period after World War II. His finely crafted novels of modern life won him the Nobel Prize for literature in 1976.

Bellow was born on July 10, 1915, in Lachine, Quebec, Canada. His parents, who were Jewish, had gone there two years before from Russia, where his father had been a businessman. Saul was the youngest of four children. Until he was 9, the family lived in Montreal. In 1924 the family moved to Chicago, which he later considered his hometown.

Bellow attended Chicago schools. He graduated with honors from Northwestern University and started graduate studies at the University of Wisconsin. But he left in his first year, determined to become a writer.

His first two novels, *Dangling Man* (1944) and *The Victim* (1947), are rather grim stories. His next novel, *The Adventures of Augie March* (1953), shows the humor for which he became known. It won the National Book Award. *Henderson the Rain King*, about an American in Africa, followed in 1959.

In 1962, Bellow became a professor at the University of Chicago. Two later novels, *Herzog* (1964) and *Mr. Sammler's Planet* (1970), won National Book Awards. *Humboldt's Gift* (1975) won the Pulitzer Prize for fiction in 1976. *Him With His Foot in His Mouth and Other Stories* (1984) is a collection of his short stories, and *It All Adds Up* (1994) is a collection of essays. Bellow moved to Massachusetts in 1993 and taught at Boston University. He died on April 5, 2005, in Brookline, Massachusetts.

Reviewed by JEROME H. STERN
Florida State University

BELLS AND CARILLONS

A bell is a hollow cup-shaped vessel that makes a ringing sound when struck. A bell may be struck on the outside by a hammer or mallet or by means of a clapper suspended inside the bell.

Most modern bells are made of metal—usually bronze, an alloy of copper and tin. In bell casting, two molds of baked clay are made. One forms the bell's interior, and the other forms the curved outside surface. Molten bronze is poured between the two molds. When the metal is cool and hard, the molds are removed. Bells are tuned by filing metal strips from their inside surfaces.

For centuries bells have been rung to mark the passing hours. But they have also been used for many other purposes: to sound an alarm, to announce a birth or a death, to call a congregation to worship, even to ward off evil spirits. In old England, folk dancers jingled bells to awaken the spirit of spring from a long winter's sleep.

In ancient Rome, bells announced public assemblies and church services. In the Middle Ages, bells woke the city at dawn, signaling morning prayers. Through the day, bells marked the hours, the half hours, and the quarters. They pealed for weddings and tolled for funerals and were heard at Easter and Christmas.

A modern-day bell tower in Atlanta, Georgia, holds a set of carillon bells. This carillon can be programmed by computer to play a sequence of tunes.

The First Bell Music. The earliest attempts to make music with bells occurred in the Middle Ages, with the *cymbala*, or bell chime. This was a small set of bells hung from a rack.

The clock bell originated in the monastery. The bells rang from a tower, regulating not only life in the abbey but in the surrounding town as well. So necessary were the bells to a town that they became civic property.

Since the first clock bells could not ring by themselves, someone was hired to strike them at the proper times. The human bell ringer was soon replaced by clock machinery. It was then possible to ring many bells, and it became customary to ring a short tune as a warning that the hour bell was about to strike. This is known as a clock chime tune.

From Bells to Carillons. A carillon is a set of bells with a range of between two and four octaves. Usually a carillon has at least 23 bells. The first carillons were made in the 1500's in Flanders (a region in present-day Belgium and northern France). At first the bells were rung automatically; later a keyboard, operated by a **carillonneur**, was added.

The carillon keyboard consists of levers and pedals. The levers resemble small broomstick handles. The carillonneur sits at a bench and strikes the levers with clenched hands while playing the foot pedals.

The oldest carillon in the world is in the Rijksmuseum in Amsterdam. It has 24 bells cast in 1554. A famous carillon is at Saint Rombold's Cathedral in Mechelen, Belgium. It has 49 bells. The first carillon in North America was installed at Notre Dame University in South Bend, Indiana, in 1856. The largest carillon in the world is at the Riverside Church in New York City. It contains six octaves of bells, of which the **bourdon**, or bass bell, weighs more than 18 tons.

Electronic carillons imitate the sound of bells through the use of electronic equipment; they are very different from true carillons.

JAMES R. LAWSON
Carillonneur, Riverside Church (New York City)

BEN-GURION, DAVID (1886–1973)

David Ben-Gurion became the first prime minister of Israel after the country became independent in 1948. He served as prime minister and minister of defense from 1949 to 1953 and from 1955 to 1963.

Ben-Gurion was born David Gryn on October 16, 1886, in Plonsk, Poland. His father, Avigdor Gryn, was a Zionist who inspired young David with the hope that some day a homeland for the Jewish people could be established in Palestine.

In 1906 David decided that the time had come for him to go to Palestine, then a part of the Turkish Empire. The new land was strange to someone who had always lived in Poland, but he soon found work as a farm laborer. In 1910 David became editor of the Palestine Labor Party's magazine. He signed one of his articles "Ben-Gurion," Hebrew for "son of the young lion." From then on he was known as David Ben-Gurion.

When World War I broke out in 1914, Ben-Gurion was arrested by the Turks and ex-

pelled from Palestine. First he fled to Egypt and later to the United States. In America he encouraged young people to emigrate to Palestine. One of these Americans was a nurse named Paula Munweis, who eventually became Ben-Gurion's wife. In 1917 Ben-Gurion helped organize the Jewish Legion to fight with the British Army against the Turks. In 1918 he returned to Palestine.

For the next 20 years Ben-Gurion devoted himself to Zionism and politics. He helped organize Histadrut (the General Federation of Jewish Labor). In 1935 he became chairman of the Jewish Agency for Palestine, an organization that assisted Jewish immigrants who wanted to settle in Palestine.

Israel declared its independence on May 14, 1948. Under Ben-Gurion's leadership the new nation became a modern democracy as well as a home for Jews seeking refuge. Ben-Gurion died in 1973, a national hero.

Reviewed by
HOWARD M. SACHAR
George Washington University

BENIN

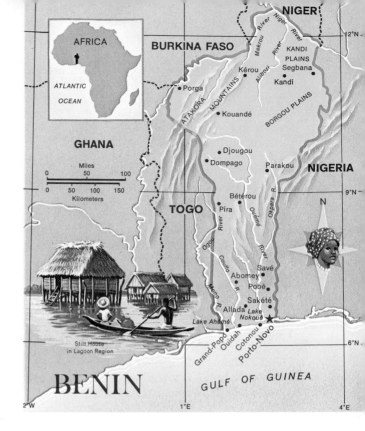

Stilt House
in Lagoon Region

BENIN

Benin, formerly called Dahomey, is a small nation situated on the west coast of Africa. It traces its history back to the powerful kingdom of Dahomey in the 1600's. Later the region came under the control of France, which governed it until 1960. Unlike the old kingdom of Dahomey, however, Benin today is one of the poorest countries in Africa.

▶ PEOPLE

Most of the people in Benin live in the southern part of the country, which has the richest soil. The northern region is more sparsely populated. Of the many different ethnic groups in Benin, the most numerous are the Fon, the Adja, the Bariba, and the Yoruba. The majority of the people follow traditional African religions, but there are considerable numbers of Christians and Muslims. French is the official language, but Fon, Yoruba, and other African languages are widely spoken.

FACTS
and figures

REPUBLIC OF BENIN (République du Bénin) is the official name of the country.

LOCATION: West coast of Africa.

AREA: 43,484 sq mi (112,622 km²).

POPULATION: 6,200,000 (estimate).

CAPITAL: Porto-Novo (official).

LARGEST CITY: Cotonou (center of government administration).

MAJOR LANGUAGES: French (official), Fon, Yoruba, other African languages.

MAJOR RELIGIOUS GROUPS: Traditional African religions, Christian, Muslim.

GOVERNMENT: Republic. **Head of state and government**—president. **Legislature**—National Assembly.

CHIEF PRODUCTS: Agricultural—corn, sorghum, cassava, yams, beans, rice, cotton, palm oil, peanuts, poultry, livestock. **Manufactured**—palm oil, palm kernel oil, copra (dried coconut meat), shea butter, castor oil.

MONETARY UNIT: African Financial Community (CFA) franc (1 CFA franc = 100 centimes).

Most of the people are farmers who produce food chiefly for their own use. The main food crops are cassava, yams, beans, corn, sorghum, rice, and peanuts. Cassava is used in making bread and tapioca (*gari*). The farmers also keep poultry, cattle, sheep, and goats. Fish are an important source of food and one of the country's exports.

Improvement in education is essential to the country's development. Most schools are in the south, but the government is trying to provide education for the scattered population in the north. Most of the schools of higher education are located in Porto-Novo, the official capital, and Cotonou, the largest city and center of government administration.

▶ LAND

Benin occupies a long, narrow strip of land that includes both lowlands and highlands. It has a short coastline on the Gulf of Guinea, a part of the Atlantic Ocean.

The country has four geographical regions. In the south is a flat coastal area along the Gulf of Guinea. Next is a region of lagoons and lakes. Farther north the land rises to a broad plateau that reaches as high as 1,500 feet (460 meters). In the far north the land is divided between the Atakora Mountains and the broad plains of Borgou and Kandi. The major rivers are the Ouémé (the country's longest), the Mono, and the Couffo. The climate in the south is hot and humid; the north is drier, with less rainfall.

▶ **ECONOMY**

Benin is a poor and underdeveloped country. Its economy is largely agricultural. The major industries are those that process the chief export crops. Palm products supply most of the country's exports. Palm oil is used in making soap and margarine. Copra (dried coconut meat), shea butter (the fat of shea tree nuts), cotton, peanuts, and castor oil are among the other important agricultural exports.

▶ **HISTORY AND GOVERNMENT**

The three great kingdoms of Ardra, Jakin, and Dahomey flourished in the early 1600's. During the 1700's, the strong kings of Dahomey gained control of Ardra and Jakin.

In 1738 the Yoruba from Nigeria seized Abomey, the capital of the kingdom of Dahomey, and forced the Dahomean rulers to pay tribute for nearly 100 years. In the late 1800's, the great Dahomean king Gezo reorganized the Dahomean Army (which included a famous band of female warriors) and succeeded in shaking off Yoruba control.

In 1894, France forcibly deposed the last of the Dahomean kings, Béhanzin, and annexed the territory to French West Africa. Gradu-ally France began to give Dahomey and its other French African territories more control over their own affairs. Dahomey elected its own legislature in 1952. In 1960 it proclaimed its independence.

Dahomey then suffered years of political instability. Military coups through the early 1970's led to frequent changes of government. In 1972, Major (now General) Mathieu Kérékou came to power and established a Communist-style government, which he later renounced. In 1975 he changed the name of the country from Dahomey to Benin.

Kérékou governed as president and head of Benin's sole political party, the People's Revolutionary Party, until 1990, when anti-government demonstrations forced him to resign. In 1991, in the first free elections in more than twenty years, former prime minister Nicephore Soglo was elected president. Kérékou regained power in 1996, however, defeating Soglo in a runoff election for president. In 2001, Soglo withdrew from the presidential race, charging Kérékou with election fraud.

L. GRAY COWAN
Columbia University

BENJAMIN, JUDAH PHILIP. See LOUISIANA (Famous People).

BENNETT, RICHARD BEDFORD. See CANADA, GOVERNMENT OF (Profiles).

BENNY, JACK. See ILLINOIS (Famous People).

BENTHAM, JEREMY. See ENLIGHTENMENT, AGE OF (Profiles).

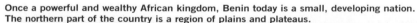

Once a powerful and wealthy African kingdom, Benin today is a small, developing nation. The northern part of the country is a region of plains and plateaus.

BENTON, THOMAS HART (1889–1975)

Thomas Hart Benton was a leader of the movement in American art known as **regionalism**. The subject of much of his work is life in the small towns and rural areas of the American Midwest.

Benton was born on April 15, 1889, in Neosho, Missouri, into a politically prominent family. He studied at the Art Institute of Chicago from 1906 to 1907 and then went to Paris, where he became familiar with the latest trends in modern art. He returned to the United States in 1912. Gradually he rejected European modernism in favor of a realistic style and distinctly American themes.

After serving in the navy during World War I (1914–18), Benton traveled through the South and Midwest, painting the people and places he saw. Works such as *Boomtown* (1927), *Louisiana Rice Fields* (1928), and *Cotton Pickers* (1932) convey the vitality of the men and women who work the land and populate the towns and cities of America.

Benton used many of these same images in his murals, which he began to paint in the 1930's. Some of the best known are in the New School for Social Research, New York City (1930); the State Capitol, Jefferson City, Missouri (1935); and the Truman Library, Independence, Missouri (1959).

In 1935, Benton moved to Kansas City, Missouri, where he lived until his death on January 19, 1975. His autobiography, *An Artist in America*, was published in 1937.

Reviewed by KENNETH HALTMAN
New Britain Museum of American Art

In *Arts of the West*, Thomas Hart Benton portrayed activities that he considered to be typical of the people of a particular region: the American West.

BEOWULF

Beowulf is the longest and greatest poem that has come down to us from Old English, the ancient form of modern English. Only one manuscript of *Beowulf* has survived. It dates from about A.D. 1000, but the poem was probably composed about A.D. 700.

In the poem, Beowulf, a hero of a Germanic tribe from southern Sweden called the Geats, travels to Denmark to help defeat a terrible monster. Why was a poem about Danish and Swedish kings and heroes preserved in England? The English people are descendants of Germanic tribes called the Angles, Saxons, and Jutes. These tribes came from what is now southern Denmark. Thus, *Beowulf* tells a story about the old days in their homeland. The opening lines state:

Hwæt! We Gardena in geardagum
þeodcyninga þrym gefrunon
hu ða æþelingas ellen fremedon.

In modern English, this reads:

What! We have heard of the glory of the spear-
Danes in the old days,
of the people's kings,
how the princes did deeds of valor.

Old English poetry such as *Beowulf* is very different from modern poetry. It was probably recited, for few people at that time were able to read. Instead of rhyme, poets typically used **alliteration**—a technique in which the first sound of each word in a line is the same, as in "Peter Piper picked a peck of pickled peppers." A line of Old English poetry usually has three words that alliterate. The meter, or rhythm, of the poetry works together with the alliteration: The stress in a line falls on the first syllables of the words that alliterate, as in the line "**weo'x** under **wo'lc**num, **weo'rð**myndum þah." (He grew under the sky, he prospered in his glory.)

Beowulf, the hero of an Old English epic poem, had many adventures, including battles with dragons and other beasts. The poem was originally recited aloud.

Old English poets also used **kennings**, poetic ways of saying simple things. For example, a poet might call the sea the swan-road or the whale-road; a king might be called a ring-giver. There are many kennings in *Beowulf*. In fact, some scholars think the name Beowulf itself may be a kenning. It may mean "bee-wolf," a term for a bear, which attacks beehives the way a wolf attacks other animals.

▶ THE STORY

The story of *Beowulf* tells how King Hrothgar built a great hall called Heorot for his people. In it he and his warriors spend their time singing and celebrating, until a monster named Grendel, angered by their singing, attacks the hall and kills and eats many of Hrothgar's warriors. Hrothgar and his men, helpless against Grendel's attacks, have to abandon Heorot.

Beowulf, a young warrior, hears of Hrothgar's troubles and, with his king's permission, goes to help Hrothgar. Beowulf and his men spend the night in Heorot. After they fall asleep, Grendel enters the hall and attacks them, eating up one of Beowulf's men. Beowulf grabs Grendel's arm in a wrestling hold, and the two crash around in Heorot until it seems as though the hall will fall down with their fighting. Beowulf's men draw their swords and rush to his help, but

there is a magic around Grendel that makes it impossible for swords to hurt him. Finally, Beowulf tears Grendel's arm from his body, and Grendel runs home to die.

The next night, after celebrating Grendel's death, Hrothgar and his men sleep in Heorot. But Grendel's mother attacks the hall, killing Hrothgar's most trusted warrior in revenge for her son's death. Hrothgar and Beowulf and their men track the monster to her lair under an eerie lake. Beowulf dives in and swims to the bottom. He finds Grendel's mother in a hideous cavern, along with her son's body and the remains of many men that the two have killed. Beowulf and Grendel's mother begin a fierce battle. Beowulf's sword breaks, but he finds another in the cavern, and with it he kills Grendel's mother. Taking Grendel's head with him, he returns to Heorot and is given many gifts.

Beowulf returns home and eventually becomes king of his own people. One day, late in Beowulf's life, a man steals a golden cup from a dragon's lair. When the dragon sees that the cup has been stolen, it leaves its cave in a rage, burning up everything in sight. Beowulf and his warriors come to fight the dragon, but only one of the warriors, a young man named Wiglaf, stays to help Beowulf. Beowulf kills the dragon with Wiglaf's help but dies from the wounds he has received. The dragon's treasure is taken from its lair and buried with Beowulf's ashes. And with that the poem ends.

Most scholars believe that *Beowulf* was written by a Christian poet. Grendel is called a descendant of Cain, and he and his mother have similarities to the devils and demons in medieval Christian stories. But the *Beowulf* poet was also very knowledgeable about pagan beliefs. The descriptions of Grendel and his mother, for example, owe as much to pagan beliefs about trolls as they do to Christian beliefs about demons. Beowulf's cremation at the end of the poem also refers to a pagan practice. But, even though Beowulf was a pagan, the poem's Christian audience could admire his heroic deeds. *Beowulf* is thus a product of the poet's knowledge of both Christian beliefs and the ancient history of his people. In combining them as he did, the *Beowulf* poet created a wonderful story.

DAVID E. GAY
Folklore Institute, Indiana University

BERG, ALBAN (1885–1935)

The Austrian composer Alban Berg was a leading figure in modern music. He combined contemporary techniques with traditional musical forms to create works of great power and emotion.

Berg was born in Vienna on February 9, 1885. He received no formal training in music until the age of 19, when he met the composer Arnold Schoenberg, who became his friend and teacher. Berg adopted Schoenberg's twelve-tone method of composition—in which every melody and harmony in a piece is drawn from a particular arrangement of twelve tones—for many of his later works.

Berg's early compositions included works for piano, string quartet, and orchestra. But his masterpiece is the opera *Wozzeck*, which had its premiere in Berlin in 1925. Based on an 1837 play by German dramatist Georg Büchner about a real-life criminal case, the opera was a worldwide success.

Berg died in Vienna on December 24, 1935, before completing his second opera, *Lulu*. The work, his only twelve-tone opera, was first performed in 1937. A completed version based on Berg's manuscripts had its premiere in Paris in 1979.

Of Berg's instrumental works, the most important is probably his last completed work, a concerto for violin and orchestra (1935). Also notable are *Three Pieces for Orchestra* (1914–15), *Chamber Concerto* (1925) for violin, piano, and 13 wind instruments, and *Lyric Suite* (1926) for string quartet.

Reviewed by KENNETH NOTT
Hartt School, University of Hartford

BERGMAN, INGMAR. See MOTION PICTURES (Profiles: Directors).
BERGMAN, INGRID. See MOTION PICTURES (Profiles: Movie Stars).

BERING, VITUS (1680–1741)

In the early 1700's, many people still believed that a bridge of land connected Asia and North America. Vitus Bering, a Dane in the service of the czar of Russia, discovered that this land bridge did not exist. His explorations helped map what was at that time a little-known part of the world and led to the discovery of Alaska.

Bering was born at Horsens, Denmark, in 1680, and entered the Russian Navy when he was 23. In 1724, Czar Peter the Great named him to lead an expedition to the Kamchatka Peninsula on the northeast coast of Siberia.

The long journey across Siberia was filled with great hardships. After more than three years, the expedition finally reached a little village on Kamchatka. Bering had a ship built and in 1728 set sail across an uncharted sea, now called the Bering Sea. He discovered an island, which he named St. Lawrence Island. Then he sailed north through the strait (now called Bering Strait) that separates Asia and North America. The discovery of this strait proved the two continents were not linked.

Bering returned to Russia in 1730 to report his findings and to plan a new expedition. In 1741 he sailed from Kamchatka again with two ships—his, the *St. Peter*, and the *St. Paul*, which was commanded by Aleksei Chirikov. The ships soon drifted apart, and on July 15–16 both Chirikov and Bering sighted the southern coast of Alaska from different points. The *St. Peter* stopped briefly at Kayak Island. But before exploring farther, Bering, who was ill, decided to return to Kamchatka for the winter. On the return voyage the *St. Peter* was buffeted by violent storms and wrecked on an uninhabited island off the coast of Kamchatka. Here, on December 8, 1741, Bering died and was buried. The island now bears his name.

Reviewed by HELEN DELPAR
Editor, *The Discoverers: An Encyclopedia of Explorers and Exploration*

BERLIN

The city of Berlin has long been a center of German political, economic, cultural, and intellectual life. Twice during the course of history it has served as the capital of a unified Germany.

Berlin first became the national capital in 1871, when the various German states were united into a single country. However, in the years that followed the defeat of the Nazi German regime in World War II (1939–45), Berlin—like Germany itself—was divided into two parts. East Berlin became the capital of East Germany (the German Democratic Republic), while West Berlin became one of the federal states of West Germany (the Federal Republic of Germany). During these years, the small university town of Bonn served as the capital of West Germany.

With the reunification of East and West Germany in 1990, however, the division of the city was ended, and Berlin once again became the official capital.

A sunny day draws Berliners to an outdoor café. In the background, the ruins of the old Kaiser Wilhelm Memorial Church stand as a stark reminder of the destruction of World War II.

Location, Area, and Population. Berlin is situated in northeastern Germany, on the Spree and Havel rivers. Its location has made it a traditional crossroads of trade between eastern and western and northern and southern Europe. Lying on the great sandy plain of the North German lowlands, the city has an average elevation of only about 112 feet (34 meters) above sea level.

Berlin makes up an urban area of about 441 square miles (1,142 square kilometers). With a population of nearly 3.5 million, it is the largest city in Germany and one of the ten largest cities in Europe. Yet the city's numerous parks, forests, lakes and other waterways give some of its districts a rustic, or country-like, setting.

Places of Interest. In the center of the former West Berlin the ruined tower of the Kaiser Wilhelm Memorial Church stands as a stark reminder of the destruction of World War II. Next to it is the new, modernistic church building, completed in 1961. The two structures are situated at the eastern end of the Kurfürstendamm, an elegant avenue of fashionable shops, restaurants, and theaters.

The reconstructed Reichstag, the old parliament building, is a landmark of historical importance. The original building was burned in 1933, soon after the Nazis took power. The present German parliament (or legislature) meets there on festive public occasions. Nearby is a Soviet war memorial, the Tiergarten, and the new Congress Hall. The Tiergarten, a park near the center of the city with a zoo and aquarium, is especially popular with Berliners. Other new buildings include the Berlin Philharmonic concert hall, the opera house, and several museums.

For years the wall that divided the city attracted millions of visitors. It was torn down in 1990, and all that remains of this relic of the Cold War is a swath of open space.

The Brandenburg Gate, one of Berlin's best-known monuments, is situated in the historic center of the city, in what was formerly East Berlin. A triumphal arch some 85 feet (26 meters) high, it faces the Tiergarten and stands at the western end of a tree-lined boulevard, Unter den Linden ("Under the Linden Trees"). This thoroughfare was once the site of military parades and the funeral processions of German rulers. Most of the government buildings, palaces, and foreign embassies that at one time lined the avenue were destroyed during World War II, but those that could be saved were restored.

At the eastern end of Unter den Linden is a giant square, which the East Germans named Marx-Engels-Platz, after the two major figures in the founding of Communism. It is also the site of the former royal palace. The huge Palace of the Republic, which once housed the East German parliament, stands nearby. Numerous museums are located on the appropriately named Museum Island.

Cultural Life. Berlin has been a cultural center of Germany for much of its modern history. During the Weimer period (1919–33), it was the entertainment capital of the world. Its numerous cabarets, theaters, and motion pictures enjoyed an international reputation, lost during the Nazi era that followed.

Top: East German border guards looked on calmly in 1989 as West Germans celebrated the coming reunification of the long-divided city. A reunited Berlin was soon followed by the reunification of Germany itself. *Right:* A poster for the German silent film classic *Metropolis* dates from 1926, when Berlin was famed as the popular entertainment capital of the world. *Far right:* This war memorial was dedicated to the thousands of Soviet troops killed in the 1945 battle for Berlin.

The city's division into eastern and western sectors from 1949 to 1990 meant that each developed its own distinct cultural life. Attempts were made, however, to preserve a common heritage. The great pre-war museum collections, for example, were divided between East and West Berlin's museums.

Berlin has recaptured some of its past glory through its Philharmonic Orchestra concerts, opera houses, theater groups, a yearly cultural festival, and jazz and rock performances. The Free University and Humboldt University play an important role in the city's intellectual life. Its many museums include the world-famous Pergamon Museum, noted for its collection of classical art.

The Economy.   Before World War II, Berlin was a center of commerce and banking as well as an important industrial city. By the 1950's, West Berlin had recovered from the war's destruction and was in the midst of an economic boom. At the same time, East Berlin was integrated into the Communist economic system of East Germany. The standard of living was considerably higher in the West than in the East.

The major industries in the Greater Berlin area involve the production of electrical and electronic equipment, machinery and motor vehicles, engineering products, processed foods, chemicals, and clothing. The city also has the largest number of scientific and technological research institutions in the country.

Since the reunification of Germany in 1990, the federal government has provided substantial economic assistance to the former eastern sector.

The City's Origins.   The city of Berlin developed out of two small trading settlements, Kölln and Berlin, which are first mentioned in documents of the 1200's. The two settlements merged in the 1300's. In 1486, Berlin became the seat of the electors (or rulers) of what was then the small state of Brandenburg. The Thirty Years' War (1618–48) laid waste to the city, but it was rebuilt by the Great Elector Frederick William.

Capital.   In 1701, Berlin became the capital of the kingdom of Prussia, which had grown out of the original core of Brandenburg. In spite of military occupation by foreign armies during the wars of the 1700's and 1800's, Berlin, along with Prussia, grew steadily in importance. When the German states united around Prussia to form the German Empire in 1871, Berlin became its capital.

During World War II, much of Berlin was destroyed by bombing and in the

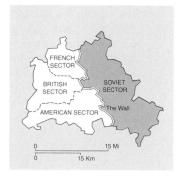

Above: Berlin was divided among the four victorious Allied powers in 1945, at the end of World War II. In 1949 the U.S., British, and French sectors were joined to form West Berlin. The Soviet sector became East Berlin. The city remained divided until 1989–90. *Left:* When the Soviet Union blockaded West Berlin in 1948–49, cutting off all land access to that part of the city, its people were supplied through a massive airlift by U.S. and British planes.

As onlookers cheer, a young Berliner adds his own blows to the crumbling wall that for nearly thirty years had physically divided the city. Erected in 1961, the Berlin Wall was designed to stop the flood of Germans escaping from Communist East Germany to West Germany, which had become a drain on the East German economy. The wall was also a symbol of the division of Germany itself, which lasted until 1990, when both Germany and Berlin were again united.

heavy ground fighting that took place in the closing weeks of the war in Europe. On May 2, 1945, Soviet armies captured the city. By agreement, U.S., British, French, and Soviet forces each occupied a sector of Berlin (see map). Germany as a whole was divided along the same lines. The United States, Britain, and France occupied the western part of the country (which later became West Germany). The Soviet Union controlled the eastern part (later to become East Germany). Berlin itself lay deep within the Soviet area of occupation of Germany. An inter-Allied governing authority administered the city jointly.

Blockade and Airlift. In 1948, Berlin became a focal point of the Cold War, the period of hostility that developed between the Soviet Union and the nations of the West after the war. The Soviets informally withdrew from the governing authority and tried to force the Western powers to end controls over their three sectors. When this failed, the Soviets cut off all land and water communications between western Germany and the three western sectors of Berlin in an effort to gain control over the entire city.

In response, the Western Allies launched a massive airlift of food and other supplies to the isolated western sectors. The blockade lasted eleven months, until May 1949, when the Soviets, not having gained their objective, lifted it.

The City Divided. In 1949 separate East and West Germanys were established. The U.S., British, and French sectors of Berlin were joined to form West Berlin; the Soviet sector became East Berlin. But the four Allied powers still had final control over the city.

In 1953 a revolt by workers in East Berlin against the East German government was crushed by Soviet tanks. Increasing numbers of East Berliners fled to West Berlin in subsequent years, until 1961, when the East German authorities erected a fortified wall, physically separating the two parts of the city.

Reunification. The easing of political tensions and a new agreement between the Western Allies and the Soviet Union in 1971 eased travel restrictions for Germans. Nevertheless, the Berlin Wall remained a symbol of a divided city and nation for nearly twenty more years. In November 1989, however, following widespread protests by its own people, the East German government opened the guarded crossing points of the wall.

As East Berliners poured into West Berlin in celebration, the dismantling of the wall and of a divided Germany was already underway. On October 3, 1990, the two Germanys were united, the special privileges of the four powers ended, and a separate West and East Berlin ceased to exist.

GERARD BRAUNTHAL
University of Massachusetts, Amherst

BERLIN, IRVING (1888–1989)

The American songwriter Irving Berlin helped define the modern American popular song. During his long career he wrote some 1,500 songs. Many—"Always," "Blue Skies," "Puttin' on the Ritz," and countless others—have become classics, recorded again and again by new generations of singers.

Berlin was born Israel Baline in Tyumen, Russia, on May 11, 1888, the youngest of eight children. He moved with his family to New York City at the age of 5. He had barely begun school when his father died, and he sold newspapers and sang in the streets to help support his family. He learned to play piano by ear and began to compose melodies by trial and error. He became Irving Berlin when his first song was mistakenly credited to "I. Berlin," and he decided to change his first name as well.

In 1909, Berlin got a job writing lyrics for a music publisher; he became world famous two years later for writing "Alexander's Ragtime Band," which sold more than one million copies of sheet music. Berlin formed his own music company in 1919. During the 1920's the composer developed his unerring touch for

ballads. In 1935 he wrote *Top Hat*, the first of many film scores. In 1939 he composed "God Bless America," which became one of the country's best-loved patriotic songs.

Among Berlin's greatest successes was the song "White Christmas," which won an Academy Award in 1942 and became a modern Christmas carol. He also wrote hit Broadway musicals, notably *Annie Get Your Gun* (1946), with its rousing showstopper, "There's No Business Like Show Business."

Berlin's last major work was the Broadway show *Mr. President* (1962). He died in New York City on September 22, 1989, at 101 years of age.

Reviewed by CHARLES MORITZ
Editor, *Current Biography*

BERLIOZ, HECTOR (1803–1869)

Louis-Hector Berlioz, an innovative French composer, was born near Grenoble, France, on December 11, 1803. Because of pressure from his father, a physician, Hector went to Paris in 1821 to enroll in medical school. While there he attended many opera performances. He also studied music at the Paris Conservatory.

In 1824 the young student abandoned medical studies but continued to compose music. When his parents refused to support him, Hector taught music lessons and wrote articles. He completed his most individual work, *Symphonie fantastique*, in 1830. That year he also won a prestigious music prize that required him to live in Italy.

After his return to Paris in 1832, Berlioz met the Irish actress Harriet Smithson, whom he married the following year. Because his unusual compositions failed to win any recognition in France, Berlioz was forced to earn a living as a music librarian and by writing essays and music criticism.

Finally, Berlioz did begin to win fame outside France. In 1843 he made a triumphant tour of Germany, conducting his own compositions. He had equally successful tours to Austria, Hungary, Russia, and England.

In Paris, though, his genius continued to go unrecognized. His great opera, *The Trojans at Carthage*, was only a partial success at its first performance in 1863. Discouraged, Berlioz stopped composing and writing. He died in Paris on March 8, 1869.

Since then his reputation has steadily grown. Berlioz is now regarded as one of the world's foremost composers, one of the first great orchestral conductors, and a very skilled writer on musical topics.

Reviewed by MARGERY MORGAN LOWENS
Peabody Conservatory of Music
The Johns Hopkins University

Bermuda is made up of many small islands situated in the western Atlantic Ocean. Their mild, sunny climate and natural beauty make the islands popular with vacationers, most of whom come from the United States.

BERMUDA

Bermuda, or the Bermudas, is a group of about 300 coral islands situated in the western Atlantic Ocean, about 670 miles (1,075 kilometers) southeast of Cape Hatteras, North Carolina. Most of the islands are small and only about 20 are inhabited. Also called Somers Islands, Bermuda is a British crown colony. The islands' natural beauty and their mild, sunny climate have made tourism the most important economic activity. Most vacationers come from the nearby United States.

The People. Bermuda has a population of about 58,000. About two thirds of the people are of black African or mixed ancestry, descendants of slaves brought to the islands in the 1700's. White Bermudians are largely of British ancestry. English is the official language. Most of the people are Christians, with the Anglican Church the largest Protestant denomination. The capital is Hamilton.

Part of the islands' charm is the unhurried tempo of life. Until 1946 automobiles were not permitted, horse-drawn carriages and bicycles being used instead. Even today the size and number of automobiles are limited.

The Land. Shaped roughly like a fishhook, Bermuda has a land area of about 21 square miles (54 square kilometers). The largest island, Bermuda (or Main Island), the site of Hamilton, is about 14 miles (23 kilometers) long. It is connected by causeways and bridges with other important islands. There are no natural lakes or streams, and Bermudians are dependent on collected rainwater for drinking.

The Gulf Stream gives Bermuda an unusually mild climate for a region so far north of the equator, allowing palm trees and other tropical vegetation to flourish. The average yearly temperature is about 70°F (21°C). Ocean breezes keep the summers from being oppressively hot.

Economy. Tourism, the mainstay of the economy, accounts for about half of Bermuda's income and provides about 65 percent of all employment. Some crops are grown for local use, and cut flowers, particularly Easter lilies, are cultivated for export. There is some light industry, chiefly ship repairing, boat building, and the manufacture of pharmaceu-

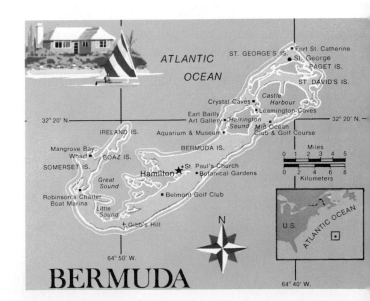

BERMUDA

ticals (medical drugs). Ship registry, finance, and insurance have become important sectors of the economy. Bermuda must import much of its food, fuel, and other necessities.

History and Government. The islands take their names from two ships' commanders—the Spaniard Juan de Bermúdez, who first sighted the islands in the 1500's; and Sir George Somers, whose ship, carrying English colonists to Virginia, was shipwrecked there in 1609. The first permanent English settlement of the then-uninhabited islands was made in 1612, at St. George. In 1815 the capital was transferred to Hamilton. The tourist industry developed in the 1900's. In 1941, during World War II, the British granted the United States a 99-year lease for naval and air bases on the islands. Several hundred U.S. military personnel are stationed on the islands.

Bermuda's constitution, which was amended in 1979, gives the colony considerable self-government. The British monarch is represented by an appointed governor, who is responsible for the islands' foreign affairs, de-

WONDER QUESTION

What is the Bermuda Triangle?

It is a triangular area of the Atlantic Ocean, with Bermuda, southern Florida, and Puerto Rico making up its approximate corners. It is also known, more ominously, as the Devil's Triangle, because of the numerous ships and airplanes that reportedly have vanished in the region, usually without trace. Some authors have sought to explain the disappearances as due to mysterious weather conditions in the area of the triangle. But this has not been borne out by any evidence.

fense, and police. The legislature consists of an appointed Senate and an elected House of Assembly. The leader of the majority party in the assembly serves as prime minister.

Reviewed by THOMAS G. MATHEWS
Secretary General, Association of Caribbean
Universities and Research Institutes

BERNINI, GIOVANNI LORENZO (1598–1680)

The sculptor, painter, and architect Giovanni Lorenzo Bernini was Italy's leading artist during the 1600's. His works, which include many of Rome's buildings, statues, and fountains, greatly influenced the development of Italian art of the baroque period.

The strong and graceful lines in the statue of King Louis XIV of France show both Bernini's technical skill and his ability to produce dramatic effects.

Bernini was born on December 7, 1598, in Naples. His father, a sculptor, received a commission from the pope and moved his family to Rome about 1605. Except for a short trip to Paris in 1665, Bernini spent his entire life in Rome. In 1639 he married Caterina Tezio; they had eleven children.

At 20, Bernini received his first important commission: a series of statues for the villa of Cardinal Borghese. Among them is the famous *David*. This figure, with its dramatic pose and expressive, flowing lines, sums up the ideals of the baroque style. Another of his great sculptures is the *Ecstasy of St. Teresa*, in the Cornaro chapel.

Some of Bernini's most powerful works were created for St. Peter's Basilica, including the square in front of the church, with its stately rows of columns and 162 statues.

Bernini died on November 28, 1680. He had been a painter, theatrical designer, and decorator. But he remains most famous for his sculpture and architecture.

Reviewed by HOWARD HIBBARD
Columbia University

BERNOULLI FAMILY

The Bernoulli family included several generations of prominent mathematicians and scientists. Because of religious persecution, the family fled Holland in 1583 and eventually settled in Switzerland. From the late 1600's to the mid-1700's, the Bernoulli family dominated European mathematics. The three most famous members of the family were Jakob I, Johann I, and Daniel. (Several Bernoullis had the same first names, so Roman numerals are often used to distinguish among them.) Jakob I and Johann I were the sons of Nikolas Bernoulli, a minor local official in Basel. Daniel was the son of Johann I.

Jakob (I) Bernoulli (1654–1705), the first member of the family to gain fame as a mathematician, was born in Basel, Switzerland. Jakob received a theology degree in 1676, but his real interest was mathematics. He traveled in Europe until 1683. Then he devoted his time to giving lectures, writing papers, and teaching himself more about mathematics. In 1687 he became professor of mathematics at the University of Basel, a position he held until his death. While at Basel, Jakob played an important part in developing both differential and integral calculus. His main contribution was showing how calculus could be applied to problems in many fields. Jakob also advanced the field of probability. A mathematical dispute with his brother Johann I led to their developing the calculus of variations.

Johann (I) Bernoulli (1667–1748), brother of Jakob I, received a degree in medicine from the University of Basel in 1694. He was drawn to mathematics as well, and in 1695 he gave up medicine to teach mathematics at the University of Groningen in the Netherlands. He returned to Basel after the death of his brother in 1705 and became professor of mathematics at the university. Johann's contributions to mathematics were greater than those of Jakob I. He became known for his work in both differential and integral calculus. He is also considered a cofounder, with his brother, of the calculus of variations. Johann's interests also extended to other fields, including physics, chemistry, and astronomy, and he sought to apply mathematical principles to these subjects.

Daniel Bernoulli (1700–82), son of Johann I, was born in Groningen. Of all the Bernoullis, he was perhaps the greatest mathematician. Daniel also had the widest interests, which included medicine, biology, physics, mechanics, and astronomy. Daniel originally planned a career in business and medicine. Like other family members, however, he was drawn to the field of mathematics. Between 1725 and 1732, he taught mathematics at the Academy of Sciences in St. Petersburg, Russia. He then went to the University of Basel, where he taught anatomy, botany, and then physics. Daniel's most important work was in mechanics. He was a founder of the science of hydrodynamics, the study of moving fluids. One of his main contributions in this area is Bernoulli's Principle, which states that the pressure in a fluid decreases as its velocity, or speed, increases. (This principle is explained in the article AERODYNAMICS in Volume A.) Daniel is also noted for his work in calculus and probability theory, especially as it applies to games. He is also considered one of the founders of the kinetic theory of gases, which helps explain the property and behavior of gases. Between 1725 and 1749, Daniel won many prizes for his work on astronomy, gravity, tides, magnetism, and ocean currents.

Several other Bernoullis were gifted mathematicians and scientists. **Nikolaus II** (1687–1759), nephew of Jakob I and Johann I, taught at many universities, including Padua and Basel. He was known for his work in probability theory. **Nikolaus III** (1695–1726), son of Johann I and brother of Daniel, also made contributions in probability theory while teaching at the Academy of Sciences in St. Petersburg, Russia. **Johann II** (1710–90), another son of Johann I, succeeded his father as professor of mathematics at Basel. He is known for his contribution to theories of heat and light. **Johann III** (1746–1807), son of Johann II, was known for his work in science. He became the royal astronomer at the Berlin Academy. **Jakob II** (1759–89), another son of Johann II, succeeded his uncle Daniel as professor of mathematics and physics at the Academy of Sciences in St. Petersburg. **Christoph** (1782–1863), grandson of Johann II and nephew of Johann III and Jakob II, was a naturalist who taught at the University of Basel.

Reviewed by BRYAN BUNCH
Coauthor, *The Timetables of Science*

BERRA, YOGI. See MISSOURI (Famous People).
BERRIES. See GRAPES AND BERRIES.
BERRY, CHUCK. See ROCK MUSIC (Profiles).

BESSEMER, SIR HENRY (1813–1898)

The industrial city of Bessemer, Alabama, is named in honor of Sir Henry Bessemer, the English inventor who made the steel industry possible. In 1855 and 1856 he patented a method of purifying iron so that it could be made into steel cheaply and easily. This method, called the Bessemer process, and a machine called the Bessemer converter are still used in steel manufacturing.

Henry Bessemer was born January 19, 1813, in the village of Charlton in southern England. His father, also an inventor, had a factory there for casting type. Young Henry spent his spare time in his father's workshop, learning to make use of his natural mechanical ability.

When he was 17 years old, Bessemer went to London, where he cast metal into artistic figures that were exhibited by the Royal Academy. Then he turned to embossing designs on cards and cloth. In 1833 he invented a method of canceling tax stamps so that they could not be used again.

During his busy life Bessemer worked out and patented 114 inventions. One of the most profitable was a method of making gold paint. The money from this invention enabled him to experiment and develop his steelmaking process, his most important invention.

The Bessemer process practically created the modern steel industry. Before the invention of this process, steel could be made only in small batches. As a result, it was very expensive. Bessemer's discovery made possible large-scale production of steel. It has been ranked with printing, the magnetic compass, and the steam engine as an invention that changed the world.

In 1879, Bessemer was knighted in reward for his tax-stamp canceling process. He died in London on March 15, 1898.

Reviewed by DAVID C. COOKE
Author, *Inventions That Made History*
See also IRON AND STEEL.

BETHUNE, MARY MCLEOD (1875–1955)

Mary McLeod Bethune rose from poverty to become a famous educator, a leader of women, and an adviser to presidents. She was born on July 10, 1875, near the small town of Mayesville, South Carolina. Her parents, Patsy and Sam McLeod, were recently freed slaves who made their living as farmers.

Even after the Civil War ended, there were not many schools for African American children in the South. Mary was 11 years old before a mission school was opened in Mayesville. She completed her education at the Moody Bible Institute in Chicago. When she was turned down for a post as a missionary in Africa, she went home to the South to teach. After her marriage to Albertus Bethune, a teacher, she moved to Florida. In 1904, she opened a school for African American girls in Daytona Beach.

The Daytona Normal and Industrial Institute for Negro Girls was only a shack, but its goals were high. The school's motto, "Enter to learn, depart to serve," described the aim of its founder, which was to educate girls to become teachers.

The early years of the school were difficult. Mary Bethune raised money by selling food to winter visitors in Daytona Beach. Before long, the institute received donations that made it possible to add a high school, a small hospital, and then a college. The institute was merged with a boys' school in 1923 and became Bethune-Cookman College in 1925.

In 1935, Mary Bethune founded the National Council of Negro Women. She helped President Franklin D. Roosevelt start the National Youth Administration, which provided employment for young people. She was a member of the President's unofficial "Black Cabinet," which advised him on ways to improve conditions for African Americans. During World War II, she served as a special assistant to the secretary of war to help end discrimination in the armed services.

The last years of Mary Bethune's life brought her many honors and awards. She died in Daytona Beach on May 18, 1955.

DANIEL S. DAVIS
Author, *Struggle for Freedom:
The History of Black Americans*

BHUTAN

The tiny landlocked kingdom of Bhutan lies along the southern slopes of the Himalaya mountains of south central Asia. For most of its history, it was a forgotten and seldom-visited part of the world. Even today much of Bhutan remains largely undeveloped and remote from modern life. In its foreign and economic affairs, Bhutan has traditionally been guided by India.

▶ PEOPLE

Bhutan's people can be divided into three main groups. The Sharchops, who live in the east, are believed to be Bhutan's earliest inhabitants. Their ancestors came from northern Burma and northeast India. They speak a number of Tibetan dialects and practice a sect of Mahayana Buddhism, the state religion. The Ngalops, who live in the northwest, are descended from Tibetan immigrants who first came to Bhutan in the A.D. 800's. They speak Dzongkha, the nation's official language, and follow the Drukpa Kargyupa branch of Tibetan Buddhism. The Lhotshampas, who live in the south, are descended from Nepalese immigrants who began settling in the south near the end of the 1800's. Most speak Nepali and practice Hinduism.

Most of Bhutan's people live in small rural villages. Settlements often cluster around a *dzong*, or fortresslike monastery. A typical village house consists of a two-story building made of stone or mud brick. The family lives on the upper floor, while farm animals occupy the lower floor.

The Bhutanese (*below*) are largely of Tibetan origin. Most live in small, rural villages situated in the fertile valleys of the Lesser Himalaya mountains (*left*).

▶ LAND

Bhutan has four land regions—the Great Himalayas in the north, the Lesser Himalayas in the central region, and the Outer Himalayas and Duārs Plain in the south.

Except for a few scattered Buddhist monasteries, the Great Himalayas are uninhabited. Bhutan's highest peak, Kula Kangri, rises 24,784 feet (7,554 meters) in this region. Most Bhutanese live in the valleys of the Lesser Himalayas. These valleys can be as high as 8,000 feet (2,400 meters) above sea level. South of the Lesser Himalayas is a narrow strip of land known as the Duārs Plain. The southern part of the plain is covered with tall grass and bamboo. The northern part is rugged and heavily forested and shelters many wild animals. Few people live on the plain because of the dense vegetation and malaria-ridden swamps.

The climate of Bhutan is as varied as the land. In the northern interior, the high elevation makes for bitterly cold winters. The southern lowlands have a tropical climate.

▶ ECONOMY

Bhutan's economy is based on farming and raising livestock. Most farms are situated in the fertile valleys of the Lesser Himalayas. The land is cultivated in a series of terraces, each bordered by a stone embankment. Rice, maize (corn), wheat, barley, and potatoes are the chief crops. Dairy animals, pigs, and poultry are valuable to the economy. Yak and sheep are raised in the higher altitudes and cattle in the central valleys. Yak are mainly used as beasts of burden. Bhutan's unusual commemorative stamps are highly prized by collectors worldwide.

▶ MAJOR CITIES

Thimphu, a modern city in the west central part of the country, replaced Paro as the capital of Bhutan in 1962. It is home to approximately 45,000 people. The city was founded near the large fortified monastery of Tashichhodzong, which dates from the 1200's. Today the monastery serves as a meeting place for the national legislature.

▶ HISTORY AND GOVERNMENT

Bhutan may have been inhabited for about 4,000 years, but no information was recorded until about the A.D. 500's. At that time Bonism, or the worship of things in nature, was introduced by Lha-Tshesangma of Tibet. Buddhism began to spread after the arrival of Guru Padma Sambhava in 747.

According to old Tibetan manuscripts preserved in Buddhist monasteries, about 1639 a Tibetan lama, or priest, named Sheptoon La-Pha became the first man to proclaim himself king of Bhutan. During the 1700's and 1800's, the *penlops* (regional governors) acquired great power, and the king became a figurehead. In 1907 the most powerful of the *penlops*, Ugyen Wangchuk, became king. His descendants continue to rule Bhutan. The present king, Jigme Singye Wangchuk, came to the throne in 1972.

Bhutan has an unwritten constitution. The legislative body, the Tshongdu, operates according to royal decree. Most of its members are elected directly by the people for 3-year terms. Some seats are reserved for religious organizations. Remaining members are appointed by the king. The king is assisted in his duties by the Royal Advisory Council and the Council of Ministers. Democratic reforms enacted in 1998 gave the legislature the power to remove the king from the throne.

P. P. KARAN
University of Kentucky

Reviewed by GARY T. WHITEFORD
University of New Brunswick

FACTS and figures

KINGDOM OF BHUTAN is the official name of the country.

LOCATION: South central Asia.

AREA: 18,147 sq mi (47,000 km²).

POPULATION: 2,050,000 (estimate).

CAPITAL AND LARGEST CITY: Thimphu.

MAJOR LANGUAGES: Dzongkha (official), Nepali.

MAJOR RELIGIOUS GROUPS: Buddhist, Hindu.

GOVERNMENT: Monarchy. **Head of state**—king. **Head of government**—chairman of the council of ministers. **Legislature**—Tshongdu (National Assembly).

CHIEF PRODUCTS: Agricultural—rice, corn, wheat, barley, potatoes, citrus fruits, livestock, timber. **Manufactured**—cement, wood products, processed fruits.

MONETARY UNIT: Ngultrum (1 ngultrum = 100 chetrum).

BHUTTO, BENAZIR (1953–)

Benazir Bhutto was the first woman to head the government of a Muslim country. She inherited the political mission and passion of her father, Zulfikar Ali Bhutto, former Pakistani president and prime minister, and is the leader of the party he founded, the Pakistan People's Party (P.P.P.).

Benazir Bhutto was born in Karachi on June 21, 1953, into a wealthy landowning family that had been prominent in politics for three generations. She was educated at Radcliffe College in the United States and Oxford University in England.

In 1977, Bhutto's father was ousted as prime minister in a military coup. He was imprisoned and later executed. Benazir, who had assumed with her mother, Nusrat, leadership of the P.P.P., spent most of the next four years under house arrest. In 1984 she went into exile in England. After military rule ended in Pakistan, she returned home in 1986 to popular acclaim. In 1988 elections, the P.P.P. won the largest number of seats and she became prime minister. Accused of corruption,

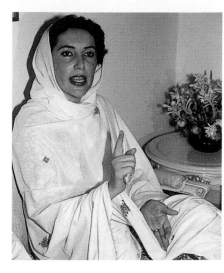

she was removed from office in 1990. But she returned as prime minister after her party's strong showing in the 1993 elections.

In her domestic policy, Bhutto worked to free women from the restraints of traditional Pakistani society. In international affairs she refused to give up Pakistan's nuclear weapons development and signed an arms agreement with China. In 1996, Bhutto was ousted once again following another corruption scandal. She left Pakistan and was later tried in absentia (in her absence) and sentenced to two separate prison terms, in 1999 and 2002.

ARTHUR CAMPBELL TURNER
University of California, Riverside

BHUTTO, ZULFIKAR ALI (1928–1979)

The career of Zulfikar Ali Bhutto, former president and prime minister of Pakistan, was cut short by his death. But, coming to power at a crucial time for his country, he forever changed the landscape of Pakistani politics.

Bhutto was born on January 5, 1928, in Larkana. His father, Sir Shahnawaz Khan Bhutto, was a distinguished figure in the politics of the period. Zulfikar received a degree in political science from the University of California, Berkeley, and a law degree from Oxford University. Returning home in 1956, he practiced law but soon became more interested in politics.

Bhutto served as a delegate to the United Nations and in 1958, at the age of 30, was named minister of commerce. With intelligence, administrative ability, and charm, he advanced rapidly. He became foreign minister in 1963 but resigned from the government in 1966 over policy differences. In 1967 he founded the Pakistan People's Party (P.P.P.), which was his permanent legacy.

The political crisis that resulted from the breakaway of East Pakistan (now Bangladesh) in 1971, following a civil war, helped propel Bhutto to power. Elected president in 1971, he became prime minister under a new constitution in 1973. He launched far-reaching reforms at home and made Pakistan strongly independent in its foreign relations. However, a certain ruthlessness about him alienated many people. This, added to accusations of corruption, brought his rule to an end in 1977, when the army, headed by General Mohammed Zia ul-Haq, seized power.

Bhutto was imprisoned, charged with conspiracy to murder an opponent, and condemned to death. In spite of international appeals to spare him, he was hanged in Rawalpindi on April 4, 1979. He became a martyr to his followers and to his daughter Benazir, who would succeed him.

ARTHUR CAMPBELL TURNER
University of California, Riverside

See also PAKISTAN (History).

BIBLE

The Bible, a collection of diverse books written in ancient times, is one of the world's most famous pieces of literature. The English word "Bible" comes from the Greek word *biblia*, meaning "books," and aptly describes this library of religious writings. The books form the sacred scripture of Jews, Christians, and, to some extent, Muslims. The Bible has had more influence on art, drama, language, and other literature than any other single collection of books. It has been translated into more languages and published in more editions than any other single collection, and it has remained a best seller up to modern times.

The Bible may be divided into three major sections: the Old Testament, the New Testament, and the Apocrypha. "Testament" comes from the Latin word *testamentum*, meaning "will," "covenant," or "agreement," and described for ancient Israelites and early Christians the type of relationship they had with their God.

The Old Testament, composed of 39 books, makes up the sacred literature of Judaism. Christianity also accepts these books, as well as the 27 books of the New Testament. The remaining 14 books, the Apocrypha, are sometimes referred to as the Inter-Testament, since they fall chronologically between the Old Testament and the New Testament. Acceptance of this part of the Bible has varied among Christian groups.

▶ TRANSMISSION AND TRANSLATION

The handing down of biblical materials is properly called transmission. Since the Old Testament is the earliest part of the Bible, its transmission must be considered first. The ancient Hebrews, whose literature this was, began to tell of their God and his relation to them long before they began to write. As a

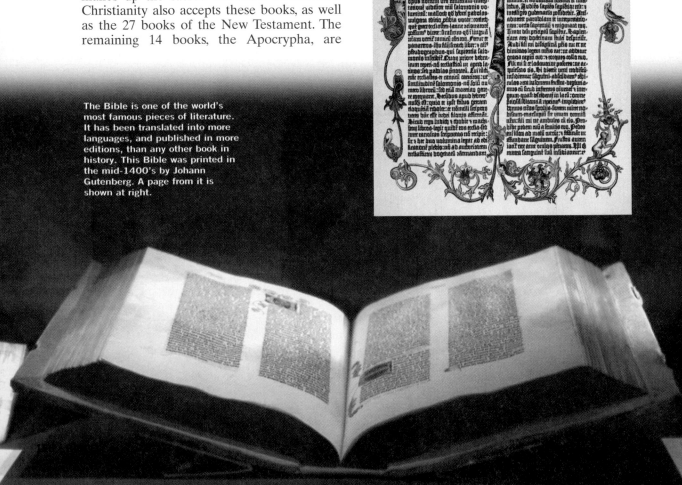

The Bible is one of the world's most famous pieces of literature. It has been translated into more languages, and published in more editions, than any other book in history. This Bible was printed in the mid-1400's by Johann Gutenberg. A page from it is shown at right.

result, the material that finally became the Bible began in oral form. Later, some of the material was put into written form, and other material was written and added. The collections grew and were reworked through the centuries as people believed that they had new insights from God or about God.

Eventually "books" were put together and became fixed in written form. These were finally accepted as authoritative for religious use. The list of such accepted books is called canon (from a word meaning "rule"). The Apocryphal books were not incorporated into the official canon of the Hebrew Bible.

The most famous early Christian translation of the Bible, called the Vulgate, was made by Saint Jerome in the early A.D. 300's.

Transmission of the New Testament was considerably different because people had begun to communicate in writing by the time Christianity began. As a result, written accounts of Jesus' life and ministry, the missionary work of the Apostles, and similar material soon spread throughout the Roman Empire. Letters to churches were also circulated. Over time, individual collections of these materials were made, and books were formed. Eventually, the whole collection known as the New Testament came into being and was accepted as canonical by the early Christian Church. There is also a New Testament Apocrypha, but it was never widely used.

Languages of the Bible

Most of the Old Testament was written in Hebrew, except for portions of Ezra and Daniel, which were written in Aramaic. The New Testament books were first recorded in Greek ("everyday," or Koine, Greek). The Bible was eventually translated from these languages into many other languages, including English. The various translations are called versions—thus there are as many versions of the Bible as there are translations of it. Some have become very famous.

The earliest translations were obviously of the Old Testament. The most important of these was probably the Greek translation called the Septuagint. Its name, which means "seventy," was derived from the tradition that it had been done by 70 scholars (actually 72—6 from each tribe of Israel) at the request of one of the Ptolemies of Egypt in the 200's B.C. About a century earlier the Samaritans, who also followed Jewish law, had made a translation of the first five books of the Hebrew Bible (the Pentateuch). In the early Christian period, another important translation, called the Peshitta, was made from the Hebrew Bible by Syriac-speaking Christians. Jewish scholars also made Aramaic translations called Targums. These were paraphrases with commentary made for popular use in Aramaic-speaking Jewish communities.

The Latin Version. Early Christians adopted the Greek version of the Old Testament because Greek was a language that could be understood by most of them. After a while, however, people wanted both the Old Testament and the New Testament in Latin, which was becoming more widely used. One very early Latin translation was made (using the Greek Old Testament for that part of the Bible), called the Old Latin, or Itala. The most famous early Christian translation, however, was made by Saint Jerome in the early A.D. 300's. Since this was in the common ("vulgar") language of the day, this version is still called the Vulgate. Jerome used both the Hebrew and Greek versions for his translation. The Church accepted Jerome's translation, and it became the official version of the Bible, although the older Latin translation of certain books remained in use. The most famous edition of this version is the Sixtine edition, done at the order of Pope Sixtus V in 1590.

King James I of England called a conference in 1604 to reconcile his country's religious parties. Out of this came the well-known King James Version of the Bible.

Other Translations. Christian missionaries traveled throughout the ancient world, carrying the Bible with them. Hebrew, Greek, and Latin versions were translated into the language of the people among whom they worked. As a result, translations appeared in Arabic, Gothic, Coptic, Ethiopic, Armenian, and many other languages.

All these translations were written by hand. When the printing press was invented about 1450, the production of individual translations of the Bible, as well as editions in the original languages, was tremendously advanced. Further changes occurred in the 1500's, when the Christian church split into Roman Catholic and Protestant branches as the result of the Protestant Reformation. From that time, Catholics and Protestants each made their own translations.

Many printed editions of the Bible appeared. One of the most significant was Martin Luther's German translation, which set the pattern for many others. About the same time, an English printed edition was issued by William Tyndale but was quickly suppressed by the authorities in England. About 1535, however, Myles Coverdale published an English translation, probably in Zurich. This time the Church was less opposed to a "popular" version, and Coverdale's Bible became widely read. A whole series of English Bibles then began to appear, with the names of translators (Matthew's Bible, Taverner's Bible) or of the cities of publication (the Geneva Bible) or even with descriptive titles (the Great Bible, because of its size) to identify them. Finally an approved Bible called the Bishops' Bible (a revision of the Geneva Bible) was published in England in 1568.

In France a group of English-speaking Roman Catholics also wanted a translation of the official Latin version. As a result, an English translation of the Vulgate was completed between 1582 and 1610. It is called the Rheims-Douai Version, in honor of the two cities in which it was done.

The King James Version. In 1604, King James I of England called a conference at Hampton Court to reconcile his country's religious parties. Out of this gathering came the King James Version of the Bible, published in 1611. This is perhaps the best-known English Bible and is still in use today.

As English changed and more new copies of ancient biblical manuscripts (texts) were found, revisions of the King James Version were made. The English Revised Edition was completed in 1881; the American Revised Edition (or American Standard Version) appeared in 1901; and the Revised Standard Version was published between 1946 and 1952. At the same time many independent translations were made of all, or part, of the Bible. These include many translations into modern speech as well as many versions for special use.

▶ **OLD TESTAMENT**

In Hebrew the Old Testament is divided into three separate sections: the Law, the Prophets, and the Writings. These divisions are not followed exactly in the English Bible but make the contents of the Old Testament easier to summarize.

The Law

Traditionally attributed to Moses, the first five books of the Old Testament make up the Law, or Pentateuch. In Hebrew they are named after the first word of each book, but in English the names are derived from the Greek Bible: Genesis, Exodus, Leviticus, Numbers, and Deuteronomy. These books trace the relationship of man to God, in a series of agreements, beginning with creation. They continue through the division of people into nations and the days of Abraham. Then the record of the Hebrews' special relation to God is told, from the time of Abraham's call by God into the land of Canaan.

Abraham and his descendants, the patriarchs, traveled through Canaan until the family of Joseph finally entered Egypt. There they were ultimately enslaved, made their escape under Moses (the Exodus), and fled to the Sinai Peninsula, between the Mediterranean Sea and the Red Sea. At Mount Sinai the people, now properly called Israelites, received the Law from God and prepared to enter the Promised Land. Because of arguments among some of the people, they were all forced to wander for forty years in the desert wilderness. At the end of that time the Israelites were permitted to enter Palestine under the leadership of Joshua.

This group of five books contains a great variety of literary styles and types. Some of the stories illustrate great religious truths: the creation, the fall of man, the flood, the Tower of Babel, the Passover and Exodus, the giving of the tablets of the Law, and other short narratives. Certain books contain great poetry: the Song of Lamech, the Blessings of the Patriarchs, the Song of Moses, and the Blessing of Moses. Others tell about specific people: Noah and his scoffing neighbors, Abraham's faith, Lot's inquisitive wife, the cunning of Jacob, and the frustration of Balaam when all his curses against Israel became blessings. The land, the nations, and the local customs are also described: the wilderness experience, the fire and smoke at Mount Sinai, the varied inhabitants of Canaan, the building of the Ark of the Covenant, the casting of metals and weaving of cloth, the marriage of Rebekah and Isaac, and other details.

Long lists of ancestors and descendants, codes of law, and rules for festivals and sacred ceremonies are also presented. Yet with all this diversity, the entire Pentateuch is held together by the religious faith that the God of Israel cared for his people and that he had made a covenant, or agreement, with them. Obedience to the covenant brought Israel to the promised land, but disobedience to its terms brought disaster.

The Prophets

Next in the Hebrew Bible is the group of books called the Prophets because it contains

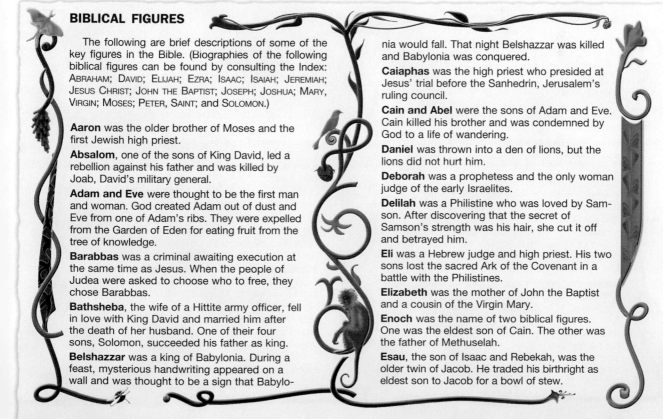

BIBLICAL FIGURES

The following are brief descriptions of some of the key figures in the Bible. (Biographies of the following biblical figures can be found by consulting the Index: ABRAHAM; DAVID; ELIJAH; EZRA; ISAAC; ISAIAH; JEREMIAH; JESUS CHRIST; JOHN THE BAPTIST; JOSEPH; JOSHUA; MARY, VIRGIN; MOSES; PETER, SAINT; and SOLOMON.)

Aaron was the older brother of Moses and the first Jewish high priest.

Absalom, one of the sons of King David, led a rebellion against his father and was killed by Joab, David's military general.

Adam and Eve were thought to be the first man and woman. God created Adam out of dust and Eve from one of Adam's ribs. They were expelled from the Garden of Eden for eating fruit from the tree of knowledge.

Barabbas was a criminal awaiting execution at the same time as Jesus. When the people of Judea were asked to choose who to free, they chose Barabbas.

Bathsheba, the wife of a Hittite army officer, fell in love with King David and married him after the death of her husband. One of their four sons, Solomon, succeeded his father as king.

Belshazzar was a king of Babylonia. During a feast, mysterious handwriting appeared on a wall and was thought to be a sign that Babylonia would fall. That night Belshazzar was killed and Babylonia was conquered.

Caiaphas was the high priest who presided at Jesus' trial before the Sanhedrin, Jerusalem's ruling council.

Cain and Abel were the sons of Adam and Eve. Cain killed his brother and was condemned by God to a life of wandering.

Daniel was thrown into a den of lions, but the lions did not hurt him.

Deborah was a prophetess and the only woman judge of the early Israelites.

Delilah was a Philistine who was loved by Samson. After discovering that the secret of Samson's strength was his hair, she cut it off and betrayed him.

Eli was a Hebrew judge and high priest. His two sons lost the sacred Ark of the Covenant in a battle with the Philistines.

Elizabeth was the mother of John the Baptist and a cousin of the Virgin Mary.

Enoch was the name of two biblical figures. One was the eldest son of Cain. The other was the father of Methuselah.

Esau, the son of Isaac and Rebekah, was the older twin of Jacob. He traded his birthright as eldest son to Jacob for a bowl of stew.

those books that the Jews considered the work of men speaking for God. The word "prophet" comes from the Greek word *prophetes*, "one who speaks forth." This division of the Bible is composed of the Former Prophets—Joshua, Judges, I and II Samuel, I and II Kings—and the Latter Prophets—Isaiah, Jeremiah, Ezekiel, and the Book of the Twelve. This last "book" contains the books of Hosea, Joel, Amos, Obadiah, Jonah, Micah, Nahum, Habakkuk, Zephaniah, Haggai, Zechariah, and Malachi. Some books that are generally found among the prophetical books in the English Bible are not included in the Hebrew Bible under that title but are placed among the Writings. Certain prophetic books also have slightly different names in the Hebrew and Greek Bibles and in the versions used by Roman Catholics and Protestants.

The prophetical books of the Old Testament contain a vast array of religious ideas, individual styles and approaches, and relate to many historical situations. Many of the beliefs of Judaism and Christianity have come from these books, and they have had a great influence on our literature. In English, for example, many expressions commonly used today are found in the Old Testament: "the fat of the land," "a man after his own heart," "the skin of my teeth," "one among a thousand," "angels' food," "eat, drink, and be merry," "see eye to eye," "holier than thou," "no new thing under the sun," and "to everything there is a season."

The Former Prophets. The Former Prophets are books that consider the history of Israel from the conquest of Canaan under

The creation of Adam and Eve is described in Genesis, the first book of the Bible.

Esther, a Jewish woman who married the king of Persia, helped prevent the Persians from killing the Jews. This is celebrated in the Feast of Purim.

Gideon was a Hebrew judge who raised an army and saved Israel from the Midianites. Under his leadership, the tribes of Israel were united.

Hagar was one of Abraham's wives. They had a son, Ishmael. At the insistence of Abraham's first wife, Sarah, Hagar and Ishmael were cast out into the desert.

Hezekiah was a king of early Judah who instituted religious reforms, restored religious spirit, and abolished idolatry.

Ishmael, the son of Abraham and Hagar, was exiled into the wilderness with his mother. The Arab peoples are said to be descended from him.

Jacob, the younger twin son of Isaac and Rebekah, inherited the covenant given by God. He passed this covenant to his sons, who founded the 12 tribes of Israel.

Jephthah was a judge of Israel. Called to lead his people in battle, he vowed, if victorious, to sacrifice the first of his household to greet him on his return. He sacrificed his little daughter, his only child, in fulfillment of this vow.

Joel, an early Hebrew prophet, predicted a plague of locusts and events associated with the coming of the Messiah.

Jonathan was the eldest son of King Saul. A heroic military leader, he was a loyal friend of the future king, David. Jonathan was killed along with his father in the wars against the Philistines.

Judas Iscariot, one of Jesus' disciples, betrayed Jesus for 30 pieces of silver. He led soldiers to Gethsemane and identified Jesus with a kiss.

Lazarus was the brother of Mary and Martha. After he died, he was resurrected by Jesus.

Leah was the first wife of Jacob, who was supposed to marry Leah's sister Rachel. Their father tricked Jacob and substituted Leah for Rachel on the wedding night.

Martha, the sister of Mary and Lazarus, was gently reprimanded by Jesus for complaining that Mary listened to him instead of helping prepare their meal.

Mary Magdalene was a Galilean woman from whom Jesus cast out demons. She became a devoted follower of Jesus and was present at the Crucifixion.

Methuselah, the grandfather of Noah, was said to have lived 969 years.

Joshua down to the release from prison of Jehoiachin, Israel's last king, by the Babylonian king, Evilmerodach, about 561 B.C. Here is the great saga of the wars fought, the settlement of the land, the rise of the monarchy under Saul, and the history of King David. Here, too, is the story of Solomon's reign and the building of the first Temple, the split of the united monarchy into the kingdoms of Israel in the north and Judah in the south, the fall of Jerusalem, and the Babylonian exile.

This part of the Bible is probably the most interesting to read as literature because it is a connective history and contains stirring tales of battles, stories of great people, the life of David, and tales of court in-

Moses destroying the tablets inscribed with the Ten Commandments. The first five books of the Bible are attributed to Moses.

trigues and plots. It also tells of the sad downfall of the two kingdoms of Judah and Israel. Also, since Hebrew literature was in its classical period at this time, one can find some of the best examples of both poetry and prose.

The Latter Prophets. The Latter Prophets are not as easy to summarize, since each has its own specific message. Isaiah, Jeremiah, and Ezekiel make up the Major, or Greater, books because they are the longer ones in this section of the Bible. Historically these prophets span the period from King Uzziah in the 700's B.C., to the time of the exile during the 500's B.C. Isaiah is concerned with the religious and political problems of Judah in his day as relations with As-

---

Naomi and her family left their home in Bethlehem because of famine. After her husband and two sons died, she returned home with her daughter-in-law Ruth. She arranged Ruth's marriage to Boaz.

Nathan, a Hebrew prophet, served as advisor to King David and King Solomon.

Nicodemus was a member of the Jewish ruling council. He became a secret disciple of Jesus and after the Crucifixion took expensive spices to cover the body of Jesus for burial.

Nimrod, the great-grandson of Noah, was a famous hunter and a king of ancient Babylon.

Noah built a great ship, the ark, and filled it with two of every kind of animal. When the flood came, Noah and his family were safe on the ark.

Pontius Pilate was the Roman governor of Judea who condemned Jesus to death.

Rachel was the best-loved wife of Jacob and the sister of Leah. Rachel bore Jacob two sons, Joseph and Benjamin.

Rebekah was the wife of Isaac. They had twin sons, Esau and Jacob. She helped Jacob, her favorite son, receive Isaac's blessing, which rightfully belonged to Esau.

Rehoboam, the son of King Solomon, caused Solomon's united kingdom to be divided into Israel and Judah. He then ruled Judah for some 17 years.

Ruth was the faithful daughter-in-law of Naomi. Her loyalty was rewarded by marriage to Boaz. Their first son was the grandfather of King David.

Salome, the daughter of Herod Philip and Herodias, danced for Herod Antipas, ruler of Galilee and Perea. As a reward, she demanded the head of John the Baptist.

Samson, a judge of Israel, had great strength, the source of which was his hair. When Delilah cut his hair, the Philistines captured him, blinded him, and chained him to their temple. As Samson's hair grew, his strength returned and he destroyed the temple, killing himself and many Philistines.

Samuel was Israel's last judge, a role that incorporated military, political, judicial, and spiritual leadership.

Sarah was the wife of Abraham and the mother of Isaac. After giving birth to Isaac, Sarah became jealous of Hagar, Abraham's other wife, and urged Abraham to banish Hagar and her son Ishmael into the desert.

Saul was the first king of Israel. Defeated and wounded in battle with the Philistines, Saul committed suicide rather than be captured.

syria became more and more difficult. A great promise of new hope for Israel has been added to Isaiah's words (Deutero-Isaiah) as a fitting climax to his book. Isaiah's "call" to prophecy (Chapter 6) is one of the most impressive accounts in ancient Hebrew literature.

Jeremiah lived at the end of the monarchial period, during the trying days of Jerusalem's destruction. He, too, speaks against the religious and social decay of the day, but gives to the people going into exile the promise of a new covenant. God, says Jeremiah, has now made a covenant with Israel that shall not be kept on tablets of stone, but shall be in the heart of every man, no matter where he goes. This was a message of great hope to a people saddened by the loss of their great city and forced to live in a strange land.

Ezekiel might be called the planner of Judaism because he gave the Israelites in exile a plan that allowed them to keep their faith

A favorite story from the Old Testament is the tale of Noah, who built an ark to prepare for a great flood.

alive in difficult times. With the writings of Ezekiel, the religion of Israel became known as Judaism and was closely linked with the Law and the Temple. The God of Israel became known as the Holy One in Israel, and Jews tried to honor this holiness by observing the proper religious ritual and duties.

Not less important, however, are the Minor, or Lesser, Prophets. Their books are just "smaller in size," which is the meaning of the Latin word *minor* used to describe them. In the Hebrew Bible the Book of the Twelve just fills one scroll of writing material, so these prophetical books have been put together for that reason. Here, again, each prophet has his own particular message, and each is a separate book in itself.

Amos is really the oldest of the prophetic writers and is the first literary, or written, prophet. Amos, Hosea, and Micah all preach against the social, political, and religious abuses of their individual periods, and each one declares that God will punish his people for their evil. Nahum, Zephaniah, and Habakkuk give their attention to specific foes of Israel—the Assyrians, the Scythians, and the Neo-Babylonians—and use those threats to the nation to stress the need for the people to trust and obey God. A little later, in the 500's B.C., the prophet Obadiah uses the example of the fall of Edom, one of Israel's neighbors, to illustrate the action of God in the world and to stress hope for the future of his own people.

Jonah, with the famous story of the great fish, urges the Jews, now restored to their homeland, to reform themselves. In the same way, the prophets Haggai, Zechariah, and Malachi speak to the new generation. In Joel, the last book among the prophets in terms of date, hope is again given to the people during a new time of national disaster.

The Writings
The final division of the Old Testament in the Hebrew Bible might be called Miscella-

Abraham's faith was tested when God ordered him to sacrifice Isaac, his only son.

neous. In the section known as the Writings are the books that Jewish leaders considered to be of religious worth, but not of the same type as those in the other two divisions. Books in this category include Psalms, a collection of hymns or religious poems said to be composed by David; Proverbs, which gives advice on everyday living; Job, in which the whole meaning of human suffering is considered; the Song of Solomon, a love song, once seen to have religious application; and Ruth, a story of deep personal devotion and a protest against racial bigotry. The Writings also include Lamentations, a series of sorrowful reflections on the exile and the plight of the people; Ecclesiastes, a book of "wisdom," or religious philosophy; Esther, which explains the festival of Purim; Daniel, a book of stories of heroes, which urges religious faithfulness in a time of oppression; and I and II Chronicles, Ezra, and Nehemiah, which summarize Israel's history up to the exile and describe the events that followed.

In this part of the Bible, too, the individual books are all different, and each one has its own special characteristics. Each has had its own influence on religious thought and world literature.

▶ **APOCRYPHA**

The Apocrypha were written between the 200's B.C. and A.D. 100. Although they have come down to us in Greek, Latin, and other translations, including the King James Bible, fragments of the Apocrypha in the original Hebrew and Aramaic have been found among the Dead Sea Scrolls from caves in northwest Jordan.

For Catholics most of the Apocryphal books are sacred. For Protestants and Jews the Apocrypha are respected as instructive writings, but not as divinely inspired.

Between the 200's B.C. and A.D. 100, Judaism was split into many sects, and the rabbis wanted to unite the people. Their solu-

King David was thought to be the author of the Book of Psalms, a collection of religious poems still used in services today.

tion was to exclude all books written after the fall of the Persian Empire in the 300's B.C. By doing this, they removed the authority of all the later writings that were splitting the community. This is why the Old Testament does not include any books that were thought to come after Alexander's conquest in the 300's B.C.

The Apocrypha begin with the First Book of Esdras. This book concerns the return of the Jews from their Babylonian exile to Palestine in the days of the Old Testament leaders Ezra and Nehemiah. The most famous passage in this book is the tale of the Three Guardsmen (3:1–5:6), which shows that truth is the most powerful force in the world.

The Second Book of Esdras justifies God's ways through divinely inspired visions.

The Book of Tobit is a story about virtue and love. It has enough magic to make the tale doubly interesting. The dog appears as man's pet and companion in Tobit for the first time in Jewish literature.

The Book of Judith is about the trials of the Hebrew people. The heroine Judith saves her people by cutting off the head of the enemy general, Holofernes.

There are six additions to the Book of Esther. These additions, examples of how reverent the Apocryphal books are, add religious tone to the Old Testament Book of Esther, which never mentions the name of God.

Wisdom Literature

The most important literary books in the Apocrypha are known as Wisdom Literature. These books seek to improve people through virtuous and sensible living so that they may be respected and successful. The first of these Apocryphal books is the Wisdom of Solomon, which praises "Lady Wisdom." This is not a woman of flesh and blood, however, but wisdom treated as a divine person.

A fragment of the Dead Sea Scrolls. Almost every book of the Old Testament is represented in these ancient religious manuscripts.

The other book of Wisdom Literature is in many ways the finest composition in the Apocrypha. It is called Ecclesiasticus or the Wisdom of Jesus, Son of Sirach ("Jesus" is simply the Greek form of the old Hebrew name "Joshua"). Ecclesiasticus is a reverent as well as a practical teacher. While he advises people to pray to God to avoid misfortune and illness, he reminds them that God created physicians and medicines for their benefit (38:1–15). He praises justice and notes the rewards of good character.

Other Books

It is believed that the Book of Baruch came from the pen of Baruch, the secretary of the Prophet Jeremiah. Of all the Apocryphal books, this comes closest to Old Testament prophecy. It ends with an appendix, the Letter of Jeremiah, in which the prophet tells the Jewish exiles in Babylonia to avoid worshiping idols.

There are three additions to the Old Testament Book of Daniel. The first, the story of Susanna, tells how Daniel saved Susanna from the false accusations of two evil elders. The second, the story of the Three Children, tells about Shadrach, Meshach, and Abednego who, according to the Book of Daniel, were thrown into a furnace. It is typical of Apocryphal literature to fill gaps in the "authoritative" books. Since the Book of Daniel does not say what happened to the people after they were thrown into the furnace, a later author took advantage of the opportunity to finish this story. The third addition is the story of Baal and the Dragon. It tells how Daniel proved to the king of Babylon that idols are false and God is the one true God.

The Prayer of Manasseh is supposed to be the prayer that was recited by the repentant King Manasseh of Judah (according to II Chronicles 33:18). This work is considered to be of high religious and literary quality.

The Apocrypha end with First and Second Maccabees. First Maccabees, covering the years 167–134 B.C., is a reliable historic account of the Jewish war against Antiochus Epiphanes and the developments that followed. Antiochus, whose empire included Palestine, tried to force the Jews to conform to Greek culture at the expense of their ancestral religion. The Jews rebelled under the leadership of the Maccabean brothers. Their victory is celebrated during Hanukkah.

Second Maccabees is more emotional than First Maccabees and is concerned with its special kind of Jewish viewpoint. Second Maccabees covers the period 175–160 B.C. It is not a continuation of First Maccabees but another account covering some of the same years.

▶ NEW TESTAMENT

The Bible's New Testament is the heritage of Christians. It states a new relation between humanity and the God of Israel, in the person of Jesus of Nazareth. He is seen by the writers of the New Testament as the long-awaited Messiah of Israel and of the whole world and is known as Christ, the Greek word for "Messiah."

The New Testament was written mainly in the days of the Roman Empire and covers the period from the last part of the reign of King Herod (37–4 B.C.) to just after the destruction of Jerusalem in A.D. 70. This period is often referred to in Christian writings as the "fullness of time," because of the significance of Jesus' coming. But it was a "full time" historically as well. The Roman government had brought peace to most of the civilized world; Greek language had made international communication easy; and the old pagan gods were becoming less important. This resulted in an atmosphere that welcomed a new faith.

Followers of Jesus, called the Apostles, began to spread the story of the risen Lord to the world. The Apostles themselves went from town to town, preaching and teaching. From this the New Testament was born. First came collections of Jesus' own words, followed by stories about his life and work, as well as letters to various individuals or groups explaining Christianity.

This material first evolved into written form, then into collections of books, and finally into the collection of canonical books. It was soon considered equal in importance, in the religious sense, to the Old Testament, which Christians shared with Jews. Thus the New Testament was also regarded as holy, or sacred, literature for Christians.

Like the Old Testament, the New Testament is a collection of diverse books under one cover, with several divisions. In the New Testament the two main divisions are Gospels and Epistles, plus a single book called Revelation.

The Gospels

The Gospels consist of four books that tell the story of Jesus—what he is supposed to have done and said, and how he acted. They were written to preserve Jesus' sayings and works for future generations and appeared relatively soon after his death (probably all before A.D. 100).

These books bear the names of their writers: Matthew, Mark, Luke, and John. Of the many books written about Jesus, the early church considered these to be the most au-

The New Testament recounts the life and teachings of Jesus of Nazareth, known as Christ—the "Messiah."

thoritative. Thus they attributed them to Apostles or to close associates of the Apostles. They are called Gospels because that word means "good news"—the good news of Jesus' message and life for the world.

The Gospel of Mark stresses the human side of Jesus and explains many Jewish customs and words for Gentile readers. It is therefore referred to as the human Gospel or the Roman Gospel (to explain that it was written for non-Jewish readers). It begins the story of Jesus with his baptism by John the Baptist in the river Jordan and ends with his appearances to the Apostles after his Crucifixion.

The Gospel of Matthew, on the other hand, is sometimes called the "Jewish" Gospel because of how it is arranged. In this book Jesus' teachings are classified for easy reference, just as the Jewish teachers in that period classified their teachings. There are five such divisions in Matthew: Jesus' ancestry and birth, which introduces his baptism and temptation and leads up to his first sermon; stories of healing, with instructions to the disciples; Jesus' relation to John the Baptist and to other religious leaders, with a series of parables (teaching stories); more healing stories, the feeding of the multitude and the story of the Transfiguration; and the Judaean ministry of Jesus, the triumphal entry into Jerusalem, parables and other teachings, and a conclusion that tells of his death and resurrection.

The Gospel of Luke is really a letter and should be read with Luke's other book, The Acts of the Apostles. Both books form what is called an apologia, or defense, of Christianity to the non-Christian world. Luke begins his Gospel with an account of Jesus's birth, followed by a brief narrative of his boyhood, his ancestry, and his work. Since Luke tells so many stories about Jesus' ministry to the common people, this Gospel is often spoken of as the "social" Gospel. In the Book of Acts the history of Jesus' message is continued, as it was carried out into the Gentile world by the Apostles and other missionaries. Again Luke is concerned with the effect of this message on people and their lives. The book therefore tells about the early Christian church as it grew from Jerusalem and other early centers of the ancient world.

The Gospel of John is very different. It is not so much a story about Jesus as it is an interpretation of who and what he was. The language is more philosophical and is therefore harder to read. In early Christian art John was depicted as an eagle because his writings soared to such great height. John likes to contrast light and darkness, for example, in speaking about Jesus' relation to the world, and he uses many similes and metaphors. He begins his Gospel "In the beginning ..." and shows how God entered the world because of his love for humanity. This view of Jesus is called the Incarnation (that is, God becoming man and living among people), and John stresses its reality and meaning for the world.

The Epistles

At about the same time that the Gospels were being written, important church leaders such as Paul, James, and John began writing the Epistles, or Letters. Among other things, these addressed questions that were asked, problems that came up, and disputes that arose as people began joining the Christian sect. The Epistles were carefully preserved by those who received them, often recopied, and were gradually collected. Since they dealt with important matters, they were finally joined with the Gospels and became part of Christianity's official literature.

The Epistles are traditionally classified into Pauline Epistles (attributed to the Apostle Paul) and General, or Catholic (in the sense of worldwide), Epistles, which were not addressed to any particular church. To these are added the Epistle to the Hebrews, whose author is unknown, and Revelation.

The Pauline Epistles include the letters to individual churches—Romans, Galatians, I and II Thessalonians, I and II Corinthians, Philippians, Colossians, and Ephesians—along with letters to two young church leaders named Timothy and Titus. Most of these letters are concerned with specific problems Paul wished to discuss with particular churches or groups, as well as answers to questions they had asked him. However, one additional letter, known as Philemon, concerns a runaway slave.

In the letter to the Romans, Paul presented a system of Christian belief as he saw it, in order to instruct the people. To the Galatians, Paul wrote about the independence of Christians from some aspects of the Jewish law and gave warnings about falling away from the teachings that he himself had given them. Moral and theological problems arose in Thessalonika and Corinth, and Paul's letters to those people consider those issues, as well as matters of Church discipline and his own authority to deal with them.

The letters to the Philippians, Colossians, and Ephesians stress the need for loyalty to Jesus' teachings and for loyalty within the Church itself. By this time some teachers had arisen in the Church who wished to modify or change the teachings of Jesus' original disciples. As a result, Paul was often called upon

The first four books of the New Testament, the Gospels, were written by Matthew, Mark, Luke, and John. Their goal was to preserve Jesus' sayings and works for future generations.

to decide issues of faith and warn people against false ideas. The letters to Timothy and Titus reflect similar problems. They are called pastoral letters, since Paul was giving advice to young men in charge of churches about conduct, theological problems, and settling problems within their churches. The letter of Philemon stands by itself in the Pauline collection because it did not result from any question asked of Paul, but from his own interest in a runaway slave, Onesimus. Paul sent Onesimus back to his master, Philemon, with a message stressing Christian brotherhood and freedom in Christ.

The **General Epistles** consist of seven letters. They are known by their writers' names but were not addressed to any particular groups. Like Paul's letters, these also arose from specific problems or theological disputes in the church. The letter of James stresses good works and faith as a way for Christians to remain active and faithful. The two letters of Peter try to answer questions about suffering (I Peter) and stress morality as an important Christian virtue (II Peter). John's first two letters deal with problems arising out of false teachings by insisting on the "reality" of Jesus as human, but also asserting his divinity. These letters thus mirror a controversy in the early church concerning the nature of Jesus. Such controversies are termed Christological because they were about interpretations of Christ. The third letter of John is administrative and considers matters of church government and authority. Jude returns to the matter of false teachings and again insists on the Christian interpretation of Jesus' life and ministry.

Many of the General Epistles relate to matters of interpretation, both of theological and administrative affairs. The early church was growing rapidly, and many new converts

In the New Testament's final book, Revelation, Jesus Christ is resurrected and enthroned. Full of hidden symbols, the book predicts the triumph of Christianity over evil.

knew nothing about the Old Testament viewpoints, from which much of Christianity's thinking had come. In addition, groups began to arise within the church that wished to modify or change the words of Jesus, or to offer new interpretations. As these issues arose they had to be settled, reconciled, or denied by the early church leaders.

Epistle to the Hebrews. The anonymous letter to the Hebrews is unusual not only because it is unsigned, but because its author's name appears unknown to the early church. Like the Gospel of John, it is a more philosophical letter. Its purpose was to urge faithfulness to Christianity in a time of great persecution. It accomplishes this by using much of the Old Testament to trace the history of faith down to the writer's own time, with Jesus seen as the fulfillment of the ancient promises of God.

Revelation, also called the Revelation of John, is an apocalypse. That is a particular type of writing, full of hidden symbols and word pictures that often focus on some indefinite "end of time." The symbols used were meant to be familiar to Christians but hidden from non-Christians. The word pictures helped to bring the author's ideas to life— people could "see" what he was trying to say.

When Revelation was written, Christians were apparently undergoing persecution. The author therefore urged them to remain faithful, for Christianity would finally triumph over evil through Jesus, the Christ. Rich in beautiful allusions, this book has had a great effect on other Christian literature through the ages.

Reviewed by KEVIN MADIGAN
Harvard Divinity School

See also BIBLE STORIES.

BIBLE STORIES

The Bible is great literature. Many writers have retold its stories for boys and girls. The following selections from the Old and New Testaments were adapted by Walter Russell Bowie.

▶ **NOAH'S ARK**

From the years far back, before the Bible was written, there had been handed down the tale that one time the earth had grown so wicked that there seemed nothing for God to do but to wash it clean and to start again.

God had to find someone fit to make the new start, and the one he found was Noah. God told Noah that there was going to be such a flood as had never been seen before. The waters would be so wide and deep that they would cover all the earth. God said that Noah must build a boat that would be big enough to take in all his family and also two of every sort of bird and animal he could find in the whole world. The boat was to be like a floating house, and it should be called the ark. It needed to be big, considering all that was going to be in it!

So Noah began to build the ark. It was a hard job to build such a tremendous boat, and it must have been all the harder when the neighbors stood around and laughed. "Who ever heard of building a boat in a dry meadow?" they asked. There the sun was shining down, and there was not enough water to float a stick, much less a thing like this huge ark. Noah must be crazy! But Noah kept on working.

Then one day it began to rain. Noah and his family went into the ark and took with them a male and female of every kind of living thing that came walking and running and creeping and flying from the face of the earth. As the water came up higher, the ark was lifted up and floated above the meadows.

When it started to rain, Noah, his family, and a male and female of every kind of animal went into the ark.

Goliath, armed with a sword, a spear, and a shield, came toward David. David drew back his arm and whirled his sling with deadly aim.

It kept on raining, and it rained harder. Day after day the water poured out of the sky as if the earth had been turned upside down and the ocean put on top. Forty days and forty nights it rained.

All the other people and creatures had climbed up to the tops of the hills to try to be out of the reach of the flood. But at last every spot of earth was covered, and nothing was left alive except Noah and his family and what they had with them in the ark.

At last the rain stopped and the sun came out, but for a hundred and fifty days the ark floated on the waters, above the empty earth. Then, little by little, the flood began to go down. One day Noah felt the bottom of the ark jolt on something, and there it was, scraping the top of the highest mountain that had been in all that part of the earth—Mount Ararat. No other land could be seen around it, but Noah knew that before long the rest of the earth would begin to be uncovered.

Noah went into the part of the ark where the birds were. He took a dove and opened a window and let the dove fly away. But presently the bird came fluttering back in the window again, because it had not found a single dry spot anywhere to rest.

A week longer Noah waited. Then he sent the dove out again. This time when the dove came back it carried in its bill a green olive leaf. Noah knew by this that somewhere the earth and the trees were rising above the water. Once more he sent the dove out. This time the dove did not come back at all, and Noah knew that it had found a place to build its nest.

Then at last the ark itself settled down on solid ground. Noah opened the doors, and he and his family and all the beasts and birds and everything else came flying and running and scrambling out, glad to be back on the earth again.

Noah thanked God, and when he looked up he saw a rainbow in the sky. The rainbow was God's sign—the sign of his promise that "while the earth remaineth, seedtime and harvest and cold and heat and summer and winter and day and night shall not cease."

▶ DAVID AND GOLIATH

About that time the Philistines collected an army again and marched up into a valley in the land of Israel. They had with them a man who was as huge as a giant. His name was Goliath. On his head he wore a helmet of brass, and he had armor on his body and on his legs. His spear was as thick as a wooden beam, and his armorbearer went before him with his great shield.

Every day Goliath came out into the valley between the camp of the Philistines and the camp of Israel and dared any man to come and fight him. But nobody dared, not even Saul. So Goliath shouted and strutted and shook his spear. "I defy the armies of Israel," he cried. "Give me a man that we may fight together!"

Now the three elder sons of Jesse, the brothers of David, were in Saul's army. David had gone back to Bethlehem for a while to take care of his father's sheep. One day, while the armies of Israel and of the Philistines were watching each other, Jesse decided to send his soldier sons some food—parched corn and bread and cheese. He told David to carry the food to the camp and give it to his brothers, and to find out how they were.

Early the next morning David left the sheep in charge of another shepherd, and started off. When he reached the camp of Israel there was a great stir in both armies, and a noise of shouting as of a battle about to begin.

David ran ahead until he found his three brothers. As he stood there talking with them, out came Goliath. He was shouting, as he always did, "What are you here for? I am a Philistine, and you are servants of Saul. Choose a man on your side, and let him come out and fight me. If he can kill me, we will be your slaves; but if I kill him, you shall be slaves to us. I defy you!"

The men around David drew back. None of them had any idea of going out to fight Goliath. They said to David, "You see that man? Whoever kills him will be rich. And Saul will give him his daughter to marry, and will make his family great in Israel."

As David looked at Goliath, he was filled with anger and contempt. "Who is this Philistine," he said, "that he should defy the armies of the living God?"

Eliab, his oldest brother, heard David say that, and was annoyed. "Why did you come down here?" he demanded. "And who have you left to keep those few sheep in the wilderness? I know your pride, and I know that you have come down here just to watch us fight."

David asked Eliab what he had done to make him speak like that. There was reason for his being there, and he would show it, too. He was not going to be frightened by Goliath, or by anyone else.

Presently the army began to talk of this young man, David, who had turned up in the camp, and word about him came to Saul. Saul sent for him. Here was the same lad who had been his armor-bearer and had played for him on the harp!

"Nobody need be troubled about Goliath," David said to Saul. "I will fight with this Philistine."

"You cannot fight with this Philistine," said Saul. "You are only a boy, and this man has been a fighter ever since he grew up."

But David had a different idea. "I have kept my father's sheep," he said, "and once there came a lion, and another time a bear, and took a lamb out of the flock. I went out after those beasts and killed them, and saved the lambs. Both the lion and the bear I killed, and this heathen Philistine shall be like them, since he has defied the armies of the living God. The Lord God who saved me from the paw of the lion and from the paw of the bear will save me from this Philistine."

Saul looked at David and thought for a moment. Then he said, "Go, and the Lord be with you." He put his own armor on David, helmet and breastplate and all, and he gave David his own sword. But David said he could not do anything in that heavy armor. He had never worn armor before, and he did not know how to handle a sword. He took them off, and gave them back to the king. Then David went down to a brook that ran through the valley. There he chose five smooth stones. He put these into the shepherd's bag which he wore at his waist. In one hand was his shepherd's staff, and in the other, his sling. With these David went out to meet the giant Philistine.

On came Goliath, with the man who carried his shield walking in front. When Goliath caught sight of David, he laughed. "Am I a dog," he shouted, "that you come to me with a stick?" And he cursed David by all his gods. "Come on," he said, "and I will give your flesh to the birds and beasts!"

But David answered: "You come to me with a sword, and with a spear, and with a shield; but I come to you in the name of the Lord of Hosts, the God of the armies of Israel, whom you have defied. This day the God of Israel will deliver you into my hands. I will kill you, and take your head from your body. The carcasses of the army of the Philistines I will give this day to the birds and the beasts, that all the earth may know that there is a God in Israel. Yes, all these people shall know that the Lord does not save with the sword and spear. The battle is the Lord's, and he will give you today into our hands."

The Philistine came on with heavy steps. David ran toward him. Putting his hand into his bag, David took out a stone and fitted it into his sling. His arm drew back and whirled with deadly aim. Out from the sling the smooth stone shot, and whistled through the air. It caught Goliath between the eyes and sank into his forehead. Goliath, the giant, pitched forward on his face.

As he fell, David ran and stood over him. He drew Goliath's own sword out of its sheath and cut off his head.

When the Philistines saw that, they fled in panic. The Israelites, shouting, poured after them along the valley and down across the country as far as the gates of Ekron. Then the army of Saul came back and took everything that was in the tents of the Philistines. But all David wanted was the armor of Goliath.

The sailors threw Jonah overboard. He had hardly touched the water when a whale came up and swallowed him.

▶ JONAH

Jonah was commanded by God to go and preach to the great and wicked city of Nineveh. This was the very city from which armies had often come to make war against the people of Israel.

Jonah did not want to go to Nineveh. Instead, he went down to the city of Joppa on the sea. There he found a ship that was going in the opposite direction from Nineveh. He paid his fare, went on board, and sailed away.

The ship had not gone far before a tremendous storm arose. The sailors were frightened and they began to pray. They threw overboard much of the cargo to lighten the ship and give it a better chance to keep afloat when the great waves broke over it. In spite of all the commotion, Jonah was asleep down below the decks. The captain went down and awoke him, and asked him to pray to God that they all might be saved.

But the sailors thought that this storm had come because there was an especially wicked person on the ship. They drew lots to see who it might be. The lot fell upon Jonah. Then the sailors asked him who he was, and what he had done, and why he was on the ship.

Jonah admitted that he was running away from God and from what God had told him to do.

The sailors tried to bring the ship to land. When they could not do this, they took Jonah and threw him overboard.

Hardly had Jonah touched the water, when up came a huge fish, like a whale, and swallowed him. Inside the fish, Jonah had plenty of time to think about God and to change his mind.

After three days, the fish came close to shore and cast up Jonah, unhurt, on the dry land. Now again Jonah heard the voice of God speaking in his heart. Once more it told him to go to Nineveh and preach there. This time he went. He preached that Nineveh and all its people would be destroyed unless they repented of their wickedness.

To Jonah's surprise, the people of Nineveh listened and repented. They fasted and put on sackcloth in sorrow for their sins. Even the king took off his royal robes, dressed himself in sackcloth, and sat down in ashes as a sign of being ashamed for the city's sins. And he gave a command that all the people should pray to God, and that everyone should turn away from whatever wickedness he had been doing.

But instead of being glad that his preaching had had such a great and wonderful result, Jonah was annoyed. He did not like Nineveh. He had not wanted to go there in the first place, and he did not want any good to come to Nineveh because of him. He began to complain to God. He said he had known that God was merciful and slow to anger and full of love and kindness, but he had not wanted God or anyone else to feel that way toward Nineveh. So far as he was concerned, he would rather die than see Nineveh blessed by God. So Jonah went outside the city. He made himself a little shelter and sat there alone and pouted, waiting to see what would happen.

It was very hot in the sun where Jonah sat. When God made a gourd vine to grow and cover Jonah's thin shelter with its cool green leaves, Jonah was pleased. But the next morning worms began to eat the gourd vine, and it withered.

When the sun rose there came a sultry east wind. The sun beat down so hot on Jonah's head that he fainted, and again he wished that he were dead.

At last God spoke to Jonah in a way to bring him to his senses. "You are angry because your gourd vine is withered," he said.

Jonah blurted out, "Yes, I am angry. I do well to be angry."

Then said the voice of God: "You did not make this gourd vine in the first place, and you did not make it grow. It was a thing that came up overnight and lasted only a day. And you are angry because it is gone. Yet here is Nineveh, the great city with more than a hundred thousand people in it and all the cattle upon which they depend, and you want to have it all destroyed."

So the Book of Jonah ends, and at least some men among the people of Israel began to appreciate its meaning: that God has pity upon all peoples, and that men must have pity too.

▶ DANIEL IN THE LIONS' DEN

Belshazzar was slain, and Darius, the king of Media, took his throne.

At first Daniel was honored by the new king even more than he had been honored before. Darius appointed a hundred and twenty princes as governors in the kingdom. Three of these he put in authority over all the others, and among these three Daniel stood first, so that he was next to the king.

That made the princes jealous. They did not want Daniel to be greater than they were. So they began to whisper among themselves, and to try to plan a way to get rid of Daniel. They knew that they could not find Daniel doing wrong. Everything that he did for the king was done well. But suppose they could persuade the king, without his thinking much about it, to make some law that Daniel would think was wrong. They knew that Daniel would not obey such a law. Then, if the king had solemnly declared that anyone who disobeyed it should be punished, they would have Daniel in a trap.

So the princes went to the king. They said to him that it was a dangerous thing to have people of other religions in his kingdom. Why could not everyone think as the king thought and believe what he believed? They suggested that the king give an order that for the next thirty days no one in the kingdom should pray to any god, or act as though even in heaven there could be anyone more important than the king.

The king, without stopping to understand just what might happen, gave the order and signed it with his royal seal. Then the princes who had persuaded him to do that persuaded him also to say that a law, signed and sealed in that fashion, would always be the law, and never could be changed.

Now they were ready to have their revenge on Daniel. When the law had been proclaimed, they watched to see what he would do. Daniel did just what they thought he would do. Law or no law, he went into his house at his regular times to pray. With the windows wide open, he knelt down, with his face turned toward Jerusalem, the Holy City, and prayed to God, just as he had always done.

The men who were trying to trap Daniel went off to tell the king. Had not the king made a law that for thirty days no one in his kingdom

Daniel was thrown into a den of lions, but the lions did not hurt him.

should pray to any god or make any petition to anyone except the king himself? And had it not been declared that any person who dared to disobey that law should be thrown into a den of lions? Well, there was one man who had paid no attention; one man who had gone right on praying as though what the king ordered did not matter.

"Who has done this?" the king wanted to know. And the princes told him it was Daniel.

Now the king was exceedingly sorry and distressed. All day long he thought and tried to find some way by which he could save Daniel. But he had made the law. Besides that, he had been persuaded into declaring that it should be one of the laws of the Medes and Persians that never could be changed. There was nothing left for him to do but to give the order that Daniel should be brought and thrown into a den of lions.

And so Daniel was put into the den where the lions were. The gate was fastened, and sealed with the king's own seal, so that no friend of Daniel could come and let him out.

The king grew more and more distressed. That night in his palace he would not eat, and he would not let any musicians play. When he lay down on his bed he could not sleep. Early the next morning he got up and went to the mouth of the den. In a miserable voice, hardly hoping for anything, he called, "Daniel, servant of the living God, has your God been able to save you from the lions?"

To his amazement and joy, he heard the voice of Daniel from the den, saying, "God has sent his angel and shut the lions' mouths so that they have not hurt me."

The king was filled with great joy. He ordered that Daniel should be taken out of the lions' den immediately. And there he was, safe and sound, not even scratched.

When the king thought of the men who had planned to have Daniel thrown into the den of lions, he ordered that they and everybody connected with them should be thrown in there themselves.

▶ **THE BOY JESUS**

When Jesus was twelve years old, he went with Joseph and Mary to Jerusalem to celebrate the Feast of the Passover. This was the greatest festival of the Jewish year. It had begun far back in the time of Moses, when the people of Israel were slaves in the land of Egypt. They had worked there making bricks for the temples and for the great monuments which Pharaoh, king of Egypt, commanded to be built. The story of all that happened then is written in the Old Testa-

ment Book of Exodus. The Feast of the Passover was the glad reminder of the way in which Moses helped the people of Israel to escape from Egypt and led them across the Red Sea to Palestine, the Promised Land. Everyone was happy when this festival came. It made men proud to remember God's help long ago, and it filled them with belief that God was with them still.

Jewish families always wanted to celebrate the Passover in Jerusalem, where the Temple was. Thousands and thousands of people, beyond anybody's counting, went up to the Holy City at Passover time. All of them were happy at the thought that they were going to see Jerusalem, the Holy City. They sang the beautiful old songs called the "pilgrim songs," which had first been written hundreds of years before.

One of them began:

"I was glad when they said unto me,
Let us go into the house of the Lord.
Our feet shall stand within thy gates,
    O Jerusalem."

And another song began:

"As the mountains are round about Jerusalem,
So the Lord is round about his people from
    henceforth even for ever."

Hardly anything could have been so exciting to Jesus as this first journey to Jerusalem. Joseph's family and their friends walked together in the midst of the growing crowds. The neighbors went too, and people from other towns along the way joined them. They stopped now and then by the roadside to eat the food they had brought with them. It was much more than one day's journey from Nazareth to Jerusalem. So at night they made a place to sleep on the ground and lay down under the open skies and the stars.

The Passover was in the spring, when the fruit trees were blossoming and the fields were bright with flowers. The road from Nazareth to Jerusalem led across the wide Plain of Esdraelon. Jesus knew the stories of the heroes who had walked on that same ground. Gideon had been there with his three hundred men; and David, and Jonathan, and Saul. Many armies had marched across it. Here and there in the earth one might come upon a broken sword blade or a piece of rusty iron from a chariot that had lain there for hundreds of years, left from some battle with the Philistines or the Egyptians or the terrible armies of the Assyrians.

After the pilgrims to Jerusalem had crossed the Plain of Esdraelon, they did not keep straight on. Instead, they crossed the Jordan River and

The young Jesus talked with the oldest and wisest teachers in the Temple court.

went through the country on the east side of the river. Jesus knew that this was because the people of Israel despised the Samaritans, who lived in the country just beyond the Plain of Esdraelon, and did not want to go into the Samaritans' land.

Along the valley of the Jordan River the roads ran south as far as the fords opposite the old city of Jericho. Here the travelers went back across the river. Then they began to climb up through the steep hills that led toward Jerusalem. Up and up they went, until at last they came to where they could see the Holy City.

Outside the walls of Jerusalem, and also within the walls, were green gardens that belonged to rich men's houses. On the highest hill was the splendid palace which Herod the king had built. But the most glorious thing was the Temple. It was even more magnificent than the Temple of Solomon which had stood on the same ground long before. The walls and columns were of colored marble, and great gates opened from each court to the court beyond. At the end of the farthest court there stood the holiest part of the Temple, so beautiful that hardly any other building in the world could be compared to it. Its marble walls were richly carved, and its roof was of shining gold.

Now that Joseph and Mary and Jesus had reached Jerusalem, they made ready for the Passover. Each family ate the Passover supper by itself. As the evening grew dark, a lamp was lighted, and the old, old prayers were said. Then the family ate a roasted lamb, and bread that had no yeast in it. They ate with their belts tightened and their sandals tied, because they were remembering the night when Moses had told the Hebrew people to be ready to leave

Egypt the instant he should give the word. The people of Israel were no longer in Egypt, but again they were not free. Rome ruled over them. Roman soldiers were there in the castle on the hill, next to the Temple. Many men who kept the Passover were hating the Roman rule and wishing to get rid of it.

Jesus may have been thinking that what they needed more was to get rid of their hatred and bitterness. Certainly he was thinking much about God and asking himself how he could know surely what God wanted for his people.

When the days of the Passover were finished, the people from Nazareth started for home. Again there was the great throng of friends and neighbors journeying along together. Joseph and Mary thought that Jesus was walking with some of the other groups. But when evening came and they stopped to camp for the night, they could not find Jesus anywhere. Then they were frightened. They went straight back to Jerusalem, looking for him. At last they came to the Temple. In one of the Temple courts some of the wisest teachers—teachers who knew most about the sacred books and the law of God— used to sit and let people ask them questions. There, in the midst of them, Mary and Joseph found Jesus. They were glad, and yet a little annoyed. Why had Jesus stayed there and let them be so worried?

"Son," said Mary, "why did you treat us so?"

Jesus was surprised. He thought they should have understood where he would be. "Did you not know," he answered, "that I must be in my Father's house?"

BICKERDYKE, MARY ANN BALL. See OHIO (Famous People).

Bicycling is enjoyed by people of all ages. Cyclists take to the road for recreation, fitness, transportation, and competition.

BICYCLING

Bicycling is fun because it gives you the freedom of the road—freedom to travel almost anywhere under your own power. People have traveled around the world by bicycle. Cyclists have ridden to the heart of China, up mountains in Africa, and across the Australian desert. But it is not necessary to do anything quite so exotic to have fun on a bicycle. You can explore your neighborhood, your town, and your state by bicycle, discovering places and things you might never see from a car.

Millions of Americans of all ages ride bicycles. Almost half of them are under the age of 16. They ride for many reasons. For children, a bicycle provides personal transportation—to school, to the store, and to friends' homes. Many adults consider the bicycle a means to better fitness. Bicycling strengthens the heart and lungs without putting severe strain on the body.

The chance to explore new places at a leisurely pace is another reason for bicycling. Bicycle tours are popular throughout the world, and many countries have special bicycle paths and trails. In the United States, cycling groups such as those organized by the American Youth Hostels and the League of American Bicyclists offer supervised outings for cyclists. Bicycling is also a competitive sport, with races for just about every kind of bicycle and rider.

▶ TYPES OF BICYCLES

The most familiar bicycles are probably those designed for riding on roads. They usually weigh about 25 pounds (11 kilograms) and have ten or more speeds, or gears, to make pedaling easier on hills and in other situations. They have narrow tires, and hand brakes operated by levers on the handlebars. Racing bikes are similar but lighter, weighing about 20 pounds (9 kilograms).

The turned-down handlebars on some racing and touring bikes shift the body forward, into an efficient pedaling position. Similar but heavier and sturdier bicycles, with one to five speeds and level handlebars, are popular for short trips. The high-riser, with raised handlebars and a banana-shaped seat, is a popular children's bicycle. The BMX (bicycle motocross) bicycle, which looks similar to a high-riser, is favored by many young riders because it has a strong frame and fat tires and can take a lot of heavy use. These bicycles have coaster brakes, which are operated by pedaling backward.

Mountain bikes, also known as all-terrain bicycles (ATB's), are similar to BMX bicycles. ATB's are strongly built, with wide, knobby tires and up to 18 speeds. They were designed to be ridden on dirt trails, but many are now used on roads. Other bicycles include folding bicycles, which can fit in the trunk of a car, and tandem bicycles, which carry two

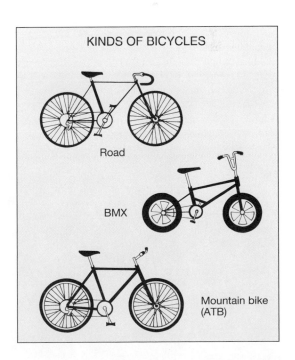

KINDS OF BICYCLES

Road

BMX

Mountain bike (ATB)

people, one behind the other—each with a separate set of pedals. Still another type of bicycle is the recumbent, on which the rider sits in a reclining position and reaches forward in order to pedal.

Bicycles are available in different sizes, based on the diameter of the wheels and on the frame size, or distance from the top of the seat tube to the pedals. Adults are usually comfortable with 26- or 27-inch wheels, while 16 and 20 inches are typical sizes for a child's bicycle. (In countries that use the metric system, the corresponding sizes are 70 and 40 or 50 centimeters.) To choose the correct frame size, straddle the bicycle. For touring models, there should be about 1 inch (3 centimeters) or so between your body and the horizontal bar that runs from the seat to the handlebars. For ATB's, there should be about 3 to 4 inches (8 to 10 centimeters). The seats of most bicycles can be adjusted to make the fit precise.

▶BICYCLE RACING

The four main types of bicycle racing are road, track, off-road, and BMX racing. Road races are run over streets and highways, which are sometimes closed to other traffic. The racers use lightweight ten- to 15-speed bicycles with hand brakes. Track races are run on closed, banked tracks called velodromes. Cy-

Left: Track races take place on oval tracks called velodromes. The distance around the track ranges from about 1/10 of a mile to 1/3 of a mile (0.2 to 0.5 kilometer). *Below left:* Road racers ride over streets and highways on lightweight bikes. The course may be as short as 6.2 miles (10 kilometers) or as long as the Tour de France, which covers about 2,500 miles (4,000 kilometers). *Below:* BMX (bicycle motocross) is an off-road sport run on a bumpy, curvy dirt track, usually less than 1/4 mile (400 meters) long.

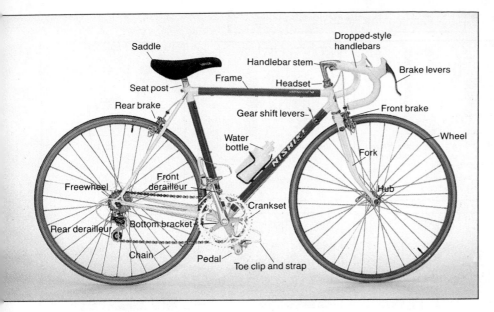

Saddle
Handlebar stem
Dropped-style handlebars
Brake levers
Frame
Seat post
Headset
Rear brake
Gear shift levers
Front brake
Water bottle
Wheel
Fork
Front derailleur
Freewheel
Hub
Crankset
Rear derailleur
Bottom bracket
Chain
Pedal
Toe clip and strap

A well-maintained bicycle is a safe bicycle. Every time you ride—Check tire pressure; make sure brakes work; test lights, horn or bell; give a quick visual check for anything obviously wrong. Every week—Pump up tires and check pressure with gauge; check tires for cuts, bulges, or glass. Every two weeks—Clean and lubricate chain. Every month—Lubricate moving parts of derailleurs and brakes and check for worn brake pads; check adjustment of brakes and derailleurs and all bearings (headset, hubs, bottom bracket and pedals); check wheels for wobbling. Every year—Clean and lubricate both wheel hubs, bottom bracket, headset and pedal bearings; tighten all nuts and bolts.

clists compete on single-speed bicycles with no brakes. Off-road races, ridden on ATB's, are one of the newest cycling events. BMX racing, popular with young riders, is done on short dirt tracks with jumps, bumps, and curves.

Probably the best-known bicycle race in the world is the Tour de France. First held in 1903, this yearly race lasts up to 25 days and covers about 2,500 miles (4,000 kilometers) or more across the French countryside. In 1986, Greg LeMond became the first cyclist from the United States to win the race. The most successful cyclist to compete in the Tour de France is the American Lance Armstrong, who won the race a record seven times (1999–2005).

The international governing body of bicycle racing is the Union Cycliste Internationale (UCI), based in Switzerland. USA Cycling (USAC), located in Colorado Springs, Colorado, is the governing body of most forms of competitive cycling (road, track, mountain, collegiate) in the United States. It chooses and trains cyclists to represent the United States in all international competitions, including the Olympic Games, and it sponsors competitions and training programs for riders of all ages across the nation. BMX cycling is overseen by the National Bicycle League (NBL) or the American Bicycle Association (ABA).

▶ **THE HISTORY OF BICYCLES**

Sketches of a bicycle were made in the 1400's by the Italian artist and inventor Leonardo da Vinci. But the first working vehicle was designed by Baron Karl von Drais, of Germany, in 1818. It had no pedals—he pushed himself along with his feet. Similar machines were soon developed and came to be called **velocipedes**, from Latin words for speed and walking. In 1839, Kirkpatrick Macmillan, a Scottish blacksmith, added foot cranks connected by rods to the rear wheel of a velocipede. Later, Ernest Michaux, of France, put rotating pedals on the front wheel.

The first U.S. bicycles were produced after 1876 by Colonel Albert Pope of Massachusetts. They were **ordinaries**, a type of bicycle with a high front wheel and a tiny rear wheel. They cost more than $300 (over $1,500 in today's dollars). In the 1890's the **safety** bicycle replaced the ordinary. It had wheels of equal size and was driven by a chain. Basic bicycle design has changed little since then, but great improvements and refinements have been made.

Bicycling reached its peak in the United States in the late 1890's, when cyclists supported the Good Roads Movement for better highways to ride on. But as more cars took to the roads, bicycling declined. It became popular again in the 1970's, as a result of a gasoline shortage and increased interest in fitness.

Rules of the Road for Bicyclists

Follow lane markings. Do not turn left from the right lane. Do not go straight in a lane marked "Right turn only."

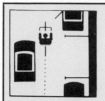

Ride in a straight line whenever possible and ride with traffic. Keep to the right, but stay about a car-door width away from parked cars.

Obey traffic signs and signals. Bicycles must behave like other vehicles if they are to be taken seriously by motorists.

Use hand signals. Hand signals tell motorists what you intend to do. Signal as a matter of law, of courtesy, and of self-protection.

Choose the best way to turn left. There are two ways to make a left turn: (1) Like a car. Look, signal, move into the left lane, and turn left. (2) Like a pedestrian. Ride straight to the far-side crosswalk. Walk your bicycle across.

Scan the road behind. Learn to look back over your shoulder without losing your balance or swerving left. Some riders use rearview mirrors. Always look back before changing lanes or changing positions within your lane, and only move when no other vehicle is in your way.

Ride a well-equipped bicycle. Always use a strong headlight and taillight at night and when visibility is poor. Be sure your bicycle is adjusted to fit you properly. For safety and efficiency, outfit it with bells, rearview mirrors, fenders (for rainy rides), and racks, baskets, or bicycle bags.

Go slow on sidewalks and bicycle paths. Pedestrians have the right-of-way. By law you must give pedestrians audible warning when you pass. Do not cross driveways or intersections without slowing to a walker's pace and looking very carefully for traffic (especially traffic turning right on a green light).

▶**BICYCLING SKILLS**

The traffic laws of every state say that people who ride bicycles have the same rights and duties as people who drive cars. In other words, a bicycle is a vehicle, and a bicyclist is a vehicle operator. Thus every bicyclist must know and follow the rules of the road.

Some important rules and tips for safe cycling appear in the boxes above. In addition, cycling is safer if you take these steps:

• Ride on routes with few cars, slow traffic, and easy intersections and on streets that have room for cyclists and motorists.

• Wear bright clothing that makes you stand out during the day. At night, wear white or reflective clothing (and make sure your bicycle is outfitted with a headlight, taillight, and reflectors). But remember that riding at night is dangerous, and avoid it.

• Wear a hardshell bicycle helmet with a sticker of approval from the American National Standards Institute (ANSI) or the Snell Memorial Foundation. It will shelter your head from the weather and make you more visible to motorists, and it may save your life. The USCF and other racing organizations require riders to wear helmets in their events.

• Ride a safe bicycle. A well-maintained bike is dependable and easy to ride. You can have a bicycle shop overhaul your bicycle once a year. Once a week or so, check to be sure that all nuts and bolts are tight, that the brakes stop the bicycle quickly, that the chain is lubricated, and that the pedals and handgrips (or handlebar tapes) are tight. Check the tires for cuts and wear, and be sure they are inflated to the pressure shown on the sidewalls. See that the wheels spin freely and that there are no broken spokes.

Cycling is more fun, as well as safer, when you practice good cycling skills, wear a helmet, and ride a well-maintained bicycle.

JIM FREMONT
Education Director, Bicycle Federation of America

BIENVILLE, JEAN-BAPTISTE LE MOYNE, SIEUR DE. See LOUISIANA (Famous People).

How to rack balls for eight ball

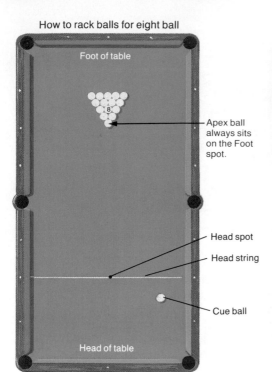

Foot of table

Apex ball always sits on the Foot spot.

Head spot

Head string

Cue ball

Head of table

How to rack balls for rotation

Foot of table

Foot spot

How to rack balls for nine ball

Foot of table

Foot spot

Cue

Rack and object balls

Cue ball

Chalk

The various forms of the game of billiards are played on a rectangular cloth-covered table. Equipment includes a leather-tipped stick known as a cue, a white cue ball, and colored balls called object balls. The balls are racked (arranged) in different positions for different forms of the game.

BILLIARDS

Billiards is the general term for a number of different games played on cloth-covered rectangular tables on which balls are struck by sticks, called **cues**. The playing surface is always twice as long as it is wide and is lined by raised rubber cushions. On each turn, the leather tip of the cue is used to strike a white ball, called the **cue ball**, and drive it into what are called **object balls**. Points are scored in some versions by making the cue ball hit two or three object balls, sometimes striking the cushions in between hits; in other versions the goal is to drive object balls into openings, or **pockets**, in the cushions.

▶ FORMS OF THE GAME

The style of play most popular in the United States is called **pool**, or sometimes **pocket billiards** to separate it from the carom, or pocketless, games. Pool is played on a table 4½ feet (1.4 meters) wide by 9 feet (2.7 meters) long, or smaller. The most often played games are **eight ball**, **nine ball**, **rotation**, and **straight pool**. In England, Canada, Australia, and India, the favorite game is **snooker**. It is similar to pool but is played on a much larger table (usually 6 by 12 feet, or 1.8 by 3.7 meters) with smaller balls and smaller pockets.

▶ RULES OF GAMES

Only the highlights of major games are given here. In every game described, players shoot until they miss, they win the game, or they commit a foul. Examples of fouls are jumping a ball off the table or hitting the cue ball twice on a single stroke.

Eight Ball. The balls are **racked** (arranged with the aid of a triangular frame that is then removed) as shown in the diagram with the 8 ball in the center. One player is chosen to **break** the balls by driving the cue ball into the rack from a position behind the **head string**. When a ball goes into one of the pockets, the shooter is restricted for the rest of the game to the balls in the same group, either those numbered higher than eight (the stripes) or those numbered lower than eight (the solids), while the opponent must aim at only those balls in the other group. Each player tries to **pocket** all the balls in his or her group, which means driving them into any of the pockets with the cue ball. Once that is done, the player can shoot at the 8 ball, the pocketing of which wins the game. Pocketing the 8 ball out of order loses the game.

Nine Ball. In the last 20 years, nine ball has replaced straight pool (see below) as the game of choice for tournaments and matches for expert players. The balls, numbered one through

The bridge (position of the hand) must be solid to give firm guidance to the cue.

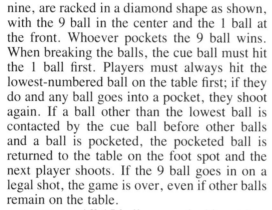

The cue stance should be relaxed and comfortable. The feet should form a line at about a 45-degree angle to the line of aim. The head should be directly over the cue, sighting as if through a gun sight. Keep the left arm straight and the feet in a comfortable position.

Another form of the bridge involves placing the fingers firmly on the table and using the thumb to guide the cue.

nine, are racked in a diamond shape as shown, with the 9 ball in the center and the 1 ball at the front. Whoever pockets the 9 ball wins. When breaking the balls, the cue ball must hit the 1 ball first. Players must always hit the lowest-numbered ball on the table first; if they do and any ball goes into a pocket, they shoot again. If a ball other than the lowest ball is contacted by the cue ball before other balls and a ball is pocketed, the pocketed ball is returned to the table on the foot spot and the next player shoots. If the 9 ball goes in on a legal shot, the game is over, even if other balls remain on the table.

Rotation. All 15 balls are racked in a triangle with the 1 ball in front and the 2 ball and 3 ball at the other corners. The 1 ball must be hit first on the break. On each shot, the cue ball must hit the lowest-numbered ball first; if it does and any ball goes in, the player shoots again. All balls pocketed during a player's turn at the table are totaled and credited to the player. Each ball is worth its number; for example, the 10 ball counts ten points. Since the numbers from 1 to 15 add up to 120 points, whoever scores 61 points or more wins.

Straight Pool. This game is considered the best test of skill by many top players. On each shot, the player must indicate which ball is intended for which pocket, a form of play termed "call shot." The numbers on the balls have no significance. Each legally pocketed ball counts one point, and a game consists of an agreed-on number of points. When only one ball remains on the table, the other 14 are racked in a triangle with the front ball missing. If the player can pocket the remaining ball and break the rack at the same time, that player can continue shooting.

Straight Billiards. Straight billiards is more popular than any other cue game in Europe, North Africa, Latin America, and Asia. A pocketless table and only three balls are used, a cue ball for each player and a red ball (sometimes two red balls). To start, the red ball is placed on the foot spot, one cue ball on the head spot, and the other cue ball 6 inches (15.2 centimeters) to one side of the head spot. A point is scored if the shooter can make the cue ball hit the other two balls, and the game is over when an agreed-on number of points is reached. By keeping the balls close together and near a cushion, experts can make hundreds, even thousands, of points in a row.

Three Cushion. In this difficult but beautiful game, points are scored by making the cue ball hit the other two balls; however, before it hits the second ball, it must contact three or more cushions. Many of the greatest players in the world prefer this game over all others. National championships are held in many countries, including the United States, and a world championship is held every year.

▶ **TIPS FOR SUCCESS**

To become a good player, much practice is necessary and a great amount of thought and skill is required. The best way to learn is to take lessons from an accomplished player or to watch pool or billiards tournaments. You can also improve your game by reading books or magazines and by watching videotapes. These are readily available in libraries, bookstores, and billiard supply stores.

ROBERT BYRNE
Author, *Byrne's Standard Book of Pool and Billiards*

BILLINGS. See MONTANA (Cities).

BILL OF RIGHTS

The Bill of Rights—the first ten amendments to the Constitution of the United States —ranks alongside the Constitution and the Declaration of Independence as one of the nation's most treasured documents. Since its adoption in 1791, the Bill of Rights has served as the cornerstone of basic American freedoms. Its laws specify the fundamental rights and most cherished liberties of the American people and protect them from the whims of popular majority opinions and abusive government officials.

The Bill of Rights became part of the Constitution of the United States on December 15, 1791. On the 150th anniversary of this event in 1941, President Franklin Roosevelt proclaimed December 15 as Bill of Rights Day. He wanted to make Americans aware of their rights and to remind them of their duties as citizens of the United States. On this day in 1991, Americans recognized the 200th anniversary of these important amendments that have proved so essential to the American political tradition.

The Bill of Rights, on display at the National Archives in Washington, D.C., summarizes the basic rights and freedoms of American citizens.

▶ WHY THE BILL OF RIGHTS WAS ADDED TO THE CONSTITUTION

At the Constitutional Convention of 1787, delegates rejected a motion made by George Mason, author of the Virginia Declaration of Rights (1776), to preface the Constitution of the United States with a bill of rights. The failure to mention basic rights soon became a major issue in the subsequent debates over whether or not the proposed Constitution would be ratified, or approved.

When the Constitutional Convention ended, delegates went back to their respective states to hold their own ratifying conventions. Each state would decide for itself whether or not to approve the new framework for the American government.

The debate over the need for a bill of rights was sparked by a proposal made by a dissenting minority in the Pennsylvania ratifying convention. Some delegates believed that guarantees of certain basic rights and liberties were missing from the proposed Constitution. They called for a number of amendments that would secure a wide range of liberties, such as the free exercise of religion, freedom of speech and press, and protection against unreasonable searches and seizures. Majorities in the ratifying conventions of New Hampshire, Massachusetts, New York, Maryland, Virginia, North Carolina and South Carolina also called for numerous amendments to the proposed Constitution. Although the substance of these recommended amendments differed from state to state, most contained provisions that would limit the powers of the new federal (national) government and protect the people from inconsistent and oppressive rule.

"....a bill of rights is what the people are entitled to against every government on earth, general or particular, and what no just government should refuse, or rest on inferences."

From a letter Thomas Jefferson wrote to James Madison, December 20, 1787.

The Anti-Federalists (those who were opposed to ratifying the Constitution) argued that the broad powers of the new federal government would threaten the powers of the individual states and the liberties of the people. However, the Federalists (those who supported ratification) argued that a bill of rights was unnecessary. Alexander Hamilton, for example, maintained that because the proposed federal government would possess only specifically assigned and limited powers, it could not endanger the fundamental liberties of the people. "Why," he asked, "declare that things shall not be done which there is no power to do? Why, for instance, should it be said that the liberty of the press shall not be restrained, when no power is given by which restrictions may be imposed?"

Nevertheless, the Federalists had to pledge their support for the addition of a bill of rights to the Constitution once the new government began operations. Otherwise they would risk endangering the Constitution's ratification in certain key states and face the possibility of another constitutional convention.

▶ DRAFTING THE BILL OF RIGHTS

James Madison, the "Father of the Constitution," may also be considered the "Father of the Bill of Rights." In his campaign for a seat in the House of Representatives under the new Constitution, he promised his voters that he would energetically push for the adoption of a bill of rights. True to his word, he took the lead in the First Congress in pressing for the desired amendments.

On June 8, 1789, drawing from proposals made by the various state ratifying conventions, Madison proposed to the Congress nine amendments to the Constitution, containing nineteen specific provisions (many of which are now contained in the Bill of Rights). Madison and members of a House committee then went through the complex process of drafting a bill that would secure the necessary two-thirds approval of both houses of Congress. The House and the Senate modified some of Madison's proposals, eliminated others entirely, and added some new ones as well.

As it finally emerged from Congress, the proposed Bill of Rights consisted of twelve amendments and was offered to the states for ratification. The first two proposed amendments were never ratified by the states. (One was related to the size of the House of Representatives and the other to laws regarding the compensation, or payment, for senators and representatives.) On December 15, 1791, Virginia ratified the remaining ten amendments, and the Bill of Rights officially became part of the Constitution.

▶ WHAT THE BILL OF RIGHTS SAYS

The first eight amendments of the Bill of Rights set forth specific guarantees and liberties. The Ninth Amendment acknowledges that the American people have rights that are not even specified in the Constitution or the Bill of Rights. (The Federalists argued for this particular amendment, stating that it would be impossible to list all of the rights and liberties that should be protected.)

The Tenth Amendment emphasizes the national character of the United States constitutional system. It declares that the states or people retain those "powers not delegated to the United States by the Constitution."

Most people, however, believe that their most important rights are those guaranteed by the First Amendment. Commonly called "First Amendment freedoms," these are the fundamental freedoms of religion, speech, and press, as well as the right of the people to assemble and to petition a government.

Other vital provisions contained in the first eight amendments also deal with the rights of individuals. They are designed to protect people against inconsistent or abusive government, particularly in criminal proceedings.

For example, the Fourth Amendment protects individuals from unreasonable searches and seizures (either of themselves or of their property and possessions) by law enforcement officials.

The Fifth Amendment prohibits double jeopardy, which means that someone cannot be tried twice for the same crime. The Fifth Amendment also states that people cannot be compelled to testify against themselves (self-incrimination), and it guarantees "due process," which means people accused of a crime must be properly notified of the charges and given a fair hearing.

The Sixth Amendment establishes the right of an accused person to a public trial by jury. The accused also has the right to have a lawyer, to confront hostile witnesses, and to obtain witnesses in his or her defense.

Finally, the Eighth Amendment prohibits the infliction of "cruel and unusual punishments" (either mental or physical) on those convicted of a crime.

The remaining amendments (the Second, Third, and Seventh) do not cover individual rights in criminal proceedings but address other specific concerns. The Second Amendment is the most noteworthy and controversial of these remaining amendments. After noting the need for a "well regulated militia" (a body of citizen soldiers called to serve during times of emergency or war), this amendment declares that the people's right ". . . to keep and bear Arms, shall not be infringed."

The Third Amendment prevents the government from making citizens shelter soldiers in their homes. This amendment was drafted in response to abuses by British forces during the Revolutionary War.

The Seventh Amendment was included to meet the demands of many Anti-Federalists who wanted to insure trial by jury in civil suits.

▶THE ORIGINS OF THE BILL OF RIGHTS

The Virginia Bill of Rights (proclaimed in 1776, only days before the Declaration of Independence) was the first of ten such declarations by the states during the Revolutionary War period (1775–83). All of these declarations contained provisions that eventually found their way into the national Bill of Rights. Major portions of the First, Fourth,

The Bill of Rights

The First Ten Amendments to the Constitution of the United States
(Ratified December 15, 1791)

Amendment 1
Congress shall make no law respecting an establishment of religion, or prohibiting the free exercise thereof; or abridging the freedom of speech, or of the press; or the right of the people peaceably to assemble, and to petition the government for a redress of grievances.

Amendment 2
A well regulated Militia, being necessary to the security of a free State, the right of the people to keep and bear Arms, shall not be infringed.

Amendment 3
No Soldier shall, in time of peace be quartered in any house, without the consent of the Owner, nor in time of war, but in a manner to be prescribed by law.

Amendment 4
The right of the people to be secure in their persons, houses, papers, and effects, against unreasonable searches and seizures, shall not be violated, and no Warrants shall issue, but upon probable cause, supported by Oath or affirmation, and particularly describing the place to be searched, and the persons or things to be seized.

Amendment 5
No person shall be held to answer for a capital, or otherwise infamous crime, unless on a presentment or indictment of a Grand Jury, except in cases arising in the land or naval forces, or in the Militia, when in actual service in time of War or public danger; nor shall any person be subject for the same offense to be twice put in jeopardy of life or limb; nor shall be compelled in any criminal case to be a witness against himself, nor be deprived of life, liberty, or property, without due process of law; nor shall private property be taken for public use, without just compensation.

Amendment 6
In all criminal prosecutions, the accused shall enjoy the right to a speedy and public trial, by an impartial jury of the State and district wherein the crime shall have been committed, which district shall have been previously ascertained by law, and to be informed of the nature and cause of the accusation; to be confronted with the witnesses against him; to have compulsory process for obtaining witnesses in his favor, and to have the Assistance of Counsel for his defence.

Amendment 7
In Suits at common law, where the value in controversy shall exceed twenty dollars, the right of trial by jury shall be preserved, and no fact tried by a jury shall be otherwise re-examined in any Court of the United States, than according to the rules of the common law.

Amendment 8
Excessive bail shall not be required, nor excessive fines imposed, nor cruel and unusual punishments inflicted.

Amendment 9
The enumeration in the Constitution, of certain rights, shall not be construed to deny or disparage others retained by the people.

Amendment 10
The powers not delegated to the United States by the Constitution, nor prohibited by it to the States, are reserved to the States respectively, or to the people.

Fifth, Sixth, and Eighth amendments, for example, can be traced directly to the Virginia Bill of Rights.

The origins of many of the other rights and liberties contained in the Bill of Rights can be found in the English tradition, dating as far back as Magna Carta (1215), a document that marked the first step toward constitutional law in England. For example, the clause in the Fifth Amendment, which declares that individuals cannot be deprived of their "life, liberty, or property, without due process of law" is rooted in Chapter 39 of Magna Carta.

England's Petition of Right (1628) and Bill of Rights (1689) further expanded individual liberties and placed increased limitations on the ruler's powers and authority. English liberties and rights, such as trial by jury and protection against self-incrimination and unreasonable search and seizure, were, in fact, included in the charters establishing the American colonies. They were considered to be the "rights of Englishmen."

▶ ENFORCING THE BILL OF RIGHTS

The courts, both state and national, are responsible for enforcing the Bill of Rights, when instances of abuse are brought to their attention through proper legal channels. The Supreme Court of the United States, however, has the final word in determining whether or not the principles contained in the Bill of Rights have been violated.

Making such a determination is seldom an easy matter. The Court, for example, must answer such questions as, What constitutes "unreasonable" search and seizure? What limits can be placed on the free exercise of religion for reasons of public morality, safety, or health? Under what circumstances may speech be legally curtailed to prevent violence or property damage?

Originally, the Bill of Rights applied only to the laws and activities of the national government. It was not until after the Civil War that the Bill of Rights' provisions were applied to the states. The 14th Amendment (1868) was the first to declare that no state "shall . . . deprive any person of life, liberty, or property without due process of law."

Today, for all intents and purposes, the fundamental rights and liberties guaranteed by the Bill of Rights apply with equal force to both the national and the state governments.

▶ STATE BILLS OF RIGHTS

All of the fifty state constitutions contain a bill of rights. The Illinois Bill of Rights borrows from the Declaration of Independence in stating, "All men are by nature free and independent and have certain inherent and unalienable rights among which are life, liberty, and the pursuit of happiness." Some states' declaration of rights are even far more detailed than the national Bill of Rights. The California Declaration of Rights, for example, says, "A person may not be disqualified from entering or pursuing a business, profession, vocation, or employment because of sex, race, creed, color, or national or ethnic origin."

▶ THE CANADIAN BILL OF RIGHTS

The Canadian Charter of Rights and Freedoms, officially proclaimed by the Canada Act on April 17, 1982, applies to both the national and provincial governments. Sections of the charter deal with distinctly Canadian concerns, such as declaring the French and English languages to have equal status in official government proceedings.

The charter details major rights and liberties under the headings of **Fundamental Freedoms** and **Legal Rights**. The fundamental freedoms correspond to those found in the First Amendment in the American Bill of Rights, but they are more extensive. In addition to freedom for the press and media, peaceful assembly, and freedom of speech and religion, they include freedom of association, conscience, thought, belief, and opinion.

The legal rights of the charter are similar to those found in the Fourth, Fifth, Sixth, and Eighth amendments in the American Bill of Rights. These include, among others, protection against self-incrimination, double jeopardy, unreasonable search and seizure, and cruel and unusual punishment.

GEORGE CAREY
Author, *The Federalist: Design for a Constitutional Republic*

See also FEDERALIST, THE; FIRST AMENDMENT FREEDOMS; UNITED STATES, CONSTITUTION OF THE; UNITED STATES, GOVERNMENT OF THE; UNITED STATES, HISTORY OF THE.

BILLY THE KID. See NEW MEXICO (Famous People).

BILOXI. See MISSISSIPPI (Cities).

BINARY SYSTEM. See NUMERALS AND NUMERATION SYSTEMS.

BINGHAM, HIRAM. See HAWAII (Famous People).

Biochemists use computer models to help determine the molecular structures of proteins and other components of cells.

BIOCHEMISTRY

Biochemistry represents the meeting of two different sciences, biology and chemistry. Biology is the study of living things, while chemistry is the study of the organization and interactions of matter. Biochemists investigate the chemistry of living systems.

Biochemists examine four major biological molecules: carbohydrates, lipids (fats), proteins, and nucleic acids (such as DNA). Biochemists try to understand how cells create and break down these molecules, what jobs each type of molecule does in the cell, and how it does it. For example, they study how DNA is copied when cells divide and what happens when this process goes wrong.

Biochemistry as a unique science has its roots in the early 1800's. Until this time biology and chemistry were thought to be completely distinct disciplines. A scientific viewpoint referred to as vitalism said that the biological reactions that occurred within cells were unique and that these reactions were too complex to be described using chemistry. Then a German chemist named Friedrich Wöhler performed a pioneering biochemical experiment that showed that urea, a compound found in living organisms, could be created from nonliving matter through chemical reactions in the laboratory.

Wöhler presented his findings in 1828, but another 70 years passed before it was shown that the same reactions that take place inside cells can take place after cells are broken open. The ability to study cellular processes in a test tube revolutionized our understanding of cell biology, and the era of biochemistry was born.

▶ WHAT BIOCHEMISTS STUDY

Biochemists study all the cellular processes necessary for life. Some biochemists focus on understanding the roles of specific biological molecules, such as proteins or lipids, in living cells. Others try to understand how organisms make energy from the nutrients they obtain. Still others investigate how different cells communicate with each other or how cells defend themselves from invaders. Finally, some biochemists study DNA, the basis of life, and how genetic information is copied, expressed, and passed on.

Protein Biochemistry

Proteins are the worker molecules of cells. They are made of building blocks called **amino acids**. Twenty different amino acids make up the many different proteins in the body. Just as many words can be formed from the 26 letters of the alphabet, thousands of proteins can be formed by arranging the

Animal Cell

PEOPLE AND EVENTS IN THE HISTORY OF BIOCHEMISTRY

Friedrich Wöhler

1828

The birth of modern biochemistry is credited to Friedrich Wöhler (1800–82), a German chemist who demonstrated that he could produce the organic compound urea from the inorganic compound ammonium cyanide.

1854–57

Louis Pasteur (1822–95) established that the process of fermentation is carried out by micro-organisms. He called the substances within micro-organisms that carry out this conversion "ferments." (Ferments are now known as enzymes.) Pasteur is best known for his discovery that most infectious diseases are caused by germs.

Louis Pasteur

1932

Gustav Embden (1874–1933) and Otto Fritz Meyerhof (1884–1951) characterized the pathway that cells use to break down glucose for production of energy. Dr. Meyerhof had previously been awarded the Nobel Prize in physiology or medicine in 1922 for his work on the link between oxygen consumption and muscle metabolism.

1937

Hans Adolf Krebs (1900–81) identified the cellular pathway that takes the end product of glucose metabolism and converts it to carbon dioxide while at the same time generating many high-energy molecules. This cyclic pathway bears his name and is also known as the tricarboxylic acid (TCA) cycle. Dr. Krebs won the Nobel Prize in physiology or medicine in 1953 for his discovery of this pathway.

amino acids in different ways. Our genes are the blueprints that tell cells how to assemble amino acids in the correct order to make a particular protein. Biochemists study proteins to try to understand what amino acids are present and how the properties of the amino acids control protein structure and function.

Sometimes mistakes in genes can cause the amino acids in proteins to be "misspelled."

This can result in disease. Sickle-cell anemia is caused by a mistake in a gene that contains instructions for making **hemoglobin**, the oxygen-carrying molecule of blood. This mistake results in a single amino acid change in the protein. The effect of this change is that the hemoglobin molecule no longer binds oxygen properly. The person's red blood cells become stiff and sometimes bend into a sickle shape. The sickle-shaped cells can become stuck in the narrow blood vessels of the body and block the flow of blood.

By studying proteins, biochemists hope to be able to understand why misspelled proteins behave the way they do and come up with drugs or other methods that will correct the problems.

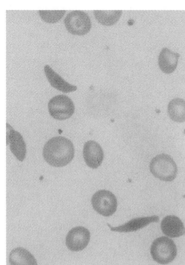

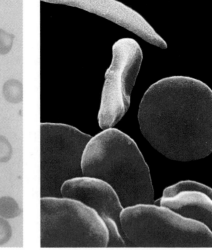

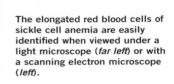

The elongated red blood cells of sickle cell anemia are easily identified when viewed under a light microscope (*far left*) or with a scanning electron microscope (*left*).

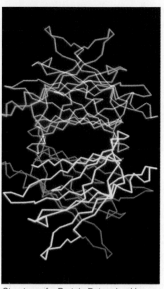

Structure of a Protein Determined by X-Ray Crystallography

1944

Oswald Avery, Colin MacLeod, and Maclyn McCarty published the initial description that the genetic material of cells (the genes) was made of DNA.

1945

A revolution in our understanding of the structure of proteins came from the use of a technique called X-ray crystallography. Linus Carl Pauling (1901–94) was a pioneer in this technology. He was awarded the Nobel Prize in chemistry in 1954 for his work on protein structure.

1953

The double-helix model for DNA was proposed by James Watson (1928–) and Francis Crick (1916–2004). They were awarded the Nobel Prize in physiology or medicine in 1962 for their determination of the structure of DNA.

1987

The polymerase chain reaction, a technique for rapidly copying small regions of DNA, was developed by Kary B. Mullis (1944–). He won the Nobel Prize in chemistry in 1993 for the development of this revolutionary technology.

Kary B. Mullis

DNA

2000

The sequencing of the entire human genome was completed by the Human Genome Project and a private company.

Lipid and Membrane Biochemistry

Lipids are a class of molecules that include fats, oils, steroids, waxes, and other related compounds. The body stores lipids to use for energy. They are also important parts of cell membranes and serve as the building blocks for different structures. Some lipids act as signaling molecules—substances that carry a message between cells or from one part of the cell to another. Lipid biochemistry aims to determine what types of lipids are present in biological systems and in what amounts. It also explores whether these amounts can be influenced by the kind and quantity of lipids in the diet.

The goal of membrane biochemistry is to define the composition and function of cell membranes. Cell membranes are made up of both lipids and proteins. Different types of cells have different membrane components. Understanding these differences is important for learning how cells "talk" to one another, how viruses invade different types of cells, and how drugs are able to do their work.

Nutrition and Metabolism

The science of nutrition explores how the nutrients in the foods we eat are used by the body. Carbohydrates, fats, and proteins are the nutrients the body uses to generate energy that is needed for many important cellular functions.

Chemical energy is obtained from food by the processes of metabolism. **Metabolism** refers to the chemical reactions through which organisms change food into energy and living tissue.

Understanding metabolism can be important for preventing disease. The disease phenylketonuria (PKU) is the result of a defect in the metabolism of the amino acid phenylalanine. If a person with PKU eats proteins that contain a high level of phenylalanine, abnormal breakdown products of the amino acid can accumulate and become toxic. Because biochemists understand the series of steps by which phenylalanine is metabolized, they are able to recommend a diet that prevents the toxic buildup.

Endocrinology

One important way the different organs and cells of the body communicate is through the action of the endocrine system. Tissues that make up the endocrine system release messenger molecules called **hormones** into

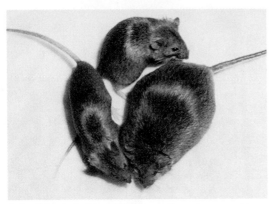

Scientists study the metabolisms of an obese mouse and its skinny siblings (*above*) to try to learn why some people gain weight more easily than others.

the blood. Hormones travel to distant cells in the body and signal them to do a particular task. Endocrinology is the study of how the body sends and responds to those signals.

Puberty is the time of life when the body changes from child to adult. The physical changes that take place during puberty are the result of changes in the production and release of many hormones. The body must tightly control the timing of both production and release of hormones. Failure to properly make and release hormones can lead to serious health consequences. For example, making too much growth hormone in early childhood results in gigantism (growth to an abnormally large size). Other hormones are needed throughout life. Failure of the pancreas to produce the hormone insulin results in diabetes.

Endocrinologists try to understand hormone production, release, and signaling so they can correct them when things go wrong. Using modern biochemical tools such as protein purification and gene splicing, scientists can manufacture human hormones in the laboratory. In the case of insulin, this allows diabetics to receive the missing hormone so that their bodies can function more normally.

Immunology

The immune system defends the body against invasion by foreign substances. These foreign substances may be bacteria, viruses, chemicals, animal hair, food, pollen, or drugs. Immunology is the science that studies how the body recognizes and gets rid of these foreign invaders.

Once exposed to a foreign substance, an individual's immune system can "remember" what the foreign substance looks like. When exposed again, the body quickly responds and the invader is eliminated. This memory is the basis for the practice of immunization against diseases such as measles, mumps, and tetanus. By understanding the response of the body to different invaders, immunologists can help design better vaccines as well as treatments for diseases such as AIDS that affect the immune system.

Pharmacology

When a person takes aspirin to get rid of a headache, the drug acts to inhibit certain biochemical pathways, thereby preventing the events that lead to the sensation of pain. Pharmacology involves studying the ways in which drugs interact with living systems.

Many things can affect the ability of drugs to exert their effects on the body. Some drugs can be taken by mouth, while others must be injected. Once a drug is given, one needs to know how long the drug remains active in the body, how metabolism may change the activity of the drug, and how the drug is eliminated. Pharmacologists work to develop the safest and most effective drugs possible.

▶ THE TOOLS OF BIOCHEMISTRY

Biochemists use specific tools to analyze proteins, lipids, carbohydrates, and nucleic acids. Some of these tools are specialized for the examination of a particular molecule. Many are useful for the study of more than one type of molecule.

Chromatography

Chromatography is a process by which complex mixtures of compounds can be separated into their individual parts. The mixture is passed through a selective substance that separates the components by size or some other property. For example, a mixture of proteins can be separated by size using a column (tube) filled with beads pierced with tiny holes. When a solution of proteins is passed through the column, small proteins will pass into the holes in the beads, and their rate of travel through the column will be slowed. Larger proteins will be unable to enter the beads and will move more quickly through the column.

1. A mixture of large and small proteins is applied to a column containing porous beads.

2. The larger proteins (red) cannot enter the beads and pass through the column first.

3. The smaller proteins (purple) can enter the beads, and their progress through the column is slowed. They exit the column after the larger proteins.

Electrophoresis

Many biological compounds, such as proteins and DNA, can be recognized according to size by separating the molecules through a semi-solid "gel" under the influence of an electric current. This is called **electrophoresis**. In general, the smaller the molecule, the faster it will move through the gel.

DNA Sequencing

DNA is the genetic information of an organism. DNA is composed of four chemically distinct building blocks, or nucleotides—adenine, guanine, cytosine, and thymine. It is important to know the sequence of these nucleotides.

Sequencing of DNA can be done using either chemicals or enzymes. The original tool for sequencing DNA, developed by Alan Maxam and Walter Gilbert, used chemicals to cut the DNA at certain nucleotides. Because of the hazardous nature of the required chemicals, the Maxam and Gilbert technique is not routinely used anymore. The enzyme sequencing tool developed by Frederick Sanger uses the actual process of DNA synthesis to insert specially modified nucleotides into the DNA. When these modified nucleotides are incorporated into the DNA, further DNA synthesis is halted. The DNA is separated by electrophoresis, and the modified nucleotides can be visualized.

DNA sequencing methods were used in the Human Genome Project to analyze the entire human genome. It is hoped that knowledge of the complete human genome sequence will enable scientists to learn more about disease, how the body works, and what makes humans unique.

The Polymerase Chain Reaction (PCR)

The PCR is a powerful technique used to copy small stretches of DNA millions of times. PCR works by first heating a double-stranded DNA sample so that it denatures, or separates, into two single-stranded pieces of DNA. Then an enzyme called DNA polymerase synthesizes (makes) two new strands of DNA, using the first two strands as guides. This results in two pieces of double-stranded DNA, each made up of one old strand

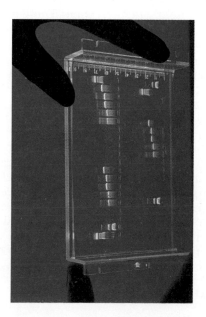

DNA separated by electrophoresis can be viewed by staining it with a special dye that causes it to glow in ultraviolet light. Each glowing band on this gel (*left*) is a piece of DNA.

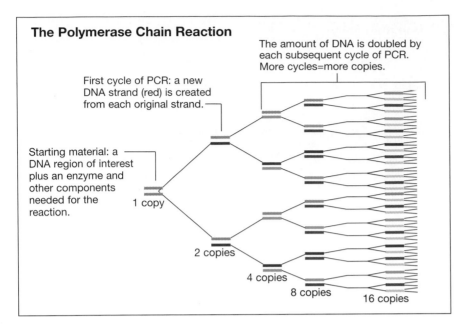

The Polymerase Chain Reaction

Starting material: a DNA region of interest plus an enzyme and other components needed for the reaction.

1 copy

First cycle of PCR: a new DNA strand (red) is created from each original strand.

2 copies

4 copies

8 copies

16 copies

The amount of DNA is doubled by each subsequent cycle of PCR. More cycles=more copies.

and one new strand. The cycle of denaturing and synthesizing DNA is repeated many times. With each cycle, the number of copies of DNA is doubled. After 20 cycles, the amount of DNA may be increased more than a million times.

The PCR has many practical uses. Forensic scientists use PCR to analyze small amounts of biological material left at crime scenes. Once the DNA in these materials is amplified, it can be compared to DNA of victims or suspects for identification purposes.

Genetic Engineering

Many diseases are caused by defects in important genes. For example, severe combined immune deficiency (SCID), also known as "boy in the bubble" disease, is a serious hereditary disorder characterized by a very weak immune system. Patients with this disease must be kept away from anything that might cause an infection, and so they spend much of their time in a germ-free isolation "bubble." SCID is caused by a defect in the adenosine deaminase (ADA) gene, which is crucial for the body's immune response.

Scientists are now able to identify the genes responsible for inherited disorders using molecular biology and molecular genetics. With these tools it is possible to determine the function of the protein encoded by a normal gene and discover what it is that is wrong with an abnormal gene that leads to disease.

Modern tools of molecular genetics allow doctors to reintroduce normal copies of genes into individuals carrying damaged or missing genes. This is referred to as **gene therapy**. The first trial of gene therapy in humans was carried out by scientists at the National Institutes of Health and involved the administration of a good copy of the ADA gene to a young girl with SCID.

▶ FUTURE OF BIOCHEMISTRY

In the future, biochemistry will probably see its most important advances in the research areas of pharmacogenomics and proteomics. Both of these fields of scientific investigation are in their infancies.

Pharmacogenomics combines the sciences of pharmacology and genetics. Every individual has some differences in the sequence of one or more genes when compared to the same genes from someone else. Some of these differences have no effect. Others may change the way the resulting protein functions. These protein differences can cause significant changes in how a person responds to a drug. Drug companies aim to understand these genetic differences in drug response and use them to design drugs for specific individuals based upon their genetic makeup.

Proteomics is the study of proteins using tools similar to those used in the study of genes and genomes. Most diseases are caused by changes or defects in certain proteins. Using large-scale screening techniques, scientists in the field of proteomics hope to analyze differences in proteins under selected conditions—for example, comparing diseased cells to normal cells.

MICHAEL W. KING
Indiana University School of Medicine

See also BIOLOGY; BODY, HUMAN; BODY CHEMISTRY; CHEMISTRY, HISTORY OF; GENETICS; LIFE.

BIODIVERSITY. See CONSERVATION; ECOLOGY.

BIOGRAPHY, AUTOBIOGRAPHY, AND BIOGRAPHICAL NOVEL

Biography is both a craft and an art. As a craftsman the biographer begins with research, gathering all the available information about a person's life. There are first the surface facts about a chosen subject. Then the biographer looks beneath the surface for evidence of inner truths—what the man or woman thought, felt, desired, suffered.

The biographer as an artist sets down the meaning of a person's life. With his research at hand, the writer chooses the facts he will use. Sometimes it is the bulk of detail; sometimes it is the essence, or pith. With this task of selection comes the task of writing the story in a clear, convincing way. The artist must so construct his book that every portion of the person's life fits into an understandable, moving whole. The writing must have style; the structure must have architectural form. That is the meaning of art.

▶ **BIOGRAPHY OLD AND NEW**

Modern biography, as an independent and popular literary form, is fairly new. Writing about individual lives, however, is an old practice. The Bible is full of stories about the prophets and saints. The earliest Greek biographical writing was done by Xenophon, who wrote about Socrates in the 4th century B.C. Plutarch's *Parallel Lives* (about A.D. 100) is still famous. The best-known Latin biographer is Suetonius, author of *Lives of the Caesars* in A.D. 120. Tacitus set down an account of the life of his father-in-law, Agricola, in A.D. 97–98. The purposes of these early Greek and Roman biographers were mixed. Some tried to tell the history of a dynasty or of a war. Others attempted to justify a moral or philosophical system. As a result the human story was sometimes lost.

Modern biographers' aims are varied. Some wish to tell an exciting, dramatic, and often inspirational human story. Others study the life of a person so that we can profit by another's experience and better understand ourselves and the world about us. Still others wish to make the past more alive. Instead of writing about the impersonal forces of history, the biographer tells of the impact of an individual on the life of his times. There is Lytton Strachey's *Eminent Victorians,* which describes an interesting age in England. Douglas S. Freeman's *George Washington* portrays the beginning of the American nation. Hendrik Willem van Loon's *R.v.R.,* a biography of Rembrandt, serves as an introduction to art. René Jules Dubos' *Louis Pasteur* gives us a picture of the scientist at work.

Biography may be written out of love or hate but never out of indifference. It may take years to write. It may require thousands of hours of study in libraries, law courts, halls of records, city halls, museums, family archives. Frequently many miles must be traveled to visit the places where the subject lived and worked, to interview men still alive who can add to the body of knowledge. This concentrated effort can be achieved only by people who love deeply—such as the biographers of Jefferson or Michelangelo or Edison—or by those who hate deeply, such as the biographers of Torquemada or Hitler or Mussolini.

Often the search is frustrating. For a conscientious biographer the easily available material won't be half enough. A researcher is a detective. He hunts down clues, pursues scraps of evidence, never gives up looking for material he senses must exist. In his hero's life there are always blank spaces that must be filled in if the biography is to be complete and true. To a good biographer everything is findable. When he comes up empty-handed, he must return to the quest with fresh ideas and renewed courage. For it is not enough to know everything a man did. It is also important to know why he did what he did—his reasoning, his fears, his failures before he achieved something important.

Once all his material is collected, the biographer faces a new challenge. The reader must feel that he is in the hands of a thorough and honest workman. Therefore, the biographer has to be objective. He has to tell the complete truth, based on his findings. He must not conceal his hero's faults, omit his shortcomings, bury his failures. He must not allow his own prejudices to take over. What is known as his "principle of selection," that is, his choice of materials to use, must be strictly ethical. Otherwise the reader will sense that something is wrong. He will feel that he is being deceived.

But when he reads an honest, well-balanced biography, such as Benjamin Thomas' *Abraham Lincoln* or Muriel Rukeyser's *Willard Gibbs* or Carl Van Doren's *Benjamin Franklin,* he will know that the strands of each story are accurately woven.

Biography is one of the most enjoyable forms of reading and learning. While reading biographies, one can sit at home yet roam the realms of time and space with *Genghis Khan* (Harold Lamb), *Napoleon* (Emil Ludwig), *Aristotle* (W. D. Ross), and *Madame Curie* (Eve Curie). A good biographer will become as one with the person he is writing about. This union enables the reader, in turn, to live another's life in his imagination.

▶ **AUTOBIOGRAPHY**

Autobiography is a very different medium. "Auto" comes from the Greek for "self," "one's own." An autobiography is the story of a person's life written by himself. Sometimes an autobiography is ghostwritten, that is, written by someone else, frequently with journalistic experience. Sometimes the real writer is completely unknown. Sometimes there is an "as told to . . ." approach.

Autobiography is a difficult art form, yet it looks easy. Perhaps that is what tempts so many thousands to try it.

A man sometimes writes his own story because he has experienced some kind of self-discovery. The discovery may be about his relationship to life, to his fellow man, or to God. Others write about their struggles against great odds and their eventual success. The autobiographies of Alfred E. Smith and Helen Keller show a refusal to be held down or defeated. Some autobiographies, like those of Booker T. Washington and Jane Addams, glow with an individual's dedication to a life of serving mankind. Greatness of character, which seems to spring from selflessness and courage, often reveals itself in an autobiography. The best of these life stories raise the stature of the human race. They inspire the reader and deepen his understanding.

Not all autobiographies are written for noble purposes. Many are written for selfish reasons—to get money, attention, sympathy, or revenge. Yet all too often the writer of autobiography conveys the exact opposite of the impression he had hoped to impart.

Every kind of American has written an autobiography. As a group, clergymen are more interested in writing about themselves than any other single category. Authors and politicians follow close behind. Industrialists, scientists, and engineers tend to remain silent. In between come the educators, the reformers, the military and the professional men. It has become fashionable for actors and athletes to have their stories ghostwritten.

▶ **THE BIOGRAPHICAL NOVEL**

In recent years a third biographical form has become increasingly popular and important. It is called the biographical novel. This is biography presented in the form of a novel, with dialogue, suspense, and plot structure. The biographical novelist can use his creative imagination to develop these aspects of the novel. But he must do so only within the framework of truth. The novelist will have found the truth in documents—diaries, letters, journals, notes, recorded deeds.

The biographical novel is thus the fruit of a marriage between the research of biography and the fictional devices of the novelist. Books like *I, Claudius* (Robert Graves) and *The Romance of Leonardo da Vinci* (Dimitri Sergeevich Merezhkovski) are fine examples of the biographical novel. It offers a more emotional approach to life, with more personal interpretation by the author. Facts can be forgotten, but rarely an emotional experience. The biographical novelist tries to catch up his readers in the emotions of his hero. Emotions felt while reading a biographical novel can be almost as unforgettable as the emotions one experiences in real life.

Not every life will fit into the form of the biographical novel. Dramatic elements must be present, along with an overall pattern into which the parts can be fitted. Many lives, important in their achievement, do not lend themselves to the nature of the novel. Other lives seem to have been lived as though the subject were constantly aware that he was creating a dramatic structure.

Biography, autobiography, and the biographical novel are personal books. They tell the story of men's lives, in order to help us understand mankind.

IRVING STONE
Author, *Lust for Life, The Agony and the Ecstasy*

BIOLOGICAL CLOCK

As the sun rises on a warm, sunny day, the trumpet-shaped flowers of the morning glory unfold. It is in the afternoon, as the morning glories close, that the buds of moss roses uncurl. When darkness comes, moss roses curl shut. Only then do evening primrose flowers open, pale and ghostly in the night. In the morning, before daylight, they close again.

The opening and closing of the flowers is one of the natural cycles, called **biological rhythms**, that occur in living things. The biological rhythms of the morning glories, moss roses, and evening primroses occur within a single day. Such rhythms are called *circadian rhythms*, from the Latin words *circa* and *diem*, meaning "about a day." But not all biological rhythms are based on a day. Some, such as the beating of the heart, occur every few seconds. Other rhythms are repeated each month and still others are repeated each year.

Scientists use the term **biological clock** to describe the internal timing mechanism that controls biological rhythms. Where is this biological clock and what is it? In animals, the brain is thought to play a role; however, plants, fungi, and microscopic organisms lack brains and still exhibit biological rhythms. There is increasing evidence that chemicals produced by living things trigger the cycles. These chemicals, in turn, are controlled by factors outside the living organism including the light-dark cycle of a day and the changing seasons of a year. Yet, even if an organism is shut off from all clues in the environment, it will still display biological rhythms.

▶BIOLOGICAL CLOCKS IN NATURE

The biological rhythms of seashore organisms are often linked to the rise and fall of the ocean's tides. Clams, mussels, and barnacles feed by filtering food from the water. When the tide is in, their shells open and they feed. As the tides go out, the shells close and the animals are protected from the drying air.

The migration of animals is an event that is triggered by a signal from an animal's biological clock. One of the most dramatic examples of a migration is the journey some birds make in spring and autumn. These migrations are associated with changes in day length. As days grow longer, birds leave their winter feeding grounds in the south. By the time they reach their northern destination, the plants they depend on for food are flourishing there. When the birds reach their summer feeding grounds, another biological rhythm is triggered: They are ready to mate and raise young. As autumn approaches, days shorten, temperatures drop, and plants begin to die. Birds' biological clocks signal the return to the south where there is food and warmth.

Like flowers, birds, and other animals, humans have biological clocks that control their biological rhythms. Humans have daily, weekly, monthly, and seasonal biological rhythms. Body temperature, blood pressure,

The jimsonweed, which blooms at night, is a desert flower with a biological rhythm opposite that of most flowers. *Right:* Throughout the hours of daylight, the flower of the jimsonweed remains tightly closed. *Far right:* After the sun has set, the funnel-shaped flower slowly opens.

sleeping and waking, and the levels of many chemicals in the body have a 24-hour rhythm. Many illnesses appear to have a yearly rhythm. Colds, flu, and pneumonia are most common in autumn and winter. Measles most often occur in spring and summer.

▶ CHANGES IN BIOLOGICAL CLOCKS

When people travel by plane across several time zones, their internal clocks are no longer in tune with where they are. This is called jet lag. Its effects are worse when people travel to a place with a later time (that is, west to east) than when they travel to a place with an earlier time (east to west). People with jet lag feel cranky and tired. They may also be clumsy and forgetful. It takes several days for the body's biological clock to reset to the new time zone.

People who work night shifts also experience problems with their biological clocks. They are generally not as productive or alert as people who work during the day, and they have more accidents on the job. They also have more health and sleep problems than people who work day shifts.

In recent years, scientists have made important discoveries about what controls circadian rhythms. The first human gene involved

At a signal from their biological clocks, monarch butterflies gather in huge swarms to make a yearly migration that covers thousands of miles.

in regulating the body's internal clock was identified in 2001. Also, certain hormones, such as melatonin, have been found to play a key role in resetting the body's clock. Exposure to bright light can change the body's natural production of melatonin. Such change affects not only sleep-wake cycles but also a person's mood. Light-sensitive chemicals in the eyes and skin appear to be involved. Sleeping aids containing synthetic melatonin are now available to help overcome the effects of jet lag and shift work.

▶ MEDICAL APPLICATIONS

Other exciting breakthroughs are being made with new medical treatments. Certain medical problems are associated with different times of the day. Heart attacks and strokes happen most often during the waking hours before noon. Asthma and ulcer attacks occur most often between midnight and 8 A.M. Thus, heart medication taken right after waking may help protect a person with heart disease. Medication for asthma and ulcers is available in time-release tablets. When these tablets are taken at night, an individual is helped most during the high-risk time.

Biological clocks control the many familiar rhythms of life. As scientists learn more about these rhythms, especially those in humans, new solutions can be found to make travel more comfortable, working conditions safer, and medical treatment more effective.

KARIN L. RHINES
Coauthor, *Discover Science*

See also HIBERNATION; HOMING AND MIGRATION.

Workers who switch between night and day shifts, such as these firefighters, experience problems with their biological clocks similar to the effects of jet lag.

BIOLOGY

You only have to look around and listen to see and hear the evidence of life. Outside, squirrels romp among the trees gathering nuts, bees dart busily in and out of flowers carrying their valuable cargo of nectar and pollen, and birds fly from ground to nest, chirping as they go. Besides those plants and animals that are readily seen, there are countless tiny living creatures in the soil, water, and air. For centuries, people have been interested in the lives of organisms around them. This interest and the observations that were generated from it were the foundation for the science of biology. Biology is the study of living things in all their forms.

▶ THE STUDY OF LIFE

Biology is a creative, dynamic, and constantly changing science. It is influenced by our social, cultural, and historical settings. Our concerns about global warming, AIDS, and overpopulation did not concern early **biologists**, the scientists who study living things. They just wanted to know which plants and animals were present in different parts of the world.

But no matter what period of time they live in, biologists examine their environments. In their searchings, they are stirred by their curiosity to ask similar questions: How do living and nonliving things differ? How was such a variety of living things produced on Earth? What makes something able to survive in its environment and reproduce? How are creatures such as a massive elephant and a microscopic bacterium alike, and how do they differ? How do all the organisms on Earth interact with one another to make the Earth what it is? How will human beings be affected by changes in the world? Wherever the search for answers to these and other questions leads biologists, it always begins with the same question: Is it a living thing?

▶ HOW BIOLOGISTS DETERMINE WHAT IS LIVING

We somehow know that a human being, a rose, and a worm are living things, while a rock and a cloud are not. Yet what are the differences between them that determine which is living and which is not? Biologists have identified a common set of characteristics that are shared by all organisms.

The world around us vibrates with the pulse of life. Biologists have identified 1.5 million species and estimate that there are perhaps as many as 50 million species of living things populating our Earth.

Organisms Are Made of Cells. All organisms are composed of the same building blocks called cells. Most cells are so small that they can be seen only with a microscope. A cell is truly the basic unit of life—it contains all the necessary components to carry on the activities of life. Like a tiny factory, a cell constructs its own tools, machinery, rooms, and even its own building. It can even repair itself and generate its own energy or power. Some simple life-forms, such as bacteria, consist of a single cell and are called unicellular. In contrast, complex life-forms, such as a whale or an oak tree, have trillions of cells and are called multicellular organisms.

Organisms Need Energy. An organism needs energy to perform the vital tasks that keep it alive. It gets that energy from its environment. Just as you eat food to get energy, other living things use materials in their environment for energy.

Ultimately, the sun is the main source of energy. Its energy flows through nearly all forms of life. Green plants and certain microorganisms capture the energy of sunlight. Through a process called **photosynthesis**, they convert the light energy into food for themselves, into energy-rich sugar molecules, and into new cells. We see the effects of this process as trees grow and produce new leaves.

Many living things, including human beings, cannot perform photosynthesis. They get their energy by eating plants and animals that have eaten plants. The chemicals, or nutrients, in the food are broken down to release the trapped energy using chemical reactions. The released energy can then be used to do work and make new cell parts. The sum of all these chemical reactions that fuel the activities of a cell is called **metabolism**.

Organisms Maintain Their Internal Environment. To stay alive and work efficiently, an organism must keep the conditions within its body in a consistently steady state. In multi-cellular organisms, this process is called **homeostasis**, from the Greek words meaning "to stay the same." Cells must continuously adapt to preserve this steady state. For example, cells cannot function if the temperature changes drastically. Your heart and brain cells must be kept at the proper temperature to work even if the temperature outside is very hot or very cold. Your body can sweat to release heat if you are hot and can metabolize more food to generate additional heat energy if you are cold.

Changes do occur in the life of an organism, such as growth and development, but these processes do not happen because homeostasis has failed. They are changes that are programmed into the life cycle of an organism. Amazingly, an organism can grow, develop, and change, yet all the while maintain a constant environment in which its cells can function.

Organisms Grow and Develop. An organism, whether it is a baby chick, a pet dog or cat, or your brother or sister, grows and develops as it ages. As living things grow, they increase in size. This occurs because of an increase in the size of cells, the number of cells, or both. Most plants and animals start out very small and grow until they reach adult size. If you measure your height over several years, you know that you are changing and getting taller. Some organisms, such as most trees, grow continuously through life, though they grow at a slower rate as they get older.

Growth of an organism is not constant throughout its life, nor do all parts of an organism grow at the same rate. Most organisms do not become adults, however, just by growing taller and larger. An adult chicken or rooster does not look like a baby chick. The chick changes its appearance as it develops, or matures. Growth and development occur in a characteristic way for each type of organism. Some changes are obvious: We see plants sprouting from seeds, or tadpoles losing their tails as they mature into frogs. You started life as a single fertilized egg, then grew and developed many specialized types of cells that formed heart, muscle, bone, or brain. The specialized jobs of these different cells are an important part of development.

Organisms Reproduce. For life to continue on our planet, new organisms must be produced constantly to replace those that die. This process of producing new individuals of the

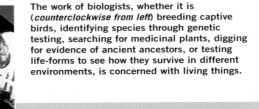

The work of biologists, whether it is (*counterclockwise from left*) breeding captive birds, identifying species through genetic testing, searching for medicinal plants, digging for evidence of ancient ancestors, or testing life-forms to see how they survive in different environments, is concerned with living things.

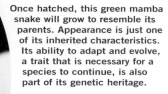

Once hatched, this green mamba snake will grow to resemble its parents. Appearance is just one of its inherited characteristics. Its ability to adapt and evolve, a trait that is necessary for a species to continue, is also part of its genetic heritage.

same kind, or offspring, is called reproduction.

A fundamental principle of biology is that life comes only from living things. In simple creatures, such as bacteria and amoebas, reproduction is usually asexual, or not sexual. A bacterium grows to twice its size, and then it usually reproduces by splitting in half to form two new bacteria. During this process, the bacterium copies its hereditary material, or genes, and directs one complete set of genes into each new daughter cell. The passing on of the genetic material is similar to passing a blueprint of the organism's characteristic traits from one generation to another.

Most plants and animals carry out sexual reproduction, in which an egg (the female sex cell) and sperm (the male sex cell) unite to form a fertilized egg that can develop into a new organism. Sexual reproduction produces offspring that show traits contributed by both the mother and father. While we all have inherited the general characteristics of a human being, the details may differ. We may have inherited the hair color of our mother and the eye color of our father. This slight variation or diversity in life is essential for the processes of adaptation and evolution to take place.

Organisms Adapt and Evolve. Organisms can sense and respond to changes in their world. If you touch something hot, you move your hand away quickly. If a baby hears a loud noise, it cries. If a plant is placed in a room with only one window, it grows toward the sunlight. Even simple, single-celled bacteria living in your intestine will make different molecules if you drink milk rather than eat bread.

Special sensing molecules and organs help us respond to light, sound, chemicals, and other signals in our environment. A response may protect you against some danger or discomfort. For example, you know to run for cover if it starts to rain heavily when you are outside. Changes in our environment can be sudden and dramatic, such as those that occur when a flash flood or earthquake rips apart the landscape, but usually they occur much more slowly. In order to survive, an organism must adjust, or adapt, to such changes. As winter sets in, you will see the fur of the arctic fox turn white and thick. This change in coat color is an adaptive response, so that in a snow-covered environment the fox will not be as easily seen by its enemies.

Some variations or differences occur in each organism that affect its ability to adapt. In a den of polar bears, there may be one animal with changes in its genes that spur the production of a fur coat that is thicker than that of the other bears. If the climate becomes colder, as it did in the ice ages, these changed animals will be more likely to survive and leave offspring. A selection process occurs in which nature determines who will survive and reproduce. This process is called **evolution**.

If changes in nature occur more rapidly than do genetic changes and adaptations, a species may become extinct. The giant trees in the petrified forests are examples of organisms that could not adapt when desertlike conditions occurred. We must remember that our activities can sometimes change an environment faster than nature can adapt. Destruction of the rain forest, global warming, and pollution of our air, soil, and water are all concerns because of their impact on living things.

Organisms Are Organized. Within the structure and function of a living thing, there is an orderly arrangement. This can be observed when examining the structure of an organism: An organism is made up of molecules that make up cells; the cells make up tissues, and the tissues make up organs. A pattern emerges as we look at the levels of life's structures. The various components of life become increasingly complex in their organiza-

tion and interactions. We find that the complex levels build on the simpler ones.

All members of a species that live in one area are called a population. When different populations living in the same area interact with one another, they make up a **community**. The various plants, fish, insects, and frogs that live in a lake are an example of a community.

Biologists who study **ecosystems** are examining how communities of living things interact with the nonliving parts of their environment. Over time, the organisms and the environment can be changed by these interactions. A coral reef is an example of a marine ecosystem. It is made up of corals, sponges, fish, algae, and many other populations. Ecosystems can be grouped together

The populations that make up a community vary depending on its environment. For example, the living things that form the community inhabiting an African savanna (*right*) are very different from those of a garbage dump (*above*). However, each community functions in much the same manner, as members interact and fight for survival.

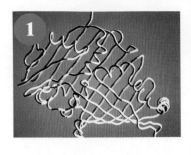

into still larger units. The **biosphere** is the most complex, since it makes up all of the ecosystems on Earth. You are part of the biosphere since it includes all of the organisms and their environments. We must remember that no individual can function at a single level. What we learn and do can affect all life on Earth.

▶ **BIOLOGISTS AT WORK**

The diversity of living things offers scientists a variety of career options and a broad range of work settings. In their work, biologists can focus on specific types of living organisms. **Botanists** study how plants grow and reproduce. They do important work in such areas as agriculture, forestry, conservation, landscaping, and botanical gardening. For example, biotechnological research has developed plants that resist drought, disease, and insects. **Zoologists** study animals. Some zoologists specialize, or focus, their work and study only certain types of animals. For example, **ornithologists** study birds, while **marine biologists** study animals that live in the oceans. Another branch of biology includes scientists called **microbiologists**. They study microscopic organisms. Their research on

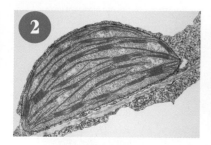

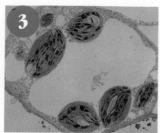

Each living thing is fashioned in the same orderly manner, from the simple to the complex. This biological organization can be seen in a tree. Many atoms make up a chlorophyll molecule (1), the light-absorbing green pigment that drives the food-making process of photosynthesis. Chlorophyll and other molecules necessary for photosynthesis are organized within a chloroplast (2). Chloroplasts and other structures are found within the functioning unit called a cell (3). Similar cells are grouped within an organism to form tissues (4) that perform specific functions. Many different tissues are organized to form the leaves (5) and other parts of a tree (6).

bacteria, fungi, and viruses, which are all micro-organisms, has a great impact on what is known about diseases in plants and animals, food production, recycling of chemicals in nature, and pollutants.

Some biologists study parts of organisms. **Biochemists** study the molecules and chemical reactions that occur in organisms. These scientists identify the substances in plant and animal cells that affect processes such as metabolism and disease. Other scientists who look at normal and diseased cells and tissues include **cytologists** and **pathologists**. The study of inheritance and genes is the work of **geneticists**. With new sophisticated instruments and techniques, the DNA molecule, which forms the genetic code, can be studied, changed, and transferred among cells. **Molecular biologists** are scientists that use this new technology in their work.

The functions of organs and systems in organisms are studied by **physiologists**. Because living creatures have many organ systems, it is not unusual that physiologists will specialize. For example, a **neurophysiologist** studies the nervous system, while a **cardiovascular physiologist** studies the functions of the heart and circulatory system.

Other biologists study living things in their natural environments. **Ecologists** study how living organisms relate to each other within their environment. Their work affects our natural resources, such as forests, water, and wildlife. Scientists who are interested in creatures that lived in prehistoric times, when the ecology of our world was different, are **paleontologists**. **Evolutionary biologists** study the diversity and history of living things resulting from evolution.

Different biologists often work together to get a more complete understanding of an organism—how its parts work together and how the organism interacts with its environ-

People and Events in the Early Development of Biology

Ancient Times
Left: An Egyptian tomb painting of a grain harvest shows the work of early biologists. Agriculture develops as people observe and experiment with living things, such as plants, to ensure a steady supply of food.

●*Left:* Declaring that "every natural event has a natural cause," the Greek physician Hippocrates (460–377 B.C.) challenges the ancient belief that events, such as diseases and other occurrences, are punishments from the gods or spirits.

●*Above:* The Greek philosopher Aristotle (384–322 B.C.), later considered the founder of biology, searches to find out all that can be known about the natural world. Dedicated to observation, logic, and objectivity, he creates theories that dominate the natural sciences for close to 2,000 years.

Early 1500's
Left: With his contribution of more than 750 sketches of the body in all its stages, including the developing fetus, Italian artist and scientist Leonardo da Vinci (1452–1519) leads the way in the study of human anatomy.

---

ment. One example would be a partnership formed by a paleontologist and an evolutionary biologist who are studying the same dinosaur. The findings of the paleontologist may reveal what the dinosaur looked like, what it ate, and where it lived, while the findings of the evolutionary biologist may disclose how different circumstances forced the dinosaur to change and evolve over time.

▶ **THE HISTORY OF BIOLOGY**

From the earliest written records, we know our ancestors observed nature and learned how to use plants and animals in beneficial ways. They trained, or domesticated, certain animals for food and tasks, such as moving loads, and developed techniques for planting crops. The early Chinese, Egyptians, and Arabs also learned how to prepare medicines from plants. A fascination with the human body is evident from historical drawings that show common practices, such as the Egyptian practice of embalming the dead.

The Golden Age. The golden age of the Greeks, about 2,400 years ago, was a time of major advances in biology. While others around them believed that natural events were caused by gods or spirits, the ancient Greeks explained their world by looking at the patterns and laws of nature. The teachings of the Greek physician Hippocrates, who lived in the 400's B.C., greatly affected the practice of medicine. He described many conditions and procedures, from the noises in the chest associated with infections to dramatic surgery on the head. Hippocrates emphasized the importance of recording both successes and failures of a treatment and, most important, the responsibility a physician has to care for people. Physicians today still take a modern version of the Hippocratic oath—an oath that was written in Hippocrates' honor and reflected his high ideals.

Another important Greek scientist and philosopher was Aristotle (300's B.C.). He very accurately described and classified many plants and animals and their behaviors. Galen, a Greek physician who practiced medicine in Rome about 100 B.C., extensively described the anatomy and functions of the

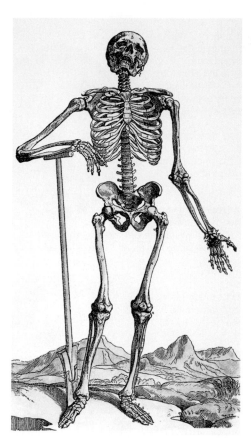

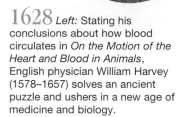

1543 *Left:* With *On the Structure of the Human Body*, Belgian physician Andreas Vesalius (1514–64) produces the first scientific anatomy text. The book, which is based on Vesalius' dissections of the human body, revolutionizes the study of both anatomy and medicine.

1628 *Left:* Stating his conclusions about how blood circulates in *On the Motion of the Heart and Blood in Animals*, English physician William Harvey (1578–1657) solves an ancient puzzle and ushers in a new age of medicine and biology.

1665 *Top:* In *Micrographia*, English scientist Robert Hooke (1635–1703) publishes his observations made using a compound microscope, describing the minute compartments of cork tissue as "cells."

1683 *Left:* The Royal Society publishes the pictures of "little animalcules" made by Dutch naturalist Anton van Leeuwenhoek (1632–1723). He is the first to see and describe single-celled microbes.

human body. He obtained this knowledge from treating the gladiators who had been injured during their battles and by dissecting animals. Progress in science slowed after the Greeks' early contributions. During the Dark Ages and most of the Middle Ages, little scholarly work occurred that added to what was known about the nature of life.

The Renaissance. The Renaissance, meaning "rebirth," was a period (A.D. 1300–1600) of intense interest in science and nature. Naturalists described and classified many plants and animals on the Earth. Great artists contributed beautiful and accurate drawings of various organisms that are still available for us to see today. Among them were the Italian artists Botticelli, Michelangelo, and Leonardo da Vinci. This was also the time when the first scientific textbook on human anatomy appeared. Written by Andreas Vesalius, *On the Structure of the Human Body* was published in 1543. One of the most important contributions of the time was made by William Harvey, an English physician. It was in 1628 that he published the results of his experiments showing how blood is pumped by the heart and how it circulates throughout the body. Up until that time, it was thought that blood ebbed and flowed out of the heart, much like a tide.

Microscopic Discoveries. The invention of the microscope opened up a whole new world for exploration. During the middle and late 1600's, great discoveries were made by those who pioneered in the use of the microscope. Among the pioneers were Marcello Malpighi, the Italian anatomist who observed blood moving through the capillaries, and Robert Hooke, an English scientist who published the book *Micrographia* (1665), in which he made detailed drawings of the many creatures he had studied using the microscope. More than any other person of his time, Dutch biologist Anton van Leeuwenhoek furthered the use of the microscope, making more than 400 microscopes himself. Using one of the simple microscopes he made, Van Leeuwenhoek was the first person to observe single-celled organisms. His drawings of small life-forms in pond water and his studies of cells influenced many scientists.

1735 *Left:* With the publication of his *Systema Naturae*, Swedish botanist Carolus Linnaeus (1707–78) transforms biology. In the book, he classifies the living world according to shared characteristics and relatedness, giving each plant and animal its own scientific name made up of two words.

Late 1700's *Below left:* The oxygen experiments of French chemist Antoine Lavoisier (1743–94) expand the understanding of body processes, including respiration and the conversion of food to energy.

1839 *Below:* Working independently of each other, German scientists Theodor Schwann (1810–82) and Matthias Schleiden (1804–81) develop the cell theory, proposing that all plants and animals have the same basic unit of life—the cell.

1856 *Above right:* Austrian monk Gregor Mendel (1822–84) begins experiments in genetics using garden peas. Through his work in the monastery garden, he discovers the basic laws of heredity.

1859 *Right:* British naturalist Charles Darwin (1809–82) offers a new theory of nature in *On the Origin of Species*, stating that new species evolve from more primitive species through a process he calls natural selection.

The Cell Theory. It was in the 1830's that two Germans, working separately, came to the same conclusion about the makeup of living things. Botanist Matthias Schleiden and physiologist Theodor Schwann established a general theory about cells. The cell theory recognized that cells are the basic units of life and that all organisms are made of cells and all cells come from pre-existing cells. This revolutionary idea made biologists rethink how organisms are made and how they function.

Classifying Life. With the beginning of world travel in the mid-1700's, biologists searched for previously unknown forms of life. Thousands of new plants and animals were collected each year. However, problems arose among these naturalists because there was a variety of ways to name new discoveries. This made it very difficult for biologists to communicate among themselves about their discoveries. A Swedish botanist named Carolus Linnaeus developed a new system of classification that solved many of these problems.

He described the rules and characteristics to use for the grouping of plants and animals. Linnaeus put organisms with similar characteristics in the same group and suggested that the group be called a **species**. He also suggested that similar species be linked into a larger group, called a **genus**. For example, lions, tigers, and jaguars each represent a different species. However, they are similar enough to be considered members of the same genus.

▶ THE GROWTH OF MODERN BIOLOGY

As biologists studied more animals and plants, they saw that there was some order in living organisms—from simple to more complex. They began to question the belief that each species in life had remained unchanged since the world began. The scientists saw that farmers could make new varieties of plants and animals by breeding two different types of organisms. Biologists also wondered why there were so many species with few differences. Eventually biologists realized that species can change over time and that some species had gradually developed or evolved from other species.

The Theory of Evolution. Several biologists in the early 1800's contributed to the understanding of how species evolved. In 1859, the British naturalist Charles Darwin presented his explanation. Darwin described his ideas on evolution in his widely read book, *On the Origin of Species*. His ideas came largely from the variation among species of plants and animals that he observed during his expeditions to the Galápagos Islands. For example, Darwin saw 13 species of finches on different islands of this group. Each bird resembled those on the other islands in general appearance, but each had a differently shaped and sized beak. The beak of each type of bird was well suited for getting the food found on its island. Darwin proposed that evolution had occurred among the birds, and he tried to explain how the changes resulted. His theory of evolution proposed that inheritable traits can vary among individuals of the same species. An organism will produce more offspring than the available natural resources. The offspring will compete for food and other necessities of life. Those born with favorable traits will survive and reproduce. The environment will select organisms with beneficial traits, a process he called **natural selection**. This theory became the theme that unified biology in the twentieth century.

The Principles of Heredity. Also occurring in the mid-1800's was the development of the principles of heredity. Gregor Mendel, an Austrian monk, performed experiments using pea plants that showed there is a pattern to how traits are passed from parents to offspring. Mendel's choice of pea plants was important because he could easily get the seeds, the plants grew fast, and many offspring were produced. Mendel also carefully thought through his experiments and kept good records. He showed that traits are produced by basic hereditary units that can be transmitted from generation to generation.

▶ **BIOLOGY TODAY**

Only in the 1900's have scientists learned that hereditary traits are passed on by means of information stored in cellular molecules called **deoxyribonucleic acid (DNA)**. We now know that the traits are due to DNA segments, called genes. These genes affect protein molecules in the cells and thus the properties and processes of cells. The structure of the DNA molecule was discovered in 1953 by James Watson, an American biologist, and Francis Crick, a British biophysicist. Knowing the structure of DNA molecules helped biologists understand how changes in these molecules, called **mutations**, could affect genes and their functions.

Many exciting breakthroughs in genetics and molecular biology have occurred since the 1950's. An understanding of DNA has made it possible to change genes and use them in beneficial ways. New laboratory instruments allow scientists to identify the many genes that are present in the DNA of living things. Potential benefits of this knowledge include the correction and prevention of diseases in organisms. With careful safeguards, biologists can change bacteria into "chemical factories" by adding new genes that can produce useful substances such as hormones, drugs, and vaccines. Today's developments in molecular biology are as exciting as the discoveries of new organisms by our early naturalists.

Scientists are also getting a better understanding of how cells and organs work and "talk" with each other. Neurobiologists are exploring the brain and its signaling system of nerve cells and chemicals. The study of the immune system is another area of intense biological research. Immunologists are studying how immune cells and molecules interact to

James D. Watson (left) and Francis H. C. Crick (right) worked together to unravel the mystery of DNA structure, paving the way for the understanding of life processes at the molecular level.

How a Biologist Explores Nature

See For Yourself

Some biologists observe nature, either directly or with instruments, and compare the general patterns or changes they see. The scientists may then think and wonder about what their observations mean. These thoughts can lead to a **hypothesis**, or an "educated guess," as scientists attempt to explain their observations. A hypothesis is tested using further observations or experiments. The results are analyzed to see if they support or reject the hypothesis, and then a conclusion about the experiment can be made. Scientists may ask new questions based on the results of their investigations and test other factors or variables that might affect their results.

But biologists are not the only people who examine nature; nature influences the work of many different people. The artist Leonardo da Vinci was a keen observer of nature. He studied the shape and design of living things, especially human beings. One of his famous studies of the human form is the drawing of a Vitruvian man. In it he showed the proportions that he believed to be typical for most people. The results of his work are still

used today, not just by artists, but by people in such diverse fields as architecture and medicine. We can use Leonardo's observations to form a hypothesis, test it, analyze the results, and come to a conclusion in much the same way a biologist would.

1. **Forming a hypothesis.** In Leonardo's drawing, the Vitruvian man is set standing inside a square with his arms outstretched to the sides. Knowing that the length of a square is the same as its width, we can develop a hypothesis about the human proportions depicted: The height of a person is equal to the distance across the individual's body with arms extended out to the sides.
2. **Testing the hypothesis.** In order to test the hypothesis, the height and width measurements of a group of people, such as your classmates, need to be taken. You will need a ruler or tape measure as well as paper and a pencil to record your data. For each individual, measure the height (for the

most accurate height measurement, shoes should be off) and then the width across the body with arms outstretched and hands open. Record your findings (in inches) for each member of your group.

3. **Analyzing the data.** After you have recorded all your data, you need to analyze it and find out if the results support the hypothesis. If there is 5 percent or less difference between the measurements, they can be considered equal. To determine this for an individual using 60 inches for height and 58 inches for body width, the calculations would be 60 − 58 = 2, then 2 ÷ 60 = .033, or 3 percent difference. This individual's measurements would be considered equal.
4. **Reaching a conclusion.** When you examine the results of your experiment, do they support or reject the hypothesis? What is your conclusion? Does the height of a person equal the distance across the individual's body with arms extended out to the sides?

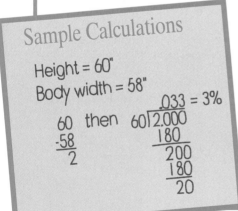

Sample Calculations

Height = 60"
Body width = 58"

60
−58
2

then

$$60\overline{)2.000} = .033 = 3\%$$
180
200
180
20

defend the body. Basic research in this area will provide a better understanding of organ transplant rejections and of diseases such as AIDS. Understanding the brain and the immune system will be some of the great challenges for future biologists.

As the human population continues to grow, the work of biologists becomes even more important. Understanding human beings and how they interact with their environment will help us better manage our world so that life on Earth can continue to exist.

CYNTHIA V. SOMMER
University of Wisconsin at Milwaukee

See also BIOCHEMISTRY; CELLS; DARWIN, CHARLES ROBERT; EVOLUTION; FOSSILS; GENETICS; HARVEY, WILLIAM; KINGDOMS OF LIVING THINGS; LIFE; MEDICINE; MICROBIOLOGY; PHOTOSYNTHESIS.

Left: Vividly colored glowing corals are animals that live on the Great Barrier Reef off the eastern coast of Australia. Above: Some species, or kinds, of fireflies have light-emitting glands in their abdomens that are used to flash mating signals.

BIOLUMINESCENCE

Light from fireflies and other living things is called **bioluminescence**. There are many bioluminescent things in nature—plants, animals, and bacteria.

The glowing plants include only a few kinds, such as certain toadstools and molds. But animals that light up are more numerous; they range from tiny one-celled sea creatures to sponges, clams, worms, and insects. The most numerous glowing forms of life are found in the salt water of oceans. The most familiar forms are found on land—fireflies, glowworms, and fox fire fungus.

Bioluminescence is called "cold" light to distinguish it from incandescence, or heat-giving light. (For example, electric light bulbs, oil lamps, and candles give off "hot" light.) Living plants and animals could not produce incandescent light without being burned up. Their light is caused by chemicals combining in such a way that little or no measurable heat is given off.

The substance that gives off the light in living things is called luciferin. This "glowing" chemical was named in 1887 by one of the earliest scientists to study living light, Raphaël Dubois, of France. Dubois named this chemical substance "luciferin," meaning "light bearer." Through his experiments using the glowing fluid taken from a clam, Dubois found that the light was caused by a team of chemicals working together. Luciferin would not light up except in the presence of a second chemical, which Dubois called "luciferase."

Scientists have since learned that living light is produced when luciferin and oxygen combine in the presence of luciferase. Other substances are also needed to produce light in some living things, such as adenosine triphosphate (ATP) in fireflies. It is the additional substances that give the light a range of color from yellow to blue, green, and red.

In some cases, the function of the light seems obvious. Marine fireworms use glowing light as mating signals. During the mating season, the female fireworms come up from deep waters to the surface of the sea and glow. Seeing the light, the males join the females. A mating dance follows and then both sexes release their reproductive cells into the water.

Bulblike organs, called photophores, on the bodies of many deep-sea fish attract mates or prey and illuminate the search for them in the darkness of the ocean depths. Some luminescent fish zigzag through the water with lights flashing to confuse predators and escape being eaten. In other cases, such as the many blind light-emitting deep-sea species, the light seems to have no function.

Much remains to be learned about the chemistry of bioluminescence. Perhaps some day enough will be known to produce this cold light for everyday use instead of the energy-wasting electric light we use now.

W. D. McElroy
Author, *Light: Physical and Biological Action*

Large herds of zebras and wildebeests roam across the vast grasslands, or savannas, of Africa, grazing on the abundant plant life that includes a variety of grasses.

BIOMES

The hot, humid rain forest, the dry desert, and the icy tundra all have something in common: Each one is a biome. A biome is a community of specific types of plants and animals that covers a large area of the earth's surface. Each biome is made up of many **habitats**—the places where a particular plant or animal normally lives and grows. The type of biome in a region is generally determined by the kind of climate in that region. Deserts cover dry regions. Rain forests cover hot, humid regions. Tundras cover cold and dry regions.

On every continent except Antarctica, most of the different kinds of biomes can be found. Each place has unique species of plants and animals, yet the plants and animals of a particular biome, all around the world, tend to be similar. For example, spine-covered cacti are common plants in the deserts of the American Southwest. In African deserts, similar prickly plants called euphorbs grow in abundance. Euphorbs and cacti have both adapted to living in the hot, dry desert biome. Similarities among plant species in biomes around the world allow scientists to identify the different kinds of biomes. Scientists also study a biome's **ecology**; that is, the interactions of living things with the environment and with each other.

▶ **KINDS OF BIOMES**

This article covers the major land biomes—grasslands, deserts, chaparral, deciduous forests, coniferous forests, tundra, and tropical rain forests. Aquatic biomes also exist in rivers, lakes, and oceans. You can find out more about the organisms in these biomes in the articles ALGAE, FISH, OCEAN, and PLANTS.

Each biome (except deserts) is named after a **climax vegetation**—one that has become dominant over a long period of time. The plants and animals that it supports together make up a **climax community**.

Grasslands

Known as prairies in North America, savannas in central Africa, steppes in central Asia, and pampas in South America, grasslands are among the richest biomes. Major agricultural crops, including corn, wheat, oats, and barley, were all bred from grasses—the main plants in the grassland environment.

Grasslands are found in climates slightly drier than the climates that support deciduous forests. Average rainfall in the grasslands varies from 10 to 40 inches (254 to 1,016 millimeters) annually. Fires, which can destroy deciduous forests, cause grasslands to thrive. Burned grasses enrich the soil and allow new plants to grow. Some grassland wildflowers cannot sprout unless their seeds are exposed to a fire's searing heat. Fires also keep certain plants from growing that would change the grassland environment, such as deciduous trees.

Grasslands that receive the most rain produce tall, dense grasses, as in America's tallgrass prairies. Grasses there can reach heights of 12 feet (3.7 meters). Early settlers riding through the grasslands had to stand up in the stirrups of their saddles to spot their cows grazing in these tall grasses. Grasslands that receive the least precipitation have short grasses. Short-grass prairies are dotted with clumps of grasses that grow less than 2 feet (0.6 meters) tall. Grasslands also include wildflowers, which add vibrant color to the green backdrop. An occasional shrub or tree dots the landscape, springing up in places where there is adequate moisture.

The dominant grassland animals are grazers. In Africa, millions of gazelles, zebras, and wildebeests migrate across the savannas, each grazing on a different part of the grass plant. Predators, including lions, tigers, and hyenas, stalk the old and sick grazing animals. Vultures feed on the decaying carcasses while insects strip the bones clean. In their natural state, grasslands support the largest herds of animals in the world.

Deserts

Regions that receive less than 10 inches (254 millimeters) of rain each year are generally classified as deserts. Desert rains are infrequent. Sometimes it will only rain once or twice a year. When it does rain, a great quantity of rain may fall so rapidly that a quick, heavy flood (called a flash flood) occurs. Deserts also tend to have extreme variations in temperatures. Days are very hot, but temperatures plummet at night, sometimes dipping down below freezing. Desert plants and animals have to be quite hardy to adapt to these difficult conditions.

Succulents, plants that store water in their leaves or stems, are among the major plants of the deserts. Cacti and euphorbs are two different types of succulents. Shrubs with small leathery or waxy leaves also thrive in some desert environments. These plants may shed their leaves and remain dormant through the desert's harshest seasons. Some desert plants live short lives, sprouting, flowering, setting seed, and dying in the few days during and after a heavy rain. The seeds of these plants lie dormant in the sand for months or years until adequate rain once again falls.

Desert animals must also find ways to adapt to the extreme dryness and heat. Many rest in their underground burrows during the day and only come out at night. Others, such as certain iguanas and other types of lizards, are active during the day. They spend most of their time out of the sun, venturing from the shade of one plant only to scurry to the shade of another. Some animals can survive with very little water. The kangaroo rat is one animal that does not need water to drink. It gets its water from the seeds and leaves it eats.

Chaparral

Scattered along certain coastal areas is the chaparral biome. The Mediterranean coast, the coast of southern California, the coast of central Chile, the southern tip of Africa, and the southern coast of Australia all are covered by chaparral. Like the desert, the chaparral gets little rainfall. Some regions average as little as 10 inches (254 millimeters) of rain a year, all of which falls during the winter months. However, warm, moist air from the oceans helps balance the chaparral environment and prevents conditions from being as severe as those in the desert.

The main plants of the chaparral are tough evergreen shrubs with small leathery leaves. Animals adapted to a dry climate, including lizards, rodents, rabbits, hawks, and owls, inhabit the chaparral. Deer and songbirds migrate to the chaparral during the wet winters, when food is more plentiful.

The scattered evergreen shrubs of the chaparral, which are the plants found most often in this dry coastal biome, help prevent soil erosion.

During the hot, rainless summers, brush-fires often rage across the chaparral. However, chaparral plants are well adapted to what would be a disaster in other places. Many species produce fire-resistant seeds. Others send shoots from the base of charred stumps. It takes as little as ten years for a burned area of chaparral to recover completely.

Deciduous Forests

Spanning eastern North America, central Europe, eastern China, and the southeast coast of Australia, deciduous forests grace the land. Such forests are made up of trees that grow and shed their leaves in a distinct seasonal pattern. In spring the trees bud, in summer they grow, in autumn they lose their leaves, and in winter they stand dormant. Ample rain falls throughout the year, averaging about 40 inches (1,016 millimeters) annually. In this constantly changing environment, many different types of plants and animals flourish.

Deciduous forests, such as the maple-beech forests of North America, tend to have rich soil that supports numerous types of plants. Shrubs grow in the shade of the leafy maple and birch trees. Ferns, flowers, and mosses carpet the floor of the deciduous forest. Mushrooms and other fungi grow on rotting leaves and logs.

Animal life, too, is quite abundant in these woods. Earthworms and insects tunnel through the dark, moist soil. Songbirds flit among the tree branches and on the ground. Amphibians, such as newts and salamanders, scurry through the thick cover of fallen leaves. Deer browse and rodents burrow. Predators, such as foxes, weasels, and bobcats, stalk their prey. Such activity, especially during the summer months, makes deciduous forests inviting places in which to study wildlife.

In the winter, when the trees have shed their leaves and the woods stand under a blanket of snow, life in the forest slows down. Many living things adapt to the cold by becoming dormant. Some mammals hibernate, burrowing in dens for a long

Snowy owl

Pronghorn antelope

Black bear

American elk

Raccoon

Rufus hummingbird

Bell's vireo

Mountain Biomes

A mountain can create as many as four different communities similar to those found in major biomes around the world. As the climate changes with the altitude, so does the community.

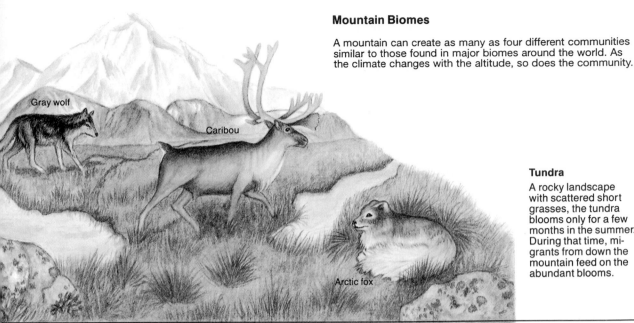

Tundra

A rocky landscape with scattered short grasses, the tundra blooms only for a few months in the summer. During that time, migrants from down the mountain feed on the abundant blooms.

Grasslands

The coniferous forest meets the grassland at the tree line. In summer, many animals migrate above the tree line. In winter, however, the harsh weather drives most animals down from the grasslands to the forests below.

Coniferous Forests

The colder, drier coniferous forest lies upslope from the deciduous forest. Many animals shelter in the coniferous forest during the winter months. They move up to the grasslands during the summer.

Deciduous Forests

The deciduous forest carpets the foothills of the mountain. The forest provides ample food for many types of animals, including hummingbirds, vireos, deer, raccoons, and squirrels.

period of inactivity. Others, including three quarters of the birds, migrate, spending the winter in warmer climates. A few, including sparrows, raccoons, and rabbits, stay through the winter, searching out food as best they can.

Coniferous Forests

Coniferous forests are forests that are largely made up of cone-bearing trees. There are two distinct types of coniferous forest biomes: the temperate coniferous forest and the northern coniferous, or boreal, forest.

The temperate coniferous forest is found in moist, coastal environments, including the northern Pacific coast of North America and the eastern coast of Australia. These forests contain the largest trees in the world—the giant sequoia trees of California, which are also called redwoods, and the towering eucalyptus trees of Australia. The boreal forests are much more extensive than the temperate coniferous forests. They stretch across the northern reaches of North America, Europe, and Asia. In these regions, winters are long and cold. The short, cool summers allow only a brief growing season.

Pine, spruce, hemlock, and fir trees are the most common trees in the boreal forests. All have needle-like leaves that help prevent water loss in the cold, dry winter air. The soil in

coniferous forests tends to be acidic, and few types of plants can grow in it. Blueberry shrubs and heather plants, however, thrive in the acidic soil.

Many different types of animals live in the boreal forests, especially in the warmer summer months. Moose, elk, and deer browse on tree leaves. Migratory birds eat the plentiful insects, which hatch in the late spring and summer. Porcupines gnaw on pine bark. Snowshoe hares, whose coats change so that they blend in with both summer's fallen leaves and winter's blanket of snow, dart from under cover. Wolverines and bears stalk their prey.

Tundra

North of the boreal forest lies the tundra. Under this treeless region is a layer of frozen ground more than 1,000 feet (305 meters) thick, called permafrost. The soil on top of the permafrost thaws for only eight weeks during the short Arctic summer. The small flowering plants and dwarf trees of the tundra have to grow, bloom, and set seed quickly to survive. The outburst of growth in the tundra during the summer creates a colorful carpet of low-lying flowers that dazzles the eye. Adding to the colorful display are the numerous types of lichens, which are really a combination of algae and fungi living and growing together, that cover the rocky landscape.

Not many animals spend the long winter months in the tundra. Some small rodents, such as lemmings, have adapted to the harsh winter environment. Arctic foxes, wolves, and polar bears also stay feeding on whatever they can find during the quiet winter months.

When summer comes, the tundra once again teems with life. Herds of caribou and also reindeer graze on the tundra's quick-growing grasses. Flocks of migrating birds make the tundra their destination. Many birds feed on the numerous insects that hatch in the ponds and puddles of the tundra's soggy ground. As summer fades away, the caribou and many other mammals travel to the forests and the birds fly south. The tundra again becomes a snowy, silent world.

Tropical Rain Forests

Tropical rain forests are damp, humid places where lush, leafy plants abound. In most tropical rain forests, annual rainfall averages between 80 and 200 inches (2,032 and

During the summer months, a wide variety of animals—elk, moose, birds, rabbits, and insects—populate the coniferous forest, feeding on tree leaves and grasses.

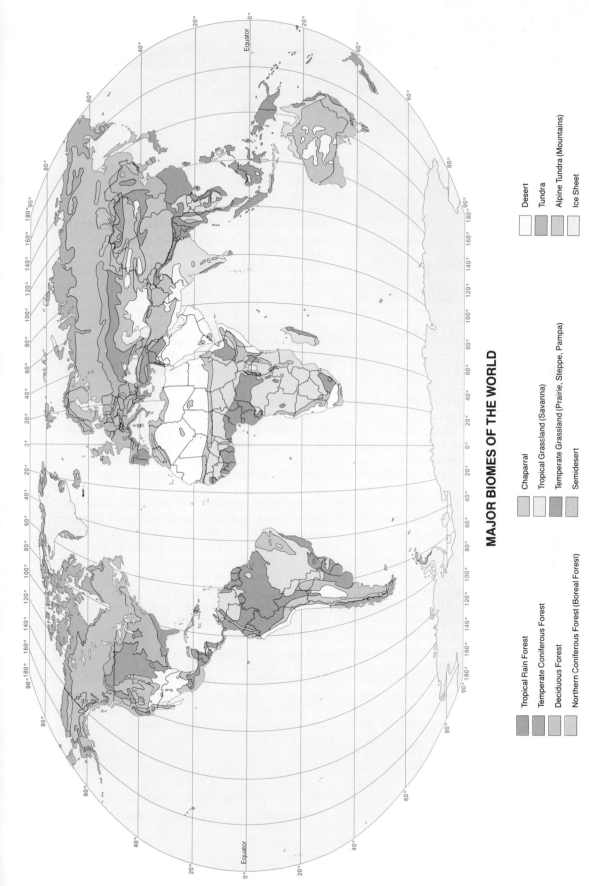

MAJOR BIOMES OF THE WORLD

Tropical Rain Forest

Temperate Coniferous Forest

Deciduous Forest

Northern Coniferous Forest (Boreal Forest)

Chaparral

Tropical Grassland (Savanna)

Temperate Grassland (Prairie, Steppe, Pampa)

Semidesert

Desert

Tundra

Alpine Tundra (Mountains)

Ice Sheet

A biome includes a large geographic area that has characteristic plants and animals. The major biomes of the world are shown on the map above. Each biome has a certain type of climate and soil to which plants and animals of the region have adapted.

The continued destruction of the rain forest may lead to such dramatic climate changes that life in all of the other biomes around the world will be threatened.

5,080 millimeters). The rain falls evenly year-round. Temperatures hardly vary, hovering just below 80°F (27°C) day and night. This steady environment has the greatest variety of plant and animal species of all the biomes.

The leafy branches of tall trees, 75 to 100 feet (23 to 30 meters) in height, spread out to form a canopy that shades and shelters the tropical rain forest. Beneath the canopy, lower trees form leafy umbrellas 40 to 60 feet (12 to 18 meters) tall. A few smaller trees grow 20 to 30 feet (6 to 9 meters) above a shrub layer that is at most 10 feet (3 meters) tall. The floor of the rain forest receives so little light that only plants able to grow in almost total shade can live there. Thick jungle growth occurs only along river edges or other places where light easily penetrates to the ground.

The most lively part of the tropical rain forest is the canopy and upper layers of trees. Colorful flowers use the higher tree branches as platforms to reach the sun. These plants, called epiphytes, send no roots into the soil. They get their nutrients from the small amounts of dirt and dust that collect in the forks of tree branches. They gather moisture from the misty air. Some epiphytes, called bromeliads, have overlapping leaves that form a cup at their base. The bromeliad cup can hold several quarts of water to nourish the plant. These miniature ponds are the breeding grounds for snails, insects, and tiny frogs.

Larger animals, including lizards, birds, monkeys, and leopards, inhabit the rain forest. Although a few rain forest animals search for roots and seeds on the ground, most dwell solely in the trees.

▶ THE CHANGING BIOMES

These descriptions of biomes apply to regions that have not been disturbed by human activity. But in many places throughout the world, nature's biomes have been altered. Forests are cut down for farms. Domestic animals are set loose on grasslands, crowding out the animals that naturally live there. Desert land is irrigated to grow crops. Oil rigs in the Arctic tundra destroy large patches of the slow-growing plants.

The disruption of the biomes can cause tremendous problems for people living in the regions. In the dry grasslands of the Sahel, in western Africa, domestic goats and sheep have overgrazed the land. The thin layer of topsoil has blown away and the Sahel is becoming a desert. This process, called desertification, threatens other parts of the world.

In other places, disturbing the biomes may cause serious problems in the future. People in Central America, South America, and Southeast Asia have been burning down the tropical rain forests to make farmland and cutting down the trees for lumber. Each year millions of acres of rain forest are destroyed. The loss of these lush lands may seriously disrupt the global climate. Plants need carbon dioxide to grow and they take this gas from the air. Without the rain forests, the amount of carbon dioxide in the air will increase tremendously. This gas holds heat close to the earth, warming the atmosphere and the earth's surface. This warming is called the **greenhouse effect**. With the destruction of the tropical rain forests, the greenhouse effect could cause our planet to heat up at an unhealthy rate.

Environmental groups and government agencies around the world are working to protect the world's biomes. In this way, the earth's precious natural resources can be preserved for future life.

ELIZABETH KAPLAN
Author, *Biology Bulletin Monthly*

See also DESERTS; ECOLOGY; FORESTS AND FORESTRY; GRASSES; PRAIRIES; RAIN FOREST; TUNDRA.

BIOSPHERE. See LIFE (Living Things and Their Environments).

BIOTECHNOLOGY

Biotechnology is the application of biological knowledge for practical purposes, most often in agriculture and medicine. The area of biotechnology that is advancing most rapidly is genetic engineering.

▶ **GENETIC ENGINEERING**

Genetic engineering is the manipulation of DNA to produce a desired trait in an organism. A simple form of genetic engineering, selective breeding, has been used for thousands of years to produce crops and farm animals that better suit human needs. In selective breeding, farmers choose plants or animals that have the most desirable traits and breed them together to produce offspring with the same traits. For example, teosinte is thought to be the early ancestor of corn. It is a prickly plant that has tiny cobs and miniature husked kernels. Over 8,000 years of selective breeding, Native Americans turned teosinte into an appealing food plant. The breeding brought together numerous mutations (changes) in the plant that favored larger and more abundant kernels, thus producing corn.

Selective breeding is not an exact science. Although some desirable genes are gained in the offspring, others are lost. In contrast, in modern genetic engineering the transfer of genetic information is controlled; therefore, the results are more predictable and exact.

Using genetic engineering, scientists can create organisms with new characteristics in a single generation by adding the desired genes. The genes might increase the leanness of livestock, slow the speed of ripening so that fruit does not rot, prevent berries from freezing, repel bugs that would otherwise destroy a crop, or provide resistance to an herbicide so that the plant survives while weeds are killed. Genetic engineering is unique in that the added gene can come from any other plant or animal. For example, a gene that prevents potatoes from freezing comes from an arctic fish (the sea flounder).

Genetic engineering techniques are also used in medicine for the production of protein drugs. Examples of protein drugs include insulin (for diabetes), growth hormone (for dwarfism), and erythropoietin (for increasing the production of red blood cells in patients with kidney failure). To make a protein drug, biologists first identify a gene that encodes (has the instructions for making) a useful protein. Then they use gene splicing methods to create bacteria that make large quantities of that protein, which can then be purified and used therapeutically.

Genetic engineering is also used to produce some vaccines. A vaccine works by pre-exposing the body to a disease-causing organism, inducing the body to produce antibodies. When the real pathogen infects the body, the antibodies quickly identify the invader and help the body kill it off. Older vaccines are made from weakened or killed forms of a pathogen and can be difficult to manufacture. With genetic engineering, harmless bacteria are used to produce a protein that is normally made by the disease-causing virus or bacteria. When injected into the body, this protein promotes an immune response the same way a traditional vaccine would but is easier and cheaper to produce. (Also see VACCINATION AND IMMUNIZATION.)

Other uses of genetic engineering are more unusual. Scientists have created and grown cells in the laboratory that have successfully

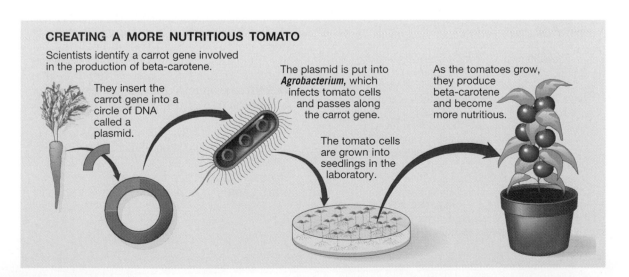

CREATING A MORE NUTRITIOUS TOMATO

Scientists identify a carrot gene involved in the production of beta-carotene.

They insert the carrot gene into a circle of DNA called a plasmid.

The plasmid is put into *Agrobacterium,* which infects tomato cells and passes along the carrot gene.

The tomato cells are grown into seedlings in the laboratory.

As the tomatoes grow, they produce beta-carotene and become more nutritious.

"turned on" a gene normally found in spiders. The gene encodes a silk protein that in nature contributes much of the strength to spider webs. The company behind this research hopes to use the high-strength silk to make bulletproof vests that are cheaper, stronger, and lighter than those now in use.

▶ **THE ENVIRONMENT**

Biotechnology applications may reduce environmental risk and damage. Several companies are trying to use bacteria to make biodegradable plastics that could decrease our reliance on petroleum products. And the insect-resistant crops mentioned above could reduce the use of toxic pesticides. Finally, ethanol and methane produced by yeast or bacteria might one day be major sources of renewable energy.

▶ **RISKS AND REGULATIONS**

Despite the many new products, biotechnology is not perfect. New products come with risks, particularly when the products are living organisms that can react to an added gene in an unexpected way. For example, pigs with an added growth hormone gene have developed problems with their joints. Other potentially harmful effects are less direct. The use of a bacterial toxin gene in many crops may lead to toxin-resistant insects, making this valuable organic insecticide useless. And some people worry that altered crops will become the only species cultivated in a given area. This lack of biodiversity raises the risk that a single toxin-resistant pest could wipe out the entire crop.

WONDER QUESTION

What is golden rice?

The goal of the golden rice project was to create a new version of rice that makes beta-carotene, a source of vitamin A. (Beta-carotene is yellow, so rice that contains beta-carotene is golden in color.) The diet of people in poorer countries often lacks sufficient vitamin A. By creating rice that contains beta-carotene, the sponsors of the golden rice project hope to prevent some of the 1 to 2 million deaths and approximately 500,000 cases of irreversible blindness that are caused by vitamin A deficiency every year. Golden rice was produced by adding three genes to the rice genome—two from daffodil flowers and one from bacteria.

To reduce many of the safety concerns, genetically modified plants and protein drugs must be tested extensively before they are released and marketed. Even so, some companies that sell genetically modified crops fear that the public will react negatively to any food made from a genetically modified organism (GMO). Therefore, they are reluctant to label such foods. In turn, the lack of labeling has allowed GMO's to enter silently into the diets of most people in the developed world through such common products as corn chips and cooking oil. Regulatory agencies in many nations are generating labeling guidelines for GMO foods.

Another controversial area in biotechnology is cloning. It has been used to make an exact copy of a particularly valuable animal, such as one that has a very high milk yield. This kind of cloning is relatively uncontroversial. But there is concern over human applications of cloning. For now, cloning a human is unlikely. But human embryos have been cloned for stem cell research. Stem cells are valuable because they can develop into any other type of cell in the body. They could be used to grow replacement tissues or even new organs. However, some people object to any form of human cloning. Advances in cloning are forcing society to decide whether any kind of human cloning is acceptable.

▶ **THE FUTURE OF BIOTECHNOLOGY**

Current research emphasizes the technology part of biotechnology. In bioengineering, artificial limbs and organs have been created. In tissue engineering, artificial tissues have been grown from living cells. They may be used to replace failing natural tissues. Identification devices have been developed that recognize a fingerprint or the iris of the eye. Findings about the nervous system have led to the development of an implant that restores partial hearing to some deaf and extremely hard of hearing people. The implants translate sounds into electrical impulses that directly turn on nerve cells in the ear. Further integration of electronics and the body seems likely.

WILLIAM WELLS
News editor, Rockefeller University Press
See also GENETICS.

BIOTERRORISM. See TERRORISM.

BIRD, LARRY. See BASKETBALL (Great Players).

Each day, no matter what kind of environment you are in, you will see some kind of bird. It may be a pair of courting swans (*left*), a proud sparrow hawk with its prey (*below left*), or some helpful oxpeckers plucking parasites off a black rhinoceros (*below*).

BIRDS

Throughout the ages, birds have been a source of wonder to all who have observed their soaring flight or listened to their sweet song. As a group, birds are unique—they are the only animals covered with feathers. This evolutionary development separates birds from all other animals.

Birds can travel faster than any other animal —the fastest bird can fly more than 100 miles (161 kilometers) per hour! Although all birds have feathers and wings, not every bird can fly. Some birds walk, run, or swim instead of flying.

Birds are **vertebrates** (animals with a backbone), as are fish, amphibians, reptiles, and mammals. Like many vertebrates, birds lay eggs from which their young hatch. They are warm-blooded animals; that is, their body temperature always remains about the same no matter what the temperature of their surroundings. They differ from other vertebrates in that they are toothless and have a hard beak, or bill, that they use to get and eat food.

The more than 9,000 kinds, or species, of birds belong to the class of animals called Aves. Because of their superb flying skills, birds have been able to reach virtually every area of the world: forests, mountains, oceans, and deserts. Birds have adapted to a great variety of habitats, living in places too harsh for people or any other animal. The large snowy owl is able to survive in the Arctic, where temperatures dip below $-50°F$ ($-46°C$) during the long winter. Its thick feather coat even covers its bill and feet. Birds are able to live in the middle of the world's oceans. The albatross family lives most of its life on the wing, soaring over the open ocean searching for food. It only comes to shore to build a nest and to breed.

▶BIRDS AND PEOPLE

Birds as Food. Humans have hunted birds since prehistoric times. Along with hunting birds, early humans also gathered bird eggs and nestlings (babies).

People eventually learned to tame and raise birds, and over time this has led to the domes-

Probably the greatest use of feathers was by native Hawaiians. Helmets, staffs, and huge feather cloaks (*above left*) were made for royal chiefs from the feathers of native honeycreepers. Since ancient times, people have engaged in the sport of hunting with trained birds of prey, such as the eagle (*above right*). Macaws (*left*) and other brightly colored tropical birds are among the most prized bird pets.

tication of several species: ducks, chickens, turkeys, and pigeons. Domestic ducks, a form of the mallard, appeared in Egypt around 1500 B.C. and spread quickly to Europe. Greylag geese were also domesticated at about the same time. Even earlier, people in Southeast Asia had tamed the red junglefowl, a bird recognized today as a chicken. Native Americans in Mexico and Central America successfully domesticated the wild turkey. Pigeons were domesticated in Europe and were used as food and to carry messages since Roman times. Birds, both wild and domestic, continue to be an important source of food today.

Products from Birds. The people of many societies used, and some still use, the feathers and skins of wild birds. Eagle feathers were exchanged much like money in some native North American tribes. The feather cloak of the Hawaiian king Kamehameha I took at least a hundred years to make and used about

450,000 feathers from more than 80,000 birds! It is not surprising that the king collected taxes from his subjects in honeycreeper feathers. The Inuit people of the Arctic use waterfowl feathers for pillows and clothing. The skins, especially eider skins, are used to make warm and waterproof blankets. On the other side of the world, the aborigines of Australia still wear feathers of cockatoos and emus as decoration.

Birds in Religion, Art, and Literature. Birds are powerful symbols used to represent everything from peace (the dove carrying an olive branch) to wisdom (the wise owl) to politics (the bald eagle that is the national symbol of the United States).

From the earliest times, birds have played almost as great a role in people's religion and art as in their diet. The religious paintings of early humans on the walls of Lascaux Cave near Montignac, France, include birds among the animals depicted. Ancient Egyptians used birds in their art. Painting and sculptures of birds adorn buildings and tombs of royalty.

Birds are also found in early literature. The Bible mentions almost forty species of birds—most often doves—in ways that show a knowledge of their habits and an appreciation of their grace and beauty. The religion of the Egyptians has many gods, including real and imaginary birds. They believed in the legendary phoenix, a bird that serves as a symbol of immortality. The ibis was so sacred that they were often mummified and buried with royalty in their family tombs.

Birds as Pets. Birds are also popular pets. Except for dogs and cats, more people have pet birds than any other animal. People share their homes with an amazing variety of birds, including finches, waxbills, and parrots.

The great horned owl fans its feathers in a defensive threat display. Along with their use as a defense measure, feathers keep birds warm and help them fly.

▶ WHAT MAKES A BIRD A BIRD?

All animals share certain characteristics, such as having the ability to move about and needing food to live. Some animals even share the same methods for performing these tasks and securing those substances that are necessary for life. However, birds are unique. There is no other animal with the same combination of features.

Feathers

Other animals have wings and can fly, but no other creature is covered with feathers. Feathers, which are formed in special skin cells from a protein called keratin, perform many different jobs. Body, or contour, feathers smooth and streamline the bird's body so it can move easily through the air or water. Contour feathers also protect the bird's skin from wind and, sometimes, from water. Beneath the contour feathers are tiny down feathers. Down acts as an insulator to help the bird

maintain its body temperature even in temperatures below zero. In addition to contour and down feathers are filoplume feathers, which provide information on the position of movable feathers, and bristles that form eyelashes, which provide sensory information in much the same manner as a cat's whiskers.

Molting. Molting is a process that involves shedding thousands of feathers, and then growing new ones. Most birds molt twice each year: before the spring migration and after nesting. Replacing all of a bird's feathers is a

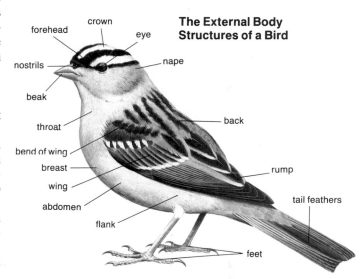

The External Body Structures of a Bird

forehead
crown
eye
nostrils
nape
beak
throat
back
bend of wing
breast
wing
rump
abdomen
flank
tail feathers
feet

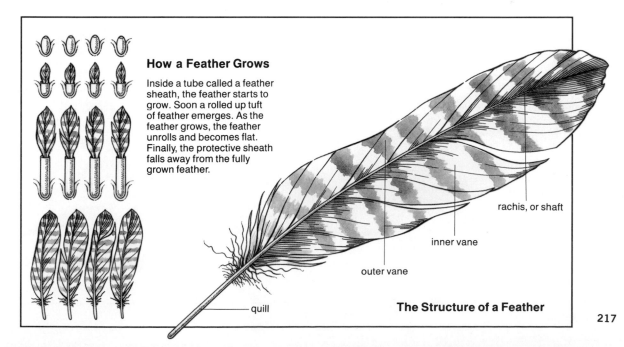

How a Feather Grows

Inside a tube called a feather sheath, the feather starts to grow. Soon a rolled up tuft of feather emerges. As the feather grows, the feather unrolls and becomes flat. Finally, the protective sheath falls away from the fully grown feather.

rachis, or shaft

inner vane

outer vane

quill

The Structure of a Feather

217

major undertaking—it takes a lot of energy to molt. Feathers are so important to birds that many birds do not nest a second time; instead, they save their energy for the molting process.

The spring molt replaces flight feathers that will be needed to make the long journey north to the breeding grounds. The males of many species molt their drab winter plumage and replace it with spectacular breeding colors—bold reds, yellows, oranges, and blues—that will help attract a mate.

After nesting, most species molt for the second time. The bright colors needed to attract a mate and defend a territory are now dangerous. Standing out makes it difficult to hide from and escape from predators. Ducks and geese even lose their ability to fly because they molt all of their flight feathers at once. During this period of flightlessness, and before they grow a new camouflage plumage, they hide in remote marshes.

Flight

The dominant forces that affect a bird's flight are lift and propulsion. The shape of a bird's wings helps create lift: Air moves more quickly over the curved top of the wing than it does under the flattened bottom of the wing. This difference in speed creates lower air pressure over the wing than under the wing. Because air moves from a high-pressure area to a low-pressure area, the higher pressure bottom air moves toward the lower pressure top air, lifting the wing upward. A bird can increase

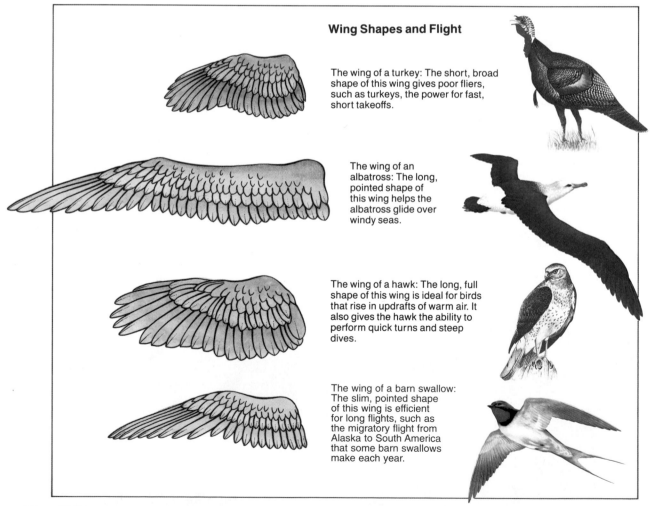

Wing Shapes and Flight

The wing of a turkey: The short, broad shape of this wing gives poor fliers, such as turkeys, the power for fast, short takeoffs.

The wing of an albatross: The long, pointed shape of this wing helps the albatross glide over windy seas.

The wing of a hawk: The long, full shape of this wing is ideal for birds that rise in updrafts of warm air. It also gives the hawk the ability to perform quick turns and steep dives.

The wing of a barn swallow: The slim, pointed shape of this wing is efficient for long flights, such as the migratory flight from Alaska to South America that some barn swallows make each year.

During the flight of the mallard duck, the bird is thrust forward by the flapping wing strokes.

or decrease the lifting force to travel up or down by tilting the forward edge of its wing upward or downward.

Propulsion, which is a forward-moving force, is created by long wing feathers that close together and overlap so air cannot pass through. In much the same manner as a boat paddle pushes against water, the closed structure of the wing pushes down against air, propelling the bird forward. On the return stroke, the wing feathers separate and allow air to pass between them.

Wing feathers are not the only feathers that aid flight. The long, strong tail feathers are used much as the tail fin of an airplane to steer while the bird is flying. The tail feathers also act as a brake when landing.

There are three basic types of flight: flapping, gliding, and soaring. Most birds use flapping flight, that is, after they take off, they continue to fly by flapping their wings. When gliding, birds keep their wings extended and coast downward. During soaring flight, birds use the energy of rising columns of warm air, called thermals, to move without having to flap their wings. With wings extended, a soaring bird circles lazily as the thermal current lifts it higher and higher. Other air movements, such as prevailing winds, are also used by birds to soar.

Walking and Running

When most people think of how birds get from place to place, they think of flight. However, there also are birds that walk, run, hop, or swim. Some birds, such as the ostrich, emu, and rhea, have evolved into flightless, swift-running birds. Typically, birds that nest and feed on the ground walk and run by moving one foot forward at a time. Most birds that nest in trees hop on both feet when they are on the ground. Some birds run and hop.

The snow goose (*above left*) uses its feathered wings for flight. Rapidly beating wings power this pair of grebes (*above*) across the water's surface during a courtship dance. The male peacock (*left*) fans its lush plumage to attract females.

A bird's legs and feet match their habits and environment. Legs serve as good shock absorbers and can launch the bird from the ground during takeoff. There is a great variety in the length of their legs. The swift-running birds have very long legs. Other birds, such as water-loving penguins, have very short legs that make walking on land difficult. Most birds have four toes—three pointing forward and one pointing backward. Some climbing birds, such as woodpeckers, have two toes pointing backward that help them to cling to tree trunks. The osprey has an outer toe that can point either forward or backward. In swifts, all the toes face forward.

Toes for grasping perches, climbing, capturing prey, and carrying and manipulating food are tipped with sharply curved and pointed nails. Strong toes for running and scratching have thick blunt nails. Toes for swimming and paddling are sometimes webbed or they may have fleshy lobes attached to them. South American jacanas appear to walk on water. Their extremely long toes spread out the bird's weight so that the bird can be supported by the underwater weeds growing near the water's surface.

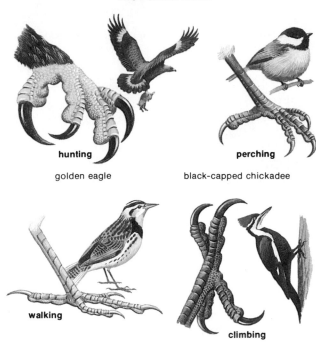

hunting

golden eagle

perching

black-capped chickadee

walking

eastern meadowlark

climbing

pileated woodpecker

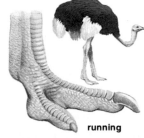

swimming, three webbed toes

common goldeneye

running

ostrich

The long-legged ostrich (*left*) can reach speeds of 40 miles (64 kilometers) per hour. The blue-footed booby performs a tapping dance during courtship (*below*). On its stilt-like legs, the flamingo (*below right*) wades into deep waters to feed.

Food and Feeding

Birds use their bills, flexible necks, feet, and ability to fly in order to find, secure, and eat their food. They feed on a wide variety of food—from fruit and seeds to dead animals.

A bird's bill is made up of upper and lower halves, called mandibles. The mandibles are the visible part of the bill and are made of layers of keratin, the same protein found in feathers. In most birds, the bill is black.

Bills come in a variety of shapes and sizes. Birds of prey have powerful, hooked bills to tear apart their victims. Wading birds, such as the heron, have long, sharp, daggerlike bills that they use to spear fish and frogs. Shorebirds have long, slender bills to probe mud for food. Seed-eaters have strong wedge-shaped bills to crack open the hard shells of seeds. The sawlike edges on the bill of a fish-eater, such as the merganser, is ideal for grasping and holding slippery prey.

Along with food, birds need water. Some birds, such as fruit- and insect-eaters, may get the water they need from the food they eat. Others find a water source and scoop water up in their bills. Still others have devised special ways to get water. The sand grouse lives in some of the driest deserts on earth. They travel long distances to a water source, soak the special feathers on their bellies, and carry water back to the nest. The young grouse suck on the feathers to get the water.

The Bills of Birds

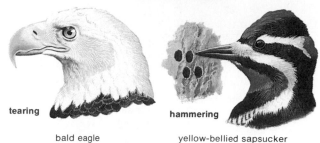

tearing
bald eagle

hammering
yellow-bellied sapsucker

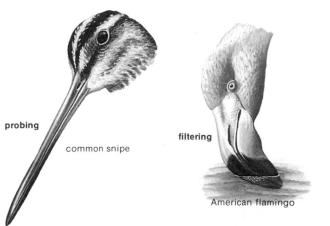

spearing
black-crowned night heron

cracking
common redpoll

probing
common snipe

filtering
American flamingo

Many birds, such as the blue jay (*left*), feed on seeds and nuts; others, such as the western gull (*below left*), eat small water animals and insects; still others, such as the bald eagle (*below*), prey on larger animals—fish, frogs, and even other birds.

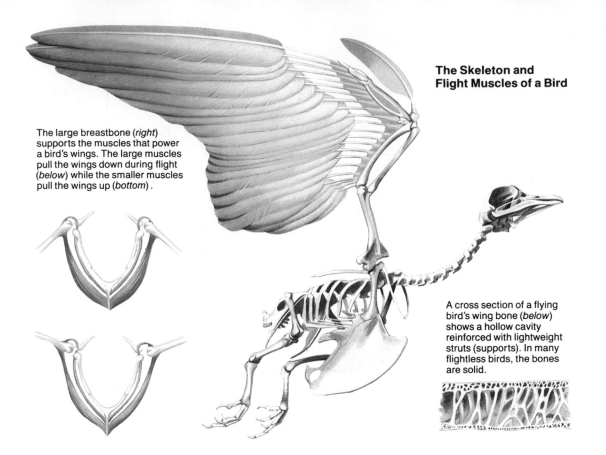

The Skeleton and Flight Muscles of a Bird

The large breastbone (*right*) supports the muscles that power a bird's wings. The large muscles pull the wings down during flight (*below*) while the smaller muscles pull the wings up (*bottom*).

A cross section of a flying bird's wing bone (*below*) shows a hollow cavity reinforced with lightweight struts (supports). In many flightless birds, the bones are solid.

▶ THE BODY SYSTEMS OF BIRDS

There are many physical features that are shared by birds and mammals. For instance, both groups of animals have backbones, are warm-blooded, and have four limbs. However, the body systems of birds are adapted to flight.

Bones and Muscles

Over time, the skeleton of the bird has developed into an airy, lightweight, yet strong, frame. Since the earliest birds, many body parts, such as teeth, have disappeared—lightening the frame. Other parts, such as the vertebrae of the back, have become fused (joined) —giving the frame more strength.

While a bird's many neck vertebrae are shaped so that the neck is extremely flexible, most of the rest of the skeleton has become stiffened. Birds have a large breastbone, or sternum, that protects the internal organs and provides strong support for the attached muscles that power flight. The heaviest, strongest bone is the coracoid. Together with the ribs, it holds the sternum and the rigid backbone apart when the flight muscles contract.

The largest muscles in a bird are the pectoral (breast) muscles. These muscles may account for as much as one fifth of a bird's entire weight. They are attached to the long bone of the wing. When they contract during flight, the wings are pulled down. Smaller muscles, called the supracoracoideus, contract during flight and the wings are pulled up.

Digestive System

Since birds have no teeth, the digestive system must grind up food so that the energy stored in it can be used. A hollow digestive tube extends from the mouth through the entire length of the body to an external opening called the cloaca. The tube is divided into the throat (pharynx), esophagus, stomach, small intestine, and large intestine.

Food passes from the mouth through the pharynx into the esophagus. Some birds, such as pigeons, doves, and hawks, have a portion of their esophagus enlarged to form a storage pouch called a crop. The crop allows birds to feed quickly and digest its meal later in safety.

Nearly all birds have a stomach made up of two parts. The first part of the stomach, called the proventriculus, secretes strong digestive juices, which in some birds are strong enough to digest bones! The second part of the stomach, called the gizzard, has strong muscular walls that act like teeth to grind and pulverize foods. In addition to the muscular walls, birds often swallow small pebbles and grit that get trapped in the gizzard and aid in the grinding process.

From the stomach, food passes into the small intestine where the nutritious end products of digestion are absorbed into the bloodstream. The remaining indigestible matter travels into the large intestine where it is stored until it is eliminated from the body through the cloaca.

Metabolic System

A bird's metabolic system guides all the chemical changes that provide energy for vital processes and activities such as new cell growth and maintenance of body temperature. Birds, which have a higher body temperature, a faster heart rate, and a greater need for oxygen than mammals, must eat a great deal of food to get the necessary energy to fuel the body functions. Small birds have a relatively higher metabolic rate, and therefore higher energy needs, than large birds. An ostrich can go several days without food, however, a small hummingbird needs so much energy that it must feed almost constantly during the day.

Birds are endothermal, or warm-blooded. That means they have an internal furnace, fueled by food, that generates heat and allows them to keep their bodies at a constant temperature, even though the temperature of their en-

The tiny hummingbird (*above*) requires between fifty and sixty meals a day to sustain its high metabolic rate. With wings beating at a rate of between fifty and eighty times a second, the hummingbird can hover (*right*) without rest for four hours at a time.

vironment changes. Birds are also able to regulate their body temperature by conserving or losing heat through a variety of ways—feathers help retain heat, while panting helps get rid of heat.

Circulatory System

A bird's circulatory system consists of a four-chambered heart and blood vessels. With each beat, or stroke, of the heart, a large volume of blood is carried throughout the bird's body by vessels called arteries. Blood is then returned to the heart by vessels called veins. Birds are nature's best athletes. With their powerful hearts, they can keep up extraordinary levels of physical exertion for long periods. A ruby-throated hummingbird's heart is about 3 percent of its total body weight, but it is strong enough to supply fuel and oxygen to the flight muscles for a nonstop flight across the Gulf of Mexico.

The high metabolism of birds requires rapid circulation of the blood because waste products build up quickly in the cells and must be removed before they reach a toxic level. Typically, small birds have a higher metabolism than large birds and therefore have a faster heart rate.

The Internal Body Structures of a Bird

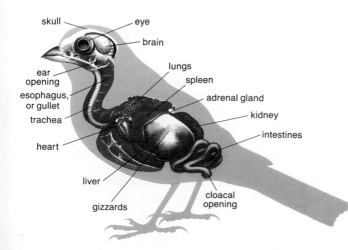

skull
eye
brain
lungs
spleen
ear opening
esophagus, or gullet
adrenal gland
trachea
kidney
heart
intestines
liver
cloacal opening
gizzards

How Birds See

The owl, whose eyes are on the front of its head, has a wide overlapping field of vision in front and good depth perception.

The falcon, whose eyes are on the sides of its head, has a narrow overlapping field of vision in front.

The woodcock, whose eyes are far back on the sides of its head, has a narrow overlapping field of vision both in front and behind.

Respiratory System

The high metabolism and athletic life-style of birds require a great deal of oxygen. Four organs work together to carry oxygen to the cells: nostrils, trachea, lungs, and air sacs. With each breath, air moves through the nostrils, down the trachea and into the lungs and air sacs. From the lungs, oxygen passes into the bloodstream and then to the body cells. The air that passes into the air sacs cools the internal organs and helps maintain body temperature. Nearly all of the air in the lungs is replaced with each breath. When flying, birds require ten to twenty times more oxygen than at rest. To supply the extra oxygen, birds increase their breathing rates.

Nervous System

The nervous system of a bird consists of the brain, sense organs, and nerves. Nerves carry messages from sense organs, such as the eyes, to the brain. Nerves also carry messages from the brain to the muscles. The term "birdbrain" may need to be forgotten. Researchers have found that although birds lack a cerebral cortex—the brain structure associated with intelligence in mammals—they can still pass messages between higher and lower brain regions. This functionality helps explain how birds are capable of complex behaviors.

As a group, birds have the best vision of all animals. Their large eyes, which sometimes weigh more than their brain, provide keen sight and excellent color perception. Birds that are most active at night, or nocturnal, also have well-developed sight. Range of vision depends on whether the eyes are on the sides of the head or on the front of the head.

Hearing is also well developed in birds, with some night birds having especially acute hearing. Only a few birds, such as the kiwi, have a highly developed sense of smell. The kiwi is nearly blind and relies on its sense of smell to find food.

Reproductive System

The reproductive system includes the sex organs and a series of tubes, or ducts, which act as passages for the sex cells produced within the organs. The male sex organs, called the testes, produce sperm; the female sex organs, called the ovaries, produce eggs. When birds mate, sperm from the testes pass from the male to the female. The sperm fertilize the eggs. After an egg is fertilized, it begins to travel down a narrow tube called the oviduct toward the external opening, or cloaca. On the way down the oviduct, it first receives a coating of the protein called albumen (the egg white). Further down the oviduct, the albumen is surrounded by a shell composed of calcium. As the egg nears the end of the oviduct and before it is laid, it also may receive various colored pigments.

▶ THE BEHAVIOR PATTERNS OF BIRDS

Birds have both learned behaviors and instinctive behaviors. Some instinctive behaviors help birds recognize enemies. Great kiskadees display an instinctive behavior related to coral snakes, which eat young birds. Even though they have never seen a snake, hand-raised great kiskadees are frightened by sticks that have been painted to look like coral snakes. Newly hatched herring gulls know by instinct to peck at the red spot on the bill of their parents in order to be fed. Pecking becomes more accurate as the baby gulls learn to anticipate the position of their parents' bills when they return with food.

Bird-watching

Birds are fascinating creatures. You do not have to be an ornithologist to enjoy watching birds. Many amateurs have contributed to the understanding of birds by recording their observations and reporting interesting or significant sightings to their local bird club. Information provided by amateur bird-watchers can then be used to compile information about population changes within a specific area or to document the introduction of a new species into an area.

Some people simply watch birds at a backyard feeder; others hike the forests, fields, and marshes to get a close look at birds. Whichever way you decide to bird-watch, recording what you observe is fun as well as helpful. Information that will help you recall a bird sighting includes the date, time of day, location, weather conditions, and persons with you (if any). Some observations to keep track of are the species, number of birds, and behaviors of the birds you see. Quick sketches of plumage or flight patterns can also be made. Along with a notebook and pencils, supplies such as field guides, binoculars, camera, and tape recorder (for recording bird calls) are all useful.

Birds also learn very well. Young birds learn to recognize predators by observing the behavior of other birds. Many species of birds make loud, scolding calls when they discover predators such as owls, cats, or snakes. Flocks of birds attack and usually drive away the predator—a behavior called mobbing. Inexperienced birds quickly learn to associate danger with mobbing. Some birds learn how to build better nests as they get older and more experienced.

Living in a Community

Flocks. Birds that stay all winter in northern regions have little time to do anything but find food, water, and shelter. Some species form large social groups called flocks. Among these species, some form flocks in the winter, some remain in flocks year-round, and others never form flocks at all. Living in a flock has two big advantages: It is easier for the many eyes of the group to find food and to spot predators. A bird in a flock is much less likely to be killed by a hawk than a lone bird singled out for attack. Usually all the birds in a flock do the same thing at the same time—they sleep together, feed together, and sometimes even breed together.

Dominance. Often winter birds living in small flocks establish a system of dominance, which is sometimes called a **pecking order**. Pecking order is organized so that each bird pecks another bird lower in standing within the group and submits to pecking by birds of higher rank.

In flocks with dominance systems, the highest ranking bird gets first choice of food, water, even mates, while others wait their turn. Dominance helps all the birds in the flock to survive by reducing competition. Being lowest bird in the pecking order is better than fighting over every scrap of food with all the members of the flock.

Defense. Birds use a variety of methods to protect themselves and their offspring against

Birds have different bathing behaviors that keep their feathers free of parasites and dirt. A swan (*above left*) thrashes its wings in water, while the helmeted guinea fowl (*above right*) digs a small pit in the ground and shuffles its feathers in the dirt.

Not all species of birds have the same activity cycle. Great gray owls (*left*) rest during the day and hunt during the night. Egrets (*below*) follow the typical cycle —they feed during the day and rest during the night.

For most birds, defending territory is the focus of the males' day. Threat displays by the sage grouse (*right*) warn intruders that they had better leave the territory. Occasionally, fighting erupts. Brown pelicans (*below right*) use their beaks to peck and grab at the enemy.

enemies. Some birds that are colored or patterned so that they blend with their surroundings can often remain undetected if they stay still. This type of **protective coloration**, or natural camouflage, not only helps a bird avoid enemies, but it also helps a bird get close to prey without being seen.

Other birds may flee or hide. As a last resort and if it cannot escape or hide from danger, a bird will fight using its beak, legs, or wings, depending on its species. Sometimes, a bird will try to distract an intruder from its nest by making a noisy disturbance or pretending to be hurt and, therefore, easy prey. Once the intruder follows the "wounded" bird away from the nest, the "wounded" bird flies off.

Establishing a Territory

In general, male birds migrate north before females. They need to arrive early to stake claim to a territory. A territory is a fixed area that is defended continuously for a period of time. Most birds defend territories during breeding; some defend territories all year long. Both males and females defend territories, but most often it is the male who works hardest to defend the territory. Birds establish, maintain, and defend breeding territories in order to attract mates, find appropriate nest sites, and find enough food to raise hungry nestlings.

Communicating

Bird song may sound beautiful, but birds do not sing to make music; birds sing to attract mates and to tell other males to stay off their territory.

Birds are capable of an enormous variety of vocalizations. Traditionally they are divided into two groups: calls and song. Calls are

short, simple vocalizations such as calls of distress, feeding, flight, flocking, and warning. Songs are long vocal displays with specific repeatable patterns. Normally only males can sing. However, some females, such as northern cardinal females, sing quite well.

Birds can sing more than just one specific song. Birds generally have between 5 and 14 songs, but some species have many more. Northern mockingbirds and wrens are capable of producing hundreds of songs. Besides helping males to defend their territories and attract mates, songs can warn others about potential dangers; can say "Here I am . . . where are you?"; and can tell other birds the species, age, sex, and experience of the singer.

No two birds sing exactly the same song. Subtle differences in the pitch and timing of songs are used to recognize individuals. Birds are able to identify their mates, young, parents, and neighbors. Penguins returning to nesting colonies that may have tens of thousands of birds are able to locate their mates by picking out their unique call from the deafening chorus of the colony.

During courtship, the male sage grouse (*left*) inflates its neck pouches and lets out booming calls to attract females. The male frigate bird (*right*) seeks the attention of a female by inflating his huge red throat pouch and keeping it inflated, sometimes for many hours, until he has lured a female to his side. During courtship, a pair of great blue herons (*below*) collect twigs and sticks and build their nest together.

▶ THE LIFE CYCLE OF BIRDS

A year in the life of a bird is controlled by a series of rhythms and cycles. Every year birds pass through the phases of breeding, molting, and migrating. What is amazing is that birds do these things with astonishing precision. This is because they have an internal biological clock that controls their daily and annual schedules and regulates when they sleep, feed, migrate, breed, and molt.

Mating

In spring, males arrive at the breeding ground before females. After establishing a territory, they defend it against neighboring males and sing to attract a mate. When the females arrive, they may choose a mate in one of several ways. Northern mockingbirds prefer males with a large number of different songs. Red-winged blackbirds select males with the best territories. Regardless of how the choice is made, a strong tie known as a pair bond is formed between the male and female. Canada geese and bald eagles form pair bonds with their mates that last their entire lives. At the other extreme, ruby-throated hummingbirds form a pair bond for only a few minutes. In most birds, the pair bond lasts the entire summer, as the birds build a nest, incubate eggs, and raise fledglings to adulthood.

Most birds are monogamous, which means they only have one mate at a time. Some birds have more than one mate at a time; they are called polygamous. Promiscuity is a form of mating without bonding. The male and female come together briefly to mate and then part. The female builds the nest and cares for the young alone.

Nesting

All birds lay eggs and care for them in one way or another. The place where birds lay their eggs is called a nest. Nests hold and cushion eggs before they hatch. Some birds, such as murres, do not build any type of nest to hold their eggs. They simply lay them on bare cliff ledges overlooking the sea. Other birds build elaborate structures to hold the eggs. Some nests are used year after year.

Birds must choose the safest possible place to nest if the young and the adults are to survive. The nest must provide protection from predators, who like to eat eggs, nestlings, and even adults sitting on the nest. The nest must also protect the eggs from bad weather.

Types of Nests. Although birds build nests in a variety of places, using many different

types of materials, members of the same species generally build similarly styled nests.

The first birds probably built nests that were just a slight depression scratched in the ground or fallen leaves. This type of nest is called a scrape and is still used by many birds today. Shorebirds, terns, nighthawks, and falcons are some of the species that make scrapes. Other birds, like belted kingfishers and petrels, nest in a scrape at the end of long burrows they have dug deep within stream banks or the ground.

When most people picture a bird's nest, they think of a cup-shaped nest. These cup nests are the most common type and can be built almost anywhere. Warblers, American robins, and blackbirds all build cup nests.

Other birds are well equipped to chisel out a home in a dead tree. Woodpeckers, parrots, and hornbills dig nest cavities. Cavity nests are widespread among birds because they provide especially good protection. Male hornbills seal the female into their nest cavity and she does not leave until the chicks have hatched!

Many species build flat platform nests in just about every type of habitat imaginable—from treetops to water environments. Bald eagles build the largest tree nests of any bird. These large platform nests are used year after year and can be more than 9 feet (3 meters) wide! Great blue herons also make large tree nests and place them close together in what are called colonies. Grebes build floating platforms, anchoring them to plants growing in shallow water. The horned coot of South America even builds its own island! Thousands of small stones are piled up over several years, making a custom-designed nesting island that may weigh as much as a ton.

One of the most unusual nests belongs to the dusky

Nests come in many forms. The northern flicker (*above*) has settled into a cavity it has made in a giant cactus. The nest of the Caribbean flamingo (*left*) is a cone of mud about 1½ feet (.5 meter) high. The eggs are laid in a small depression formed at the top of the cone. Nestlings within their snug cup-shaped nest (*below left*) call for food. The cup-shaped nest is the most common type of nest. At one time the mud nests of the cliff swallow (*below*) were only found at cliff sites; today they can be found under the eaves of buildings and under concrete bridges.

scrub fowl of Australia. Males of this species build gigantic mounds of rotting leaves, sticks, and grass that can sometimes measure 36 feet across (11 meters) and more than 16 feet (5 meters) high! The female lays her eggs in the mound, where they are warmed by the heat generated from the rotting vegetation and by the sun. The male dusky scrub fowl carefully checks the temperature of the mound with his bill and adds or removes layers of vegetation as needed.

Eggs and Egg Laying

Once an egg is fertilized, it develops quickly in the female's oviduct and is surrounded with a protective eggshell. As soon as the egg is fully formed, it is laid before the next one has grown very large. Usually females lay an egg each day, or every few days, until the group of eggs, called a clutch, is complete. Most birds wait until all the eggs are laid, then they sit on the eggs to warm them with their bodies. They will warm the eggs in this manner, in the process called incubation, until the eggs hatch. In this way, all the young birds hatch at about the same time.

Other birds, like owls, start incubating as soon as the first egg is laid. The eggs hatch at different times and the young are much different in size.

Eggs vary tremendously in size and color. The flightless ostrich lays a gigantic egg that can weigh up to 4 pounds (1.8 kilograms). It is so big and the shell is so thick that few animals can break it open. On the other hand, the tiny Cuban bee hummingbird's egg is only ¼ inch (.5 centimeter) long and weighs ¹⁄₁₀₀ ounce (.25 gram). More than 5,000 hummingbird eggs would fit inside an ostrich egg!

Often eggs are perfectly colored to blend in with their background. Ground-nesting birds usually have pastel gray, blue, or green eggs that are speckled with shades of brown or black.

Eggs show countless variations, not only in size and color but in shape. The shape of eggs varies from long and elliptical, or oval, to nearly round. Most eggs are shaped like the familiar chicken egg. Streamlined birds, such as swifts and hummingbirds, lay long, elliptical eggs that help females keep their efficient body shape. Murres, which nest on narrow

Bird Eggs

Blue grouse   Mountain plover   American crow   European starling   Golden-fronted woodpecker

Ostrich

American robin   Northern cardinal   Bobolink   Black-chinned hummingbird

The shape, color, and size of egg that a bird lays varies with each species. Some eggs are round, others are oval; some eggs are glossy white, some are black, still others are speckled with color. The ostrich lays an egg that weighs about 3 pounds (1 kilogram), while the hummingbird lays an egg that is only ¹⁄₁₀₀ ounce (0.35 gram).

When temperatures soar, the heron (*left*) partially extends its wings to provide cooling shade for the eggs in its nest. The trumpeter swan (*right*) turns the eggs to make sure they are warmed evenly. Eggs may be turned from once every few minutes to about once an hour. The cowbird lays its eggs in other birds' nests. Here (*below*), a yellow warbler cares for cowbird nestlings.

cliffs, have eggs shaped like toy tops. These eggs roll in a tight circle, which is important if rolling out of the nest means a fall of several hundred feet. Cavity-nesting birds tend to lay round eggs that pile neatly in the bottom of the nest hole. Shorebirds lay four pointed eggs that fit together like pieces of a pie.

Incubation. A few days before a bird lays its first egg, the bird loses some of the feathers on its belly. The blood vessels in the area also enlarge and form what is known as a brood patch. When a bird incubates its eggs, it settles itself down so that its brood patch is in direct contact with the eggs. In general, brood patches develop only in the birds that incubate. If both sexes incubate, both develop brood patches.

Birds that nest in places where the temperatures are above 100°F (38°C) need to keep their eggs cool. Some birds will stand over the eggs, shading them with partially opened wings. Mourning doves nesting in Arizona have been found to use their brood patches to cool their eggs down to body temperature. The birds pant heavily while incubating, to get rid of the extra heat.

The incubation period of an egg is the time from the start of incubation until hatching of the egg. In general, larger eggs need longer incubation periods. The wandering albatross, one of the largest flying birds, needs 75 to 82 days of incubation. Small finches and warblers need only 11 to 12 days.

Some birds neither build nests nor take care of their young. Instead, they lay their eggs in the nests of other species, and rely on them to incubate the eggs and rear the offspring. This

behavior is called brood parasitism. Some birds, such as cuckoos, are always brood parasites, while others, such as redhead ducks, are irregular brood parasites.

Redhead ducks are irregular brood parasites, which means that sometimes they have their own nests and incubate their own eggs, and sometimes they lay eggs in the nests of different duck species. Honeyguides, found in Asia and Africa, are totally parasitic and have lost all courtship and nesting behaviors. Honeyguides usually lay a single egg in the nest of a closely related species. Newly hatched honeyguides, while still blind and featherless, will eliminate the other nestlings that compete with them for food. They use the sharp hook on the tip of their beaks to bite and kill the other nestlings or, one by one, they push the host's young out of the nest.

Hatching of a Chick

When the offspring inside the egg is fully developed, hatching begins. The chick uses the egg tooth on the tip of its beak to peck an opening in the shell. Pushing through the opening it has made, the chick tumbles out of the shell. Depending on the species, hatching may take as little as five hours or as long as four days.

The brown-headed cowbird, which is widespread throughout North America, is also a brood parasite. Cowbird eggs have been found in the nests of more than 150 species. The abundance of cowbird parasitism has been an important factor in the decline of some birds, such as the endangered Kirtland's warbler.

Hatching. Inside the egg, the growing bird develops a short, pointy structure on the tip of the upper beak called an egg tooth. When the incubation period is complete, the fully developed offspring uses its egg tooth to break out of the shell. Small birds, such as warblers, finches, and sparrows, may complete the hatching process in five hours. Larger birds, especially seabirds, may take as long as four days.

Imprinting. Birds exhibit a very special type of learning called imprinting. Imprinting only occurs during a critical period early in life, and once something is learned by imprinting it cannot be changed or forgotten. For instance, the moving object that a duckling follows in the first 24 hours after hatching is accepted as its "mother." Usually the moving object is the adult female duck; however, it has been shown that a duckling will follow and imprint on humans or even a moving box with a ticking alarm clock inside.

Later in life, birds will select mates and other members of their flock based on what has been imprinted. Baby birds raised by people do not imprint correctly and never select an appropriate mate for nesting. Birds also imprint on the type of nest and its location, which is important information when they need to select a good spot to build their nest.

Because these peregrine falcon chicks are being raised by humans, they will not learn how to perform some of the tasks necessary for their survival in the wild.

Care of the Young

Feeding. A nestling bird is an ugly thing. It is all belly and head with two large bulging eyes. Almost immediately, a nestling can lift its wobbly head and open its mouth. The inside of the mouth is usually brightly colored, providing a food target for the parents. On either side of the nestling's mouth are sensitive nerve endings. When touched, the mouth automatically snaps shut. The combination of the nestling's wide-open mouth and constant begging for food is powerful stimuli for the adults. The instinct to feed young is so strong that they will occasionally feed other birds' young.

Some birds are altricial—that is, they are helpless when they are born. They are born featherless and blind. At first, altricial nestlings cannot maintain their own body temperature. If the parents are gone too long, they grow cold. Fortunately, in a few days, the nestlings grow a coat of downy feathers. They also take in huge quantities of food and grow very rapidly. A common cuckoo, which is only about 0.07 ounces (2 grams) at hatching, weighs about 3.5 ounces (100 grams) after three weeks. By the time it leaves the nest, its weight is almost that of the adult female. Young albatrosses and petrels weigh much more than either parent when they leave the nest. Their tremendous fat reserves are slowly used up after the parents abandon them and return to sea. By the time young albatrosses have reached normal adult weight, they are ready to leave the nest and soar over the ocean in search of food.

Precocial birds spend more time in the egg than altricial birds do, so they are better developed when they hatch. However, they grow more slowly than altricial birds after hatching. The killdeer is typical of most precocial birds. It is born with its eyes open, a thick layer of down, and well-developed legs and bill. Shortly after hatching, it is able to run around and find its own food.

In the Nest

Life in the nest is not easy. Very few of the young live long enough to nest themselves. Eight or nine out of every ten birds die during their first year. For most species, weather and predators are the greatest threats to young

To satisfy the seemingly boundless appetite of nestlings, a parent bird makes many trips to and from the nest—sometimes as many as 900 trips per day.

The 27 Orders of Living Birds

Psittaciformes
gray parrot

Colliformes
blue-naped mousebird

Apodiformes
ruby-throated hummingbird

Passeriformes
blue jay

Coraciiformes
carmine bee-eater

Gruiformes
crowned crane

Rheiformes
common rhea

Tinamiformes
variegated tinamou

Casuariiformes
Australian cassowary

Columbiformes
victoria crested pigeon

Anseriformes
wood duck

Falconiformes
bald eagle

Apterygiformes
brown kiwi

T. BOYER

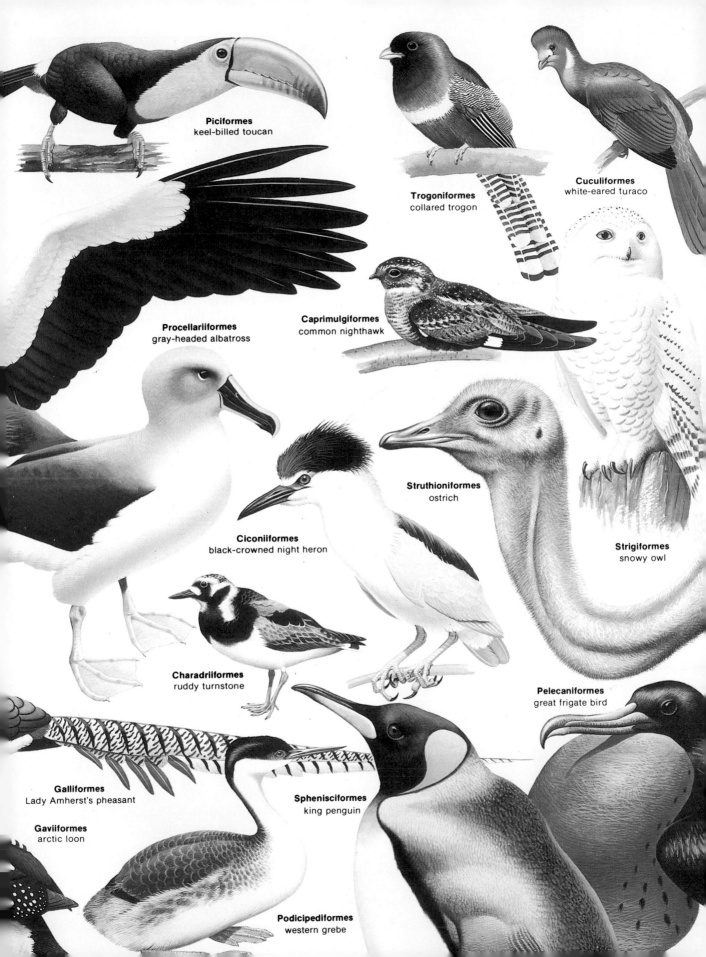

Piciformes
keel-billed toucan

Trogoniformes
collared trogon

Cuculiformes
white-eared turaco

Procellariiformes
gray-headed albatross

Caprimulgiformes
common nighthawk

Struthioniformes
ostrich

Strigiformes
snowy owl

Ciconiiformes
black-crowned night heron

Charadriiformes
ruddy turnstone

Pelecaniformes
great frigate bird

Galliformes
Lady Amherst's pheasant

Sphenisciformes
king penguin

Gaviiformes
arctic loon

Podicipediformes
western grebe

birds. Bad weather can reduce insect populations and thus reduce the birds' food supply, or it can interfere with the parents' ability to find food for their young. Mammals, especially raccoons, foxes, and squirrels, can be very destructive. Nestlings can also suffer heavy losses from parasites, such as mites and blow fly larvae. These insects attach themselves to the skin of the nestlings and feed on their blood, weakening them so much that they are unlikely to survive.

Regardless of their regular diet, the adults feed their young foods rich in proteins. Young birds, like children, need large amounts of protein in order to grow. Even hummingbirds, which as adults feed mainly on flower nectar, bring small insects to their young. Some birds have unique ways of feeding their young. Pigeons and doves (a member of the pigeon family) feed their young on pigeon's milk, a

The trumpeter swan is an attentive parent that sometimes carries its young, called cygnets, on its back. More often, however, the swan simply escorts its brood from one place to another.

material high in fat and protein that is formed in their crop (the storage portion of their stomach). Pelicans catch and store fish in their huge mouths and let their young dip into the enormous pouch and help themselves to the food there. Cormorants swallow the heads of their young and the young feed right from the adult's stomach.

The large amount of food brought to a nest full of young results in the production of much waste. If not removed, this material would foul the nest, attract predators and parasites, or cause disease. Many young birds eliminate undigested food and wastes in a small membrane called a fecal sac. The sacs are then eaten by the adults or carried away.

Before long, the nest becomes overcrowded with the rapidly growing nestlings and soon it can no longer hold them. Then it is time for the baby birds to leave the nest; this is called fledging. In some birds, the young make their first flight when they fledge. In others, the fledglings (baby birds) simply move out of the nest to a nearby limb.

The masked booby (*left*) carefully preens its offspring, combing through the feathers to remove dirt and parasites. Spreading its wings to create shade, the egret (*below*) protects its downy offspring from the hot sun. In a few species of birds, such as the emperor penguin (*below right*), the male has much of the responsibility for taking care of the offspring. Here, the emperor penguin chick huddles under the warm belly of its parent.

By fall, the young birds that were born in late spring have learned a great deal. They have practiced flying and can now find their own food, although they still may beg for their parents to feed them. In many cases, they have been on their own for months. Many birds nest more than once in a summer. The young from the first nest fend for themselves while the parents start a second brood. In some birds, the young from the first nest stay with the parents and help raise their siblings.

The Migration Cycle

There are ancient records of the appearance and disappearance of birds. Early naturalists did not know if birds migrated or hibernated. People told stories of swallows that were found frozen in marshes and would fly away when thawed. Now we know that billions of birds make astonishing migrations, traveling to distant places to breed and winter. Each spring, an estimated 5 billion birds migrate from the Central and South America to North America in search of nesting sites. An equal number leave the warmth of Africa and set out for breeding grounds in Europe and Asia. The migration of birds is truly one of the most spectacular feats in the natural world.

Residents and Migrants. Some birds never make a long-distance migration. These birds are called residents. Other birds fly incredible journeys to spend winters in tropical areas. These birds are called migrants.

There are advantages and disadvantages to both resident and migrant life-styles. Residents face long, cold winters and scarce food supplies. If a bird cannot find enough food to burn for energy during the long, cold winter night, it will freeze to death. It is much easier to survive the winter in the warm tropical forests of Central and South America. However, long-distance migrations are dangerous. Many birds are killed during migration by storms and man-made hazards, such as radio and television towers. Many forest areas have been destroyed to provide land for construction and development, so good places to stop and rest during migration are harder and harder for birds to find.

Migration. As fall approaches, the days get shorter and the nights grow cooler. With nesting over, things begin to change. The territories that were defended so vigorously in the beginning of summer no longer matter. Many species have urges to join large flocks of birds —for safety and to prepare for the migration to come.

Whether in a flock or not, birds feed heavily at this time of year to build up the fat reserves they will need to fly back to their wintering grounds. Before long, the alarm goes off on their biological clocks and it is time to migrate south.

Some birds migrate by day, others migrate at night. Hawks ride the thermals created as the sun warms the ground below. Humming-

With winter on the way, snow geese leave their nests in high Arctic regions to form large flocks for the journey southward. They fly during the day and night, coming down at regular intervals to rest and feed.

birds migrate alone and during the day, stopping to feed as needed. However, most small land birds, including flycatchers, thrushes, warblers, and orioles, migrate at night when temperatures are cooler and the tremendous quantities of heat generated by flapping flight muscles are quickly lost to the cool night air. Predation is less likely at night and the daylight hours can be used to find food and refuel for the next night's journey. As the day dawns, large flocks of migrating songbirds descend into patches of woods in what is known as a fallout, to rest and feed.

Many birds, especially duck and geese, follow narrow paths as they migrate north and south. These paths are called flyways. The main migration routes in North America run north to south, much as most of the mountain ranges and major rivers do. In Europe and Asia, birds migrate east to west as they travel from their breeding grounds to wintering ground.

In spring the days grow longer, and once again the changing daylight sets off the bird's biological clock. It is time to molt and begin preparations for the migration north. Longer days do more than just trigger the molting process. The increasing day length also triggers an increase in appetite and an increase in fat storage, which help to prepare the bird for spring migration.

After traveling all the way to the tropics, why do birds not stay and nest there? The costs of migration are great, but the benefits

Under clear skies and with a good tail wind, Canada geese can cover many hundreds of miles in a single nonstop flight.

Each year in their migratory journey between the Arctic and the Antarctic, Arctic terns log up to 25,000 miles (40,225 kilometers) of travel.

of returning north to breed are even greater. The tropics are full of predators that would quickly gobble up young birds. In North America, there are not as many reptile and small mammal predators.

Birds also migrate north to breed because there is an extremely large supply of the insects that are needed to feed growing young. In the long days of the northern summer, birds have time to find plentiful amounts of food for their young. In the Arctic, the mid-summer sun never sets, allowing birds to hunt 24 hours a day.

How Birds Migrate

How do birds know where to go? How do they find their way? Why do some birds travel during the day, while others travel during the night? These are questions that **ornithologists** (scientists who study birds) have tried to answer for at least a century. Birds have an astonishing ability to return to an exact location after wintering in South America or Africa. Homing pigeons can return to their home loft from places hundreds of miles away.

Recently ornithologists have started to learn how birds know where they are and navigate during their great migrations. Near your house, it is unlikely that you would ever get lost. You know the way because you recognize landmarks; birds also use landmarks to find their way. But they also have other ways of navigating when they fly out of their neighborhood. They have several sources of information that tell them which way to go. Migrating birds can use the sun by day and the stars by night. Research shows that they can even use the earth's magnetic field (the same field detected by a compass) and that they sometimes use odor clues, and maybe even low-frequency sounds.

However birds find their way, they are rarely very late. One of the extraordinary things about migration is its precision. Birds that travel across a continent, or farther, arrive at their destination within a few days of the same time each year.

A bird's internal clock is mostly responsible for the start of migration, but weather is also a factor. Many species, such as American robins, time their arrival to match the spring thaw. Birds are sensitive to changes in atmospheric pressure. Strong favorable winds cause birds to migrate in large numbers.

The Birds Around Us

Some birds spend most of their lives in deserts, others can be found along seacoasts, still others are found in woodlands and forests. In the following section, a variety of birds are shown in the kind of habitat, or environment, in which they can typically be found. The habitats include seacoasts, deserts, woodlands and forests, grasslands, polar regions, tropics, and residential areas. Below is an alphabetical listing of the birds presented and the habitats in which they live.

Bird	Habitat	Bird	Habitat
American kestrel	Grasslands	Hairy woodpecker	Woodlands and forests
American oystercatcher	Seacoasts	Herring gull	Seacoasts
American robin	Residential areas	Hoatzin	Tropics
Baltimore oriole	Residential areas	Long-billed curlew	Seacoasts
Blue jay	Residential areas	Mockingbird	Residential areas
Bobwhite	Grasslands	Phainopepla	Deserts
Bohemian waxwing	Woodlands and forests	Purple finch	Woodlands and forests
Burrowing owl	Grasslands	Quetzal	Tropics
Cactus wren	Deserts	Red-tailed hawk	Deserts
Chipping sparrow	Residential areas	Ruffed grouse	Woodlands and forests
Common cormorant	Seacoasts	Sandpiper	Seacoasts
Common pigeon	Residential areas	Scarlet ibis	Tropics
Common tern	Seacoasts	Snowy owl	Polar regions
Eastern meadowlark	Grasslands	Tawny owl	Woodlands and forests
Emperor penguin	Polar regions	Toco toucan	Tropics
Gila woodpecker	Deserts	Wandering albatross	Polar regions
Great hornbill	Tropics	Western kingbird	Grasslands
Great skua	Polar regions	Wilson's storm petrel	Polar regions
Greater roadrunner	Deserts	Yellow warbler	Woodlands and forests

Birds of the Seacoasts

Many birds are found along the coasts of the world's continents. Some are shorebirds; that is, they live most of the time on the shore. The most widely distributed and — probably the best-known shorebird is the gull. Gulls are scavengers — they forage along the shore for dead animals and even search through garbage dumps for food. They also hunt the shallow waters for fish or clams and other mollusks. The gull must break the mollusk's shell to get to the soft meat inside. It does this by carrying the mollusk aloft, then dropping it on rocks or other hard surfaces. Other birds found along the coasts are seabirds; they live most of the time at sea, coming ashore only to breed and nest. Terns are seabirds that stay at sea for long lengths of time, sometimes months or even years. Some seabirds spend so much time flying that they have lost the ability to walk on land or to swim. Not all of a seabird's time is spent flying; seabirds also soar and glide.

Herring gull

Common tern

Long-billed curlew

Common cormorant

Sandpipers

American oystercatchers

Birds of the Deserts

Only the hardiest of birds survive in the desert. The days are very hot, and during the night the temperatures plunge, sometimes even dipping below freezing. The desert is also a dry place. Because it is so dry, desert birds must get their water from the foods they eat. Rather than eating dry seeds and other plant products, most desert birds eat insects or small animals, such as lizards, snakes, and tree frogs, that supply the moisture they need. It is difficult to escape the hot desert sun. Few birds build nests on the hot ground; most build nests in the scattered thickets of low trees and shrubs. Cacti and prickly, thorny shrubs are the favorite nesting sites of the cactus wren. The nest is built deep among the protective spines of the cactus. Within the nest, the cactus wren is shaded from the sun. The Gila woodpecker excavates a cavity in the giant saguaro cactus. The bird uses the same hole for several years. When the nest is abandoned, other birds take it over.

Red-tailed hawk

Gila woodpecker

Phainopepla

Cactus wren

Greater roadrunner

Birds of the Woodlands and Forests

Woodlands and forests provide habitats to many different kinds of birds. Some birds are found in dense forests of evergreen trees; others prefer the open areas among the scattered thickets of shrubs and leafy trees of the woodlands. Some birds build their nests high in the treetops, while others make their nests in the lower branches or on the ground. The ruffed grouse builds its nest on the ground in thick woods and dense cover — at the base of a tree or rock, under a log, or in dense brush. The hairy woodpecker, which digs a cavity in a tree or tree stump, is a year-round resident whether it is found in woodlands, wooded swamps, or mountain forests. It is active even on the most frigid winter days. One part-time resident of wooded areas is the yellow warbler. It builds its nest in shrubs or low trees close to streams and lakes. After raising its young, it heads for warm southern climates.

Tawny owl

Bohemian waxwing

Purple finch

Ruffed grouse

Hairy woodpecker

Yellow warbler

Birds of the Grasslands

Whether they are called prairies, savannas, pampas, or steppes, grass-lands provide an abundant source of food and water for a variety of birds. The rich food supply supports birds that eat plant matter, such as grasses and seeds, as well as those birds that eat small animals, such as insects and spiders. Some birds, such as bobwhites, seek the dense cover pro-vided by the tall grasses to hide their ground nests. While nesting, the bobwhite jealously guards its territory deep within the grassland. The meadowlark is also a ground nester that forms its nest from surrounding grasses. However, it prefers to be in more open areas. Perched at the edge of a field, the meadowlark can be heard singing its cheerful song. The burrowing owl does not burrow into the ground to make its nest; in-stead, it searches for the abandoned burrow of other animals, such as the prairie dog.

American kestrel

Western kingbirds

Burrowing owl

Bobwhites

Eastern
meadowlark

Birds of the Polar Regions

The polar regions, the Arctic and Antarctic, are the coldest regions of the Northern and Southern hemispheres. Not all polar birds stay in this harsh environment all the time. Some birds leave the polar regions during the freezing winters and return during the spring to breed and rear their young; others leave to spend months at sea. Birds within these regions have developed in special ways that allow them to withstand the severe environment. Some have specialized body features. The emperor penguin is a flightless bird with short flipperlike wings, webbed feet, and a stiff rudderlike tail. Although it does not fly, it is an excellent swimmer. It also has a thick layer of body fat that serves as insulation against the cold. The skua is a seabird that breeds in the polar regions. Part of its special adaptation is its method of feeding: The skua is a predatory bird that pirates the prey captured by gulls and terns.

Wandering albatross

Great skua

Wilson's storm petrel

Emperor penguin

Snowy owl

Birds of the Tropics

The tropics are damp, humid places where lush, leafy plants abound. Day and night, the temperatures hover just below 80°F (27°C). This steady environment has the greatest variety of animal species, including birds, of anywhere on earth. The brilliantly colored male quetzal is one of the most beautiful birds in the world. Humid mountain forests are home to the quetzal. Some tropic birds, such as the hoatzin, are found feeding on the plentiful supply of leaves and fruit in the dense vegetation that lines the rivers and streams of South American rain forests. Other tropic birds live in the thick canopy formed by the leafy branches of tall trees. There they feast on a great variety of insects and other small animals such as frogs and lizards. The rain forests of India and Indochina are home to the great hornbill. The ibis, which is a wading bird that can be found in most of the warmer areas of the world, nests in huge coastal colonies.

Quetzal

Scarlet ibis

Great hornbill

Toco toucan

Hoatzin

Birds of Residential Areas

The variety of habitats in which birds are found includes patches of grass and trees within the noisy city and in the trimmed backyards and gardens of the suburbs. The mockingbird can be heard singing its varied song, composed of other birds' songs, animal calls, and other common sounds. The cooing of pigeons is a familiar sound in cities as well as in less populated areas. Pigeons are quite social and often breed in colonies and gather in flocks during the nonbreeding season. In some places, the robin is a year-round sight; in other places it is only a resident during the warmer months. The blue jay is a big, bold, dashing bird. Its presence does not go unnoticed. It is a noisy bird that is abundant in backyards and wooded areas.

American robin

Blue jay

Baltimore oriole

Chipping sparrow

Mockingbird

Common pigeon

▶ THE HISTORY OF BIRDS

Since the days when dinosaurs roamed the land, millions of years ago, birds have inhabited the earth. They have become one of the most widely distributed of all the wild creatures. Many evolutionary changes have occurred on the path that has led those first primitive forms to modern-day birds.

The First Birds

Most scientists now believe that birds evolved from small two-legged dinosaurs known as theropods. The earliest known bird is *Archaeopteryx*, which lived about 150 million years ago. Fossils of this ancient bird were discovered in 1861. *Archaeopteryx* was about the size of a blue jay. It had wings and feathers, but unlike modern birds, it also had a long bony tail and teeth. The bone structure of its legs suggests that it was a good runner, and scientists believe *Archaeopteryx* could fly, but not very well.

There are two theories about how birds began to fly. One idea proposes that early birdlike creatures first climbed trees to find food and safety. Over a long period of time they developed flight—first by jumping, then gliding, and finally flying between tree branches. Another theory suggests that flight began when small birdlike dinosaurs ran quickly along the ground and stretched their arms out for balance, occasionally leaping up to catch insects or other prey. With this running start, some began to be able to lift off from the ground. The true origins of flight may be a combination of both theories.

Modern Birds

As the ability to fly evolved, birds developed the higher metabolism necessary to provide the fuel for the flight muscles; they also developed the trait of warm-bloodedness. Some experts believe that feathers may have developed as an insulating covering to conserve body heat and that feathers became an aid to flying later. Others argue that feathers emerged to help primitive birds fly and later became useful in keeping the body at a constant temperature.

Fossil evidence discovered in China has contributed to the debate. In 1996 a fossil of a dinosaur with feathers was identified. Since then more than 1,000 specimens have been discovered. These fossils are not as old as the *Archaeopteryx* fossils, however, so these feathered dinosaurs cannot be the ancestors of the first birds. Thus, the origin of feathers remains a mystery.

By the end of the Cretaceous period, 65 million years ago, the toothed birds had vanished and a wide variety of bird life had evolved. The ancestors of modern birds, such as penguins, rheas, loons, tropic birds, and even some perching birds, were already flying across the skies and swimming in the seas. Fifty-three million years ago there was a marked change in the life on earth. Gone were the dinosaurs and the early reptiles that had dominated the environment. Birds, warm-blooded and able to fly, spread and multiplied quickly, taking advantage of every available habitat on earth.

The Decline of Birds

In the past 20 million years or so, there have been more bird extinctions than evolutions of new species. Humans have caused the decline of many birds, in direct and indirect ways.

Environmental pollution caused by humans is a constant threat to the welfare of birds. This bird is a helpless victim of an oil spill.

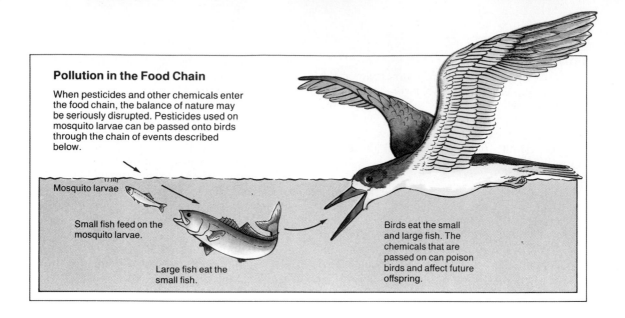

Pollution in the Food Chain

When pesticides and other chemicals enter the food chain, the balance of nature may be seriously disrupted. Pesticides used on mosquito larvae can be passed onto birds through the chain of events described below.

Mosquito larvae

Small fish feed on the mosquito larvae.

Large fish eat the small fish.

Birds eat the small and large fish. The chemicals that are passed on can poison birds and affect future offspring.

At one time, the hunting of birds for food and feathers destroyed a large part of the bird population. Barrel after barrel of salted birds and bale after bale of feathers were shipped to market. In 1878, a single Michigan hunter shipped 3 million passenger pigeons to market. Eleven years later, the passenger pigeon was extinct in that state.

The popularity of bird pets has also contributed to the decline of birds. The international trade in species from Africa, Asia, and South America is one of the major causes of a decline in their numbers—especially hard hit are the world's parrots. Of this beautiful bird family, 78 species are in danger of extinction. Conservationists estimate that for every bird that reaches the pet shop alive, another four perish during the trip to the market.

People have introduced into new lands animals, such as rats, cats, and mongooses, that are bird predators. Cattle, rabbits, pigs, and sheep do not kill birds directly, but they destroy the habitats that birds live in.

The most damage to bird populations has been caused by the human destruction of habitats: Woods and forests have been cut down, marshes drained, and swamps filled to provide more land for development, farming, and grazing.

The Future of Birds

The combination of hunting, destruction of natural habitats, and environmental pollution has proved to be too much for many plants and animals. More than one hundred known birds have become extinct, although many more species must have disappeared before they were even discovered.

Conservationists describing the status of birds categorize them as endangered, threatened, or rare. A species is considered endangered when the population has been so severely reduced that it is unlikely to survive if the cause of the bird's decline is not stopped. Endangered species are in immediate danger of extinction. Threatened species are likely to move into the endangered category in the near future. Rare species have small populations that are not yet in trouble, but could be quickly driven toward extinction.

The need for effective measures on behalf of the world's birds has never been more urgent. Humankind needs birds. We no longer depend on them for food, but we still need them. Birds are part of a healthy, thriving planet. Coal miners used to bring a canary into the mines with them to warn them when the air became too poisonous to breathe. Birds are like the coal miner's canaries for the whole planet. When they can no longer survive, we are in danger. Saving the birds is in our own best interest. By preserving the environment for birds, we take the first steps in saving all life on earth, including our own.

Todd A. Culver
Education Specialist
Cornell Laboratory of Ornithology

See also ANIMALS; BIRDS AS PETS; ENDANGERED SPECIES; HOMING AND MIGRATION; OSTRICHES AND OTHER FLIGHTLESS BIRDS.

Although ducks are most often raised for their commercial value, their lively manner makes them a popular zoo animal and an affectionate companion.

BIRDS AS PETS

Everyone has a different idea of what kind of animal makes a good pet. Some people want an animal that is friendly and will be a good companion; others want an animal that is entertaining—one that can talk, do tricks, or sing; and still others want an animal that is inexpensive to keep. It is possible to have all these things when the pet you have is a bird.

Birds have been popular pets for centuries. Records show that pigeons were tamed in Egypt nearly five thousand years ago. Canaries were luxury pets of wealthy Europeans about five hundred years ago. Alexander Wilson, a pioneer and scholar of American bird life, kept a Louisiana parakeet as a companion. Wilson even took the bird on long horseback journeys exploring the West. The parakeet rode in Wilson's pocket during the day and perched beside his campfire at night.

One of the best features of keeping a pet bird is that most kinds take up little space. They usually live in cages that fit easily in small homes or apartments. Pet birds keep themselves clean and need little daily care. There are also many unusual and interesting varieties to choose from.

▶PARAKEETS

The parakeet is among the most popular of all house pets, feathered or furred. It is called by several names. Budgerigar, or "budgie" for short, is its Australian name, for parakeets originally were native to Australia. In the Far East, these birds are known as shell parakeets.

Parakeets belong to the parrot family. There are certain characteristics that help identify such birds. The feet have two toes in front and two behind. The bill is thick, strong, and hooked. The body is short and compact, with a short neck, large head, and thick tongue. The plumage (feathers) comes in a variety of bright colors. Parakeets are hardy birds and long-lived. These pets also have the wonderful ability to imitate a human voice.

The best place to buy a parakeet (or other cage bird) is at a reliable pet store. There you can learn the age and the sex of the bird you are buying. You can also ask for advice on the correct size and type of cage.

These birds can eat boxed mixtures of small-sized seed like wheat, millet, and canary seed. Many of them have tastes for certain snacks. With some it is apples; others enjoy bits of vegetable greens. Drinking water must always be within reach.

▶PARROTS AND MYNAHS

A parrot or a mynah bird does not have to say anything really funny to be amusing. The way these birds talk is funny enough. They seem to know what they are saying and why they are saying it. Of course this is not true.

WONDER QUESTION

Can people get parrot fever?

Parrot fever, also known as psittacosis, can be passed along to people from infected birds. Although the disease occurs most often in members of the parrot family, it is also found in other birds such as pigeons. In people, the disease is an infection somewhat like pneumonia. It can spread to humans when they handle sick birds or come into contact with infectious articles (bird droppings, perches, cages). The best way to avoid it is to buy pet birds from a reliable dealer, keep their cages clean, and never handle sick birds.

Choosing a Bird

Everyone wants to have a healthy pet. Before selecting a bird, it is important to watch the bird during its normal activities. Look for one that has bright, fully opened eyes and is completely feathered without any bald spots or deformities, such as crooked toenails or overgrown beaks. A bird that looks tamer than the others in its cage may actually be quiet and inactive because it is sick. Other signs that may mean a bird is ill include an unwillingness to eat, runny nose, ruffled feathers, coughing and sneezing, and excessive scratching.

They merely imitate sounds they have heard. But it makes them seem almost human.

Pet parrots need a great deal of attention. They must be given roomy living quarters and a well-balanced diet. As with other pet birds, proper seed foods for them will be found at pet shops. But parrots have a definite need for more than seeds. Greens, fruits, and nuts are all important for a parrot. On their own, parrots are likely to sample any food that is around—meat, eggs, cheese, or cake—even though it may not be good for them.

The Amazon parrot, with blue markings on its face, and the African gray are two of the most popular parrots. Both can be taught to speak clearly and often to sing and whistle.

If you are shopping for a parrot, you will find a wide range in price. Some are young and completely untrained, while others are older and used to talking and living with people. Be prepared to care for a parrot for a long time. Depending on the type of parrot, these birds can live from 25 to 50 years.

The mynah bird is quick to imitate human talk. It is also likely to startle its owner with a piercing squawk or scream. Native to Southeast Asia, mynahs are members of the starling family. There are several kinds of mynahs, some as small as robins, some as large as crows, but all are bright and perky. Again, proper food (mynah birds like a soft mixture) is to be found at pet shops. Once a day they should be given fruit, such as cut up bananas, apples, and grapes.

▶CANARIES

Like parakeets, canaries are mostly seed-eaters. They are easily cared for with foods you find at pet shops, with additional snacks of fresh greens and bits of apple or orange. Since its song is one of the canary's best features, the smart canary shopper will look into this before buying a bird.

There are many kinds of canaries, but all of them may be grouped into two main types of singers—the choppers and the rollers. The choppers are the kind of canary most often found in pet shops. They may be sold when only 5 or 6 months old and without training in singing. The chopper sings loudly with high-pitched, short notes. The rollers are usually older and are often given careful training so that their song is at its best. The roller performs with soft, sweet, rolling trills. The male is always the singer.

With its cheerful yellow color and its soft, sweet trill, the roller canary is one of the most popular of all pet birds. Canaries, which belong to the finch family, are native to the Canary Islands, off the coast of Africa. Over time, breeders have developed different varieties—some are known for their melodious songs, others are known for their distinctive appearance.

Native to Central and South America, the scarlet macaw is a large long-tailed parrot. It is valued as a pet because it is easy to tame and lives a long time.

▶ PIGEONS

People who keep pigeons may own dozens of these birds. They are mainly used for racing or to produce the squabs, or young pigeons, that people eat as a luxury food.

Pigeons are kept in many city areas as well as in the country. Pigeon fanciers sometimes keep them in special houses, or lofts, on the roofs of buildings—if city laws permit. From the rooftops the birds can be released for exercise flights. Wherever they are kept, pigeons need air and light and protection from drafts and mice. Seed mix that can be bought from a pet shop is their chief food. If you feed them by hand, they become very tame and friendly. A pair of pigeons may be purchased for a small amount of money, but a single champion racing bird may be expensive.

▶ BACKYARD BIRDS

Chickens, ducks, and geese are birds that are usually thought of as farm birds, but any one of them may be tamed and kept as a backyard pet. A chicken is interesting to watch and to hear. It has a varied and unmistakable "language" all its own. Ducks and geese, too, make interesting and unusual pets.

DOROTHY E. SHUTTLESWORTH
Author, *Exploring Nature With Your Child*
Founder, *Junior Natural History Magazine*

BIRTH CONTROL

When a man and a woman have sexual intercourse and do not want the woman to become pregnant, they use birth control, or **contraception**, to try to prevent pregnancy. Deciding when to have a child and how much time should pass between the birth of one child and the birth of the next is important. It allows parents to have children when they are ready to love and care for them and be responsible for their many needs.

▶ METHODS OF BIRTH CONTROL

To understand how birth control works, you must understand some basic facts about human reproduction. About once every 28 days an egg cell, or ovum, is released from one of a woman's ovaries and begins to travel down a narrow fallopian tube toward the uterus. This is called **ovulation**. If this ovum is not fertilized by a sperm cell from a man, it will quickly die and pass out of the uterus during a normal menstrual period. But if sexual intercourse takes place while the ovum is in the fallopian tube, one of millions of sperm cells deposited in the woman's vagina by the man's penis may unite with the ovum. This is called **conception**—fertilization of the ovum. The fertilized egg may then attach itself to the inner lining of the woman's uterus, and a new life will begin to develop—the woman is pregnant. Some nine months later a baby will be born.

Barrier Methods. Barrier methods of birth control prevent pregnancy by blocking sperm from reaching the ovum so conception cannot take place. The **condom** is a sheath of thin latex rubber that is rolled down over the penis before intercourse to trap ejaculated sperm. A **diaphragm** is a dome of thin rubber that is inserted into the vagina before sex. It covers the opening of the uterus, blocking the entrance of any sperm. A condom for women was introduced in the 1990's. It looks similar to a diaphragm with a long polyurethane sheath attached. The **vaginal sponge** and the **cervical cap** can be inserted into the vagina; they function much like a diaphragm. Barrier methods of birth control are best used with a **spermicide**—a chemical that kills sperm cells. Condoms can be bought at a pharmacy; diaphragms and cervical caps must be fitted by a doctor. The vaginal sponge is not currently available in the United States; it is marketed in Canada. When used properly, barrier contraceptives are about 80 to 90 percent effective. In addition to preventing pregnancy, condoms reduce the risk of contracting a sexually transmitted infection.

Hormonal Methods. Hormonal methods of birth control work by changing a woman's body chemistry so that eggs are not released from the ovaries. Some forms also make it hard for any fertilized egg cell to attach itself to the uterus lining and grow. In the United States the most widely used hormonal method of birth control is "the pill." Contraceptive pills containing hormones are taken by mouth every day and block ovulation as long as the pills are taken. **Hormonal implants** release tiny amounts of hormones into the woman's body daily. The implants are inserted under the skin of the upper arm and work for up to five years. **Injectable hormones** are given every one to three months and prevent pregnancy during that time.

Hormonal methods of birth control must be prescribed or administered by a doctor, who can discuss and monitor any side effects that may occur. When used properly, they are about 99 percent effective. Fertility returns shortly after the hormones are stopped.

Intrauterine Device (IUD). An intrauterine device is a small coil of metal or plastic that is inserted by a doctor into the woman's uterus. It prevents any fertilized egg cell from attaching itself in the uterus. Younger women who use IUD's are sometimes bothered by infections, cramping, or unusual menstrual bleeding. IUD's are used more easily by older women who have already had children. They are over 97 percent effective for preventing pregnancy.

Natural Birth Control. Natural birth control methods attempt to prevent conception without the use of artificial devices. The **Fertility Awareness Method (FAM)**, or rhythm method, depends upon avoiding sexual intercourse on the days before, during, and after ovulation—about 12 days each month—so that no sperm are present to fertilize the egg cell. It can be difficult to pinpoint the time of ovulation, so the FAM, like another natural birth control technique—withdrawing the penis from the vagina just before sperm are ejaculated—can be unreliable.

Emergency Birth Control. "Morning after pills" can be used to prevent pregnancy after intercourse when a birth control method failed or no method was used. The pills contain hormones that delay ovulation or keep a fertilized egg from attaching to the uterine wall. The pills are available from a doctor. They are about 75 percent effective. Side effects include nausea and vomiting.

Sterilization. **Sterilization**—surgically cutting and tying off or sealing the woman's fallopian tubes (tubal ligation) or the man's sperm tubes (vasectomy)—is a way to prevent pregnancies permanently. These operations can seldom be reversed.

▶ **HISTORY OF BIRTH CONTROL**

Birth control is a fairly recent idea in human history. Centuries ago large families were important for survival. Many babies died in infancy and childhood, and people had large families to be sure that enough children would survive to help gather food and have children of their own.

In the 1700's and 1800's, medical and scientific discoveries enabled many diseases to be controlled and food supplies to be increased. Large families were no longer necessary for survival. People lived longer, and the world's population began to grow rapidly.

In 1798 Thomas Malthus, an English economist, predicted that the world's population would quickly outgrow the available food supply. He recommended people stop having so many children.

Malthus' prediction proved to be wrong. But as the world population increased rapidly in the early 1900's, the idea of family planning took root. Methods of contraception began to be developed, and a worldwide movement to encourage birth control began.

Margaret Sanger, a trained nurse, became a leader of that movement in the early 1900's. She published pamphlets and books about family planning and helped pass laws that allowed doctors to teach birth control methods. Sanger also established clinics to advise and educate people and founded the National Birth Control League. These were combined to form the Planned Parenthood Federation of America in 1942.

▶ BIRTH CONTROL TODAY

The world now has more than 6 billion people, and the number is increasing rapidly, especially in developing countries. Different countries support birth control in different ways. In Europe and the United States, many birth control methods are readily and legally available. In China, rigid laws control family size. In India, vigorous efforts are being made to make birth control available to millions of people.

Not everyone favors the use of birth control, however. The Roman Catholic Church forbids artificial methods of birth control, believing that sexual love in marriage should never be separated from the possibility of conception. Only **abstinence** (refraining from sexual intercourse) or the Fertility Awareness Method of family planning are considered acceptable. Some people fear that governments may impose birth control in order to obtain political control over their people. Others charge that teaching birth control encourages people to have sex before marriage—an idea that is not supported by scientific evidence.

Doctors and other knowledgeable people you respect can help you understand the different methods of birth control and how they may affect your life and your health.

ALAN E. NOURSE, M.D.
Author, *Birth Control* and *Teen Guide to Birth Control*

See also REPRODUCTION (Human Reproduction).

BIRTHSTONES. See GEMS.
BISHOP, BERNICE PAUAHI. See HAWAII (Famous People).
BISMARCK. See NORTH DAKOTA (Cities).

BISMARCK, OTTO VON (1815–1898)

Otto Eduard Leopold von Bismarck-Schönhausen—the statesman responsible for bringing about the unification of Germany—was one of the most skillful and practical politicians the world has ever known. He was born on April 1, 1815, at Schönhausen, in the German state of Prussia. His father belonged to the Prussian landowning class known as the Junkers.

As a boy, Bismarck attended a boarding school in Berlin. Later, he studied law at the universities of Göttingen and Berlin. After graduating in 1835, Bismarck worked in the Prussian civil service and served in the army. He then returned home to help his father manage the family estates. He became religious, partly because he married the devout Johanna von Puttkamer in 1847. That same year, he became a member of the Prussian Diet (parliament), where he represented the conservative traditions of the Junkers.

In 1848, a wave of change swept across Europe. Germany was still a collection of independent states. Liberals tried to turn the country into a constitutional monarchy headed by the king of Prussia. But the king refused to accept the crown from an elected parliament.

In 1851, Bismarck was Prussia's delegate to the German Diet (assembly) at Frankfurt-am-Main. There he spoke for Prussia's interests against those of Austria—then the most powerful German state. In 1859 he was named Prussian ambassador to Russia and, later, to France.

In 1862 the new king of Prussia, William I, clashed with his parliament. When the lower house refused to approve money for military reforms, King William appointed Bismarck prime minister and minister of foreign affairs. Bismarck skillfully silenced parliament and gained the power to put his ideas on foreign and domestic policy into effect. Prussia and Austria defeated Denmark in 1864 in a war over the tiny northern states of Schleswig and Holstein. These two regions had large German populations but were linked to the Danish crown. Prussia then fought the Seven Weeks' War (1866) against Austria and gained control of both Schleswig and Holstein.

In 1867 Bismarck set up the North German Confederation, dominated by Prussia. As chancellor of the confederation, he soon became known as the Iron Chancellor. The nickname came from an 1862 speech in which he had said that "the great questions of the time are decided not by speeches and majority decisions…but by iron and blood."

Bismarck had made Prussia the strongest German state. In 1870 he helped provoke the Franco-Prussian War, which united the German states against a common enemy. In 1871, France was defeated and forced to cede the province of Alsace and most of Lorraine to Germany. The new German Empire was born. It included all the German states except Austria. King William of Prussia became Kaiser (Emperor) William I of Germany.

Bismarck had reached his goal of a united Germany under Prussian leadership. He formed alliances that kept a balance of power in Europe and helped nations settle their differences peacefully. Within Germany, Bismarck played his political rivals off against each other. Although he never accepted democratic views, he put through sweeping social reforms to gain liberal support. But King William II, who came to the throne in 1888, had his own ideas on running the empire. After much conflict, Bismarck resigned in 1890. His retirement from public life marked the end of an era in European history.

Bismarck died on July 30, 1898. His tombstone bears the words "A true German servant of Emperor William I."

Reviewed by GERARD BRAUNTHAL
University of Massachusetts, Amherst

See also FRANCO-PRUSSIAN WAR.

BISON. See BUFFALO AND BISON.
BLACK, HUGO. See ALABAMA (Famous People).
BLACK AMERICANS. See AFRICAN AMERICANS.
BLACKFOOT INDIANS. See INDIANS, AMERICAN (On the Prairies and Plains).
BLACK HAWK. See ILLINOIS (The Black Hawk War).

BLACK HOLES

Black holes are regions in space where a dense concentration of matter has produced an enormous gravitational field so strong that nothing—not even light—can escape it. Even though a black hole cannot be seen directly, most astronomers think that black holes litter space and that they often lurk in the centers of large galaxies.

How Black Holes Form. A star burns by converting hydrogen into helium. This produces radiation (such as heat and light) that pushes the star's matter outward. Stopping the matter from expanding indefinitely is the star's gravity, which is determined by its mass. When a star dies, its supply of hydrogen is exhausted. Its gravity compresses it into a tiny, very dense object. Smaller stars, about the size of our sun, collapse into a white-hot ball called a white dwarf. Larger stars, three times the mass of the sun or more, collapse into an even smaller and denser object known as a black hole.

An artist's impression of an X-ray binary star system consisting of a black hole (bottom) and a normal orange-red star (top). Gas is pulled from the atmosphere of the star by the black hole's strong gravitational field, into which it spirals in the form of an intensely hot, X-ray-emitting disk.

Finding Black Holes. Black holes do not allow light to escape and are therefore invisible. However, there are ways to detect them. Black holes may influence nearby stars. A black hole may be part of a binary—two stars that circle each other. If a black hole takes the place of one of the stars, the remaining star seems to dance around an invisible partner. When scientists began looking for black holes, they hoped to find one that was part of a binary and strong enough to steal gas from its companion. Such a black hole would pull the gas into a swirling disc, squeezing and heating it to millions of degrees, forcing it to emit X-rays. The first X-ray binary that seemed to include a black hole was Cyg X-1. Eventually, other binaries provided even stronger evidence of black holes.

Researchers believe black holes inhabit the centers of many galaxies. These black holes could have been formed when the galaxies were young and their inner regions were crowded with large stars. When these stars died, they became individual black holes that combined to create a single, massive black hole. Gases were swirled and heated, producing the radiation we often see coming from the centers of galaxies. This radiation includes radio waves, visible light, and X-rays.

Although black holes are associated with destruction, they may be a creative force. A black hole may not swallow all the nearby gas that it heats. Some of the superheated gas may be ejected into space. If a jet of high-speed, superheated gas from a black hole hits a dense gas cloud, the cloud may collapse, triggering the birth of a star. Black holes may even play a role in galaxy formation.

SETH SHOSTAK
SETI Institute

See also ASTRONOMY; GRAVITY AND GRAVITATION; MILKY WAY; QUASARS; STARS; UNIVERSE.

BLACK KETTLE. See INDIANS, AMERICAN (Profiles).

BLACKMUN, HARRY A. See ILLINOIS (Famous People).

BLACK MUSLIMS. See AFRICAN AMERICANS (Separatism, Militancy, and Black Power).

BLACK PANTHER PARTY. See AFRICAN AMERICANS (Separatism, Militancy, and Black Power).

BLACK SEA. See OCEANS AND SEAS OF THE WORLD.

BLACKWELL, ELIZABETH
(1821–1910)

As a young woman, Elizabeth Blackwell earned her living as a teacher. But she was not happy in her work. She longed for independence and became a supporter of women's rights. Searching for a career that would offer her independence and that would also allow her to help people, Blackwell decided to become a doctor.

Blackwell was born on February 3, 1821, in Bristol, England. She and her family moved to the United States in 1832. It was in the United States that Blackwell applied to medical school. However, women were not welcome in the medical profession, and Blackwell was repeatedly denied admission. Finally she was accepted by the Geneva Medical College in Geneva, New York.

Most of her fellow students respected her, but the doctors at a hospital where she went for training treated her less kindly. "When I walked into the wards they walked out," she later wrote. Still, Blackwell did not give up. She graduated from medical school in 1849, the first woman in the United States to do so. She then went to Europe to continue her studies.

Blackwell returned to the United States in 1851, but no hospital would allow her to practice medicine. In 1853 she set up her own clinic in New York City. In 1857 she opened the New York Infirmary for Women and Children, a hospital run mostly by women. In 1868 she founded the Women's Medical College, the first of its kind in America. In 1869, she returned to England and helped found the London School of Medicine for Women. She died in Hastings, England, on May 31, 1910, at the age of 89.

KARYN L. BERTSCHI
Science Writer

BLAINE, JAMES GILLESPIE. See MAINE (Famous People).

BLAIR, BONNIE. See ICE-SKATING (Profiles).

BLAIR, TONY (1953–)

Tony Blair was the first Labour prime minister in British history to win two full terms in office, in 1997 and 2001. He increased that record by winning a third term in 2005.

Anthony Charles Lynton Blair was born on May 6, 1953, in Edinburgh, Scotland, but grew up in England. After graduating from Oxford University in 1975, he practiced law in London, where he met Cherie Booth, also a lawyer. The couple married in 1980 and had four children.

Blair became a member of Parliament from Sedgefield in 1983. In the House of Commons, he was active in the areas of trade, industry, employment, education, and energy. He rose rapidly in the Labour Party's ranks and in 1994 was named party leader. Under Blair's leadership, the Labour Party broadened its working-class appeal to include the middle classes. Blair called his party New Labour, and in 1997 he campaigned to "modernize" Britain. He won that election with a 179-seat majority in the Commons.

Blair supported the establishment of separate legislatures for Scotland and Wales. He also worked toward ending violence between Catholics and Protestants in Northern Ireland. In foreign affairs, Blair joined the United States in launching air strikes against Iraq; repaired relations with other European Union (EU) members; and backed an air assault on Yugoslavia by the North Atlantic Treaty Organization (NATO).

After the September 11, 2001, attacks on the United States, Blair became U.S. president George W. Bush's strongest ally in the war against terrorism. And in 2003, despite unpopular public opinion, he supported the war to topple the Iraqi dictator, Saddam Hussein. (For more information, see the article IRAQ WAR in Volume I.)

WARREN HOGE
London Bureau Chief, *The New York Times*

BLAKE, WILLIAM (1757–1827)

William Blake, the English poet and artist, was born on November 28, 1757, in London. His father was a shopkeeper, and the family lived simply. William was taught at home by his mother. Sometimes William would speak of visions he had seen. Once he returned home from a walk and told his parents that he had seen angels in the treetops.

When he was 10, William was able to go to a drawing school. He began to write poems at the age of 12. At 14, he was apprenticed to an engraver so that he could learn a trade.

In 1782, Blake married Catherine Boucher. Blake trained his wife to help him produce hand-colored engravings of his poems and drawings. Blake's drawings enlarge and complete the meaning of his poems.

Blake's chief prose work is *The Marriage of Heaven and Hell* (1790–93), a satire. But he is best loved for his collections of poems called *Songs of Innocence* (1789) and *Songs of Experience* (1794). The latter contains one of his most famous poems, "The Tiger."

Blake's comments on the ugliness, cruelty, and injustice of the world as he saw it play as much a part in his works as do his comments on the beauties and joys of life. He believed that the world of the imagination was more real than the world that people could see or touch. His art and poetry, increasingly filled with symbols from his visions, brought alive the world of his own imagination.

After about 1818, Blake did little writing, but he continued to produce engravings and watercolors. He died in London on August 12, 1827. His genius was not fully appreciated until long after his death.

EDMUND FULLER
Author, *Man in Modern Fiction*

BLEEDING. See FIRST AID.

BLIGH, WILLIAM (1754–1817)

British naval officer William Bligh commanded the H.M.S. *Bounty*. The scandalous mutiny aboard that ship in 1789 immortalized his name in the annals of maritime history. Bligh was born in the old Devon County seaport of Plymouth, England, on September 9, 1754. At the early age of 22, he became sailing master of the H.M.S. *Resolution* on Captain James Cook's third great Pacific voyage of exploration (1776–80).

In 1787, Bligh was given command of the H.M.S. *Bounty* and ordered to sail to the South Pacific to collect breadfruit plants in Tahiti. The plants were to be transported to the British West Indies and used to feed the slaves on the colonial plantations.

The infamous mutiny on the *Bounty* occurred on April 28, 1789, when Bligh's crew became fed up with his bullying ways. The ship's second lieutenant, Fletcher Christian, took command of the *Bounty* and cast Bligh adrift in a small boat with 18 loyal crew members. After a stormy and miraculous passage

that covered 3,900 miles (6,240 kilometers) in 43 days, Bligh and his men landed safely on the island of Timor in Southeast Asia. Christian, in the meantime, had sailed eastward with 8 other mutineers and 17 Tahitians and settled on uninhabited Pitcairn Island (where some of their descendants still reside).

The British searched in vain for Christian and his group, but three of the mutineers who had settled in Tahiti were found and hanged for their crime. Bligh was absolved of all blame for the loss of the *Bounty*. His last important appointment was as governor of the British penal colony in Australia (1805–08). He retired as a vice admiral and died in 1817.

SAM MCKINNEY
Author, *Bligh: A True Account of Mutiny Aboard His Majesty's Ship Bounty*

BLINDNESS

Some people cannot read the words printed on this page. This is because they are blind. People without eyesight face difficulties in everyday life that can be hard for sighted people to imagine. Try putting toothpaste on a toothbrush with your eyes closed. How would you cook a meal if you could not see? Most of the things we learn by watching others must be taught to people without sight.

Blindness is not simply being without eyesight. There are many degrees of blindness. Some blind people can distinguish light and dark. Others can recognize the direction of a light source.

People who have limited eyesight are said to be visually impaired. Their eyesight may be limited in one or more ways. Some visually impaired people can recognize large objects, such as chairs or tables, but cannot see details on those objects. Some individuals cannot see to the left or right, some have several blind spots in their vision, and some individuals cannot distinguish colors or contrasts.

There are approximately 2.5 million people in the United States alone who are severely visually impaired. Three quarters of these people are 65 years of age or older. This is because many of the causes of eyesight loss are associated with aging.

▶ **THE DEGREES OF BLINDNESS**

People who study eyesight loss have established guidelines for identifying blindness and visual impairment. The guidelines are based on **visual acuity**, which means the amount of details an individual can see. A person is said to be visually impaired if he or she has a visual acuity of 20/70 or less when wearing corrective lenses (eyeglasses or contact lenses). This means that what a person with normal vision can see at 70 feet away, a visually impaired person can see at only 20 feet away.

A person is considered to be blind if his or her visual acuity is 20/200 or less with corrective lenses. This means that what a person with normal vision can see at 200 feet away, a blind person cannot see at all or at no more than 20 feet away.

These measurements are always determined by the stronger eye. Some people have no eyesight in one eye but some vision in the other eye. They are not considered blind or visually impaired unless the stronger eye meets the above guidelines.

There is one additional measure of blindness that has to do with a person's **visual field**. Visual field refers to how great an area a person can see. It is measured in degrees of an angle. If a person with normal vision looks straight ahead, he or she should be able to see nearly all the objects in a half-circle (180 degrees). Individuals who have a visual field of no greater than 20 degrees are considered to be blind.

▶ **CAUSES OF BLINDNESS**

There are many causes of blindness and visual impairment. Some people are born with this condition. Their blindness or visual impairment is said to be **congenital**, meaning "born with."

Accidents can also cause eyesight loss. Wearing protective eyeglasses or goggles during activities such as using power tools, playing racquetball, or working with chemicals can help prevent such accidents.

Disease is a very common cause of blindness and visual impairment. **Cataracts**, an ailment usually found in elderly people, causes a clouding of the lens in the eye. If you look through a piece of waxed paper, you can experience what some people with cataracts see.

Glaucoma is a disease that causes increased fluid pressure inside the eye. It can cause blindness and also tunnel vision. If you close one eye and look through a paper towel tube with the other eye, you will see what tunnel vision is like. If detected early, glaucoma often can be treated with special eye drops or surgery.

Diabetes causes a swelling and leaking of the blood vessels inside the eye. This can cause blurred vision. If the blood vessels break, the blood interferes with light passing through the eye. This can cause visual impairment or total blindness.

In developing nations, there are additional diseases that cause eyesight loss. **Onchocerciasis**, commonly referred to as "river blindness," is an eye infection caused by a parasite. This disease is common in tropical areas such as Central America and parts of Africa. In some villages, 10 percent of the total population is blind because of this disease.

What to Do When You See a Blind Person

If you see a blind person who seems to need help, offer your assistance. Tell the person who you are and that you are speaking to him or her. If the person says that help is not needed, believe it and simply go on your way.

If the person accepts your help, let him or her take your arm at the elbow. When you lead a blind person, you should always walk slightly in front. If a blind person is using a guide dog, do not pet or distract the animal. The guide dog is a working dog and is not a pet.

Do not be afraid to use words like "see" and "look." Such words do not make blind people uncomfortable. If a person is blind, that does not mean he or she cannot hear. Remember to speak in a normal tone of voice.

When you leave a blind person, tell him or her that you are leaving. Let the person know that you may meet again. "See you soon!"

Using an abacus, the student works on math problems from a braille textbook. Braille is a touch method of reading letters, numbers, and other symbols.

BRAILLE ALPHABET AND NUMERALS

a	b	c	d	e	f	g	h	i	j
k	l	m	n	o	p	q	r	s	t
u	v	w	x	y	z
1	2	3	4	5	6	7	8	9	0

Xerophthalmia is the major cause of blindness in young children in many developing countries. It is caused by a severe lack of protein and vitamin A in the diet. This disease is found in overpopulated regions of south and east Asia, Africa, the eastern Mediterranean, and parts of Latin America. In India alone, more than 60,000 children under the age of 6 go totally blind each year due to this disease.

▶ COPING WITH BLINDNESS

Two of the biggest challenges that a blind or visually impaired person must face are moving about independently and communicating with others.

Moving about without sight—or with very limited sight—requires a unique set of skills. Blind people must use their sense of hearing, smell, and touch to learn about their environment. This is called **orientation**. For example, a blind person in the city listens for traffic sounds to know when to cross a street. The person may smell flowers in a park or food from a restaurant to help them know where they are.

To move about safely, blind or visually impaired people can rely on a variety of aids. A long cane, also called a prescription cane, is used when walking to warn of objects, stairs, or street curbs in a person's path. Scientists have developed a laser cane, which can also detect objects at head or chest level. When it senses an obstacle, the cane gives out a warning sound.

Blind teenagers and adults can learn to use a guide dog to move about. Both the dog and the handler attend a special school to learn how to work together. Guide dogs serve the same purposes as the long cane. They help the person move around obstacles or stop before stepping up or down.

Blind and visually impaired people have the same need for information about the world as people with sight. To meet that need, there are many useful aids.

Braille is a touch method of reading. The braille alphabet was developed in France by Louis Braille in the 1800's. The letters of the braille alphabet are based on a system of six raised dots that can be read by the fingertips. There are also special braille symbols for mathematical, musical, computer, and foreign language materials. Braille can be produced by using heavy paper with special braille typewriters.

Large-print books and magazines are useful to people with less severe visual impairments. Audio tapes are frequently used for both leisure and educational reading. Some computers have speech devices that can talk to the user, telling what is happening on the screen.

Two recent developments help blind and visually impaired people gain more immediate access to current information. Talking Newspaper programs allow people to call on the telephone and have the newspaper read aloud to them. Audiodescription Services provides a description of the action, mannerisms, and

What is a Talking Book?

The world of books is open to the blind today through books prepared in braille and through long-playing recordings of books, called talking books. The largest producer of braille textbooks is the American Printing House for the Blind in Louisville, Kentucky.

The Library of Congress of the United States, Division for the Blind and Physically Handicapped, in Washington, D.C., has hundreds of thousands of braille volumes and talking books. Hundreds of new library titles are recorded and brailled each year. Throughout the country there are libraries that act as distributing centers for these books and records. They are mailed postage-free.

Technological advances, such as talking computers and electronic braille machines, have opened up new career opportunities for blind and visually impaired individuals.

other nonverbal communications shown on television programs.

▶ **EDUCATION AND EMPLOYMENT**

The first school for children who were blind was founded in France in 1784 by Valentin Hauy. By 1833 there were three special schools for blind children in the United States. Public school began to educate blind children in the early 1900's. Today, about 90 percent of all the children in the United States who are blind or visually impaired are educated in their neighborhood or community schools. Blind and visually impaired children must learn the special skills needed by people without sight. They also must learn basic concepts in special ways. Because so much of what we learn is through observation, visually impaired children need a great deal of hands-on experience. Concepts such as up and down, streets, rainbows, clouds, and stars are meaningless words unless taught with models or accurate verbal descriptions.

Any career that does not depend on sight is open to a blind or visually impaired person. People without sight can become teachers, farmers, computer programmers, government workers, accountants, or lawyers. Young people can work at jobs such as delivering newspapers, counseling children at summer camp, and serving food at fast food restaurants.

▶ **AGENCIES AND ASSOCIATIONS THAT HELP**

The American Foundation for the Blind helps blind and visually impaired people achieve equal access to opportunities that will help them live independent and satisfying lives. This organization helps pass laws that will help people with limited sight, publishes information about blindness, and provides a directory of consumer groups, agencies, schools, and services that can help. Its headquarters is in New York City.

Three United Nations agencies are concerned with blindness in both industrialized and developing nations. These are the United Nations Education, Scientific and Cultural Organization (UNESCO), the World Health Organization (WHO), and the United Nations Children's Fund (UNICEF).

KATHLEEN MARY HUEBNER
Director, National Consultants Department
American Foundation for the Blind

See also EYE; KELLER, HELEN.

BLOOD

A crimson river flows through the human body, carrying materials that are essential to the life of each and every body cell. This river of life is blood. Each beat of the heart propels the vital fluid to the body's cells. Without blood, we could not exist.

The amount of blood in an individual's body depends for the most part on size, making up about 7 percent of a person's body weight. The average 160-pound (73-kilogram) adult has about 5 quarts (4.8 liters) of blood, while the average 80-pound (36-kilogram) child has about 2.5 quarts (2.4 liters).

Blood supplies the body's cells with food and oxygen and carries away carbon dioxide and other cell waste products. It also carries the hormones that help regulate body functions and removes excess heat from cells, which helps keep the body temperature within a steady range. Antibodies and other chemicals produced by blood cells fight infections and heal injuries. In addition, the water that body cells need for their chemical reactions is transported by the blood. The ability to perform all these tasks truly makes blood the river of life.

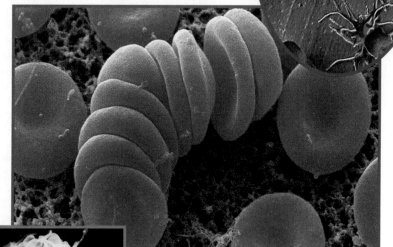

Every 60 seconds, a life-giving cycle takes place as blood courses through our bodies. Fluid plasma and solid matter—platelets (*right*), red blood cells (*below*), and white blood cells (*bottom*)—form the complex mixture that is blood.

▶ WHAT BLOOD IS MADE OF

Blood is a complex mixture of solid matter (cells and cell fragments) and fluid. The fluid portion of blood is called **plasma**. It makes up about 55 percent of the blood volume. The solid matter, which makes up about 45 percent of the volume, consists of **red blood cells** (or **erythrocytes**), **white blood cells** (or **leukocytes**), and cell fragments called **platelets**.

Plasma. Plasma, which is about 92 percent water, is a straw-colored fluid. The majority of substances dissolved in plasma are proteins, such as albumins, globulins, and fibrinogen. Other important substances found in plasma include minerals, nutrients, and waste products.

Red Blood Cells. Red blood cells, shaped like tiny round disks with flattened centers, make up most of the solid portion of blood. It is the **hemoglobin**, an iron-containing protein, found inside these cells that gives blood its red color. There are more red blood cells in an individual's body than any other kind of cell—about 25 trillion in the average adult. If they were stacked one on top of another, they would reach 31,000 miles (50,000 kilometers) into the sky!

White Blood Cells. There are about 5,000 to 10,000 white blood cells in 1/30,000 of an ounce (1 microliter) of blood—about one for each 700 red cells. White blood cells are jelly-like blobs that can change their shape. These large cells ooze along on their own and can even leave the bloodstream, squeezing out through tiny gaps in the blood-vessel walls. There are five main kinds of leukocytes: **neutrophils** make up the largest percentage of white blood cells, followed by **lymphocytes**,

Red blood cells squeeze single file through thin-walled capillaries as they carry their load of oxygen to all the cells of the body.

monocytes, eosinophils, and basophils.

Platelets. Blood platelets are tiny bodies, much smaller than red blood cells. They are formed as broken fragments of megakaryocytes, which are giant cells found in bone marrow. Unlike other cellular components of the blood, platelets have no nucleus. There are normally from 250,000 to 400,000 platelets in 1/30,000 of an ounce (1 microliter) of blood.

▶ HOW BLOOD WORKS IN THE BODY

The river of blood that courses through the body journeys along a path that stretches 60,000 miles (97,000 kilometers). As it flows, it functions as a vehicle of transportation, protection, and regulation.

Transportation. Networks of tiny blood vessels called capillaries carry oxygen to the cells. In the lungs, inhaled oxygen passes through the thin walls of capillaries surrounding the air sacs and combines with hemoglobin in the red blood cells. The bright red, oxygenated blood flows into the heart, which pumps it out into a network of blood vessels that go to all parts of the body.

When the blood reaches its destination, the hemoglobin releases its oxygen, which then passes out of the capillaries and into the cells. The cells' waste products, including carbon dioxide and urea, move out of the cells and into the capillaries to be carried away in the bloodstream. When the blood reaches the lungs again, carbon dioxide passes

out through the capillary walls and into the air sacs, to be breathed out. Urea, along with salts and other substances, is filtered out as blood passes through the kidneys and leaves the body in the urine.

After a meal, the blood picks up nutrients from food digested in the stomach and intestines: amino acids from proteins, sugars from starches, and small particles of fats, as well as vitamins and minerals. The blood carries these nutrients to cells, where they are used as fuel, to build and repair tissue, or stored for future needs.

Hormones that aid digestion are also carried in the blood. For example, the hormones insulin and glucagon control how much glucose, the body's main fuel, is taken up or released by cells. They also keep the amount of glucose in the blood at a consistent level.

Fighting Disease. The white blood cells help defend the body against disease-causing micro-organisms and other threats. Neutrophils are the first to attack invading mi-

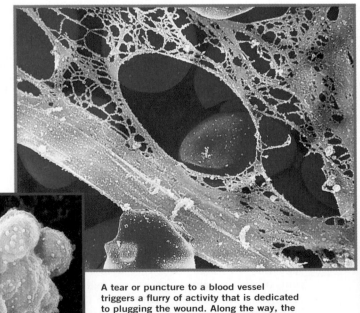

A tear or puncture to a blood vessel triggers a flurry of activity that is dedicated to plugging the wound. Along the way, the plasma protein fibrinogen is converted to fibrin. The sticky, threadlike fibrin gradually spins a loose net (*above*) that catches platelets and blood cells. Platelets (*left*) deliver chemicals that link the threads together, helping to form the clot.

crobes. The neutrophil's body flows around a bacterium and digests it. Eosinophils help fight parasites and allergic reactions. Basophils release chemicals that help in inflammation and healing. Monocytes leave the bloodstream to fight microbes in infected tissues. They mature in the tissues and become macrophages, swelling in size as they gobble up bacteria. Some lymphocytes (**B cells**) make the specialized proteins, called **antibodies**, that help to attack germs. Others (**helper T cells**) release substances that direct the activities of the antibody-producing cells. Still others (**killer T cells**) attack the germs directly. Some T lymphocytes search out and destroy outlaw body cells that could grow into cancerous tumors.

Regulating the Internal Environment. The blood helps to regulate the body temperature by carrying excess heat away from body cells. Heat is radiated out into the air from capillary networks in the skin. In cold weather, these capillaries contract, reducing the amount of heat lost from the body.

▶ **THE BLOOD SUPPLY**

Red blood cells live an average of 120 days before wearing out. Many worn-out red cells are captured and destroyed in the liver and spleen. White blood cells, too, wear out. They also can be poisoned by the microbes they gobble up while defending the body.

New blood cells are formed in the bone marrow. Special blood-forming marrow cells called **stem cells** can develop into red blood cells, one of the various kinds of white blood cells, or platelets. A hormone produced by the kidneys, **erythropoietin**, stimulates the bone marrow to produce new red blood cells. Other hormones help to regulate the volume of blood and the concentration of salts and other substances in the blood plasma.

Blood platelets normally live for only about five to eight days. If a platelet comes in contact with the rough edge of a cut blood-vessel wall, it tears, spilling out chemicals that help control bleeding. Some cause the blood vessel to contract; others start chemical reactions that convert the plasma protein **fibrinogen** to **fibrin**, a jellylike substance. Threadlike strings of fibrin form a sticky mesh on which platelets and blood cells are caught. Together they form a clot, which plugs up the hole and stops the bleeding.

BLOOD TYPES

It was in 1901 that the Austrian doctor Karl Landsteiner discovered that red blood cells have special proteins (antigens) on their surface that can react with antibodies, causing the red cells to clump together. People do not have antibodies to their own red blood cell proteins, but their plasma may contain antibodies to antigens of a different blood type. If blood of different types is mixed, the red cells may clump (*pictured below*), clogging the blood vessels.

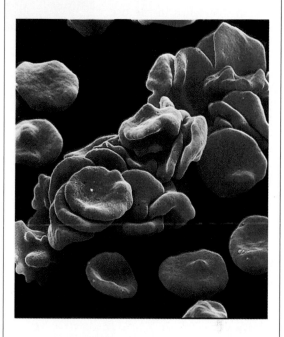

Landsteiner found two main types of antigens, A and B, which are transmitted by heredity from parents to their children. There are four possible blood types: A, B, AB (both antigens), and O (neither antigen). In addition to the A-B-O blood groups, researchers have found many other blood groups, including the Rh and M-N blood groups. Those who have the Rh antigen, called the Rh factor, on their red blood cells are Rh positive; those who do not are considered Rh negative.

The other blood groups, such as the M-N, also have red-cell antigens. But unlike the A-B-O and Rh blood groups, these antigens rarely produce a strong antibody response. This means they are much less likely to cause dangerous reactions during transfusion procedures.

DISORDERS OF THE BLOOD

Blood disorders result from a variety of conditions, including too many or too few blood cells. In **anemia**, there are not enough red blood cells to supply the body with the oxygen it needs. A diet lacking iron or B vitamins, both of which are needed to produce hemoglobin, or the lack of intrinsic factor, a stomach protein that helps in the use of vitamin B_{12}, can cause anemia. In **aplastic anemia**, the bone marrow has been damaged, perhaps by radiation or certain drugs, and is unable to produce new blood cells. **Sickle-cell anemia** is a hereditary disorder in which defective hemoglobin causes the blood cells to have a

The deformed cells, rigid and twisted, that are present in sickle-cell anemia are the result of an error in the genetic coding of the hemoglobin molecule.

characteristic sickle or crescent shape. When sickling occurs, cells clump together and block small blood vessels, depriving tissues of blood and resulting in joint pain and fever. Several types of the anemia known as **thalassemia** are also caused by abnormal hemoglobin, resulting in destruction of red blood cells.

Leukemia is a cancer of the bone marrow or lymph nodes, resulting in the production of large numbers of abnormal white blood cells that cannot fight infection. Damage to the bone marrow may stop the formation of white blood cells, producing **leukopenia** (a lack of white blood cells). Without an adequate number of white blood cells to patrol the body, disease-causing invaders can multiply unchecked, causing infections in many parts of the body.

Blood clotting is a very complex process, involving more than a dozen different chemicals. A hereditary lack of one of the "clotting factors" can cause **hemophilia**, a condition in which even a minor cut can result in severe blood loss. Damage to the bone marrow can result in **thrombocytopenia**, a lack of blood platelets. The amount of time it takes for blood to clot increases as the amount of platelets decreases. The person with thrombocytopenia may have many small purplish patches on the skin, due to bleeding from torn capillaries.

In **infectious mononucleosis**, the Epstein-Barr virus infects B lymphocytes. Some of them become abnormal and are attacked by killer T cells, producing swollen lymph nodes and fever. The AIDS virus, HIV, does the most damage to the helper T lymphocytes. As these blood cells are destroyed, the body loses its ability to fight infections.

ALVIN SILVERSTEIN
VIRGINIA SILVERSTEIN
Coauthors, *The Circulatory System*

See also BODY, HUMAN; CIRCULATORY SYSTEM; HEART.

Did you know that...

the first successful blood transfusion was performed more than 500 years ago by the Incas of South America? When an Inca was injured and suffered a great blood loss, the victim was given blood from a healthy individual. Inca doctors used a hollow tube to link the injured person with the blood donor.

Doctors in other parts of the world also tried to perform transfusions, but the recipients often died when they did. Medical experts think the treatment worked for the Incas because it is likely that they all had the same blood type. Having the same blood type would mean that they could give and receive blood among themselves without the risk of a dangerous transfusion reaction.

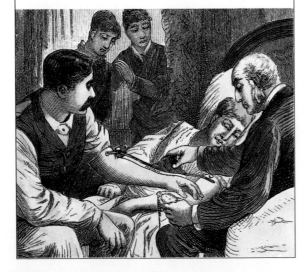

BLUEPRINT

The blueprinting process was discovered by Sir John Frederick Herschel, an English astronomer, in 1842. It was originally called cyanotype and involved coating paper with a special chemical, which resulted in a print of white lines on a Prussian blue background.

The blueprint was used mainly for copying drawings and other clerical work done by architects, engineers, and shipbuilders who needed quick, long-lasting records of designs and figures. It was the simplest, cheapest, and most permanent photographic print and could be easily made by almost anyone.

To make a blueprint, a chemical coating is applied to a piece of paper. When the sensitized paper has dried to a bronze color, it is placed in contact with a drawing, covered with a sheet of glass, and exposed to sunlight for about an hour. After a final cold-water wash, the paper becomes bright blue and the lines of the image are white.

Blueprints were widely used until the 1960's when other techniques were developed. The sepia print and the whiteprint—an image of blue, brown, or black lines on a

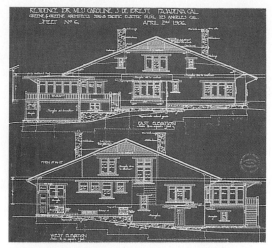

A blueprint like this one serves as a detailed plan for the building of a house. Copies used by everyone in the construction process show both the builder and the owner the exact specifications they have agreed upon.

white background—were faster to make and easier to mark up and read. Architects and engineers continue to use these alternative reproduction methods. No one is sure, however, if they will last as long as blueprints, which survive for many decades without fading.

DONNA ROBERTSON
Director, Barnard College Architecture Program

BLUES. See JAZZ.

BLUME, JUDY (1938–   )

The American writer Judy Blume is best known for books that deal frankly with issues and problems confronting young people. Her books consistently appear on lists of young readers' favorites.

Blume was born Judy Sussman in Elizabeth, New Jersey, on February 12, 1938. She was an imaginative child who studied dance and earned high honors at school. After graduating from New York University in 1960, she lived in suburban New Jersey with her husband, John Blume, and two children. Looking for a creative outlet, she tried

Judy Blume's fiction deals frankly with issues confronting young people. Her books are sometimes controversial with adults but always popular with her young readers.

writing pop songs and making banners. Finally, she began to write stories, taking a college course in writing for children.

Her first successful book was *Are You There, God? It's Me, Margaret* (1970). It tells of a sixth-grader's preoccupation with religion and with her own developing body. Blume dealt with the issue of parental divorce in *It's Not the End of the World* (1972) and with teenage sex in *Forever* (1975). In all her works she attempted to be completely honest with her readers, saying, "Problems only get worse when there are secrets, because what kids imagine is usually scarier than the truth."

Other books by Judy Blume include *Superfudge* (1980), *Just As Long As We're Together* (1987), *Fudge-A-Mania* (1990), *Here's to You, Rachel Robinson* (1993); three novels for adults; and *Letters to Judy* (1986), a collection of letters from her young readers.

Reviewed by CHARLES MORITZ
Editor, *Current Biography*

BLY, NELLIE (1864–1922)

Nellie Bly was once the most daring and celebrated newspaper reporter in the United States. She helped pioneer a sensational eyewitness reporting style that broke new ground for women and journalism. Bly acquired international fame by traveling around the world in record time—72 days, 6 hours, and 11 minutes. Her trip, completed in 1890, sought to outdo the fictitious record of Phileas Fogg, the hero of Jules Verne's popular novel, *Around the World in Eighty Days.*

Nellie Bly was born Elizabeth Cochran on May 5, 1864, in Cochran's Mills, Pennsylvania. She began her journalism career in 1885 as a reporter for the Pittsburgh *Dispatch.* It was there she took the pen name Nellie Bly.

As a novice reporter, Bly took many risks for a woman in her day. She wrote controversial articles on divorce, slum housing, and dangerous factory conditions. Newspapers around the country picked up her articles.

In 1887, Bly moved to New York City and joined Joseph Pulitzer's *World.* For her first assignment, she pretended to be insane to gain admission to the notorious asylum on Blackwell's Island. She wrote a blistering account of her experiences and exposed the asylum's appalling treatment of its patients. Her story sparked a statewide reform effort.

Such stunts became Bly's trademark. She later posed as a prostitute and as a criminal to gain firsthand information on prison life. Her most famous exploit, however, was her 72-

News reporter Nellie Bly became an international celebrity when she completed a record-breaking 72-day trip around the world in 1890. This photograph was taken the day she returned from her journey.

day trip around the world. She recorded her adventures in *Nellie Bly's Book: Around the World in 72 days,* published in 1890.

In 1895, Bly married Robert L. Seaman, a Brooklyn industrialist. After his death in 1904, Bly took over his manufacturing company, where she provided health care and equal wages to men and women. At the age of 50 she resumed her newspaper career but failed to achieve a major comeback. Nellie Bly died of pneumonia on January 27, 1922.

ELIZABETH EHRLICH
Author, *Nellie Bly*

BOARDSAILING

Boardsailing is a modern sport that combines features of two ancient activities, sailing and surfing. It is sometimes called windsurfing because the first sailboard, built in 1968, was named Windsurfer by its inventors, Americans Hoyle Schweitzer and Jim Drake.

Certified schools offer one- or two-day boardsailing courses that help beginners learn correct techniques. With six to eight hours of practice, beginners can learn enough of the basic skills at such schools to enjoy sailing in gentle breezes on smooth water.

Experienced boardsailors have many exciting challenges. There are races from local to international level, including the Olympic Games. Freestyle is a form of gymnastics on the sailboard. Wave jumping combines the speed of surfing and sailing to gain enough momentum to fly off the crest of a large wave and then fly or somersault through the air.

Equipment. A sailboard resembles a surfboard. It may be about 12 feet (3.6 meters) long for sailing and racing or shorter for freestyle and wave jumping. It is equipped with a **mast** attached by a **universal joint**—a device that allows the mast to turn and tilt in all directions. A bar, called the **boom,** curves around both sides of the sail at a height at which the sailor can grip it when standing on the board. The triangular sail usually has an area of from 55 to 65 square feet (5 to 6 square meters). It has a clear plastic window, allowing the sailor a view of the water on either side.

Controlling the Sailboard. When the sailboard is at rest, the mast and the sail lie flat on the water. The sailor stands on the board and pulls them upright with an attached line. The sailor then holds the boom. **Tacking** (turning the board toward the direction from which the wind is blowing) is done by tilting the mast toward the back of the board. **Jibing** (turning away from the wind) is done by tilting the mast forward.

Safety. Boardsailors must follow the general rules found in the article SAILING in Volume S. They must know how to swim and should always wear life jackets. It is important to have a companion nearby to give assistance if required.

Boardsailors must guard against hypothermia—chilling of the body that can cause death. This chilling can be caused by exposing the wet body to wind even when the air and water seem warm. The first symptoms are numbness in the hands and feet and uncontrollable shivering. If this occurs, the sailor must immediately get out of the water, dry off, and get warm. Wet suits are worn by most boardsailors. These suits hold a thin layer of water next to the body, where it is warmed and acts as insulation.

Competition. Boardsailing races are held on triangular, slalom, or long-distance courses. Triangular courses are used in Olympic competition (known as sailboarding), which was instituted for men in 1984 and became a part of women's competition in 1992. Slalom racecourses have six marks set close enough together to test the sailors' ability to tack and jibe. Distance races usually cover 5 to 15 miles (8 to 24 kilometers) and test both skill and endurance.

RHONDA SMITH-SANCHEZ
World Champion

BOAS, FRANZ (1858–1942)

Franz Boas was a pioneer of anthropology, the study of the origin and development of people and their cultures. Before Boas, many believed that some cultures were advanced while others were primitive. Boas did not accept this. He believed that cultures were different from one another because of the differences in their environments. He established that each culture should be judged on the basis of its own environment and history, and not by the standards of others.

Boas also had a great influence on how anthropologists work. He established the importance of field work—the recording of data based on personal observation. He showed that information about language, art, folklore, and mythology was as important to one's evaluation of a culture as the physical details about the people and their surroundings.

Franz Boas was born on July 9, 1858, in Minden, Germany. His parents encouraged his interest in science, and he attended the University of Kiel. His interest in anthropology developed during a scientific expedition to Baffin Island in the Arctic (1883–1884), where he had an opportunity to observe the local Inuit culture. Many of his ideas were shaped by several trips he made to the northwest coast of North America, over a period of time from 1886 to 1931, to study several Indian cultures, including the Kwakiutl.

In 1887 Boas decided to live permanently in the United States and he became a citizen in 1891. At first he worked for the magazine *Science*. Later, he taught and did research at Clark University in Massachusetts and at Chicago's Field Museum of Natural History. Finally, he settled in New York City to work at the American Museum of Natural History and to study and teach at Columbia University. Boas founded a department at Columbia that produced many of the great anthropologists of the 1900's, including Ruth Benedict, Margaret Mead, and Edward Sapir. He also published many books and several important studies on American Indian folklore and art.

Franz Boas died in New York on December 22, 1942.

RACHEL KRANZ
Editor, Biographies
The Young Adult Reader's Adviser
See also ANTHROPOLOGY.

BOATS AND BOATING

Boating is a fast-growing sport. Every year more young skippers pilot their craft on fresh-water lakes and rivers and on the bays and inlets at the ocean's edge. To keep pace with the rapid growth of boating, hundreds of marinas have been built to provide shoreside berths, or places to anchor small craft. *Marina* is a Spanish word meaning "seacoast," and is used in English to describe a modern boat basin with piers and slips for docking boats, launches, and yachts. In a marina large and small boats are repaired, serviced, and stored. Shore electricity, telephones, fresh water, ice, and fuel are available at dockside. Pleasure-boat owners may shop here for supplies and food and drink all within walking distance of their boats. Every type of craft may be seen at a marina. There are sailing dinghies and two-masted schooners, outboard runabouts and big cabin cruisers with facilities to sleep six or more people.

The 14- to 18-foot (4.3- to 5.5-meter) runabouts are the most popular small powerboats. They are wonderful for fishing or for just having fun on the water. The larger ones, fitted with powerful outboard engines, are used for towing water-skiers.

Before beginners learn to run one of these craft or even go for a ride in a dinghy or other small rowboat, they should know the basic rules of safety for themselves and their boat.

▶**SAFETY RULES FOR YOUNG SAILORS**

(1) Learn to swim. If you cannot swim, wear a life jacket.

(2) Do not go out in a boat alone. Young children should always be accompanied by an adult.

(3) Do not go out in bad weather, or when a storm is forecast, or in a fog. Beginning boaters should stay close to shore.

(4) Never overload your boat.

(5) Sit quietly when boating. Do not scuffle while aboard a boat. Do not change seats when the water is rough or when the boat is in deep water.

(6) Do not try to swim ashore from an over-turned boat even if you are a good swimmer. Hold on to the boat and wait for help.

(7) Wear sneakers or rubber-soled shoes to avoid slipping, and wear a hat to protect yourself from the sun.

(8) Before diving off a boat into strange water, test for depth, rocks, and weeds. Swim in a safe place.

▶ THE RULES OF BOATING

It is important to know the rules of any sport, but in boating not knowing the rules can mean disaster. The important rules of boating concern whistle signals, the lights for different kinds of boats, and rights of way.

Signal Talk

One blast of a boat's whistle or horn means "I am going right." Two blasts mean "I am going left."

Motorboats are forbidden to respond using a cross signal—that is, answering one whistle with two blasts or two blasts with one. Instead, they are required to answer with the same signal to indicate that the other boat's signal has been understood. Whistle or horn signals, however, are not exchanged between sailboats.

Four or more blasts mean danger. If the skipper disagrees with a signal or does not understand it, the danger signal should be given and the boat stopped. The boat should not proceed until the proper signals have been given, answered, and understood.

Lights Required After Sunset

Class A boats, which are under 16 feet (4.9 meters) long, and Class 1 boats, which are 16 to 26 feet (4.9 to 7.9 meters) long, have a combination red and green light at the front, or **bow** of the boat. The red light indicates the **port**, or left side, and the green light indicates the **starboard**, or right side.

Each color should be visible from dead ahead and should show for 10 points around the horizon on each side for a distance of 1 mile (1.6 kilometers). (On a compass, 32 points represent a complete circle.) A white light at the rear, or **stern**, of the boat should show all around the horizon and be visible for about 2 miles (3 kilometers).

Class 2 boats, which are 26 to 40 feet (7.9 to 12.2 meters) long, and Class 3 boats, which measure 40 to 65 feet (12.2 to 19.8 meters), have separate red and green side lights. These boats must also have a white 20-point light at the bow, as well as a white 32-point stern light, which is placed higher than the bow light.

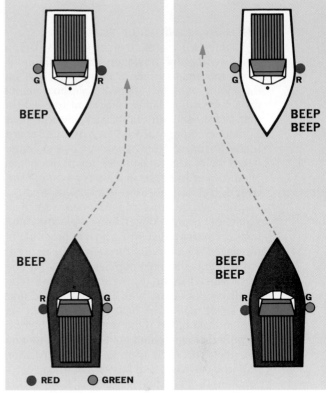

When boats approach head on, one blast of the whistle means "going right" (starboard). It is answered by one blast from the approaching boat. Two blasts mean "going left" (port), and are answered by two blasts.

Right of Way

The first rule of the seaway is "Keep to the right." For instance, when two boats are about to meet head on, each skipper should give one blast on the whistle and turn the boat to starboard (right). The boats will then pass port side to port side (left side to left side). This and other passing situations are shown above and on pages 268–69.

Sailboats always have the right of way over powerboats, unless a sailboat is overtaking a powerboat. In any dangerous situation, even though a boat may have the right of way, it is best to turn or back away to avoid collision. Pamphlets on piloting rules are available from the U.S. Coast Guard office in Washington, D.C., or from local coast guard offices. In Canada, boating information is available from the Canadian Coast Guard, headquartered in Ottawa, Ontario.

Good boating safety also requires having certain emergency equipment, including a fire extinguisher, a first-aid kit, life jackets, and buoyant cushions. A compass is also important for boats that navigate offshore.

▶THE MANY ACTIVITIES OF BOATING

People swim from all types of boats. Before going swimming, however, the boat should be either moored to a pier or lying at anchor, and the motor must be stopped. The boat should have a boarding ladder placed at one side so that swimmers can climb back into the boat. Someone should always remain on board, ready to throw a life preserver if a swimmer needs help. Children under ten years of age should wear life vests and never swim in water over 5 feet (1.5 meters) deep. Skin diving is another activity that can be done from most kinds of boats. Waterskiing, on the other hand, requires a fast powerboat in order to pull the water-skier rapidly through the water.

Fishing is the most popular activity for boaters. Most fishing from runabouts and other small boats is done with light poles and lines and small reels. The boat can be stopped and the bait cast out into the water, or the bait can be pulled along behind the boat as it is moving —a method called trolling. Deep-sea fishing requires big boats and heavy fishing tackle. A

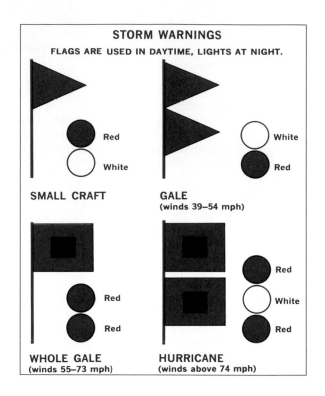

STORM WARNINGS
FLAGS ARE USED IN DAYTIME, LIGHTS AT NIGHT.

SMALL CRAFT — Red / White

GALE (winds 39–54 mph) — White / Red

WHOLE GALE (winds 55–73 mph) — Red / Red

HURRICANE (winds above 74 mph) — Red / White / Red

Left: Sailboats always have the right of way over powerboats. *Center:* Red to red (port to port) means safe to go ahead. *Right:* When you see both red and green lights, blow one blast and pass red to red (port to port).

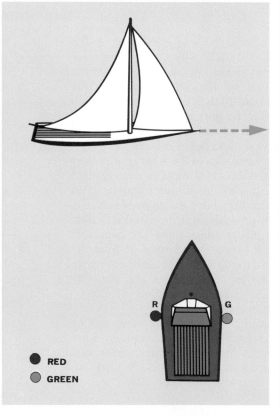

RED
GREEN

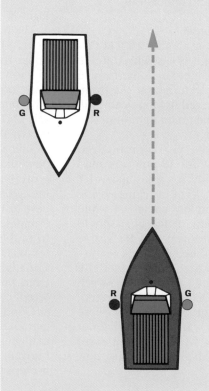

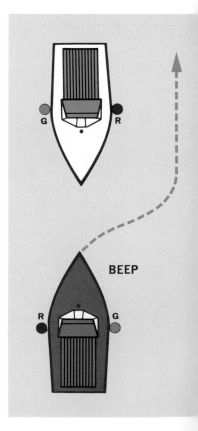

BEEP

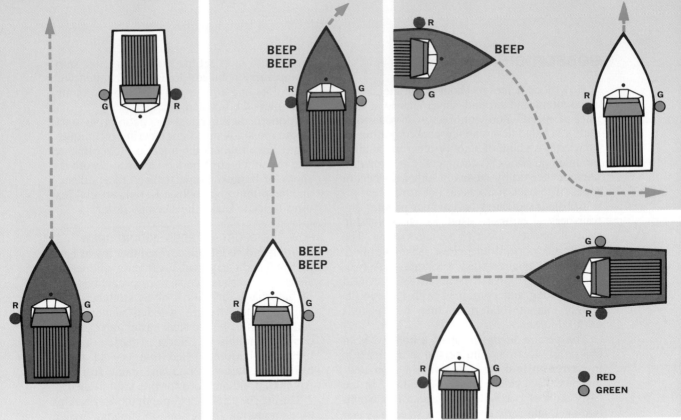

Left: Green to green means safe to proceed. *Center:* Boat astern asks to pass. Lead boat answers and moves to starboard. *Upper right:* Red to starboard gives other boat right of way; signal and go astern. *Lower right:* Green off your port bow gives you right of way.

boat with a "flying bridge," a piloting platform at the top, is used to fish for large game fish, such as marlin or sailfish. When one of these fish is hooked, the skipper must be able to twist and turn the boat quickly to keep the fishing line tight and prevent it from getting under the boat. The person fishing is often strapped into a special chair and may require several hours to land a large fish.

Camping is another activity that almost every boat owner can enjoy. Even a canoe or small runabout can carry the tent, sleeping bags, portable stove, and supply of food that will make a satisfying trip.

▶POWERBOAT RACING

A more specialized boating activity is powerboat racing. Most racing requires special boats and motors. Racing boats are classified according to the size of the boat and the type of motor. The largest competition boats are the 25- to 40-foot (7.6- to 12.2-meter) **hydroplanes**. (Hydroplanes are light, flat-bottomed boats.) These boats have powerful engines that enable them to reach speeds of 200 miles (320 kilometers) an hour. Jet-powered speedboats can reach speeds of almost 300 miles (480 kilometers) an hour.

Racing boats compete in a variety of contests in the United States and throughout the world. The famous Gold Cup race, for example, is held at various cities in the United States. The marathon is a long-distance event often raced on a river. Powerboat races are also held on the open ocean. These races provided a rugged test of boats, their equipment, and their drivers.

Racing requires expert boating skills. However, newcomers to boating can have a great deal of fun using their boats for exploring, for nature studies, for photography, and for simply being on the water. As Kenneth Grahame wrote in *The Wind in the Willows*, "There is nothing half so much worth doing as simply messing about in boats. . . . in or out of 'em, it doesn't matter."

TOM BOTTOMLEY
Author, *Cruising for Fun*

See also DIVING; FISHING; ROWING; SAILING; SKIN DIVING; SWIMMING; WATERSKIING.

BOBSLEDDING

How does it feel to shoot down the side of a mountain and around sharp curves at high rates of speed? You would know if you rode a racing bobsled down an ice-packed bobrun. A bobsled is a plank of steel or other metal alloy mounted on two sets of runners. The front runners are steered by means of either a wheel or ropes. The back runners do not turn.

Bobsleds can carry two or four people. The four-person bobsled used in championship races is about 12 feet (3.5 meters) long. The weight of the sled and crew cannot be more than 1,389 pounds (630 kilograms). A two-person racing bobsled is about 8½ feet (2.5 meters) long and combined with its crew its weight cannot total more than 827 pounds (375 kilograms).

The person in the front of a bobsled is in charge of steering. The person in the back is in charge of braking. On a four-person sled, the other two riders sit in the middle. In the early days of bobsledding, these riders would bob back and forth to make the sled go as fast as possible. This is how bobsledding got its name.

The bodies of today's bobsleds are often made of graphite or other very lightweight material. The body of the bobsled helps protect the riders and the steering mechanism. Streamlined design helps cut down wind resistance, making faster speeds possible. Push handles on each side of the sled are used by the crew to help get the sled off to a fast start. Competitive bobsleds are usually painted with the colors and emblem of the club or country that enters the bobsled in a race.

Modern racing bobsleds incorporate some of the most advanced engineering techniques. Many have runners mounted in rubber that act like the shock absorbers on a car to absorb the shock of bumps. Some bobsled racers design and build their own bobsleds, with special features to try to make the sleds go faster.

▶HOW THE SPORT OF BOBSLEDDING GREW

Long ago people discovered that it was easy to travel and carry loads over snow and ice on sleds. The earliest sleds were probably made of flat boards or animal skins stretched over frames. Later, narrow wooden runners were added. This made the sleds faster and easier to control. Indians of North America used a light, flat-bottomed sled that curved up in front. The name "toboggan" came from the Algonkian Indian word for this kind of sled.

During the 1880's, people in the Swiss Alps tried mounting toboggans on runners, which made them go faster. In fact, they went so fast that they often ran off course, out of control. Members of the Toboggan Club at St. Moritz, a famous winter resort in Switzerland, found that by making these sleds much heavier they could be controlled better. This was the birth of the bobsleigh, or bobsled, as it is called today. A special bobrun was built at St. Moritz, and the first race was held there in 1898.

A United States bobsled crew pushes off for a fast start in an Olympic race.

The first national championship bobsled races were held in Austria in 1908, and bobsledding became a world event in the first Olympic Winter Games, held in France in 1924.

▶ BOBRUNS

There are 16 bobruns in the world. The first bobrun in the United States was built in Lake Placid, New York, for the 1932 Winter Olympic Games. The longest bobrun, in Nagano, Japan, is 5,781 feet (1,762 meters) long. Other bobruns are located in St. Moritz, Switzerland; Calgary, Canada; and Cortina d'Ampezzo, Italy.

Bobruns are composed of a series of curves and straightaways. The walls are made of reinforced concrete covered with a mixture of ice and snow. Using concrete eliminates the need for building walls of large ice blocks. The base of the bobrun is also made of concrete. A refrigeration system under the concrete keeps the run cold. When water is sprayed onto the run, it freezes quickly into ice, making the run extremely fast.

Bobruns are also used for luge and skeleton competition. The luge is a small sled on which the athlete rides on his or her back. The skeleton is also a small sled, but it resembles the "skeleton" of a bobsled, and the athlete rides it headfirst down the run.

Spectators watch a two-person bobsled climbing high on the sidewall as it takes a curve.

▶ BOBSLED RACING

There is room for only one sled at a time on a bobrun. A bobsled race is therefore a race against time. Each sled is timed with the aid of electronic eyes.

Bobsled racers push their sled from a starting point and leap on it after crossing the starting line. As the sled crosses the starting line, electric eyes cause a clock in the timing booth to start running. Other electric eyes along the bobrun mark the sled's time at intermediate points. At the end of the run a final pair of electric eyes stops the clock in the timing booth. The clock is able to time each run to 1/100 of a second.

Championship races consist of four heats, or runs, for each sled. The sled with the shortest total time for the four heats is the winner. The fastest times on the bobrun at Lake Placid are less than 1 minute for a four-person sled and less than 1 minute and 4 seconds for a two-person sled. Bobsleds often reach speeds of about 90 miles (145 kilometers) an hour.

Bobsled racing is governed by the Fédération Internationale de Bobsleigh et de Tobogganing (International Bobsleigh and Tobogganing Federation). During races, a jury of three people is in charge of the bobrun and the sleds. If anything should happen to the bobrun during the event, this jury would decide what to do. Bobsled championships are held at the Winter Olympics, as well as at world championship races each year. North American championships are usually held each year also.

▶ BOBSLEDDING FOR FUN

It is not necessary to be a racer to enjoy bobsledding. The bobrun at Lake Placid is open for public pleasure riding. Paying passengers can ride with experienced bobsledders who do the steering and braking. People who want to drive a bobsled must have a license. To obtain one, they must first pass a physical examination. They are then taught by expert drivers. If they pass the driving tests, they are granted licenses.

STANLEY BENHAM
Former World Bobsled Champion
Reviewed by JOHN J. FELL
Bobsled Chairman, XIII Olympic Winter Games

BOCCACCIO, GIOVANNI. See RENAISSANCE (Profiles).

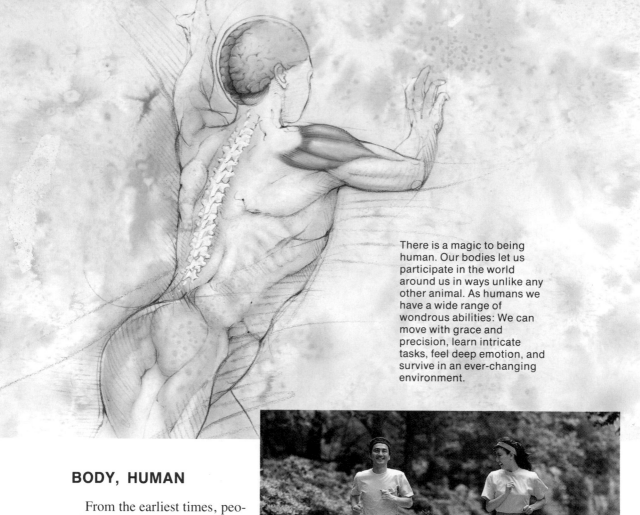

There is a magic to being human. Our bodies let us participate in the world around us in ways unlike any other animal. As humans we have a wide range of wondrous abilities: We can move with grace and precision, learn intricate tasks, feel deep emotion, and survive in an ever-changing environment.

BODY, HUMAN

From the earliest times, people have tried to understand how the human body is made and how it works. Scientists have tried to unlock its secrets to improve health and to help fight disease. Artists have used the human body as a source of inspiration to create art. Athletes and performers have studied the human body to better their performing abilities.

Those who have studied the human body often compare it to a machine. Like a machine, the body needs energy to do its work. A machine such as an automobile engine burns fuel, usually gasoline, to obtain energy. The fuel combines with oxygen from the air, and energy is released. The body's fuel is food. The food is combined with oxygen that is breathed in. Energy is released.

There are many other likenesses between machines and the human body. But it is the differences that make us better than machines.

The body can grow. Machines cannot. Cameras can "see" and computers can "learn" in a way. But machines cannot feel, see, think, and learn as humans do. The body can repair worn-out parts and even produce new humans. Most important, the human body has a very special quality—it is alive.

▶BODY CHEMISTRY

The human body consists of chemical elements—substances that cannot be broken down into simpler substances by ordinary means. The most common chemical elements in the body are carbon, hydrogen, nitrogen, and oxygen; the body also contains many others, such as sodium, calcium, iron, phosphorus, and potassium.

Every element is made up of units called **atoms**. When two or more atoms combine, a microscopic structure called a **molecule** is formed. Some molecules are composed of atoms of only one element. For example, a molecule of oxygen (O_2) consists of two atoms of oxygen. When an atom combines with one or more atoms of different elements, **compounds** are formed. Water (H_2O), for instance, is a compound consisting of molecules that contain two atoms of hydrogen joined with one atom of oxygen.

The compounds of the body must be arranged in a very special way to produce life. The most basic compound in the human body is water. It is necessary for most of the chem-

serve important chemical functions. Nucleic acids carry the instructions that pass human traits from one generation to the next.

▶**THE LIVING CELL**

The cell, which is a collection of compounds, is the basic unit of life in all living things. A cell can take in food, get rid of wastes, and grow. The human body is made up of billions of cells. This tells you something about the size of cells. Most of them are too small to be seen without a microscope. But they are alive. Throughout life, the body continues to grow new cells. These new cells replace those that have worn out.

Most cells have three main parts. A thin skinlike covering, called the **cell membrane**, encloses each cell. Inside the cell is a soft jelly called **cytoplasm**. Within the cytoplasm lies the **nucleus**, which is sometimes called the "control center" because it directs the activities of a cell.

ical reactions that occur. In addition to water, there are four other main compounds in the body: carbohydrates (such as starch), lipids (or fats), proteins, and nucleic acids.

These four compounds are large, complex structures that contain the element carbon. Carbohydrates provide the energy for all of the body's activities. Lipids store extra fuel and serve as building material for the cells of the body. Proteins also perform several duties. Some proteins are used to build cells, others

The cell membrane acts not only as a wrapper but as a sieve: It lets some materials pass into the cell while keeping others out. Food and oxygen carried to the cell must pass through the cell membrane. Wastes given off by the cell when it has burned the food and oxygen pass through the sievelike membrane back into the blood and are carried away.

The cytoplasm makes up most of the cell. Within the cytoplasm are many tiny structures called **organelles**. These are the organs of the

During cell division, two sets of chromosomes are pulled apart toward opposite poles. Completion of the process yields two genetically identical cells.

cell. The **mitochondrion** is one type of organelle. It transforms substances from the food we eat into energy that the cell can use. Cells that are very active such as muscle cells have lots of mitochondria. Another type of organelle is the **lysosome**. It digests and gets rid of unwanted material.

The nucleus is a solid ball in the center of the cell. It contains rodlike structures called **chromosomes**. Each cell has 46 chromosomes—half are inherited from the mother and half from the father. The chromosomes are made up of **genes**. Genes are the basic units of heredity—that is, they carry the characteristics that are inherited from an individual's parents. The fact that a boy has blue eyes like his

mother or brown hair like his father is determined by the genes that he has inherited from his parents.

The genes also control what cells do. The genes carry their instructions, or master plans, in a special language called the **genetic code**. The genetic code is formed using a chemical substance called **DNA** (*d*eoxyribo*n*ucleic *a*cid). All living plants and animals use the same genetic code; however, it is the different master plans carried in the genetic code that make every living thing different from all other living things.

Cells not only grow larger, they also reproduce new cells. New cells serve two functions: They help the body grow and they replace injured or dead cells. Cells reproduce by dividing—one cell divides to make two cells. First the nucleus reproduces by dividing into two parts. Then each part becomes a new cell complete with chromosome-containing nucleus, cytoplasm, and cell membrane. When cells divide, each of the two **daughter cells** are exactly like the **parent cell**.

Cells get their nourishment from blood. They convert some of the nourishment to energy. This is called **energy metabolism**. They may also use part of the food for making new cell materials. In some kinds of cells, such as fat cells, food is stored for later use.

▶THE ORGANIZATION OF THE HUMAN BODY

The human body has more than a hundred different kinds of cells. Each has a special form that makes it fit with the special job it

The Living Cell

The adult human body contains some 100 trillion cells teeming with activity. Although all the cells do not look alike, they do share the same basic structure and some characteristic parts.

Cell membrane

Ribosomes

Endoplasmic reticulum

Cytoplasm

Chromosomes

Golgi apparatus

Lysosome

Mitochondrion

Centriole

Nucleolus

Nucleus

Cells of the Body

Cells are the building blocks of life. The many different kinds of cells that make up the human body come in all shapes and sizes. Cartilage cells (*right*) form the major supporting tissues of the body. The regularly arranged epithelial cells (*below right*) make up the outer surface of the skin. A cross section of bone (*bottom left*) shows the spidery form of bone cells. Each nerve cell (*below left*) has projections that carry electrical signals to the cell and others that carry electrical signals away from the cell to other parts of the body.

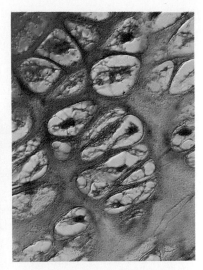

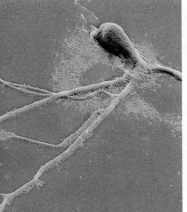

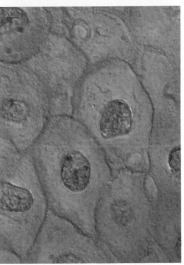

has to do. Cells of one kind are usually joined to make **tissue**. Blood cells are an exception. They are not joined. They travel alone through the blood vessels.

A tissue is a fabric of the same kind of cells. For example, muscles are tissue made up of muscle cells; nervous tissue is made up of nerve cells. There are four main kinds of tissue: **Epithelial tissue**, which covers the surface of the body; **connective tissue**, which helps support and join together parts of the body; **muscle tissue**, which makes body movement possible; and **nervous tissue**, which carries nerve signals throughout the body.

Different kinds of tissue are combined in the body's organs. An **organ** is a body part that does one or more special jobs for the rest of the body. The heart, lungs, stomach, brain, and skin are all organs.

A group of organs working together is called a **system**. For example, the heart, blood, and blood vessels make up the circulatory system. The nose, throat, windpipe, and lungs make up the respiratory (breathing) system. The kidneys, bladder, and connecting tubes make up the urinary system. The systems of the body are like members of a team. Each one has a specific job, but together they make it possible for the body to work, play, grow, and carry out many other functions.

Your skin—the only body organ that is exposed to the outside world—is the largest organ of your body. Skin is a tough, elastic, waterproof protection for the entire body. Even your eyes have a transparent layer of skin, called the conjunctiva, covering them. The skin of an average adult covers an area of about 22 square feet (2.04 square meters) and weighs 8 to 10 pounds (3.6 to 4.5 kilograms).

While the skin is the largest organ of the entire body, the liver—which in an adult weighs about 3 pounds (1.4 kilograms)—is the largest organ inside the body. It is also one of the most active organs. Its tasks include processing nutrients, such as proteins and carbohydrates; metabolizing drugs and hormones; and storing blood, vitamins, and minerals.

▶ BODY SYSTEMS AND ORGANS

Body systems help the body remain alive: The skin protects the body; the body obtains oxygen through the respiratory system; the digestive system processes food so it can be used for energy and growth; the heart and blood vessels circulate oxygen and other substances throughout the body; the kidneys eliminate waste materials; and the reproductive system produces offspring. Together the nervous system and endocrine system form a command system that links all of the other body systems.

The Skin

The skin is the largest organ of the body, and it does many jobs. It holds fluids inside the body. It protects the body from air, water, dirt, and germs. By giving off heat, it helps to regulate body temperature. It contains nerves that are sensitive to things such as touch and temperature that provide information about the world around us.

The skin is made up of two layers of tissue. The top protective layer is called the **epidermis**; the inner layer is called the **dermis**. The thickness of the skin varies on different parts of the body. For example, the skin on the soles of the feet is thicker than that on the face.

In addition to forming a protective covering for the body, the epidermis also forms the fin-

The Skin

Skin — the largest organ of the body — contains such structures as sweat glands, blood vessels, and nerve endings and performs many vital functions, including protecting the body from dirt and germs and helping to control body temperature.

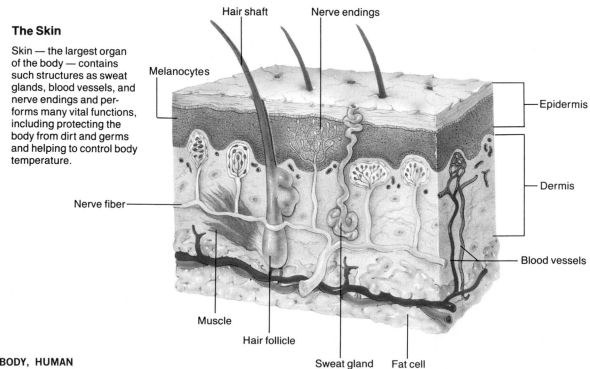

Hair shaft · Nerve endings · Melanocytes · Epidermis · Dermis · Nerve fiber · Blood vessels · Muscle · Hair follicle · Sweat gland · Fat cell

Some people, such as the young boy above, are born with clumps of melanocytes in their skin. These people end up with freckles.

The pigment melanin acts as an umbrella to help protect the skin of these sunbathers (*left*) from ultraviolet rays that could damage cells.

gernails and toenails. Fingernails and toenails are collections of dead cells. That is why it does not hurt when you cut your toenails and fingernails.

The outermost layer of the epidermis is called the **stratum corneum**, and it is made up of a tough protective layer of dead cell material called **keratin**. When you look at a person's skin, all you are actually seeing is dead cells. The stratum corneum is thickest on the soles of the feet and on the palms of the hands. Collections of keratin, called corns, form to protect the foot from ill-fitting shoes.

The epidermis also has special cells called **melanocytes**, some 60,000 in every square inch of skin. Melanocytes produce a dark pigment called **melanin**. Melanin gives skin its color. People with black or brown skin have more melanin in their skin than people with white or yellow skin. Melanin protects the body from the damaging effects caused by the sun. When the skin is exposed to sunlight, the melanocytes produce additional melanin. This is what creates a suntan.

The dermis contains sweat glands, blood vessels, nerves, and cells called **hair follicles**. Each hair follicle contains a hair root. The hair root produces hair cells. These cells die and form the hair that projects from the skin's surface. Hair is present on most parts of the body's surface except for the palms of the hands and soles of the feet.

Each person's handprint is a unique pattern of loops, arches, and swirls formed by the ridges and grooves of the skin.

The Skeletal System

The framework that holds the human body erect is the **skeleton**. The skeleton, which is made mostly of bones, has two major jobs. It supports the body—without a skeleton you would be like a jellyfish—and it protects delicate organs, such as the brain and heart.

The skeleton must also be able to move. The parts of the skeleton that let bones move are called **joints**. Bones fit together at joints and are held fast by tough cords or straps, called **ligaments**. Some joints can be moved freely; others cannot be moved at all. When you run, you move your legs at the hip and knee joints. When you throw a ball, you move your arms at the shoulder and elbow joints. The bones in your spine help you stand straight. They do not move as freely as other joints, but they let you bend. Except for the bones in the jaw, the bones in your skull, which protect your brain, do not move at all.

Bone is made up of two types of living tissue. The outer layer of bone is dense hard (or compact) tissue; the inner layer is lightweight spongy tissue. The holes in the spongy tissue are filled with **marrow**. Some of the marrow is yellow and stores fat. Other marrow is red and produces blood cells. Because bone is living, growing tissue, it must be fed. The outside of bone is covered with a thin skin called a periosteum, which holds the tiny blood vessels that carry food to the bone.

The Skeletal System

The human skeleton is a hard, strong, living framework for the body's tissues. It provides the support needed so that we can stand upright and move about freely. It also holds internal organs in place and shelters them from injury.

Cross Section of a Bone

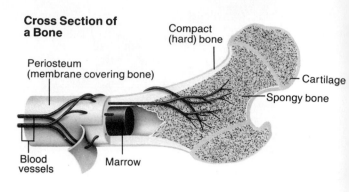

Compact (hard) bone

Periosteum (membrane covering bone)

Cartilage

Spongy bone

Blood vessels

Marrow

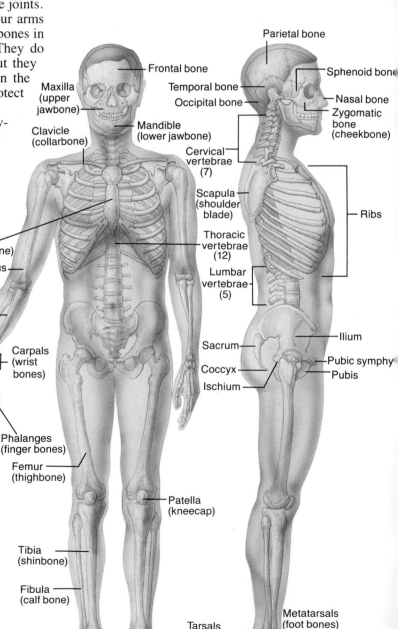

Parietal bone

Frontal bone

Temporal bone

Occipital bone

Sphenoid bone

Nasal bone

Zygomatic bone (cheekbone)

Maxilla (upper jawbone)

Mandible (lower jawbone)

Clavicle (collarbone)

Cervical vertebrae (7)

Scapula (shoulder blade)

Ribs

Thoracic vertebrae (12)

Sternum (breastbone)

Humerus

Lumbar vertebrae (5)

Ulna

Radius

Ilium

Sacrum

Carpals (wrist bones)

Coccyx

Pubic symphy

Pubis

Ischium

Metacarpals (hand bones)

Phalanges (finger bones)

Femur (thighbone)

Patella (kneecap)

Tibia (shinbone)

Fibula (calf bone)

Tarsals (anklebones)

Metatarsals (foot bones)

Phalanges (toe bone

The Muscular System

Bones are the framework of the body, but they cannot move by themselves. **Muscles** are the body's movers. For every bone that can move, there are muscles called **skeletal muscles**, that move it. Skeletal muscles are firmly attached to the bones by hard, ropelike tissue called **tendons**.

Muscles have the unique ability to contract, or get shorter. They are able to do this because each muscle cell contains special proteins. It is the proteins that are extended or shortened when the muscle relaxes or contracts. The process of relaxing or contracting is controlled by the central nervous system.

When a skeletal muscle shortens, it pulls on the tendons that are attached to the bone, and the bone moves. Muscles pull, but they cannot push. So they must work in pairs. If you bend your arm, one set of muscles contracts and pulls your forearm up. To straighten your arm, you relax the first set of muscles. A second set pulls in the opposite way, straightening your arm.

The skeletal muscles are under a person's control. They work because you decide to walk, pick up a ball, or take off your sweater. The body also has another body system that works without conscious orders from you. These muscles, called **smooth muscles**, contract automatically. They are found in many parts of the body and are not attached to bones. Smooth muscles do jobs like controlling the pupil of the eye and propelling food through the digestive tract.

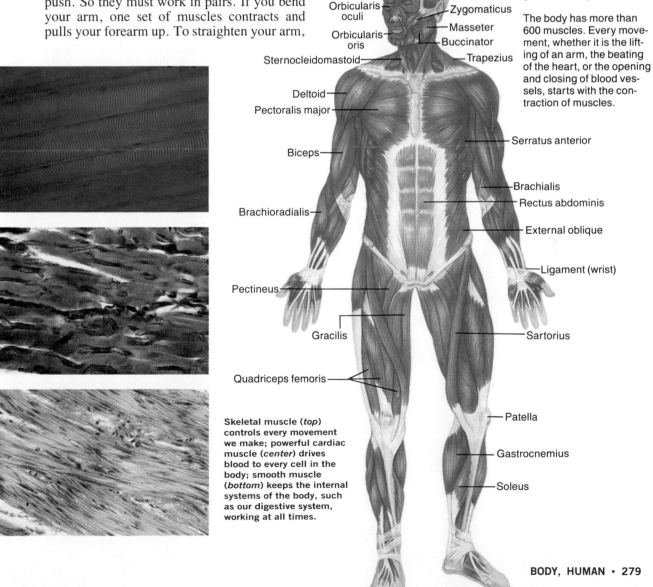

The Muscular System (Front view)

The body has more than 600 muscles. Every movement, whether it is the lifting of an arm, the beating of the heart, or the opening and closing of blood vessels, starts with the contraction of muscles.

Frontalis — Temporalis — Orbicularis oculi — Zygomaticus — Masseter — Orbicularis oris — Buccinator — Sternocleidomastoid — Trapezius — Deltoid — Pectoralis major — Serratus anterior — Biceps — Brachialis — Rectus abdominis — Brachioradialis — External oblique — Ligament (wrist) — Pectineus — Gracilis — Sartorius — Quadriceps femoris — Patella — Gastrocnemius — Soleus

Skeletal muscle (*top*) controls every movement we make; powerful cardiac muscle (*center*) drives blood to every cell in the body; smooth muscle (*bottom*) keeps the internal systems of the body, such as our digestive system, working at all times.

The Muscular System (Back view)

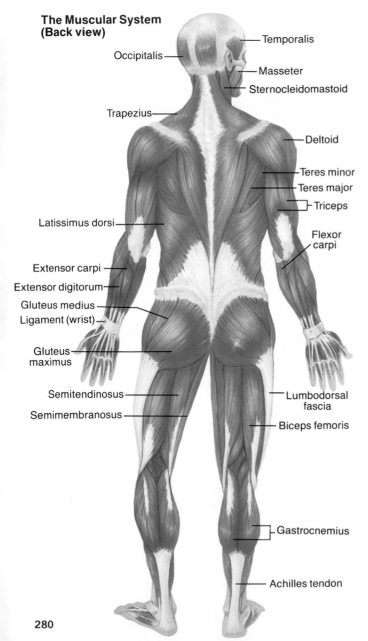

Occipitalis
Temporalis
Masseter
Sternocleidomastoid
Trapezius
Deltoid
Teres minor
Teres major
Triceps
Latissimus dorsi
Flexor carpi
Extensor carpi
Extensor digitorum
Gluteus medius
Ligament (wrist)
Gluteus maximus
Semitendinosus
Semimembranosus
Lumbodorsal fascia
Biceps femoris
Gastrocnemius
Achilles tendon

The heart is made up of another type of muscle, called **cardiac muscle**. Cardiac muscle is made up of fibers that resemble skeletal muscle. However, cardiac muscle also resembles smooth muscle in that it contracts automatically without conscious control.

The Digestive System

To do work, muscles and other tissue need water and fuel to burn. This fuel comes from the foods we eat and drink. But food cannot be used directly as fuel. Foods must be broken up and changed before they can be used as an energy fuel. This process of converting food to fuel is called **digestion** and takes place in the digestive system.

Digestion begins in the mouth where the teeth are used to break food into small pieces. The saliva that is in the mouth gets the food moist and makes the food easier to swallow. Saliva also contains amylase, an enzyme that starts breaking the starch in food into sugar. Then the moist ball of food is carried to the back of the mouth by the tongue.

Swallowing starts food on its journey through the 25- to 30-foot (8- to 9-meter)-long tube that coils through the center of the body and makes up the digestive system. Muscles force the food into the **esophagus**, the section of the digestive tube that connects with the stomach. Other muscles force the food down the esophagus.

Next, the food enters the pouchlike stomach portion of the tube. Here the food is churned and broken down further. Glands in the stomach add the chemical substances hydrochloric acid and pepsin to the food mixture. Pepsin is an enzyme that breaks down meats and other proteins. The acid sterilizes the food and makes the pepsin work better. A mucous slime, which coats the stomach and protects it from injury by the acid, is also secreted. The stomach works on the food for one to four hours. By then, the food is almost liquid.

From the stomach the food is pushed into the **small intestine**. The small intestine is so called because it is about 1 inch (2.5 centimeters) in diameter. However, it can be very long —about 20 feet (6 meters) in length. The small intestine does the main job of digestion. And it is from the small intestine that food starts its journey to the cells.

In the small intestine, more protective mucus is secreted. Food mixes with juices from the liver and pancreas. The liver makes liver bile, which helps to digest fats; the pancreas secretes enzymes that digest protein, fat, and carbohydrates. The small intestine also makes some digestive enzymes. As the food is digested, it becomes liquid. The starches are broken down into simple sugars. Proteins are split into smaller particles. Fats are changed to fatty acids and glycerol.

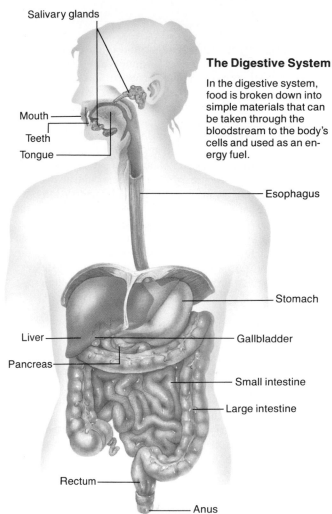

The Digestive System

In the digestive system, food is broken down into simple materials that can be taken through the bloodstream to the body's cells and used as an energy fuel.

Salivary glands

Mouth

Teeth

Tongue

Esophagus

Stomach

Liver

Gallbladder

Pancreas

Small intestine

Large intestine

Rectum

Anus

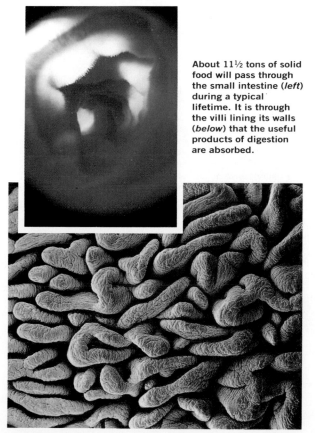

About 11½ tons of solid food will pass through the small intestine (*left*) during a typical lifetime. It is through the villi lining its walls (*below*) that the useful products of digestion are absorbed.

These digested materials pass through the cell membranes of the intestinal cells into the bloodstream. To make sure that none of the small particles are wasted, the small intestine is lined with hundreds of microscopic fingerlike projections called **villi**. These projections reach out and capture the food particles. Because particles can pass through the sides as well as the top of the villi, there is more space for food to be absorbed. Food particles travel from the villi into the bloodstream, then into the cells.

Most of the blood from the intestine passes through the liver before it enters the heart. The liver is like a large chemical factory. It changes many of the food particles. Some of the sugar is changed to a starchy substance called **glycogen** for storage in the body. When body cells need more sugar, the liver changes glycogen back to sugar and releases it into the bloodstream. Other products are used by the liver to manufacture proteins and process fats to be used as fuel. The liver also acts as a storage warehouse. It stores vitamins such as vitamin A and D.

Whatever food is left undigested after its journey through the small intestine moves into the **large intestine**. The large intestine is much wider than the small intestine and also much shorter. It is about 6 feet (2 meters) long. In the large intestine, water and minerals are removed from the undigested material, leaving solid waste material. Most of the body's waste comes from what is left of the food after the body uses what it needs. The solid wastes are then stored in the large intestine until they pass out of the body as bowel movements.

The Respiratory System

Cells have two important needs: They must have oxygen to produce energy, and they must get rid of the waste gas, called carbon dioxide, that forms when energy is produced. The respiratory system provides both of these services for the body's cells.

Oxygen enters the body from the air that is breathed in. Usually the air is taken in through the nose. But at times, when the body needs extra oxygen, air can be also taken in big gulps through the mouth. The moist lining of the nose contains many small hairs that clean the air as it moves through the nose. There are also many blood vessels in the lining of the nose, and the warm blood heats the air.

From the nose, air travels through the **pharynx** (the cavity located behind the nose and mouth), to the **larynx** (or voice box), the **trachea** (or windpipe), and finally, the lungs. Together these structures form the respiratory system.

The larynx contains folds of gristle-like tissue called the **vocal cords**. When air moves through the vocal cords, the cords vibrate and

The life-sustaining exchange of gases, oxygen and carbon dioxide, takes place within the lungs' approximately 300 million tiny air sacs called alveoli.

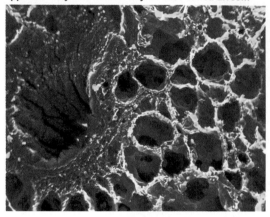

The Respiratory System

During the process called breathing, the respiratory system supplies the body with oxygen. With each breath, oxygen, which is needed to produce energy, enters the lungs and carbon dioxide, a waste product, is breathed out.

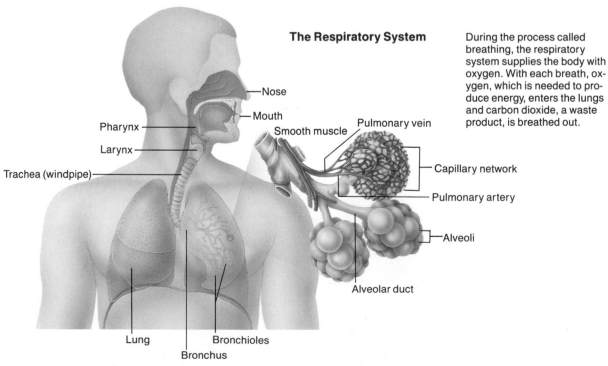

Nose
Mouth
Pharynx
Smooth muscle
Pulmonary vein
Larynx
Trachea (windpipe)
Capillary network
Pulmonary artery
Alveoli
Alveolar duct
Lung
Bronchioles
Bronchus

produce sounds, such as talking. Like the strings on a violin, the vocal cords can be tightened or loosened to produce higher- or lower-pitched sounds. The larynx also serves a protective function. When water or other materials enter the throat, the folds close so that the material cannot go into the lungs.

Air moves from the larynx to the trachea. The trachea is a ridged tube that is about 1 inch (2.5 centimeters) in diameter. The ridges, which are made up of firm gristle-like material, keep the trachea from collapsing during the act of breathing. In the upper part of the chest, the trachea divides to form two tubes. Each tube, called a **bronchus**, branches into smaller and smaller bronchial tubes that look like the branches on a tree. Each of the tiniest branches opens into a grapelike cluster of air-filled sacs, called alveoli. The air sacs are covered with a network of capillaries, which are the small blood vessels that connect veins and arteries.

Waste-carrying blood is pumped from the heart into the capillaries of the air sacs. Here a quick exchange takes place. Oxygen moves out of the air sacs into the blood. The waste gas carbon dioxide moves out of the blood into the air sacs and then is breathed out of the body. The oxygen is picked up by the red blood cells and carried back to the heart. From there it is pumped throughout the body.

Aided by the work of muscles, air is moved into and out of the lungs during the process of breathing, or **respiration**. Muscles in the chest wall and a muscle called the **diaphragm**, that separates the chest from the abdomen change the size and shape of the chest. With each breath taken in, the chest muscles contract, lifting the front and sides of the ribs and the breastbone to make a bigger space in the chest. When the diaphragm contracts, it flattens out and makes the space even bigger. As the chest expands, so do the lungs and air rushes in to fill them. With each breath let out, the muscles relax, the space becomes smaller, and air is pushed out of the lungs.

Breathing is automatic. That means you do not have to think about breathing to actually breathe. You continue to breathe even when you are sleeping. People do have some control over their breathing. You can take large or small breaths and you can breathe faster or slower. You can even hold your breath. But you cannot stop breathing altogether.

The Circulatory System

The circulatory system, which includes the heart, blood, and blood vessels (arteries, veins, and capillaries), moves life-giving blood throughout the body. Many thousands of miles of vessels travel through the body, supplying oxygenated blood to the body's tissues and organs.

Blood acts as a transport vehicle, carrying nutrients and oxygen to cells. Blood also picks up unneeded waste materials from the cells, carries important immune cells throughout the body, and picks up and carries heat from the inside of the body out to the skin, where it is released into the air.

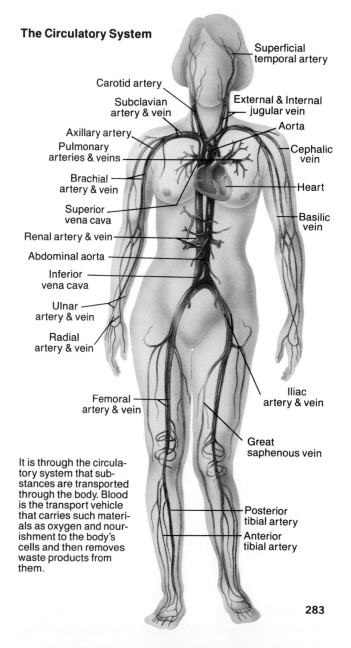

The Circulatory System

Superficial temporal artery

Carotid artery

Subclavian artery & vein

External & Internal jugular vein

Axillary artery

Aorta

Pulmonary arteries & veins

Cephalic vein

Brachial artery & vein

Heart

Superior vena cava

Basilic vein

Renal artery & vein

Abdominal aorta

Inferior vena cava

Ulnar artery & vein

Radial artery & vein

Iliac artery & vein

Femoral artery & vein

Great saphenous vein

Posterior tibial artery

Anterior tibial artery

It is through the circulatory system that substances are transported through the body. Blood is the transport vehicle that carries such materials as oxygen and nourishment to the body's cells and then removes waste products from them.

283

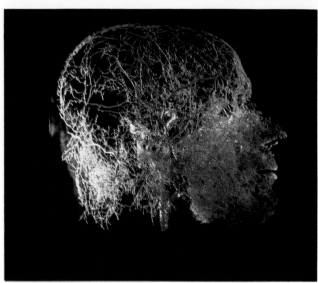

An elaborate and extensive network of blood vessels brings a rich supply of oxygenated blood to the face, head, and brain.

About half of the body's blood is made up of a thin, clear light yellow liquid called **plasma**. It flows through the blood vessels carrying many dissolved materials and solid blood cells. Most of these blood cells are red blood cells. Some 25 trillion red cells move through the bloodstream.

The red blood cells carry out specific jobs. Their main job is to carry oxygen from the lungs to cells in the body. These blood cells have powerful protein molecules called **hemoglobin** that carry the oxygen. Each hemoglobin molecule contains an iron atom that acts as a magnet, snapping up oxygen in the lungs, then clinging tightly to it. When the red cells reach the tissues, the hemoglobin releases the oxygen. Red blood cells also pick up carbon dioxide in the tissues and carry it back to the lungs, where it is removed from the body.

White blood cells are also transported in the blood. These cells kill dangerous bacteria and fight disease. **Platelets** are the third kind of solid material carried in the blood. They are the repair force. More than a trillion strong, platelets start the clotting process when a blood vessel is torn or cut.

The red and white blood cells and the platelets are all made in the bone marrow. Red blood cells live about four months. White blood cells live a much shorter time—some live only a few days. Platelets are not actual cells. They are pieces of larger cells. They live about eight to ten days. The bone marrow replaces blood cells and platelets as they die or are destroyed.

The force needed to push the blood through the many miles of vessels is supplied by a powerful muscular pump: the heart. It lies in the middle of the chest, between the lungs.

The heart is divided into four parts called **chambers**. There are two chambers called **atria** at the top of the heart and two chambers called **ventricles** at the bottom. The atria act as receptacles for blood as it enters the heart and the ventricles act as pumps to force blood out of the heart. The heart pumps the body's 4 to 6 quarts (4 to 6 liters) of blood through many thousands of miles of blood vessels, most of them tiny.

From the heart, blood is pumped into the lungs where carbon dioxide and other wastes are removed, and oxygen from the air breathed in is added to the blood. The oxygen-rich blood returns to the heart to begin its travels to the body's cells.

The Heart

The heart is a hollow muscle that functions as a pump to distribute oxygen-rich blood throughout the body. The round-trip of blood traveling between the heart and a part of the body may take about a minute.

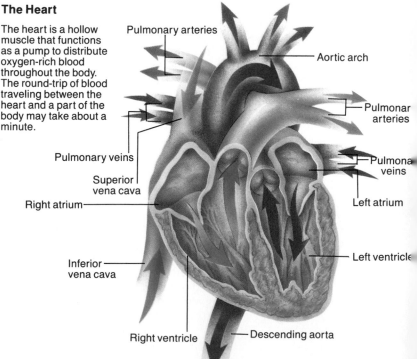

Pulmonary arteries

Aortic arch

Pulmonary arteries

Pulmonary veins

Superior vena cava

Right atrium

Pulmonary veins

Left atrium

Inferior vena cava

Left ventricle

Right ventricle

Descending aorta

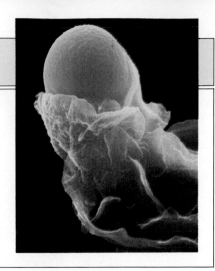

there are more red blood cells in the body than any other kind of cell? Some 25 trillion of the plump, round dimpled cells course through the bloodstream. The sole task of these tiny cells is to bring oxygen to all of the body's tissue and remove carbon dioxide.

Each of the cells travels approximately 173,000 times between the lungs and other tissues before it dies. The red blood cell has a life span of about 120 days. At that time, the aging cell is caught by a macrophage (*pictured at right*) and digested.

When the oxygen-rich blood leaves the heart, it travels in vessels called **arteries**. The **aorta** is the biggest artery in the body. It travels from the heart through the chest into the abdomen. Other large arteries branch from it, and still other arteries branch from them. Blood flows from the smallest arteries into tiny thin-walled tubes called **capillaries**. The oxygen and nutrients from digested food are carried in the blood and pass through the walls of the capillaries to the cells. In much the same manner, the waste materials from the cells pass back into the blood through the walls of the capillaries.

From the capillaries, the waste-carrying blood moves into tiny vessels called **veins**. The tiny veins lead into bigger veins. The bigger veins lead into still bigger veins until the blood finally flows into the large **vena cava**, the vein that enters the heart. From the heart, the waste-carrying blood is pumped into the lungs where the waste gases are removed from the blood and oxygen is added. The oxygen-rich blood returns to the heart and once again begins its travels.

The Urinary System

In order to function properly, the body must be able to get rid of its gaseous, solid, and liquid waste materials. Carbon dioxide, the waste gas, is eliminated through the lungs; solid wastes are eliminated through the large intestine. Some liquid waste evaporates from the skin as sweat; however, most of the liquid waste is removed by the urinary system as **urine**. The two kidneys, the bladder, and the tubes that connect them are the structures of the urinary system.

The Urinary System

Removing liquid waste and regulating fluid balance are the tasks of the urinary system. Each hour, as blood passes through the kidneys, about 2 ounces (57 grams) of urine are produced.

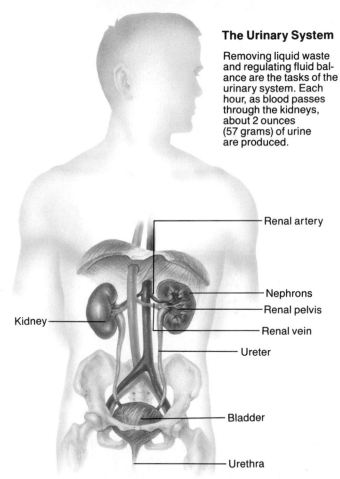

Renal artery

Nephrons

Renal pelvis

Renal vein

Kidney

Ureter

Bladder

Urethra

A **kidney** is bean-shaped and dark red in color. It is about 4 inches (10 centimeters) long. The kidney is like a waste purification system. Within each kidney there are about a million capillary clumps. These capillaries are like sieves. They have small openings that allow water and waste particles, but not blood cells, to leave the blood. The liquid containing waste is collected in small tubes that surround the capillary sieves.

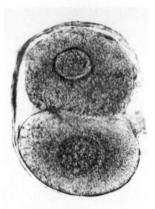

From the tubes, the waste then moves through the kidney and is processed further. Some small particles, such as sugar and salt, are taken back into the body; other waste particles are added to the urine. One familiar substance that is in the waste liquid is water. Water makes up more than 95% of urine. By removing water, the kidneys help keep the balance of water in the blood just right.

After the waste liquid has been processed in the kidney, it moves through the connecting tubes into the bladder. The bladder stores the urine until it is eliminated from the body.

The Reproductive System

The process of reproduction involves the creation of a new human being. It begins when a male's reproductive cell, called a **sperm**, joins with a female's reproductive cell, called an **ovum**. The joining of the sperm and the ovum is called **fertilization**.

Within a fertilized egg are all the instructions that are needed to direct the growth of a new human being. The baby develops as the joined cells divide and form the many organs that make up a new human being. Because the two reproductive cells contain the parents' genes, the baby that is formed will tend to look like both its parents.

The reproductive structures that develop in male babies, both inside and outside, are different from those that develop in female babies. Males and females also produce different chemical messengers, or **hormones**. During puberty and adolescence, these hormones produce noticeable body changes.

In the male, the reproductive structures include the **testes**, two walnut-sized structures

The Reproductive System

The reproductive structures of the male and female, which differ, provide the means to produce a new generation of human beings. The process begins when the male sex cell and the female sex cell unite.

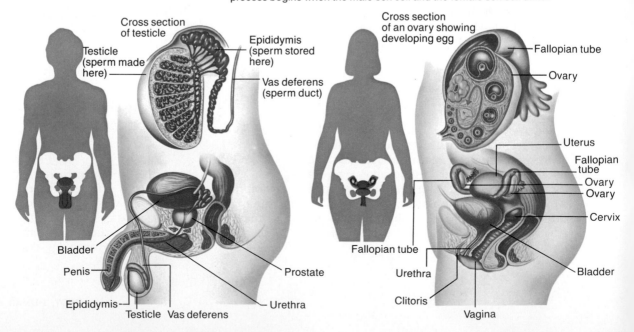

Cross section of testicle

Testicle (sperm made here)

Epididymis (sperm stored here)

Vas deferens (sperm duct)

Cross section of an ovary showing developing egg

Fallopian tube

Ovary

Uterus

Fallopian tube

Ovary

Ovary

Cervix

Bladder

Penis

Prostate

Fallopian tube

Bladder

Epididymis

Urethra

Urethra

Testicle   Vas deferens

Clitoris

Vagina

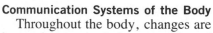

Fertilization takes place when one of the sperm cells thrashing around the egg (*opposite page, far left*) penetrates its gelatinous covering. A new life grows cell by cell as the fertilized egg divides (*opposite page, left*). The fetus floats within a wet, dark world. Now at 4 months (*right*), all its organs have been formed, and the time remaining before birth will be simply a time of growth.

that hang between the legs in a loose skin sac called the **scrotum**. The testes produce and store sperm. The sperm that are produced in the testes are transported through narrow tubes to the **penis**, which is the external reproductive organ of the male. The penis is used for both transporting sperm into the female reproductive system and eliminating urine.

In the female, the internal reproductive structures include the **ovaries** (which produce the ovum) and the **uterus** (which is where babies grow until they are ready to be born). Women have two ovaries. Each ovary is connected to the top of the uterus by a small tube called the **fallopian tube**. At the bottom of the uterus, a canal-like structure called the **vagina** opens to the outside of the body. The external structures of the female are small folds of skin and mucous membranes called **labia**.

Women usually produce only one ovum a month. At the same time that the ovum is developing, changes occur in the uterus. It is preparing a place for the baby to grow. The inside of the uterus gets thicker and forms new blood vessels. If the ovum is not fertilized, the uterus sheds this inside layer. This is called a **menstrual period**. Most women have a menstrual period once a month.

The reproductive process involves an act called **sexual intercourse**. During sexual intercourse, millions of sperm from the penis enter the vagina. The sperm move around and look for the ovum. If an ovum is present, a sperm may join with the ovum and begin the process of creating a new human being.

Communication Systems of the Body

Throughout the body, changes are happening second by second and minute by minute. Even though hundreds of different things are going on at the same time, no part of the body acts alone. For instance, the heart does not just start beating differently. If it did, other systems in the body would act to bring the heart back to the usual rhythm. All of the body systems communicate with each other and work together in the ongoing process called **self-government**. Self-government works whether you are awake or asleep.

When you run, both legs must move at the right time. You breathe more often, your heart beats faster, and your cells use more energy. Messengers travel from one part of the body to another telling each part what needs to be done and when it needs to be done.

There are two types of messenger systems that work together in the body. One system uses electrical signals; the other system uses chemical signals. Most of the body's electrical messages are sent through the **nervous system**. The many kinds of chemical messages are carried in hormone messengers that travel through the bloodstream and other body fluids. The most common are hormones that are produced by the **endocrine system**.

Although each person is a unique mix of genetic information, individuals within a family tend to share a likeness of features.

The Nervous System

The structures of the nervous system include the brain, spinal cord, **neurons** (or nerve cells), and sense organs (such as the eyes and ears). The brain acts as a central computer for the nervous system, processing many types of orders, sensations, emotional feelings, and thinking behaviors.

Neurons have a cell body that contains a nucleus and wire-like projections called **nerve fibers**. They have input fibers that receive information and a single long output fiber that sends information. Nerve fibers from all over the body go to the brain and fibers from the brain go to all parts of the body.

Within the nervous system, electrical signals are used as messengers. Neurons have been programmed to recognize specific incoming signals. When the correct signal arrives, the nerve cell "fires." Some nerves work like calculators—they add up the incoming signals until they get the correct answer and then they fire.

When a nerve fires, information leaves the nerve through the output fiber. Many of these fibers communicate with other nerves, many of which are in the brain. Some communicate with muscle cells; others communicate with glands, blood vessels, and organs of the digestive tract.

The Nervous System

The complicated tasks of detecting, interpreting, and acting on information from the body's external and internal environments are performed by the nervous system.

Cerebrum · Cerebellum · Brain stem — Brain
Spinal cord — Cervical nerves
Thoracic nerves
Radial nerve
Median nerve
Ulnar nerve
Lumbar nerves
Sacral and coccygeal nerves
Femoral nerve
Sciatic nerve

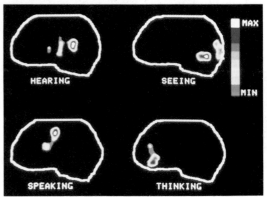

Scans of the brain while an individual is awake show the level of activity in areas of the brain that are dedicated to hearing, seeing, speaking, and thinking.

Different parts of the brain do different things. The **brain stem** is the part of the brain that connects with the spinal cord. Its nerve cells carry messages between the spinal cord and other parts of the brain. These nerves are in charge of the muscles and glands that work day and night. Even as you sleep, nerves in the **medulla**, a part of the brain stem, keep your heart beating and your lungs breathing.

The **cerebellum** controls body movement and balance. Information about many of the habits and skills you have learned is stored there. Once you have learned these behaviors they become automatic. The cerebellum issues orders that enable you to, among other things, walk, ride a bicycle, and play the piano.

The **cerebrum**, the largest part of the brain, is where thinking, learning, remembering, deciding, and being aware occur. Sensations of seeing, hearing, smelling, tasting, and touch-

The structures of the nervous system work together to produce conscious and automatic activities. Without the contributions of each part, it would be impossible to engage in such activities as playing the violin (*above*) or jumping hurdles (*right*).

ing are centered there. So are body feelings. The cerebrum enables you to enjoy things, speak intelligently, make up a poem, even design a rocket.

The different parts of the brain work together to accomplish a task. For example, suppose you decide to take a bike ride. The cerebrum, which is the thinking part of your brain, makes this decision. It decides where you will ride, how fast you will pedal. It orders the muscles to work. After that, the cerebellum and other parts of the brain take over. These make the muscles work smoothly and together. The medulla matches the action of the heart and the lungs to the energy needs of the muscles. As you pedal harder, your heart beats faster and you breathe more often.

The Sense Organs. Because we get information about the outside environment through the senses of sight, hearing, smell, taste, and touch, they are often referred to as external senses. Along with the external senses that tell us about the outside world, there are some senses that tell us what is going on inside of our bodies. These senses, called internal senses, let us know such things as when we are hungry or thirsty, whether we are in pain, and if we are sitting up or lying down.

There are **receptors** for every sensation. Receptors are special nerve structures such as those in the eye that let you see. Each receptor processes only one kind of information. That is why you cannot see with your ears or hear with your eyes. The sensory information is sent to the brain through input fibers. The eyes report on a wide range of sensory information, such as the size, shape, color, position, and movement of objects.

The seeing process begins when light coming from an object reaches the eyes. The rays of light go through the **lens** to the **retina**, a sort of screen at the back of the eyeball. From there the message is sent to the brain, and the person sees.

Because the two eyes are a small distance apart, they report slightly different images.

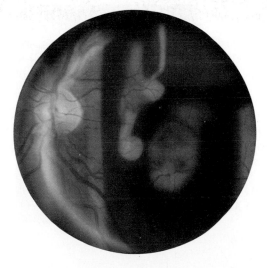

The human eye observes its surroundings as an upside-down image and sends this message along nerve fibers to the brain. The brain interprets this information so that we perceive the world with objects right side up.

The Eye

The eye provides visual information by changing light waves into nerve impulses that are interpreted in the brain.

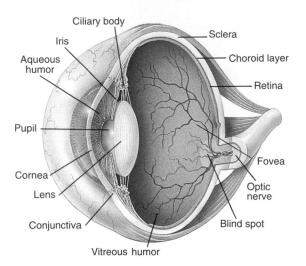

Ciliary body
Iris
Aqueous humor
Pupil
Cornea
Lens
Conjunctiva
Vitreous humor
Sclera
Choroid layer
Retina
Fovea
Optic nerve
Blind spot

The Ear

Sound waves received by the ear are conducted through its structures and converted to nerve impulses before traveling to the brain.

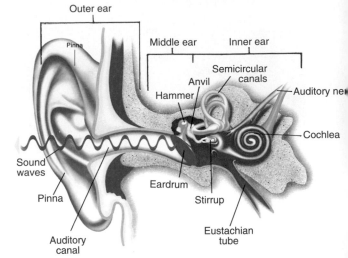

Outer ear
Pinna
Middle ear
Inner ear
Semicircular canals
Anvil
Hammer
Auditory nerve
Cochlea
Sound waves
Eardrum
Pinna
Stirrup
Auditory canal
Eustachian tube

However, the two images merge, and the important result is that we see things in depth and can therefore judge distances.

Having an ear on each side of our head helps us to judge the direction from which a sound comes. We hear when something sends out vibrations called **sound waves**. The sound waves enter the ear and hit the eardrum, causing a vibration that moves some small bones inside the air-filled cavity of the skull's temporal bone. The bones send a message along the hearing nerves to the brain.

Smelling and tasting work closely together, and much of what most people call tasting is actually smelling. Taste is a chemical sense. As food becomes wet in the mouth and dissolves, a chemical reaction takes place and taste receptors are activated. These receptors, usually called **taste buds**, are contained within the small bumpy structures, or **papillae**, on the tongue. Once activated, taste buds send messages to the brain about whether the flavor of the food is sweet, sour, bitter, or salty. Some tastes seem stronger on certain tongue areas. The tongue also has receptors that report on heat, cold, texture, and pain.

Anything that has an odor is giving off tiny particles of gas, which mix with the air. By breathing, you draw these particles into your nose, where the particles of gas are moistened. Nerve cells sense the wet particles and send a message to the brain. Then you smell whatever the odor is.

Through different kinds of nerve cells in the skin, the brain learns about pain, pressure, heat, cold, and touch. The sense of touch tells whether things are rough or smooth, hard or soft, sharp or rounded. When you feel your way through the dark, you are using your sense of touch. The same sense tells you when and how the skin is being stroked and about something that is pulling on the skin.

The nerve cells of the skin are scattered all over the body, but some parts of the body have especially large collections of them. The fingertips are such parts—you can get much more information by feeling something with your fingertips than with your elbow.

Sometimes the information that is reported by our exter-

The tongue's surface is covered with small budlike projections that house the taste buds.

nal senses seems more obvious and important than information reported by our internal senses. However, the internal senses make us aware of feelings such as hunger, pain, movement, and fatigue. The internal senses help maintain a steady, healthy environment inside the body. They do this by responding to specific chemical and physical changes in internal systems, such as the digestive, respiratory, and nervous systems.

None of the senses work alone. We do not see with just our eyes or hear with just our ears. The senses are reporters. They take in information and send it to the brain. Each kind of information reaches a particular part of the brain, and in a way that scientists do not understand, the brain turns nerve impulses into sounds, tastes, and smells. Not until the messages reach the brain do we actually see, hear, taste, and so on.

Sometimes when one sense does not work, other senses tend to become sharper to make up for the loss. People who are blind tend to develop keen senses of hearing and touch. And people who are deaf tend to develop sharper senses of sight and touch.

The Endocrine System

The endocrine system produces powerful chemical messengers called hormones. Similar to the nervous system, the endocrine system works automatically and we cannot control it. Hormones are most often manufactured by patches of cells called **glands**. Glands that are part of the endocrine system include the thyroid, parathyroid, adrenal, pituitary, and sex glands. However, there are hormone-secreting endocrine tissues in organs such as the brain, kidneys, stomach, and pancreas. Wherever the endocrine secretions are produced, they pass directly into the bloodstream and remain in the body.

Some glands do not produce hormones. Instead, they secrete substances such as saliva or sweat. Such glands are called exocrine glands. Substances such as saliva and sweat perform specific tasks close to where they are released. Their secretions leave the body either from the skin or through the digestive tract.

When sense receptors send conflicting messages to the brain, such as during weightlessness, the mechanism that keeps our internal processes stable is disrupted.

The **thyroid gland** is an example of an endocrine gland that keeps the body working normally. It is a rather large gland in the neck. Its hormone stimulates cells to produce more energy. The thyroid hormone controls the rate at which cells burn food and thus the rate at which they produce energy. It also affects growth and development of the mind. Four tiny glands that function as one make up the

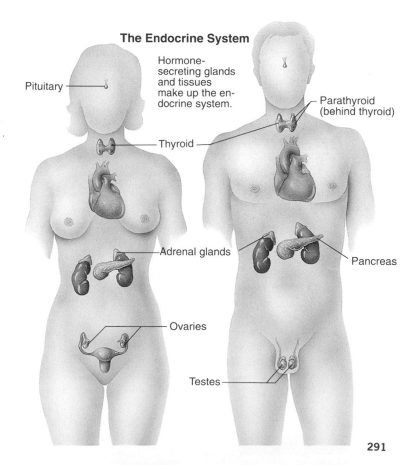

The Endocrine System

Hormone-secreting glands and tissues make up the endocrine system.

Pituitary

Parathyroid (behind thyroid)

Thyroid

Adrenal glands

Pancreas

Ovaries

Testes

Many things contribute to a healthy and well-functioning body and mind, including work, play, and companionship.

parathyroid, which lies close to the thyroid. The parathyroid secretes hormones that control blood calcium and are important in several body processes, such as bone growth and muscle and nerve function.

Another type of endocrine gland is the **adrenal gland**. There are two adrenal glands—one is located on the top of each kidney. Each adrenal gland has two parts, and each part does a different job. Whenever a person is in danger, one part of the gland releases a hormone called **adrenalin** that prepares the body for quick action. Suppose something happens to give you a sudden fright. Your heart begins to pound. Your face turns pale, and the pupils in your eyes open wider. Your muscles tense. You feel "butterflies" in your stomach. This is what adrenalin does to the body.

The other part of the adrenal gland produces hormones too. These hormones help keep your blood sugar up between meals, regulate the salt levels in your blood, and prevent tissue damage due to injury or infection.

The **pituitary gland** is a pea-sized gland at the base of the brain. It is sometimes called the master gland because it makes hormones that control other endocrine glands. For example, one of its hormones controls the action of the adrenal glands. Another makes the thyroid gland work harder.

The pancreas is one of the organs that has endocrine tissue. **Insulin**, which is produced by specialized pancreatic cells, helps to control blood sugar. It carries the message that tells fat cells and muscle cells to take sugar out of the blood.

Hormones and other chemical messengers act through receptors. The chemical messengers fit into the receptors in a lock and key fashion. Each hormone and chemical messenger (the key) has its own specially shaped receptor (the lock). Insulin has a different shape of receptor than the thyroid hormone. Hormones travel throughout the body but will communicate only with cells that have the right kind of receptor.

▶**YOUR BODY**

The human body is a complex arrangement of separate parts. Each part performs its own specific task, yet each is dependent on the other to maintain one unique living being: you. Learning about the human body and how it works also helps us examine ourselves and the world around us. When we examine the human body, we find that there are differences that make each person unique and special. However, the basic truth is that we are each of us more alike than we are different.

CAROL MATTSON PORTH
Author, *Pathophysiology: Concepts of Altered Health States*

See also BLOOD; BODY CHEMISTRY; BRAIN; CELLS; CIRCULATORY SYSTEM; DIGESTIVE SYSTEM; DISEASES; EAR; EYE; GLANDS; HEART; IMMUNE SYSTEM; KIDNEYS; LIVER; LUNGS; LYMPHATIC SYSTEM; MUSCULAR SYSTEM; NERVOUS SYSTEM; PHYSICAL FITNESS; SKELETAL SYSTEM.

BODYBUILDING

Bodybuilding is a system of exercises for developing the muscles in order to change the body's appearance. It is also a sport in which contestants are judged for their muscular development.

Bodybuilding grew out of weight lifting. Training with weights produces bigger and stronger muscles because of the body's ability to adapt to stress. Lifting a weight heavier than a muscle is accustomed to lifting causes that muscle to get stronger. Once the muscle adapts to the new level of stress, you must increase the amount of weight you are using in your training in order to force the muscle to continue to adapt. This is called **progressive-resistance training**—you progressively increase the weight, or resistance, to keep pace with the increasing strength of your muscles.

The purpose of weight lifting is to lift as much weight as possible. But the aim of bodybuilding is to use weights, or some other form of resistance to muscular effort, to change the way the body looks. The bodybuilder is not concerned with how much weight he or she can lift but rather with the full contraction of each muscle involved in an exercise. Of course, bodybuilding training does make you stronger. But more important to the bodybuilder is the size, shape, proportion, and definition of the muscle structure. These create the unique physique of a bodybuilder.

▶ **PRINCIPLES OF BODYBUILDING**

There are certain basic principles of bodybuilding training. The first is progressive-resistance training. The bodybuilder also tries to isolate and train each muscle of the body. Using weights or some other form of resistance, the bodybuilder subjects each of the muscles to a series of "sets" that are made up of a specific number of "reps," or repetitions. For example, to build up the biceps, a bodybuilder may do an exercise called "curls," which alternately contract and expand the biceps muscles. Using weights the bodybuilder may do 5 sets of 20 repetitions of curls. Contracting the muscles over and over, with the proper balance of sets and repetitions, is what gives the bodybuilder's muscles the shape and definition that weight lifters lack.

Bodybuilders used to work their whole bodies in each exercise session. Then they

This bodybuilder is doing an exercise called curls to develop her biceps—a muscle in the upper arm. Bodybuilding has become increasingly popular among women.

found that they got better results by training certain body parts one day and others the next. They also learned more about diet and nutrition. They are now able to create maximum muscle mass together with minimum body fat, so that every individual muscle fiber seems to be visible.

Top-level bodybuilding competitors train for many hours each day. As with any athlete, proper rest and nutrition are extremely important. Anything—even emotional factors—can change the way the bodybuilder's physique appears during the day of a contest.

▶ **THE FIRST BODYBUILDING CONTESTS**

The forerunners of modern bodybuilding contests were "physical culture" competitions, which took place in the United States during the 1920's and 1930's. In these contests a variety of athletes, including swimmers, runners, boxers, gymnasts, and weight lifters, were judged on the look of their physiques and on their ability to perform athletic feats. The weight lifters began to dominate these contests because their huge muscles created such an overwhelming impression. Eventually all the competitors in these events were weight lifters, and the modern bodybuilding competition was born.

A competition called the Mr. America contest was held in 1939, but the first of the modern Mr. America bodybuilding events was held in 1940. Competitors were still required to perform some sort of athletic feat, as in the old physical culture contests. But the mass, proportion, and overall development of the contestants' physiques made it clear that they were really bodybuilders and not just weight lifters or physical culturists.

MODERN BODYBUILDING CONTESTS

In modern bodybuilding contests, the judges look at each competitor in order to evaluate the shape and proportions of the body, as well as how much muscle definition the competitor has achieved. The contestants are asked to do a series of poses that reveal the relative quality of the various parts of their physiques. Each also does a posing routine of his or her own choice. This routine is designed to emphasize the especially well-developed parts of the competitor's body.

Presenting the body properly through posing is a difficult art. It involves more than just flexing the muscles. The way a bodybuilder poses can impress or disappoint the judges. In addition, posing for long periods of time requires great endurance. Bodybuilders must practice posing in order to avoid becoming exhausted on stage.

In the late 1970's, the first bodybuilding contests for women were held. Before that time, contests for women were actually physical-culture beauty contests. Today women bodybuilders are held to the same high standards of physical development as men.

BODYBUILDING ORGANIZATIONS

The world governing organization of bodybuilding is the International Federation of Bodybuilders (IFBB), which has more than 120 member nations. The major events sanctioned by the IFBB are the World Amateur Bodybuilding Championships (Mr. Universe), the men's and women's World Professional Championships, the World Mixed-Pairs Championship (in which men and women compete together as teams), and the Mr. Olympia contest, in which the top champions come together each year to see who is the best.

FAMOUS BODYBUILDERS

The first bodybuilder who became well known to the general public was Steve Reeves, an American Mr. Universe winner who played Hercules in a series of "muscle movies" in the 1950's. In the 1970's and 1980's, two other bodybuilders gained celebrity through movies and television: Lou Ferrigno, an American, who played in "The Incredible Hulk" on television, and Austrianborn Arnold Schwarzenegger, who won the Mr. Olympia contest seven times. Both men starred in *Pumping Iron* (1977), a movie about bodybuilding.

BILL DOBBINS
Founding editor, *Flex* magazine

Left: Arnold Schwarzenegger strikes a pose, displaying the physique that won him numerous bodybuilding titles. Right: A bodybuilder examines her muscular development.

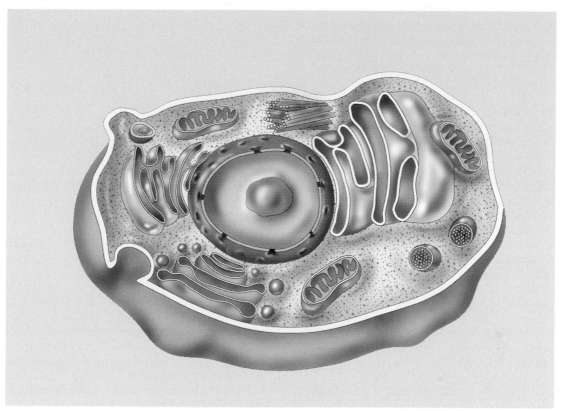

Hundreds of different types of cells make up the human body. Although these cells play different roles, they all share certain cellular processes.

BODY CHEMISTRY

The human body is made from hundreds of different types of cells interacting in precise ways. Cells group together to form organs such as the brain, liver, and heart. The organs are held together with a "glue" called the extracellular matrix. And the entire body is covered and protected from the outside by the largest organ, the skin.

Each different cell type carries out highly specialized functions that no other cell type can. For example, rod cells in the eye capture light from objects, allowing us to see. Liver cells could never do this, but they are responsible for storing certain vitamins, detoxifying the blood, and other tasks.

Although different cell types are needed for specific jobs, many tasks are common to all cells. For example, every cell in the body must make energy and produce proteins, and every cell carries out these functions in the same way.

▶ COMPOSITION OF THE BODY

Each cell is a tiny sack containing many structures and chemical compounds. Water is the most abundant chemical compound in cells. Although it is a simple molecule, water is absolutely necessary for the chemical reactions that take place in cells to occur. Water dissolves other chemical compounds so they can perform their functions, and water itself is used in many cellular chemical reactions. Salts are another kind of simple chemical compound found in cells.

Cells contain four main types of **macromolecules**—carbohydrates, lipids (fats), proteins, and nucleic acids. These complex molecules form the basic structures of cells. They perform various functions and may be broken down to provide energy. Carbohydrates and lipids are made from carbon, hydrogen, and oxygen. Proteins and nucleic acids also contain nitrogen. In addition, nucleic acids contain phosphorus. The relative number of atoms of each element and the way these atoms are arranged create the different types of macromolecules. For example, lipids contain mostly carbon and hydrogen. They contain very little oxygen compared to carbohydrates.

Carbohydrates

Carbohydrates provide a major source of fuel for the body. They include sugars, starches, and cellulose. Sugars are also called **saccharides**. Saccharides are classified by the number of sugar units they contain. They may be mono-, di-, tri-, or polysaccharides ("poly" means many). **Sucrose** (table sugar) is a disaccharide formed by combining two monosaccharides, glucose and fructose.

Glucose is the main source of energy for cells. It can be obtained from most carbohydrates in the diet. Because it is such an important source of fuel, the body stores glucose in the form of **glycogen**. Glycogen is a polysaccharide formed by linking thousands of glucose units to create a highly branched structure. It is stored mainly in liver and muscle cells.

Plant cells store glucose in the form of **starch**. Starch is similar to glycogen but it has fewer branches. **Cellulose** is another carbohydrate produced by plants. It is also made of glucose units, but they are linked together in a different way. Because of this, humans cannot digest cellulose, which is classified as a fiber. However, some animals, such as ruminants, are able to digest cellulose—with the

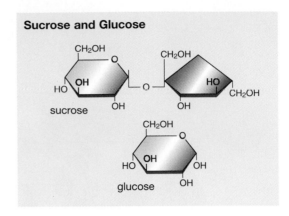

Sucrose and Glucose

help of micro-organisms in their guts—to obtain glucose for energy.

Lipids

Lipids are oily substances that do not mix with water. Lipids include fats, oils, waxes, steroids, and other related compounds. Lipids perform many functions in cells. They serve as sources of energy, structural components, and signaling molecules.

Fatty acids are the most abundant lipids in the body. Fatty acids are long chains of carbon and hydrogen atoms with an acid group on one end. The body stores fatty acids in the adipose tissue (fat cells) to use for energy. They are stored in the form of **triglycerides**, which are molecules made up of three fatty acids attached to a backbone called glycerol. When they are needed for energy the fatty acids are released into the blood, taken up by other tissues, and broken down to produce energy molecules.

A well-known body lipid is cholesterol. Cholesterol is an important part of cell membranes, and it is the building block for the steroid hormones. The body needs cholesterol to function properly. But excess cholesterol can build up in the arteries, eventually clogging them. A diet high in cholesterol and saturated fats may lead to excess cholesterol in the body.

Proteins

The cells of living organisms contain thousands of proteins and each protein performs a specific function. Proteins are made from building blocks called amino acids. Animal cells use 20 different amino acids to make proteins. Cells produce proteins by assem-

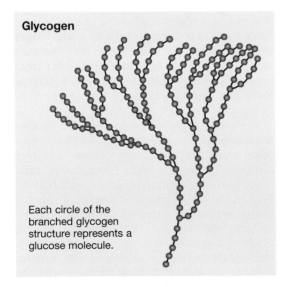

Glycogen

Each circle of the branched glycogen structure represents a glucose molecule.

bling amino acids into long chains. Our genes determine the order and the number of amino acids in each chain. Some proteins are made from a single chain of amino acids; others have more than one chain acting together.

Proteins can be classified as either structural or functional. As their name suggests, structural proteins make up the structures of the body. Your hair, fingernails, and toenails are made from a protein called **keratin**. Another structural protein, **collagen**, acts as a glue to hold cells together to form tissues and organs and to keep the skin attached to the body structures underneath.

Functional proteins perform the many tasks that are necessary for cells to survive. One of the most important functional proteins in animals is **hemoglobin**, the oxygen-carrying protein found in red blood cells. Hemoglobin takes up oxygen as blood passes through the lungs and delivers it to tissues throughout the body.

Enzymes are a special type of functional protein. An **enzyme** is a compound that speeds up the rate of a chemical reaction but is not changed by the reaction. Enzymes play a role in almost every chemical reaction that occurs in cells.

Nucleic Acids

Nucleic acids are long chainlike molecules that contain genetic information. **Deoxyribonucleic acid (DNA)** is the molecule that makes up our genes. **Ribonucleic acid (RNA)**

is an intermediate molecule involved in the transfer of information from genes to make proteins.

Nucleic acids are made from building blocks called **nucleotides**. Each nucleotide is formed from a sugar and a base. DNA and RNA differ from one another by the type of sugar contained in their nucleotides. Ribonucleotides, which make up RNA, contain the

Structures of Lipids

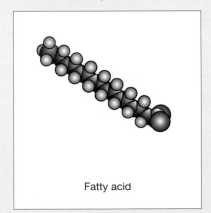

Fatty acid

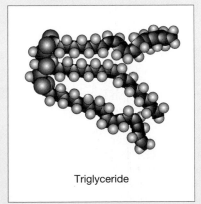

Triglyceride

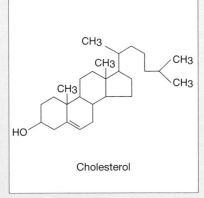

Cholesterol

Carbon atoms are shown in black, hydrogen atoms are shown in blue, and oxygen atoms are shown in red.

Hemoglobin

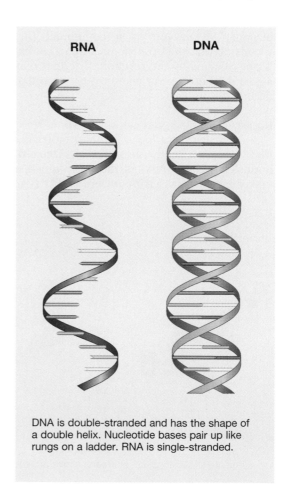

The hemoglobin molecule is made up of four protein chains encoded by two different genes.

sugar ribose. Deoxyribonucleotides, which make up DNA, contain deoxyribose, a sugar with one less oxygen molecule than ribose. The different bases found in nucleotides are adenine, cytosine, guanine, thymine, and uracil (abbreviated A, C, G, T, U). Thymine is found only in DNA and uracil is found only in RNA. The other bases are found in both DNA and RNA. It is the varying sequence of the bases that makes up the different genes.

DNA and RNA have different structures. DNA is usually double-stranded. This means it is composed of two chains of nucleotides that line up parallel to one another with the bases of the nucleotides meeting in the middle like the rungs of a ladder. The two chains, or strands, twist to form a structure known as a double-helix. RNA is usually single-stranded.

▶ **BIOCHEMICAL PROCESSES WITHIN THE CELLS OF THE BODY**

Metabolism refers to the chemical changes in living cells by which molecules are broken down to create energy or synthesized to produce new cellular materials. For example, fats and carbohydrates taken in through the diet are converted into forms that cells can use for energy. Proteins are also taken in through the diet. The body breaks proteins down and uses the amino acids to build new proteins. The creation of new proteins is directed by our genes.

Production of Energy

In our homes we require energy in the form of electricity to power our lights and appliances. The body needs energy to carry out all the functions necessary for life. A special nucleotide called **adenosine triphosphate (ATP)** is the energy molecule of cells. In order to make ATP, cells break down complex compounds such as fats and sugars.

As indicated earlier, the sugar glucose is the major source of energy for cells. Cells break down glucose to form ATP. This requires many enzymes and many different steps. For each 6-carbon glucose molecule, the cell produces 6 molecules of carbon dioxide, 42 molecules of water, and 36 molecules of ATP.

Flow of Genetic Information

We inherit half our genes from our mother and half from our father. Therefore, every in-

RNA   **DNA**

DNA is double-stranded and has the shape of a double helix. Nucleotide bases pair up like rungs on a ladder. RNA is single-stranded.

DNA Contains the Information Needed to Make Proteins

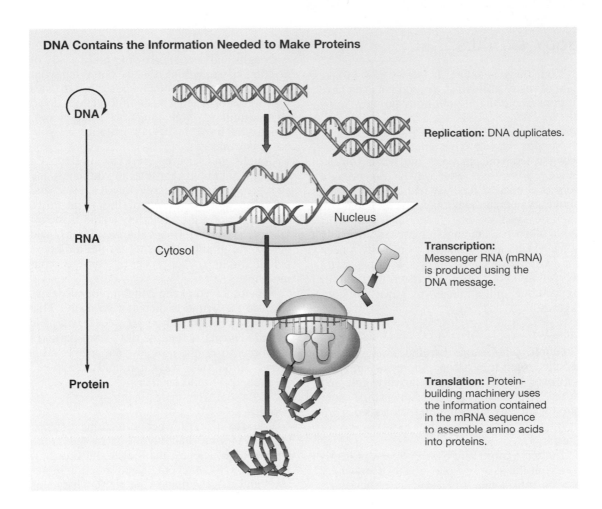

DNA

RNA

Protein

Replication: DNA duplicates.

Nucleus

Cytosol

Transcription: Messenger RNA (mRNA) is produced using the DNA message.

Translation: Protein-building machinery uses the information contained in the mRNA sequence to assemble amino acids into proteins.

dividual is a mix of the properties of his or her parents. We can get our eye color from our mother and our hair color from our father. But how does inheriting a particular gene result in blue eyes or any other physical trait? Genes contain the information that directs the cell machinery to make proteins. The different proteins of the body form the physical features seen by the outside world.

Every animal begins as a single cell and becomes a complex organism through the process of cell division. Before cells divide they must duplicate their genes so that each cell has the same number of genes as the original. Cells copy their DNA using a process called **replication**.

Once formed, each cell must then make proteins. Several steps are needed to create a protein from a DNA "blueprint." DNA is found in the nucleus of cells. But the protein-building machinery is found outside the nu-

cleus in an area of the cell called the **cytosol**. RNA is created to take the information contained in the DNA to the protein-building machinery. This type of RNA is called **messenger RNA (mRNA)**. Messenger RNA is made using DNA as a template in a process called **transcription**. The mRNA contains the same sequence of nucleotides as the DNA.

In the cytosol, the protein-building machinery uses the code contained in the mRNA to assemble amino acids in the correct order for a given protein. This process is called **translation**. Two other kinds of RNA are part of the protein-building machinery. Thus, it can be seen that DNA makes RNA that makes proteins; this is the flow of the genetic information in our genes. It is an essential process for cells to survive.

MICHAEL W. KING
Indiana University School of Medicine

See also BIOCHEMISTRY; CELLS.

BODY SIGNALS

Your body is smart. It knows how to take care of many problems. You do not even have to think about them; your body just acts.

Yawns

No one knows what causes yawns. You yawn when you are tired and when you are bored. Sometimes you yawn just because someone nearby has yawned. Even reading about a yawn can make you yawn. When you exercise, you do not yawn, and you never yawn when you are angry or excited. Probably some yawns are caused by your body's need for extra oxygen. A big yawn brings extra oxygen into your body. However, the need for oxygen does not explain why yawns are contagious.

Snores

People who snore breathe through their mouths when they sleep. Snores occur when soft parts of the mouth and throat wiggle and flop as air goes in and out. Many people snore only when they are lying on their backs.

Blushing

There are more tiny blood vessels, or capillaries, in the skin of your face than anywhere else on your body. When you are embarrassed or angry or overheated, your body sends a message to the blood vessels in your skin to expand, or become larger. When the capillaries expand, more blood flows through them, and your skin looks red. "You're blushing!"

Coughs and Sneezes

Coughs and sneezes are your body's way of reacting to something that is bothering your throat or your nose. When something irritates your throat or when a piece of food goes down your windpipe, you cough to force it out. When you have an itch or irritation in your nose, you sneeze.

Coughs and sneezes are very similar: you take in a big breath, muscles in your chest and abdomen tighten up, your throat closes, and air bursts out. In a cough, the vocal cords close tight, and the exploding sound is the air blasting its way through the vocal cords and out of the mouth. In a sneeze, the air is expelled through your nose as well as your mouth.

Sometimes you keep coughing or sneezing, because the irritation does not go away. That is why you cough and sneeze a lot if you have a cold. During a sneeze, tiny germ particles are forced from the nose at great speeds. This is one of the main ways that colds are spread from one person to another.

Hiccups

You get hiccups when something unusual happens to your diaphragm (the muscle at the bottom of your chest that helps you breathe). When you breathe out, your diaphragm relaxes and bulges up into your chest. That helps push air out of your lungs. When you breathe in, the diaphragm tightens and flattens out. This makes a bigger space in your chest, and air rushes in.

Your diaphragm usually has a regular rhythm of relaxing and tightening. But every so often the diaphragm suddenly jerks itself tight. That sudden jerk is called a spasm.

When your diaphragm is tight, air usually goes into your lungs. But when the diaphragm spasms, a tiny flap at the back of your throat, called the epiglottis, covers up the opening of your windpipe and prevents the air from going down. The "hic" is the sound you make when the air hits the epiglottis. After a "hic" the diaphragm goes back to normal. Then the spasm may happen again.

No one knows what causes the spasms. Sometimes they happen after a scare, or from laughing very hard, or from swallowing food too fast. Hiccups usually just stop after a while, but people have invented many unusual ways to try to cure them.

Burps

Burping is the body's way of getting rid of too much air or gas in the stomach. You swallow air with everything you eat and drink. When you chew food, you mix air with it. When you drink a glass of water, you swallow air. Soda, popcorn, and toast are filled with air. Apples and oranges have gases trapped in them that are set free by the acids in your stomach.

As your stomach digests the food you swallow, the trapped air and gases rise as bubbles and pop, just like the bubbles in soda. As more and more bubbles pop, more and more air presses against the sides of your stomach. Finally the gas pushes up into your esophagus and bursts out your mouth as a burp. The scientific word for burping is eructation.

Stomach Growls

Stomach growls can happen anytime, not only when you are hungry. Usually it is not even your stomach that is growling at all; it is your intestines. When your stomach finishes mashing and grinding your food, it pushes the food into your intestines where muscles then move the food along. It is this squeezing of the liquid food out of your stomach and through the twisted narrow intestines that causes stomach growls.

Gas

Everything you swallow moves into your digestive tract. Your digestive tract is a very long tube that has two openings. One opening is at your mouth; the other is at your anus, through which you expel solid waste and gas. All the air you swallow with your meal goes right to your stomach. The swallowed air that is not burped out goes on from the stomach into your intestines. Other gases are added to this air when millions of bacteria that live in the intestines attack the food.

When air, or gas, comes to the end of the digestive tract, it is held there by a muscle that keeps the exit tightly closed. The muscle is called the anal sphincter. Sometimes a lot of air gets to the anal sphincter and puts so much pressure on it that you cannot hold the muscle tight. The gas just pushes out. Other times you can keep your sphincter tight so the gas will not come out at an embarrassing time. Still other times, you can relax your anal sphincter and push out the gas when you want to.

Goose Bumps

Sometimes you feel chilly or are frightened by something, and you get little bumps all over your body. Those are called goose bumps, or gooseflesh.

If you look closely at the goose bumps, you will see a hair coming out of each one. Each hair on your body sits in a tiny pocket in your skin (called a follicle) with a little muscle attached to it. Usually those muscles are relaxed and let the hairs lie flat on your skin. But when you are cold or frightened, the muscles tighten. That makes the hairs stand up and the skin bunch up into little bumps.

Scientists think that many years ago, people's bodies were covered with lots of thick hair. When all those hairs stood up, warm air from the body was trapped by the hairs and kept the body warm. That thick hair is not there any more, but the muscles still are. And they still pull on the tiny pockets, making hairs stand up and causing goose bumps.

SUSAN KOVACS BUXBAUM
Coauthor, *Body Noises*

BOEING, WILLIAM EDWARD. See WASHINGTON (Famous People).

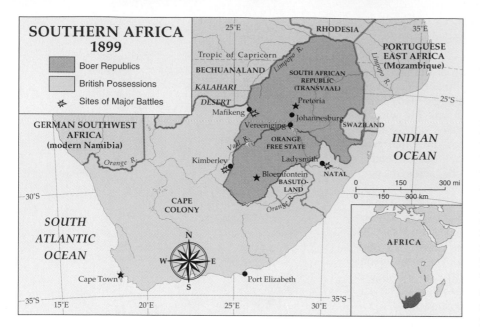

The Discovery of Gold. The discovery of gold in the Transvaal in 1886 attracted many immigrants, most of them British. Hostility between the British and the Boers increased as the British began to outnumber the Boers.

To assert control, the Boers passed restrictive measures against the newcomers, including refusing them the right to vote. But the British government insisted that the new settlers be granted full political rights.

In 1895 a band of British colonists tried to overthrow the government of the South African Republic. This action convinced the Boers that the British meant to take control of their territory. The two Boer republics formed a military alliance and mobilized their forces. The British sent troops to the border areas. When the British refused to withdraw, the Boers declared war on October 12, 1899.

The Second Boer War (1899–1902). The Boers were not professional soldiers, but their knowledge of the land aided them against the slow-moving British troops. Early in the war the Boers defeated the British in several battles. The British government was embarrassed by the defeats and stung by criticism of the war at home and abroad. It sent more troops and new generals to Africa. By 1900 the superior British force succeeded in capturing the capitals of both Boer republics. But the Boers refused to surrender, and they waged a guerrilla war for over a year. The British retaliated by burning Boer farms and putting Boer families in detention camps.

The Outcome. Finally, on May 31, 1902, the Boers signed a peace treaty at Vereeniging, and the two republics became British colonies. In 1910 they became part of the Union (now the Republic) of South Africa.

Reviewed by JOHN E. FLINT
Dalhousie University

See also SOUTH AFRICA.

BOGART, HUMPHREY. See MOTION PICTURES (Profiles: Movie Stars).

BOER WAR

The Boer War—also known as the South African War—took place between 1899 and 1902. It was actually the second of two wars fought between Great Britain, then the world's leading power, and two small African countries—the Orange Free State and the South African Republic (Transvaal).

Background. In the 1600's the southern tip of Africa was settled by employees of the Dutch East India Company. In 1814, following the Napoleonic Wars in Europe, Great Britain acquired the territory from the Netherlands and called it Cape Colony. Not wishing to live under British rule, some of the Dutch descendants, then known as Boers (from the Dutch word for "farmers"), moved northward, settling in Natal, the Transvaal, and the Orange Free State. In 1853, without giving up its sovereignty, Great Britain recognized the independence of the Transvaal, which the Boers then called the South African Republic. The Orange Free State was declared independent the following year.

The First Boer War (1880–81). Diamonds were discovered near Kimberley in 1871, leading Britain to annex the western portion of the Orange Free State. Then in 1877, Britain formally annexed the Transvaal. The Boers revolted and defeated the British in the First Boer War (1880–81). They regained their independence, but their republics remained British sovereign lands.

BOGOTÁ

Bogotá is the capital of Colombia and its largest and most important city. Located in central Colombia, on a wide plateau high in the Andes mountains, Bogotá is a city of contrasts, with skyscrapers perched next to historic buildings.

The city, which is more than 8,600 feet (2,600 meters) above sea level, is surrounded by mountains on three sides. For centuries, Bogotá was isolated by these high ranges. Formerly it took eight days to reach the city from the Atlantic coast. Now the trip can be made in one hour by airplane.

Bogotá usually bustles with activity. In the downtown sector, the main commercial district, the narrow streets are crowded with people and cars. Children walk or ride donkeys through traffic. Everywhere there are vendors and *campesinos* (farm laborers), who come to the city looking for work. Well-dressed business people and shoppers stroll by or stop at one of the many coffeehouses.

The people of Bogotá are of European, Indian, and mixed ancestry. The city's rapid growth to a population of about 6 million has

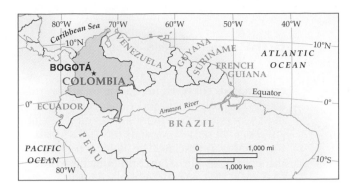

caused a housing shortage. Many new apartment houses are being built. But the slums have grown enormously, and unemployment is a problem.

Bogotá's factories process agricultural and dairy products from nearby farmlands and manufacture furniture, household appliances, construction materials, textiles, and chemicals. The city is a world center for emeralds, which are mined north of Bogotá.

Places of Interest. Bogotá has fine restaurants, hotels, and theaters. Concerts and plays are performed in the richly decorated Colon Theater, in the older part of the city. It faces the Palace of San Carlos, where the president of Colombia lived. The city is also home to several universities, including the National University of Colombia, founded in the late 1500's. Among the art galleries and museums, the National Museum and the Colonial Museum are known for collections of colonial art. The Gold Museum houses magnificent gold objects made by Indians before the country was conquered by the Spanish.

History. Bogotá was founded in 1538 by the Spanish conquistador (conqueror) Gonzalo Jiménez de Quesada. It became the capital of New Granada, which was a center of the Spanish empire in South America. The city was liberated from Spanish rule in 1819, and in 1821 it was named the capital of Gran (Greater) Colombia. This federation, which included the present-day nations of Colombia, Panama, Venezuela, and Ecuador, fell apart by 1830. Bogotá then became the capital of the Republic of New Granada, which was later renamed the Republic of Colombia.

ARLENE GOULD
Former correspondent, *Life en Español*
Reviewed by THOMAS E. SKIDMORE
Brown University

BOGS. See WETLANDS.

Bogotá, Colombia's capital and largest city, is located high in the Andes. Visitors enjoy a spectacular view of the city from atop the nearby mountain of Monserrate.

BOHR, NIELS (1885–1962)

Early in the 1900's a young Danish physicist named Niels Bohr began to study the atom. His studies turned out to be both his life's work and extremely important. First he gave science a new view of the atom's structure. Some years later he helped to release the energy of the atom. Still later he worked to control that energy for peaceful uses.

Niels Bohr was born on October 7, 1885, in Copenhagen, Denmark. His father was a scientist and professor at the university there, and Niels was raised in a home where science was naturally of interest. In 1903 he entered the University of Copenhagen. His chief concern was physics, but he was also an outstanding soccer player. By 1907 Niels had won a gold medal from the Royal Danish Academy for his scientific work.

After receiving his doctor's degree in 1911, Bohr wanted to learn more about the atom. He decided to go to England and study with J. J. Thomson and Ernest Rutherford. Both these men were leaders in atomic physics. Bohr first studied under Thomson at Cambridge University; a year later he worked with Rutherford at the University of Manchester. In 1913 Bohr returned to the University of Copenhagen as a lecturer.

It was during this year that Bohr made his first great contribution to atomic physics. By that time many scientists had attempted to explain the atom. Rutherford, for example, had provided one theory. The great German physicist Max Planck had another.

Working from the ideas of Rutherford and of Planck, Bohr set forth a new theory of his own. It dealt with atomic structure and behavior. Bohr's theory became the basis of the branch of modern physics known as quantum mechanics. For his brilliant work, Bohr received the Nobel Prize for physics in 1922.

Bohr continued teaching at the University of Copenhagen, and in 1920 he became director of the university's new Institute of Theoretical Physics. He made the institute into one of the world's major research centers. Scientists came from all over the world to study with Bohr. He was sometimes so busy with his work that he forgot about his meals. But he always managed to make time for his wife and five sons.

About 1930 the institute began important studies of the nucleus of the atom. In 1936 Bohr made another major advance in atomic physics: he gave the first correct description of a nuclear reaction. This work later helped the United States develop the atomic bomb.

Bohr arrived in the United States in 1939 to work at the Institute for Advanced Study in Princeton, New Jersey. Some of the world's leading scientists were there, including Albert Einstein. Bohr told them of the work going on in Europe in splitting uranium atoms. His reports spurred the United States to conduct research in this field.

Bohr returned to Copenhagen a few months after World War II broke out. In 1940 the Germans conquered Denmark. Bohr refused to cooperate with them and closed his institute. In 1943, when he was threatened with arrest, Bohr fled. He went first to Sweden and then to the United States.

Bohr served as adviser at the first atomic bomb laboratory, near Los Alamos, New Mexico. He soon began to worry about the far-reaching effects of the new bomb. After the first atomic bomb test, in 1945, Bohr went to Washington to plead for immediate international control of atomic weapons.

When the war ended in 1945, Bohr returned to work at his institute in Copenhagen and periodically spoke out on important nuclear issues. In 1955 he became chairman of the newly founded Danish Atomic Energy Commission. Two years later Bohr received the first Atoms for Peace award—a fitting climax to his life. Bohr died November 18, 1962.

JOHN S. BOWMAN
Author and Science Editor

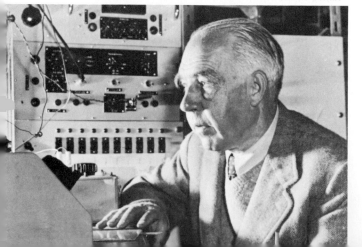

Niels Bohr helped form the modern theory of atomic structure. He later was an adviser on the atomic bomb.

BOLÍVAR, SIMÓN (1783–1830)

For nearly 300 years most of South America was under Spanish rule. Simón Bolívar vowed to free his native land, Venezuela, from Spain. When he died in 1830, he had freed not only Venezuela, but Ecuador, Bolivia, and Colombia as well.

Bolívar was born at Caracas, Venezuela, on July 24, 1783. His ancestors in Spain had belonged to the nobility, and young Bolívar was educated as an aristocrat. When he was 16, Bolívar was sent to Spain to continue his education. For the next seven years he studied and traveled in Europe. The example of the American and French revolutions stirred Bolívar deeply. He swore that he would not rest until he had broken the chains that bound his country to Spain.

In Venezuela a group of patriots, including Bolívar and Francisco Miranda, seized Caracas. On July 5, 1811, they declared Venezuela's independence. But the patriots were crushed by Spanish troops. Miranda died in prison and Bolívar fled from Venezuela.

Years of bloody fighting and heartbreaking defeat followed. Twice again Bolívar was forced to flee into exile. But his stern face and dark, piercing eyes showed a determination to win independence at all costs. In 1819 he boldly marched his patriot army over the snow-covered Andes mountains. It was winter, and in that terrible march many men and all the horses perished. But Bolívar surprised the Spanish Army and defeated it completely at Boyacá, in Colombia. The victory brought independence to Colombia. Two years later, Bolívar liberated Venezuela. And the following year, Ecuador was freed.

Venezuela, Colombia, and Ecuador were united into the republic of Gran Colombia, with Bolívar as its president.

Meanwhile, General José de San Martín, the liberator of Argentina, with Bernardo O'Higgins of Chile, had proclaimed the independence of Peru. Bolívar met with San Martín at Guayaquíl. San Martín generously gave Bolívar command of his army to complete the liberation of Peru. The next year Upper Peru was renamed Bolivia in honor of its liberator.

Bolívar soon had all the powers of a dictator, though his ideals were freedom and jus-

Simón Bolívar led his troops over the Andes mountains in 1819, surprising the Spanish Army. His victories led to the liberation of Colombia, Venezuela, and Ecuador.

tice. He encouraged the creation of constitutional government and urged that more schools and universities be built. There were slaves in South America. Bolívar had freed his, and he insisted that other slave owners do the same.

Bolívar's dream had been to see all the liberated countries united. However, each country wanted its independence. New revolutions broke out and Gran Colombia fell apart. Bolívar's enemies accused him of being a tyrant, and an attempt was made to kill him.

In 1830, weary and ill after years of war and revolution, Bolívar resigned as president of Colombia. On December 17, 1830, he died at the age of 47.

Bolívar's dream of a united South America was a failure. He died a disappointed man, with few friends and many enemies. But to the people of South America he is still *El Libertador*—the liberator.

Reviewed by ERNESTO SÁBATO
Author, *The Graves and the Heroes*

BOLIVIA

Bolivia, a landlocked country about three times the size of the U.S. state of Montana, lies in the heart of South America. It is surrounded by Brazil to the north and east; Paraguay and Argentina to the south; and Chile and Peru to the west. Bolivia has one of the highest altitudes of any country in the world, and it is dominated by the great peaks of the Andes mountains.

▶ **PEOPLE**

More than half of Bolivia's people are Quechua and Aymara Indians. The Quechua are descended from the Inca invaders who came to Bolivia in the A.D. 1200's. The Aymara trace their ancestry back more than 1,000 years to the great Tiahuanaco civilization that flourished on the banks of Lake Titicaca in the Andes.

Mestizos, or people of mixed European and Indian descent, make up about one-third of the population. A small fraction of the people are of unmixed European ancestry.

Language. Bolivia has three official languages: Spanish, Aymara, and Quechua. Spanish is the primary language of the mestizos and "whites," and it is taught in most schools. The Aymara and the Quechua speak

Above: Most of Bolivia's people are Quechua and Aymara Indians. These native people speak Spanish in addition to their own languages.
Right: Llamas are native to the Andes mountains. Sure-footed and strong, they are used by rural farmers as pack animals.
Upper right: A man paddles across Lake Titicaca in a balsa (small reed boat). Lake Titicaca is the highest navigated body of water in the world.

their native languages, but most speak Spanish as well.

Religion. More than 90 percent of Bolivians are Roman Catholic. Catholicism is the state religion, but members of all religious groups may worship freely. There is a small but growing percentage of Protestants.

Education. All children between the ages of 6 and 14 are expected to go to school. However, more than half of rural children stop their studies after a year or two, and few go on to universities. Bolivia's urban children generally attend school through the elementary level.

Some of Bolivia's schools are modern, especially the private and parochial schools. Universities are located in the cities of Oruro, Potosí, Cochabamba, La Paz, and Santa Cruz.

Rural Life. Bolivia's rural areas are inhabited mostly by Indians, along with some mestizos, whose lives are generally harsh and monotonous. Families live in one-room houses of stone or baked mud brick called adobe, and they typically depend on subsistence farming for survival. These rural farmers use traditional equipment, such as the plow drawn by draft animals, and most of the land is unsuitable for productive farming.

City Life. The populations of Bolivia's urban areas have grown rapidly in recent years, and more than 60 percent of all Bolivians now live in the cities. This growth is mostly the result of people fleeing the harsh conditions of the countryside to seek a better life in the cities.

▶**LAND**

Bolivia has three major land regions: the Andes, the Altiplano, and the lowlands.

Land Regions. The Andes form the longest mountain system in the world, and they are at their widest in Bolivia, stretching as far as 400 miles (640 kilometers) across. The Bolivian Andes are divided into two main ranges, or cordilleras. The Cordillera Oriental, or eastern range, runs through the center of the country. Deep valleys called *yungas* have been cut by rushing rivers in the slopes of the eastern range. The Cordillera Occidental, or western range, forms Bolivia's border with Chile and contains the country's highest mountain, Nevado Sajama (21,391 feet/6,520 meters). For more information, see the article ANDES in Volume A.

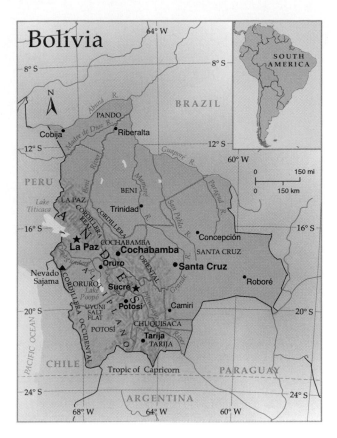

Between the eastern and western mountain ranges is the Altiplano, a high, bleak, cold, and almost treeless plateau. Its average elevation is almost 2 miles (3 kilometers) above sea level.

Bolivia's northern lowlands are heavily forested, and close to the border of Brazil the jungle grows dense. The southern lowlands are drier than those in the north and consist of great plains.

Rivers and Lakes. The Beni River and its tributaries flow north to join the Madeira River in Brazil and finally the great Amazon River. The Pilcomayo River and its tributaries are part of the river system that flows southeast to join the Paraguay River and the Río de la Plata in Argentina.

Lake Titicaca, at the northern edge of the Altiplano, is the highest navigated body of water in the world. It lies 12,500 feet (3,810 meters) above sea level, on the border with Peru. Lake Titicaca drains into Lake Poopó, farther south. There is no drainage from Lake Poopó. The water evaporates, leaving the lake very salty.

The Andes form one of Bolivia's three major land regions. The mountains are at their widest in Bolivia, reaching as far as 400 miles (640 kilometers) across.

Climate. The average annual temperature in La Paz, on the Altiplano, is only 47°F (8°C). In Trinidad, a city in the lowlands of eastern Bolivia, the average temperature is about 70°F (21°C). There is little difference in temperature between summer and winter. The dry season lasts from May to November. Between December and February there are heavy rains on the Altiplano and drenching tropical storms in the lowlands.

Natural Resources. Bolivia has a wealth of natural resources, but the country's mountainous terrain and its turbulent history have kept it from making full use of these resources. Deposits of tin, zinc, tungsten, antimony, silver, iron, lead, and gold are found on or near the Altiplano. The Cerro Rico ("rich hill") of Potosí is a mountain that is almost a solid mass of tin, silver, tungsten, and other ores. Deposits of petroleum and natural gas occur in southern Bolivia, while the country's hydroelectric potential remains untapped.

Timber is another of Bolivia's valuable and under-exploited resources. Forests cover nearly 40 percent of the land. The most valuable trees are mahogany, jacaranda, rosewood, balsa, and cedar.

▶ **ECONOMY**

Bolivia is one of the poorest nations in the Western Hemisphere. However, during the 1990's and early 2000's, the country began to successfully build a market economy. It signed free trade agreements with Mexico, and it joined the Southern Common Market (Mercosur). It also privatized the national airline, telephone system, railroad, electric power company, and oil company.

Services. Service industries represent more than 50 percent of Bolivia's economy. These services include restaurants, hotels,

FACTS and figures

REPUBLIC OF BOLIVIA (República de Bolivia) is the official name of the country.

LOCATION: Central South America.

AREA: 424,165 sq mi (1,098,587 km²).

POPULATION: 8,300,000 (estimate).

CAPITAL: La Paz (seat of government), Sucre (legal capital and seat of supreme court).

LARGEST CITY: Santa Cruz.

MAJOR LANGUAGES: Spanish, Quechua, Aymara (all official).

MAJOR RELIGIOUS GROUPS: Roman Catholic, Protestant.

GOVERNMENT: Republic. **Head of state and government**—president. **Legislature**—National Congress (composed of the Chamber of Senators and the Chamber of Deputies).

CHIEF PRODUCTS: Agricultural—soybeans, coffee, coca, cotton, corn, sugarcane, rice, potatoes. **Manufactured**—refined metal, food and beverages, tobacco, handicrafts, clothing. **Mineral**—tin, petroleum, natural gas.

MONETARY UNIT: Bolivian peso (1 peso = 100 centavos).

More tin is mined in Bolivia than any other mineral. Mining has long been the country's chief source of income.

tourism, education, and state employment.

Manufacturing. Manufacturing accounts for about 30 percent of Bolivia's economy. The main products are refined metals, food and beverages, tobacco, handicrafts, and textiles.

Agriculture. Bolivia's chief agricultural products are soybeans, coffee, coca, cotton, corn, sugarcane, rice, and potatoes. About half of Bolivia's farms are on the Altiplano, but the crops there are poor because of the high altitude, the lack of rain, and the primitive methods of cultivation. Only a very small portion of the lowlands east of Santa Cruz are under cultivation. Cattle and hogs are raised in the lowlands.

Mining. The chief source of Bolivia's industrial wealth comes now, as it has for centuries, from mining. Tin is mined in larger amounts than any other mineral, and Bolivia has long been one of the leading exporters of tin in the world. Petroleum and natural gas are increasingly important to the economy.

▶ **MAJOR CITIES**

Sucre is the legal capital and the site of the Supreme Court. Founded by the Spanish in 1538, Sucre has been known by several names. It received its present name, after Bolivia's first president, in 1839. It has a population of about 223,000.

La Paz is the administrative capital and the seat of government. It is Bolivia's second largest city, with a population of about 1 million, and it is the center of the country's commerce and culture. La Paz was founded by the Spanish in 1548 on the site of an Indian village. At about 12,000 feet (3,600 meters) above sea level, it is the world's highest capital city.

Santa Cruz is the country's largest city, with a population of about 1,034,000. The only major city in Bolivia's lowlands, Santa Cruz retains a distinctly Spanish flavor in its music, architecture, and many gardens. It is also a major center of commerce and industry.

La Paz, Bolivia's administrative capital and second largest city, is a center of commerce and culture.

Bolivian highlanders produce a great variety of crafts, including pottery, baskets, woodcarvings, and jewelry. Textile production is an ancient tradition in Bolivia, and the weavers are known for their artistry. Indians often wear distinctive clothing that identifies them as members of a particular community.

▸ GOVERNMENT

Bolivia's government is based on a 1967 constitution that was revised in 1994. A president, elected to a 5-year term, serves as both head of state and government. (Presidents may not serve two consecutive terms.) The legislature is the National Congress. It consists of two houses, the Chamber of Senators and the Chamber of Deputies. Members are elected to 5-year terms.

▸ HISTORY

The magnificent carved stone Gate of the Sun and some ruined temples are about all that remain of Bolivia's ancient Tiahuanaco (or Tiwanaku) civilization. Its people, the Aymara, ruled from about A.D. 600 to 1000. The Incas of Peru took control by 1300. But they were conquered in the 1500's by the Spanish, who then ruled for nearly 300 years.

Independence. Harsh Spanish rule led to a number of uprisings in the 1600's and 1700's, but the most important movement toward Bolivian independence began in 1809. It was inspired by Simón Bolívar's liberation of the northern part of South America from Spain. It was not until 1824, however, that Antonio José de Sucre, one of Bolívar's lieutenants, completely broke Spanish power in the region. The new nation declared its independence on August 6, 1825, and was named for Bolívar, the Liberator. (See the biography of Bolívar in this volume.)

Bolivia's first constitutional president was General Sucre. General Andrés Santa Cruz, who tried but failed to bring about a permanent union between Peru and Bolivia, succeeded him in 1829.

The next 50 years of Bolivian history were scarred by a succession of military dictatorships. The worst of these dictators was Mariano Melgarejo, who came to power in 1864 and sold or leased national territory to neighboring countries. Later wars with its neighbors cost Bolivia more of its original territory.

During the economic depression of the 1930's, demand for tin was slight and the Bolivian economy suffered. World War II (1939–45) brought a rise in the price of tin but only a short-lived improvement to the economy.

A revolution in 1952 brought the National Revolutionary Movement (MNR) to power. Victor Paz Estenssoro, an MNR leader, served as president from 1952 to 1956 and from 1960 to 1964. He nationalized (brought under government control) the country's tin mines, began a program of land reform, and extended the right to vote to all adult Bolivians. Hernán Siles Zuazo served as president between Paz Estenssoro's two terms. Paz Estenssoro was then overthrown in a military coup in 1964 by his vice president, General René Barrientos Ortuño. Barrientos was elected president in 1966. His death in an accident in 1969 led to a period of political instability as Bolivia alternated between military and civilian rule. General Hugo Banzer Suárez held the presidency from 1971 to 1978. Former president Siles Zuazo was re-elected in 1982.

Recent History. Siles resigned in 1985 because of protests against his policies, and Victor Paz Estenssoro was re-elected president after more than 20 years. He was succeeded by Jaime Paz Zamora in 1989 and Gonzalo Sánchez de Lozada in 1993. No candidate won a majority in the 1997 election, so Congress appointed a president, Hugo Banzer Suárez, as called for in the constitution. Banzer stepped down in 2001 due to illness and was briefly succeeded by his vice president, Jorge Quiroga.

In the 2002 election, no presidential candidate won a majority, so Congress appointed former president Sánchez de Lozada. But in 2003, anti-government riots, sparked by Sánchez de Lozada's market reform policies and rising energy costs, forced his resignation. He fled the country and was succeeded by his vice president, Carlos Mesa. Mesa himself was forced out in 2005, as he was seen as part of the old establishment. Eduardo Rodríguez, head of the Supreme Court, was appointed to lead the country, which appeared to be on the brink of civil war.

Reviewed by Hugo Murillo-Jiménez
Center for Latin American Studies
San Diego State University

BOMBAY (MUMBAI)

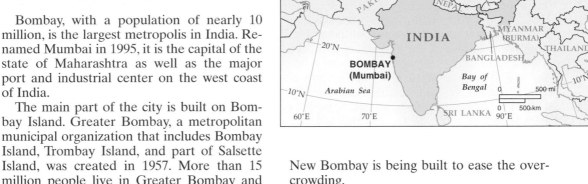

Bombay, with a population of nearly 10 million, is the largest metropolis in India. Renamed Mumbai in 1995, it is the capital of the state of Maharashtra as well as the major port and industrial center on the west coast of India.

The main part of the city is built on Bombay Island. Greater Bombay, a metropolitan municipal organization that includes Bombay Island, Trombay Island, and part of Salsette Island, was created in 1957. More than 15 million people live in Greater Bombay and its mainland suburbs. A satellite city called New Bombay is being built to ease the overcrowding.

Bombay is considered India's most sophisticated and culturally varied city. The majority of the inhabitants are followers of the Hindu religion, but the population includes Muslims, Christians, Jains, Zoroastrians, Jews, and Sikhs. The two major languages are Marathi and Gujarati, although more than fifty different languages are spoken.

The City. At the southwestern end of Bombay Island, the coast is indented. It forms a shallow body of water known as Back Bay, which opens into the Arabian Sea. To the west of the bay is a high ridge known as Mal-

Left: Fruits and vegetables are sold in Bombay's colorful Crawford Market. *Below:* The imposing Chatrapati Shivaji railway station (formerly known as Victoria Terminus) is a landmark of the British colonial period.

abar Hill, where many expensive homes have been built. The Hanging Gardens and Kamala Nehru Park, featuring a giant Mother Hubbard shoe, are also in the Malabar Hill area. The summit of the hill offers a superb view of the city. At night thousands of lights form a sparkling outline of Marine Drive, which runs along the northeastern edge of Back Bay. Marine Drive has rows of modern apartments on one side. On its other side are lovely palms and a wide promenade facing the bay.

At the entrance to the harbor is the Gateway of India, the most familiar landmark of the city. This magnificent stone arch was built in 1911 in honor of King George V and

Modern apartment houses line Marine Drive along the shoreline of Back Bay, an inlet of the Arabian Sea.

Queen Mary of England. Elephanta Island in the harbor is the site of seven magnificent Hindu cave temples built in the 700's. Other special attractions in Bombay include the Prince of Wales Museum, the Jehangir Art Gallery, the National Art Gallery, and many religious temples and shrines. Kanheri National Park, on Salsette Island, contains more than one hundred ancient Buddhist temple caves. Additional places of interest include Victoria Gardens, an aquarium, and a zoo.

Bombay's major commercial center is situated west of the waterfront, in a part of the city known as the Fort. The area includes the famed Chatrapati Shivaji railway station (formerly Victoria Terminus) and the University of Bombay. Most of the older and larger buildings in the Fort are built in Gothic and other European styles of architecture.

Economic Activity. Most of India's foreign trade passes through the port of Bombay, which is situated on the eastern edge of the island in one of the world's finest natural harbors. Its shore is lined with miles of docks, piers, and warehouses. Bombay's factories are generally located in the north, where there are also many overcrowded slums.

Bridges link Greater Bombay to the mainland, where many factories have been relocated. Chemicals, glassware, leather goods, and machinery are among the products made there. Finance, commerce, oil exploration, filmmaking, and publishing are also major activities in Bombay.

History. The Bombay area has been inhabited since prehistoric times. The harbor and islands were ceded to Portugal by the sultanate of Gujarat in 1534.

In 1662 the British king Charles II married a Portuguese princess, Catherine of Braganza. He received Bombay as part of her dowry, and it soon became the leading center of British power on the west coast of India. But the city did not grow rapidly until it replaced the Confederate South as the world's chief source of cotton during the U.S. Civil War (1861–65).

Today Bombay is more than a great port and textile center. Each year the glamour and wealth of what has been called India's most beautiful city attract huge numbers of people seeking a better life. Modern Bombay, with its skyscrapers and slums, has become one of the world's most crowded cities.

DAVID FIRMAN
Towson State University
Reviewed by the Consulate General of India

BONDS. See STOCKS AND BONDS.

BOOKKEEPING AND ACCOUNTING

No business could operate very long without knowing how much it was earning and how much it was spending. Bookkeeping and accounting are the methods business firms use to keep track of their earnings and expenses.

Bookkeeping is a formal, organized system of recording financial transactions. (Volumes in which business records are kept are often called books.) It is done according to standardized rules. These rules make it easier to detect errors in the bookkeeping. The bookkeeper's record shows how much was spent in a certain transaction and how much was gained or lost in the transaction. The information is arranged so that it may be easily analyzed, that is, examined to determine the financial condition of the business or person involved.

A bookkeeper often works under the direction of an **accountant.** While the bookkeeper's duties are mainly to keep a record of the company's business transactions, the accountant's work has a broader scope. In addition to supervising the recording of financial information, the accountant analyzes the information. The company relies on this analysis when making business decisions.

THE DOUBLE-ENTRY SYSTEM

The system used in keeping the financial records of a business is the **double-entry** system. Behind this system is the basic idea that every business transaction affects the company's financial position in at least two ways. In the double-entry system every aspect of a transaction is recorded.

Accounts

The records kept by bookkeepers are called accounts. The three main types of accounts used in bookkeeping are assets, liabilities, and capital.

Assets are anything of value owned by the company. Examples of assets are land, buildings, and equipment. Money in the company's bank account also is an asset, as are services that the company has paid for in advance.

Liabilities are debts owed to persons or to other companies. Examples of liabilities are wages owed to employees, money owed to a bank, unpaid bills for supplies, and stocks that have been sold to obtain money to run the business.

Capital, sometimes called **equity,** is the total value of everything that the company owns free of debt. Capital is equal to the company's assets minus its liabilities. For example, if a company's assets are $100,000, and its liabilities total $45,000, its capital would be $55,000.

Each of the company's assets and liabilities, as well as its capital, is given a separate account. Examples of asset accounts are the "cash" account, which is a record of money that a company owns, and the "accounts receivable" account, the record of money owed to the company. One type of liability account is the "accounts payable" account, the record of money owed by the company for such things as purchases of goods, supplies, and equipment.

In a double-entry system, each account has two sides: the left side, called the **debit** side, and the right side, called the **credit** side. One side is used for increases and the other for decreases. In asset accounts, increases are recorded on the debit side of the account, and any decrease in value is shown on the credit side. In liability and capital accounts, increases and decreases are recorded in the opposite way. These accounts are increased on the credit side and decreased on the debit side. Every business transaction affects two or more accounts—any entry made on the credit side of one account must be balanced by an entry on the debit side of another account. Debits must equal credits. Here are two examples of this system:

(1) Suppose the Acme Company decides to pay off a $25,000 bank loan. Payment of the loan decreases the liability account, so Acme's bookkeeper will debit the liability account $25,000. Acme's "cash" account, an asset account, has also been affected by the transaction. It has been decreased by the $25,000 used to pay off the loan. Thus, in order to record the transaction fully, the bookkeeper must also credit the "cash" account $25,000.

(2) Suppose Acme sells a piece of equipment for $2,000. The buyer pays $500 immediately and will pay the other $1,500 later. Acme's bookkeeper credits the "equipment" account $2,000 and then debits the "cash" account $500 and the "accounts receivable" account $1,500.

ACCOUNT: Checking

Date	Item	Debit	Credit	Balance
12/1	Balance			4,500.00
12/8	Cash Sales	1,350.00		5,850.00
12/15	Cash Sales	2,000.00		7,850.00
12/15	Old Farms Dairy		830.00	7,020.00

ACCOUNT: Accounts Payable

Date	Item	Debit	Credit	Balance
12/1	Balance			2,285.00
12/15	Old Farms Dairy	830.00		1,455.00
12/15	Sprinkles 'n' Such		300.00	1,755.00
12/25	Acme Refrigeration Co.		1,500.00	3,255.00

```
                SUE'S ICE CREAM SHOP
                   Balance Sheet
                   Dec. 31, 1989


            ASSETS

Current Assets
  Cash                        10,800.00
  Accounts Receivable          4,500.00
  Materials and Supplies       2,400.00
  Interest Receivable            500.00
                             ---------
        Total Current Assets              18,200.00

Fixed Assets
  Equipment                   20,000.00
  Shop Building               55,000.00
                             ---------
        Total Fixed Assets                75,000.00
                                         ---------
Total Assets                              93,200.00
                                         =========



            LIABILITIES AND CAPITAL

Current Liabilities
  Accounts Payable             3,500.00
  Notes Payable                6,000.00
  Mortgage Interest Payable      600.00
                             ---------
        Total Current Liabilities         10,100.00

Long-Term Liabilities
  Mortgage Payable            38,000.00
                             ---------
        Total Long-Term Liabilities       38,000.00

Capital                                   45,100.00
                                         ---------
        Total Liabilities and Capital     93,200.00
                                         =========
```

Top to Bottom: **Each of a company's assets and liabilities, as well as its capital, has a separate account. A checking account is a type of asset account, while accounts payable is a liability account. A balance sheet shows a company's financial state at a given time. Note that assets equal liabilities plus capital.**

The use of the double-entry system maintains an up-to-date record of the assets, liabilities, and owner's equity of a business. At any time an examination of the books will show just what the financial situation of a business is. An accountant periodically checks the books to see that the debit and credit entries are equal to one another. If they are not equal, it shows that an error has been made. This is called preparing a **trial balance.**

Journals and Ledgers

Separate entries of all day-to-day transactions are made in a book known as a **journal.** Typically, a journal contains columns for recording the date, the account title, the amount of money debited, and the amount credited. In modern bookkeeping, journal entries often are entered on a computer, which stores the information until it is needed.

At the end of each month, or more frequently, all journal entries are recorded, or **posted,** in a more permanent book of accounts called a **ledger.**

▶FINANCIAL STATEMENTS

Financial statements use the records kept in the accounts to give a picture of the financial activity of the company. Two types of financial statements are most commonly used to report this information: the **balance sheet** and the **income and expense statement.** (Before these statements are prepared, a trial balance is made to be certain that debits equal credits.)

The balance sheet, sometimes called the statement of financial position, is a summary that represents the financial condition of a business at a given time. It shows the company's assets at that moment, as well as its liabilities and capital.

The income and expense statement, sometimes called the profit and loss statement, shows the income and expenses of a business over a specified period of time, usually one year. From this statement the managers of the business can learn whether the company had a profit or a loss for the period covered by the report.

▶ACCOUNTING SPECIALTIES

The three main fields of accounting are public accounting, industrial accounting, and governmental accounting. Each of these fields has special characteristics.

Public accountants offer their services to the public rather than to one organization. Their work often involves advising businesses about investments or taxes. They may also help individuals prepare their income tax returns. Public accountants also perform **audits.** An audit is an examination of a business's financial record and a report on the findings. Audits are made mainly for the benefit of stockholders, creditors, and the public.

Public accountants can become C.P.A.s (Certified Public Accountants) by fulfilling certain requirements of education and experience and passing a written examination. A C.P.A. certificate is the mark of expert competence in the accounting field. This certificate is required in order to certify financial statements.

Industrial accountants are employed by single business firms. They keep the records and make the reports on which the managers of a business rely in planning the operations of the business. The accounting department is, in effect, the nerve center of a company. A gain or loss in business is almost immediately revealed in the figures of the accounting department's records.

Government accountants hold important positions at all levels of federal, state, and local government. Their duties are often similar to those of public and industrial accountants.

In modern business, accounting has such a variety of duties to perform that there are accountants who specialize in certain types of jobs. **Tax accountants** keep tax records and prepare reports that must be sent to government tax agencies. They also advise management about the taxes that the company may have to pay as a result of a business transaction. Many individuals hire tax accountants to prepare their income-tax returns.

Cost accountants deal with the costs involved in all the operations of a business. These may be the cost of a product, a service, a manufacturing process, or the operating expenses of a business. The information provided by the cost accountant helps management to budget the company's money and to plan its future operations.

More and more financial information is assembled using electronic data-processing equipment. Many personal computers can be equipped with accounting programs, so that even small businesses can have computerized record-keeping systems. Today's accountants should have some familiarity with data processing.

▶**HISTORY**

People have counted and kept records throughout history. In the ancient world, trade between merchants made necessary the creation of some kind of business records. Ancient clay tablets show that a system of positive and negative entries was used, in which the gain or loss of any business transaction was added to or subtracted from the total worth of the business.

The modern system of bookkeeping originated in medieval Italy. Records were kept according to the modern system in the city of Genoa in 1340. Some historians believe that the origins of the system can be traced as far back as the 13th century. Genoa, Lombardy, and Tuscany were all thriving business centers in Italy, and any one of them could have been the birthplace of modern bookkeeping. Gradually merchants in other countries learned of the new bookkeeping system, and it spread throughout Europe.

As the methods of the new bookkeeping system were developed, some people became specialists in this kind of record keeping. They were known as accountants. With the increase of business activity, some accountants began to offer their services to any individuals or organizations that needed accounting work done. This was the origin of public accounting. Public accounting developed mainly in the British Isles, which were a leading center of trade. As early as 1720 an English public accountant was called in by Parliament to investigate a financial scandal.

During the 19th century, corporations became the most important form of business organization. A corporation has many owners. These are the stockholders, people who have bought shares, or stock, in the business in return for a share of the corporation's profits. The stockholders depended on published financial reports to learn how well their corporations were doing and whether the executives they hired to manage them were doing their jobs properly. During this period the basic principles of modern accounting were worked out to ensure that the stockholders got thorough and accurate reports.

Stockholders soon realized that if the reports were to have any value, there had to be a set of common principles for gathering and reporting the information. Without a standard method of reporting financial information, a misleading idea about the condition of a business could be given by reporting some facts and ignoring others.

Many unqualified people claimed to be accountants and attempted to do auditing work. Just as standard accounting methods were needed, it also became necessary to establish standards by which properly qualified accountants could be trained and measured.

Today a college degree in accounting has become essential for a successful accounting career. The possible rewards make it worthwhile to get the education. The accountant's familiarity with nearly all the basic operations of a business provides a good opportunity for promotion to the management of a company. Many business executives began their careers as accountants.

EUGENE L. SWEARINGEN
Bank of Oklahoma, N.A.
Tulsa, Oklahoma

Reviewed by JOHN PETRO
Accounting Teacher

BOOK REPORTS AND REVIEWS

A **book report** is a discussion or an analysis of a book and it is one of the most common school assignments. It can be either written or delivered aloud. Book reports are helpful both to those who prepare them and to those who read or listen to them. When you are assigned a book report, you pay extra attention when reading your book, and you think carefully about what it says. Doing this helps you understand your book better and remember it longer.

Others benefit, too. By listening to or reading each other's reports, students learn about a variety of subjects and discover new books to read.

Readers outside the classroom also benefit from what others have to say about books. Newspapers and magazines regularly publish **book reviews** for readers who want help deciding what new books to read or information about books they might not have an opportunity to read. In a book review, a knowledgeable person offers comments and criticism on a recently published book.

Keep in mind, then, that your book report is a sharing experience. Even if no one but your teacher reads it, prepare it as though you were addressing a wide audience.

▶ **WRITTEN BOOK REPORTS**

Your book report, whether it is written or spoken, should include five major points of information: (1) the author, title, publisher, and date of publication of the book, (2) the type of book it is, (3) what the book is about, (4) the form and style in which the book is written, and (5) your opinion of the book.

Author, Title, Publisher, and Publication Date. The first thing your readers will want to know about your book is its title and the name of its author. Remember, also, whenever you prepare a written record of a book, to include the name of the publisher and the date the book was published. The publisher's name can be found at the bottom of the title page. The date of publication is usually located on the other side of the title page, following the word "Copyright." Put all of this information in a heading—several lines at the top of the first page of your written report.

Type of Book. All books can be classified as either fiction or nonfiction. In a library, all novels and short stories are called fiction, and all other books nonfiction. Within these two divisions, though, books can be put into narrower categories. The book you report on might be a collection of poems, a biography, a history, or a work of science fiction. Add this information to your heading.

What the Book Is About. The longest portion of your report will be devoted to the subject matter of your book. If the book is a work of fiction, you will reveal something of the story in this section. If it is a factual work, you will deal mainly with the information it contains.

In the case of a novel, your report should cover the plot, the characters, and the time and setting. It is not necessary to discuss all of these at equal length. There are many kinds of novels, and you must decide what is most important about the one you have read. For a mystery or adventure tale, in which the plot is usually the outstanding feature, your main job will be to relate the story.

Do not tell too much of it. For most people, reading a novel is a kind of adventure, where the pleasure comes from not knowing what will happen next. Your role in narrating a story is to tell your audience of readers enough about what is going on to make them want to read the book, but not so much as to take away the surprise.

Use the present tense to re-tell a story. Avoid opening phrases such as ''This book is about . . .'' Just tell what it is about. Your summary might be something like this:

The day Henry Jameson turns 12, a lot of strange things begin to happen to him. A package arrives in the mail, and he thinks it is a birthday present. But there is no card or return address, and the box contains only a key on a chain.

The following day, he receives another box, this one containing a map with directions to a place he has never heard of. Every day after that,

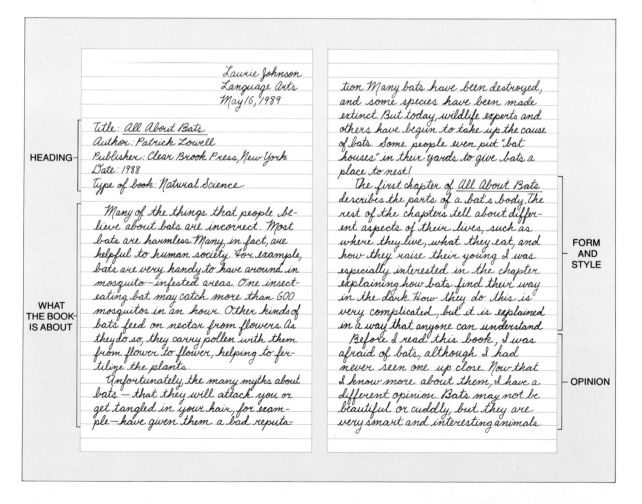

HEADING

WHAT THE BOOK IS ABOUT

FORM AND STYLE

OPINION

Laurie Johnson
Language Arts
May 16, 1989

Title: All About Bats
Author: Patrick Lowell
Publisher: Clear Brook Press, New York
Date: 1988
Type of book: Natural Science

Many of the things that people believe about bats are incorrect. Most bats are harmless. Many, in fact, are helpful to human society. For example, bats are very handy to have around in mosquito-infested areas. One insect-eating bat may catch more than 600 mosquitos in an hour. Other kinds of bats feed on nectar from flowers. As they do so, they carry pollen with them from flower to flower, helping to fertilize the plants.

Unfortunately, the many myths about bats — that they will attack you or get tangled in your hair, for example—have given them a bad reputation. Many bats have been destroyed, and some species have been made extinct. But today, wildlife experts and others have begun to take up the cause of bats. Some people even put "bat houses" in their yards to give bats a place to nest!

The first chapter of All About Bats describes the parts of a bat's body. The rest of the chapters tell about different aspects of their lives, such as where they live, what they eat, and how they raise their young. I was especially interested in the chapter explaining how bats find their way in the dark. How they do this is very complicated, but it is explained in a way that anyone can understand.

Before I read this book, I was afraid of bats, although I had never seen one up close. Now that I know more about them, I have a different opinion. Bats may not be beautiful or cuddly, but they are very smart and interesting animals.

a package arrives with a mysterious object that seems to be connected in some way with what he has received before. He feels as though he is on a treasure hunt, and when, after many weeks, he finally puts all the clues together, he learns something about his ancestors that no one in his family had ever suspected before.

For other novels, you will want to concentrate more on the characters than on the events. To describe a character clearly, imagine that you are telling someone about an old friend. Tell what she looks like and how she behaves. Tell, too, how she feels inside and what she thinks:

Everybody in Maria's family says that she is "the plain one." Her hair is no special color, her eyes are small, her teeth are too big, and her ears stick out. Maria's two sisters, Jane and Laura, are "the beauties." That is what all their aunts call them, adding in a low voice, "Maria is the plain one." After a while, Maria thinks of herself that way, too. She spends most of her time in her room, making up strange fantasies about people she's never met.

In a novel of this type, the plot focuses on changes that cause the character to be different at the end of the book from the way she was at the beginning. Keep this in mind when you tell the story:

When Maria goes to Oklahoma to visit a grandmother she has never known before, she finds herself in a household where what you say is more important than how you look. There are some "beauties" in Grandmama's family, and some "plain ones" like Maria, but nobody cares about any of that. What matters is how you tell a story, and when Maria relates some of the fantasies she had made up, everybody listens. For the first time in her life, Maria is admired, and pretty soon she begins to admire herself.

Some novels are written to inform readers about a specific culture or historic era. When reporting on this kind of book, concentrate on its setting and time:

Raj Sahni lives in a rural village just west of New Delhi, in present-day India. Life is not easy for Raj. In the summer months, the temperature goes over 100°F in the shade, and in the monsoon season that follows, rain falls for days on end. Very little has changed over the generations in Raj's village. Many people live in mud houses with thatched roofs, and goats and water buffalo wander about on the streets. Raj's father plants corn and wheat in the same fields his father and grandfather farmed before him. Raj, though, wants to do something different when he grows up. He wants to be a doctor in the small hospital down the road from his house.

If, instead of a novel, your book is a collection of short stories, mention a common theme among them, if there is one, and then tell about one or two stories in detail:

All the stories in *After and Beyond* tell of supernatural happenings. The most frightening is "The Strange Return of Mr. Jensen," in which a baker disappears from his shop one day in late 19th century London and is not heard from for nearly ten years. During that time, his family, many of his former customers, and the police try to track him down. When a little girl finally discovers where he is and what he has become, they all wish they had never looked for him in the first place. "What Became of Jody?" and "The Lost Butler" are also about people who have disappeared and later return in strange and frightening forms.

Follow the same rules when you report on a collection of poems:

Wingsongs is a collection of poems about things that fly, such as airplanes, geese, bees, angels, and pterodactyls. Some of the poems are funny, some are scary, and some are full of unusual images. In "Washday," a flock of geese is compared to a clothesline of wash flapping in the wind. In "Pterrible Beast," the poet makes up crazy words and spellings to describe a pterodactyl.

For a report on a biography, a history, or a science book, you will be relating facts rather than imaginary events. Works of this sort usually contain a great deal of information, and you may have difficulty remembering it all. Keep a notepad at your side as you read, so that you can write down important points and their page numbers as you come across them. Do not attempt to report on all the material in the book. Offer a general statement about the subject, and follow that with a few specific details.

If your book is a biography, begin by explaining why its subject was important and what he or she accomplished. Use the past tense when you report on real events:

Harriet Tubman was often called "Moses" during her lifetime because she led her people out of slavery and into freedom. A runaway slave, she returned to the South over and over to help hundreds of other slaves escape to a new life.

A report on a book of history or science should also open with a general statement, this time offering an introduction to the subject:

The Boston Tea Party of 1773 was an act of rebellion engaged in by Boston citizens who opposed British taxation of tea.

Or, for a science book:

Many of the things that people believe about bats are incorrect. Most bats are harmless. Many, in fact, are helpful to human society.

Use your notes to provide further details about your subject. You might conclude this section of your report on a biography this way:

Harriet Tubman lived to be more than 90 years old, and she devoted most of these years to helping other blacks. Before the Civil War, she worked with the Underground Railroad to rescue slaves. During the war, she helped the Northern army locate enemy camps in the South, and she nursed runaway slaves and black soldiers in hospitals. After slavery was abolished, she set up the John Brown Home in Auburn, New York, where she took care of sick and poor blacks.

Form and Style. Every book has a form and style all its own. The form of a book refers to its structure, or the way it is organized. A novel, for example, might be written in the form of a diary. A biography might be written in the form of an exchange of letters. The style refers to the way the author expresses himself or herself. Styles vary from book to book the way personalities vary from person to person. Some books are written in very formal prose, others in the language you hear around you all the time. You can combine a discussion of the form and the style in a single paragraph:

Each chapter of *The Plain One* is introduced by a letter written by Maria to her grandmother, long after she has returned home from her visit to Oklahoma. The chapter then tells in detail what the letter refers to. The letters are written in simple, everyday language. The chapters often sound like poetry, with long descriptions of cornfields and the Oklahoma sky.

Your Opinion. There are many reasons for liking or disliking a book. The plot of a novel may be exciting, or it may be slow moving. The dialogue may sound authentic, or it may sound false. The facts in a history book may be clear and understandable, or they may be hard to follow. At times, you will like some aspects of a book and dislike others. Whatever your opinion, be specific in stating it. Do not say only that the book was interesting or boring. Tell why:

When I read *The Plain One*, I felt that I myself was Maria. I suffered with her when her family ignored her at home, and I triumphed with her when her storytelling won her so much admiration in Oklahoma. The other characters, though, seemed much less real. They all spoke alike, and they sounded like people on a television show, not like people in the real world.

▶**ORAL REPORTS**

When you present an oral book report, you should give the same basic information that you would provide in a written report. This time your audience will be listening to, rather than reading, what you have to say. However, you will still have to write out in advance everything you want to tell them. Do not read this written report word for word to your audience. Instead, prepare index cards, each containing a few phrases that will remind you of what your full-length report said. Make one card for each major idea in your report. An index card for the biography of Harriet Tubman might read like this:

Harriet Tubman often called Moses
Led her people to freedom
Runaway slave
Returned to South over and over
Helped hundreds of slaves escape

Glance down at your cards when you need to, but look at your audience as much as you can. Stand up tall and speak in a slow, clear voice. Keep reminding yourself that your audience wants to hear what you have to say. Those who have not read your book will want to hear about something new. Those who have read it will want to compare your understanding of it with their own.

SYLVIA CASSEDY
Author, *In Your Own Words:
A Beginner's Guide to Writing*

BOOKS

It is difficult to imagine a civilization without books. Their importance in human history cannot be exaggerated. Valuable ideas and discoveries throughout our history have been recorded in books. Using information from books, scholars and scientists have explored and expanded almost every subject known to us. Without books there would be no modern medicine, no modern science or technology, no television, no space flights to the moon, no teachers, and no schools. In short, without books, life as we know it would not be possible.

Information about fields and crops are etched on this clay tablet, which dates from about 2800 B.C. Clay tablets could be moved from place to place but they were heavy and not very practical.

▶ BEFORE BOOKS

The human need to record and pass along stories and information is as old as the human race. For thousands of years, some of our early ancestors preserved their beliefs, legends, and daily activities by painting pictures on walls of caves and other rock surfaces protected from the weather. Unfortunately, in order to "read" these stories, one had to go to the source—a wall could not be carried or placed on a library shelf.

The Need for Books

About 10,000 years ago, people began raising crops in addition to hunting animals and gathering edible plants. As farming expanded and became more complicated, there was a need to count, measure, and record holdings —sheaves of grain, numbers of cattle, bins of rice, and so on. Therefore, people developed simple symbols to help them count and keep track of their animals and crops.

Over time a creative people called the Sumerians, who also built the world's first cities, invented a simple form of writing that was made up of three-cornered marks. This form of writing is called **cuneiform**, which means "wedge-shaped." Using sticks, the Sumerians drew their farm and business records on small slabs, or tablets, of soft, damp clay that were then hardened in the sun. The tablets could be stored and carried, and when they were no longer useful, they were simply thrown away.

The more important Sumerian texts were baked in ovens much like fine pottery and then stored in the world's first libraries. In recent times, thousands of these clay tablets have been discovered; many were found in perfect condition under the dry desert sands.

▶ THE FIRST BOOKS

The next advance in the history of books occurred in Egypt, around 3500 B.C. The ancient Egyptians had developed a lovely, but complex, picture writing called **hieroglyphics**, or "sacred writing." In order to reproduce this complicated writing, they invented papyrus sheets. These thin cream-colored sheets were made from the papyrus plant—a tall reed that grew in flooded marshes along the Nile River. To make the sheets, the reeds were split open

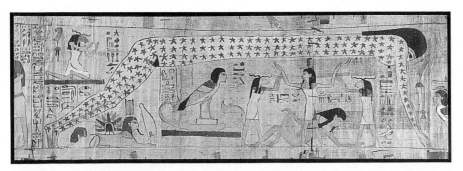

This Egyptian papyrus, which dates from about 2500 B.C., illustrates the creation of the universe.

and cut into strips. Then the strips were flattened and joined together. Brushes and reeds were used to illustrate and write on the long rolled pieces of papyrus, which were called **scrolls**.

Papyrus-making became a major industry in Egypt; blank rolls and scrolls were exported to every corner of the known world, especially to Rome and Athens. Although Egypt was the largest producer, excellent quality papyrus was also grown in other places in the eastern Mediterranean.

Ancient Greece—Books Begin to Travel

The best customers for Egypt's papyrus were the Greeks, particularly the people of Athens, then the world capital of learning. Scribes, people who made copies of scrolls, were busy individuals in Athenian communities, and their work required large amounts of papyrus.

Greek scholars, teachers, actors, and musicians, who often traveled from job to job and from town to town, usually carried with them

many Greek ideas, seized large numbers of Greek books, and moved entire Greek libraries to Rome.

The Romans also wrote their own books on thin wooden boards. Eventually, they decided to join several boards together by punching holes along one side and passing rings through the holes to connect the pages. This kind of wooden book became known as a **codex**, which in Latin *(caudex)* means "tree trunk."

In order to write in an early codex, the pages were first coated with gesso, a liquid mixture of chalk and glue. When the gesso dried to a hard finish, a thin coat of black wax was applied. Then with a pointed instrument called a stylus, the writer scratched the lettering through the wax. The early codices were used mainly as notebooks.

The crude early codices made of wood were soon replaced by ones made of flat papyrus pages that were cut to uniform sizes and bound between two boards. These codices were very popular, largely because they were so easy to use and to carry. When an opened codex was

Wooden boards were spread with gesso and a thin coat of black wax. Using a sharp, pointed tool, it was easy to scratch symbols on the waxed surface. The tablets could be joined together, making a wooden book, or codex. These codices replaced the clay tablets and papyrus scrolls of earlier times.

the latest papyrus scrolls of poetry, geometry, philosophy, music, manners, and morals.

The Greeks greatly advanced writing and the making of books by inventing an alphabet of 24 symbols, called letters. Each letter represented a particular sound in the spoken language. It is far easier to write down a language made up of letters than one based on pictures.

Moving Toward Modern Books

Around 146 B.C., the expanding Roman Empire conquered Greece. The victorious Romans were dazzled by the cultural richness of classical Greece, and they readily adopted

placed on a table, it stayed open, unlike a scroll, which had an annoying tendency to roll back up the moment it was put down. It was also easier to locate sections of a text in a codex. Today, codex is the technical term for any book made up of many pages bound together and not in the form of a roll or scroll.

Parchment Replaces Papyrus

The next step toward the modern book was the use of **parchment**, or processed and stretched animal skin. Parchment was not a new material, but its potential was realized with the invention of the Roman codex.

A "page" from an Indian palm-leaf book. People in India, China, and Nepal sometimes wrote on the backs of palm leaves. When the leaves were fastened together, they could be spread for reading.

Parchment is actually a very smooth thin leather. It is prepared from a sheep's or goat's skin that has been carefully cleaned, bleached white, stretched flat, and then rubbed smooth with pumice, a lightweight volcanic material that works like a fine sandpaper. An especially desirable creamy white parchment called vellum was made from calfskin.

Parchment was more expensive than papyrus, which was made from a plant that grew wild and required much less preparation. But parchment had several advantages over papyrus. It was a tougher material and less likely to tear or decay. Ink could be erased from parchment, unlike papyrus, and parchment could be painted and decorated with bright colors and gold leaf. Parchment also had two usable sides. A single page of parchment could carry twice as many words as a page of papyrus, which had only one usable side.

The codex, with its double-sided parchment pages, was in many ways the first truly modern book—one of Rome's many gifts to the world.

▶ BOOKS OF THE ORIENT

Thousands of miles east of Egypt, Greece, and Rome was the "celestial kingdom" of China. The Chinese developed their language, writing, and books in ways similar to those of their Western counterparts, even though there was very little contact between the two widely separated areas.

The ancient Chinese, like the Sumerians and the Egyptians, began to write with pictures instead of an alphabet. Over the centuries Chinese writing developed into elegant **pictograms** with thousands of separate characters. With some changes, this writing system is still used by the Chinese people today.

The earliest Chinese books were written on the backs of palm leaves and on flattened pieces of wood and bamboo. The Chinese never used the roll or scroll. Instead, their palm-leaf and bamboo books were strips fastened at one end much like a fan and then spread like a fan to be read. The Chinese did not use pens or styluses. They painted their pictograms with brushes and shiny black ink.

The Chinese had no papyrus or parchment, and they desired a better, more practical material than palm leaves or bamboo as a writing surface. They tried using panels of silk cloth for their finest poetry, but silk pages were not durable and were very expensive. Their search for a better material finally ended in A.D. 105 when a Chinese dignitary named Ts'ai Lun invented the world's first sheets of real paper. He concocted a pulp of wood chips, silk and cotton rags, hemp rope, and even old fishing nets, and then molded it into sheets. The Chinese were immediately aware of the great value of paper and they kept the art of papermaking a secret for hundreds of years. Eventually, however, the technique was carried east in the 100's and west in the 200's.

Using their paper, the Chinese at first made books that were written by hand. Later, they developed a printmaking technique, called **woodcut**, which enabled them to illustrate their texts more easily and also allowed them to make multiple impressions of the pages.

The invention of paper changed the format of Chinese books—full-size pages were glued together and accordion-folded. This style of book was the Chinese standard for well over a thousand years, until the introduction of the printing press from Europe.

This illustration of a man collecting bamboo pulp is from a Japanese edition of a Chinese encyclopedia on traditional technology, written about 1637.

▶ MEDIEVAL MANUSCRIPTS

After the fall of Rome in 476, nearly all the making and selling of books stopped as a cultural and political decline, called the Dark Ages, occurred throughout Europe. Later, books began to be made again in small Christian communities called **monasteries**.

Dedicated monks of religious orders began to make exact, handwritten copies, or **manuscripts**, of the most significant Greek and Roman books that had survived. The monks diligently copied the old books—mostly Bibles and other religious and philosophical works—from dawn to dusk, six days a week, year after year. They worked in rooms called **scriptoria** whose windows faced the sun. The presence of such rare manuscripts made the monks very fearful of fire, so the scriptoria were unheated and candles were not allowed.

By the Middle Ages, around the year 1100, monks were making beautiful **illuminated manuscripts**—radiantly colored codices with ornamental borders of animal and plant designs. Nuns sometimes inked in the delicate, perfectly formed letters. But hand-copying, however beautiful, was a very slow process. Even the most diligent monks could not produce enough books to satisfy the growing demand for them.

▶ THE PRINTING PRESS

At the height of the Middle Ages, the first colleges and universities were opening in cities across Europe. Students wanted and needed books. Secular professional copyists, called **stationers**, began to make hurried, unattractive manuscripts for the students, but still there never seemed to be enough books. This situation changed—rapidly and forever—with the invention of the printing press.

The printing press was invented by Johann Gutenberg in the small city of Mainz in Germany around 1450. Gutenberg's press used tiny pieces of metal type to print each letter of the alphabet. The printing press soon replaced the slow work of the manuscript copyist. The printer with his ink-stained hands could create thousands of copies of a book in the time it would take a copyist or stationer to make just one.

The next 50 years were explosive. By 1500 there were printing presses in some 300 European cities. More than 10 million copies of thousands of books had been printed. In order

Illuminated manuscript pages like this one from the *Belleville Breviary* (1343) are as colorful and hauntingly beautiful as the stained-glass cathedral windows of the same period.

to illustrate so many books quickly and easily, Europeans adopted the Chinese woodcut technique. A drawing was carved into a block of wood, and the block was locked into the press with the text. Then the text and illustration were printed as a complete page again and again.

For the first time in history, books were plentiful and popular. Millions of ordinary people developed an intense desire to learn to read now that books were available.

All of the books printed before 1501 are called **incunabula**, the Latin word for "cradle," because this was the infancy of modern bookmaking. By 1500 the printing press itself was so mechanically perfected that it would change very little over the next 400 years.

The form, look, and feel of the books we read today were also worked out and adopted worldwide during the late 1400's. Italian book designers and printers were especially adept at creating typefaces, layouts, and illustrations that were pleasing to look at and to read.

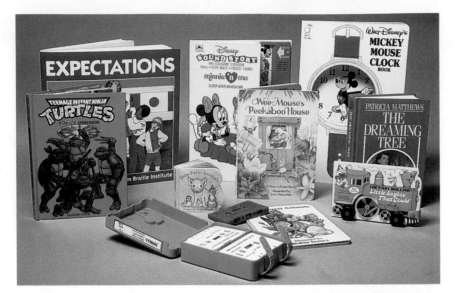

Left: Some unusual types of books include large-print books for the visually impaired, and talking books, shape books, and pop-up books. *Below:* Children's books in braille, such as this one, are available in many bookstores and libraries.

▶ **MODERN BOOKS**

Most modern books resemble those made 450 years ago—paper pages are bound between a front cover and a back cover. There have been, however, a few variations in the materials, and even in the format, used in books over the last 200 years.

In the 1800's the first paperback books were published. Printed on cheap paper with paper covers, they only cost a dime. Just about anyone could read about the exploits of cowboys in the Wild West and other adventurers. Paperback editions of the classics as well as popular fiction and nonfiction were also printed. The paperback book industry is still a big business today.

Since the 1930's when they were first introduced, books on audio tape have become increasingly popular. Well-known actors and sometimes the authors themselves are recorded as they read entire novels or nonfiction books. More recently, children's stories have been recorded to give pre-readers more exposure to language and literature.

Other innovations in children's books have included cloth books with pages that cannot be torn; plastic books that can be taken into the bathtub; wipe-off books that can be colored with crayons and then wiped clean with a cloth; and pop-up story books with flat pages that become three-dimensional when they are turned.

The newest types of books are electronic books. These are books that can be read on a computer screen. Researchers are even developing electronic paper and electronic inks. These will be used to create books whose content can be changed completely when connected to the Internet or cued by a radio signal. Imagine owning books with ever-changing stories!

▶ **BOOKMAKING TECHNOLOGY**

The technology involved in making books has changed dramatically with the advent of phototypesetting, computers, and four-color printing processes used in reproducing illustrations and photography. The paper used for the pages of books has also been improved to ensure its durability and longevity.

JACK KNOWLTON
Author, *Books and Libraries*

See also GRAPHIC ARTS; ILLUMINATED MANUSCRIPTS; ILLUSTRATION AND ILLUSTRATORS; LIBRARIES; PRINTING; WOODCUT PRINTING.

BOOKS: FROM AUTHOR TO READER

Books are one of the miracles of humanity. They make our thoughts, our feelings, our dreams, and our knowledge permanent, and they make them available to everyone.

Millions of books are printed each year in the United States. Have you ever wondered how these books were made? Let us look at the bookmaking process for the type of book you might buy in a bookstore or borrow from your local library. We will begin with the author's manuscript.

▶ FROM AUTHOR TO PUBLISHER

Imagine that you have written a story called *It Rained Every Day,* about a family on vacation. Like most authors today, you have used a word processor to prepare your manuscript. In the past when authors wrote poems, stories, novels, or other material, they prepared handwritten copies of their work. Typewritten copies or printed copies from word processors or computers are much easier to read, and the people who make books prefer them.

You have worked very hard and long on your story and think it is good. Friends and family who have read it agree. They urge you to try to have *It Rained Every Day* made into a book. Fine! But now that the story is finished and you have prepared the manuscript, what do you do?

▶ FINDING A PUBLISHER

When your manuscript is finished, you must find a publisher who is interested in making it into a book. The best way to find a publisher is to go to the library and look at *Literary Market Place (LMP).* This reference book lists hundreds of different publishers with their addresses, phone numbers, and the names of some of the people who work there. You want to find publishers who publish children's trade books. **Trade books** are fiction and nonfiction works sold in bookstores, and that is where you want your book to end up. Other publishers listed in *LMP* may specialize in textbooks, reference books, or other types of publishing.

February 9, 1992

Ms. Julia Lee, Editor
Children's Book Department
Crabapple Publishing Co.
669 Fifth Avenue
New York, NY 10020

Dear Ms. Lee:

I am enclosing my manuscript, IT RAINED EVERY DAY, which I would like you to consider for publication.

IT RAINED EVERY DAY is about a brother and sister who fight all the time. When they go on vacation with their family, the weather is bad every day. The brother and sister learn that if they keep fighting each other, their vacation will be really ruined. This is the story of how the vacation is saved.

I hope you will enjoy reading the manuscript. I look forward to hearing from you.

Sincerely,

Mary Smith

Mary Smith
8 Lafayette Street
Belmar, NJ 07719
(908) 555-6704

MS/ms
Enc: ms and SASE

Above: Be sure to enclose a one-page letter and a self-addressed, stamped envelope with any manuscript you send to a publisher.

Left: A young author works on her manuscript. Changes in her manuscript are easy to make on a word processor.

Contacting a Publisher

After selecting a number of trade book publishers, the next step is to write a short, one-page letter to the children's book editor at one of them. In this letter you should tell the editor a little about yourself and your book. Send the letter and a copy of your manuscript to the editor in a sturdy envelope. Include a stamped, self-addressed envelope so that the editor can return your manuscript if he or she decides not to publish it.

A book contract is carefully checked before it is sent to an author.

Publishers receive thousands of manuscripts every year, so months may go by before you hear from the editor. The manuscript may be returned with a rejection note, saying that the publisher is not interested. If so, send it to another publisher. Imagine, however, that the editor wants to publish your manuscript as a book. What happens next?

Book Contracts

If the editor is interested in your book, one of the first things he or she probably will do is telephone you and offer you a contract. At this point the editor will want to discuss an advance and a royalty, as well as some of the other terms of a contract.

Advances and Royalties. An **advance** is an amount of money the publisher agrees to give you before your book is published. Usually, the publisher pays half the advance when a contract is signed and the other half when the manuscript is delivered and the editor agrees that it is acceptable. Advances for first novels usually range from $1,500 to $4,000. Well-known authors receive advances many times greater than that.

A **royalty** is a percentage of the price of each copy of your book that is sold. Part of the royalty is used to pay off the money you received as an advance. When the advance has been paid off, an author begins to receive royalty payments twice a year based on the sales of the book.

Contract Clauses. A book contract contains many clauses, or conditions, dealing with such things as territorial and subsidiary rights, warrants, and permissions. It will also include the date on which you, the author, promise to deliver the final manuscript.

Clauses dealing with **territorial rights** specify the countries in which your book can be sold. The contract may state that you agree to sell "world rights," or the rights to sell your book in any country. Or it may agree to sell rights for only certain countries.

Subsidiary rights allow your book to be sold for such things as a paperback edition, a book club edition, a movie or television version, translations into foreign languages, a large print edition, or a serialization in a newspaper or magazine.

Contracts also include **warrants**, or guarantees. One warrant states that you guarantee your work to be original and of your own creation. Another states that the book contains no recipe, formula, or instruction that may be harmful to someone reading your book. Suppose, for example, that you write about a person eating a particular wild plant. If someone reads your book, eats this plant, and becomes ill because the plant is poisonous, this person might sue. The warrant helps protect the publisher from such a lawsuit, and reminds you, the author, of your responsibility to be sure such information is carefully checked and that appropriate warnings are included in your book when they are necessary. The contract will also include a warrant stating that you have not invaded the privacy of another person or written anything that is libelous—that is, that discredits someone's character.

Contracts may also include clauses concerning permissions. **Permissions** are written consents from others saying that you may use materials they have created. Songs, poems, photographs, and excerpts from interviews are all examples of materials that usually require written consent for their use. Contracts normally state that the author must pay any fees required to obtain such permissions.

The Importance of Agents

Dealing with publishers and book contracts can be quite complex. For this reason, it is usually advisable for writers to hire literary agents to represent them in negotiations with editors and publishers. Agents often are able to get better terms in contracts than writers can get negotiating alone. In return for their services, agents will charge commissions of 10 to 15 percent of the income writers earn from their books.

Literary agents are professionals who know the publishing business and the people who work in it. Because of this, the manuscripts of writers with agents are usually given more careful consideration by publishers than ones by writers without agents. Getting an agent is not easy, however. It is almost impossible to find an agent who will take on a young, unknown writer before he or she has been published. Once a writer has been offered a contract, it is much easier to get an agent. Nevertheless, unknown writers can try to find agents by submitting letters of inquiry and samples of their work to them.

▶ THE EDITORIAL AND DESIGN PROCESS

Once a contract has been signed, the publisher begins work on your manuscript of *It Rained Every Day* to make it into a book. The publishing process is quite complex. It involves many stages and a variety of people both inside and outside the publishing company. Since several parts of the process may be going on at the same time, the people involved in making a book work closely together to ensure the book's completion.

The two divisions of a publishing company that are initially involved in creating a book from manuscript are the editorial department and the art department. The publishing professionals working in these departments include the editors, managing editors, copy editors, proofreaders, art directors, designers, and illustrators.

The Editor

Most manuscripts undergo changes after they have been submitted to the publisher. The person responsible for improving a manuscript is the editor. The edi-

tor will read the manuscript and then return it to the author with suggestions for changes, or revisions. These constructive suggestions are not meant as criticisms but are aimed at making the book better. The editor will point out flaws or errors and propose ways the manuscript could be improved. Perhaps he or she will suggest a different ending, or question whether a character's actions make sense. The editor might even suggest that certain parts of the manuscript be rewritten.

Although editing is their primary role, good editors do more than just edit. They must be knowledgeable about new trends, new ideas, and what is being written elsewhere. They must also be on the lookout for new, talented writers and must encourage published writers to continue working. They might also develop ideas for books themselves and try to find writers who can turn those ideas into books.

After a manuscript has been revised and approved, the editor prepares to put it into **production**. The editor estimates the length of the book; sets a date for publication; and determines other specifics, such as the size of each page (the **trim**), the kind of binding, and the

On this page of the copyedited manuscript, note the content changes—"fork" to "spoon" and "plate" to "cereal bowl"—as well as the corrections in grammar and punctuation.

CHAPTER ONE

Paula Jones grit her teeth. The screen door slammed. Her brother Pete was gone, and she was left at the breakfast table with her parents and her little brother, Ted.

She slammed down her ~~fork~~ spoon. "It isn't fair," she said. "It's Pete's turn to do the dishes. I did them last night."

Her mother stood up. "It's not fair, you're right. I'll do the dishes, but I hope you'll help us with unpacking and setting things up. It's a shame to waste our first day of vacation working, but we have to get organized before we can have fun."

"I'll help." Ted stood up, his ~~plate~~ cereal bowl in his hand. He reached for his half-full glass of milk, grabbed it tightly, and set it in the ~~plate~~ bowl. Holding the ~~plate~~ bowl and glass of milk with one hand, he began piling silver into the ~~plate~~ bowl. It wobbled, and the milk sloshed against the sides of the glass. A knife fell onto the floor. Ted lurched for it, but the glass tilted, and milk splashed onto the table.

Ted looked miserable, Paula thought. He's always trying to help and makes a mess because he's so little. Paula remembered when she was six...

all: they had cereal... see changes below

how many "sides" does a glass have?

quantity of books to be printed. The editor also prepares a brief description of the book—to be used later for advertising purposes—and a brief biographical note about the author.

The editor's responsibility does not end when a book goes into production. He or she generally reviews the progress of a manuscript during the publishing process to see that everything is proceeding as planned.

An editor often uses a word processor to make changes the author has agreed to in the manuscript.

The Managing Editor

When an editor puts a manuscript into production, the first person to receive it is generally the managing editor. Managing editors are familiar with all aspects of the bookmaking process. Although their duties may vary from publisher to publisher, they are usually in charge of **trafficking** the manuscript. This means making sure that the manuscript is complete, sending it to the appropriate people at the right time, and keeping track of schedules and deadlines. It often takes from nine months to a year for a manuscript to be made into a book and placed in bookstores. The managing editor makes sure that each person involved in the process does his or her job properly and on time.

The Copy Editor

One of the first people to receive a manuscript from the managing editor is the copy editor. Copy editors are responsible for checking a manuscript for accuracy and style—that is, consistency in spelling, grammar, and word usage. The copy editor's most important tools are a collection of specialized reference books that he or she refers to while working.

While working on a manuscript, the copy editor keeps an alphabetical list of proper names and unusual spellings on a piece of paper called a **style sheet**. This style sheet will be used later to double check the accuracy of the manuscript. The copy editor rewrites passages that are not grammatical, corrects misspellings, and punctuates the book according to accepted rules of punctuation. The copy ed-

itor also checks for consistency, making sure that words are spelled the same way throughout the book.

Copy editors are trained to doubt every fact in a manuscript and to check these facts in a variety of source books. For example, if a manuscript says that a character caught a rainbow trout in the ocean, the copy editor will suggest that the author choose another type of fish after checking and learning that rainbow trout are only found in freshwater streams.

In making corrections and changes, copy editors use marks called proofreader's marks. These are special marks used throughout the bookmaking process to ensure that instructions are conveyed accurately.

The Proofreader

One member of the editorial staff—the proofreader—does not become involved in the bookmaking process until much later. The proofreader begins working on a book after the manuscript has been set into type by a typesetter. At that point the proofreader will carefully check typeset copies of the manuscript against the copyedited manuscript to catch any errors and mark them so that they will be corrected. You will read more about typesetting and the job of proofreaders later in the section on composition.

The Art Director

The art director in a publishing house is responsible for overseeing all aspects of a book's design. This includes assigning artists to work on a book, supervising design staff, and often choosing a design for a book's cover. The art director, as well as other artists involved, works with the editorial staff to make sure that the design of a book is appropriate for its content and its intended audience. The art director becomes involved in the publishing process when he or she is given a copy of the manuscript by the editor. At that point, the art director assigns the work to staff members of the art department or to outside artists.

The Book Designer

The design of a book—the physical arrangement of all the materials that make up the book—is the responsibility of the book designer. The primary goal of the book designer is to translate an author's words into a visual design that helps a reader understand the author's ideas.

Determining Book Length. One of the first things the book designer does with the manuscript of *It Rained Every Day* is make a **cast off** or **character count**. A character is any letter, numeral, space, and punctuation mark in the manuscript. A cast off is necessary for calculating how long the finished book will be. An average young person's novel of 160 to 192 pages may contain more than a quarter of a million characters!

Choosing Type. Once the cast off has been done, the designer chooses a typeface and type size that he or she considers most appropriate. The designer also considers the length of each line of type, the space between the words, the space between lines, and the margins around the outside of the type. These elements all help to determine how easy or difficult the book will be to read.

Baskerville

Size 14 pt. ABCDEfghijklmno

Size 18 pt. ABCDefghijkl

Size 24 pt. ABCdefghi

Helvetica

Size 14 pt. ABCDEfghijklmno

Size 18 pt. ABCDefghijkl

Size 24 pt. ABCdefghi

Above: Baskerville and Helvetica are two of the many typefaces used for books. Note the differences in the shapes and sizes of the letters in these examples.

Left: A designer discusses the layout of a book with the art director.

One

Paula Jones grit her teeth. The screen door slammed. Her brother Pete was gone, and she was left at the breakfast table with her parents and her little brother Ted.

She slammed down her spoon. "It isn't fair," she said. "It's Pete's turn to do the dishes. I did them last night."

Her mother stood up. "It's not fair, you're right. I'll do the dishes, but I hope you'll help us with unpacking and setting things up. It's a shame to waste our first day of vacation working, but we have to get organized before we can have fun."

"I'll help." Ted stood up, his cereal bowl in his hand. He reached for his half-full glass of milk, grabbed it tightly, and set it in the bowl. Holding the bowl and the glass of milk with one hand,

he began piling silver into the bowl. It wobbled, and the milk sloshed against the side of the glass. A knife fell onto the floor. When Ted lurched for it, the glass tilted, and milk splashed onto the table.

Ted looked miserable, Paula thought. He's always trying to help and makes a mess because he's so little. Paula remembered when she was six.

This two-page layout shows how the text and art will look when the manuscript for *It Rained Every Day* is printed into a book.

The placement of the title, the author's name, and the name of the publisher on the book jacket is important because the book may be placed on a shelf rather than on a table or in a window of a bookstore.

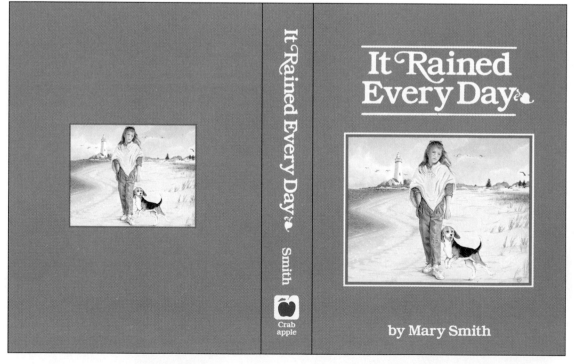

Front Matter and Back Matter. The book designer is not only concerned with the main text, or body, of the book. He or she also designs the material that comes before, and sometimes after, the text. The material at the front of the book, called the **front matter**, normally includes a half-title page, a title page, a copyright page, and often a dedication page. Some books may have additional front-matter pages such as a frontispiece (a page with a map or illustration), a preface, an author's note, a table of contents, or an introduction. Nonfiction books often include **back matter**, such as an appendix, a glossary, a bibliography, and an index.

Layouts. After a design has been created, the designer prepares special sheets, called **layouts**, that show how the book will look. Layouts include detailed plans for every element of the book. Frequently, the designer will ask the **compositor**—the person setting the type—to provide samples that show how these different elements will look after the book is printed. After reviewing the layouts and samples, the designer and editor may decide to make changes in the design.

Preparing for Typesetting and Printing. When the design has been finalized, it is the designer's job to mark the manuscript with coded instructions for setting type. These instructions tell the compositor exactly how to set all the type throughout the book, including the main text, page numbers (folios), headings at the top or bottom of the page, and all front- and back-matter materials.

Before a book is printed, the designer may sometimes be asked to prepare a mechanical. A **mechanical** is a detailed assembly of the book, with every element in place. The mechanical is then photographed and the film is used in the printing process.

The Jacket Designer

While *It Rained Every Day* is being edited and designed, artists are creating its artwork. This could include art for the cover of a paperback book and for the paper dust jacket that protects the cover of a hardcover book.

The cover or dust jacket of a book is very important. It protects the book and serves as an advertisement. The person responsible for designing the cover is the jacket designer. Working with the art director of the publishing house, the jacket designer tries to create an

WONDER QUESTION

What information is on a copyright page?

The copyright page contains a copyright notice, which indicates that the rights of the book are reserved as of a specific year. It also lists the full address of the publisher, the edition number, and the Library of Congress Cataloging in Publication (CIP) notice. The CIP is the official catalog card information to be used at the Library of Congress in Washington, D.C., and at many other libraries.

Another important piece of information on the copyright page is the International Standard Book Number (ISBN). This is an identification number, assigned to every book published, that is used in ordering books. Several parts of the ISBN stand for specific things. The first digit indicates the language of the book; a zero stands for English. The next three digits indicate the publisher; each publisher is assigned a three-digit code. The next group of five digits is the number of the book. The last digit is a checking number.

attractive, eye-catching, and informative cover that is appropriate for the book and conveys all necessary information, including the title and the author's name.

When the jacket designer has created a design, he or she often prepares a **comp**, a mock-up of what the design will actually look like after it is printed. If the editor and art director approve the design, the jacket designer will then prepare a mechanical to be used in the printing process.

The Illustrator

Many books, especially those for young readers, have artwork in the interior of the book as well as on the cover. The artist who creates the original art to be used in the interior of a book is called an illustrator.

While the manuscript of *It Rained Every Day* is being prepared, the editor and art director choose an illustrator to work on the art. Following their guidelines, the illustrator prepares sketches to show what the finished art will look like. These sketches are checked by the editor or an assistant to make sure they are appropriate to the text and that all the details are correct. For example, a section of a story may say that a girl has red hair, wears blue jeans, and is walking with her dog, so the illustration for this portion of the story should show the same things.

If an illustration does not match the text, something will have to be changed. Sometimes the art can be changed. However, since it is often costly and time-consuming to change a piece of art, the editor might ask the author to revise the text as long as it will not hurt the author's storyline or ideas.

▶ THE PRODUCTION PROCESS

After the editorial and art and design departments have completed their work, the actual production of a book begins. This part of the bookmaking process involves several stages, including composition, or typesetting, color separation, printing, and binding. Most of the work at these stages is done outside the publishing house.

Control over the process during these stages is maintained largely by the publishing house's production department and a production manager or supervisor. The role of the production manager or supervisor is a complex and very important one. It is that person's responsibility to select outside groups to work on various production aspects of the book, to act as liaison between these groups and the publishing house, to choose the paper to be used for the book and its cover, to coordinate production schedules, and to maintain control of production budgets.

Composition

During the composition process a compositor, or typesetter, changes a typewritten manuscript into pages of type that can then be printed and made into a book. In the past, typesetting was done manually and involved arranging individual pieces of metal type to create a page. Today, computer technology has made most typesetting much easier, as well as faster and cheaper.

As the typesetting proceeds, the compositor prepares **galley proofs**, which are long sheets of paper showing the typeset material. These galley proofs are sent to the publisher for approval. A proofreader compares a master set of galley proofs against the original, copy-edited manuscript to find any errors. The author receives a set of galley proofs as well and may request certain changes. These changes are added to the master set, which is then sent back to the compositor for corrections.

The compositor then prepares other stages of typeset material to be checked by the editor and designer. These stages include page proofs, repros, and blues. **Page proofs** are corrected galley proofs that have been broken up into pages. They show how the type on each page of the book will appear. The editor checks page proofs for any additional changes or corrections. **Repros**, or reproduction proofs, show any further changes in typesetting. They are printed on a special coated paper that will be photographed and used in the printing process. Repros are used by the designer to make any mechanicals that might be required. **Blues**, or blueprints, are the last stage in the typesetting process. They are made from photographic film that has been prepared for use in the printing process. Blues show how all the parts of each book page will be assembled, with art, text, and any other

On this galley proof, note the proofreader's correction marks. A "pe" indicates a printer's error; an "aa" indicates an author's or editor's change in the text.

One

Paula Jones grit her teeth. The screen door slamed. Her brother Pete was gone, and she was left at the breakfast table with her parents and her little brother Ted.

She slammed down her spoon. "It isn't fair," she said. "It's Pete's turn to do the dishes. I did them last night."

Her mother stood up. "It's not fair, you're right. I'll do the dishes, but I hope you'll help us with unpacking and setting things up. It's a shame to waste our first day of vacation working, but we have to get organized before we can have fun.

help." Ted stood up, his cereal bowl in his hand. He reached for his half-full glass of milk, grabbed it tightly, and set it in the bowl. Holding the bowl and glass of milk with one hand, he began piling silver into the bowl. It wobbled, and the milk sloshed against the side of the glass. A knife fell onto the floor. Ted lurched for it, but the glass tilted, and milk splashed onto the table.

Ted looked miserable, Paula thought. He's always trying to help and makes a mess because he's so little. Paula remembered when she was six . . .

elements in place as they will appear in the finished book. Corrections can be made at this stage, but they are very expensive.

Color Separation

Printing colored illustrations in a book or on a cover is a much more complicated and expensive process than printing black type. In order to print color, it is necessary first to separate a color image into four process colors—yellow, magenta (red), cyan (blue), and black. The principle behind this is the same as mixing paints. Mixing the three primary colors—red, yellow, and blue—produces all other colors. Black is used to add highlight and depth.

Records or separations of the different hues of each color illustration or photograph are made. They are produced by a process that uses photographic film or by one that uses an electronic scanner and a computer program. The separations are then used to make printing plates that, when printed, will produce a full-color image on the printed pages of the book or cover.

A designer carefully checks the color plates. If the colors are not right, the color separator can change color hues.

A color illustration or photograph is first separated into four process colors—yellow, cyan (blue), magenta (red), and black.

yellow   cyan (blue)   magenta (red)   black

When the four colors are printed together, they make up more colors. For example, a combination of yellow and blue produces green, and a combination of blue and red produces purple.

yellow blue   yellow red   blue red   red purple   black
green   orange   purple   orange   brown
                                          yellow blue
                                          green

This example shows how 32 pages are printed on one sheet of paper. Sixteen pages are printed on each side. Some pages are upside down. They are arranged so that they will fall into the proper sequence when the sheet is folded. This arrangement is called an imposition.

25	8	5	28
24	9	12	21
29	4	1	32
20	13	16	17

27	6	7	26
22	11	10	23
31	2	3	30
18	15	14	19

When the separation has been done, the separator will send a proof to the publisher for approval. If the colors do not seem right, the color separator can make adjustments and change color hues.

Printing

The printing process involves transferring all typed images and art onto large sheets of paper, which can then be folded and bound into a finished book. In the past, printing was done by hand on manually operated printing presses. Today, modern machines do the work.

When the printer receives the film prepared by the compositor, the film is exposed to flexible metal sheets. This process is similar to the way a photograph is developed from a negative. The images on the film are transferred to the metal sheets, which are then treated with chemicals. When these sheets are placed on cylinders in the printing press and passed by ink, the images are transferred to the sheets of paper that become the pages of the finished book.

The pages of a book come off the printing press on large sheets of paper. From 4 to 64 pages may be printed on each side of these sheets, but the usual number is 16 or 32. The pages do not follow each other in order. In-stead, they are arranged so that they will fall into the proper sequence when the sheets are folded. This arrangement is called an **imposition**. When all the pages have been printed, the book is ready for the next stage of the production process.

Binding

Binding is the final stage of the production process. After printing is finished, the printed sheets are sent to a bindery where they are folded, arranged in the correct sequence, and put within the book's cover.

At the bindery, the large printed sheets are put into a folding machine to be folded, gathered, and trimmed by special knives. Each folded section is called a **signature** and is usually made up of groups of 16 or 32 pages. Putting the signatures together in the proper sequence is called **gathering**.

Next, the signatures are sewn together by a large sewing machine. There are three methods of sewing a book. In **saddle sewing**, the book is stitched only through the center from back to front. With this method, books will open flat, but they are not very strong. In **Smyth sewing**, each signature is first individually sewn through its fold. Then the signatures are placed next to each other and sewn together across the back. Smyth-sewn books

Left: **Two press operators check the color printing press.**
Below: **The signatures—folded groups of 16 or 32 pages —are sewn or glued together before they are bound into a book.**

open flat, and they are much stronger than saddle-sewn books. In **side sewing**, stitching runs through all the signatures from the side. Side-sewn books cannot open flat, but they are the strongest type of books.

Some books, such as paperbacks, are not sewn. Instead, a method called **perfect binding** is used. In this method, the folded rear edge of each signature is trimmed and the pages are glued directly to the cover. Perfect binding is not always durable.

After sewing comes smashing and gluing. In **smashing**, a powerful compressor squeezes all the signatures so that the sewing does not cause a bulge along the rear edge of the book. Smashing is usually followed by gluing, in which a mechanical roller and brush force glue between the rear edges of the signatures. This increases the book's strength.

After smashing and gluing, the pages of the book are trimmed and cut again in preparation for attaching the cover. The covers for most books are made of special cloth that can withstand wear and tear and be cleaned easily. This cloth is attached to heavy cardboardlike material called **binder's board**, which acts as a backing to stiffen the cover. After the covers are attached and the book's dust jacket is put on, it is ready to be shipped to the publisher's warehouse.

▶**MARKETING AND SELLING**

After a long complicated process, your book, *It Rained Every Day*, has finally been published. Congratulations! Soon you will receive your first copy, hot off the press.

Long before you see this first copy, however, your publisher will have begun planning how to market and sell your book. It was listed in the publisher's catalog with a photograph of the book jacket and a summary of the story. Advance news about the book was sent to book reviewers and booksellers, and plans were made to exhibit the book, along with other new books, at special conventions and traveling exhibits throughout the country.

When the first copies of *It Rained Every Day* are available, some are sent to book reviewers. Book reviews in newspapers, magazines, or on radio and television are free advertising and can be very important in generating interest in the book. Copies may also be sent to groups, such as library associations, that include booklists in their publications.

Most bookstores have a department where you can find many kinds of books for young readers, including picture books, storybooks, books on special topics such as history, science, or sports, and dictionaries and encyclopedias.

Publishers employ other techniques to market books as well. These may include paid advertisements in magazines and newspapers, posters that are displayed in bookstores or other places where books are sold, special bookmarks, and public appearances by the author (if he or she is well known).

Marketing promotes your book and creates interest in it. Selling the book is what earns money for you and the publisher. Several months before your book was published, it was presented at one of the publisher's sales conferences. At this conference your editor enthusiastically described your book to sales representatives, whose job it is to sell it to bookstores and other booksellers. Once in the hands of booksellers, the long process of publishing *It Rained Every Day* is finally over.

OLGA LITOWINSKY
Executive Editor, Books for Young Readers
Simon & Schuster

See also CALDECOTT AND NEWBERY MEDALS; CHILDREN'S LITERATURE; PRINTING; PROOFREADING; PUBLISHING.

BOONE, DANIEL (1734–1820)

Daniel Boone has become a legend as one of America's greatest pioneers and frontier heroes. He was a dead shot with a rifle and a skillful hunter who could glide through forests as swiftly and silently as an Indian.

Daniel was born on November 2, 1734, at Oley, a frontier settlement in Pennsylvania. By the age of 12, he was hunting game for the dinner table with his first rifle. Indians roamed the nearby woods. Daniel knew that if he were caught by Indians on the warpath against intruders on their land, he would either be tomahawked or taken prisoner. So he learned how to walk through the forest without making a sound.

In 1751 the Boones settled in North Carolina. In 1755, during the French and Indian War, Daniel joined British General Edward Braddock's expedition against the French. The British, who were unused to Indian ways of fighting, were ambushed and slaughtered, but Daniel and a hunter named John Finley (or Findley) escaped into the woods. Finley told Daniel about a mysterious land, west of the Appalachian Mountains, that the Indians called Kentucky. He said its forests were thick with turkeys, bears, and deer, and buffalo thundered across its prairies. These stories inspired Daniel to go to Kentucky.

First Daniel returned to North Carolina to marry 17-year-old Rebecca Bryan, whose family lived near the Boones. For the next ten years they rarely lived very long in one place.

Daniel often was away hunting deerskins and beaver pelts, which he sold to support his growing family.

Finally, in 1769, Daniel set out across the Appalachian Mountains, and for the next two years he explored Kentucky. Then he went back to North Carolina to gather several families who would return with him to establish a settlement. On the journey back to Kentucky, the pioneers were attacked by Indians, and Daniel's son James and several others were killed. The settlers turned back.

In 1775, still determined, Daniel cleared the Wilderness Road, through the Cumberland Gap, into Kentucky and built a fort called Boonesborough on the Kentucky River. Then he returned home to lead another group of pioneers across the mountains to settle there. Daniel's wife and daughter were among the first women settlers in Kentucky.

In 1778, Daniel was captured by Shawnee Indians. Their chief, Blackfish, was so proud to have caught the famous frontiersman, he "adopted" Daniel as his son and named him *Shel-tow-ee*, meaning "Big Turtle." For several months, Daniel lived among the Indians. One day he overheard the Indians plan a raid on Boonesborough, but he was able to negotiate a plan with the Shawnee to surrender his men as prisoners. His quick thinking saved the lives of countless numbers of other settlers. Later, when Daniel discovered the Indians were planning yet another attack on Boonesborough, he made a daring escape and reached the fort in time to warn the settlers.

Daniel later held several public offices, including lieutenant colonel of the militia and representative of the Kentucky state legislature. However, he lost all claim to the land he had been the first white man to explore and settle, because he had not followed the proper procedures to obtain legal title to it.

In 1799, feeling Kentucky had become too crowded with people, he moved westward to Missouri to find, as he put it, "more elbow room." He died in Missouri on September 26, 1820, at the age of 86.

Reviewed by DANIEL ROSELLE
State University College (Fredonia, New York)

BOOTH, JOHN WILKES (1838–1865)

John Wilkes Booth, the infamous assassin of President Abraham Lincoln, came from one of America's most famous theatrical families. His father, Junius, and his brother, Edwin, both were actors of considerable reputation, and John followed in their footsteps.

Booth was born in 1838 near Bel Air, Maryland, on a farm worked by slaves. As a young man during the Civil War, he strongly sympathized with the Confederate cause. In 1864, as the war turned ever more in favor of the Union, Booth and several other conspirators hatched a plan to kidnap Lincoln and strike a blow against Union morale. They also hoped to exchange the president for Confederate prisoners of war. However, nothing came of their immediate plans. After Confederate General Robert E. Lee's surrender at Appomattox on April 9, 1865, Booth and his followers' kidnapping plot turned toward murder. In addition to Lincoln, their targets included Vice President Andrew Johnson and Secretary of State William H. Seward.

On the evening of April 14, Lincoln, his wife, and two young friends attended the play *Our American Cousin* at Ford's Theatre in Washington, D.C. Booth entered their private box with a small pistol and shot the president in the back of the head at point-blank range. Witnesses reported that Booth then jumped down to the stage, shouting, "*Sic semper tyrannis!*" (Thus always to tyrants), Virginia's state motto. Lincoln never regained consciousness and died the next morning in a rooming house across the street from the theater. As the president drew his last breath, his Secretary of War Edwin Stanton uttered, "Now he belongs to the ages."

In his leap to the stage, Booth had broken his left leg above the ankle, but he managed to escape with one other conspirator. Union soldiers caught up with him several days later and cornered him in a barn near Port Royal, Virginia. Refusing to surrender, Booth was shot to death. His last reported words were, "Tell mother I died for my country."

For the president's murder, eight conspirators were quickly brought to trial and sentenced. Four were hanged: George Atzerodt, Davy Herold, Lewis Paine, and Mary Surratt (who owned the boardinghouse in which the conspiracy reportedly took place).

After shooting President Abraham Lincoln, John Wilkes Booth leapt to the stage of Ford's Theatre and escaped. Lincoln died the following morning.

The other four were sentenced to life imprisonment, including Dr. Samuel Mudd, who had set Booth's fractured leg after his escape from Ford's Theatre.

Many conspiracy theories regarding Lincoln's assassination arose after his death. One story, for example, implicated Secretary of War Stanton as a co-conspirator; others claimed repeated "sightings" of Booth as late as the 1890's. Such stories take advantage of the fact that, unlike in detective mysteries, many questions regarding historical events can never be answered with certainty.

It is possible that the Confederate government was involved in the assassination plot, but Lincoln's murder was more likely the work of a small group of conspirators living in a society deeply disturbed and divided by war. In Lincoln's last speech, he made reference to extending to blacks the right to vote. For John Wilkes Booth, it appears that this was a consequence he could not endure.

GABOR S. BORITT
Director, Civil War Institute,
Gettysburg College

BORAH, WILLIAM EDGAR. See IDAHO (Famous People).

BORDEN, SIR ROBERT LAIRD. See CANADA, GOVERNMENT OF (Profiles).

BORGIA FAMILY. See RENAISSANCE (Profiles).

BORGLUM, GUTZON. See IDAHO (Famous People).

BORLAUG, NORMAN. See IOWA (Famous People).

BORMAN, FRANK. See SPACE EXPLORATION AND TRAVEL (Profiles).

BORNEO

Borneo is the world's third largest island. Only Greenland and New Guinea are larger. With an area of about 287,000 square miles (743,000 square kilometers), Borneo is larger than many nations of the world.

Borneo straddles the equator at the western end of the Pacific Ocean. To the north, across the South China Sea, is the mainland of Asia.

Politically, Borneo is divided among three separate nations—Indonesia, Malaysia, and Brunei. Kalimantan, the largest region of Borneo, belongs to Indonesia. Sabah and Sarawak belong to Malaysia and together are known as East Malaysia. Brunei, a tiny, oil-rich nation, is situated on the northwestern coast of the island.

▶ PEOPLE

Borneo has a population of more than 14 million. The great majority are Dayaks, a native people who belong to a number of different tribes. Malays and Chinese make up the next largest ethnic groups. Many people from the crowded nearby island of Java, encour-

aged by the Indonesian government, have resettled on Borneo in Kalimantan.

Language. Major languages spoken in Borneo include Bahasa Indonesia and Bahasa Malaysia (the official languages of Indonesia and Malaysia). Various Dayak dialects, English, and Chinese are also spoken.

Religion. Many Dayaks practice traditional native religions. Most of the other people of Borneo are Muslims.

Rural Life. The Dayaks, who form the majority of residents in the interior, tend to follow older, more traditional ways of life. The people hunt, fish, and plant crops on small plots cleared from the forest.

▶ LAND

Land Regions. Borneo consists of a flat, swampy coastal lowland and a mountainous interior, with dense tropical rain forests and many rivers. Mount Kinabalu, the island's highest peak, rises 13,455 feet (4,101 meters) above sea level. The Kapuas mountain chain, which runs generally east and west, forms the backbone of the island. The Schwaner Mountains run in a northeast and southwest direction.

Rivers and Coastal Waters. The island of Borneo is located in the western Pacific Ocean. The South China and Sulu seas lie to the north, the Celebes Sea to the east, and the Java Sea to the south. The Karimata Strait separates Borneo from the island of Sumatra in the west.

Borneo's many rivers include the Baram, Kayan, Mahakam, Barito, Kahayan, Kapuas, and Rajang. Since travel is often difficult in the rugged interior, the rivers provide an important means of transportation.

Climate. Borneo has a tropical climate, with generally high temperatures and humidity and considerable rainfall. The temperature seldom falls below 70°F (21°C), except in the cooler highland areas, and often reaches a high of 96°F (36°C). Depending on elevation and exposure to rain-bearing monsoon winds, Borneo receives from 100 to 200 inches (2,500 to 5,000 millimeters) of rainfall a year.

Wildlife. Borneo is famous for its wildlife. Hundreds of species of birds add brilliant color to the forest. Reptiles include several varieties of poisonous snakes; crocodiles live in the rivers. The larger forest animals include two-horned rhinoceroses, honey bears, wild

Borneo

Many houses along the coast of the island of Borneo are built on stilts because the land is low and easily flooded.

pigs, wild oxen, deer, elephants, monkeys, and gibbons. One of the shiest creatures is the orangutan, a large ape whose name means "man of the forest" in Malay.

Natural Resources. Forests cover most of the island. The trees, which may grow to a height of 120 feet (37 meters), grow so thickly that little sunlight can penetrate their cover. Timber is one of Borneo's most valuable natural resources. Teak and other valuable hardwoods grow in the interior.

Petroleum and natural gas are Borneo's most important minerals. Brunei is the single most important petroleum-producing area on the island. Coal, bauxite, iron, gold, and other minerals are also mined.

▶ ECONOMY

Agriculture and Forestry. The majority of Borneo's people earn their living from agriculture. Rice is the most important food crop; other crops include corn, sweet potatoes, yams, cassava (manioc), and beans. Clearing land for cultivation frequently is carried out by the slash-and-burn method, in which vegetation is first cut and then burned away. In 1997–98, many such fires raged out of control when the normal monsoon rains did not arrive, destroying thousands of acres of forest and blanketing Borneo with dense smoke.

Borneo's chief commercial agricultural product is rubber. Copra (dried coconut), tobacco, pepper, and hemp (for making rope) also are produced in large quantities.

Manufacturing and Mining. Borneo has limited industry. Most of it involves the drilling for and refining of petroleum and the processing of agricultural products and timber.

▶ MAJOR CITIES

Almost all of Borneo's cities and towns are located in the coastal areas. Banjarmasin in Kalimantan is Borneo's largest city. Other large cities, also in Kalimantan, are Pontianak, Balikpapan, and Samarinda. Kuching is the capital of Sarawak, and Kota Kinabalu the capital of Sabah. Brunei's capital city is Bandar Seri Begawan.

▶ HISTORY

Borneo has a long history. Traders from India arrived in Borneo at least 2,000 years ago. Chinese settled on the island in succeeding centuries. There were also early contacts between Borneo and what are now the Indonesian islands of Java and Sumatra.

Europeans first arrived in the region in the 1500's. The Dutch became the most successful colonizers, gaining control of what is now Kalimantan by the early 1800's. By the mid-1800's the British were dominant in the northwestern quarter of the island, in what are now Sabah, Sarawak, and Brunei.

During World War II (1939–45), Japanese troops occupied most of the coastal areas of Borneo. When Indonesia gained its independence from the Netherlands in 1949, it acquired Dutch-controlled Borneo. Sabah and Sarawak became part of Malaysia in 1963. Brunei remained a British protectorate until 1984, when it won complete independence.

PHILLIP BACON
University of Houston
Author, *Golden Book Picture Atlas of the World*

See also BRUNEI; INDONESIA; MALAYSIA.

BOSNIA AND HERZEGOVINA

Bosnia and Herzegovina
18° E
46° N
N
CROATIA
Danube River
Sava River
Una R.
Bosanska Gradiška
Derventa
Prijedor
KOZARA MTS.
Brčko
Bihać
Sanski Most
Banja Luka
Doboj
MAJEVICA MTS.
Bijeljina
Kljuć
Tuzla
Jajce
VLAŠIĆ MTS.
Drvar
Travnik
Zenica
Vareš
CROATIA
44° N
DINARIC ALPS
Bugojno
Srebrenica
44° N
MONTENEGRO
Sarajevo
Pale
Konjic
Goražde
Jablanica
0 20 40 mi
0 20 40 km
Mostar
16° E
Maglic
SERBIA AND
BJELAŠNICA MTS.
EUROPE
Trebinje
Adriatic Sea
ASIA
ALBANIA
42° N
42° N
AFRICA
18° E

Bosnia and Herzegovina (or Hercegovina) is a nation in the Balkans region of southeastern Europe. Once a republic of the former nation of Yugoslavia, the country declared its independence in 1992.

People. The country has a population of about 4 million. Sarajevo, the capital and largest city, has a metropolitan population of about 500,000.

The people are sharply divided into three ethnic communities—the Bosniaks (who are mostly Muslim in religion), the Serbs (mostly Serbian Orthodox), and the Croats (mostly Roman Catholics). The nation's official language is Serbo-Croatian.

Land. Bosnia takes its name from the Bosna River and Herzegovina from *Herzog*, the German word for "duke." The land is largely mountainous. About half is forested and one-quarter is suitable for farming. Most of the rest is used as pasture for livestock.

Economy. The country's economy is based chiefly on agriculture. Wheat and other grains are major food crops. A variety of fruits and vegetables are also grown. The forests provide timber and other wood products.

History and Government. An independent Bosnia emerged in the 1300's, but it later fell to the Ottoman Turks and then Austria-Hungary. After World War I (1914–18), Bosnia and Herzegovina became part of a newly created Yugoslav kingdom. And after World War II (1939–45), Yugoslavia fell to the Communists.

In 1991, Yugoslavia began to break apart with the collapse of Communism in Eastern Europe, and Bosnia and Herzegovina proclaimed its independence in 1992. Bosnian Serbs, supported by Yugoslav forces, then expelled large numbers of Muslims and gained control of much of the republic. But in 1995 the intervention of NATO forces led to a peace accord, signed in Dayton, Ohio. A new constitution divided the country into two parts: one Muslim-Croat and the other Serb. Three presidents—one Bosniak, one Croat, and one Serb—are elected by popular vote to 4-year terms and rotate the chairmanship every eight months. All groups are proportionately represented in the legislature.

Reviewed by Janusz Bugajski
Center for Strategic and International Studies

FACTS and figures

BOSNIA AND HERZEGOVINA is the official name of the country.

LOCATION: Southeastern Europe.

AREA: 19,741 sq mi (51,129 km²).

POPULATION: 4,000,000 (estimate).

CAPITAL AND LARGEST CITY: Sarajevo.

MAJOR LANGUAGE: Serbo-Croatian.

MAJOR RELIGIOUS GROUPS: Muslim, Serbian Orthodox, Roman Catholic.

GOVERNMENT: Federal republic. **Head of state**—chairman of the presidency. **Head of government**—chairman of the council of ministers. **Legislature**—Parliamentary Assembly, made up of the National House of Representatives and the House of Peoples.

CHIEF PRODUCTS: **Agricultural**—wheat, corn, fruits, vegetables, livestock. **Manufactured**—steel, vehicles, textiles, tobacco products, wood furniture. **Mineral**—coal, iron ore, lead, zinc, bauxite (aluminum ore).

MONETARY UNIT: Marka (1 marka = 100 fening).

BOSTON

Boston is the capital of the Commonwealth of Massachusetts. The city is located in the northeastern United States on a peninsula, where the Charles River flows into a large, well-protected bay of the Atlantic Ocean, forming one of the world's finest natural harbors. Founded in 1630, Boston is at once an old city and a new one. Because many of the major events of the American Revolutionary War took place in or near Boston, it has come to be known as the "Cradle of Liberty."

With a population of about 589,000, Boston is the most populous city in New England. The city encompasses 51 square miles (132 square kilometers), which is far greater than its original colonial size. Its growth was due in part to a clever landfill project that was undertaken in the late 1800's. The project took soil from Boston's hills to create the Back Bay section and the waterfront area along the Charles River basin. Boston's growth also resulted from the annexation of several bordering towns. The modern city of Boston is made up of many neighborhoods, including Charlestown,

Dorchester, Roxbury, Back Bay, Beacon Hill, the North End, Allston-Brighton, the Fenway, Jamaica Plain, Roslindale, West Roxbury, Mattapan, and Hyde Park.

Boston's average temperatures range from 31°F (–1°C) in the winter to 71°F (22°C) in the summer. The average yearly precipitation is 43 inches (1,090 millimeters).

Business and Industry

Boston was one of the first industrial cities in the United States. Today the city's economy is based largely on service industries. The five most important are financial services (banking, insurance, and real estate), health care, high technology, education and consulting, and tourism. Together they provide more than half of all employment in the region.

Transportation

Boston's public transportation system, the oldest in the United States, provides a criss-cross of subway lines, trolleys, buses, and trains, which makes it easy for residents of outlying neighborhoods to travel into the center of the city.

Boston is the major seaport and air terminus for Massachusetts and New England. The port of Boston has 25 miles (40 kilometers) of docking space. Boston's Logan International Airport provides passenger and freight services.

Urban Renewal

In the 1960's an extensive project was undertaken to bring new life to the decaying

Skyscrapers and historic landmarks grace the modern Boston skyline. Situated on the Charles River, the city was founded by English Puritans in 1630.

Colorful Quincy Market is a lively place where residents and tourists alike go to shop, dine, and be entertained. Both the market and Faneuil Hall (rear) were successfully restored in the late 1970's.

this day maintains a national reputation for academic excellence. In 1636, across the Charles River in neighboring Cambridge, Harvard University opened its doors.

Today, there arc more than 65 colleges and universities serving 250,000 students in the Greater Boston Area. Among these are Harvard University, Radcliffe College, the Massachusetts Institute of Technology (MIT), Boston University, Boston College, Northeastern University, Brandeis University, Emerson College, Tufts University, and the University of Massachusetts.

Libraries. Many world-class libraries are located in Boston. Among them are the Athenaeum, which owns George Washington's book collection; the Boston Public Library, considered one of the finest in the United States; and the library at Harvard, the world's largest university library, with more than 9 million volumes.

Museums. Famous Boston museums include the Museum of Fine Arts, the Children's Museum, the Museum of Science, the Computer Museum, the John F. Kennedy Presidential Library and Museum, and the Isabella Stewart Gardner Museum.

Music and Dance. The Boston Pops Orchestra and the Boston Symphony Orchestra delight audiences at Symphony Hall. The Boston Opera and the Boston Ballet have earned worldwide recognition and perform regularly to full houses.

downtown area. Today, Boston's skyline includes many new skyscrapers and prominent landmarks, such as the Prudential Center, the Government Center, and the John Hancock Mutual Life Insurance Company tower.

Education, Culture, and Recreation

For its size, Boston has an unusually large number of educational, cultural, and recreational facilities. It is a major center for the publication of books, textbooks, and magazines. The city's major newspapers are the *Boston Globe*, the *Boston Herald*, and the *Christian Science Monitor*, which is distributed internationally.

Schools. In 1635, Puritan settlers established the Boston Latin Academy, the first free public school in the United States, which to

---

BOSTON "FIRSTS"

A partial list of many "firsts" that occurred in Boston illustrates the city's importance in American tradition, culture, and technological development.

1639	First post office.
1653	First public library.
1686	First schoolbook printed.
1704	First American newspaper published, the *Boston News-Letter*.
1776	First proclamation of the Declaration of Independence, Old State House, July 18.
1845	First sewing machine.
1846	First anesthesia demonstration.
1857	First American literary magazine published, the *Atlantic Monthly*.
1873	First university to open all departments to women (Boston University).
1874	First words spoken by telephone.
1897	First subway for trolley car operation.
1900	First Davis Cup tennis match.
1903	First modern World Series, won by the Boston Red Sox over the Pittsburgh Pirates.
1929	First computer, developed at MIT.
1944	First automatic digital computer, patented at Harvard.

Parks. Boston Common (the oldest public park in the United States), the Public Garden, the Arnold Arboretum, the Charles River, and Boston Harbor provide beautiful settings within the city for outdoor activities, such as bicycling, jogging, picnicking, and sailing.

Sports. Fenway Park is the home of Boston's professional baseball team, the Boston Red Sox. The city also supports professional teams in basketball (the Boston Celtics), football (the New England Patriots), and ice hockey (the Boston Bruins). Perhaps the one sporting event most identified with the city is the Boston Marathon. Held on Patriot's Day (the third Monday in April), it is the oldest sporting event in the United States and attracts more than 6,000 competitors every year.

▶ **HISTORY**

Ten years after the Pilgrims arrived at Plymouth on the *Mayflower*, English Puritans followed them to New England in search of religious freedom. In 1630, under the leadership of John Winthrop, the first governor of the Massachusetts Bay Colony, the Puritans founded Charlestown and later Boston on the other side of the Charles River.

Although the Indians who inhabited the area called it "Shawmut," the Puritans first re-named it "Trimountaine" for the three hills that dominated the landscape. (To this day, the official symbol of the city includes the "trimount.") The name Boston was later adopted because many of the Puritans had come from a town by that name in England. In 1632, Boston became the capital of the Massachusetts Bay Colony.

For two hundred years after the Puritans arrived, Boston remained populated almost exclusively by their descendants. However, beginning in the 1840's, great waves of European immigrants voyaged to the United States in search of a better life. Many of those who settled in Boston came from Ireland to escape the great famine caused by a four-year blight to their potato crops. Today the Irish form the largest ethnic group in Boston, followed by the Italians. Blacks account for about 22 percent of Boston's population.

Throughout the 1800's, Boston witnessed many religious, literary, philosophical, and social changes. The Christian Science religion was established at The Mother Church, and King's Chapel was the birthplace of American Unitarianism. William Lloyd Garrison made his first antislavery speech in 1829 at the Park Street Church. The Old Corner Bookstore became a favorite meeting place for distin-

Every year millions of people take a walk along the famous "Freedom Trail" to visit Boston's most important historic landmarks, many of which date from colonial days.

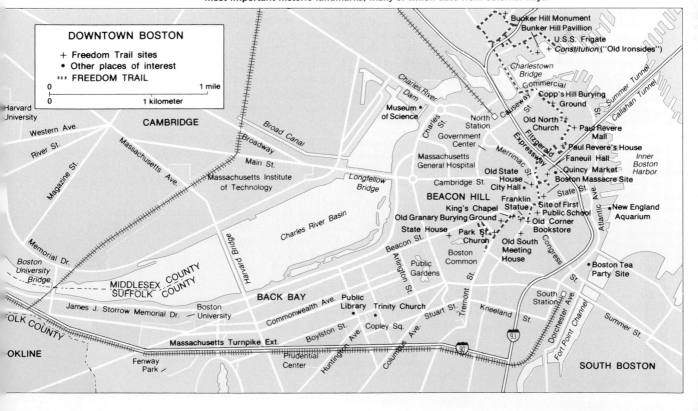

guished writers, such as Henry Wadsworth Longfellow, Ralph Waldo Emerson, and Henry David Thoreau.

Places of Interest

Each year more than 2 million visitors—as well as countless area residents—take a 2-mile (3.2-kilometer) walk along a well-marked path called the "Freedom Trail" to visit the Boston of old. Colonial Boston seems to come alive when one visits the sites of many of the events that led up to the American Revolutionary War (1775–83). Of special interest are the site of the Boston Massacre (1770), where British troops fired at a crowd of American colonists, killing five; the Old South Meetinghouse, where in 1773 the "Sons of Liberty" planned the infamous Boston Tea Party; and Christ ("Old North") Church, where in 1775 Robert Newman hung the "two if by sea" lanterns that sent Paul Revere and William Dawes on their famous midnight rides to warn the Minutemen.

Other sites along the Freedom Trail include Paul Revere's house, the site of Benjamin Franklin's birth, the Old State House, and Fan-

euil Hall. Since 1742, Faneuil Hall has been used as an all-purpose marketplace (first floor) and meeting hall (second floor). In front of Faneuil Hall is Quincy Market. Today, more than 14 million residents and tourists every year come to visit its 175 shops, restaurants, food markets, and art galleries.

Boston also has a "Black Heritage Trail," a walking tour that explores the history of Boston's black community. The trail begins at the Museum of Afro-American History and includes visits to the African Meeting House (the oldest church established by blacks in the United States) and the Robert Gould Shaw and 54th Regiment Memorial, a monument to one of the black regiments that fought for the North during the Civil War.

Boston's rich historic and cultural heritage makes it an exciting city for its residents as well as its 10 million annual visitors. The unusual variety of attractions makes Boston deserving of another of its popular nicknames—the "Hub of the Universe."

ANNE N. BONNER
Director of Communications and Public Relations
Greater Boston Chamber of Commerce

BOSTON MASSACRE.   See REVOLUTIONARY WAR.
BOSTON TEA PARTY.   See REVOLUTIONARY WAR.

BOTANICAL GARDENS

Botanical gardens are museums that maintain collections of living plants for scientific and educational purposes and for public display. **Botanists** (scientists who study plants) carry out research in the laboratories and test plots of botanical gardens to learn more about how plants grow, how new plants can be developed, and how plants can be useful to people as a source of food and other products.

Sharing knowledge of plants with the public is an important function of botanical gardens. Visitors will find all the plants labeled with their scientific and common names. Botanical gardens may have libraries and information services and may publish books and pamphlets on botanical subjects. School classes might visit local botanical gardens for guided tours or workshops. Sometimes students actually tend small garden plots there to learn about plants.

Most large botanical gardens include greenhouses or conservatories—glass buildings

where temperature, humidity, and light can be controlled. These artificial environments can copy natural ones, making it possible to grow plants from many different regions and climates of the world. In one room a tropical rain forest might be created; in another, desert plants can grow in a sunny, dry climate; and yet another room can display the conditions found in a marshy bog.

Some botanical gardens have theme gardens, such as a butterfly garden with flowers that attract those insects. A Japanese garden would have the plants arranged in typical Japanese fashion. A Shakespeare garden would have plants mentioned in Shakespeare's plays or sonnets. Frequently there is an herb garden and often an herbarium—a place where dried plants and parts of plants are preserved and cataloged for study.

One of the most interesting of all botanical gardens is in Uppsala, Sweden, home of Carolus Linnaeus. This great botanist of the

1700's devised a system of classifying and naming plants and animals. He managed the Uppsala Gardens from 1742 to 1777. Today the gardens have been restored to match Linnaeus' original design. A biography of Linnaeus is included in Volume L.

One of the greatest botanical gardens in the world today is the Royal Botanic Gardens at Kew, near London, England. The facility is sometimes known as Kew Gardens. In the 1800's it introduced plants brought back from the voyages of Captain Cook, including coffee, cotton, and cinnamon trees.

One of the best-known botanical gardens in the United States is the New York Botanical Garden in the Bronx, New York, which has more than 13,000 species of plants. The Missouri Botanical Garden in St. Louis is the oldest in the United States.

Canada has a number of well-known botanical gardens, among them the Montreal Botanical Garden in Quebec and the Royal Botanical Gardens in Ontario.

LUCY E. JONES
Director of Education
Brooklyn Botanic Garden

Carefully arranged and labeled gardens offer an opportunity to study as well as enjoy plants in a natural setting. The Royal Botanical Gardens in Hamilton, Ontario, is known for its late-blooming tulip collection.

BOTANY

Have you ever wondered what is inside a flower? Or what the veins in a leaf are for? If you have, you have asked the same sorts of questions as those asked by a botanist. A botanist is a scientist whose field is botany—the study of plants.

Plants form the basis of all life on earth. Only plants can capture the energy of the sun and use it—in a process called photosynthesis—to make food. Animals cannot do this and so must depend on plants for food. We also depend on plants for the oxygen they give off during photosynthesis.

This essential world of plants is a large and varied one. There are about 300,000 different kinds of plants that have been identified. They range in size from tiny mosses as small as ⅜ inch (1 centimeter) to the giant redwoods, the largest living things on earth. Some plants, such as carrots, are rooted in soil. Others—orchids, for example—grow in air. Some plants reproduce from seeds, others from underground stems.

Botany includes every aspect of plant life. A botanist may study the plant itself—its structure and the function of its various parts. Other botanists may study the development of plants on earth—when they first appeared, how they changed over long periods of time, and how they are related to one another.

Some botanists study plants in relation to their environment. They may, for example, try to determine how soil and water affect the growth and reproduction of plants.

A botanist may specialize in one area of botany, but whatever his or her specialty, the work can benefit people. Thus, botanists may discover plants that yield important new medicines, or they may help to improve crops by developing better varieties of plants.

Reviewed by NANCY R. MORIN
Missouri Botanical Garden

See also ALGAE; BACTERIA; CACTUS; CELLS; FERNS; FLOWERS; FUNGI; GENETICS; GRASSES; KINGDOMS OF LIVING THINGS; LEAVES; LIFE; MOSSES; PHOTOSYNTHESIS; PLANT PESTS; PLANTS; REPRODUCTION; TREES; WEEDS.

BOTSWANA

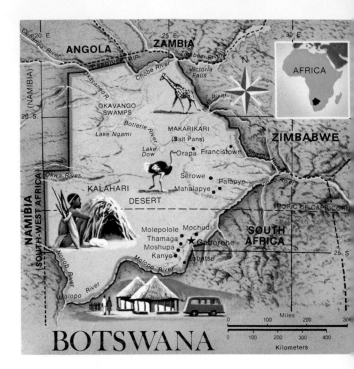

BOTSWANA

Botswana is an arid, landlocked country in southern Africa. Formerly known as Bechuanaland, it was a British dependency before gaining independence in 1966. Much of Botswana's land is desert or grassland suitable only for grazing cattle.

▶ PEOPLE

Most of the people are Tswana, who belong to the large Bantu family. The Tswana are cattle herders and farmers. A number of San, a distinct people of southern Africa, inhabit the Kalahari Desert, where they live primarily as hunters and food gatherers. Many of the people practice traditional African religions. Others are Christian. The most widely spoken languages are Setswana, a Bantu language, and English, which is the official language. Botswana has few cities. The largest city is Gaborone, the capital. Most of the people live in villages, some of great size.

▶ LAND AND ECONOMY

Most of Botswana is a vast plateau. In the northwest the Okavango River overflows to create an area of large swamps. Southern Botswana forms part of the great Kalahari Desert.

FACTS and figures

REPUBLIC OF BOTSWANA is the official name of the country.

LOCATION: Southern Africa.

AREA: 231,804 sq mi (600,372 km²).

POPULATION: 1,500,000 (estimate).

CAPITAL AND LARGEST CITY: Gaborone.

MAJOR LANGUAGES: English (official), Setswana.

MAJOR RELIGIOUS GROUPS: Traditional African religions, various independent Christian churches.

GOVERNMENT: Republic. **Head of state and government**—president. **Legislature**—National Assembly.

CHIEF PRODUCTS: Agricultural—cattle, sorghum, millet, corn. **Mineral**—diamonds, copper, nickel.

MONETARY UNIT: Pula (1 pula = 100 thebe).

The north and east receive most of the slight rainfall and generally have the only land suitable for cultivation. Most of the population is concentrated in the east.

Botswana's economy is based on cattle raising and mining. Meat and hides, diamonds, copper, and nickel are the chief exports. Farming is limited to a few food crops.

▶ HISTORY AND GOVERNMENT

Europeans knew little about what is now Botswana before the early 1800's, when British missionaries arrived there. For many years the region was torn by tribal warfare and by clashes between the Tswana and the Boers of South Africa. In 1885 the native chiefs asked Great Britain for protection against the Boers, and the territory—then called Bechuanaland—became a British protectorate. Botswana gained its independence in 1966.

The government consists of a president and a legislature called the National Assembly. There is also an advisory body, the House of Chiefs. Elections are held every five years.

Since independence, Botswana has had continuously elected democratic governments. It has followed a moderate course in African affairs and a policy of non-alignment in its international relations.

HUGH C. BROOKS
St. John's University (New York)

BOTTICELLI, SANDRO (1444?–1510)

The poetic paintings of the Renaissance master known as Botticelli often describe the beginnings of things. With grace and delicacy Botticelli depicted not just love but the birth of the love goddess, not simply faith but the birth of Christ, not only the beauty of nature but the blooming of spring. He turned for subject matter to history and religion, to poetry and legend.

Botticelli's life is somewhat like a legend. Little about it can be proved since much of what we know has come down through the ages by word of mouth. He was born in Florence and died there when he was about 65. His real name was Alessandro Filipepi, but he took the name Botticelli from his older brother, whose nickname was *Botticello,* meaning "little barrel." By 1460 he was probably studying with the well-known artist Fra Filippo Lippi. By the time he was 25, Botticelli had already become teacher to Lippi's son and was considered one of the best painters in Florence.

Among his many admirers was Pope Sixtus IV. In 1481 the Pope invited Botticelli to Rome to help decorate the Sistine Chapel, which had recently been completed. Botticelli's contributions to the chapel include wall paintings illustrating the life of Moses.

The Medici family, rulers of Florence, were the greatest supporters of artists and scholars in all Italy. Botticelli received encouragement from them and may even have lived in the Medici palace. The scholars there were fascinated by the poetry and philosophy of ancient Greece. As his painting the *Primavera* shows us, Botticelli, too, was entranced by the creators of ancient mythology. The spiritual quality of his religious paintings can also be seen in his portrayals of the gods and heroes of ancient Greece.

In his later years Botticelli was influenced by the monk Savonarola, who preached against the vanity and extravagance of the Florentines. Botticelli became very religious and painted only religious subjects.

Botticelli's paintings are famous for their dancing lines, flowing forms, and delicate details, admirably represented in the *Primavera.* His golden-haired Venus, goddess of love, has in her eyes the faraway look of one lost in a daydream, which appears so often in Botticelli's work.

Reviewed by ARIANE RUSKIN BATTERBERRY
Author, *The Pantheon Story of Art for Young People*

Primavera ("Spring") by Sandro Botticelli, painted around 1478. This famous picture, on a huge, rectangular wooden panel, hangs in the Uffizi Gallery, Florence.

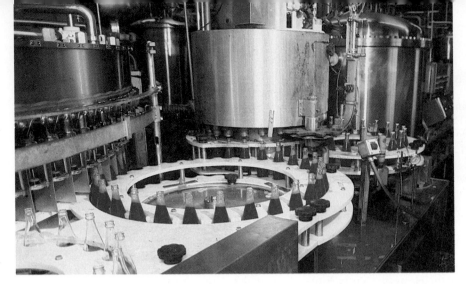

Bottling is an automated process. Conveyor belts carry bottles to washing, filling, capping, and labeling machines. Machines also pack the bottles in cartons, which are conveyed to shipping areas.

BOTTLES AND BOTTLING

Bottles are made in an endless variety of forms—tall, squat, round, and slender. They range in size from tiny perfume bottles that hold less than an ounce to large industrial bottles that hold many quarts. Some bottles are designed from a practical standpoint. They have very broad bases to keep from being toppled over or long, narrow necks to make pouring easy. Other bottles are shaped in odd and interesting ways for advertising purposes. Many bottles are so beautifully designed that they may be used solely as ornaments.

Glass bottles came into use very slowly over a span of many hundreds of years. The Egyptians learned how to make glass before 3000 B.C. Around 1500 B.C. they began to make bottles by forming molten (melted) glass around a core of sand or clay. When the object had been fashioned and decorated, the core was scraped out. Making bottles in this way was so difficult and expensive that glass bottles were a luxury item for 1,500 years. Then the Romans developed cheaper and quicker methods of production. Using blowpipes, skilled Roman workers blew the molten glass into bubbles. By blowing the bubble inside a mold, they found they could produce bottles of uniform size and shape.

After the fall of the Roman Empire in the 5th century A.D., glass bottles again became a scarce and sought-after luxury in Europe. They were collected and displayed like prize paintings.

Bottles became more of an everyday item in the 18th century, but they were still made by hand by the same methods the Romans used nearly 2,000 years before. Even with the help of molds, an experienced glassblower and a crew of assistants could only turn out about 250 bottles a day.

Some of our most familiar glass containers date from the 19th century. The first baby bottle was patented in 1841. John L. Mason put his famous mason jar on the market in 1858. Dr. Hervey D. Thatcher perfected the milk bottle in the mid-1880's.

Glass manufacturers experimented with various ways to automate the bottle-making process. In 1865 the pressing and blowing machine was invented. In this machine a plunger forces the molten glass against a mold. Then compressed air blows the glass into its final shape.

The first fully successful automatic blowing machine was invented in 1903. The Owens Bottle Machine, invented by Michael Owens, was the first real advance in the manufacture of glass containers since the invention of the blowpipe. Today, modern versions of blowing machines make a variety of products—including jelly glasses, fruit jars, and soft-drink bottles—efficiently and inexpensively.

Bottling

After bottles have been made, they must be filled and prepared for shipment to stores. This task, called bottling, involves a number of steps. These are washing, filling, capping, labeling, and packing. Today almost all the work is done by machines. Conveyor belts move the bottles from one machine to another in an orderly parade, like marching soldiers.

The bottles must first be cleaned. This is especially important with returnable glass containers that are used over and over again. Some bottles are reused as many as 30 times before they are broken or lost.

The clean bottles move along a conveyor belt to a rotary filling machine. Rotary filling machines can fill up to 2,000 containers per minute. A platform lifts each bottle up and presses it tightly against one of many filling valves. The contents pour in. The full bottle is then lowered and moved on to the capping machine. The capping machine presses a cap onto the mouth of each bottle. These may be cork- or plastic-lined caps or screw caps. One type of cap used in the soft-drink market is a closure made of aluminum and rolled onto the lip of the bottle. Other bottles have corks inserted in the neck. After capping comes labeling, if required. This is done by a labeling machine that has sets of automatic "fingers." The fingers pick up a label, put glue on it, and press it onto the correct place on the bottle.

After being washed, filled, capped, and labeled, bottles are ready to be packed for shipment to stores. Packing is done by machines that drop the bottles into cases or cartons, seal the boxes, and send them on their way to the shipping platforms.

Recycling

Glass bottles have been replaced for some uses by disposable plastic, metal, and cardboard containers. However, government legislation in many states has discouraged discarding glass, plastic, and metal beverage containers by requiring that deposit fees be paid at the time of purchase. The fees are refundable only if the container is returned.

Bottles and other glassware that are not reusable can be recycled and used to make new glass containers. The used glass is sorted by colors. It is crushed into small pieces and added to a mixture of sand, limestone, and soda ash. This mixture is melted in a furnace and formed into new bottles and other products. By recycling bottles, we conserve the energy resources used in making new bottles. We also limit the costs and other problems of disposing of discarded bottles.

Reviewed by JANET F. FLYNN
Glass Packaging Institute

BOURKE-WHITE, MARGARET. See PHOTOGRAPHY (Great Photographers).
BOUTROS-GHALI, BOUTROS. See UNITED NATIONS (Profiles).
BOW AND ARROW. See ARCHERY.
BOWELL, SIR MACKENZIE. See CANADA, GOVERNMENT OF (Profiles).

BOWIE, JAMES (1796?–1836)

James (Jim) Bowie was a fighter in Texas' struggle for independence from Mexico. Much folklore has been passed down about his adventures. It has been said that he rode alligators, speared wild cattle, and smuggled slaves for profit along the Gulf Coast with the pirate Jean Laffite.

Born about 1796, Bowie grew up in the backwoods of Louisiana. He was said to have invented the bowie knife after he cut his hand on a butcher knife while fighting Indians. He had a crosspiece placed between the handle and the blade to prevent the hand from slipping forward.

In 1828, Bowie settled in San Antonio, Texas, which then belonged to Mexico. About 1832 he joined the Texas independence movement and later became a colonel in the Texas army. In 1836 he and fewer than 200 other Texans were besieged at the Alamo by Mexican General Santa Anna and his large

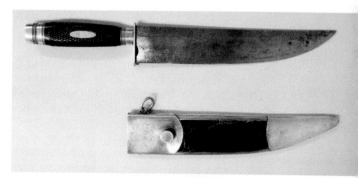

Folklore credits Jim Bowie with the invention of the bowie knife. A metal guard, or crosspiece, separates the blade and handle. Frontiersmen nicknamed this razor-sharp, all-purpose tool the "Arkansas Toothpick."

army. Although sick with pneumonia, Bowie killed several of the attackers before he was fatally wounded on March 6, 1836. All of the other defenders of the Alamo lost their lives there as well.

Reviewed by DANIEL ROSELLE
State University College (Fredonia, New York)

People of all ages enjoy the game of bowling. It has existed in some form for thousands of years and is played throughout the world.

BOWLING

The game of bowling has been played for more than 7,000 years. Objects similar to our modern tenpins were discovered in the grave of an Egyptian whose burial has been placed at 5200 B.C.

Just how the sport came to be called bowling is not known. The word "bowl" may have come from the Saxon *bolla* and the Danish *bolle*, meaning "bubble," and through usage, "round."

In its earliest form bowling was a crude recreation and was played with primitive equipment in any space that provided suitable conditions. Today we have automatic pinsetters, automatic scorers, and smooth, well-balanced balls and pins. We bowl in air-conditioned centers amid attractive surroundings. Bowling is very popular with people of all ages.

▶ EQUIPMENT FOR THE GAME

The basic idea of bowling is to roll a ball down a wooden lane and knock down the ten pins set in a triangle. The American Bowling Congress and the Women's International Bowling Congress set the following standards for the equipment used in bowling tenpins.

The length of a bowling lane is 60 feet (18 meters) from the foul line to the head pin. The width of the lane is 42 inches (107 centimeters), and the approach must be 15 feet (4.5 meters) from the rear edge to the foul line. Tenpins are 15 inches (38 centimeters) in height and must weigh not less than 3⅜ pounds (1.5 kilograms). The distance between pins set for play is 12 inches (31 centimeters) from center to center. A bowling ball cannot

weigh more than 16 pounds (7 kilograms). Its circumference must be no more than 27 inches (69 centimeters).

The correct clothing for bowling is important. Since the sport involves activity of the entire body, clothing should allow freedom of movement of arms, shoulders, and legs.

Special bowling shoes should be worn on the lanes. One of these shoes has a leather sole and one has a rubber sole. The leather sole allows you to make the necessary slide on the last step of your approach. The rubber sole is used as a brake to control the slide. The shoes can be rented for a nominal fee. The use of a bowling ball is included in the price of the game.

A three-finger ball is recommended for beginners. Grip is very important. If the distance between the holes is too wide or too narrow, it strains or cramps the hand, reducing ball control. Bowling balls come in weights of 6 to 16 pounds (3 to 7 kilograms). Use a ball weight with the right feel. Never use a ball that is too heavy, for it will tend to make you drop your shoulder and thus put you off balance before you release the ball. Start with a lightweight ball and gradually work up to the heavier weights.

▶ **PLAYING THE GAME**
The Four-Step Approach

The most popular style of bowling is called the four-step approach. Although five-step and three-step approaches are used, the four-step has proved to be the best for most bowlers.

Champions agree that every bowler eventually develops his or her own style, but for beginners the illustrated way to learn the four-step delivery is strongly recommended.

To determine where you should begin your approach, go to the foul line and place your left foot so that the toes are from 2 to 6 inches (5 to 15 centimeters) on the near side of the line. Then turn around, take one long step, one full step, one half step, and one small step. Again turn around and face the pins. This position indicates approximately where you should start your four-step delivery. If you are left-handed, start with your right foot on the near side of the line.

Timing

In bowling, timing is very important. It consists of the ability to coordinate the forward motion of your body with the pendulum swing of your arm.

Converting Spares

If you knock down all the pins on your first try, it is scored as a strike. If you knock down all 10 pins with two balls, it is scored as a spare. Spares are important in bowling, both to beginners and to expert bowlers. They can make the difference between a 190 and a 90 bowling average.

Spares fall into four categories: right-side spares; left-side

Bowling Alley

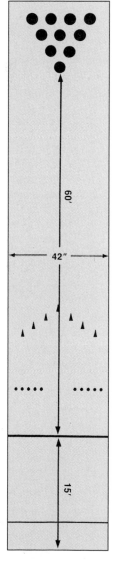

FOUR-STEP APPROACH: (A) Face pins, holding ball just above waist. (B) Step 1, right foot, is short. Push ball forward smoothly. (C) Step 2 is a half step, ball passes right leg. (D) Ball is at top of backswing on a full-size step 3. (E) On step 4, left foot glides to foul line, ball is released well beyond foul line. (F) Follow through.

spares; spares that can be converted with your strike ball; and splits, the most difficult spares. Study the illustrations that show how to convert spares—that is, to knock down all the pins that remain standing after your first bowl. In spare situations where your strike-ball delivery is required, you should take the position you normally apply to your first ball. Splits are very difficult, but with the proper determination, concentration, and confidence, you will find yourself converting more spares than you are missing.

Scoring

A game consists of ten frames. Each bowler rolls two balls per frame unless he or she strikes, which makes a second ball unnecessary. The symbols used for scoring are **X**, strike; */*, spare; *–*, possible spare not converted; **O**, split that is difficult to convert; and **Ø**, split that has been converted.

For a strike a player receives ten pins plus the total number of pins knocked down (called a **pinfall**) by his or her next two balls. A spare entitles a player to ten plus a pinfall on the next ball.

▶ BOWLING ORGANIZATIONS AND COMPETITION

Bowling is played in more than 100 countries, and more than 10,000 bowling tournaments are conducted in the United States each year. There is competition for bowlers of all ages and all degrees of ability.

The men's Professional Bowlers Association sponsors more than 35 tournaments each year. At most of these events, young amateur bowlers can compete with the pros in junior Pro-Am competitions. There is also a tournament circuit for a women's bowling association, the Professional Women's Bowling Association (PWBA).

The American Bowling Congress (ABC) is the official organization for adult male bowlers. The Women's International Bowling Congress (WIBC) is the counterpart of the ABC for adult women bowlers. The Young American Bowling Alliance regulates youth and collegiate bowling in the United States.

▶ OTHER BOWLING GAMES

Germans of the Middle Ages played a game in which balls were rolled to knock over wooden clubs, or *kegels*. The players were called *keglers*. From Germany this game spread to other parts of Europe. Varying numbers of pins were used, but the most common game in Germany and the Netherlands was (as it is today) ninepins. The pins were set up to form a diamond.

Early Dutch settlers in New York played ninepins. By about 1840, ninepin bowling had become such a popular gambling game that some states issued laws against playing it. In order to get around the laws against playing ninepins, a tenth pin was added. Tenpins is the most popular form of bowling in the United States today.

Fivepins, developed about 1909, is a favorite form of bowling in Canada. The pins are 12⅜ inches (31 centimeters) tall and are arranged in a V shape. The balls are 5 inches (13 centimeters) in diameter and weigh 3½ pounds (1.6 kilograms). A bowler rolls three balls in each of the ten frames.

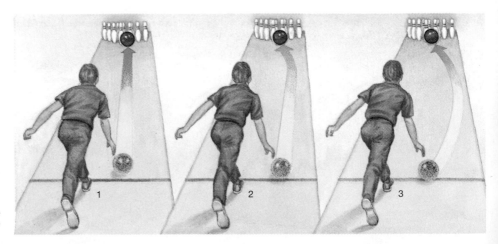

DELIVERING BALLS:
(1) Straight: Thumb on top, fingers underneath.
(2) Hook: Twist wrist left, remove thumb first, lift and spin with fingers.
(3) Curve: Same as hook, less twist of wrist.

Another bowling game, popular in New England and eastern Canada, is candlepins. It is played with long, tapering pins.

Duckpins

The game of duckpins is a variation of bowling in which smaller pins and smaller balls are used. It is popular in the eastern part of the United States.

The game is played on a regulation bowling alley, but the ball used in duckpins is no more than 5 inches (13 centimeters) in diameter and weighs 3¾ pounds (1.7 kilograms). It is completely smooth, without holes for the player's fingers. The ten bottle-shaped pins are 9¹³⁄₃₂ inches (24 centimeters) high. Some duckpins have a band of rubber around the middle.

Each player bowls three balls in a frame, rather than two. Even though there are three chances to score in each frame, the total score is usually lower than in regular bowling because the ball is so much smaller and lighter.

In duckpins you hold the ball comfortably and firmly, but not very tightly. The ball is rolled straight off the tips of the fingers, without any twisting motion. After the ball has been bowled, the back of your hand should be turned down.

Bowls, or Lawn Bowling

The game called bowls is the most popular form of bowling in Great Britain, Australia, New Zealand, and some other Commonwealth lands. In the United States and Canada it is called lawn bowling, or bowling on the green, to avoid confusion with tenpins.

Bowls is usually played on a smooth, level grass court. The object is to roll balls, which are themselves called bowls, as close as possible to the jack, a white ball 2½ inches (6 centimeters) in diameter. Bowls are made of a composition material or very hard wood and weigh not more than 3½ pounds (1.6 kilograms) each. They are about 5 inches (13 centimeters) in diameter. One side of a bowl bulges less than the other, giving it what is called **bias**. This causes the bowl to lean to one side and curve as it loses rolling speed. A player can roll his or her bowl so that it will approach the jack in a curve from either side.

In singles or doubles games, each player uses four bowls; in triples, three bowls. When

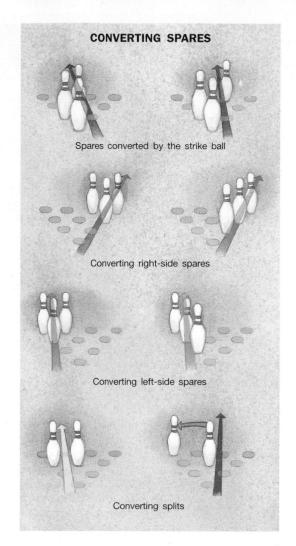

CONVERTING SPARES

Spares converted by the strike ball

Converting right-side spares

Converting left-side spares

Converting splits

full teams of four play, each person rolls two bowls.

Similar games were played with balls of stone long ago. A game called bowles was popular in England in the 1200's or earlier. The bowls were generally of wood, and by the 1500's they were made with bias. From England the game spread to Scotland and to the British colonies.

Bowls was played in Jamestown, Virginia, as early as 1611. It was also enjoyed by early New Yorkers in a small area at the lower end of Manhattan that is still called Bowling Green. Lawn bowling grew in popularity in the United States during the 1900's.

ARTHUR K. SERBO
Brunswick Division, Brunswick Corporation
Reviewed by CHUCK PEZZANO
Author, *PBA Guide to Better Bowling*

BOXING

Boxing is a sport in which two opponents fight each other with their fists. A boxer tries to score more points than his or her opponent by the use of skills in which the boxer has been trained. In amateur boxing, especially, skill is more important than strength.

Boxers wear gloves made of soft leather padded with sponge rubber. Gloves usually weigh from 8 to 10 ounces (230 to 280 grams). A boxer's hands are wrapped in soft cotton or linen for protection from the impact of his or her own blows. Amateur boxers wear headgear to protect their heads and ears from injuries. All boxers use a rubber mouthpiece that helps prevent injuries to the teeth.

The space in which a boxing match (bout) takes place is called a ring. It is generally 18 to 20 feet (5 to 6 meters) square, closed in by lengths of muslin-wrapped rope. The ropes are 2, 3, and 4 feet (0.6 meter, 0.9 meter, and 1.2 meters) above the floor of a platform on which the ring is mounted. A canvas floor covering is laid over thick padding. The cornerposts and turnbuckles that hold the ropes are also heavily padded.

The length of a round in men's amateur and professional boxing is 2 or 3 minutes. There is a 1-minute rest period between rounds. During this period the fighters go to corners of the ring opposite one another and are tended by their cornermen. Amateur matches are three, four, or six rounds. Professional championship bouts can be as many as twelve rounds. A timekeeper marks the beginning and end of each round by sounding a bell.

The referee is a very important third person in the ring during a bout, seeing that the rules are obeyed and separating the boxers if they clinch one another. Blows below the beltline, on the kidneys, or on the back of the neck (rabbit punches) are fouls. So too are pushing, head-butting, or hitting an opponent when he or she is down (on the floor; getting up; or outside, between, or hanging helpless over the ropes).

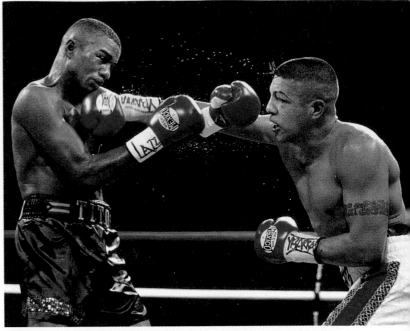

The sport of boxing, also called pugilism, has existed in various forms for thousands of years. A boxing match, or bout, tests the skill and strength of each fighter.

If a fighter is knocked down, the other fighter must go to a neutral corner—a corner of the ring not occupied by either fighter between rounds. The fighter who is down must get back up within the ring before the referee counts to 10 at 1-second intervals. If the fighter does not do this, the opponent is declared the winner by a knockout (KO). Until 1963, if a round ended before the count reached 10, the boxer who was down was said to have been "saved by the bell" because he or she could recover between rounds and continue. In 1963, though, the rules were changed. The count continues despite the bell, and the fight can end if the count is completed. In some bouts, the count may continue even after the bell has sounded, ending the final round. If a downed boxer gets up before the count of 10, both fighters are usually forced to wait for a count of 8 before action can continue.

The referee can stop a fight if it appears that a boxer is too hurt to continue. This is called a technical knockout (TKO). A physician must be on hand to determine whether an injured fighter should continue. It is also a TKO if a fighter is knocked down three times in one round. But this rule does not apply to professional championship bouts.

If there is no knockout or technical knockout in a professional bout, three judges decide the winner based on points awarded. They note the effectiveness of the fighters' punches, how well they defend themselves, and how aggressive they are. Points are deducted for repeated fouls such as low blows or holding. In case of a tie, a bout is declared a draw. In amateur boxing (under Olympic rules), five judges determine the winner by registering scoring blows on a computer.

▶ **AMATEUR AND PROFESSIONAL BOXING**

Many youth and athletic clubs provide instruction in basic boxing skills. They stress sound body condition, proper training, knowledge of the rules, and principles of fair play. They match only opponents of nearly equal size and experience.

Olympic and other international amateur boxing is governed by the International Amateur Boxing Association (IABA). In the United States, USA Boxing is the chief governing organization.

Men's professional boxing—fighting for cash prizes (purses)—is regulated mainly by the World Boxing Association (WBA), the World Boxing Council (WBC), and the International Boxing Federation (IBF). However, these organizations often disagree on which boxer is champion of his division. Professional boxing in Canada is regulated by the Canadian Boxing Federation (CBF) and by various provincial and local boards.

▶ **BOXING PAST AND PRESENT**

Boxing has a very long history. Archaeologists have found an ancient Sumerian stone carving that shows two boxers in combat. Greek and Roman athletes fought with their hands wrapped in a kind of leather covering called a cestus. A Roman boxer was called a *pugil*, from which we get the word "pugilism," another name for boxing.

Revival in England

Little more is known about fistfighting until the 1600's. Then in England the name "boxing" was given to a contest in which men boxed, or beat, one another with their bare fists. In 1719, James Figg became the first British champion. Figg opened a boxing school in London, and interest in the sport spread quickly. Men often fought for prizes, hence the term "prizefighting." Jack Broughton, a champion from 1743 to 1750, drew up the first London Prize Ring Rules.

Boxers of the bareknuckle era stood toe to toe and wrestled, shoved, or struck each other until one man was knocked down. That marked the end of a round. After a brief rest the fight began again. When one man could no longer fight, his opponent was the victor.

In 1865 the Marquis of Queensberry drew up rules that are the basis for those in use today. The rules provided for 3-minute

WEIGHT LIMITS

Weight Class	Amateur	Professional
Light Flyweight	106 lb (48 kg)	108 lb (49 kg)
Flyweight	112 lb (51 kg)	112 lb (51 kg)
Bantamweight	119 lb (54 kg)	118 lb (53 kg)
Featherweight	125 lb (57 kg)	126 lb (57 kg)
Lightweight	132 lb (60 kg)	135 lb (61 kg)
Light Welterweight	141 lb (64 kg)	140 lb (53 kg)
Welterweight	152 lb (69 kg)	147 lb (67 kg)
Middleweight	165 lb (75 kg)	160 lb (72 kg)
Light Heavyweight	178 lb (81 kg)	175 lb (79 kg)
Heavyweight	201 lb (91 kg)	Over 200 lb (90 kg)

The names assigned to some weight classes can vary depending on the sanctioning organization or on whether the bout is amateur or professional.

HEAVYWEIGHT CHAMPIONS*

1882–92	John L. Sullivan	1932–33	Jack Sharkey	1964–67	Muhammad Ali	1992–93	Riddick Bowe
1892–97	James J. Corbett	1933–34	Primo Carnera	1968–70	Disputed	1993–94	Evander Holyfield
1897–99	Robert Fitzsimmons	1934–35	Max Baer	1971–73	Joe Frazier	1994	Michael Moorer
1899–1905	James J. Jeffries	1935–37	James J. Braddock	1973–74	George Foreman	1994–95	George Foreman
1905–06	Marvin Hart	1937–49	Joe Louis	1974–78	Muhammad Ali	1996	Mike Tyson
1906–08	Tommy Burns	1949–51	Ezzard Charles	1978	Leon Spinks	1996–2000	Evander Holyfield
1908–15	Jack Johnson	1951–52	Joe Walcott	1978–79	Muhammad Ali	1999–2000	Lennox Lewis
1915–19	Jess Willard	1952–56	Rocky Marciano	1979–85	Larry Holmes	2001	Hasim Rahman
1919–26	Jack Dempsey	1956–59	Floyd Patterson	1985–86	Michael Spinks	2001–03	Lennox Lewis
1926–28	Gene Tunney	1959–60	Ingemar Johansson	1986–90	Mike Tyson	2004–05	Disputed
1928–30	None	1960–62	Floyd Patterson	1990	James Douglas		
1930–32	Max Schmeling	1962–64	Sonny Liston	1990–92	Evander Holyfield		

*Various champions have been recognized by the World Boxing Association (WBA), World Boxing Council (WBC), and International Boxing Federation (IBF). Those listed are considered to have the best claims to the title.

Championship titles in these profiles are recognized by a majority of boxing's main sanctioning organizations—the World Boxing Association (WBA), the World Boxing Council (WBC), and the International Boxing Federation (IBF)—and so indicate the most legitimate claim to the titles. When not recognized by a majority, titles are identified by the organization they are recognized by. Before the early 1960's, only the WBA named champions.

For information on the American boxer Muhammad Ali, see the article ALI, MUHAMMAD in Volume A.

Jack (William Harrison) Dempsey (1895–1983), born in Manassa, Colorado, was known as the Manassa Mauler for his brutal attacks in the ring. He learned to fight as a youth living on freight trains and in mining camps. He won the heavyweight crown in 1919 by defeating the reigning champion Jess Willard. Dempsey defended his title five times, but he finally lost it to Gene Tunney in 1926. In a famous 1927 rematch, Dempsey knocked Tunney to the canvas in the seventh round but at first refused to go to a neutral corner while the standard count of 10 was given. With the extra time it took to put Dempsey into a corner, Tunney was able to recover and

eventually win the fight. Dempsey was inducted into the International Boxing Hall of Fame in 1990.

George Foreman (1949–   ), born in Marshall, Texas, was one of the most recognizable and colorful boxers of recent times. He first achieved fame in 1968 when he won the heavyweight gold medal at the Olympic Games. He held the heavyweight championship in 1973 and 1974, and he was named *Ring Magazine*'s Fighter of the Year in 1973 and 1976. After a nine-year retirement, Foreman regained the heavyweight champi-

Jack Dempsey (left)

onship in 1994 at the age of 45—the oldest boxer to hold the title. He held the title until March 1995. Foreman was inducted into the International Boxing Hall of Fame in 2003.

Joe Frazier (1944–   ) was born in Beaufort, South Carolina. His first major victory came when he won the heavyweight gold medal at the 1964 Olympic Games. Frazier became the undisputed heavyweight champion in 1971 when he defeated Muhammad Ali in what has been called the "Fight of the Century." He lost the title to George Foreman in 1973, and his most famous comeback attempt was in "The Thrilla in Manila" fight against Ali in 1974. He was defeated in the brutal bout, and his later attempts to recapture

Joe Frazier (left)

rounds with a 1-minute rest period between rounds. They required fighters to wear "fair-sized" boxing gloves, banned wrestling holds, and set the 10-second count for a knockout. With the adoption of the Queensberry rules, boxing gradually became acceptable in the United States, where it had been illegal. Heavyweight bouts were the most popular.

The Modern Era

In 1892, John L. Sullivan, the last of the bareknuckle champions, was defeated by James J. (Gentleman Jim) Corbett in the first heavyweight title bout fought with gloves under the Queensberry rules. Three other great heavyweight champions of the early modern era were James J. Jeffries, who retired undefeated in 1905; Jack Johnson, who became the first black champion in 1908; and Robert Fitzsimmons, who was also a middleweight and light heavyweight champion during his career.

As the 1900's progressed, boxing began drawing huge crowds. The heavyweight division produced some of the greatest names in the sport, beginning with William Harrison (Jack) Dempsey and James J. (Gene) Tunney in the 1920's. From the late 1930's to the late 1940's, Joe Louis was the heavyweight champion. The 1950's saw the emergence of Rocky Marciano (who retired undefeated in 1956), Floyd Patterson, and Ingemar Johansson.

Foremost among the greats of the 1960's and 1970's was Muhammad Ali. He won his first heavyweight crown in 1964, and he would go on to become the first boxer to win the title three different times. (For more information, see the biography of Ali in Volume A.) Two other top champions during the 1970's were Joe Frazier and George Foreman.

During the 1980's, Larry Holmes, Michael Spinks, and Mike Tyson dominated the heavyweight division.

the title also failed. During his career, Frazier was named *Ring Magazine*'s Fighter of the Year three times (1967, 1970–71). He was inducted into the International Boxing Hall of Fame in 1990.

Marvin Hagler (1954–), born in Newark, New Jersey, liked his nickname Marvelous so much he eventually made it his legal first name. He was middleweight champion from 1980 to 1987, defeating such opponents as Roberto Duran and Thomas Hearns. *Ring Magazine* named Hagler Fighter of the Year in 1983 and 1985, the same years he won the Edward J. Neil Trophy for being the top boxer. He was inducted into the International Boxing Hall of Fame in 1993.

Evander Holyfield (1962–), born in Atmore, Alabama, was called the Real Deal. Before moving up to the heavyweight level, he was world cruiserweight champion in 1987–88. Holyfield was then heavyweight champion three different times, from 1990 to 1992, 1993 to 1994, and 1996 (WBA) to 2000, a feat matched only by Muhammad Ali. He was named *Ring Magazine*'s Fighter of the Year three times (1987, 1996–97).

Sugar Ray (Ray Charles) Leonard (1956–), born in Wilmington, South Carolina, was called Sugar after famed boxer Sugar Ray Robinson. He emerged on the boxing scene when he won the light welterweight gold medal at the 1976 Olympic Games. Twice named *Ring Magazine*'s Fighter of the Year (1979, 1981), Leonard is the only boxer to win titles in five different divisions (light heavyweight, super middleweight, middleweight, junior middleweight, and welterweight). During the 1980's he was considered the best boxer of any division. Leonard was inducted into the International Boxing Hall of Fame in 1997.

Evander Holyfield (right)

Joe Louis (Joseph Louis Barrow) (1914–81) was born in Lafayette, Alabama. Known as the Brown Bomber, Louis was heavyweight champion from 1937 to 1949—longer than any other boxer in the history of the sport. He defended his title a record 25 times while being named *Ring Magazine*'s Fighter of the Year four times (1936, 1938–39, 1941). He retired in 1949, although he later made an unsuccessful comeback attempt. He was inducted into the International Boxing Hall of Fame in 1990.

Floyd Patterson (1935–), born in Waco, North Carolina, was only 17 years old when he won the middleweight gold medal at the 1952 Olympic Games. Four years later, at the age of 21, he became the then youngest heavyweight champion when he defeated Archie Moore for the crown. After losing the championship to Ingemar Johansson in 1959, Patterson became the first boxer in the sport's history to recapture the heavyweight title when he defeated Johansson in a 1960 rematch. Patterson lost the title to Sonny Liston in 1962, and he never regained it. He was inducted into the International Boxing Hall of Fame in 1991.

Sugar Ray Robinson (Walker Smith) (1921–89), born in Detroit, Michigan, is considered one of the best boxers ever to step into the ring. Robinson took the name Sugar because his style of boxing was once called "sweet as sugar." He was welterweight champion from 1946 through 1950 and middleweight champion from 1951 through 1952, in 1955, and from 1957 through 1958. Robinson was twice named *Ring Magazine*'s Fighter of the Year (1942, 1951). He retired in 1965 and was inducted into the International Boxing Hall of Fame in 1990.

In the 1990's, Evander Holyfield held the heavyweight crown three different times. Riddick Bowe, George Foreman, Mike Tyson, and Lennox Lewis also held the title.

There have been notable champions in other weight classes too. Lightweights Joe Gans, who held the title from 1902 to 1908, and Benny Leonard, who held the title from 1917 to 1925, are two of boxing's greats. Henry Armstrong was the first boxer to win three different titles—featherweight (1937–38), lightweight (1938–39), and welterweight (1938–40). Sugar Ray Robinson held the middleweight title five times (1951–58) and he was also a welterweight champ (1946–51). Rivals Willie Pep and Sandy Saddler ruled the featherweight class (1946–57). Roberto Duran won lightweight, welterweight, and junior middleweight titles between 1972 and 1984. Sugar Ray Leonard held welterweight, junior middleweight, middleweight, super middleweight, and light heavyweight titles.

Women and Boxing

Women have been boxing since the 1720's in England. Until recently, however, women's bouts did not receive much attention, acceptance, or respect.

A women's boxing match was televised for the first time in 1954, featuring the famed boxer Barbara Buttrick. It was not until 1988, however, that a national boxing association (Sweden's) sanctioned, or gave official approval to, women's boxing. During the 1990's, interest in women's boxing grew. USA Boxing developed guidelines in 1993 for the inclusion of women's boxing in its organization. The Amateur International Boxing Association (AIBA), the governing body of international amateur boxing, officially recognized women's boxing in 1994.

Professional organizations include the International Female Boxers Association (IFBA), the International Women's Boxing Federation (IWBF), and the Women's

Although women have boxed for many years, the sport of women's boxing did not receive wide acceptance and popularity until the 1990's.

International Boxing Federation (WIBF). The same weight divisions used in men's boxing, except the superheavyweight, are used in women's. The rules for women's bouts differ slightly from those of men's bouts.

While much publicity has surrounded former champions' daughters, such as Laila Ali, Jacqui Frazier-Lyde, and Freeda Foreman, other women have established themselves as champions in the sport. These include Christy Martin, Lucia Rijker, Deirdre Gogarty, Valerie Mahfood, Mia St. John, and Kathy Collins.

ROCKY MARCIANO
Former World Heavyweight Boxing Champion
Reviewed by EDWARD SCHUYLER
Boxing Writer

BOYD, BELLE. See SPIES (Profiles).

BOYLE, ROBERT (1627–1691)

Robert Boyle is often considered the father of modern chemistry. A self-taught scientist, he was one of the first to use careful scientific methods during his experiments.

Boyle was born on January 25, 1627, at Lismore Castle in Ireland. His father was the Earl of Cork, a wealthy, landowning Englishman. Boyle went to Eton, the famous boys' school, at the age of 8. When he was 11, he went abroad with a tutor. He spent most of the next six years in Switzerland and Italy. During this time Boyle developed an interest in science and began to study the works of Galileo.

When his father died in 1644, Robert Boyle inherited a rich estate in England. Upon arriving there, he was in a position to do anything he wanted. Having what he called "an unsatisfied appetite for knowledge," he decided to explore the unknowns of science. Since there were no textbooks and few teachers, Boyle had to proceed on his own. He set up a laboratory and worked alone but hired assistants when he needed help. One assistant was Robert Hooke, who became an important scientist himself.

Boyle conducted experiments in biology, chemistry, and physics. He studied how animals breathe, how blood circulates, and how matter burns, boils, and freezes; and he theorized that matter was composed of atoms, or, as he called them, "corpuscles."

Boyle's work with an air pump he invented is probably best known. The pump could both compress air and produce near vacuums. With it Boyle could control the quantity of air in a closed container. His experiments demonstrated the essential role of air in burning, breathing, and the transmission of sound. During these experiments Boyle discovered that when pressure on a given quantity of air is increased, the volume of air becomes smaller. This finding became the basis of what is now known as Boyle's law: If the temperature and quantity of a gas remain constant, the volume varies inversely with the pressure.

By 1645, Boyle was meeting with other scientific researchers in London. The Royal Society, which is still one of the world's leading organizations for the encouragement of science, grew out of these meetings.

Boyle, a deeply religious man, learned Greek and Hebrew in order to read the Bible in the original text, and he wrote books on religious matters. He also financed translations of the Bible and supported missionary work abroad.

Boyle never married. He was often ill, but his interest in science was so strong that he worked steadily almost until his death in London, England, on December 30, 1691.

JOHN S. BOWMAN
Author and Science Editor

BOYS & GIRLS CLUBS OF AMERICA

Boys & Girls Clubs of America is a national federation of clubs that offer a wide range of programs and activities for young people. More than 2,200 clubs are located in communities throughout the United States. Each year, these clubs assist some 3 million children, many of whom are from underprivileged backgrounds.

Clubs are located in cities, suburbs, and rural areas. Some clubs are in specially designed centers equipped with swimming pools, learning centers, computer laboratories, and gymnasiums. Other clubs operate programs for young people in schools, homeless shelters, shopping malls, reservations, and military bases.

Programs

Boys & Girls Clubs provide programs for children 6 to 18 years of age, conducted by a full-time professional staff. (A small fee is charged for joining the club.) Programs emphasize character and leadership development, educational enhancement, career preparation, health and life skills, the arts, and sports, fitness, and recreation.

SMART (Skills Mastery and Resistance Training) Moves, an alcohol, drug, and pregnancy prevention program, provides girls and boys with the information and skills they need to be able to make smart choices in their everyday lives. Kids in Control is a safety awareness program focusing on safety habits and skills. Torch Clubs are leadership development groups for youth ages 11 to 13. In this program, youngsters elect officers and plan and carry out their own activities and community service projects. In the Career

Boys & Girls Clubs offer members a broad range of recreational and educational activities, including arts and crafts.

Explorers Club, youngsters visit various businesses, government agencies, and colleges while receiving information about career choices. Through the National Fine Arts Program, members can create art using techniques such as pastels, watercolor, collage, and sculpture. Other programs provide instruction on arts and crafts, music, and sports.

History

The first Boys Club was established in 1860 in Hartford, Connecticut. The national organization, originally named Federated Boys' Clubs and later Boys' Clubs of America, was founded in 1906. The purpose was to provide leadership and programs for its member clubs, while helping to establish new clubs in disadvantaged communities. In 1956, the organization was chartered by Congress. In 1990, the organization's name was changed to Boys & Girls Clubs of America.

Boys & Girls Clubs of America headquarters are located in Atlanta, Georgia. The organization continues to work across the country, reaching more and more young people as new branches are opened.

ANDREA K. JOHNSON
Boys & Girls Clubs of America

Did you know that...

many famous personalities are former Boys & Girls Club members? Well-known alumni include newscasters Bernard Shaw and Dan Rather; actors Denzel Washington, Bill Cosby, Jennifer Lopez, and Danny DeVito; sports figures such as football's Randall Cunningham, Junior Seau (Tiana Seau, Jr.), and Wayne Chrebet; baseball's Joe DiMaggio, Alex Rodriguez, and Frank Thomas; basketball's Michael Jordan, Shaquille O'Neal, Anfernee "Penny" Hardaway, and Earvin "Magic" Johnson; and track and field's Jackie Joyner-Kersee.

Camping is one of the many ways in which Boy Scouts work and play to develop mental and physical fitness. Approximately 16,000,000 Scouts and leaders participate in Boy Scout programs throughout the world.

BOY SCOUTS

Not long ago, a 12-year-old Boy Scout was leaving a tidal pool when he saw two small children bobbing helplessly in the water. The Scout rescued the children from the pool and began mouth-to-mouth resuscitation. One child began to breathe, but the other did not. The Scout instructed people on the beach to continue working on the second child while he called for an ambulance. Both children lived, thanks to the Scout's actions.

This is but one of hundreds of real cases in which Boy Scouts have saved lives by using the skills they learned in Scout training. This worldwide organization teaches young men leadership and good citizenship. It teaches them the skills that enable them to live up to their Scout motto, "Be prepared."

Boys get much more from Scouting besides training for emergencies. They find fun and fellowship with other boys and the men who lead them. They find adventure in hiking, camping, boating, and other outdoor sports. They gain useful knowledge and skills and have many chances to take part in the life of their community and nation.

▶ **THE BOY SCOUTS OF AMERICA**

The Boy Scouts of America has more than 5,000,000 members. The organization provides a long-term program for a boy from the time he enters the first grade until his 21st birthday. In the first grade, a boy may become a Tiger Cub; in the second grade a Cub Scout; at age 11 a Boy Scout; and at age 14 a Varsity Scout or Explorer.

Tiger Cubs

Introduced by the Boy Scouts of America in 1982, the Tiger Cub program is for boys in the first grade. They join with an adult partner, usually a parent, and they participate together in a program of activities and fun with the family and as part of a Tiger Cub group. Group leadership is shared among all of the adult partners.

Tiger Cub Promise: "I promise to love God, my family, and my country, and to learn about the world."

Tiger Cub Motto: "Search, discover, share."

Cub Scouts

Cub Scouting is a program for boys in second through fifth grades.

Many of a Cub Scout's activities and achievements take place in the home with the encouragement of adults in the household. He starts out as a Bobcat. By completing twelve achievements, he earns his Wolf Badge. Then, for earning credits in a variety of activities of his choice, he receives arrow points to wear below his badge. When he completes the second grade (or is 9 years old), he begins to work for the Bear rank. On completion of the third grade (or when he is 10 years old), he may join a Webelos den and earn the Webelos badge and the highest Cub Scout award, the Arrow of Light. Webelos activity badges are awarded for learning special skills. "Webelos" stands for "*We'll Be Loyal Scouts.*"

A Cub Scout belongs to a den with boys from his neighborhood. The den meets each week under the guidance of its adult den leader, who is helped by a Boy Scout called the den chief. Several dens make up a Cub pack, which has an adult leader called the Cubmaster. The pack meets once a month, often in the form of a group outing.

The Cub Scout uniform is dark blue with yellow trim. A different color neckerchief is worn by the Cub Scout to designate his grade or age. Yellow indicates second grade; blue, third grade; and plaid, fourth- and fifth-grade Webelos Scouts.

Cub Scout Motto: "Do your best."

Cub Scout Promise: "I, [name], promise to do my best to do my duty to God and my country, to help other people, and to obey the Law of the Pack."

Law of the Pack: "The Cub Scout follows Akela. The Cub Scout helps the pack go. The pack helps the Cub Scout grow. The Cub Scout gives goodwill." ("Akela" means "good leader.")

Boy Scouts

A boy may become a Boy Scout at age 11. By understanding the Scout Oath and Law and by passing a few simple tests, he may join and be called a Boy Scout. Skill awards and merit badges lead him on to Tenderfoot, Second Class, and then on to First Class rank. Scouts may earn merit badges in any of more than 100 different fields. Certain merit badges help him achieve the ranks of Star (6 merit badges), Life (11), and Eagle Scout (21), the highest rank in Scouting.

SCOUT UNIFORMS, INSIGNIA, AND BADGES

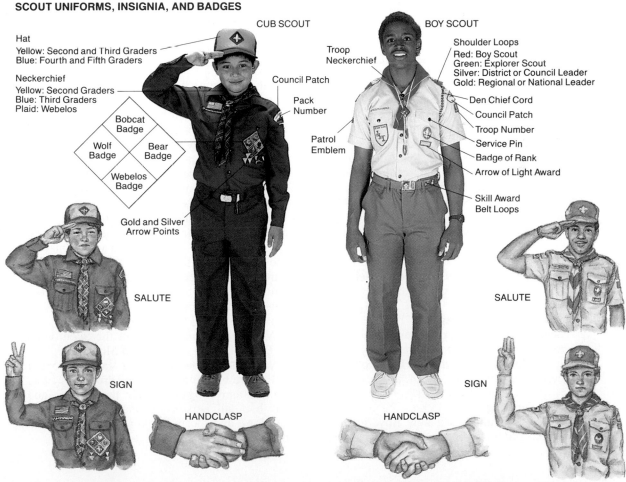

CUB SCOUT

BOY SCOUT

Hat
Yellow: Second and Third Graders
Blue: Fourth and Fifth Graders

Neckerchief
Yellow: Second Graders
Blue: Third Graders
Plaid: Webelos

Bobcat Badge

Wolf Badge

Bear Badge

Webelos Badge

Gold and Silver Arrow Points

Council Patch

Pack Number

Patrol Emblem

Troop Neckerchief

Shoulder Loops
Red: Boy Scout
Green: Explorer Scout
Silver: District or Council Leader
Gold: Regional or National Leader

Den Chief Cord

Council Patch

Troop Number

Service Pin

Badge of Rank

Arrow of Light Award

Skill Award Belt Loops

SALUTE

SIGN

HANDCLASP

SALUTE

SIGN

HANDCLASP

Scouts wear insignia showing their rank, den or patrol, and service and achievement awards. Webelos Scouts may wear blue or khaki and tan uniforms.

Agribusiness   American Business   American Cultures   American Heritage   American Labor   Animal Science   Archery   Architecture   Art   Astronomy

Athletics   Atomic Energy   Aviation   Backpacking   Basketry   Beekeeping   Bird Study   Botany   Bugling   Camping

Canoeing   Chemistry   Citizenship in the Community   Citizenship in the Nation   Citizenship in the World   Coin Collecting   Communications   Computers   Consumer Buying   Cooking

Cycling   Dentistry   Dog Care   Drafting   Electricity   Electronics   Emergency Preparedness   Energy   Engineering   Environmental Science

Farm Mechanics   Fingerprinting   Firemanship   First Aid   Fish and Wildlife Management   Fishing   Forestry   Gardening   Genealogy   General Science

Geology   Golf   Graphic Arts   Handicap Awareness   Hiking   Home Repairs   Horsemanship   Indian Lore   Insect Study   Journalism

A Scout must earn a number of awards, or merit badges, in order to qualify for each new rank. The colorful badges can be earned in many different subject areas.

A small group of Boy Scouts forms a patrol. Several patrols make up a troop. The troop usually meets once a week with its adult leader, the Scoutmaster. Hiking and camping are part of the adventure that Scouts enjoy. They learn how to take care of themselves in the open and how to help others in case of accidents. They also learn to be useful citizens.

Scout Oath or Promise: ''On my honor I will do my best to do my duty to God and my country and to obey the Scout Law; to help other people at all times; to keep myself physically strong, mentally awake, and morally straight.''

Scout Motto: ''Be prepared.''

Scout Slogan: ''Do a good turn daily.''

Scout Law: A Scout is trustworthy, loyal, helpful, friendly, courteous, kind, obedient, cheerful, thrifty, brave, clean, and reverent.

Varsity Scouting

Varsity Scouting is a new Boy Scouts of America program for young men 14 through 17 years of age. It is the ''varsity'' of Boy Scouting, just as the varsity is the senior team in school sports.

Varsity Scouts are members of a Varsity Scout team. They are under the leadership of an adult Varsity Scout coach. The youth leader of the team is the Varsity Scout team captain. There are youth squad leaders and a youth program manager for each of the five program fields of emphasis.

The fields of interest—advancement, high adventure, personal development, service, and special programs—challenge a young man to use the basic skills learned in Boy Scouting. Participation in Varsity Scout activities and requirements lead to earning the Varsity Scout letter. Advancement toward the Eagle Scout rank is continued in Varsity Scouting.

Varsity Scouting ideals are the Scout Oath or Promise, Law, Motto, and Slogan.

Varsity Scout Pledge: ''As a Varsity Scout, I will: Live by the Scout Oath (Promise), Law, Motto, and Slogan; Honor the dignity and worth of all persons; Promote the cause of freedom; and Do my best to be a good team member.''

Landscape Architecture · Law · Leatherwork · Lifesaving · Machinery · Mammal Study · Masonry · Metals Engineering · Metalwork · Model Design and Building

Motorboating · Music · Nature · Oceanography · Orienteering · Painting · Personal Fitness · Personal Management · Pets · Photography

Pioneering · Plant Science · Plumbing · Pottery · Public Health · Public Speaking · Pulp and Paper · Rabbit Raising · Radio · Railroading

Reading · Reptile Study · Rifle Shooting · Rowing · Safety · Salesmanship · Scholarship · Sculpture · Shotgun Shooting · Signaling

Skating · Skiing · Small-Boat Sailing · Soil and Water Conservation · Space Exploration · Sports · Stamp Collecting · Surveying · Swimming · Textile

Theater · Traffic Safety · Truck Transportation · Veterinary Science · Waterskiing · Weather · Whitewater · Wilderness Survival · Wood Carving · Woodwork

Exploring

Exploring is a division of the Boy Scouts of America for young men and women from high school age to 21. Young adults—and they need not have been Scouts—may join a general- or special-interest Explorer post or Sea Explorer ship. Exploring offers a choice of activities and a chance for adventure, career experience, education, and recreation. Explorers plan their own programs with the help of an adult adviser or skipper. Young women became full members in 1971.

More than half of all posts are organized around a career interest such as law enforcement, medicine, banking, space exploration, computer programming, or other occupation.

▶THE BOY SCOUT ORGANIZATION

There are about 16,000,000 Scouts and leaders in the world today. They are found in 116 countries. They have different uniforms, badges, and customs, but their aims and ideals are alike. The motto ''Be prepared'' is known in many languages. The headquarters of the Boy Scouts World Bureau is in Geneva, Switzerland.

World jamborees are held every four years. These are huge camps that bring Scouts from many nations together in friendship. The first world jamboree was held in England in 1920. Many countries also hold national jamborees. The Boy Scouts of America held its first jamboree in 1937. Canada held its first in 1949.

United States

The National Council of the Boy Scouts of America is made up of representatives who come from more than 400 local councils across the country. This body elects an Executive Board, which is the governing body of the Boy Scouts of America. The national office is in Irving, Texas. A full-time staff, headed by the Chief Scout Executive, publishes handbooks and magazines for boys and leaders and prepares video and other materials for training leaders. It also controls the manufacture and sale of uniforms and equipment through local Scouting distributors.

The staff of the national organization provides assistance to local councils made up of volunteers who offer to help Scouting in a city, county, or larger area. The council must have, among other things, a camp for its members. A group of professional Scouting administrators work full time in area councils.

Scouting reaches boys and young men and young women through churches, schools, and other organizations. Each group that receives a charter to operate a troop or other Scouting unit offers a meeting place, good leaders, and other needed support.

Although uniforms and customs in different countries may vary, the aims of Scouting are alike worldwide. Here a group of Canadian Wolf Cubs enjoy a fishing trip.

Today there is an active interest in Scouting in the inner cities. Many city youngsters join Scouting for its outdoor activities, such as camping and water-safety programs.

Scouting for the Handicapped. Today about 100,000 physically or mentally disabled Scouts are active in various programs throughout the United States. Anyone who has been certified as disabled by a proper medical authority may enroll in Scouting and remain in its program beyond the regulation age limits. This provision allows all members to advance in Scouting as far as they wish.

Canada

In 1914, the Canadian General Council of the Boy Scouts Association was formed. In 1961 this name was changed to Boy Scouts of Canada. In 1990, the organization began accepting girls and was renamed Scouts Canada. Today there are more than 200,000 Canadian scouts divided into five age groups: (1) Beavers, age 5 to 7; (2) Wolf Cubs, 8 to 11; (3) Scouts, 11 to 14; (4) Venturers, 14 to 17; and (5) Rovers, 18 to 26 years old. The mission of Scouts Canada is "To contribute to the development of young people in achieving their full physical, intellectual, social, and spiritual potential as individuals, as responsible citizens, and as members of their local, national, and international communities ...."

▶ **HISTORY OF SCOUTING**

Boy Scouting was started by Robert Stephenson Smyth Baden-Powell, an Englishman born in 1857. As an army officer, Baden-Powell made up many training games and contests, which he later described in a book called *Aids to Scouting*. He became a hero during the Boer War in South Africa (1899–1902). On his return to England, he found that some leaders of boys had started using his scouting games and contests. He then worked out a scouting program for boys that was built around the ideals of the Scout Promise and Law. Guided by Baden-Powell's *Scouting for Boys* (1908), troops of Boy Scouts were formed in many countries.

In 1910, Baden-Powell, Chief Scout of the world, retired from the British army to devote all his time to Scouting. He died in Kenya in 1941.

Shortly after Scouting started in Britain, William D. Boyce, a Chicago publisher, became lost in a London fog and was aided by an English Scout. This led Boyce to become interested in Scouting. On February 8, 1910, he founded the Boy Scouts of America.

Reviewed by Boy Scouts of America

BRAHE, TYCHO (1546–1601)

Tycho Brahe, the great Danish astronomer, was born on December 14, 1546. He grew up in Knudstrup, a village in Denmark that is now part of Sweden. In 1559, his aristocratic family sent him to Copenhagen to study law. But after witnessing an eclipse of the sun, he went against his family's wishes and began studying astronomy on his own.

Brahe was not only stubborn but also hot-tempered. In his student years, he fought a duel with another young nobleman, who cut off part of his nose. Brahe replaced the part with one of gold and silver.

In 1572, Brahe became the first European to sight a supernova—a star that suddenly explodes and becomes brilliant. The star was in the constellation of Cassiopeia. Brahe's fame as an astronomer drew the attention of King Frederick II of Denmark, who built him an observatory, called Uraniborg, and paid him a salary. There, for 21 years, Brahe made careful observations of the stars, sun, moon, and planets—all without the use of the telescope, which had not yet been invented. In 1599, Brahe was invited by the Holy Roman emperor, Rudolph II, to continue his studies in Prague.

Brahe died there two years later, on October 24, 1601. But his work lived on, thanks to his assistant, a young German astronomer named Johannes Kepler. Brahe believed that the sun revolved around Earth, and the other planets revolved around the sun, all in perfectly circular paths, or orbits. However, using Brahe's measurements, Kepler was able to show that all planets in the solar system, including Earth, revolve around the sun, in oblong, or elliptical, orbits.

JOHN S. BOWMAN
Author and Science Editor

See also KEPLER, JOHANNES.

BRAHMS, JOHANNES (1833–1897)

Johannes Brahms was one of the most important composers of the 1800's, producing works in nearly all the forms of music popular in his day. During his life he composed chamber music, numerous works for piano, four symphonies, and over 100 songs. In his music, Brahms combined classical traditions with the warmth of the romantic style.

Brahms was born on May 7, 1833, in Hamburg, Germany. At an early age he showed unusual musical ability. By the time he was 16, however, Brahms decided that his chief interest was composing music rather than performing it.

In his early 20's, Brahms met the great composer Robert Schumann, who recognized his talent as a composer. In 1853 Schumann wrote a famous magazine article entitled "New Paths" in which he hailed Brahms as the coming genius of German music. Schumann also had great influence as a music critic, and his praise of Brahms helped the young composer become better known.

Passed over for a conducting position in Hamburg, Brahms moved to Vienna, Austria, in 1862. His abilities were quickly recognized there, and he soon won an appointment as a choral conductor. During the 1860's, Brahms composed the *German Requiem*, which brought him much recognition. From 1872 to 1875 Brahms was musical director of the famed Viennese Society of the Friends of Music.

In 1876 his first symphony, which he had begun to compose 22 years before, was finally performed. Three years later Brahms introduced his violin concerto. The great second piano concerto was finished in 1881, and in 1885 Brahms completed the fourth and last of his symphonies.

In 1894 Brahms was offered the post he had wanted all his life, conductor of the Hamburg Philharmonic Orchestra. But he felt he was too old for the position and declined the offer. He died on April 3, 1897.

Reviewed by KARL GEIRINGER
Author, *Johannes Brahms*

BRAIN

Inside your head is a spongy, jelly-like organ that allows you to throw a ball, taste a pizza, talk to a friend, and remember your telephone number. This organ is your brain: It controls just about everything you do.

The brain is your body's most complicated organ. It receives and processes sensory information from the outside world and sends messages to control muscles and glands. Your brain is also where you plan ahead, learn, and experience thoughts and emotions.

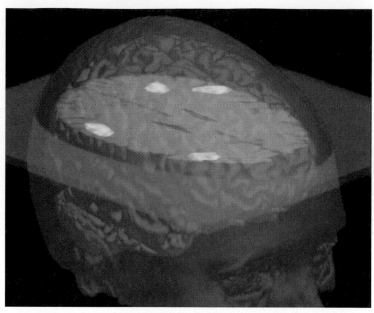

This computer-enhanced view of a person's brain was created using an MRI scanner. The device detected active areas (shown above as bright spots) as the person thought about a series of letters.

▶ CELLS OF THE BRAIN

The brain is composed of two main types of cells: nerve cells, or **neurons**, and glial cells, or **glia**. Neuroscientists—researchers who study the brain and nervous system—estimate that the brain has 100 billion neurons and ten to fifty times as many glia.

Neurons and glia have different functions. Neurons are responsible for sending information throughout the nervous system. Neurons are some of the oldest cells in the body because they can last a lifetime. Some neurons are the longest cells in the body, stretching all the way from the tip of your toe to your brain. Glia, from the Greek word for "glue," do not transmit information. Instead, they insulate neurons, clean debris away from them, carry nutrients to them, and provide structural support for the nervous system.

The basic types of neurons are the same in humans and other vertebrates (animals with a backbone). These types can be classified according to their function. **Sensory neurons** respond to a stimulus (plural: stimuli) such as light, temperature, sound, smell, or touch. **Motor neurons** are responsible for controlling muscles. **Interneurons** relay information between sensory neurons and motor neurons.

Although neurons vary in size and shape, depending on their location in the nervous system, they all have four specialized features: a cell body (or soma), dendrites, an axon, and a synaptic terminal.

The **cell body** is the central part of a neuron. It contains a control center, called the nucleus, and other structures, called organelles, that are important for the cell's function. Cell bodies can vary in size from 4 microns (millionths of a meter) to 120 microns in diameter—about the width of a human hair.

Threadlike extensions called **dendrites** branch out from the neuron's cell body. Dendrites, from the Greek word meaning "tree," contain structures called **receptor sites** for detecting signals, or impulses, coming from other neurons. The dendrites bring information to the cell body.

Also extending from the cell body is a single **axon**. The axon carries nerve impulses away from the cell body toward the **synaptic terminal**. At the synaptic terminal, information from one neuron is transmitted to another neuron. This area is called the **synapse**. An axon can branch several times to form synapses with many different neurons.

▶ NERVE CELL COMMUNICATION

Neurons send messages using an electrochemical process—that is, one that involves both electricity and chemistry. For instance, when you throw a ball, neurons in your brain send messages to the spinal cord, which then relays the messages to the nerves and muscles in your arm. These messages are electrical signals that travel on electrically charged chemicals called **ions**. In the nervous system, important ions are sodium, chloride, calcium, and potassium. When there are different numbers of ions inside and outside a nerve cell, there is a difference in positive and negative electrical charges called a **potential difference**. If some of these ions switch places and move inside or outside the cell, the potential difference can be reversed. When this happens, the neuron generates a brief electrical signal. This signal is called an **action potential**, or a nerve impulse.

Action potentials travel down the axon without a change in the electrical signal. Depending on the size of an axon and whether it is insulated with glial cells, action potentials can travel down an axon at rates between 0.4 mile and 268 miles per hour (0.2 meter and 120 meters per second). That is as slow as a turtle or as fast as a race car! A single neuron can generate hundreds of action potentials each second. It is the pattern of these signals that makes up the messages transmitted throughout the nervous system.

At the synaptic terminal, action potentials cause the release of chemicals called neuro-transmitters, such as dopamine, norepinephrine, epinephrine, acetylcholine, and serotonin. These chemicals are released from tiny sacs, called **vesicles**, at the end of a neuron's axon and float across the synapse to the dendrite, cell body, or axon of another neuron. There they may attach themselves to receptor sites. In response to this chemical signal, the receiving neuron's **excitability** changes. In other words, the neuron will be either more or less likely to pass on the signal.

▶ **BRAINS AND NERVOUS SYSTEMS**

Single-celled organisms, such as the amoeba, do not have a nervous system or a brain. However, these types of animals do react to light, heat, and food. Simple multicellular animals, like the sea anemone and jellyfish, have a primitive nervous system but no collection of cells that can be called a brain. Instead, the nervous system of these animals is made up of a collection of interconnected nerve cells called a nerve net.

In general, larger animals have bigger brains. In adult humans, the brain measures about 3.1 pounds (1.4 kilograms) in weight, 5.5 inches (14.0 centimeters) in width, 6.6 inches (16.7 centimeters) in length, and 3.7 inches (9.3 centimeters) in height. For a per-

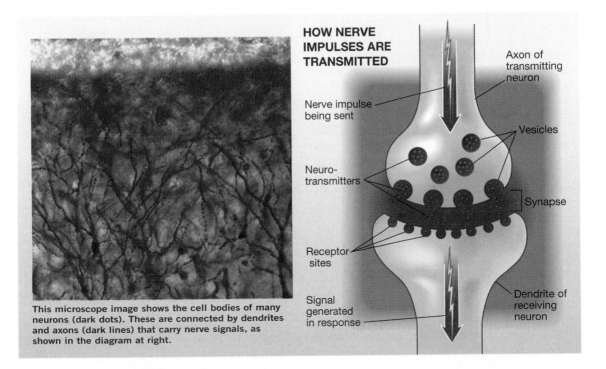

This microscope image shows the cell bodies of many neurons (dark dots). These are connected by dendrites and axons (dark lines) that carry nerve signals, as shown in the diagram at right.

HOW NERVE IMPULSES ARE TRANSMITTED

Axon of transmitting neuron

Nerve impulse being sent

Vesicles

Neuro-transmitters

Synapse

Receptor sites

Signal generated in response

Dendrite of receiving neuron

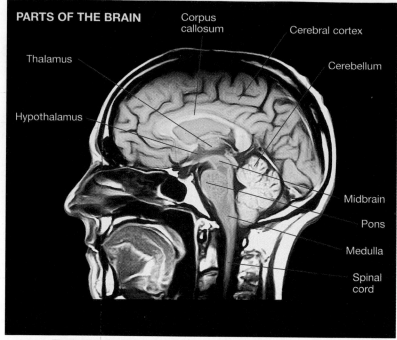

PARTS OF THE BRAIN

Thalamus

Hypothalamus

Corpus callosum

Cerebral cortex

Cerebellum

Midbrain

Pons

Medulla

Spinal cord

The brain's three main parts—the cerebrum (brown), cerebellum (green), and brain stem (blue)—can be seen in this colored image. Other structures within these parts and the beginning of the spinal cord are also visible.

First, there is the skin of the head—the scalp. Under the scalp are the bones of the skull. Between the skull and the brain are three special coverings called the **meninges**. The outermost layer is called the dura mater, which is tough and thick. The middle layer is called the arachnoid. The innermost layer, located on top of the brain, is called the pia mater. A clear, colorless liquid called the **cerebrospinal fluid** flows between the pia mater and arachnoid. This fluid supports the brain, cushions it against sudden impacts, removes waste products, and distributes chemicals called hormones to other parts of the body. The fluid also flows through cavities in the brain called ventricles.

The brain consists of three main parts: the cerebrum, the brain stem, and the cerebellum. Although different areas of the brain may play a role in specific functions, areas in these three parts interact to coordinate how we perceive, move, think, and feel.

Cerebrum

The cerebrum (the Latin word for "brain") is the largest part of the brain, making up about 85 percent of the total brain weight in humans. It looks like a large pinkish-gray walnut that is wrinkled and divided into left and right halves, or **cerebral hemispheres**. It includes the cerebral cortex, the basal ganglia, the amygdala, and the hippocampus.

The **cerebral cortex** makes up the outermost layer of the cerebrum. It is rather thin, varying in thickness from about $1/16$ to $3/16$ of an inch (1.5 millimeters to 4.5 millimeters). The cerebral hemispheres are connected by a thick band of over 300 million nerve fibers called the **corpus callosum**. The wrinkles of the brain are the result of bumps and grooves on the cerebral cortex. Each bump on the brain is called a gyrus (plural: gyri), also called a convolution. Each gyrus is separated by a groove called a sulcus (plural: sulci).

Although most people have the same patterns of gyri and sulci, no two brains are exactly alike. The folding of the cerebral cortex

son who weighs 154 pounds (70 kilograms), the brain makes up 2 percent of the total body weight but uses about 20 percent of the body's total oxygen supply.

On average, men's brains are larger than women's brains. However, it is important to note that there is no relationship between intelligence and brain size: A genius does not necessarily have a larger-than-average brain. In fact, the great physicist Albert Einstein had a brain that weighed just over 2.7 pounds (1.2 kilograms).

The brain connects with the rest of the body's nervous system, which is divided into two main parts: the **central nervous system** and the **peripheral nervous system**. The brain and spinal cord make up the central nervous system. The peripheral nervous system is composed of twelve pairs of cranial nerves that extend from the brain, 31 pairs of spinal nerves that extend from the spinal cord, and nerves that connect to all parts of the body. (For more information, see the article NERVOUS SYSTEM in Volume N.)

▶ ORGANIZATION OF THE BRAIN

The brain is isolated and protected from the outside world by several layers of tissue.

increases how much of it can fit in the skull. The total surface area of the human cerebral cortex is about 2½ square feet (2,200 square centimeters), about the size of a full page of newspaper.

Each hemisphere of the cerebrum is divided into four regions, or lobes, by various sulci and gyri. The **occipital lobes** are located at the back of the brain and are concerned with vision. The **temporal lobes**, located on the lower sides of the brain, play a role in hearing. The **parietal lobes**, found on the upper sides of the brain, are responsible for perceptions related to touch, pressure, temperature, and pain. The **frontal lobes** are found in front of the temporal and parietal lobes and are important for reasoning, planning, parts of speech, movement, emotions, and problem solving.

Deep inside the cerebrum are a group of structures called the **basal ganglia**. These areas are important for controlling movement. The **amygdala** is sometimes included as part of the basal ganglia. It is important for memory and emotional behavior. Another structure within the cerebrum is the **hippocampus**. It is important for transferring memories from short-term memory to long-term memory.

The amygdala and the hippocampus are sometimes grouped together with other brain structures and referred to as the **limbic system**. It was once thought to be the seat of all emotions, but scientists now know that it interacts with other parts of the brain (notably the cortex) in forming memories and emotional responses. The limbic system also shares various types of sensory information, such as smell, with other parts of the brain. That is why smelling something familiar, such as perfume or fresh-baked bread, often brings back strong memories and emotions associated with it.

Brain Stem

The brain stem is subdivided into many parts, including the thalamus, hypothalamus, midbrain, pons, and medulla.

Located at the front end of the brain stem, the **thalamus** is a group of structures that processes information from all of the senses except smell (which is processed by an area in the brain just above the nose called the olfactory bulb). This sensory information passes through the thalamus before it reaches the cerebral cortex. The thalamus also contains cell groups important for motor function, or movement.

Below the thalamus at the base of the brain lies the **hypothalamus**. The hypothalamus is responsible for regulating basic functions such as drinking and feeding, body temperature, sleep, and emotions. The pituitary gland extends down from the hypothalamus and acts as a master-control organ for other glands in the body.

The **midbrain** contains areas important for auditory (hearing) and visual reflexes. It constricts the pupils in our eyes when we step out of a dark room and into the bright sunlight, for instance. Other parts of the midbrain are involved with pain and movement. The **pons** (Latin for "bridge") contains areas that relay motor information from the cerebral cortex to other places in the nervous system. The **medulla** regulates certain invol-

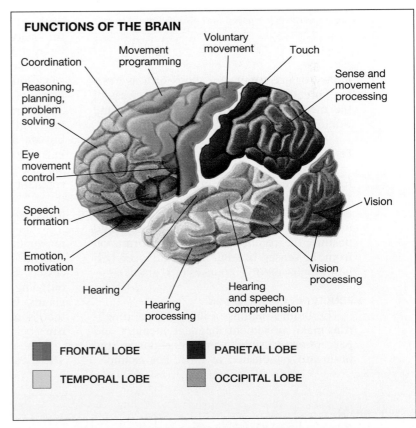

FUNCTIONS OF THE BRAIN

Coordination

Movement programming

Voluntary movement

Touch

Sense and movement processing

Reasoning, planning, problem solving

Eye movement control

Speech formation

Emotion, motivation

Hearing

Hearing processing

Hearing and speech comprehension

Vision

Vision processing

■ FRONTAL LOBE   ■ PARIETAL LOBE

□ TEMPORAL LOBE   ▨ OCCIPITAL LOBE

Here are some simple tips and good advice to keep your brain functioning at top efficiency:

1. Eat a well-balanced diet. The brain requires energy and proper nutrients to work efficiently.

2. Get enough sleep. To avoid drowsiness and irritability, get a good night's rest. Your brain will react faster and be better at performing complex mental tasks.

3. Avoid head injuries by wearing a helmet when you bike, skate, snowboard, or ski. Head injuries account for almost two-thirds of all bicycle-related deaths. Bicycle helmets reduce the risk for head injury by as much as 85 percent and reduce the risk for brain injury by as much as 88 percent. Also, always wear a seat belt in the car. Seat belts significantly reduce the severity of injury and decrease the number of deaths in car accidents.

4. Never use illegal drugs. Drugs such as cocaine, marijuana, heroin, LSD, and amphetamines alter the function of neurotransmitters in the brain and often lead to addiction and other mental and physical problems.

untary, or autonomic, functions such as heart rate, breathing, and digestion. Other areas of the medulla are important for sleeping and waking.

Cerebellum

The cerebellum (Latin for "little brain") is found at the back of the brain above the pons and midbrain. It plays a role in movement and the learning of motor skills. To coordinate movement and maintain balance and posture, the cerebellum receives information from the senses. In adult humans, the cerebellum weighs about 5.3 ounces (150 grams).

▶ FUNCTIONS OF THE BRAIN

The brain's billions of interconnected neurons make movement, language, memory, and perception possible. Some functions of the brain are established at birth. For example, babies are born with a set of reflexes that help them survive. Other more complicated behaviors develop as we grow, learn, and communicate with other people.

The Senses

The nervous system is equipped with special receptors to provide the brain with information about the environment. These receptors convert outside signals such as light, sound, and pressure into electrical impulses. Receptors are specialized for one particular type of signal. For example, receptors in the eye respond to light, but not to sounds. Electrical impulses generated by receptors are relayed to the central nervous system, where a perception of the signal is formed.

It is often said that humans have only five senses: touch, taste, sight, hearing, and smell. However, the inner ear has receptors that provide information related to balance, and joints and muscles have receptors that provide information about body position. Some animals have additional sensory systems or a greater sensitivity to particular information than humans do: fish can detect changes in water pressure; snakes can see infrared light; the platypus can detect electrical currents; bats can hear high-frequency sounds.

The nervous system also monitors sensory signals inside the body. Sometimes we are not aware of such internal sensory signals. For example, information related to body temperature and blood pressure is sent to the brain, but we are often not conscious of such signals. These signals are monitored by the brain and used to maintain a normal internal environment in the body.

Motor Behavior

A major function of the brain is to control movement, or motor behavior. Incoming sensory information sent to the brain can be processed by the brain and converted into outgoing signals to control muscles and glands. It is the pattern of outgoing signals that is ultimately responsible for an organism's behavior.

Some movements do not require the brain. These automatic movements, called spinal reflexes, require processing only in the spinal cord. For example, when an area on your knee is lightly tapped, your leg will kick before the message is relayed to your brain. Although the information eventually does get to the brain, it is not required for the kick to occur.

More complex movements, such as talking, throwing a ball, or dancing, involve multiple areas of the brain. These brain areas include those involved with memory, perception, and planning. Neurons in an area of the cerebrum called the primary motor cortex send signals to neurons in the spinal cord to control muscles.

The basal ganglia and cerebellum are two other brain areas important for movement, particularly planned movements and those requiring smooth control.

Learning and Memory

The brain is in a constant state of change. As we learn new skills and make new memories, we actually change the physical structure of the nervous system, as our neurons make new connections. This is true not just in humans but in other animals as well. While exploring their environment, organisms learn about the world around them and form memories of events that have taken place. The ability to form new memories is essential for an organism's survival.

Memories are stored in the brain in stages. Small pieces of new information are processed in short-term memory for only a few minutes. Memories may then be transferred to a more permanent form in long-term memory.

The hippocampus, within the cerebrum, plays an important role in this transfer. Although damage to the hippocampus does not affect old memories, it can result in the inability to form new memories. For example, people with damage to the hippocampus can remember their own names, but they cannot remember the names of people whom they have just met.

The exact mechanisms by which the brain stores information are not known. It is likely that other areas of the brain, especially those in the cerebral cortex, are also important for memory. Electrical stimulation of parts of the cerebral cortex can evoke memories of past experiences.

Sleep

About one-third of your life is spent sleeping. During sleep, you are not conscious of the world around you. Although you appear to be inactive, your brain is not at rest. Using a machine called an **electroencephalograph** (EEG) to measure brain activity, scientists have discovered that at times during sleep, the brain displays patterns of activity similar to those when we are awake.

Sleep follows a predictable pattern of stages each night. There are two basic forms of sleep: slow wave sleep and rapid eye movement (REM) sleep. After falling asleep, people pass through a series of stages of slow wave sleep, each characterized by different patterns of brain activity. People then enter REM sleep, which is characterized by brain activity similar to wakefulness. This cycle is repeated at intervals of about 90 minutes. During REM sleep, most skeletal muscles are completely paralyzed. In the 1950's, scientists found that during REM sleep, people's eyes dart back and forth rapidly. Also, if people were awakened during REM sleep, they often reported that they were dreaming.

WONDER QUESTION

Is it true that we use only 10 percent of our brains?

No. This is a common misconception. Although different parts of the brain are more or less active during different activities, there is no evidence that we use only a small portion of our brains. Damage to a small area of the brain can cause devastating effects, such as amnesia, paralysis, or loss of language. This suggests that every part of the brain serves an important function, upon which other parts of the brain depend.

On the other hand, some people—especially children—can recover after suffering major damage to the brain or even losing part of it. Such remarkable recoveries do not suggest that we need only a fraction of our brain, however. Rather, they illustrate the tremendous capacity of the brain to "rewire" itself: Cells in the remaining parts of the brain form new connections and take over the functions of those parts that were removed.

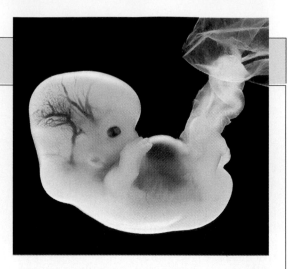

Although all of the brain mechanisms responsible for sleep are not known, circuits involving the brain stem, hypothalamus, and cerebral cortex are important for sleep and wakefulness. (For more information, see the articles SLEEP in Volume S and DREAMING in Volume D.)

▶ DETECTING BRAIN DISORDERS

Brain disorders affect millions of people and have a tremendous impact on society. Some disorders such as Parkinson's disease, Huntington's disease, and Alzheimer's disease cause neurons in parts of the brain to break down, or degenerate. Epilepsy, which affects about one out of every hundred people, is caused by the massive release, or dis-

charge, of electrical signals by neurons. This discharge can result in seizures, often characterized by periods of unconsciousness or uncontrolled shaking of the body. Brain tumors are caused by the rapid growth of cells and can be life-threatening.

Also life-threatening are strokes, or "brain attacks." Strokes are the third leading cause of death in the United States. A stroke occurs when the blood supply to part of the brain is blocked. The lack of nutrients and oxygen to the brain causes neurons to die. People who suffer a stroke may have memory problems, lose their ability to speak, or become partially paralyzed.

Mental illnesses such as schizophrenia, depression, and anxiety disorders affect mood and thought patterns. These illnesses are also brain disorders. Although the causes of these disorders are not completely understood, many drugs that target specific neurotransmitters have been developed to treat people suffering from mental illnesses.

Mapping the Brain

A variety of methods are used to diagnose brain disorders. Early neuroscientists learned about the human brain by observing the behavior of people who had brain damage. In the 1860's, for example, French surgeon Paul Broca discovered the importance of the left cerebral hemisphere in language by examining the abilities of people with damage to specific areas of the brain.

The electroencephalograph (EEG) was used in human subjects for the first time in the

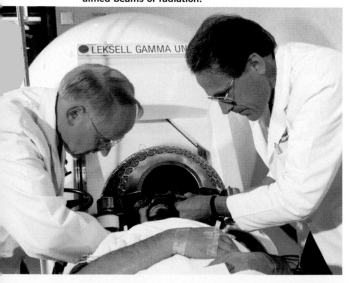

Doctors prepare a patient for entry into a machine that will destroy a life-threatening brain tumor with precisely aimed beams of radiation.

1920's by German psychiatrist Hans Berger. It is an important tool that measures the electrical activity of the brain through contacts called electrodes taped to the scalp. The EEG is still used today in sleep research and in the diagnosis of illnesses such as epilepsy.

In the 1940's and 1950's, the pioneering American-Canadian neurosurgeon Wilder Penfield applied small electrical shocks to the human brain. These shocks caused different sensations, movements, and even memories in the patients. Experiments by Penfield provided detailed maps of the workings of the cerebral cortex. These maps aid surgeons during the removal of brain tumors.

Seeing Inside the Brain

Technological advances now allow scientists to peer inside the living human brain to see the brain in action. These procedures are safe and painless. Scientists using these methods can determine which part of the brain is damaged after an injury or because of disease, and they can develop new methods to treat brain disorders. Brain imaging methods also help scientists understand normal brain behavior as well as mental illnesses such as schizophrenia and depression.

In the 1970's, researchers began using computers to help visualize the structure of the brain. **Computed tomography**, or CT, scanning (also called computerized axial tomography, or CAT, scanning) provides images of the brain formed by multiple beams of X rays that pass through the various tissues of the brain. The CT method has been used to locate brain tumors and other structural abnormalities in the brain. The structure of the brain can also be viewed using **magnetic resonance imaging** (MRI). MRI uses powerful magnets to detect small changes in the atoms of the brain and provides a more detailed view of the brain than CT can.

Unlike CT and MRI, **positron emission tomography** (PET) provides a functional image of the brain—that is, one that shows how the brain functions. During a PET scan, a small dose of a radioactive substance is injected into a person's bloodstream. Scanners around the head detect a form of radiation called gamma rays produced by the radioactive substance. Areas of the brain that contain more of the substance emit more gamma rays. Therefore, PET can be used to determine which parts of the brain are more active than other parts.

▶ UNDERSTANDING THE BRAIN

Scientists have learned a great deal about the brain. Nevertheless, some of the most basic questions about the brain remain unanswered: Why do we sleep? What is consciousness? What is the best way to treat neurological and mental disorders? How do we remember, and why do we forget? What

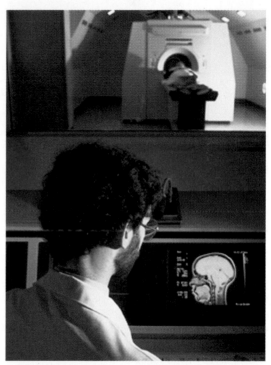

A technician looks at a computer screen showing the brain of a patient whose head is positioned inside an MRI scanner (in the background).

is the neural basis of drug addiction? These and other questions promise to challenge scientists as they attempt to understand the workings of the most complicated structure in the world: the brain.

ERIC H. CHUDLER
Editor, *Neuroscience for Kids* Web site
Research Associate Professor
University of Washington

See also BODY, HUMAN (The Nervous System); MENTAL ILLNESS; NERVOUS SYSTEM.

BRAKES. See HYDRAULIC AND PNEUMATIC SYSTEMS; RAILROADS.

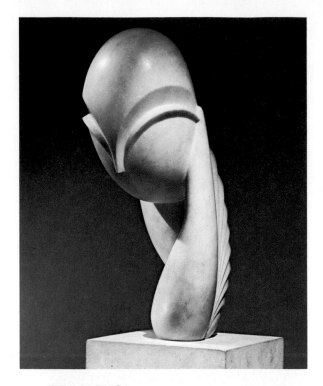

BRANCUSI, CONSTANTIN (1876–1957)

Constantin Brancusi was one of the great sculptors of the 1900's. His life was outstanding in its simplicity and devotion to art. For many years he lived alone in his studio in Paris, surrounded by his work.

Brancusi was born in a village in western Romania on February 19, 1876, the son of land-owning peasants. When he was 11 years old, he left his home to seek his fortune. He worked at odd jobs for five years and then went to Craiova.

In 1895 he entered the Craiova School of Arts and Crafts and studied sculpture for the first time. From then on, his education was paid for by scholarships and grants. He graduated from the Bucharest School of Fine Arts in 1902 and in 1905 enrolled in the École des Beaux-Arts (School of Fine Arts) in Paris. His work quickly gained respect.

Brancusi's first sculptures showed the influence of the French sculptor Rodin. Brancusi worked in Rodin's studio in 1906 but left after a short time, stating, "Nothing can grow in the shade of a great tree." His work became personal and inventive. In much of his sculpture, natural shapes are reduced to simpler forms.

He sometimes produced multiple versions of a theme—a smooth, simple egg or a bird with elegant lines—seeking to express its purest form. *Bird in Space* was one such example. Brancusi created several variations of this sculpture, in marble and bronze, over a number of years.

From 1908, Brancusi's work was almost entirely of wood or stone—carved often in large, simple shapes—and of bronze cast from the carvings and frequently polished to a mirror finish.

Brancusi died on March 16, 1957. His studio in Paris, as he left it, serves as a museum of his work.

Reviewed by MARK ROSENTHAL
Philadelphia Museum of Art

BRANDEIS, LOUIS D. See KENTUCKY (Famous People).
BRANDO, MARLON. See MOTION PICTURES (Profiles: Movie Stars).

BRANT, JOSEPH (1742–1807)

Joseph Brant was a Mohawk Indian chief and war chief of the Six Nations of the Iroquois. He is known for the help he gave the British during the Revolutionary War.

Joseph, the son of a Mohawk chief, was born in 1742 in what is now the state of Ohio. His Indian name was Thayendanegea, which means "he places two bets." When Joseph was 12, he met Sir William Johnson, the British superintendent of Indian affairs. The next year he accompanied Johnson in a French and Indian War campaign. A few years later,

Johnson sent him to school in Connecticut. Joseph became a member of the Anglican Church and began to translate religious works into the Mohawk language.

When the Revolutionary War began, Brant and most of the members of the Six Nations remained loyal to Britain. Brant received the rank of captain in the British Army. He plunged into the conflict and led Indian forces against settlements on the New York frontier. After the war he led members of the Mohawk tribe into Canada, seeking a new home for his people. The British Government granted him a large tract of land in what is now Ontario.

Brant made two trips to England and was presented to King George III. In 1793 he attended a great conference of Indian tribes. He urged the Indian people to live in peace with the settlers. But many of the tribes deserted him and continued to wage war.

Brant died on November 24, 1807. Brantford, Ontario, was named for him.

JOHN S. MOIR
University of Toronto

BRAQUE, GEORGES (1882–1963)

Georges Braque's interest in art began when he was a child in Argenteuil, France, where he was born on May 13, 1882. His father was an interior decorator and an amateur painter. Georges watched and copied his father, and art became the center of his life.

The Braque family moved to the city of Le Havre in 1890, and Georges continued to draw and paint and study. Ten years later he went to Paris, where a great revolution in art was taking place. Braque's first paintings were done in the Impressionist style, but by 1906 he was exhibiting with a new group called *les fauves* ("the wild beasts").

In 1907, Braque met the great young painter Pablo Picasso. They became close friends and for years worked together, experimenting with modern techniques. They helped develop **cubism,** a kind of painting that shows many sides of an object at once. In 1912, Braque invented *papier collé,* or **collage,** a technique of gluing scraps of paper and other objects onto a flat surface, as part of a picture.

During World War I, Braque was seriously wounded while serving in the French Army. After the war he began to work more slowly and thoughtfully. After 1917 he struck out on his own, although he continued to work with cubism, simplifying it as the years passed. He painted many still lifes, often using the table in his studio as a subject.

Braque did not limit himself to painting. He also created stage scenery, book illustrations, and sculpture. In the 1950's he designed a ceiling for the Louvre museum in Paris. Braque died in Paris on August 31, 1963.

Reviewed by PHILIP LINHARES
Director, Mills College Art Gallery

BRASS.   See BRONZE AND BRASS.
BRASS INSTRUMENTS.   See WIND INSTRUMENTS.

Le Guéridon ("The Pedestal Table") is one of several paintings by Braque using a small, round-topped table as the center of a still life.

BRAZIL

The faces of Brazil reflect the country's ethnic and cultural diversity. *Clockwise from below:* University students in Rio de Janeiro; women of Bahia state in traditional dress; a group of youngsters in São Paulo; brokers at São Paulo's stock exchange; a man from a Japanese community in São Paulo; and an Awa Gaja Indian in Maranhão state.

Brazil is one of the world's giant nations. It is the largest and most populous country in South America, containing almost half the continent's area and more than half its people. Among the nations of the world, Brazil ranks fifth in area, after Russia, Canada, China, and the United States. It ranks sixth in population.

When Portuguese traders arrived in the 1500's, they found certain trees with wood the color of live coals—*brasa* in Portuguese. They called the trees brazilwoods and named their country after them. Brazilwood yields red and purple dyes, which were highly prized in Europe for coloring cloth.

Brazil was ruled by Portugal for over 300 years before gaining its independence peacefully in 1822. Following the reign of two emperors, Brazil dissolved the monarchy in 1889. Today it is a federal republic, made up of a number of states, territories, and the federal district of Brasília, the national capital.

Brazil is a land of great variety and contrast. Vast jungles and tropical rain forests, great rivers, and mountains cover much of the interior of Brazil, while rapidly growing modern cities crowd the long coastline of the Atlantic Ocean.

▶ PEOPLE

Brazil's population is unevenly distributed. Most of its people are concentrated on the eastern edge of the country along the Atlantic coast between the Amazon River and the border with Uruguay and Argentina.

Most Brazilians are of mixed European, African, and Indian ancestry, although many people have come from Japan, the Middle East, and Europe, especially Portugal. People of mixed racial ancestry, called mestizos, are found mostly in the small towns and rural areas of the interior, although in recent decades, thousands have migrated to the cities in search of work and a better way of life. A small number of Indians still live in remote areas of the tropical rain forest.

Language. The Spanish greeting "*Buenos días*" is the way to say "good morning," "hello," or "good day" in every South American country except Brazil. In Brazil, people say "*Bom dia,*" which is Portuguese for the same greetings. Brazil is the only Portuguese-speaking nation in the Western Hemisphere. But because there are many Brazilians, Portuguese has become a major world language. Brazilian Portuguese is much like the language spoken in Portugal except that it is spoken with a different accent and intonation. A visitor from Portugal would also have to learn new words that have been added to the language by Africans and Indians.

Many educated Brazilians also speak Spanish, and many are fluent in English and French. German and Italian are spoken by several million in the southern states.

Religion. Most Brazilians are Roman Catholics. This gives Brazil the distinction of having the largest Catholic population of any nation in the world. There are also many Protestants in Brazil. In fact, Evangelical Protestants represent the country's fastest-growing religious group. Smaller numbers of Buddhists and Jews make their homes in

Brazil. An unusual mixture of African religions and Roman Catholicism known as *candomblé* is practiced by many Brazilians of African descent in the cities and the Northeast.

Education. Brazilian law requires all children to attend elementary school for at least three years. Elementary school pupils can be recognized easily by their uniforms. Boys

Above: A *candomblé* ceremony takes place in Bahia state. Many Brazilians of African descent practice *candomblé,* which is a mixture of African religions and Roman Catholicism. *Left:* Evangelical Protestants are the fastest-growing religious group in Brazil.

wear khaki or white shirts and navy-blue shorts. Girls wear navy-blue skirts and white blouses. They study Brazilian history, arithmetic, science, social studies, and Portuguese. English and French are taught as second languages in the higher grades.

Secondary school consists of four years of junior high school, called *ginásio,* and three years of senior high school, called *colégio.* Most secondary schools are privately run, and only affluent Brazilians can afford to send their children to them.

Advanced education is available at technical schools, state colleges, and at national and Catholic universities. State and federal universities charge no tuition, and admission is based on results of a nationwide competitive

Carnival is a four-day holiday celebrated in all Brazilian cities and towns. The best-known festival is held in Rio de Janeiro and draws people from all over the world.

remote villages. However, because many of the people of Brazil are under 18 years of age, more schools are needed every year.

Food and Drink. The national dish of Brazil is called *feijoada*. It contains black beans, pork sausage, tripe (stomach of cow or other cud-chewing animal), spices, and greens, and is served with rice. Brazilians also use farinha as a condiment. This is made from the root of cassava, or manioc, a tropical plant that is native to Brazil. When it is cooked and dried, people sprinkle it on soups, meat, and stews and use it as flour in bread and puddings.

Every region of Brazil has its own special foods. *Charque* (dried and salted beef) is traditional in southern Brazil. In the Northeast and along the Amazon River, fish dishes are popular. The cowboys (*gaúchos*) of the southern grasslands eat a form of barbecued beef. Oranges, pineapples, bananas, papayas, mangos, and other varieties of tropical fruit are plentiful and popular.

Coffee is Brazil's main beverage. Brazilians like to drink *cafezinhos*, tiny cups of sweet, steaming hot coffee several times a day. Another beverage is *maté*, an herbal tea. It is sometimes served in a hollowed-out gourd and drunk with a straw.

Holidays and Other Special Events. Brazilians share in the many Catholic holidays, such as saints' days, when festivals, pageants, and dances are held. The most famous of these holidays is Carnival— the four-day festival that occurs just before

Maté, an herbal tea, is a popular Brazilian beverage. In the far south, it is traditionally served in a hollowed-out gourd and sipped through a silver straw.

examination, the *vestibulário.* Students often take a year off after graduating high school to prepare for this entrance examination. Once admitted to the university, students specialize at once, choosing among schools of architecture, business, law, medicine, engineering, and humanities. Some students enter military academies; others prepare to be diplomats in Brazil's highly regarded Foreign Ministry school.

There are still not enough schools for the fast-growing population. The number of people who are able to read and write has been increased greatly through a massive government program of school construction and teacher training. In addition, adult education courses are being given in some of the larger cities. There are also mobile schools that bring teachers, books, and school supplies to

Futebol (soccer) is Brazil's national sport. Thousands of fans watch the game at Maracanã Stadium in Rio de Janeiro.

Lent. Carnival is celebrated in all Brazilian towns and cities. The best-known festival is held in Rio de Janeiro. Schools and businesses close, and the whole city is given over to parades, street dances, and masked balls. Strolling musicians play music such as samba, *marcha*, and *frevo*. Confetti and streamers fill the air. *Cariocas*, as the people of Rio are called, and tourists join in this huge citywide celebration during which no one sleeps and nearly everyone dances to the throbbing samba rhythms.

Sports. Nearly all Brazilians are sports fans. Boating, sailing, and swimming are popular activities, but Brazilians delight in a good *futebol* ("soccer") match. *Futebol* is the national sport, and every school and town has its own team. Professional soccer players are national figures in Brazil, just as baseball players are in the United States. In recent years, however, the biggest stars have left to play in Europe, although every four years they return to form the *Seleção Brasileira*, the all-star Brazilian World Cup team. Brazilians have also excelled internationally in automobile racing and yachting, as well as in basketball and volleyball.

Libraries, Museums, and the Arts. Brazil has very few public lending libraries although large cities have libraries that house both books and archives of documents. Of the country's museums, São Paulo's Museum of Modern Art has a fine collection, as does the Museum of Contemporary Art. In Rio are the National Historical Museum and National Museum of Fine Arts. The National Museum in Brasília displays historical artifacts. In Belém, at the mouth of the Amazon, the Goeldi Museum displays anthropological artifacts. Rio's Municipal Theater features opera, ballet, and concerts. Manaus, in the heart of the Amazon Basin, has an opera house that was built in the late 1800's and has been restored as a tourist site.

Urban and Rural Life. Approximately three-quarters of the people live in urban areas. Affluent Brazilians live in luxurious high-rise apartments or houses surrounded by high walls. They can afford to buy a variety of goods and almost always have maids and servants. For other city dwellers, however, the problem of poverty is severe.

Rural areas, which are mostly poor, consist of small, sleepy towns surrounded by farm-

FACTS and figures

FEDERATIVE REPUBLIC OF BRAZIL (República Federativa do Brazil) is the official name of the country.

LOCATION: Eastern South America.

AREA: 3,286,478 sq mi (8,511,965 km²).

POPULATION: 165,000,000 (estimate).

CAPITAL: Brasília.

LARGEST CITY: São Paulo.

MAJOR LANGUAGE: Portuguese (official).

MAJOR RELIGIOUS GROUP: Christian (Roman Catholic, Evangelical Protestant).

GOVERNMENT: Republic. **Head of state and government**—president. **Legislature**—National Congress (consisting of the Chamber of Deputies and the Federal Senate).

CHIEF PRODUCTS: Agricultural—soybeans, coffee, beans, rice, cassava, cacao, sugar, corn, oranges, bananas, pineapples, tobacco, cotton, livestock and livestock products. **Manufactured**—processed foods, textiles, steel, motor vehicles, chemicals, television sets, paper and other wood products. **Mineral**—iron ore, manganese, bauxite, chrome, nickel, gemstones, uranium, salt, lead, gold.

MONETARY UNIT: Real (1 real = 100 centavos).

Brazil

land on which people live in huts or tiny houses.

Although the family remains the center of everyday life in Brazil, widespread poverty has changed the ways many families are organized. Many families, especially in the *favelas*, or slums, are headed by single mothers. The pressures of crime, drugs, and economic hardship has forced thousands of children to live on the streets.

Poor families tend to have many children. The older children are given the responsibility of taking care of the smaller ones. Because of a housing shortage, many families—including cousins, aunts, uncles, and grandchildren—often live together under one roof. Middle- and upper-income families are usually smaller. Legal adoption is not widely practiced but families will sometimes take in children of relatives or neighbors whose parents cannot raise them. Fathers are traditionally heads of Brazilian households, but women are assuming increasingly important economic roles.

A farmer in Minas Gerais, in Brazil's eastern region, takes a moment to contemplate the sloped valley below him.

▶ LAND

Brazil, like all large countries, has a varied landscape. The country can be divided into uplands and lowlands. The two main upland areas—the Brazilian Highlands and the Guiana Highlands—cover more than one-half of Brazil. The three major lowland areas are the Amazon Basin, a small area in southern Brazil drained by the Rio de la Plata system, and the small area of the upper Paraguay river system in the southwest. There are not many high mountains.

Brazilians usually divide their country into five regions. These are the Northeast, the East, the South, the Central West, and the Amazon Basin. Each region contains several states.

The Northeast. In the region known as the Northeast are the states of Maranhão, Piauí, Ceará, Rio Grande do Norte, Paraíba, Pernambuco, Alagoas, Sergipe, and Bahia. This area, along the upper Atlantic coast, has rich, fertile soil, but the inland area, called the *sertão*, or "backland," is quite rocky. Many unusual plants grow in the *caatinga*, a tropical thorn forest of the Northeast. One, the carnauba palm, is found only in Brazil. Its leaves yield a widely used commercial wax.

The East. The eastern region is made up of the states of Rio de Janeiro, Espírito Santo, Minas Gerais, and São Paulo. A combination of favorable climate, rich soils, and abundant natural resources has made these states, with the exception of Espírito Santo, the richest and most important in Brazil.

The South. The three southern states are Santa Catarina, Paraná, and Rio Grande do Sul. This region consists of a narrow coastal plain and fertile, rolling grasslands in the interior. The coastline has many beautiful beaches. The Great Escarpment is a steep slope along the southern coast. Huge rolling grasslands are located in the south of this region, near Uruguay.

The Central West. Brazil's frontier states are Goiás, Mato Grosso ("Great Forest"), Mato Grosso do Sul, and Tocantins on the western plateau. This is a vast, thinly populated area. It is rich in plant and animal life.

Cattle are raised on the rolling grasslands of southern Brazil. These *gaúchos* (cowboys) are driving cattle across Brazil's border into Argentina.

Left: The Amazon River, which crosses northern Brazil, is the world's second longest river, after the Nile. The Amazon rain forest, the world's largest, is home to some of the rarest animals on Earth. *Below:* Workers unload fruit from boats in Belém, one of the few large cities on the Amazon River.

The Amazon Basin. The six states of Amapá, Acre, Amazonas, Pará, Rondônia, and Roraima are situated in this enormous basin formed by the Amazon River and its tributaries. It is a rich area filled with rain forests, jungles, and swamps. So much rain falls in the Amazon Basin that Brazilians divide the seasons into the "time of the big rains" and the "time of the little rains."

Rivers and Rain Forests. The Amazon River, which flows across northern Brazil, is the world's second longest river, after the Nile. Brazil has the world's largest tropical rain forest, the Amazon. The *selva*, or rain forest, is home to many rare forms of wildlife, including endangered butterflies, giant spiders, huge beetles, snakes, boa constrictors, and other animals. More than 1,000 different species of fish live in the river. One of these is the *pirarucú*, a codfish that often grows to 5 feet (1.5 meters) in length. Another is the piranha, a small, flesh-eating fish.

A second important river is the São Francisco River, which runs from the coast to the mountainous highlands of Minas Gerais. This river has provided a means of transportation to and from the eastern interior of Brazil.

Climate. Most of Brazil has a tropical climate. The Amazon basin is extremely humid; in Acre, near the border with Bolivia, temperatures hover near 95°F (35°C) most of the time. The climate along the Atlantic coast, however, is mild, aided by ocean breezes. South central Brazil has mild winters. In the far south, snow has fallen and there have been frosts that have killed coffee trees and other crops.

Natural Resources. Brazil's largest gold deposits and a mountain of iron ore have been discovered in Pará. The Amazon Basin also contains large reserves of bauxite (aluminum ore), copper, manganese, and tin. However, scientists fear that opening the Amazon to large-scale development would destroy the fragile balance of the tropical rain forest.

The country has tremendous iron reserves at Itabira and a wealth of industrial diamonds, aquamarines, beryls, topazes, and tourmalines elsewhere in the region.

▶ **ECONOMY**

Throughout Brazil's history, the economy has depended mainly on one product at a time. During the early years of settlement, sugar was the main export. When the soil on the sugar plantations began losing fertility, large deposits of gold were discovered. Throughout the 1700's, Brazil was gripped by "gold fever." As the profits from gold lessened, Brazil turned to agriculture again as the basis of the economy. But services, including tourism, are becoming an increasingly important part of the economy.

Services. Service industries employ many people and account for almost half of Brazil's economy. Leading service industries include education, finance, health care, domestic service, and businesses relating to tourism. Tourists come from all over the world, especially to Manaus, Salvador, and Rio de Janeiro.

Manufacturing. Brazil is the leading industrial nation in Latin America. Many foreign companies have built factories in Brazil, although most industrial plants are owned by Brazilians.

Food processing and textiles are the industrial giants. Industry is centered in São Paulo and Rio de Janeiro but is expanding rapidly in many other cities. Volta Redonda, for example, was once a tiny village. Today it has one of the largest steelworks in Latin America. The manufacture of automobiles, commercial vehicles, television sets, chemicals, and consumer goods is also growing rapidly in Brazil.

The most serious obstacle to industrial growth is the lack of mineral fuels such as coal and petroleum. The building of hydro-

Workers sort through cashew nuts in a Brazilian factory. Food processing is one of the country's most important industries.

electric plants on Brazil's rivers has helped provide electricity. The country is also turning to nuclear power as a source of energy.

Agriculture. Agricultural products are Brazil's chief export. The nation is among the world's leading producers of soybeans, coffee, cacao (the source of cocoa and chocolate), sugar, corn, cassava (manioc), oranges, bananas, pineapples, tobacco, and cotton. Cotton is grown in the South for export and in the East to supply Brazil's textile industry. Beans, rice, and cassava are grown widely for local use. Jute, used for making burlap, sacking, and twine, was introduced by Japanese immigrants. In spite of Brazil's rich agriculture, however, some foods must be imported.

Brazil is now a major cattle-raising nation. It exports large quantities of meat and other animal products. Hogs are also raised extensively, as are horses and other animals.

Mining and Forestry. Iron ore is Brazil's leading single export. Manganese, bauxite, chrome, and many other minerals are mined, and new mineral discoveries are constantly being made. Wood is cut for export and is also processed into wood pulp, paper, and other products. However, be-

An iron mine and smeltery in the Amazon rain forest. Brazil is one of the world's chief producers of iron ore, which is the country's leading single export.

made it easier for member nations to trade with one another. Many exports go to western Europe, Japan, and the United States. Brazil supplies many kinds of raw materials and consumer goods to other Latin American countries.

Transportation. Transportation in Brazil has always been difficult because the country is very large. Settlements, towns, and cities are far from one another, and mountains and forests often separate them. The Great Escarpment has made the construction of roads and rails slow. When Brazilians travel long distances, they have to travel by airplanes or buses because passenger railroads are inadequate. Roads on the coasts are good but crowded with traffic.

Air travel links all parts of Brazil. Brazil's domestic air network has become one of the world's busiest. There are many excellent harbors that are busy centers of world trade.

Communication. All major cities are linked by telephone. The country's telegraph system is being replaced by use of electronic mail.

Brazil has hundreds of radio stations. The *Globo* television network is the fourth largest in the world, and many Brazilians receive cable programs by satellite from all over the world.

▶ **MAJOR CITIES**

Brazil has many large and bustling cities.

Brasília is the chief city of the Central West as well as the national capi-

cause of the pollution problems from paper manufacturing, environmentalists are debating whether limits should be placed on this industry.

Fishing. Because meat, not fish, is a staple in the Brazilian diet, most fish is exported to other countries. Tuna, sardines, lobsters, and shrimp are caught in the Atlantic Ocean off Brazil's eastern coast.

Energy. Brazil has some offshore oil but otherwise must import petroleum. It relies on hydroelectric energy and nuclear power. The Itaipu hydroelectric power plant, on the Paraná River between Brazil and Paraguay, is one of the most powerful in the world.

Trade. Brazil sells its products to other countries to pay for imports of fuels and lubricants, machinery, chemicals, foods, and technology. Imports come mainly from western Europe, Japan, the United States, and Venezuela. Brazil is a partner with Argentina, Paraguay, and Uruguay in Mercosur, an economic common market established in 1991 that eliminated tariff barriers and

São Paulo's cathedral is located in the Praça da Sé, the oldest part of the city. São Paulo is Brazil's largest city.

Boats dot a harbor in beautiful Rio de Janeiro, Brazil's second largest city. Cone-shaped Sugarloaf Mountain rises in the background.

tal. It is considered an outstanding example of modern large-scale city planning. The city is shaped roughly like a giant airplane. The buildings of its central area are bordered by a V-shaped artificial lake.

São Paulo, in the state of São Paulo, is the chief industrial city of Latin America and the largest city in Brazil. This bustling, modern city is the center of the nation's textile industry. A separate article on São Paulo can be found in Volume S.

Rio de Janeiro, in the state of Rio de Janeiro, is considered one of the world's most beautiful cities. Its fine harbor, steep mountains, and magnificent modern apartment houses strung along the beaches and wide, tree-lined avenues have made Rio one of the most visited and most often photographed cities in the world. For more information, see the article on Rio de Janeiro that appears in Volume Q-R.

Belo Horizonte, in the state of Minas Gerais, is Brazil's third largest city and a major commercial and industrial area. Its name means "beautiful horizon" in Portuguese.

Salvador, in the state of Bahia, is one of the chief cities of the Northeast. **Forteleza**, in the state of Ceará on Brazil's northeastern coast, is a commercial center. **Nova Iguaçu**, in the state of Rio de Janeiro, is an industrial suburb of Rio de Janeiro city. **Curitiba**, in the state of Paraná, is a leading city and rivals São Paulo as a center of coffee production. **Pôrto Alegre**, is one of the leading cities in the state of Rio Grande do Sul in the South. **Recife**, in the state of Pernambuco on Brazil's eastern coast, has a flourishing port. **Belém**, in the state of Pará, is one of a few large cities on the Amazon River. **Manaus**, a free-trade port on the central Amazon, was very important during the 1800's, when the Amazonian forest was the world's leading source of natural rubber. The opera house and mosaic sidewalks of Manaus are reminders of the city's prosperous past.

Many operas and ballets are performed at the Teatro Amazonas, or Amazon Opera House, in Manaus. The opera house was built in the late 1800's.

▶ CULTURAL HERITAGE

The Portuguese brought a love of music and art from their home country that has become a vital part of Brazilian life. As the colony grew into a nation, many Brazilians won fame in the arts.

Sculpture and Painting. One of the first well-known Brazilian artists was a sculptor of the 1700's, Antonio Francisco Lisboa, who was known as O Aleijadinho—"The Little Cripple." Aleijadinho had leprosy. When he could no longer use his hands, he had his tools strapped to his wrists so that he could go on sculpting. His most famous works are the statues of the twelve prophets on the steps of a church in Congonhas do Campo, a small town in Minas Gerais. One of the statues is pictured in the article LATIN AMERICA, ART AND ARCHITECTURE OF in Volume L of this encyclopedia.

Brazilian painters only began to win worldwide fame in the 1900's. Among the best known are Emiliano di Cavalcanti, Lasar Segall, and Cândido Portinari, whose murals can be seen not only in Brazil but also at the Library of Congress in Washington, D.C., and at the United Nations headquarters in New York City.

Architecture. In the field of architecture, too, Brazilians have won international fame.

The dramatic capital city of Brasília is the work of Brazil's leading designers—the city planner Lúcio Costa, the architect Oscar Niemeyer, and the landscape architect Roberto Burle Marx.

Music and Dance. Brazilian dances and music, such as the samba, *baião*, bossa nova, and *lambada*, are known by millions all over the world. Several Brazilian musicians have won international fame. One is Antônio Carlos Gomes, a composer of the 1800's whose opera about a proud Indian is called *Il Guarany* (1870). Heitor Villa-Lobos composed more than 2,000 works based on the folk music of the Brazilian Africans and pioneers. Guiomar Novaes was a noted pianist.

Literature. Brazil has produced many distinguished writers. Joaquim Maria Machado de Assis is considered one of the greatest South American writers. His portrayals of life in Rio de Janeiro during the early 1800's are found in *Epitaph for a Small Winner* (1881), *Dom Casmurro* (1900), and *Quincas Borba* (1891).

Euclides da Cunha is another of Brazil's better-known writers. His most famous book, *Rebellion in the Backlands* (1902), is an essay on people and the land in the Northeast. Distinguished Brazilian writers of the 1900's include the poets Carlos Drummond de Andrade, Manuel Bandeira, and novelists Jorge Amado, Guimarães Rosa, Graciliano Ramos, Erico Veríssimo, Rachel de Queiroz, and Nélida Piñon. The sociologist-historian Gilberto Freyre is well known in other countries. His classic works are *The Masters and the Slaves* (1933) and *The Mansions and the Shanties* (1936).

▶ GOVERNMENT

Brazil is a federal republic, consisting of 26 states and the Federal District of Brasília. Each state has its own elected legislature and governor.

Brazil's legislative body is the National Congress, which is composed of the Chamber of Deputies and the Federal Senate. Deputies are elected, on the basis of population, for a term of four years. Senators serve 8-year terms, with three senators elected from each of the states.

From 1964 to 1985, the military controlled the government under a succession of generals, who suspended constitutional guarantees of rights. Civilian government was restored in 1985, and a new democratic constitution took effect in 1988. It provided for direct elections of a president and vice president to 6-year terms. The president is the head of both state and government.

▶ HISTORY

Brazil's earliest inhabitants were the Indians. More than one hundred native tribal groups inhabited the land. They did not plant crops, but hunted and gathered fruits and berries.

The Portuguese navigator Pedro Álvares Cabral claimed Brazil for Portugal in 1500. However, for some thirty years after Cabral's historic voyage, the Portuguese paid little attention to their new colony, and only a few trading posts grew up along the coast. Portugal's main interest still lay in trade with the Far East. But Portugal's attitude changed after 1530 for two reasons. A new source of wealth was needed, and other European powers were threatening to take Brazil.

Portuguese Settlement. The Portuguese king started the settlement of Brazil by giving favored

During a visit to the United States, Brazil's president Fernando Cardoso met with U.S. president Bill Clinton.

nobles grants that stretched far inland from the coast. The early settlers had difficulties with the Indians. The settlers also had to face a new and strange tropical environment and unfamiliar soil conditions. The large landowners soon discovered that if they were to run successful settlements, they needed more farm laborers. Black slaves were brought from Africa to work on plantations in the Northeast.

Meanwhile, in the East and the South, groups of people called *bandeirantes* roamed the interior in search of gold. They also sought Indians to sell as slaves to the plantation owners of the north. The *bandeirantes* found both gold and slaves. In doing so, they opened large regions for more exploration and settlement in the present states of Minas Gerais, Mato Grosso, Goiás, and Mato Grosso do Sul.

By the early 1800's, Brazil's first gold mines had been nearly exhausted, but a large part of the country was permanently settled. Farming was the major occupation. The descendants of the Portuguese settlers now thought of themselves as Brazilians rather than subjects of the king of Portugal.

Just as the first movements for Brazilian independence were developing, troops sent by French emperor Napoleon invaded Portugal. In 1808 the Portuguese royal family and more than a thousand members of the court fled to Brazil. For the next 14 years Rio de Janeiro was the capital of the Portuguese empire. At last, in 1821, the king returned to his native land and left his son, Dom Pedro, to rule Brazil. The next year Dom Pedro, following the advice of José Bonifácio de Andrada, his minister of the interior, declared Brazil independent of Portugal. Peaceful change became the pattern of Brazil's political life.

Independence. Brazil remained an empire from 1822 until 1889. Dom Pedro reigned for nine years, then turned over the throne to his 5-year-old son, Dom Pedro II, who became emperor in 1840 at age 14. Dom Pedro II ruled Brazil for 49 years, during which the nation became larger and richer. Wars with Argentina (1851–52) and Paraguay (1865–70) were settled peacefully. Railroads were built. Rubber from the Amazon jungle doubled foreign trade. And thousands of immigrants swelled the population.

But much of the nation's wealth depended on slavery, and economic growth ended when slavery was abolished in 1888. Many large landowners and slaveholders demanded an overthrow of the government. Others, who favored a republican form of government, also wanted change. The old emperor left Brazil, and by 1891, the Republic of Brazil had its first constitution.

The Republic. In the early years, the army ruled the republic, leading to further political upheaval and civil war. But by 1895 order had been restored and Brazil had a civilian government.

Brazil became increasingly important in world politics and fought on the side of the Allies during World War I (1914–18). But the fall of world coffee prices during the Great Depression of the 1930's brought new difficulties. In 1930 the president was overthrown, and Getúlio Vargas became dictator. He patterned his government after the fascist regimes in Italy and Portugal. Vargas encouraged a spirit of nationalism and worked to boost the economy. Under his rule, living conditions improved and trade grew. During World War II (1939–45), Brazil fought on the side of the Allies and sent troops to Italy.

The Second Republic. In 1945, the army forced Vargas to resign, and General Eurico Gaspar Dutra was elected to succeed him. But in 1950, Vargas was elected. In 1954, following a serious political crisis, Vargas took his own life. Juscelino Kubitschek de Oliveira then became president.

Kubitschek told the Brazilians that they would "enjoy in five years the progress of 50 years." He worked hard to live up to his promise. The government built a new capital in Brasília and helped develop hydroelectric plants and some industries. But inflation and falling world coffee prices brought new economic and social problems. In 1960, Jânio Quadros was elected president, but his attempts to improve conditions were blocked. He resigned within a year, and his vice president, João Goulart, took his place.

By 1964, Goulart's leftist policies had created an economic crisis. Discontent with his government led to a revolution, supported by the United States, that brought the military to power. Until 1985, Brazil's presidents all came from the armed forces. In 1985, Tancredo de Almeida Neves, a civilian, was elected president. Neves died before his inauguration, and the vice president, José Sarney, became president.

The 1989 elections were the first since 1960 in which Brazilians voted directly for the president. Fernando Collor de Mello won the presidency after a runoff election but was impeached in 1992 on charges of corruption. He resigned and was succeeded by his vice president, Itamar Franco. In 1994, Fernando Henrique Cardoso became president. He was re-elected in 1998, becoming the first president in Brazil's history to win a second term. As president he favored policies that made Brazil attractive for foreign investment while at the same time addressing some of Brazil's most pressing social needs.

Cardoso's primary challenge was to stabilize the country's failing economy. In order to avert a disaster, the International Monetary Fund (IMF) stepped in and gave $41.5 billion in emergency funds; in 1999 the government reduced the value of its currency. In 2001, Cardoso announced the launch of a $6 billion anti-poverty program that included health and education programs for the poor. But the economy worsened, and the IMF had to grant further loans. In 2002, Luiz Inácio Lula da Silva of the Worker's Party was elected president. Da Silva, popularly known as Lula, was a former factory worker and labor leader. He won the election by the largest margin in Brazil's history.

PETER O. WACKER
Rutgers, The State University of New Jersey
Reviewed by ROBERT M. LEVINE
University of Miami
Author, *Brazilian Legacies*

See also AMAZON RIVER.

BRAZING. See WELDING AND SOLDERING.

BREAD AND BAKING

Bread in some form is eaten almost everywhere in the world. It is called "the staff of life" because it can go far in meeting people's need for food, thereby supporting human life.

There are two main types of bread—flat and leavened. Flatbreads are rolled flat and either cooked to be flat or puffed with steam. They include tortillas and pitas as well as Indian naan and Jewish matzo.

Leavened breads are lighter than flatbreads because they contain a rising, or leavening, agent. They include white, whole wheat, and rye bread; muffins; and rolls. There are many other bakery products that can be considered forms of bread, such as cakes, cookies, crackers, and pretzels.

Bread is an important source of carbohydrates and protein for the body. Carbohydrates provide energy, and protein is used for building and repairing cells. Most breads also contain B vitamins and some minerals, including iron and calcium.

▶ BASIC INGREDIENTS

The majority of breads made in the United States, Canada, and western Europe are leavened products. These breads usually contain just four basic ingredients—flour, a leavening agent, salt, and water.

Flour. Bread contains more flour than any other ingredient. There are many different types of flour. Most are made from grains such as wheat, rye, barley, oats, corn, and rice. White flour is made from wheat that is milled (crushed and sifted repeatedly) until the outer covering has been completely removed.

There are three distinct components to each wheat kernel. First is the hull, or outer covering of the kernel. From the hull we get wheat bran. Second is the germ, or heart of the kernel. The germ is what sprouts to produce new wheat plants. Last is the endosperm. This is the starchy white material that makes up the largest percentage of the wheat kernel. The endosperm is the food for the germ as it sprouts and also the component that makes up white flour.

Different flours produce breads of different flavors and textures. This is because flours contain different amounts of gluten. Gluten is a protein found in the grain. When gluten comes in contact with a liquid (such as water or milk) and is pushed about by stirring or kneading, it develops long, elastic strands. The stretchable strands of gluten form an invisible

Breads come in many different shapes, sizes, textures, and flavors, but all are made with the same basic ingredients.

structure that enables a loaf of bread to hold its shape. It is because of the elastic nature of gluten (and the carbon dioxide gas trapped between the strands) that baked bread will bounce back when you poke it gently with your fingers.

Leavening Agent. Yeast was the first leavening agent, and it is still the most important. Yeast is a tiny one-celled fungus that is present all around us. It is found in the air, in the soil, and on the skins of fruits. Yeast cells feed on sugars and starches. They change the starch of the bread dough into sugar and use it for energy. As they do this, they give off carbon dioxide gas as a waste product. This chemical change is called **fermentation**. The gluten strands in the dough trap bubbles of

How to Bake a Loaf of Bread

Ingredients

5 to 6 cups all-purpose flour
3 tablespoons sugar
2 teaspoons salt
1 package dry active yeast ($2^1/_4$ teaspoons)
2 cups hot water (120°F/48°C)
3 tablespoons butter or margarine, at room temperature

Directions

In a large mixing bowl, combine 2 cups of flour, sugar, salt, and yeast.

Add the hot water to the dry ingredients and stir with a wooden spoon until a smooth batter is formed.

Add the butter or margarine and continue stirring until it is well combined.

Add 3 cups of flour, one at a time. After each addition, stir with a wooden spoon. The dough will become stiff.

Sprinkle flour on a clean countertop or table. This will be your kneading surface.

Mixing Ingredients

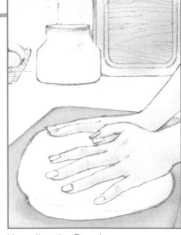

To knead the bread dough, put the dough on the kneading surface and flatten it with the palm of your hand. Pick up the edge farthest from you and fold it over the edge nearest you. Push the edges together with the heel of your hand. At the same time, push the mass of dough away from you. Then turn the dough a quarter of the way around and repeat the process.

Kneading the Dough

Knead the dough until it is smooth and has lost all its stickiness. Add more flour (up to 1 cup) if the dough is too sticky.

Letting the Dough Rise/Testing the Dough

carbon dioxide. The trapped gas expands and causes the bread to rise.

In the early days of baking, the chief source of yeast was the foam that bubbled on the tops of vats in which ale or beer was brewing. This liquid yeast is called barm. In dry form, it is known as brewer's yeast.

Today people can easily buy yeast in a supermarket. Some yeast is compressed into tiny blocks, or cakes. Other yeast, called dry active yeast, is sold as a powder in small packets for the home baker. These little beads of yeast have had all the moisture removed and remain in a dormant (sleeping) state until they come in contact with warm water. There is also fresh (non-compressed) yeast that is sold primarily to commercial bakeries.

Breads leavened by yeast are called yeast breads. Those leavened by other agents are often called quick breads because they can be baked immediately, without waiting for fermentation to take place. Baking powder is one leavening agent used in quick breads. The active ingredients in baking powder are baking soda and an acid such as tartaric acid (cream of tartar). When the baking powder is moistened, the baking soda reacts with the acid to form carbon dioxide gas. The carbon dioxide is released, resulting in a dough that is light and airy. Just as yeast causes bread dough to rise, this chemical reaction causes the batter to increase in volume as well. Baking powder is used mostly in cookies, biscuits, and pretzels. It makes these baked goods rise just enough to be light and crumbly.

Another leavening agent is a mixture of baking soda and an acidic food, such as buttermilk, molasses, or lemon juice. This mix-

Put the kneaded dough into a large buttered bowl. Cover the bowl with plastic wrap or a clean kitchen towel and place the bowl in a warm, humid place, away from any cold drafts.

Let the dough rise until it has doubled in bulk. To test when the dough is ready, gently press the tips of two fingers about 1/2-inch (1 centimeter) into the dough. Remove your fingers, and if the indentation remains, the dough is ready for the next steps. If not, allow the dough to rise a bit longer.

Baking the Loaves

Releasing the Gas

To release the retained gas, press down on the dough with a clean hand or fist.

Divide the dough in half. Place each half in a buttered loaf pan. Cover the pans and allow the dough to rise again until doubled in volume.

Preheat an oven to 350°F (177°C). (Ask an adult to help you use the oven.) When the dough in the pans has risen, place the pans in the preheated oven and bake for 45 minutes, or until the loaves are golden brown. Remove the bread from the oven. Allow the loaves to cool and remove from the pans.

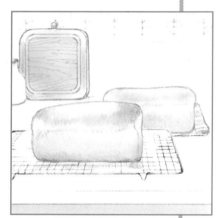

The Finished Loaves

ture is often used in making muffins and other quick breads.

Salt. Salt is an important ingredient in most baked goods. Salt enhances the flavor of the product. Baked goods prepared without salt usually taste flat and "tinny." In yeast breads, salt slows down the fermentation process. This gives the baker better control over the flavor and texture of the bread.

Liquids and Fats. For plain, ordinary bread, water is the only liquid required. A dough made only with water is called a **lean dough**. Because of its fat content, milk is sometimes used in addition to, or instead of, water. The fat in milk creates a richer-tasting loaf with a softer crust. For this reason, milk is often the preferred liquid for making sweet rolls, muffins, cakes, and cookies.

To make a rich dough, butter, margarine, vegetable shortening, or lard (rendered ani-mal fat) is added. These ingredients are called shortenings because they make the gluten strands "short," or not as elastic. A short dough will be crisp and flaky like a pie dough.

Other Ingredients. The great variety of baked goods results from the many other ingredients that can be added to the basic dough. Sugar has several functions in baked goods. It adds a sweet flavor; it attracts moisture from the air, which helps keep the baked good moist; and it aids in the browning of the crust. Sugar also provides extra food for yeast cells and speeds up their manufacture of carbon dioxide.

Eggs are used in breads such as challah and brioche and in many festive breads and cakes. Eggs add to the richness of the dough. Whole eggs, yolks, or egg whites may be used. Angel food cake calls only for egg whites.

The whites are beaten until they are stiff. Then they are carefully folded into the cake batter. Because beaten whites contain many little pockets of air, they help to create a very light cake.

Nuts and dried fruits are often included in breads, coffee cakes, and holiday cakes. The candied peel of citrus fruits such as lemons and oranges is often added as well. Sometimes fresh fruits are mixed into a dough—banana bread is an example. Finely ground nuts may be mixed with flour for an especially moist cake or quick bread with a nutty flavor. Spices such as caraway, dill, cumin,

Sugar cookies are made by rolling out a dough and cutting shapes using cookie cutters. Dipping the cookie cutters in flour helps keep them from sticking to the dough.

fennel, and anise are often used to give baked goods a particular flavor. Sweet spices such as cinnamon, cloves, nutmeg, and allspice are used in breads and cakes.

▶ **MAKING YEAST BREAD**

Two common ways of making yeast bread are the sponge method and the straight dough method. The method used by the baker will determine the final flavor, texture, and shelflife of the bread. In the sponge method, the yeast is first **proofed** (mixed) with some or all of the water and a portion of the flour. This mixture is called a sponge, *biga* (Italian), or *poolish* (French), depending on the proportions of water and flour that are used. The sponge is allowed to ferment before the remaining ingredients are added. In the straight dough method, the yeast is first proofed with the warm water, and then the remaining ingredients are added before any fermentation is allowed to start. With either method, several steps remain after the ingredients are combined—kneading the dough, letting it rise, releasing the trapped gas, allowing the dough to rise again, and baking the bread.

Kneading is the process of pushing and folding the dough to work it into a smooth, uniform texture and fully develop the elasticity of the gluten. For the gluten to develop properly, most breads made at home require about 8 to 10 minutes of kneading by hand. The time will vary depending on the type of flour used. Some home bakers also use electric mixers or specially equipped food processors to handle the kneading process.

Next the dough is allowed to rise until it has roughly doubled in volume. The dough should be placed in a warm location that is free from drafts. An ideal spot is an unheated gas oven. (The interior of an electric oven is cool and does not serve the purpose well.) The dough is covered with a clean, dry kitchen towel or plastic wrap. This prevents a dry crust from forming on the surface of the dough.

Depending on the recipe and the amount of yeast used, the initial rise will take from one hour to close to 24 hours. After the dough has finished the first rise, it is necessary to release the gas trapped within it by pressing down gently. The process of degassing the dough improves the uniformity of the final product and strengthens the gluten. Then the dough is transferred to a pan, covered again, and allowed to rise a second time.

Baking is the final stage in the breadmaking process. The dough is placed in a preheated oven either in a bread pan, on a sheet pan, or on a baking stone. To ensure even baking, it is important that the bread be heated evenly from all sides.

The heat of the oven gives the yeast its last chance to work, and most loaves will rise 10 to 15 percent within the first few minutes of baking. The yeast is killed when the internal temperature of the loaf reaches 130°F (54°C). As it takes longer for the center of the loaf to reach that temperature, most baked breads have a rounded top.

Some home bakers use bread machines to make bread. Bread machines automate the bread-making process. Once the ingredients are added to a pan and the machine is turned on, it mixes the ingredients, kneads the dough, allows it to rise, and bakes the bread.

▶ MANUFACTURING BREAD

Today the vast majority of bread eaten in the United States is produced commercially. In large industrial bakeries, the entire bread-making process is automated. Every day, machines run by computers mix thousands of pounds of flour into dough. Machines also divide the dough into pieces of the desired weight, shape it into loaves or rolls, and put it onto or into baking pans. Then conveyor belts move the dough from rising to baking to cooling without the direct involvement of human hands.

In contrast, a small but growing percentage of baked goods are produced by artisanal (traditional) baking methods. These baked goods are produced with time-honored traditions of longer fermentation, more individuality, and more specialized ingredients. The artisanal bakeries have a different focus from that of industrial bakeries. Their emphasis is on quality and healthiness rather than mass production and sameness.

At both industrial bakeries and artisanal bakeries, the actual baking takes place in large ovens. These are not typical household ovens; they can bake hundreds of loaves at a time. Larger industrial bakeries use tunnel ovens, where the bread enters the oven on a conveyor belt as raw dough and exits on the other end of the tunnel as a fully baked loaf. The larger artisanal bakeries are now using a specialized version of these tunnel ovens, but most still bake on the traditional stone or brick hearth.

▶ HISTORY OF BREADMAKING

Perhaps the most fascinating part of bread-making is its history. No one knows for sure when people first began to make bread. But many scholars believe that bread was first

Industrial bakeries use conveyor belts to move large numbers of bagels and other breads from one stage of the bread-baking process to another.

made more than 10,000 years ago, in the Middle East. About that time, people made a thick porridge of crushed wheat or barley and water. They shaped the mixture into flat disks, and then these disks were baked in ashes or on hot stones. These were the earliest flatbreads.

The first leavened bread was likely made by accident as a result of the beer brewing process, about 6000 B.C. As the brewers were working with a wild form of yeast to make their beverages, some of the yeast may have fallen into a mixture of crushed grain and water that was left out longer than usual. It is likely that basic fermentation began to take place before it was baked, thus producing a bread that was unlike any that had been baked before.

The Greeks were the master bakers of antiquity; they had more than 70 different recipes for bread. The Romans turned baking into a large-scale industry and passed many laws governing the quality and production of bread. The first bakers' guilds were formed by the Romans, as were the first price controls on the sale of bread.

White bread was the bread of the rich and privileged in Europe during the Middle Ages. It was more expensive than dark breads because the grain required more milling, sifting, and so on. Dark, sour breads were eaten by the remainder of the population. This continued to be so until the late 1700's, when the Industrial Revolution brought many changes and advances in baking. Large bread factories took the place of neighborhood bakeries. As standards of living rose and wheat became more abundant, people began to demand more refined bread. They thought that whiter bread was better in quality than dark bread. This is not true, however. The milling that produces white flour removes most of the vitamins and minerals naturally present in wheat. Since 1940, most white bread baked in the United States has been enriched with vitamins and minerals, thus replacing what was lost during the milling process. In recent decades, many people have again begun eating whole grain breads for their health benefits. Whole grain breads contain more fiber than white breads. Unlike vitamins, fiber lost during the milling process is not replaced in white breads.

▶ OTHER BAKED GOODS

Cookies, crackers, and pretzels do not look or taste alike, but they are alike in many ways. All are small and crisp, and they keep well. Each is made with the same basic ingredients—flour, a leavening agent, shortening, and liquid. Baking powder is the predominant leavening agent used.

Part of the fun of eating cookies is their shape. The dough for some cookies is simply dropped by the spoonful onto a baking sheet. They are referred to as drop cookies. For other cookies, the dough is rolled out into a thick or thin sheet, depending on the variety. The baker then uses cookie cutters of various shapes to cut out pieces of dough. These cut pieces are then placed on the baking sheet and baked. Still other varieties of cookies are made by forcing the dough through a nozzle-shaped container called a cookie press to create a unique design.

Crackers appeared in the United States about 1860. Generally, every grocery store had a cracker barrel filled with square soda crackers or round butter crackers. These grocery stores were traditionally one of the popular centers of social life in small towns during the 1800's and early 1900's. The people who gathered there to exchange news, opinions, and gossip were called cracker-barrel philosophers.

Pretzels date back to the early Christians in the Roman Empire. At that time, pretzels were used solely for religious purposes. Fat, milk, and eggs were forbidden during the Lenten season, and people ate dry pretzels instead of bread during this time. It was only in modern times that pretzels became snacks on which to nibble. In northern Europe and Scandinavian countries, the pretzel has become the sign of the baker. A large golden pretzel is usually seen hanging outside each bakery.

Other baked goods have interesting histories as well. The croissant was developed as an expression of gratitude. According to legend, a baker alerted the military forces of Vienna to the approach of the Turks in the Siege of 1683. The curved shape of the modern croissant was intended to commemorate the Viennese victory because the Turkish flag bears a crescent on it.

The size, shape, and contents of baked goods are forever changing. The basic ingredients of flour, a leavening agent, water, and salt can produce a long crusty loaf of French bread, a soft roll, a crispy pretzel, or a crunchy cracker. Knead in a little olive oil for pizza dough. Leave out the leavening agent, add some butter, and you have a flaky pie pastry. Stir in a few eggs, some sugar and spice, and you have a pound cake. Any way you slice it, this is our daily bread.

LORNA J. SASS
Author, *To the King's Taste*
Reviewed and updated by PETER FRANKLIN
Chairman of the Board
Bread Bakers Guild of America

See also FLOUR AND FLOUR MILLING; FOOD; GRAIN AND GRAIN PRODUCTS; WHEAT.

BRECKINRIDGE, JOHN C. See VICE PRESIDENCY OF THE UNITED STATES.

BRECKINRIDGE, MARY. See KENTUCKY (Famous People).

BRENNAN, WILLIAM J. See NEW JERSEY (Famous People).

BRENT, MARGARET. See MARYLAND (Famous People).

BRETT, GEORGE. See BASEBALL (Great Players).

BREYER, STEPHEN G. See SUPREME COURT OF THE UNITED STATES (Profiles).

BREZHNEV, LEONID (1906–1982)

Leonid Ilyich Brezhnev was the leader of the Soviet Union from 1964 until his death. He was the first Soviet leader to be head of state and head of the Communist Party at the same time.

Brezhnev was born in Dneprodzerzhinsk (formerly the village of Kamensk) in the Ukraine, on December 19, 1906. His father was an ironworker. Brezhnev's education exposed him to the two fields in which Communist Party leaders usually have some working knowledge—industry and agriculture. He studied first at a boys' secondary school. Later, at an agricultural school, he learned surveying. He graduated from a technical institute as a metallurgical engineer.

Brezhnev's rise in the Communist Party followed the same pattern as that of Nikita Khrushchev, who was party chief before him. Brezhnev became a member of the Young Communist League in 1923 and joined the party in 1931. He attended party schools and gained experience in agricultural and industrial positions in various parts of the country. He worked in the Ukraine with Khrushchev, who was in charge of reorganizing the party there. He was a political officer in the Red Army during World War II.

After the war Brezhnev held several high-level party positions. From 1953 to 1957, he directed an effort to open the dry regions of Soviet Central Asia to farming. When he returned to Moscow, he was named to the party's ruling Presidium. In 1960 he became chairman of the Presidium of the Supreme Soviet (head of state of the Soviet Union). This position is less powerful than that of general secretary of the Communist Party.

Brezhnev was involved in Khrushchev's dismissal in October, 1964. He had resigned his position as head of the Presidium earlier that year, and he replaced Khrushchev as party general secretary. He later strengthened his leadership. A constitution adopted in 1977 elevated the office of head of state, which he resumed and held with his party job. He died on November 10, 1982, in Moscow.

In his domestic policies, Brezhnev favored the military, and he built up Soviet forces. He also tried to improve production in industry and agriculture. He pushed some projects—such as the Baikal-Amur Mainline railroad, in Siberia—despite difficulties in construction.

Brezhnev showed both a mailed fist and a silk glove in dealing with Eastern Europe. In 1968, reform programs in Czechoslovakia seemed to threaten Soviet control there. He ordered Soviet troops to invade Czechoslovakia and dismiss its liberal leaders. The reason given was that the interests of the Soviet bloc outweighed the right to self-rule of any member country. (This policy became known as the Brezhnev Doctrine.) In contrast, when riots broke out in Poland in 1970 and 1976, Brezhnev ensured that the party leader was removed in the first case and that food prices were lowered in the second. But Soviet pressure encouraged the Polish Government to declare martial law in 1981, after workers had formed independent unions and demanded more political freedom.

Under Brezhnev, the Soviets remained on unfriendly terms with China. They gave aid to pro-Communist forces in other countries. In 1979, Soviet troops entered Afghanistan to support a Communist government.

Brezhnev expressed a policy of détente (easing tension) with the West. The Soviets negotiated on arms control. In 1975, they joined in talks in Helsinki, Finland, that set goals of peace, security, and justice for Europe, the United States, and Canada. But relations with the West were often strained.

ROBERT H. DODGE
Washington and Jefferson College

BRICKS AND MASONRY

Brick is one of the most common and useful building materials. It is also one of the oldest. Bricks are made of fired (baked) clay and can be used to build almost any type of structure.

Early forms of brick were sun-baked and were not as durable as fired bricks. Bricks have been made in many sizes and shapes since they were first used almost 10,000 years ago. At the present time, the standard brick in the United States is a rectangular block measuring about 2¼ inches (5.7 centimeters) thick by 3¾ inches (9.5 centimeters) wide by 8 inches (20 centimeters) long. Bricks are produced in many other sizes, as well as in some special shapes, including curved and sloped brick.

Bricks range in color from nearly white, through tan, red, and red-brown, to dark purple. The color is determined by the type of clay used as well as the amount of iron and other impurities in it. The method of firing is also a factor. Generally, the higher the firing temperature, the darker the brick. Bricks, like pottery, may also be glazed in various colors. Finally, coatings and mechanically applied textures can also change the color and appearance of the brick.

Bricks are extremely durable. Ordinary brick can stand the direct flames of a fire with little damage, and refractory brick (a special brick used for lining fireplaces and furnaces) can stand temperatures as high as 4000°F (2200°C). Because brick is not easily damaged by acids, it resists the chemicals created by air pollution and various industrial processes better than some kinds of stone and painted metal.

The strength of brick also varies a great deal. Brick has high compressive strength; that is, it can withstand forces that press in on it. The average brick can take a load of about 10,000 pounds (4,500 kilograms) a square inch before it is crushed. Several types of brick can stand a load as high as 20,000 pounds (9,000 kilograms) a square inch. However, brick does not have tensile strength—it cannot withstand forces that tend to pull it apart.

▶FROM CLAY TO BRICK

Bricks are made from clay, which is a common mineral substance. Some types of clay are formed by the disintegration of rocks by weathering. Other types of clay were formed during the Ice Age by the action of glaciers grinding boulders to fine powder. Clay is found over most of the earth's surface, often in lake beds and riverbeds. It is frequently mixed with other substances, such as sand and silt. Clay becomes slippery and plastic (easily molded) when it is wet. When it is dry, it becomes hard and stony.

Workers in Madagascar set bricks out to dry in the sun. Most modern bricks are machine-formed and baked at high temperatures in large ovens.

When clay is heated to about 850°F (450°C), it changes chemically so that it no longer becomes plastic when it is wet. This means that bricks of fired clay will not soften and lose their shape when they become wet, and a wall made of these bricks will not collapse into a sticky heap during a heavy rain. Bricks are baked, or burned, at 1600 to 2200°F (870 to 1200°C). At about 1000°F (540°C) the brick turns from greenish gray to its matured color (for example, red, buff, or white).

Until the 1800's bricks were made by hand. In one common method clay was dug up from the ground and exposed to the air from fall to spring. After the clay was thoroughly dried, the brickmaker spread a small quantity of it on the ground, added a little water, and mixed it into a paste. He pressed the mixture into wooden forms, or molds, which gave the bricks the correct size and shape. Then he removed the sides of the mold and laid the moist brick on the ground to be dried and hardened by the sun. In biblical times chopped straw was usually mixed with the clay to help hold it together.

Because rain might slow up the process or even ruin the soft clay, brickmakers realized that they had to find a better process of drying. As early as 2500 B.C. the technique of baking the brick in ovens, or kilns, was being used in Mesopotamia and India. (Sun-dried bricks, or adobe, are still used in regions where it seldom rains.)

Over the centuries a number of different types of kilns were invented. In older types of kilns only one batch of brick could be made at one time. Most bricks today are made in continuous kilns. Continuous kilns are designed so that they can turn out bricks 24 hours a day, all year long, if necessary. The tunnel kiln, a heated tunnel through which the bricks are pushed or pulled slowly on small railroad cars, is a leading type of continuous kiln.

A mason places a brick in a bed of wet mortar and taps it into place with the handle of his trowel. Mortar holds bricks together and makes the wall watertight.

Some Brick Bonds

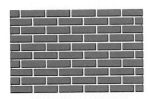

Running bond — stretchers (bricks' long sides) are laid in overlapping courses

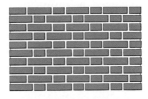

Flemish bond — stretchers and headers (bricks' short sides) alternate in each course

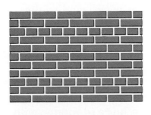

Common, or American, bond — a headers course is placed at every sixth stretcher course

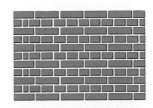

English bond — a course of stretchers and a course of headers alternate up the wall

Herringbone bond — often used for paving; bricks may be laid flat or on edge

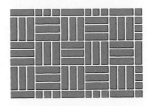

Basketweave bond — used for paving; bricks may be laid flat or on edge

391

Stonemasons carefully select rocks and fit them into this dry stone wall (built without mortar). Strings are used as guides for building the wall straight and level.

Basically the manufacture of bricks has changed little since ancient times, except that machines now perform most of the tasks that were once done laboriously by hand. The clay is now dug by power shovels. After drying, it is ground in power-driven mills and screened to get particles of uniform size.

In the **stiff-mud** process the clay is mixed with water into a stiff paste and then forced out under pressure through nozzles called **dies**. As it comes out, the clay resembles a giant square-cornered strip of toothpaste. The strip is automatically cut into pieces of the proper size by knives or wires. The soft "green" brick is then dried in heated holding areas. Finally the brick is carried on small, flat railroad cars through the kilns for firing.

The **soft-mud** process is older than the stiff-mud process. More water is mixed with the clay than in the stiff-mud process. This produces a softer paste. The soft paste is shaped in individual molds either by machine or by hand. The soft-mud process is usually slower than the stiff-mud process and is used to produce bricks that cannot be formed by other brick-making methods.

In the **dry press** process the ground-up clay is moistened with just enough water to hold it together. Powerful hydraulic presses squeeze the clay into brick shape. Bricks made by this method are as durable as bricks made by the stiff-mud process and usually shrink very little during the drying process. This process is used to make most refractory brick.

▶**MASONRY**

Masonry is the name for walls, pillars, arches, and other structures made by laying bricks, stone blocks, and other stonelike materials, such as concrete blocks, in a cementing material called **mortar**.

Long ago, primitive people discovered that they could pile naturally occurring stones together to make a rough wall. Later came the idea of trimming the stones so that they would fit together better. This made a firmer and more solid wall. At about the same time, people in regions where stone was scarce discovered how to turn clay into artificial stones—bricks. Bricks were easy to handle and build with because they were the same size and shape and did not need trimming to fit together. An important step in the development of masonry was taken when builders learned that they could use various materials to cement bricks or stone blocks together. In this way they could build rigid walls and more complicated structures, such as arches and vaults.

Brick Masonry

To make a rigid wall of brick, individual bricks are laid together in horizontal layers, or **courses**. The bricks are bound together with mortar.

The mason spreads a layer of mortar with a wide, flat tool called a trowel. The bricks are set on the mortar and pressed down lightly. If a brick is out of line, it is tapped gently into place with the handle of the trowel. Mortar is

Some Stonework Patterns

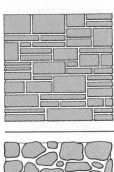

Examples of ashlar masonry

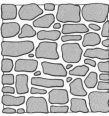

Examples of rubble masonry

also placed between each brick in a course. When the first course is laid, the mason spreads mortar on top of it and lays the second course on this mortar. This process is repeated until the wall is built.

It is important to make each course level and the wall straight. An uneven wall is not only unsightly but weak. The mason uses a straight level to make sure that the bricks are set level in the mortar. A plumb line (a string with a weight at one end) is used as a vertical guideline. A string stretched tightly from one end of the wall to the other helps the mason line up the bricks horizontally.

The thin horizontal and vertical layers of mortar between the bricks are called the **joints**. The early masons learned that they could build a stronger wall by staggering the joints, or overlapping the bricks so that the vertical joints of one course do not line up with the joints of the course below. The different arrangements or patterns in which the bricks are laid are called **bonds**. A brick laid so that its long end is exposed to view is called a **stretcher**; a brick laid with its short end exposed is called a **header**. Many builders use brick as a facing, or veneer, over the wooden frames of houses and the concrete or steel frames of large buildings.

Stone Masonry

Stones vary widely in size, shape, and composition. The two main types of modern stonework are **ashlar** and **rubble**. Ashlar masonry is constructed of cut and squared stones. They may be set in regular courses, similar to brick, or in random courses where different sizes of stone are used. Rubble masonry is composed of rough, irregularly shaped stones. Rubble stones are usually set in random patterns.

A person who works with stone is called a stonemason. The stonemason's work is more difficult and exacting than the bricklayer's. The stones have rough, jagged edges. To get a smooth surface, the stonemason trims off the projections. This is called dressing the stone and requires experience and skill.

Setting the stones in place in the walls is an art in itself. Because building stones are usually cut in large sizes (to save labor in trimming), they are very heavy. For example, a granite block 6 feet (1.8 meters) long by 3 feet (0.9 meter) wide by 1 foot (0.3 meter) thick weighs about 3,060 pounds (1,377 kilograms) —more than a ton and a half.

Obviously, such stones are too heavy to lay by hand. They must be lifted by powerful derricks and guided into place by the stone setter as they are gently lowered. If the stone is out of line, it cannot simply be tapped into line like a brick. It must be lifted up and lowered into place again.

Stone, like brick, was once a major structural material. It was used where great strength and weight were required, as in dams, bridges, fortresses, foundations, and important buildings. Today steel and concrete have taken the place of stone as a basic construction material. However, stone is still important as sheathing (outside covering) for buildings, as flooring

Built some 4,500 years ago, the Great Pyramid, in Egypt, contains more than 2 million close-fitting stone blocks averaging 2.5 tons (2.3 metric tons) each.

where there is heavy traffic, and for many decorative uses. It is valued for its many colors and textures.

▶ **HISTORY OF MASONRY**

The history of masonry goes back as far as that of civilization. Archaeologists have unearthed bricks that authorities have dated as 9,000 to 10,000 years old. These bricks were discovered at the site of an ancient settlement beneath the biblical city of Jericho. The Old Testament of the Bible contains the earliest written record of brick making.

In Egypt brick making began about 3100 B.C. Although the Egyptians had vast supplies of fine building stone, it took so much labor to quarry the stone, cut it to size, and transport it

to the building sites that stone was used only for temples, palaces, and monuments. Ordinary buildings were made of sun-baked brick.

From Egypt brick making spread to other countries around the Mediterranean Sea. The Romans became the master brickmakers of ancient times. Roman bricks were relatively thin and broad, and they were made in a variety of different shapes: rectangular, square, triangular, and semicircular.

One of the biggest problems faced by builders in the ancient world was the lack of a strong mortar to bind their bricks and stones together. Despite this, ancient builders constructed some remarkable brick temples and palaces, with walls 10 to 20 feet (3 to 6 meters) thick. The builders depended mainly on the weight of the walls to hold the bricks in place.

Masonry construction was revolutionized by the Roman discovery of concrete in the 100's B.C. With this strong cementing material, builders no longer needed to make their walls enormously thick to keep them from toppling over. In fact, the Romans' concrete was so strong that most important Roman buildings were made of concrete with a thin decorative facing of brick or stone.

Perhaps the most famous examples of ancient stone masonry are the pyramids of Egypt, some of which are more than 4,500 years old. These huge stone structures were built as tombs for rulers of ancient Egypt.

Other ancient civilizations besides the Egyptians developed great skill in handling very large blocks of stone. The Myceneans, who lived in central Greece between 2100 and 1300 B.C., built fortifications and tombs of rough stone blocks that weighed several tons apiece. The Greeks became the master stone workers of the ancient world. They were especially skilled at designing and trimming stone blocks.

The Gothic cathedrals of the late Middle Ages are the most complex structures in pure stone ever attempted. The skill of those who built these cathedrals has never again been equaled.

CARL W. CONDIT
Coeditor, *Technology and Culture*
Reviewed by CHARLES N. FARLEY
The Brick Institute of America

See also ARCHITECTURE; BUILDING CONSTRUCTION; CEMENT AND CONCRETE.

BRIDGER, JIM. See WYOMING (Famous People).

Bridges allow easy passage across rivers and other obstacles. In a city like Pittsburgh, Pennsylvania, bridges are lifelines, allowing people and goods to move into and out of the downtown area.

BRIDGES

Imagine life without bridges. Even the smallest river would be a barrier to travel and trade. To cross a broad river we would have to wade across or wait for a ferry boat. To cross a steep canyon would require trudging down one side and climbing slowly up the other. Before bridges were built, cars and trains lined up at busy crossings, waiting for traffic going in other directions.

There are more than 500,000 bridges in the United States today. Most of them are designed to carry automobile or railroad traffic, but some are intended for pedestrians only. Without bridges we would not have a modern system of highways and railroads. Most bridges are so short that they do not have names, and most travelers do not even notice going over them. There are some bridges, however, that are famous for their length, for their outstanding design, and for their beauty.

▶TYPES OF BRIDGES

A bridge must be strong enough to support its **load**, which includes its own weight as well as that of any traffic it may carry. It must have the stiffness and stability to withstand natural forces such as temperature changes, wind, and earthquakes. A bridge must also stand up to corrosion caused by moisture, polluted air, and road salt.

People have developed a variety of structures that meet these requirements. These structures include beam bridges, truss bridges, arch bridges, cantilever bridges, suspension bridges, cable-stayed bridges, and movable bridges. When deciding which kind of bridge to build, engineers consider how far the bridge must span, how deep in water or earth they must go to find solid support, and how much traffic the bridge must carry. These considerations help them choose the type of bridge and the right materials.

Beam and Truss Bridges. The simplest way to bridge a stream or other obstacle is to lay a beam across the stream so its two ends rest on opposite banks. The first bridges were probably natural bridges formed by fallen trees.

The beam may be made of wood, steel, or concrete reinforced with steel. Beam bridges resting on **abutments** (supports at each end of the bridge) are used to span fairly short distances. Longer beam bridges have additional supports, called **piers** and **trestles**, between the abutments.

Beam bridges are simple and relatively inexpensive to build. They can be found on most highways and expressways, where they are widely used at crossings.

Left: A familiar example of a beam bridge is the highway or expressway overpass. Bridged crossings permit automobile traffic to flow in different directions without stopping at intersections.

Bottom left: This long truss bridge is really a series of shorter truss bridges connected end to end. Trusses—strong triangular frameworks—can help support a bridge from above or below the roadway.

Beam   Truss

Adding a framework called a truss to a beam bridge creates a **truss bridge**. The parts of a truss are connected in a series of triangles. The truss may lie under the bridge **deck** (roadway). Or large truss arrangements may extend above both sides of the bridge deck. Truss bridges are used to span longer distances than beam bridges. Timber trusses helped support wooden covered bridges built in the 1800's.

Arch Bridges. Bridge builders can span greater distances with arch bridges than they can with beam or truss bridges. The roadway can be built above the gracefully curved arch (a **deck-arch bridge**) or be suspended from it (a **through-arch bridge**). Foundations support the load of the arch, which pushes outward and downward on them.

Arch bridges have been constructed of stone, brick, timber, cast iron, steel, plain concrete, and reinforced concrete. The construction of beautiful stone masonry arch bridges reached a peak in the early 1900's, but they are rarely built anymore. Almost all modern arch bridges are constructed of steel, reinforced concrete, or timber.

Most of the great Roman bridges were supported on arches. In the city of Rome alone, six of the eight arch bridges built over the Tiber River almost 2,000 years ago are still standing.

Cantilever Bridges. In its simplest form, a cantilever is a beam that extends or projects beyond its vertical support. A wall bracket is a familiar example of a cantilever. When secured firmly at one end (bolted to the wall), a wall bracket can support a heavy weight. To make a bridge, two cantilevers are ordinarily built projecting toward each other from opposite sides of a waterway. Each cantilever rests on a pier and is anchored to the waterway bank behind the pier. The cantilevers do not meet until they are connected in the center by a truss.

The Forth Rail Bridge in Scotland, opened in 1890, is a cantilever bridge constructed of enormous steel tubes. Some of the tubes are 12 feet (3.7 meters) in diameter. More recently, very strong reinforced concrete has been used to build cantilever bridges.

Suspension Bridges. All of the world's longest and many of the best-known bridges are suspension structures. Suspension bridges are built to span the longest distances—more than 4,600 feet (1,400 meters) between support towers. And with their tall towers and swooping cables, suspension bridges are among the most beautiful bridges.

All suspension bridges have three common parts: towers, anchorages, and cables. The majestic towers are built on firm foundations near either shore. Some stand more than 700 feet (210 meters) above the water.

The anchorages are placed on land at each end of the bridge and are where the main cables are secured. The cables may be anchored in bedrock or huge blocks of reinforced concrete. The anchorages hold the main cables against tremendous forces.

The main cables themselves are made of thousands of strong steel wires bound together. From one anchorage, the cables soar to the top of a tower, then swoop gracefully almost to road level and back up to the top of the next tower. Finally, they swoop down again to the end anchorages.

Once the main cables are in place, smaller support cables are attached to them. These support cables, called **suspenders**, hold up the framework for the roadway.

The first primitive suspension bridges were probably made with vines in a tropical region. Ropes replaced vines as civilization progressed. Bridges were later supported by wrought-iron chains strung over towers. Eventually, cables made of woven strands of iron or steel were developed, making possible the construction of modern suspension bridges.

The first modern suspension bridges were introduced by the German-American engineer

Left: The Sydney Harbour Bridge in Australia supports its roadway by a graceful steel arch. The roadway of an arch bridge can run through the arch or sit completely above it.

Below: The Forth Rail Bridge—a massive cantilever structure in Scotland—crosses the Firth of Forth, an inlet of the North Sea. The spans of a cantilever bridge project toward one another from piers and are connected by shorter truss spans.

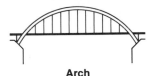

Arch

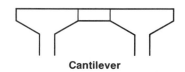

Cantilever

Suspension bridges span the greatest distances. The Golden Gate Bridge reaches across California's San Francisco Bay, stretching 4,200 feet from tower to tower. The roadway is supported by two heavy steel cables that are attached to both shores and hung across both towers.

John A. Roebling. Although Roebling had built earlier suspension bridges, the Brooklyn Bridge in New York City, completed in 1883, was his masterpiece. With its beautifully designed stone towers, the Brooklyn Bridge was one of the first all steel-cable suspension bridges. Its main span of 1,595 feet (486 meters) also made it longer than any bridge previously built.

Roebling never saw the Brooklyn Bridge completed. In 1869, before construction even began, he died following an accident. The work of building the bridge was taken over by his son, Washington A. Roebling. The younger Roebling devoted his life to the bridge's construction for the next 14 years.

Suspension bridge designs, construction techniques, and materials have improved greatly since Roebling's time. Today suspension bridges can be built with main spans nearly three times longer than the main span of the Brooklyn Bridge. The Humber Bridge over the Humber River in England, opened in 1981, holds the record for the world's longest single span—4,626 feet (1,410 meters).

Cable-Stayed Bridges. Dramatic new cable-stayed bridge designs look like suspension bridges. Both types of bridges have towers and cable-suspended roadways. But on a cable-stayed bridge, the cables supporting the roadway run straight from the towers to the bridge deck. The cables may fan out from the tops of the towers or they may be spaced at intervals along the lengths of the towers.

Suspension

But no cables run from one end of the bridge to the other. The result is a bridge that has a sleek, futuristic beauty.

Cable-stayed bridges span up to 2,000 feet (610 meters) and can cost less to build than suspension bridges of the same size.

Movable Bridges. Sometimes it is not possible or convenient to build a bridge high enough for ships to pass underneath. If this is the case, the bridge must be built so that it can be moved out of the way or raised, so that ships can pass under it. Almost all modern movable bridges are driven by electric motors. Among the most common movable bridges are drawbridges and vertical-lift bridges.

A **drawbridge** opens when one or two sec-

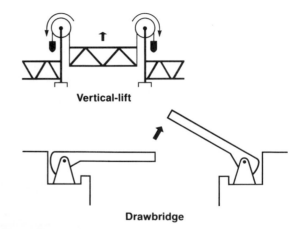

Vertical-lift

Drawbridge

tions swing upward to allow ships to pass through. The **vertical-lift** bridge has a span that can be lifted straight up into the air to allow ships to pass under.

▶ BUILDING A LARGE BRIDGE

The construction of a suspension bridge requires the talents and efforts of many people. Many types of information must be collected during the planning phase. Maps of the building site are drawn to show the shape of the land. Other maps showing the underlying soil and rock are prepared, so that proper foundations can be planned. Studies are made to estimate the amount of bridge traffic there will be. Tides, flood conditions, currents, and other characteristics of the waterway are carefully studied. Information is also gathered on natural hazards such as high winds and earthquakes.

Engineers take all the information collected and produce finished written descriptions and drawings telling what is to be built, the exact location of the bridge, the materials to be used, and how they are to be put together.

Construction starts with the foundations. No matter how strong a bridge is designed to be, it requires good foundations. The piers and abutments must be able to support the load of the bridge and traffic and to resist the forces

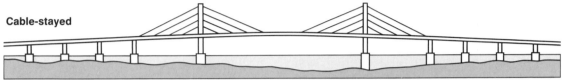

Cable-stayed

The Sunshine Skyway Bridge over Florida's Tampa Bay is a cable-stayed bridge. *Above:* During construction, roadway segments are added to both sides of a central tower, supported by cables connected directly to the tower. *Right:* Beam sections and cable-stayed sections have been joined to create a dramatic finished structure.

of wind, water, ice, and earthquakes. Piers must be solidly based on rock or firm ground.

Many bridge foundations have to be sunk into the bottom of a river or bay. To support the foundation, the builder may drive long, slender pieces of wood, steel, or concrete called **piles** through surface layers of loose material to firm soil or rock below. This is usually done with a powerful hammering machine called a **pile driver**.

Another method is to dig away the loose mud and silt and build concrete pillars or walls on firm soil or bedrock. For this underwater construction, large watertight compartments called **caissons** are sunk to the bedrock. The water is pumped out of them, and air is pumped in. The high air pressure keeps water out. Then workers enter the caisson, excavate the loose soil, and build the foundations. In the early days of bridge construction, people who worked in caissons returned too quickly to normal air pressure. Such a rapid change can cause internal injuries. Many people were seriously injured or died from this condition, which became known as caisson disease, or "the bends."

The bridge towers are constructed on the foundations, and cable anchorages are prepared on each bank of the waterway. Then the placing of the cables can begin.

John A. Roebling designed a way to string cables in place. Individual steel wires fed from each shore are looped back and forth many times over the bridge towers. Once the proper number of strands has been placed, the strands are wrapped tightly together with corrosion-resistant wire. Vertical cables, or suspenders, are attached to giant bands clamped to the newly constructed cables.

After the roadway is completed, signs, lighting, guardrails, and other finishing details are installed, and the bridge is ready to use.

SOME NOTABLE BRIDGES OF THE WORLD

Name of bridge	Location	Length of main span feet	meters	Year opened
Suspension				
Akashi Kaikyo	Kobe, Japan	6,529	1,990	1998
Storebaelt	Storebaelt Strait, Denmark	5,328	1,624	1998
Humber	Humber River, near Hull, England	4,626	1,410	1981
Verrazano-Narrows	Lower New York Bay, New York, N.Y.	4,260	1,298	1964
Golden Gate	San Francisco Bay, Calif.	4,200	1,280	1937
Mackinac	Straits of Mackinac, Mich.	3,800	1,158	1957
Second Bosporus	Bosporus Strait, Turkey	3,597	1,096	1988
George Washington	Hudson River, New York, N.Y.	3,500	1,067	1931
Brooklyn	East River, New York, N.Y.	1,595	486	1883
Cantilever				
Quebec Railway	St. Lawrence River, Quebec, Canada	1,800	549	1917
Forth Rail	Firth of Forth, Queensferry, Scotland	1,710	521	1890
Minato Ohashi	Osaka Bay, Japan	1,673	510	1974
Commodore John Barry	Delaware River, Chester, Penn.-Bridgeport, N.J.	1,644	501	1974
Greater New Orleans	Mississippi River, New Orleans, La.	1,575	480	1958
Steel Arch				
New River Gorge	New River, near Fayetteville, W. Va.	1,700	518	1977
Bayonne	Kill Van Kull, Bayonne, N.J.	1,675	510	1931
Sydney Harbour	Sydney, Australia	1,650	503	1932
Fremont	Willamette River, Portland, Ore.	1,255	383	1973
Cable-Stayed				
Tatara	Ehime, Japan	2,920	890	1999
Pont de Normandie	Le Havre, France	2,808	856	1995
Alex Fraser	Fraser River, British Columbia, Canada	1,525	465	1986
Sunshine Skyway	Tampa Bay, Fla.	1,200	366	1987
Millau Bridge	Millau, France	N/A*	N/A*	2004
Continuous Truss				
Astoria	Columbia River, Astoria, Ore.	1,232	376	1966
Oshima	Oshima Island, Japan	1,066	325	1976
Croton Reservoir	Croton, N.Y.	1,052	321	1970
Concrete Arch				
Krk	Krk Island, Croatia	1,280	390	1979
Gladesville	Parramatta River, Sydney, Australia	1,000	305	1964

*The Millau Bridge has no main span; instead, it has a total span of 1.6 miles (2.5 kilometers) supported by seven piers.

Over the years bridge builders have worked to make their bridges as safe as possible. With proper engineering, construction, and maintenance, bridges will be strong and safe. On the other hand, serious engineering flaws, faulty construction, or lack of proper maintenance can lead to bridge failure.

One such catastrophe involved the Tacoma Narrows Bridge over the Puget Sound in 1940. Only four months after it was completed, while exposed to strong winds, the suspension bridge began twisting violently. The roadway was ripped from its suspenders and plunged into the water below. The knowledge engineers gained from that and other bridge disasters led to safer designs.

To remain safe, bridges require constant inspection and maintenance. Scuba divers inspect piers for damage or erosion that may weaken the bridge's foundation. Steel bridges are painted to prevent corrosion from air pollutants and rain.

When a bridge is no longer economical to maintain, it may be demolished and replaced. Some bridges are simply abandoned, and new bridges are built nearby. In rare cases bridges are moved or are maintained as historic sites.

▶ **SOME FAMOUS BRIDGES**

One of the most famous structures in history is London Bridge, across the Thames River. The original bridge, begun in 1176 and completed in 1209, was a series of stone arches. Until the 1700's it was the only bridge across the Thames in London. The bridge became a center of London life. After the bridge was finished, houses were built on it, and in time it became lined with buildings.

Erosion of the bridge foundations was a continual problem. Some scholars think the song "London Bridge Is Falling Down" originally referred to the bridge's constant need for repairs. The old bridge continued in use, however, until the 1830's, when it was replaced by a new London Bridge, also an arch.

With the passing of time this bridge, too, had to be replaced. In the 1970's, stones from this bridge were shipped to Lake Havasu City, Arizona, where the bridge was reconstructed over an arm of the Colorado River. The present London Bridge, another arch bridge, was begun in 1968 and completed in 1973.

Venice, Italy, has about 400 bridges crossing its many canals. Located in this city is the

WONDER QUESTION

Why were some of the early bridges in America covered?

Covered bridges once dotted the American countryside from the Atlantic Coast to the Ohio River. The bridges looked like square tunnels with peaked roofs. Some people claim that the bridges were covered so that horses would not be frightened by the water underneath. Others say that they were built as a shelter for travelers in bad weather. Actually the coverings were designed to protect the wooden framework and flooring of the bridges and keep them from rotting. The pitched roofs, which shed snow, also reduced the amount of heavy snow that collected on the bridges. Wooden bridges became obsolete as traffic loads increased and modern trucks grew in size. Today only a few are still standing. Many people work to preserve the remaining covered bridges.

Bridge of Sighs, built around 1600. It is believed that prisoners sentenced to death could be heard sighing as they crossed the bridge on their way to execution.

The Quebec Railway Bridge over the St. Lawrence River in Canada is the only major bridge to have collapsed twice. When the bridge was nearly finished in 1907, part of it collapsed, killing 75 workers. Work began again on a redesigned and stronger bridge. In 1916 a new span fell while being lifted into place, killing 13 more workers. The bridge was finally completed in 1917.

The Chesapeake Bay Bridge-Tunnel is an unusual combination of trestles, bridges, and tunnels stretching almost 18 miles (29 kilometers) across the entrance to Chesapeake Bay. Most of the roadway is supported by trestles and lies about 25 feet (8 meters) above the water. The trestles join two bridge spans that rise high above the water and two tunnels that dip beneath the channel. Ships can pass under the bridges or over the tunnels.

Other significant bridges, their lengths, and the years in which they were opened are listed in the accompanying table.

Reviewed by NEAL FITZSIMONS
Principal, Engineering Counsel

See also TRANSPORTATION.

BRITISH ANTARCTIC TERRITORY. See COMMONWEALTH OF NATIONS.

BRITISH COLUMBIA

British Columbia's flag (above) and coat of arms (opposite page) feature the Union Jack, which recalls the province's traditional ties with England. The elk and bighorn sheep on the coat of arms are two animals that are found in British Columbia. The provincial bird is the steller's jay (right), and the provincial flower is the Pacific dogwood (opposite page).

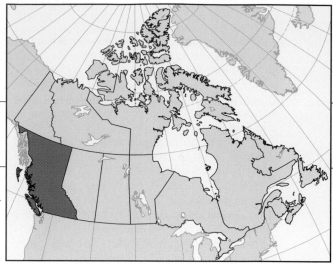

British Columbia, the most westerly province in Canada, faces the Pacific Ocean. The coast is indented with hundreds of narrow inlets. Some of them extend inland as far as 60 miles (100 kilometers). Vancouver Island and the Queen Charlotte Islands, which are part of British Columbia, lie between the coast and the open sea. The Inside Passage, a natural waterway extending from the state of Washington in the United States to Alaska, separates the islands from the mainland.

▶ THE LAND

British Columbia is the most mountainous province in Canada. Row after row of jagged peaks must be crossed to travel from one side of the province to the other. In the northeast corner are the forested, rolling plains of the Peace River district. The Rocky Mountains are the most easterly mountain range. The Rockies are cut by narrow passes such as Crowsnest, Kicking Horse, Yellowhead, and Pine. These passes are used as road and railway routes across the Rockies.

The Coast Mountains form the western rim of British Columbia's mainland. These forest-covered mountains rise steeply from the shores of the coastal inlets and the Inside Passage.

The Interior Plateau, in central British Columbia, is an area of rolling plateaus and valleys from 2,000 to 3,000 feet (600 to 900 meters) high.

The rivers of British Columbia flow directly or indirectly into two oceans—the Pacific and the Arctic. The Columbia River, with its tributaries, and the Fraser, Skeena, Stikine, and other rivers flow into the Pacific. The Peace and Liard rivers in the northeastern part of the province are tributaries of the Mackenzie River, which flows through the Northwest Territories on its way to the Arctic Ocean.

British Columbia owes much of its beauty to its many lakes. Among the best known of the natural lakes are Atlin, Babine, and Kootenay. Williston Lake, the largest lake in the province, was formed by the W. A. C. Bennett Dam on the Peace River.

Climate

British Columbia has a great variety of climates. In winter the climate along the coast is the mildest in Canada. Air masses moving eastward across the Pacific Ocean bring mild winters, cool summers, and much winter precipitation to the coastal area. Average January temperatures are above 32°F (0°C) at most coastal locations. Average July temperatures along the southwest coast are 64°F (18°C). Precipitation along the southwest coast occurs mostly as rain. The average annual rainfall on western Vancouver Island is more than 100 inches (2,540 millimeters), the heaviest in North America.

Summers are hotter and winters are colder in the interior of the province. Average January temperatures are between 5°F and 14°F (−15°C and −10°C) across the central interior. Average July temperatures are 70°F (21°C). There is much less precipitation in the interior than there is on the coast.

FACTS AND FIGURES

Location: Western Canada. **Latitude**— 49° N to 60° N. **Longitude**—114° W to 139° W.

Joined Canadian Confederation: July 20, 1871, as the 6th province.

Population: 3,907,738 (2001 census). **Rank among provinces**—3rd.

Capital: Victoria, pop. 74,125 (2001 census).

Largest City: Vancouver, pop. 545,671 (2001 census).

Physical Features: Area—364,763 sq mi (944,735 km²). **Rank among provinces**—3rd. **Rivers**—Peace, Liard, Fraser, and Columbia. **Lakes**—Atlin, Babine, Kootenay, Okanagan, and Williston. **Highest point**— 15,300 ft (4,663 m), Mt. Fairweather.

Industries and Products: Lumbering and the manufacture of forest products; mining; farming and the processing of food products; commercial fishing.

Government: Self-governing province. **Titular head of government**—lieutenant governor, appointed by the governor-general in council. **Actual head of government**— premier, leader of the majority in the legislature. **Provincial representation in federal parliament**—6 appointed senators; 34 elected member(s) of the House of Commons. **Voting age for provincial elections**—19.

Provincial Bird: Steller's jay.

Provincial Flower: Pacific dogwood.

Provincial Motto: *Splendor sine occasu* (Splendor without diminishment).

Natural Resources

Vast forests, powerful rivers, an abundance of well-distributed minerals, fertile valleys, and beautiful scenery are British Columbia's main natural resources.

Forests. The mild, wet coastal climate helps the growth of British Columbia's most abundant natural resource—the vast forests of coniferous trees. These forests cover the eastern lowlands of Vancouver Island and the Queen Charlotte Islands, as well as the lower slopes of the Coast Mountains. Forests also cover most of the Interior Plateau and the valley slopes in southeastern and northern British Columbia. The most valuable tree is the gigantic Douglas fir, which may reach a height of 200 feet (60 meters). Western hemlock, Sitka spruce, and western cedar also are commercially important.

Waterpower. Swift, snow-fed rivers provide an abundance of waterpower. The largest hydroelectric projects are near Kitimat, along the Columbia River and its tributaries, and on the Peace River.

Minerals. Coal is British Columbia's most important solid mineral product. Copper,

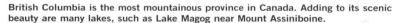

British Columbia is the most mountainous province in Canada. Adding to its scenic beauty are many lakes, such as Lake Magog near Mount Assiniboine.

Above: Farmers bale hay in the Thompson River valley in southern British Columbia, where there is much fertile soil. *Right:* Grapes ripen in vineyards in the Okanagan Valley. The wine industry is a small but growing part of the provincial economy.

gold, zinc, molybdenum, silver, and lead head the list of metallic minerals found in the province. Nonmetallic minerals include sand and gravel, stone, and sulfur. Oil and natural gas are significant mineral fuels.

▶ THE PEOPLE AND THEIR WORK

The population of British Columbia is small for its vast area. Many parts of the province are unpopulated because the land is too rugged for agriculture or forestry. More than 80 percent of the people live in or near the cities in the southwest. The remainder live in towns or small cities in the southern valleys or along roads or rail lines crossing the interior of the province.

The majority of early white settlers were of British origin, though many of them came to British Columbia from elsewhere in Canada or the United States.

In the 1880's, Chinese laborers came to British Columbia to help build the western section of the Canadian Pacific Railway. Afterward many of them settled in Vancouver and formed the largest Chinese community in Canada.

Other significant ethnic groups include Germans, East Indians, Dutch, Ukrainians, and Italians. Much of this immigration took place after World War II (1939–45). More recent immigrants have arrived from Pakistan, Malaysia, the Philippines, and Hong Kong.

Of the approximately 170,000 native peoples, about 45,000 are métis (people of mixed Indian and European ancestry). Inuit number about 1,000.

Industries and Products

The availability of waterpower has played an important part in the growth of industry in British Columbia. Forestry and the manufacture of wood products are a dominant force in the economy. The province also depends on mining and mineral industries, agriculture, and fishing. Today, service industries make up the most important sector of the economy.

Services. Service industries account for more than 70 percent of the province's gross domestic product. Finance, insurance, and real estate make up the largest portion of the service economy. Tourism is also important.

Manufacturing. The production of wood products such as lumber, paper, and furniture makes up more than half of the manufacturing in the province. Food and beverage production is also an important part of manufacturing. Other manufacturing includes the fabrication of metals, printing and publishing, and the production of transportation equipment.

Forest Industries. Approximately half of the softwood lumber produced in Canada comes from British Columbia's forests. Before 1940, most of the large sawmills were on the coast, so that lumber could easily be exported on oceangoing ships. But after 1950, production from forests in the interior increased. New pulp and paper mills were built in the interior after 1960. More recently, the forest industry has developed into large, centrally located operations complete with drying kilns and chipping facilities.

Mining. The second largest resource-based industry in British Columbia is mining. Mining activity began in the 1840's with the working of Vancouver Island's coal deposits. The gold rush of 1858 along the Fraser River and later in the Cariboo region brought the first large wave of white settlers to the mainland. Currently the most valuable minerals are copper, gold, zinc, molybdenum, silver, and lead. Oil and gas are produced in the northeastern Peace River district.

Agriculture. Most of the good farmland is found in the lower Fraser River valley, the valley around Okanagan Lake, the central Interior Plateau, and the Peace River district. The lower Fraser Valley is used for dairy farming. Other farms in that area produce vegetables, berries, and poultry for the nearby cities. Specialty crops of flowers and flower bulbs are grown on Vancouver Island and are exported to eastern Canada. The Okanagan Valley is a major apple-growing area. It also produces peaches, cherries, pears, plums, and the only apricots in Canada. Beef cattle are raised on ranches in the Interior Plateau. The Peace River district produces grain and legume seed crops, as well as cattle.

Local agricultural products are used to make canned and frozen fruit and vegetables. The wine industry is a growing sector of the provincial economy.

Fishing. Almost all the Pacific salmon—Canada's most valuable fish—are caught in the river mouths and coastal inlets of British Columbia. The large salmon canneries are south of Vancouver. In the 1980's, fish farming emerged and is now an important part of the fishing industry.

Transportation and Communication

Transportation in British Columbia has always been a problem because of the mountains, the scattered population, and the high costs of construction. The historic Cariboo Road into British Columbia's gold country, built in the 1860's, had to be cut through the rock wall of the Fraser River's canyon. The Trans-Canada Highway was completed in 1962. Modern highways reach into the settled regions of the province. The Alaska Highway starts at Dawson Creek—the end of the railway in the Peace River district—and extends about 600 miles (1,000 kilometers) through northern British Columbia before entering the Yukon Territory.

The Canadian Pacific and the Canadian National transcontinental railways connect British Columbia with the rest of Canada.

A large pulp mill operates near the Fraser River in Prince George in the central part of the province.

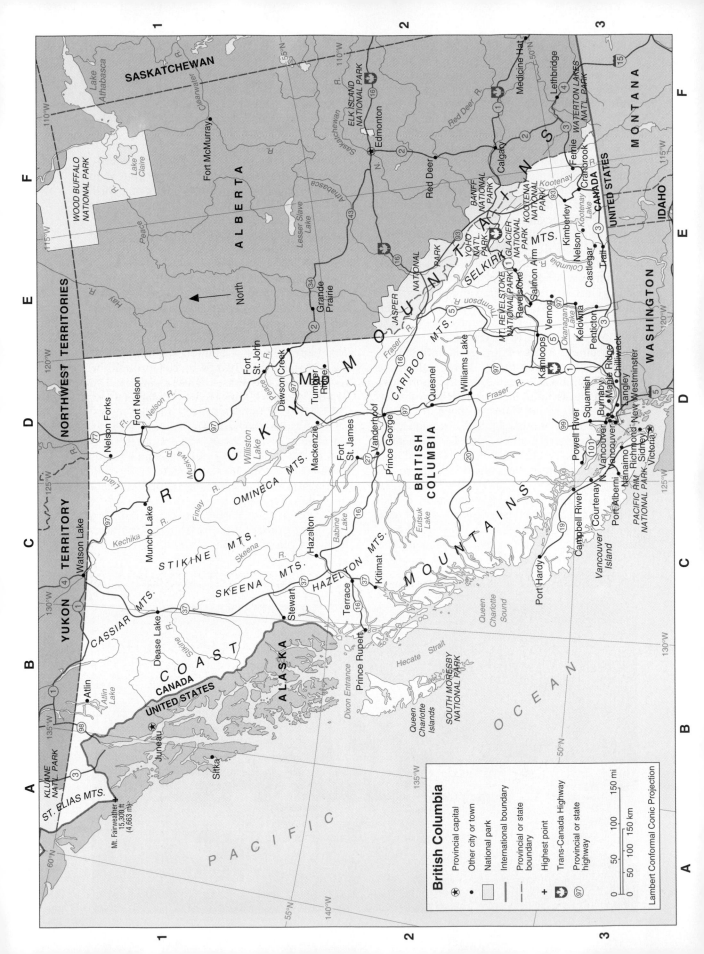

British Columbia

✪	Provincial capital
•	Other city or town
▢	National park
	International boundary
	Provincial or state boundary
+	Highest point
⊞	Trans-Canada Highway
97	Provincial or state highway

Lambert Conformal Conic Projection

0 50 100 150 km
0   50   100   150 mi

North

PACIFIC OCEAN

YUKON TERRITORY

NORTHWEST TERRITORIES

ALBERTA

SASKATCHEWAN

BRITISH COLUMBIA

ALASKA

UNITED STATES

CANADA

MONTANA

IDAHO

WASHINGTON

ROCKY MOUNTAINS

COAST MOUNTAINS

CASSIAR MTS.

STIKINE MTS.

SKEENA MTS.

HAZELTON MTS.

OMINECA MTS.

CARIBOO MTS.

SELKIRK MTS.

ST. ELIAS MTS.

Mt. Fairweather 15,300 ft (4,663 m)

KLUANE NATL. PARK

WOOD BUFFALO NATIONAL PARK

ELK ISLAND NATIONAL PARK

JASPER NATIONAL PARK

BANFF NATIONAL PARK

YOHO NATL. PARK

MT. REVELSTOKE NATIONAL PARK

GLACIER NATIONAL PARK

KOOTENAY NATIONAL PARK

WATERTON LAKES NATL. PARK

PACIFIC RIM NATIONAL PARK

SOUTH MORESBY NATIONAL PARK

Queen Charlotte Islands

Vancouver Island

Lake Athabasca

Lake Claire

Lesser Slave Lake

Williston Lake

Atlin Lake

Babine Lake

Eutsuk Lake

Kootenay Lake

Okanagan L.

Salmon Arm

Columbia R.

Kootenay R.

Thompson R.

Fraser R.

Skeena R.

Stikine R.

Finlay R.

Kechika R.

Muskwa R.

Nelson R.

Liard R.

Peace R.

Hay R.

Athabasca R.

Saskatchewan R.

N. Saskatchewan R.

Red Deer R.

Clearwater R.

Queen Charlotte Sound

Hecate Strait

Dixon Entrance

Juneau

Sitka

Atlin

Watson Lake

Dease Lake

Muncho Lake

Nelson Forks

Fort Nelson

Stewart

Terrace

Prince Rupert

Kitimat

Hazelton

Fort St. James

Vanderhoof

Prince George

Mackenzie

Fort St. John

Dawson Creek

Tumbler Ridge

Quesnel

Williams Lake

Grande Prairie

Fort McMurray

Edmonton

Red Deer

Calgary

Medicine Hat

Lethbridge

Fernie

Cranbrook

Kimberley

Nelson

Castlegar

Trail

Revelstoke

Vernon

Kelowna

Penticton

Kamloops

Powell River

Campbell River

Courtenay

Port Hardy

Port Alberni

Nanaimo

Richmond

New Westminster

Victoria

Vancouver

Burnaby

Maple Ridge

Langley

Chilliwack

Squamish

Map Page

15

16

93

1

3

2

43

34

2

97

77

4

1

98

3

37

16

27

20

5

5

99

101

19

5

97

110°W

115°W

120°W

125°W

130°W

135°W

140°W

60°N

55°N

50°N

INDEX TO BRITISH COLUMBIA MAP

The provincially owned British Columbia Railway crosses the province from Vancouver to the Peace River. It carries many of the resources from the interior to the coast.

Passenger boats and cargo vessels stop at the small coastal villages between Vancouver and Prince Rupert. Ferries make regular runs between Victoria, Nanaimo, Vancouver, and ports in Washington state. Many vessels travel from Seattle, Washington, and Vancouver through the Inside Passage to Skagway, Alaska—a voyage of about 950 miles (1,530 kilometers). There are airports in major cities, including Vancouver International Airport and Victoria International Airport.

All major towns and cities have radio stations. Television reaches all parts of the province by use of relay stations. Major daily newspapers include the *Times-Colonist* of Victoria and the *Sun* and the *Province* of Vancouver.

▶ EDUCATION

Education is free and compulsory for children from 6 to 15 years of age. Elementary school extends through the first seven grades; secondary school, from the eighth to the twelfth grade.

There are four universities. The largest is the University of British Columbia in Vancouver. The other three are Simon Fraser University in Burnaby, an eastern suburb of Vancouver; the University of Victoria in the capital city; and the University of Northern British Columbia in Prince George. Students may also obtain undergraduate degrees at regional university-colleges, while community colleges provide the first two years of post-secondary education.

Public libraries are maintained in all the larger cities, and mobile libraries serve distant

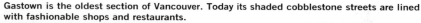

Gastown is the oldest section of Vancouver. Today its shaded cobblestone streets are lined with fashionable shops and restaurants.

communities. The library of the University of British Columbia in Vancouver and the provincial archives in Victoria are noted for their collections of historical material on British Columbia.

▶ PLACES OF INTEREST

Some of British Columbia's magnificent scenery and places of historic interest are preserved in national and provincial parks. The province also has many other attractions.

Anthony Island Provincial Park was established in the South Moresby region of the Queen Charlotte Islands. The park is a unique rain forest that is one of North America's most diverse plant and wildlife habitats. The ancient grounds and totem poles of the Haida Indians are of significant archaeological and cultural value.

Barkerville Historic Park is a restored gold rush town, dating from 1862, in the interior of the province. It became a ghost town in 1950 and was made a provincial historic park in 1959.

Butchart Gardens is a major tourist attraction close to Victoria. It was created by Jennie Butchart in 1904 in the abandoned limestone quarries surrounding the family home. Today it consists of almost 50 acres (20 hectares) of cultivated gardens overlooking Tod Inlet on Vancouver Island.

K'san Historic Indian Village is a reconstructed Gitksan Indian village at the junction of the Skeena and Bulkley rivers. It includes the oldest totem poles still in a native setting. Buildings include a carving school and workshop and a museum.

Pacific Rim National Park was established in 1971 on the central west coast of Vancouver Island. It includes the longest continuous stretch of sand beach in British Columbia.

Yoho National Park was established in 1886 on the west side of the Continental Divide. It is the site of Takakkaw Falls, which drop about 1,200 feet (360 meters). The park has many lakes and a natural stone bridge. It adjoins Banff National Park in Alberta.

Other places of interest in British Columbia include museums and more than 365 provincial parks and recreational areas.

The Maritime Museum, in Vancouver, has displays emphasizing the importance of the ocean in British Columbia's past and in its present economic life. In a drydock is the *St. Roch*, the first ship to navigate the Northwest Passage through the Canadian Arctic from west to east. The city archives and museum and a planetarium are nearby.

The Royal British Columbia Museum, in Victoria, is renowned for its displays of Native American artifacts. It also has exhibits depicting British Columbia's past, including a pioneer town, sawmill, fish cannery, and train station.

▶ CITIES

More than 80 percent of the people of British Columbia live in cities and towns with populations of more than 1,000. Since about 1900, nearly half the people have resided in or near Vancouver.

Victoria is the capital of British Columbia. It grew from a Hudson's Bay Company trading post built in 1843 and became the capital of the colony of British Columbia in 1868. Today, Victo-

Left: Visitors can pan for gold at Barkerville Historic Park. *Below:* Colorful Butchart Gardens, near Victoria, is one of the province's most popular tourist attractions.

ria's metropolitan population is about 312,000. Many of the residents do government work. The city also receives more than 3 million tourists each year.

Vancouver is the largest city in British Columbia and Canada's major Pacific seaport. It is the center of British Columbia's industry, finance, and trade, as well as the headquarters of many businesses. Vancouver has a metropolitan population of more than 1.9 million. Most of the city's residents work in service industries and commerce. For more information on this city, see the article on Vancouver in Volume U-V.

Kelowna is the largest city in Okanagan Valley. It is the supply and service center for the valley, as well as a recreation center. This flourishing city has a population of more than 96,000.

Kamloops is the largest city in the southern interior. It has sawmills, a pulp and paper mill, and an oil refinery. It is also a transportation and distribution center. It has a population of about 77,000.

Nanaimo, on eastern Vancouver Island, was an important coal-mining town in the last half of the 1800's. Its major industries today are sawmills and a pulp mill. It is the main wholesale and distribution center for central Vancouver Island. Nanaimo has a population of about 73,000.

Prince George is a forestry and transportation center for central British Columbia. It has many sawmills and three pulp and paper mills. It is also the site of the University of Northern British Columbia. Prince George has a population of some 72,000.

New Westminster, on the north bank of the Fraser River near its mouth, was founded in 1859. It was the capital of British Columbia until 1868. The city has a good freshwater port and several large sawmills. It has a population of about 55,000.

▶ GOVERNMENT

British Columbia is a self-governing province with a legislative assembly of 79 members. A lieutenant governor, appointed by Canada's governor-general, is the titular head of the province. The actual head of government is the premier of the province, who is the leader of the political party electing the most representatives to the legislature. British Columbia has six appointed senators in the Canadian Parliament and 34 elected members of the House of Commons. The voting age for provincial elections is 19.

▶ FAMOUS PEOPLE

British Columbia has been the home of many people who have contributed to the economic development of the province and to its political, social, and cultural life.

The parliament buildings in Victoria are the center of provincial government. Victoria became the capital of British Columbia in 1868.

William Andrew Cecil Bennett (1900–79) was premier of British Columbia for 20 years (1952–72), longer than any other political leader in the history of the province. As premier, he promoted the growth of the forest and mineral industries and developed hydroelectric power during the economic boom years. Bennett was born in New Brunswick. In 1941 he was elected to the provincial legislature. He became the leader of the Social Credit Party and premier in 1952, a position he held until 1972, when his party lost to the New Democratic Party.

Kim Campbell (1947–   ) became Canada's first female prime minister in 1993. She was born in Port Alberni, a city in central Vancouver Island. She has been active in federal and provincial politics. For more information, see the article on Campbell in Volume C.

Emily Carr (1871–1945) was a noted painter and writer. Born in Victoria, she was known as Canada's leading woman painter. She took as her subjects the west coast Indians and the forests of British Columbia. Her paintings are on display in Vancouver. Her prose writings include *The Heart of a Peacock* (1953) and *Pause* (1953).

Amor De Cosmos (1825–97) was born William Alexander Smith in Windsor, Nova Scotia. He took the name Amor De Cosmos, meaning "lover of the universe," during the California gold rush of 1853. He joined the gold rush in British Columbia in 1858 and in that year founded *The Colonist* (now the *Times-Colonist*), one of the oldest newspapers in western Canada. He was premier of British Columbia from 1872 to 1874.

Sir James Douglas (1803–77), sometimes called the founder of British Columbia, was born in British Guiana (now Guyana). He was associated with the fur-trading Hudson's Bay Company for more than 35 years and was instrumental in establishing Victoria as an important trading center. Sir James was governor of Vancouver Island (1851–63) and also of the mainland colony of British Columbia (1858–66). He worked to keep British Columbia and other British colonies on the Pacific coast from becoming part of the United States.

Simon Fraser (1776–1862), born in what is now Bennington, Vermont, explored much of the territory of British Columbia for the North West Company and established several fur-trading forts, including Fort George and Fort Fraser. In an extremely perilous journey in 1808, he traveled the length of the river that now bears his name. He retired in 1820 and died a poor and lonely man.

Rick Hansen (1957–   ), born in Port Alberni, began his "Man in Motion" tour from Vancouver on March 21, 1985. Paralyzed from the waist down in an automobile accident in 1973 and confined to a wheelchair, Hansen set out to ride, by wheelchair, the equivalent of the Earth's circumference—some 25,845 miles (41,585 kilometers)—to raise money to be used for spinal cord research, rehabilitation, and wheelchair sports. The 26-month tour took him through 34 countries, across 4 continents, and over 5 mountain ranges.

Mary Ellen Spear Smith (1861–1933), born in England, was one of British Columbia's most noted social reformers. Politically active from 1918 to 1928, she was instrumental in the fight for woman suffrage and reforms for women and children. The first woman to sit in British Columbia's legislature, she was also the first woman to hold cabinet rank (as a minister without portfolio), in 1928.

George Woodcock (1912–95) was a literary critic, poet, and historian. Born in Manitoba, Woodcock moved to England at an early age. There he became an associate of George Orwell, the writer. Woodcock returned to Canada in 1949 and took up residence in

British Columbia. He founded the quarterly journal *Canadian Literature* and authored several books, including a literary biography of Orwell, *The Crystal Spirit*, and a history of British Columbia.

A biography of fur trader Sir Alexander Mackenzie, who was the first white person to explore the interior of British Columbia, appears in Volume M. A biography of George Vancouver, who explored and mapped the northwest coast of North America and gave his name to Vancouver Island and the city of Vancouver, appears in Volume U-V.

▶ **HISTORY**

Before the first Europeans reached British Columbia, the land was inhabited by many Native American tribes, including the Halkomelem, Carrier, Shuswap, Gitksan, Coast Tsimshian, and Nootka. They lived by fishing and hunting. Some of them created distinctive works of art, such as the totem poles that are treasured in British Columbia today.

In 1774 the Spanish voyager Juan Pérez became the first European known to have reached the coast of British Columbia. Pérez claimed the land for Spain. Four years later Captain James Cook arrived and claimed the land for Britain. For many years Spain and Britain contested the territory, but during these years both countries carried on a lively fur trade with the Native Americans.

In 1792 Captain George Vancouver explored Puget Sound and surveyed the coastal inlets. A year later Alexander Mackenzie, a trader with the North West Company, completed the first overland journey from eastern Canada to the Pacific coast. Finally Spain was forced to give up its claim and to recognize Britain's right to the territory.

In 1808, Simon Fraser explored the river that now bears his name. By 1811, David Thompson had explored the southeast interior and the Kootenay and Columbia rivers. During these years the only European settlers were fur traders. Trading posts were established along the Columbia River and in the north. In 1843 Victoria on Vancouver Island became the center of the coastal fur trade. Settlers arrived and farming began.

In 1858 the discovery of gold in the Fraser River brought prospectors from eastern Canada and the United States. By 1861 the gold rush to the Cariboo region was in full swing. Ranching and farming began in the interior plateaus and river valleys, and sawmills began harvesting the coastal forests.

Vancouver Island and the mainland settlements were separate crown colonies until 1866, when they were united by the British government into the single crown colony of British Columbia.

In 1871 British Columbia became Canada's sixth province. In 1885 the Canadian Pacific Railway was completed, and the next year the first transcontinental train arrived at Port Moody. The water around Port Moody was too shallow for an ocean port, so the rail terminal was moved to the little sawmilling town of Granville. Later, Granville was renamed Vancouver.

During the 1890's, another mining boom brought settlers to the southeast Kootenay country. Commercial fishing began off the river mouths, and lumber from the tall forests was exported east of the Rockies to build the towns in the prairie provinces. Early in the 1900's, farming began in the irrigated Okanagan Valley, and dairy farming expanded across the lower Fraser Valley.

In the 1930's, British Columbia was hit particularly hard by the Great Depression. World War II (1939–45) restored industry and prosperity, and the province's natural resources were developed after the war.

In the 1960's, Vancouver was a center of Canada's counterculture. Music, poetry, and literature flourished, as did the radical politics of the period. Since the 1970's, the province's economy has been stronger than that of most regions in Canada. For that reason, British Columbia continues to attract immigrants from across Canada and increasingly from a number of Asian countries.

J. LEWIS ROBINSON
University of British Columbia
Reviewed by MARK LEIER
History Department, Simon Fraser University

BRITISH COMMONWEALTH. See COMMONWEALTH OF NATIONS.

BRITISH GUIANA. See GUYANA.

BRITISH HONDURAS. See BELIZE.

BRITISH ISLES. See UNITED KINGDOM.

BROADCASTING. See RADIO (Radio Programs); TELEVISION (Television Programs).

BRONCHITIS. See DISEASES (Descriptions of Some Diseases).

Anne, Emily, and Charlotte Brontë, as painted by their brother Branwell about 1835. All three sisters wrote novels about life in 19th-century England.

BRONTË SISTERS

Charlotte, Emily, and Anne Brontë and their brother Branwell lived with their father, the Reverend Patrick Brontë, in a parsonage high above the village of Haworth in Yorkshire, England. Their mother had died when Anne was a year old. There were no other children nearby for the Brontës to play with. They walked on the moors, read books, and wrote stories about imaginary places called Angria, Gondal, and Gaaldine. The stories were more real to them than their own lives.

Charlotte Brontë was born on April 21, 1816. Like her younger sisters, she wrote poetry as well as stories. In 1846 the sisters joined together to publish *Poems by Currer, Ellis and Acton Bell*. To hide their true identities, Charlotte called herself Currer, Emily was Ellis, and Anne was Acton.

The sisters had also been working on novels. Anne's and Emily's were accepted for publication, but Charlotte's novel, *The Professor*, was rejected. Finally one publisher expressed an interest in her work, so she finished *Jane Eyre*, her second novel, and sent it off. She drew on her own life in this novel. Like her main character, Jane Eyre, Charlotte Brontë was once a governess in a large house. The school where Jane Eyre taught was modeled after one that the Brontë sisters attended. *Jane Eyre*, published in 1847, was an immediate success. Her third novel, *Shirley*, was published in 1849, and her last novel, *Villette*, in 1853. *The Professor* was finally published in 1857, after her death.

Emily Brontë was born on July 30, 1818. She wrote only one novel, *Wuthering Heights*, which was published under her pen name, Ellis Bell, in 1847. It was not so popular at the time as *Jane Eyre*, but it is the most imaginative and poetic of all the Brontës' novels. Set on the wild Yorkshire moors, *Wuthering Heights* tells the love story of Catherine Earnshaw and the gypsy Heathcliff.

Anne Brontë was born on January 17, 1820. She worked for many years as a governess, and her first novel, *Agnes Grey* (1847), was about that experience. Her second novel was *The Tenant of Wildfell Hall* (1848).

Fame made little difference in the lives of the sisters, since their identities were still unknown to the public. Their father did not know of their success until much later. Their brother Branwell never knew. A failure at painting and writing, he took to drink and opium and died on September 24, 1848, at the age of 31.

Branwell's death was the first of a series of tragedies for the Brontës. Emily caught cold at her brother's funeral and became very ill. She refused all care and died less than three months later, on December 19, 1848. Her dog, Keeper, followed her coffin to the grave. On May 28, 1849, Anne also died of tuberculosis.

Charlotte lived for six more years, but life seemed empty to her without her sisters and brother. She let her real name be known after a rumor spread that Currer, Ellis, and Acton Bell were all the same person, but she was too shy to enter into society. She did travel to London occasionally. There she met literary celebrities of the day, including the novelists Elizabeth Gaskell, who later wrote a biography of Charlotte, and William Makepeace Thackeray. Charlotte married her father's curate, Arthur Nicholls, less than a year before her death on March 31, 1855.

Reviewed by JULIET MCMASTER
University of Alberta (Canada)

BRONZE AND BRASS

Sometime between 3500 and 3000 B.C., people discovered that mixing copper and tin would yield a new metallic substance, harder and tougher than either copper or tin. This new substance was bronze, and its discovery was an important event in human history.

Before the discovery of bronze, most tools and weapons were made of stone, wood, or bone. Stone could be given a sharp edge, but it was hard to shape, and it broke easily. Bone and wood, being softer than stone, were easier to shape. But they also wore out more quickly.

Copper, which was discovered around 5000 B.C., made better tools and weapons than stone, wood, or bone. It could be cast (melted and poured into a mold) or hammered into many different shapes. When a copper knife broke, it could be melted down and used to make a new knife. But copper was soft, and it bent easily.

Bronze was different. Bronze could be cast into complicated shapes more easily than copper. It would hold a sharp edge much longer. It did not bend in use or grow brittle quickly, as copper did. Durable bronze hoes and spades helped farmers to cultivate their fields better and thus grow more food. Bronze saws and chisels made it possible for carpenters to cut and trim wood accurately.

Bronze brought other changes, too. Armies equipped with bronze weapons easily crushed their more primitive neighbors. From these conquests the first empires were formed.

Archeologists believe that bronze originated somewhere in the mountainous regions of southwestern Asia. Both native copper nuggets and tin ore were found there, often in the beds of mountain streams. Tin was probably discovered shortly before bronze, when an early gold hunter tried to melt the gold out of some gravel containing tin ore. But tin—a soft, pliable white metal—was apparently not used by itself. No tin objects from that time have been found.

Metallurgy (the science of metals) was a mysterious art in those times. Primitive metalworkers experimented with new combinations of metals and ores, just as sorcerers might try new ingredients in their "magical" potions. Copper was already being alloyed with lead and antimony to make it easier to cast. When someone tried adding tin, bronze was the result.

The knowledge of how to make bronze spread gradually from the Near East to other parts of the ancient world. Eventually, people from China to the British Isles were using bronze. The period in history when bronze was the most important material for tools and weapons is called the **Bronze Age.** It lasted from about 3500 B.C. to 1200 B.C., when iron became plentiful and cheap enough for everyday use and took the place of bronze.

▶BRONZE MAKING TODAY

Bronze is made by mixing molten copper with molten tin. The most commonly used bronzes contain up to 10 percent tin.

Traces of other elements are often added to the basic copper-tin mixture to obtain bronzes with special qualities. Phosphorus, for instance, yields a hard, springy bronze that has high resistance to fatigue and corrosion. (Fatigue means that the metal becomes brittle under stresses such as repeated bending or twisting.) Phosphor bronzes are used for products in which these qualities are important, such as bearings, shafts, and diaphragms. Sil-

Brass is made by mixing molten copper and zinc. Here a machine trims the rough edges off long coils of brass. Each coil weighs six metric tons.

icon bronze is used for piston rings, metal screens, and propeller shafts for ships because it resists corrosion. Aluminum bronze is also used for engine parts and fittings for ocean-going ships.

Bronze may range in color from reddish brown to silvery white, depending on its composition. But the most usual color is golden brown. Bronze is a favorite material for statues and other works of art.

Although "bronze" really means an alloy made chiefly of copper and tin, the name is also used now for some copper alloys that do not contain any tin at all. These tinless bronzes do have some of the characteristics of true bronze, especially its typical golden brown color. Tinless bronze is often used in architectural trim for buildings, as in lobbies and storefronts.

▶BRASS

Brass, an alloy of copper and zinc, was developed much later than bronze. It appears to have been first used by the peoples of the Middle East around 700 B.C.

Much of our present knowledge of brass comes from the alchemists of the Middle Ages. Their attempts to turn common metals into gold (or at least gold-colored alloys) yielded much information about mixtures of copper, zinc, tin, and lead.

During the 18th and 19th centuries, hundreds of different copper alloys were developed. Most of them were brasses. Today brass is the most widely used copper alloy.

Brass is made in the same way as bronze except that zinc is used instead of tin. Copper and zinc cannot be melted together because copper melts at a much higher temperature than zinc. The zinc would boil away by the time the copper melted. Instead, solid ingots of zinc are added to the molten copper. The two metals may also be melted separately and then mixed.

The resulting alloy ranges in color from deep red through gold to creamy white. The zinc content ranges from 5 to 40 percent. The more zinc, the harder the brass is. Small quantities of other elements—lead, tin, silicon, manganese, or iron—may be added to produce special qualities.

Brasses are divided into two main types, based on the amount of zinc they contain. Brasses with up to 37 percent zinc are called alpha brasses, and those with more than 37 percent are called beta brasses. Alpha and beta brasses have different crystal structures and therefore different properties.

Alpha brasses are malleable, or easily worked. They are especially suited for cold-working (forming or rolling the metal without softening it by heating). Beta brasses are very malleable when hot, but at normal temperatures they are hard and not easily worked.

Low-zinc, or alpha, brasses are used for such products as water pipes, costume jewelry, cosmetics containers, and artillery shells. High-zinc, or beta, brasses are used for musical instruments, lamps, doorknobs, locks, and hinges.

A small amount of lead makes brass more easily machinable (easier to cut and drill with machine tools). Leaded brass is used in parts that must be accurately shaped, such as watch and clock parts, gears, plumbing materials, and printers' engraving plates.

▶METHODS OF WORKING

In addition to casting and machining, there are several different methods of shaping brass and bronze that also change the properties of these alloys. **Forging** increases the strength of the metal. In forging, the hot metal is pressed with great force between a set of dies. A die is a type of mold that shapes objects by squeezing them.

In **cold-rolling,** the unheated metal is passed back and forth between two heavy rollers, growing longer, wider, and thinner each time. The rolling hardens the metal, but it also creates stresses that make it brittle. **Annealing** (heating the metal and slowly cooling it) relieves the stresses and softens the metal. The cold-working process can then be repeated without danger of cracking the metal.

Seamless tubing and pipe are made by **extrusion.** The heat-softened alloy is squeezed out of a circular die with a plug in its center. As the metal is forced through the die and around the plug, it takes the shape of a hollow tube. While it is still soft, it is drawn, or stretched, to the desired size.

Reviewed by A. H. LARSON
Metals Division, Gould Inc.

See also ALLOYS; COPPER; DIES AND MOLDS; METALS AND METALLURGY.

BROOKE, EDWARD. See MASSACHUSETTS (Famous People).

BROWN, GEORGE (1818–1880)

George Brown was the owner of the most powerful Canadian newspaper of his day, the *Toronto Globe*; a leader of the Liberal Party; and one of the Fathers of Confederation.

Brown was born in Alloa, Scotland, on November 29, 1818, and went to the United States when he was 18. In 1843 his family moved to Toronto, in Upper Canada. Brown was very close to his father, Peter Brown, and together they founded the *Toronto Banner*. In 1844 they started the *Globe*. The *Globe's* strong editorials supported the struggle for responsible (cabinet) government and the right of Canadians to rule their own affairs within the British Empire.

In 1851, Brown was elected to Parliament. Canada was then a union of two provinces—Upper Canada and Lower Canada. Brown felt that the country was being controlled by Lower Canadian votes. Yet Upper Canada had the larger population. He demanded representation by population to give Upper Canada the greater number of seats in Parliament. Brown rebuilt a Liberal Party nicknamed the Clear Grits. In 1858 he became premier, but his term lasted only two days.

Brown was re-elected to Parliament in 1863. He offered to work with his chief foes, John A. MacDonald and George Cartier, to solve Canada's problems. This led eventually to a federal union, or confederation, of all the Canadian provinces. Brown played a major part at the Charlottetown and Quebec conferences, which were held to settle the design of the new union. In 1867 the British North America Act was passed, creating a united Canada.

Brown died in Toronto on May 9, 1880.

J. M. S. CARELESS
University of Toronto

BROWN, JOHN (1800–1859)

John Brown is remembered because of his strong hatred of slavery and for his use of violence in attacking it. He considered himself an instrument of God and believed that only through force and bloodshed would the slaves be freed.

Brown was born in Torrington, Connecticut, on May 9, 1800, but he grew up in Ohio. To support his 20 children, he moved from place to place working as a farmer, sheep raiser, wool merchant, and surveyor. Brown's father had taught him to hate slavery, and over the years his feelings against it grew stronger. In Pennsylvania he used his barn as a hiding place and shelter for runaway slaves.

In order to strike a direct blow at slavery, Brown moved to Kansas in 1855. The Kansas territory was then the center of conflict between slaveholders and those who opposed slavery. On May 24, 1856, Brown headed a party of eight (including four of his sons) that put to death five unarmed proslavery settlers at Pottawatomie Creek.

In December 1858, Brown led a raid into Missouri. His party seized eleven slaves and conducted them to the Canadian border and freedom. Ten months later he was ready to carry out his long-cherished plan to invade Southern territory in order to free the slaves and organize them into military companies.

On October 16, 1859, Brown and 21 followers launched an attack on the U.S. arsenal at Harpers Ferry, Virginia (now in West Virginia). A company of U.S. Marines, led by Colonel Robert E. Lee, was sent to crush Brown's band. Ten of Brown's men, among them two of his sons, were killed. Brown and six others were captured. Brought to trial for murder and treason, Brown was convicted and sentenced to hang. As he mounted the scaffold on December 2, 1859, he showed the same dignity and calm that had marked his appearance in the courtroom. To some people, Brown was a lunatic and a murderer who deserved to die. To others he was a martyr. During the Civil War, his memory inspired Union soldiers who sang: "John Brown's body lies a-mouldering in the grave, His soul goes marching on."

BENJAMIN QUARLES
Author, *Allies for Freedom: Blacks and John Brown*

BROWN, MARCIA. See CHILDREN'S LITERATURE (Profiles).

BROWN, MARGARET WISE. See CHILDREN'S LITERATURE (Profiles).

BROWNING, ELIZABETH BARRETT (1806–1861) AND ROBERT (1812–1889)

Two of England's finest poets, Robert Browning and Elizabeth Barrett Browning, are remembered as much for their romance as for their poetry. Elizabeth was born on March 6, 1806, in Durham, England. She was the first of 12 children and her father's favorite. He encouraged her to read and let her be tutored in Greek and Latin along with her brother Edward. When at 13 she composed an epic poem, *The Battle of Marathon,* he had it printed.

Elizabeth was impetuous. One day, when she was 15, she tried to saddle her pony by herself. The pony stumbled, and the saddle fell on top of Elizabeth, injuring her spine. That injury and an infected lung made her a semi-invalid. From then on she spent most of her time indoors, reading and writing.

Robert Browning was born six years after Elizabeth Barrett on May 7, 1812, in Camberwell, near London. Like Elizabeth's father, Robert's had a well-stocked library and encouraged his son to read. Like Elizabeth, Robert began writing verses at an early age. He studied art, music, languages, and literature and published his first poem, *Pauline,* in 1833.

As poetry by both Elizabeth Barrett and Robert Browning began to appear in print, they grew acquainted with each other's work. Then in 1845, Browning found himself mentioned in one of Miss Barrett's poems. He wrote to her, told her how much he admired her poetry, and said he had long wished to meet her. He had, he told her, been as far as her door, but she had not been well enough to receive him. They began corresponding, and on May 20, 1845, Browning called on Miss Barrett in the house on Wimpole Street in London, where the Barretts were living. He visited her frequently afterward, his visits carefully hidden from Mr. Barrett, who had forbidden his children to marry.

Although Elizabeth loved her father, her love for Robert Browning was stronger. On September 12, 1846, the two were secretly married. A week later they left for Italy. Mr. Barrett never forgave his daughter and returned her letters unopened.

The Brownings were extremely happy, and Mrs. Browning's health improved greatly. They both worked on their poetry, although they never discussed or showed their poems to each other until they were finished. They traveled a good deal, yet always returned to Casa Guidi, their home in Florence. It was there that their only child, Robert Wiedemann Barrett Browning, called Penini or Pen, was born on March 9, 1849.

Shortly after the Brownings' third wedding anniversary, Mrs. Browning slid something into her husband's pocket while he stood looking out a window. It was the manuscript of sonnets she had written before they were married. Browning felt they should belong to the whole world and urged his wife to publish them. To hide the identities of the lovers, he suggested she call them *Sonnets from the Portuguese.* No one would know that he sometimes called her his "little Portuguese" after the heroine of her poem "Catarina to Camoens." The sonnets are Mrs. Browning's best-known work.

For 16 years, Elizabeth Barrett and Robert Browning knew a life together of such happiness that it has become legendary. Then on June 30, 1861, Mrs. Browning died at Casa Guidi. A month later, Browning left for England with his son. He could not bring himself to return to Italy until 1878, but from then on he spent most of his time there. He died on December 12, 1889, in the palace his son and daughter-in-law had bought in Venice. His body was taken to England and buried in the Poets' Corner of Westminster Abbey.

Reviewed by REGINALD L. COOK
Middlebury College

This is a sonnet from Elizabeth Barrett Browning's *Sonnets from the Portuguese:*

How do I love thee? Let me count the ways.
I love thee to the depth and breadth and height
My soul can reach, when feeling out of sight
For the ends of Being and ideal Grace.
I love thee to the level of every day's
Most quiet need, by sun and candle-light.
I love thee freely, as men strive for Right;
I love thee purely, as they turn from Praise.
I love thee with the passion put to use
In my old griefs, and with my childhood's faith.
I love thee with a love I seemed to lose
With my lost saints—I love thee with the breath,
Smiles, tears, of all my life!—and, if God choose,
I shall but love thee better after death.

Robert Browning's *Pied Piper of Hamelin* is based on an old legend. The following excerpt tells how the rats followed the piper out of the town of Hamelin.

Into the street the Piper stept,
Smiling first a little smile,
As if he knew what magic slept
In his quiet pipe the while;
Then, like a musical adept,
To blow the pipe his lips he wrinkled,
And green and blue his sharp eyes twinkled
Like a candle-flame where salt is sprinkled;
And ere three shrill notes the pipe uttered,
You heard as if an army muttered;
And the muttering grew to a grumbling;
And the grumbling grew to a mighty rumbling;
And out of the house the rats came tumbling.
Great rats, small rats, lean rats, brawny rats,
Brown rats, black rats, gray rats, tawny rats,
Grave old plodders, gay young friskers,
Fathers, mothers, uncles, cousins,
Cocking tails and pricking whiskers,
Families by tens and dozens,
Brothers, sisters, husbands, wives—
Followed the Piper for their lives.
From street to street he piped advancing,
And step by step they followed dancing,
Until they came to the river Weser
Wherein all plunged and perished
Save one, who, stout as Julius Caesar,
Swam across and lived to carry
(As he the manuscript he cherished)
To Rat-land home his commentary,

Which was, "At the first shrill notes of the pipe,
I heard a sound as of scraping tripe,
And putting apples, wondrous ripe,
Into a cider press's gripe;
And a moving away of pickle-tub boards,
And a drawing the corks of train-oil flasks,
And a breaking the hoops of butter casks;
And it seemed as if a voice
(Sweeter far than by harp or by psaltery
Is breathed) called out, Oh, rats! rejoice!
The world is grown to one vast drysaltery!
To munch on, crunch on, take your nuncheon,
Breakfast, supper, dinner, luncheon!
And just as a bulky sugar puncheon,
All ready staved, like a great sun shone
Glorious scarce an inch before me,
Just as methought it said, come, bore me!
—I found the Weser rolling o'er me."

You should have heard the Hamelin people
Ringing the bells till they rocked the steeple.
"Go," cried the Mayor, "and get long poles!
Poke out the nests and block up the holes!
Consult with carpenters and builders,
And leave in our town not even a trace
Of the rats!"—when suddenly up the face
Of the Piper perked in the market-place,
With a, "First, if you please, my thousand
    guilders!"

413

BRUEGEL, PIETER, THE ELDER (1525?–1569)

The painter Pieter Bruegel (or Brueghel) the Elder is best known for landscapes and peasant scenes. He was born in the Netherlands sometime between 1525 and 1530. Very little is known about his early life, but he became a master in the Antwerp Painters Guild in 1551.

Bruegel looked to Italy for inspiration. He was in Rome in 1553 and returned home across the Alps by 1555. He had always been interested in landscape painting, but his travels in the Alps led him to portray nature in a grander and more unified way.

In Antwerp, Bruegel made drawings for engravings. The drawings often portrayed serious ideas in humorous form. They showed his interest in popular subjects, his observations on the foolishness of people, and his concern for freedom of religion. Bruegel's paintings were usually made for private patrons. They dealt with many themes. He was interested in the human figure. In many of his paintings, crowds of people cover the canvas, creating a brightly colored pattern. But he was also concerned with nature and how it affects people's lives. This can be seen in the five paintings that remain of a series called the *Months*. *Hunters in the Snow* (1565) is a winter scene from the series, probably representing January.

In 1563 Bruegel married and moved to Brussels. He died there on September 9, 1569. Two of his sons also became famous painters. Pieter the Younger (1564–1638) made many copies and variations of his father's works. Jan (1568–1625) was a painter whose elegant style earned him the nickname Velvet Bruegel.

LOLA B. GELLMAN
City University of New York

In *Hunters in the Snow*, the hunters are part of a vast, wintry landscape. Bruegel arranged the elements in this scene to show how nature dominates people's lives.

BRUNEI

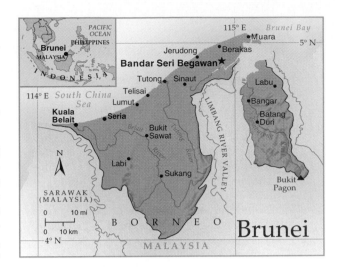

Brunei

The small southeast Asian nation of Brunei is located on the northwestern coast of the island of Borneo. Except for its border on the South China Sea, Brunei is entirely surrounded by the territory of Sarawak, a state of the nation of Malaysia. Brunei has considerable deposits of petroleum and natural gas, which have given it one of the highest incomes per person in the world.

People. The majority of Bruneians are Malays. About 15 percent are Chinese. The country also has a large number of foreign workers. Most of the people live in the capital, Bandar Seri Begawan, and in towns along the coast.

Brunei's official language is Malay. English, Chinese, and native dialects are also spoken. Islam (the religion of the Muslims) is the official state religion, although other religions are permitted.

Land. Brunei is divided into two unconnected parts, separated by the Limbang River valley of Sarawak. Dense forests cover about 70 percent of the country. The climate is tropical, with high temperatures and humidity and heavy rainfall.

FACTS and figures

NEGARA BRUNEI DARUSSALAM (Brunei, Abode of Peace) is the official name of the country.

LOCATION: Southeast Asia, on the northwestern coast of Borneo.

AREA: 2,226 sq mi (5,765 km²).

POPULATION: 345,000 (estimate).

CAPITAL AND LARGEST CITY: Bandar Seri Begawan.

MAJOR LANGUAGES: Malay (official), English, Chinese.

MAJOR RELIGIOUS GROUPS: Muslim (official), Buddhist, Christian.

GOVERNMENT: Constitutional sultanate (monarchy). **Head of state and government**—sultan.

CHIEF PRODUCTS: **Mineral**—Petroleum, petroleum refining, natural gas.

MONETARY UNIT: Bruneian dollar (1 dollar = 100 cents).

Economy. Petroleum and natural gas account for nearly all Brunei's exports and more than half its wealth. The traditional economic activities of agriculture and fishing have declined, and Brunei must import most of its food. About half the workforce is employed by the government, which provides free education, medical care, and many other social services. Bruneians pay no income tax.

History and Government. Brunei's first sultans, or rulers, date from the 1200's. By the 1500's Brunei was the dominant state in the region, but it soon declined in size and power. In 1888, Brunei became a British protectorate.

Petroleum was discovered in Brunei in the early 1900's. Commercial production of oil began in 1929, attracting the attention of the Japanese, who occupied the region during World War II (1939–45). After the war, Britain resumed its protectorate over the territory. Brunei became self-governing under its own constitution in 1959. It regained complete independence in 1984. That year, Brunei joined the Association of Southeast Asian Nations (ASEAN).

Brunei is ruled by Sultan Sir Hassanal Bolkiah, who succeeded his father in 1967. Although he governs with the aid of a cabinet, the sultan holds complete power as both head of state and government.

ROBERT O. TILMAN
North Carolina State University

BRUNHOFF, JEAN DE. See CHILDREN'S LITERATURE (Profiles).

BRUSILOV, ALEKSEI. See WORLD WAR I (Profiles: Allied Powers).

BRYAN, WILLIAM JENNINGS (1860–1925)

William Jennings Bryan was a leader of the Democratic Party for more than 20 years. He was also one of the most powerful speakers of all time. Known as the silver-tongued orator, he is best remembered for his moving Cross of Gold speech and for his work as a prosecutor in the famous Scopes "monkey" trial.

Bryan was born in Salem, Illinois, on March 19, 1860. In 1887 he moved to Nebraska, where he became interested in politics. In 1890 he was elected to the U.S. House of Representatives.

Toward the end of the 1800's, a great argument existed over what kind of money the nation should use. Silver-mine owners and farmers wanted the government to issue silver as well as gold. The farmers felt that free (unlimited) silver coinage would put more money into circulation and raise prices for crops. But people in business wanted money backed by a gold standard. At the Democratic convention of 1896, Bryan, a Free Silver Democrat, excited quarreling delegates to applause with these words from the Cross of Gold speech, "We will answer their demand for a gold standard by saying to them . . . you shall not crucify mankind upon a cross of gold." Bryan's speech won him the Democratic presidential nomination. But he lost the election to Republican William McKinley.

In 1900, Bryan again lost the presidential election to McKinley. In 1908 he ran against William Howard Taft and was defeated for a third time. Yet Bryan still had great influence, and he used it to help Woodrow Wilson win the presidential nomination in 1912. When Wilson became president, he appointed Bryan secretary of state.

In 1925, John Scopes, a high school biology teacher, was brought to trial in Dayton, Tennessee, for teaching Darwin's theory of evolution in violation of state law. Many people felt that Darwin's theory denied the biblical story of creation. A deeply religious man, Bryan went to Dayton to help in the case against Scopes. Bryan won the case. Five days after the trial, he died in Dayton on July 26, 1925.

Reviewed by PAOLO E. COLETTA
Author, *William Jennings Bryan*

BRYANT, PAUL WILLIAM ("BEAR"). See ALABAMA (Famous People).

BRYANT, WILLIAM CULLEN (1794–1878)

The American poet and editor William Cullen Bryant was born on November 3, 1794, in Cummington, Massachusetts. His father was a doctor, who encouraged his son Cullen to write. When the boy was only 13, he published a long satirical poem, "The Embargo." He wrote his most famous poem, "Thanatopsis," a meditation on death, while he was a student at Williams College.

Bryant had to leave college because he lacked funds to support himself. He was apprenticed to a lawyer and passed his bar examination before he was 20. After moving to Great Barrington, Massachusetts, he pursued a successful law career. In 1821 he married Frances Fairchild. He celebrated their romance in "Oh Fairest of the Rural Maids."

Bryant wrote sensitive descriptions of nature and the American landscape in such poems as "To a Waterfowl," "The Yellow Violet," and "Green River." Collections of his poems issued in 1821 and 1832 established Bryant as the leading American poet of his time.

In 1825, Bryant moved to New York City to begin a new career in journalism. He rose to editor in chief on the *New York Evening Post* by 1829. He worked for the *Post* for over 50 years. On its editorial pages, Bryant supported such causes as abolition and the labor movement. He helped form the Republican Party and elect Abraham Lincoln.

Bryant also continued to compose poems. In "The Flood of Years," he pondered life after death, and in "The Prairies," he described the vast American West. After his wife's death in 1865, Bryant began his popular translation of the *Iliad* and of the *Odyssey*, published in 1870 and 1872. He lived an active life until his death on June 12, 1878.

JOHN B. PICKARD
University of Florida

BUBONIC PLAGUE. See VECTORS OF DISEASE (Vector-Borne Diseases Worldwide).

JAMES BUCHANAN (1791–1868)

15th President of the United States

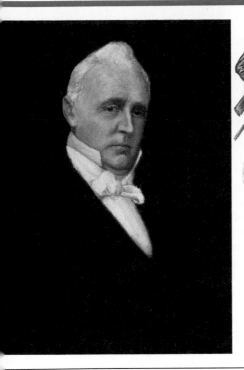

FACTS ABOUT BUCHANAN

Birthplace: Cove Gap, Pennsylvania
Religion: Presbyterian
College Attended: Dickinson College, Carlisle, Pennsylvania
Occupation: Lawyer
Marriage: None
Political Party: Democratic
Nickname: "Old Buck"
Post Held Before Becoming President: Minister to Great Britain
President Who Preceded Him: Franklin Pierce
Age on Becoming President: 65
Terms Served: One
Years in the Presidency: 1857–1861
Vice President: John C. Breckinridge
President Who Succeeded Him: Abraham Lincoln
Age at Death: 77
Burial Place: Woodward Hill Cemetery, Lancaster, Pennsylvania

James Buchanan

DURING BUCHANAN'S PRESIDENCY

Minnesota (1858), Oregon (1859), and Kansas (1861) became states. *Below:* The first transatlantic telegraph cable was laid between Newfoundland and Ireland (1858). *Left:* John Brown, attempting to start a slave rebellion, attacked the U.S. arsenal (1860) at Harpers Ferry, Virginia (now West Virginia). Brown was hanged. *Above:* The Pony Express was established (1860) to carry mail from St. Joseph, Missouri, to Sacramento, California. The first Japanese delegation arrived in the United States (1860). South Carolina seceded from the Union (1860), followed by other Southern states that together formed the Confederate States of America.

BUCHANAN, JAMES. James Buchanan, the 15th president of the United States, also served his country as a congressman, senator, ambassador, and secretary of state. But many people remember mainly two things about him: that he was the only president who never married; and that the Civil War followed his administration.

▶EARLY LIFE

Buchanan was born on April 23, 1791, in a log cabin near the frontier settlement of Cove Gap, Pennsylvania. His father, a Scotch-Irish immigrant, had come to America in 1783. When James was 6, the family moved to Mercersburg, Pennsylvania, where his father opened a general store. James's mother had little schooling, but she loved to read and she inspired her son with a love of learning.

James was able to go to school in Mercersburg. When he was not studying, he helped his father in the store. James's father was fond of his son, but he made him work hard and pay close attention to business. Mr. Buchanan taught James that he must be ready to care for his nine younger brothers and sisters if their parents should die. In later years, after his father died, James Buchanan became responsible for the care of his mother and four of his brothers and sisters.

When James was 16, his father sent him to Dickinson College in Carlisle, Pennsylvania. Young Buchanan was a serious student, but he also wanted to have a good time. He began to drink and smoke with some of the other students. Even though his marks were excellent, he was expelled for bad conduct at the end of his first term. James pleaded to be taken back and promised to turn over a new leaf. He was allowed to return and went on to graduate with honors.

Buchanan then went to Lancaster, Pennsylvania, to study law. Hard work and intelligence made him a very good lawyer. Before long he was earning more than $11,000 a year, a huge sum in those days.

In 1814, Buchanan became a candidate for the Pennsylvania legislature. But the War of

Buchanan's birthplace as it now stands at Mercersburg Academy, Pennsylvania.

Ann Coleman (1796?–1819).

1812 was raging, and the British had just burned Washington. Buchanan felt that the United States should not have gone to war against Great Britain. However, he knew it was his duty to serve his country, and he joined a volunteer cavalry company.

Buchanan returned in time for the election and won his seat in the legislature. He served a second term and then returned to Lancaster to continue his law practice.

▶ A TRAGIC LOVE STORY

As his practice grew, Buchanan became an important figure in town. He was invited to parties at some of the best homes in Lancaster. At one party he met and fell in love with beautiful Ann Coleman. In 1819 Ann and James were engaged to be married, but their happiness was destined to end quickly.

During the fall of 1819 Buchanan often had to be out of town on business. While he was away rumors spread that he wanted to marry Ann only for her money. There was gossip about another woman. All of this was untrue, but Ann was heartbroken. Because of a misunderstanding, she broke her engagement to James.

A short time later Ann died. Buchanan was so grief-stricken that he vowed he would never marry. Years later, after his death, a package of Ann's letters, yellow with age, was found among his papers. They were burned, according to his last wishes, without being opened.

▶ HE RETURNS TO POLITICS

Buchanan turned to politics to forget his sorrow. The Federalist Party was looking for a candidate for Congress. Buchanan agreed to run, and in 1820 he was elected to the House of Representatives, where he served for 10 years. During his years in Congress, Buchanan changed his political party. He joined the Jacksonian Democrats (named for Andrew Jackson), and became a leader of the Jacksonians in Pennsylvania.

In 1831 President Jackson asked Buchanan to become minister to Russia. Buchanan went to Russia the following year. While there he negotiated the first trade agreement between Russia and the United States.

On his return to the United States, Buchanan was elected to the Senate. He served until 1845, and became chairman of the important committee on foreign affairs.

Buchanan applied all his training as a lawyer to his work in the Senate. The Constitution, he said, was the basis of all political power. But the Constitution also strictly limited the powers of the federal government. Buchanan believed that a constitutional republic could adjust serious differences between its people only by compromise and legal procedure.

▶ SECRETARY OF STATE

By 1844 Buchanan had become an important political figure. Though he hoped for the presidential nomination, he gave his support to James K. Polk, who won the nomination and the election. President Polk appointed Buchanan secretary of state.

During Polk's term as president, war broke out between the United States and Mexico. Buchanan, as secretary of state, helped to arrange the treaty of peace in 1848. By this Treaty of Guadalupe Hidalgo the United States purchased from Mexico the region

Photograph of President Buchanan, taken about 1859.

President Pierce made Buchanan minister to Great Britain in 1853. Shortly thereafter Pierce instructed the American ministers in Europe to draw up proposals to "detach" Cuba from Spain. This led to the Ostend Manifesto, named after the Belgian city where the ministers met. The Manifesto defined a plan to purchase Cuba. But it also included a proposal many people condemned: that the United States would be justified in seizing Cuba if Spain refused to sell the island. Buchanan's political opponents severely denounced the Ostend Manifesto, and nothing ever came of the plan. Buchanan wrote of it: "Never did I obey any instructions so reluctantly."

While Buchanan was in England, Congress passed the Kansas-Nebraska Act, permitting slavery in regions of the Northwest from which the Missouri Compromise of 1820 had formerly excluded it. This new law marked the beginning of the Republican Party, which vowed to prevent any further expansion of slavery, and it split the Democratic Party into northern and southern groups. As Buchanan had been in England during the Congressional fight over the Kansas-Nebraska bill, he remained friendly with both sections of his party. When the Democrats met in 1856 to pick a new candidate for president, they needed someone who would be accepted by both the North and the South. Buchanan proved to be the man. This time he won the nomination and the election.

▶ PRESIDENT BUCHANAN

On March 4, 1857, Buchanan was inaugurated as president. Since Buchanan had no wife, his 27-year-old orphan niece, Harriet Lane, acted as his hostess. She was very popular, and Buchanan's administration was a great social success. White House guests included the first Japanese representatives to the United States and the Prince of Wales (who later became King Edward VII of England). The Prince arrived with such a large party that the President had to give up his own bed and sleep on a couch.

The Dred Scott Decision

But the political situation was getting worse. Two days after Buchanan's inauguration, the Supreme Court gave its historic

extending west from Texas to the Pacific Ocean.

Another problem concerned the vast Oregon territory, which both Great Britain and the United States claimed. The dispute became so bad that war threatened. But Buchanan arranged a compromise, and the Oregon Treaty of 1846 settled the Northwestern boundary between Canada and the United States.

When Polk left office, Buchanan also retired. For 4 years he lived the life of a country gentleman. He bought the famous mansion, Wheatland, near Lancaster, Pennsylvania, partly to have a suitable place to entertain political guests, but mainly to care for a growing family. Although Buchanan remained a bachelor, he had over the years become a kind of foster father to a score of nephews and nieces, seven of them orphans. They often visited him at Wheatland, and two made their home with him there, cared for in his absence by his faithful housekeeper, Miss Hetty Parker.

But Buchanan could not stay out of politics for long. In 1852 he was again a candidate for the presidential nomination. He was beaten by a little-known candidate, Franklin Pierce.

President Buchanan received the first Japanese delegation to the United States in 1860.

IMPORTANT DATES IN THE LIFE OF JAMES BUCHANAN

1791   Born at Cove Gap, Pennsylvania, April 23.
1809   Graduated from Dickinson College.
1814   Elected to the Pennsylvania legislature.
1819   Death of Ann Coleman.
1821–   Served in the United States House of Repre-
1831   sentatives.
1832–   Minister to Russia.
1833
1835–   Served in the United States Senate.
1845
1845–   Secretary of state.
1849
1853–   Minister to Great Britain.
1856
1857–   15th president of the United States.
1861
1868   Died near Lancaster, Pennsylvania, June 1.

decision in the case of the slave Dred Scott, who sued for his freedom because he had been taken to a nonslave territory. However, the court decided that Congress could not outlaw slavery in United States territories. Buchanan thought slavery was wrong, but unfortunately the Constitution then recognized it. He hoped the Dred Scott decision would calm the country. Instead, people in the North refused to accept the court's decision. Thus the North and South became more divided than ever.

South Carolina Secedes from the Union

The crisis came in December, 1860. Abraham Lincoln had just been elected president, but he did not take office until March, 1861. Until that time Buchanan was still president.

When the news of Lincoln's victory reached the South, the state of South Carolina seceded from the Union, declaring that it was no longer a part of the United States. By February, 1861, six more southern states had broken away from the Union. The split in the nation that Buchanan feared had taken place.

In this crisis Buchanan wanted to keep the remaining slave states loyal to the Union. He said he would do nothing to provoke a war but he would try to protect federal property and enforce the laws in the South. He asked Congress to call a Constitutional Convention and to vote him the men and money needed to enforce the laws. But Congress refused.

▶ THE COMING OF WAR

On March 5, 1861, Buchanan left Washington and returned to Wheatland. He was happy to leave the presidency and hopeful that the president who followed him could maintain peace and restore the Union. But 5 weeks after Lincoln's inauguration, the South fired on Fort Sumter and the Civil War began.

Buchanan spent his last years writing a book about his term as president. He died at Wheatland on June 1, 1868.

Could Buchanan have prevented the Civil War? Historians do not agree. Some say that a stronger president, one with more imagination, could have prevented the war. Others argue that the Civil War was inevitable: it would have happened no matter who was president, and if Buchanan had used force against the southern states, the war would only have started earlier.

Buchanan tried to solve the problems of the United States by acting within its laws. He failed. Whether any man could have succeeded will never be known.

Reviewed by PHILIP S. KLEIN
Author, *President James Buchanan*

See also DRED SCOTT DECISION; KANSAS-NEBRASKA ACT; MISSOURI COMPROMISE.

BUCHAREST

Bucharest (Bucureşti in Romanian) is the capital and largest city of Romania as well as its economic and cultural center. It has a population of more than 2 million. The city is situated amid the fertile plains of Walachia, one of the country's historic regions. It lies on both banks of the Dimboviţa River, a tributary of the Danube.

The City. Much of modern Bucharest was laid out and built in the late 1800's and early decades of the 1900's, in a style that owed much to French influence. During the 1930's, in fact, it was known as the Paris of the Balkans. Many changes were made to the city, however, during the long period of Communist rule after World War II.

From the northwest, a number of broad streets and boulevards lead to the city's center. Among the chief ones are Calea Victoriei and the Bulevardul Bălcescu. Other thoroughfares run in an east–west direction. Where the two intersect, there are usually large, handsome squares. The most notable are Republic Square, the nearby Palace Square, and University Square, where many of the faculties of the University of Bucharest (founded in 1694) are located. Spacious parks add to the city's attractiveness.

Bucharest's museums include the National Museum of Art; the Village Museum, with its examples of village homes from different regions; and the Georges Enesco Museum, dedicated to Romania's most famous composer. The city's vigorous cultural life is also reflected in its numerous theaters, its opera, and its symphony orchestra.

Economic Activity. Bucharest lies astride one of the major trade routes of the Balkans and has a long commercial tradition. The city and surrounding areas (where most of the factories are located) account for about one-fifth of Romania's total industrial output. The major manu-

factured products include various kinds of machinery, motor vehicles, electrical equipment, and consumer goods.

History. The name of the city first appears in written documents in the mid-1400's. Bucharest was destroyed by the Ottoman Turks in the late 1500's but rebuilt soon after. Proclaimed the capital of the first Romanian state, consisting of Walachia and Moldavia, in 1862, it remained the capital when Romania won complete independence in 1877–78.

Bucharest flourished in the years after World War I, and its population increased substantially after World War II. A considerable area of the city was destroyed in an earthquake in 1977, and under the Communist dictator Nicolae Ceauşescu, in power from 1965 until his overthrow in 1989, many older buildings were torn down to make way for redevelopment. Although the lights of Bucharest were dimmed under Communism, a slow but steady recovery took place in the 1990's, reviving the aspects of the city that made it so attractive in the past.

ARTHUR CAMPBELL TURNER
University of California, Riverside

Calea Victoriei is one of Bucharest's main streets. The spired Palace of the Republic, completed in 1937, now houses the national art museum.

BUCK, PEARL (1892–1973)

Pearl Sydenstricker Buck, American author, was born on June 26, 1892, in Hillsboro, West Virginia. Her parents, Presbyterian missionaries in China, were home on leave. They returned to China five months later.

China was Pearl Buck's home for 42 years. She learned to speak Chinese before she learned English. All her schooling was in China until she attended Randolph-Macon College and, later, Cornell University.

Her marriage to Dr. John Buck, an agricultural missionary, took her to a small town in northern China. She described the region in her best-known novel, *The Good Earth* (1931). After five years she moved to Nanking and taught English literature to university students. When revolutionary soldiers invaded Nanking in March 1927, she was rescued by an American gunboat and went to Japan. The next winter she returned to China, but by 1934 the situation was so dangerous for foreigners that she knew she must leave. She decided to make her home in Pennsylvania. She was divorced from Dr. Buck in 1935 and married Richard J. Walsh, her publisher.

Pearl Buck received many honors for her writing. *The Good Earth* won the Pulitzer Prize in 1932, and in 1938 she became the first American woman to win the Nobel Prize for literature. Her humanitarian activities were also numerous. In 1949 she founded Welcome House, an adoption agency for American children of Asian ancestry. In 1964 she established the Pearl S. Buck Foundation, which aids neglected American-Asian children living overseas. Pearl Buck died in Danby, Vermont, on March 6, 1973.

Reviewed by PAUL A. DOYLE
Author, *Pearl S. Buck*

▶ **THE GOOD EARTH**

Pearl Buck's most famous novel, *The Good Earth*, describes the daily life of a Chinese peasant family. In the following passage, Wang Lung and his wife O-Lan face disaster in the form of a plague of locusts.

And as if to cure him of the root of his ceaseless thought of his own troubles, there came out of the south one day a small slight cloud. At first it hung on the horizon small and smooth as a mist, except it did not come hither and thither as clouds blown by the wind do, but it stood steady until it spread fanwise up into the air.

The men of the village watched it and talked of it and fear hung over them, for what they feared was this, that locusts had come out of the south to devour what was planted in the fields. Wang Lung stood there also, and he watched, and they gazed and at last a wind blew something to their feet, and one stooped hastily and picked it up and it was a dead locust, dead and lighter than the living hosts behind.

Then Wang Lung forgot everything that troubled him. Women and sons and uncle, he forgot them all, and he rushed among the frightened villagers, and he shouted at them,

"Now for our good land we will fight these enemies from the skies!"

But there were some who shook their heads, hopeless from the start, and these said,

"No, and there is no use in everything. Heaven has ordained that this year we shall starve, and why should we waste ourselves in struggle against it, seeing that in the end we must starve?"

And women went weeping to the town to buy incense to thrust before the earth gods in the little temple, and some went to the big temple in the town, where the gods of heaven were, and thus earth and heaven were worshipped.

But still the locusts spread up into the air and on over the land.

Then Wang Lung called his own laborers and Ching stood silent and ready beside him and there were others of the younger farmers, and with their own hands these set fire to certain fields and they burned the good wheat that stood almost ripe for cutting and they dug wide moats and ran water into them from the wells, and they worked without sleeping. O-Lan brought them food and the women brought their men food, and the men ate standing and in the field, gulping it down as beasts do, as they worked night and day.

Then the sky grew black and the air was filled with the deep still roar of many wings beating against each other, and upon the land the locusts fell, flying over this field and leaving it whole, and falling upon that field, and eating it as bare as winter. And men sighed and said, "So Heaven wills," but Wang Lung was furious and he beat the locusts and trampled on them and his men flailed them with flails and the locusts fell into the fires that were kindled and they floated dead upon the waters of the moats that were dug. And many millions of them died, but to those that were left it was nothing.

Nevertheless, for all his fighting Wang Lung had this as his reward: the best of his fields were spared and when the cloud moved on and they could rest themselves, there was still wheat that he could reap and his young rice beds were spared and he was content.

BUCKLEY, WILLIAM F. See NEW YORK CITY (Famous People).

BUDAPEST

Budapest is the capital, largest city, and economic heart of Hungary and the center of the country's cultural life. It lies on the Danube River, which divides it into two main parts, Buda and Pest. The two sections were once separate cities. Buda, the older part, is situated on the steep hills of the Danube's western bank. Pest, the much more heavily populated of the two, is spread out along the flatter eastern bank of the river. Eight bridges link the two sections. The population of the city is more than 2 million.

The City: Buda. Buda was once the residence of Hungarian kings and the seat of their governments. It is dominated to a great extent by its hills. Two of the most notable are Castle Hill and Gellért Hill.

Castle Hill is a walled residential district, dating from the Middle Ages, where the nobility formerly made their homes. Its most impressive monuments are the Royal Palace and the Coronation Church, more commonly known as the Matthias Church. The Coronation Church, where Hungary's monarchs were crowned, was completed in 1269 and is the oldest building in Buda. Nearby is the Fisherman's Bastion, which provides an unequaled view of the opposite bank of the Danube.

Gellért Hill, to the south, has at its summit a citadel, or fortress. This was constructed by the Austrian authorities after a failed revolt by Hungarians against Austrian rule in 1848. The hill itself was named for St. Gellért (or Gerard), who, according to legend, was thrown to his death here in 1046 by opponents of Christianity.

At the northern edge of Buda is the district of Óbuda (Old Buda).

It, too, was once a separate city but is now a part of Budapest.

Pest. By contrast, the layout of Pest is distinguished by wide boulevards and avenues. Many of these extend from the Inner City, the oldest and most famous part of Pest. Within the Inner City and overlooking the Danube is the neo-Gothic Parliament building, one of Budapest's most striking landmarks. Nearby is the National Gallery, a fine arts museum. The Academy of Sciences, St. Stephen's Cathedral, the National Museum, and the various colleges of Eötvös Loránd University, the country's oldest and largest university (founded in 1635), are all situated in the Inner City.

Pest has many other museums and institutions of learning. Numerous theaters, two opera houses, and several concert halls also

Budapest, the capital of Hungary, lies on the Danube River. The domed Parliament building is in Pest, on the river's eastern bank.

reflect its rich cultural life. The Margaret Bridge links Pest with Margaret Island, a resortlike area in the Danube.

Economic Activity. Budapest is Hungary's transportation hub and an important river port as well as its industrial center. It produces a wide variety of manufactured products, including transportation and electrical equipment, machine tools, precision instruments, agricultural machinery, textiles, clothing, and pharmaceuticals.

History. Settlements have existed at or near the site of Budapest since earliest known times. The Magyars, the ancestors of the Hungarians, established the cities of Óbuda and Pest during the late 800's. In 1255, King Bela IV built his royal residence in what is now the Castle Hill section of Buda. The city reached the height of its splendor during the reign of Matthias Corvinus (1458–90). But in 1541, Buda fell to the Ottoman Turks, who ruled the region for some 145 years. During this period, Pest developed as a separate city.

Ottoman Turkish rule was replaced by that of the Austrian Habsburgs, who dominated both Hungary and Budapest for the next 200 years. The union of Buda and Pest in 1873 marked the beginning of the modern city, while the breakup of the Austro-Hungarian Empire in 1918, at the end of World War I, made Budapest the capital of a Hungarian republic.

The city suffered enormous damage in 1944–45, near the end of World War II, when many of its historic landmarks and public buildings were destroyed and its eight bridges blown up by retreating German soldiers. In 1948, after Hungary came under Communist rule, Budapest, as it had been under the Turks and Austrians, became a center of resistance to oppression. When a revolt against Communist rule erupted in 1956 and was put down with great severity by Soviet troops and tanks, the city once again suffered considerable damage. However, a peaceful revolution in 1989 led to the collapse of Communism in 1990, and a democratic government was re-established.

HELMUT KOENIG
Travel Writer

BUDDHA

Siddhartha Gautama, also known to Buddhists as **Bhagavat** (Blessed One), **Sugata** (Well-Gone), or **Tathagata** (Thus-Gone), is widely believed to be the historical Buddha. He was a Hindu prince who was probably born in the mid-500's B.C. His father ruled a small state in northern India, near the Himalayas. According to legend, Siddhartha was conceived when his mother, Maya, dreamed of a white elephant. When he was born, a sage predicted he would become either a great leader or a buddha (an enlightened, supreme, and perfect being).

Siddhartha's father did not want his son to dedicate himself to a religious life, so he tried to shield him from life's difficulties and all knowledge of sickness, pain, suffering, and death. Siddhartha spent his early years within palaces and gardens where everything was beautiful and pleasant. When he left the palace grounds, his father sent servants to clear the road of any painful sights. As a result, the young future buddha knew nothing about unhappiness.

Despite these efforts, Siddhartha did learn of unhappiness. As he was riding in his chariot one day, he came upon a frail old man. Then he saw another man suffering from a dread disease. Later he met some men carrying the body of one who had died. When Siddhartha asked about those who suffered from old age, disease, and death, he was told, "This happens to all men." For the first time he understood that unhappiness is a part of life.

Siddhartha was overwhelmed with compassion and sorrow. He realized he could no longer remain cut off from the sight of all suffering and would never be content until he understood things as they really were.

At age 29 he decided to become a religious recluse. Although he was married and had a newborn son, he renounced his old life, including a vast fortune, and left the palace. He wanted nothing to interfere with his search for understanding.

At first Siddhartha believed that giving up all worldly pleasures and eating very little food would help him in this search. After six years, however, he realized it would not. He abandoned his rigid lifestyle and decided to look for the truth within. He sat beneath a tree (which Buddhists now call the Bodhi Tree) and vowed that he would not leave until he understood the whole meaning of life. Siddhartha attained buddhahood in one day; after that he remained there for 49 days enjoying the bliss of his insight.

It is believed that at this time he could have entered **nirvana**. (For more information, see the article BUDDHISM.) However, the Buddha decided he could help others by delaying his entry into nirvana and sharing what he had learned.

The Buddha spent the next 45 years teaching. He died when he was 80. Shortly before his death he reminded his followers that they should not grieve, because all things must change. Buddhists believe that the Buddha continues to exist through his teachings.

Reviewed by ROBERT A.F. THURMAN
Jey Tsong Khapa Professor of Buddhist Studies
Columbia University

BUDDHISM

Buddhism is one of the world's oldest and most widespread religions. Scholars believe that its **sangha**, or religious community, is the oldest continuously existing human institution. Founded in India during the 500's B.C., it is based on the teachings of the historical Buddha.

Buddhism has no central authority or organizational structure. It is not based on belief in a supreme creator, although it does accept the existence of lesser deities. Buddhism centers instead on concepts known as the Three Jewels. They are the Buddha-jewel (the teacher), the **dharma** jewel (the Buddha's teachings), and the sangha jewel.

Before Communism, Buddhism was the dominant religion of Asia, and there are still many Buddhists there. Buddhists are found in lesser numbers throughout the world. Estimates on the total number of Buddhists vary considerably and range from 230–500 million. An exact figure is hard to determine because Buddhism coexists harmoniously with some other religions. For example, a Chinese Buddhist may also be a Confucian and a Taoist in some respects. Some may be Buddhists as well as Christians or Jews. A Buddhist is defined as a person who has embraced the Three Jewels. Currently, Buddhists living in areas where their beliefs are not accepted (China, for example) may not wish to identify themselves.

▶ BELIEFS

The most important Buddhist teachings are incorporated in the Four Noble Truths. They consist of the following:

One of the best-known images of the Buddha is this bronze statue in Kamakura, Japan, created in the 1200's. It draws many visitors each year.

Unenlightened life is suffering.
The origin of suffering is ignorance and desire.
Suffering can be brought to an end in enlightenment and **nirvana**.
There is a path to the attainment of enlightenment and nirvana.

Buddhists believe that everything in life is in a constant state of change. People do not realize they are actually part of the flow of the universe and struggle to maintain a sense

Many Buddhists worship at shrines and holy sites such as this one. Worshipers often make offerings of food, flowers, incense, and other items to the Buddha.

of permanence for their separate selves. However, nothing is separate or permanent—everyone dies and is reborn an indefinite number of times. The effects of one's past actions (**karma**) determine the quality of life a person experiences each time.

The perpetual cycle of death and rebirth for those struggling to maintain a separate permanence is called **samsara**. It is accompanied by misery and suffering. Only by eliminating ignorance, the misperception of reality (of the self and the world), and the desire that arises from that misperception—attachment to things, other people, even life itself—can humans end suffering and attain peace. This state of inner peace and enlightenment is called nirvana and buddhahood. Buddhists believe that those who follow the Middle Way and the Eightfold Path can attain nirvana.

Following the Middle Way means avoiding extremes of both desire and self-denial. The Eightfold Path outlines actions and ways of thinking that stress morality, compassion, and respect for others, as well as self-discipline and wisdom.

Divisions into different types of Buddhism are somewhat complex. Buddhism spread through many different cultures, leading to divisions such as Indian Buddhism, Tibetan Buddhism, Chinese Buddhism, and Japanese Buddhism. Within each of these are numerous different schools. Several main types of Buddhism developed in India: Theravada, Mahayana, and Vajrayana or Tantrayana. While all have similar basic beliefs, each is distinguished by certain traits.

Theravada Buddhism is practiced in its exclusive form mainly in Sri Lanka, Myanmar (Burma), Thailand, Cambodia, and Laos. It is considered the most conservative form of Buddhism. Theravada means "teaching of the elders," and Theravada Buddhists believe that their teachings are closest to the original doctrines and practices of the Buddha. These Buddhists believe that enlightenment is only attainable by a few—those who give up many physical and material comforts and live in seclusion as monks or nuns. The goal is to attain enlightenment and become an **arhat**, or perfect saint. The sacred writings of Theravada Buddhism include the **Tripitaka**, or Three Baskets. These are the Discipline (Vinaya), which are rules for followers; the Discourse (Sutra), which are the words of the Buddha; and the Science (Abhidharma), systematic studies of Buddhist principles and beliefs.

Mahayana Buddhism, which developed from Theravada, is practiced primarily in China, Tibet, Mongolia, Vietnam, Japan, and Korea. (Theravada itself is also found in most of these countries.) Mahayana is considered a more liberal and universal interpretation of the Buddha's teachings and emphasizes a life of compassion and service. Mahayana Buddhists believe that enlightenment is available to all. The goal of Mahayana Buddhism is to become a **bodhisattva** (a "being destined for enlightenment"), who postpones entering nirvana in order to benefit others. When the bodhisattva finally attains buddhahood, all beings are taken with him or her into a buddha-land, which is a world free of suffering. Unlike the arhat, who remains in seclusion and practices the religious life only for his or her own liberation (enlightenment), the bodhisattva is more focused on other individuals and humanity in general.

The spiritual concept of "emptiness" (**suny-ata**) is also found in the Mahayana tradition. Emptiness is part of the basic Buddhist teaching of selflessness (**anatman**), and the idea that all people and things are interconnected. The Mahayana literature consists of an expanded version of the Three Baskets. Important Mahayana scriptures (sutras) are called the Transcendent Wisdom Sutras (including versions known as Diamond-Cutter and Heart Sutras), the Flower Ornament Sutra, the Pure Land Sutra, and the Lotus Sutra.

Vajrayana (or **Tantrayana**) Buddhism is a lesser-known form of Buddhism that developed in India. It features various forms of physical and mental yoga that aim to speed the bodhisattva's progress to buddhahood. The first Vajrayana practitioners were Theravada monks with a Mahayana philosophy, whose compassion for all beings made them wish to use various methods to free beings from suffering and bring on the buddha-world more quickly.

These three main forms of Indian Buddhism—Theravada, Mahayana, and Vajrayana—spread throughout Asia in waves. Some eventually disappeared from some countries due to various circumstances. India lost almost all three forms when foreign invaders destroyed the Buddhist monastic universities and Buddhist ideas were absorbed by Hinduism. In many countries, Buddhism now exists as some combination of these three main forms and is also interwoven with the local culture, language, and religions.

Tibetan Buddhism, which originated in Tibet, is distinguished from these other types by its role in government. Only in Tibet did the monastic community also govern the nation. For much of the past 300 years Tibet's spiritual leader, the Dalai Lama, has also been its political leader. The Dalai Lama is believed to be the reincarnation of the bodhisattva of compassion, Avalokiteshvara.

Zen Buddhism is a variety of Japanese Buddhism that has become well known in the West. It originally began in China and was known as *Ch'an*. It emphasizes the Mahayana belief that each person has the potential for enlightenment. It particularly emphasizes direct experience and meditation rather than texts and explanation, as Zen Buddhists believe it is impossible to put teachings into words. Zen teachers also employ a sort of riddle called a koan. Koans are puzzles or questions that challenge one's usual thinking patterns in order to overcome barriers to enlightenment. One of the most well-known koans is "What is the sound of one hand clapping?"

Buddhist monks spend much of their time in study and contemplation. Most shave their heads and wear long robes.

▶ PRACTICES

A number of Buddhists become monks or nuns—even entering novitiate as young children. That is, they go to live in a monastery with others, give up all ownership, renounce marriage, and enter a demanding program of study and contemplation. This lifestyle can be temporary, but it is usually permanent. Other Buddhists consider it an honor to support these monastics, who depend on them for food and clothing. The monastics, in turn, provide others with spiritual guidance.

For those who are not monks or nuns, there are other ways to participate in the religious community (sangha). Many Buddhists

Wat Benchamabophit, in Bangkok, Thailand, is one of the world's most beautiful Buddhist temples. Also known as the Marble Temple, it has a majestic entrance flanked by two huge marble lions.

meditate. They may worship at shrines, at home, in public, and at holy sites, and make offerings of food, flowers, incense, and other special items to the Buddha. Taking a trip to a holy site (pilgrimage) is considered very important. Buddhists believe that all of these actions can enhance karma, lead to greater happiness in the world, and bring one closer to enlightenment.

Buddhists celebrate a number of holidays, although not all are observed on the same day by all groups. The most important holidays are the Buddha's birthday, the day the Buddha attained enlightenment under the Bodhi tree, and the day of final nirvana (passing away). (See the article BUDDHA for more information.) Most Buddhists celebrate all three of these holidays on the full moon day of the fourth lunar month, usually falling in May. In Japan, these holidays are celebrated on three different days.

▶ HISTORY

Buddhism developed at a time of social and religious change. It evolved as a reaction against the elaborate rituals and caste system (rigid division of social classes) of the ancient Indian Vedic religion. The Buddha invented monasticism to provide those seeking enlightenment with a safe haven. After the Buddha's death, his followers—monks, nuns, and others—devoted themselves to preserving and spreading his teachings (the dharma)

throughout northern India. For hundreds of years these teachings were passed on by word of mouth. When people began to write them down, they found they did not agree on everything. Some had learned one thing; some had learned another. These different beliefs led to the development of different types of Buddhism.

Meanwhile, various factors helped spread Buddhism to other areas. One was the conversion of the Indian emperor Asoka (reigned about 273–232 B.C.) to Buddhism. He not only promoted Buddhism in India but sent Buddhist missionaries abroad. As international trade developed, Buddhism also spread into what is now Pakistan, Afghanistan, and Central Asia, across the Bay of Bengal to southeast Asia, then to China, Korea, and eventually Japan.

Although Buddhism began in India, it had virtually disappeared from there by the 1300's and was replaced primarily by Hinduism and Islam. India's great Buddhist universities—Nalanda, for instance—were no longer significant. The number of Buddhist pilgrims from distant lands decreased.

In China, however, Buddhism took root in the first century A.D. and became strong, aided by the distribution of Buddhist texts that had been translated from Sanskrit (an Indian language) to Central Asian languages. By the 400's there was a great interest in viewing the original Sanskrit texts, and many Chinese Buddhist pilgrims journeyed to India. Numerous texts were translated into Chinese.

Japanese Buddhism was based on Chinese models. It first emerged in the 500's. Initially of interest mainly to scholars and members of the Japanese court, it had gained widespread popularity by the 1100's.

Buddhism was introduced in Tibet in the early 600's. By the 1200's, Tibetans had translated many Sanskrit Buddhist texts, thus preserving knowledge that would have been lost with the destruction of Indian Buddhist institutions. Later the Tibetans succeeded in converting the Mongolians to their peaceful Buddhist lifestyle.

BUDDHISM TODAY

Since the beginning of the 1900's, Buddhist practices have been increasingly challenged throughout Asia. The practice of Buddhism has been a political issue in many countries and has been discouraged by Communist governments in Vietnam, Laos, China, Tibet, and North Korea. However, some Buddhist leaders have encouraged followers to become more involved in the nationalist movements of their own countries and have sought more contact with other nations where Buddhism is flourishing.

An organization that promotes this is the World Fellowship of Buddhists, founded in 1950, which now has chapters worldwide. Another organization, the World Buddhist Sangha Council, founded in 1966, also promotes unity among Buddhists.

One of Buddhism's most visible and politically active figures is the current Dalai Lama, Tenzin Gyatso. He was recognized and installed as the Dalai Lama in 1940. He fled from Communist repression in 1959 and traveled the world spreading Buddhist teachings and representing the Tibetan people. He received the Nobel Peace Prize in 1989 for his nonviolent efforts to end the Chinese Communist domination of Tibet. Although he has been living in exile from Tibet for much of his life and is no longer Tibet's political leader, he is still the spiritual leader of all Tibetan Buddhists. The Dalai Lama has also established a Tibetan government-in-exile in India and has worked to preserve Tibetan arts, scriptures, and medicine.

Meanwhile, Buddhism continues to grow in Europe, Australia, and New Zealand. Some growth, but not as much, has also taken place in Africa and South America.

Although Buddhism has grown considerably in North America, it is still not a major religion there. Until the 1960's it was largely a religion of Chinese and Japanese immigrants. But because there are now more Asians living in North America, and more North American converts, the number of Buddhists there continues to expand.

ROBERT A.F. THURMAN
Jey Tsong Khapa Professor of Buddhist Studies
Columbia University

BUDGETS, FAMILY

Most families have far more money than they realize. The ones who get the most from their money seem to have learned how to manage the money they have very well.

A plan for spending the money is called a budget. You, as a member of a family, share in the money spent for food, shelter, clothing, medical care, education, and recreation in your family. It is important to know how much thought and planning often has to be done to provide for the family's basic needs and the individual wants of each member.

Each family must decide for itself exactly how much planning it wants to do. However, there are useful steps that any family can follow for this purpose.

Step 1. Decide whether to divide the budget into periods of 1 week, 2 weeks, or 1 month. Most people find that the time between paydays is the best budgeting period.

WEEKLY BUDGET

Fixed Expenses	Cost
Rent and Mortgage	
Insurance	
Transportation	
Taxes and Savings	
Time Payments	
Living Expenses	
Food	
Clothing	
Utilities	
Recreation	
Contributions	
Medical	
Automobile	
Others	
Total	

Step 2. List all fixed expenses. Include every bill for which the exact amount is known in advance, such as payments for rent, mortgage, insurance, the car, and any other installment purchases.

Step 3. List all regular living expenses for which the amounts vary. Estimate how much each costs during a pay period. Accurate estimates will require time and experience since the amount spent on living expenses depends on such things as how much care is shown by the shopper and the time of year it is. For example, food costs can be kept down by the person who shops and cooks wisely; more water is used in summer, and more fuel and electricity in winter. The cost of clothing and its care can be spread out over the whole year instead of spending large amounts in the fall and spring. The home-maker who knows what to look for in selecting clothing, who has a wardrobe plan that will prevent unwise purchases, and who can sew, will need less money than another person.

Step 4. List any expected major expenses too large to be paid in a single pay period. Decide how much should be set aside each payday to meet such expenses when they occur. Taxes can usually be estimated in advance, and enough money saved to pay them. Home appliances and furnishings can be bought with savings.

Step 5. Total all expenses. Compare this total with the family's income for the budgeting period. If the expenses are too high, look for ways to cut them. If there is money left, some of it should be set aside regularly in an emergency fund and some in a savings or investment program.

Step 6. Use a budget book or make a chart. Write down the family's plans for using its money. In the following weeks and months, compare this budget with what is actually spent and make any necessary changes.

Even a good budget will not help the family control its spending unless all family members co-operate. Young people who get experience in good money management as they grow up will have little difficulty in working out a family budget of their own.

KATHERINE R. CONAFAY
Author, *Family Budgets*

BUENOS AIRES

Buenos Aires is Argentina's largest city, its capital, and its gateway to the world. It is one of the largest ports in the Americas, situated on the Río de la Plata ("river of silver"), about 170 miles (275 kilometers) from the sea. The city was founded by Spanish conquistador Pedro de Mendoza in 1536. It was named by the early Spanish explorers. Buenos Aires means "good winds."

One of the largest cities in the Southern Hemisphere, Greater Buenos Aires has approximately 12 million people—about one-third of Argentina's total population. The city itself has about 3 million people. Like Argentines in general, about 95 percent of *porteños* ("people of the port"), as the city's inhabitants are known, trace their origins to Italy and Spain, with significant numbers of Eastern Europeans. Buenos Aires has one of the world's largest Jewish populations.

Buenos Aires is set on a flat plain like a huge, sprawling giant. Its highways and streets stretch out in all directions as far as

the eye can see. The city is known for its sunny plazas and wide boulevards; Avenida 9 de Julio in downtown Buenos Aires is one of the widest streets in the world. Many of the streets and avenues are bordered with flowers. The center of the city bustles with sound and movement. Busy people go about their errands, talking in Spanish and many other languages.

The City. Buenos Aires, a city of music and drama, is the home of the tango. World-famous opera stars perform at the luxurious

Avenida 9 de Julio, one of the widest streets in the world, is among the many broad, tree-lined boulevards that are characteristic of Buenos Aires.

Teatro Colón. Open-air ballet performances are held at the Palermo Gardens, where symphony orchestras play. Other attractions include the Casa Rosada presidential palace, the National Cathedral, the National Museum of Art, and the National Historical Museum. The city's inhabitants also love to watch and play sports—golf, tennis, swimming, rowing, polo, car and horse racing, and, above all, soccer.

The city is home to many important public universities, including the nation's largest, the University of Buenos Aires, founded in 1821. There are also several private institutions. The city's fine libraries include the National Library, founded in 1810.

Buenos Aires has many colorful suburban neighborhoods. People enjoy strolling past La Boca's brightly painted wooden houses or through San Telmo's antique market. A huge public transportation system of trains, subways, and buses lets people travel quickly between neighborhoods.

Economic Activity. Buenos Aires is the hub of Argentina's commerce and a great port city; ships come and go from all over the world. The Greater Buenos Aires metropolitan area is the site of an impressive concentration of manufacturing activity. Leading industries are metalworking, auto manufac- turing, oil refining, machine building, and the production of textiles, chemicals, and paper.

History. The first settlement by the Spanish in 1536 failed because of Indian attacks. Juan de Garay established the first permanent community in 1580. Buenos Aires was a modest city until the end of the 1800's. In time hundreds of thousands of immigrants made it the diverse city it is today.

By 1900, the city began a process of industrialization and social modernization. Political upheavals and military coups interrupted constitutional order in the 1930's, 1940's, 1960's, and 1970's. In the 1990's the government began free-market economic reforms, including a radical money reform. The economy grew rapidly at first but then went into a deep recession.

In 2001 Argentina suffered a financial collapse and an unprecedented political crisis. By 2002, unemployment in Buenos Aires and its suburbs surpassed 20 percent. About 16 million people—nearly half the population— were thrust below the poverty line.

Ernesto Sábato
Author, *On Heroes and Tombs*
Reviewed by William C. Smith
School of International Studies
University of Miami

BUFFALO. See New York (Cities).

Buffalo and bison are related to cattle. Water buffalo (*left*) have wide, sweeping horns and smooth coats. Bison (*above*) have smaller horns, large heads, and heavy coats.

BUFFALO AND BISON

Buffalo and bison are large, hoofed cattle-like animals. Asian and African buffalo are tropical animals. The animal that is sometimes called an American buffalo is actually a bison. There is a European bison as well.

Asian Buffalo. Asian buffalo are commonly known as water buffalo because they spend much of their time in water and mud. They have smooth coats, and their wide horns are ridged and flattened. Water buffalo range from southern Europe to Southeast Asia. They are rare in the wild but are widely used as domestic animals. Several types of buffalo survive in the wild on islands in Southeast Asia. These include the **anoa**, which is a dwarf buffalo, and the **tamarau**, which is slightly larger.

Domestic water buffalo are used for farmwork, particularly cultivating rice paddies and collecting oil palm fruits in Southeast Asia. They have also been introduced to Brazil and other hot, moist countries in South America. These animals are remarkably docile (obedient) and intelligent. Water buffalo are also used for milk production, particularly in India and southern Europe.

African Buffalo. African buffalo look similar to Asian buffalo, but they are a different group. Their horns are wide with a heavy base that is used in combat among males. The hooked ends are useful for defense against predators. The African buffalo is known for its contrary (difficult) nature. The savannah buffalo is large, black, and aggressive and is found on the savannas of eastern and southern Africa. It may form large herds and tends to stand and fight predators rather than flee. The forest buffalo is a smaller, reddish, less aggressive animal. It is found in western Africa, where it lives in small groups in dry woodlands and forests. Because of its unpredictable behavior, the African buffalo has never been domesticated but is held on some larger ranches for hunting or wildlife viewing.

Bison. Bison are found in North America and Europe. They are characterized by a large head and strong forequarters. Unlike the Asian and African buffalo, bison have a heavy coat and a "beard." Bison horns are smooth and sharp and relatively small.

North American bison are divided into two closely related types—the plains bison and the wood bison. The plains bison once lived in huge numbers on the plains of central and western North America. But millions were slaughtered for meat and clothing and to make way for settlement, so only a few remained by 1890. Conservation efforts allowed them to survive, but they are now found in the wild only in parks and reserves. Wood bison lived on grassy floodplains of northern Canada. They also were saved from extinction but are still quite rare.

North American bison have been raised domestically since the 1700's. Today bison are raised for meat, milk, and hides. The current farmed bison population exceeds 150,000 in Canada and 350,000 in the United States.

The European bison is also known as the **wisent**. Their numbers have been depleted by hunting and war and now number about 3,000 despite conservation efforts. The European bison is considered less suitable as a domestic animal because of its behavior and more specialized feeding.

ROBERT J. HUDSON
University of Alberta

See also HOOFED MAMMALS.

BUFFALO BILL   (WILLIAM FREDERICK CODY)   (1846–1917)

Buffalo Bill was the last of the famous American frontier scouts. He was a sharpshooter and an expert guide and hunter. His Wild West shows did much to establish the popular image of the Old West.

Buffalo Bill, whose real name was William Frederick Cody, was born in Le Claire, Iowa, on February 26, 1846. At the age of 14 he was carrying mail for the Pony Express. During the U.S. Civil War, he was a Union Army scout. Later he hunted bison (often called buffalo). It is said that Cody killed 69 bison in one day, and over 4,000 in 8 months. He became known everywhere as Buffalo Bill. When war with the Sioux and Cheyenne Indians broke out in 1875, Cody again became a scout for the cavalry. He is said to have fought a duel with Yellow Hand, the son of a Cheyenne chief, and killed him.

In 1883, Cody organized his famous traveling Wild West shows. These shows included a huge cast of cowboys, Indians, and sharpshooters, as well as herds of bison, elk, ponies, steers, and wild horses. Historic events such as Custer's Last Stand were re-enacted. Sitting Bull, the Sioux chief whose warriors had helped defeat General Custer's soldiers, traveled with the show in 1885. Annie Oakley, the famous sharpshooter, was another star. Thousands of people in the United States, Canada, and Europe saw the show before Cody lost it in 1913 because of debts.

Cody died on January 10, 1917. His grave and the Cody Memorial Museum are on top of Lookout Mountain in Colorado. Other Cody museums include the Buffalo Bill Historical Center in Cody, Wyoming, where scenes from the old Wild West shows are re-created, and Buffalo Bill's Ranch State Historical Park in North Platte, Nebraska.

Reviewed by THOMAS B. MORRISON
Buffalo Bill's Ranch State Historical Park

BUFFALO SOLDIERS

The Buffalo Soldiers were African American cavalrymen who fought in the Indian Wars in the American West. They belonged to the ninth and tenth regiments, which were created in 1866.

The term "Buffalo Soldiers" was reportedly first used in the summer of 1867 when the black soldiers fought against Cheyenne warriors for the first time. The Cheyenne called the cavalrymen Buffalo Soldiers because, like the buffalo, the men fought ferociously when cornered. And because the buffalo was sacred to the Native Americans of the Great Plains, the term must also have implied some respect for the soldiers. The members of the ninth and tenth regiments proudly accepted the name, and the tenth regiment's flag even had a buffalo on it.

The Buffalo Soldiers protected settlers and the builders of the Union Pacific Railroad; carried mail; escorted wagon trains; built forts and roads; and strung telegraph lines. They battled Indians who were led by such famous warriors as Geronimo, Satanta, and Roman Nose. Twelve of the cavalrymen were awarded the Congressional Medal of Honor for their services.

After large-scale conflict with the Indians ended in the early 1890's, the Buffalo Soldiers saw less combat as they encountered growing racism. In 1944, the ninth and tenth regiments were removed from active duty and their members transferred to other army units.

Members of two other black regiments, the 24th and the 25th, were also sometimes referred to as Buffalo Soldiers. Formed in the same year as the ninth and tenth, they fought in both world wars and the Korean War before being disbanded in the 1950's.

CLINTON COX
Author, *The Forgotten Heroes: The Story of the Buffalo Soldiers*

The 110-story Sears Tower in Chicago is the tallest building in the United States. Because of their height, skyscrapers must be uniquely and carefully designed.

BUILDING CONSTRUCTION

The construction of a building requires the talents and skills of many people who work with a variety of materials and processes. Architects and engineers design buildings. Workers in forests, quarries, mills, and factories produce the materials from which buildings are made. Contractors bring together the materials and the workers to assemble the buildings, and building inspectors make sure each building is constructed so it will be safe and healthy for the people who use it. Working together, these people create the fabric of our cities—buildings ranging from simple sheds to skyscrapers.

Materials of Construction

Two basic types of materials are used in buildings: structural and nonstructural. Structural materials hold up the building against such forces as gravity, wind, and earthquakes.

Such materials include stone, bricks, concrete blocks, concrete, wood, and steel. Nonstructural materials keep out the weather and finish the building in useful and attractive ways. There are many nonstructural materials used in buildings, but the most important are roofing materials, thermal insulation, glass, and gypsum.

Structural Materials. The major kinds of stone used in construction are granite, sandstone, limestone, and marble. Quarry workers cut large pieces of stone from the earth. At factories these pieces are sawed into blocks and slabs that will be used to make buildings. Stone is expensive because it is hard to cut and heavy to transport. But with its many colors and patterns, it is among the most beautiful of materials. It is also very durable.

Bricks are molded from moist clay. After drying, they are put into a kiln (a kind of oven), where they are heated to very high temperatures and converted into hard, stone-like blocks. Concrete blocks are molded from fresh concrete. Then they are hardened in a steam chamber.

People who work with stones, bricks, and concrete blocks are called masons. Any construction that uses these materials is called masonry. To make a masonry wall, masons set the blocks or stones in a thick layer of mortar, which is a mudlike mixture of sand, portland cement, and water. (Portland cement is a fine gray powder made from clay and limestone.) The mortar soon hardens into a rocklike material that holds the wall together and makes it weathertight.

Concrete is a mixture of sand, crushed stone, and portland cement. When blended with water, the cement powder hardens into a very strong adhesive that binds the sand and crushed stone into a rocklike material.

Masonry and concrete stand up well against pressing or squeezing forces known as **compression.** These materials are used in walls and columns that must withstand the compression created by the building's weight, or **load.** But masonry and concrete are brittle; they break when exposed to stretching forces, or **tension.** Nonbrittle materials that retain their strength when stretched are also necessary in building construction. Wood and steel, for example, are materials that can be used for beams and slabs that span horizontally between walls and columns.

Wood is used for structures of small or medium size. It is also used for the walls of small structures such as houses. Because wood can burn, however, it is not used in the construction of large buildings. Wood used in buildings must be kept dry and off the ground so it does not rot or become infested with insects.

Steel is a form of iron. Because of its great strength, steel is used for the frames of the tallest skyscrapers. Although it will not burn, steel will lose its strength at very high temperatures. In a large building, steel is covered with fire-resistant materials such as gypsum to protect it from becoming too hot should a fire occur in the building.

The brittleness of concrete can be overcome by embedding steel rods in it. This forms **reinforced concrete.** Beams and slabs of reinforced concrete can also span horizontal distances and are very resistant to fire.

Nonstructural Materials. Many nonstructural materials are just as important as structural materials. Roofing materials prevent rain and snow from leaking into the rooms below and causing structural damage. Buildings with sloping roofs, such as houses, typically are roofed with shingles. These are small, overlapping squares or rectangles of wood, slate, or asphalt. Flat roofs tend to hold rather than shed rainwater and snow. Because shingles have many seams, they are not watertight when used on flat roofs. Seamless sheets of asphalt or synthetic rubber must be used on flat roofs to keep water out.

Thermal insulating materials are also extremely important. They make buildings more comfortable and greatly reduce the amount of energy needed for heating and cooling. Insulating materials include loose mats of mineral fibers and lightweight boards of plastic foam.

Glass, another important nonstructural material, is made by melting sand, soda ash, and lime together. It is cast into large, smooth sheets that are cut into squares for use in windows. Gypsum is a common mineral that is made into plaster and plasterboard for walls and ceilings inside a building. Gypsum creates hard, smooth surfaces and is very resistant to fire. Gypsum plaster and plasterboard play a very important role in protecting structural materials from fire and preventing the spread of fire from one room of a building to another.

Constructing a House

Most houses are built by small crews of builders working with relatively simple tools and methods. The plans for a house may be specially drawn by an architect or team of architects to meet the needs or desires of a homeowner or builder. For an ordinary house, the builder may draw the plans or buy standard predrawn plans from a catalog. After the builder receives a building permit from the city or town building inspector, construction can begin. The first step is for an excavator to dig a hole for the foundation. Then workers construct the foundation, using concrete that has been poured into forms, concrete blocks, or wood treated with chemicals to prevent decay. The foundation must be strong enough to support the weight of the house.

Building a house: The first steps include digging for a foundation (*left*) and pouring concrete foundation walls and floors (*right*). Workers must spread and smooth the concrete for the floor before it hardens.

Sometimes the ground floor of the house is a concrete slab poured directly on the ground. More often it is made of wood. To make a wood floor, carpenters first bolt planks of wood, called **sills,** to the top of the foundation. Then horizontal pieces of lumber called **joists** are nailed to the sills. The joists are covered with sheets of plywood to create a level unfinished floor called the **subfloor.**

Walls of a house are framed with vertical pieces of lumber called **studs.** The subfloor is

Building a house: The foundation has been "capped" with a subfloor. *Above:* Workers are putting up wall frames. *Right:* The wall frames are up and the slanting roof beams—rafters—are in place. A worker is nailing sheathing to the frame. *Below:* A diagram shows the main parts of a house.

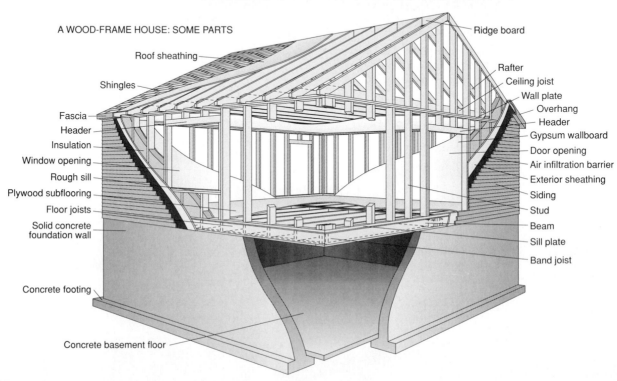

A WOOD-FRAME HOUSE: SOME PARTS

Ridge board
Roof sheathing
Shingles
Rafter
Ceiling joist
Wall plate
Overhang
Header
Fascia
Header
Insulation
Gypsum wallboard
Door opening
Air infiltration barrier
Window opening
Rough sill
Exterior sheathing
Plywood subflooring
Siding
Floor joists
Stud
Solid concrete foundation wall
Beam
Sill plate
Band joist
Concrete footing
Concrete basement floor

434

used as a kind of table on which sections of wall framing are assembled. Carpenters tilt finished sections of wall framing up into place and nail them to the floor frame. If the house is to be two stories high, the second floor joists rest on top of the first floor walls. Then the second story walls are assembled on the second floor, tilted up, and nailed down.

The attic floor and the sloping roof **rafters** are the last pieces of the house frame to be installed. The roof and all the outside walls are covered with a **sheathing** of wood boards, plywood, or sheets of wood composition board. Then carpenters can begin finishing the exterior of the house. First the roof is made watertight by nailing on the shingles. Then windows and doors that have been preassembled at a factory are installed in wall openings left for them. Finally, wood, vinyl, or aluminum siding is applied to the wall sheathing. Brick, stone, or stucco can also be used as siding.

Building a house: When the main frame is up, there is much left to do. *Below:* Pipes for water and wires for electricity must be run throughout the house. *Bottom:* A worker nails siding on the outside. *Below left:* Insulation is installed and large sheets of gypsum wallboard cover the framing inside. *Left:* Overlapping layers of shingles make the roof watertight.

435

Building a house: Finishing work (*above*) includes filling each wallboard joint with plaster and installing decorative trim. Painting or staining the house outside (*right*) makes the house look nice and protects it from the weather.

Why is a tree or an American flag sometimes placed on the highest part of a building under construction?

A tree or flag placed on, or nailed to, the highest part of a building under construction is a modern version of the ancient "topping out" ceremony. Topping out, still practiced in many parts of the world, is meant to indicate that the frame of the structure has been completed. During a topping out ceremony of long ago, a barrel of beer might be drunk while a tree or wreath was attached to the ridge of a building's newly completed roof. Today, finishing the frame of a building is still cause for celebration.

Even before the exterior of the house is finished, work inside begins. Masons may construct a fireplace and chimney. Electricians, plumbers, and sheet metal workers install the electrical wiring, the pipes and plumbing fixtures, and the heating and air conditioning systems. Workers stuff blankets of insulation into all the spaces between the exterior wall studs and ceiling joists. Insulation helps keep heat inside the house during cold weather. The interior walls are then covered with gypsum plaster or sheets of gypsum wallboard. Decorative wood trim is nailed around interior windows and doors. Finish flooring, cabinets, and lighting fixtures are the last items to be installed. Unfinished surfaces are painted, stained, varnished, and wallpapered. Driveway, sidewalk, and landscaping work can take place outside. After a final cleanup the house is ready to live in.

Constructing Larger Buildings

A larger building is much more complicated than a house. Each one is specially designed by a team of professionals that includes both **architects** and **engineers.** Architects design the exterior form, interior spaces, and surfaces of the building. Engineers, who work closely with the architects, design the foundations, the structural skeleton, the heating and cooling system, the electrical wiring, and the plumbing. The design work is complicated and takes many months. The architects and engineers work with the owner of the building to design a structure that is attractive and sturdy, and meets the owner's requirements. They also work with the city building inspector to be sure that the building is constructed according to the building code, which is a set of rules for making buildings safe and healthy. The building code may require that the building is made of fireproof materials; that enough toilets and lavatories are provided for everyone in the building; and that there are at least two safe ways for people to escape from the building in case of fire. Even in buildings that are made from materials that will not burn, the contents of the rooms may burn, causing dangerous fires. The designers must always take fire safety into account.

After the design work has been completed, the architects and engineers make blueprints of their final drawings and give them to the **building contractor.** He or she is responsible for seeing that the building is constructed exactly as it was designed. The contractor buys the materials for the building, hires many kinds of workers to put the materials together, and manages the entire construction process.

Larger buildings are much, much heavier than houses and need larger and stronger foundations. If the soil beneath a building is very firm and the building is not too tall, the foundations may be ordinary concrete **footings,** which are the flat strips and squares of concrete that lie in the ground and support the walls and columns of the building. If the soil is not so firm or the building is tall, more elaborate kinds of foundations have to be built. Sometimes the building is placed on one giant concrete footing that is as broad as the building; this is called a **mat** or **raft** foundation. Sometimes large drills may be used to bore holes several feet in diameter straight down through softer layers of soil until solid rock or a very firm soil is reached. This may lie a hundred feet (about 30 meters) or more beneath the surface of the ground. Then each hole is filled with concrete to make a type of foundation called either a **pier** or a **caisson.** It takes dozens of caissons to support a building; each one can support a single column or a part of a foundation wall. **Pile foundations** are used in some types of soft soil. Workers hammer **piles** into the ground using machines called pile drivers. Piles are long, slender pieces of wood, steel, or concrete. After the pile has been pounded firmly into the soil like a giant nail, it can support a considerable amount of weight. A cluster of piles can support each column of the building. Many clusters of piles in a line can hold up a wall.

Buildings larger than houses must be built of stronger, more fire-resistant materials than those used in houses. Large wood beams and columns can be used in structures less than five stories high. The frames of most large buildings, however, are built entirely of stronger materials such as steel or concrete.

In some large buildings, masonry or concrete walls support floors made of steel beams or concrete slabs. In smaller buildings, the floors might be made of wood joists or beams. This type of construction is called **bearing wall construction** because the walls bear, or support, the weight of the floors and roof. This weight is finally transferred to the foundation, on which the bearing walls are built.

Large buildings need sturdy foundations. Some rest on hundreds of piles, which are driven deep into the ground by powerful machines called pile drivers.

Most large buildings are held up by an open framework of vertical columns and horizontal beams. This type of construction is called **skeleton construction** because it resembles the bony structure that holds up a human body. A building's skeletal frame may be made of steel or concrete. Steel building frames are put up by people called **ironworkers.** Ironworkers use cranes to lift the heavy beams and columns into place. Then they bolt and weld the parts of the frame together. Diagonal braces are also installed to prevent the building from swaying due to wind or earthquakes.

WHY DON'T TALL BUILDINGS BLOW DOWN IN A STRONG WIND?

Tall buildings must be braced throughout their height with cross-bracing, rigid connections, or stiff structural walls called shear walls. Most tall buildings are constructed of steel or reinforced concrete. These materials are flexible—that is, they can bend slightly without breaking. When strong winds blow, the steel and concrete buildings give way to the force of the wind by bending a little. For example, the Sears Tower in Chicago was designed to sway as much as 10 inches (25 centimeters). If tall buildings did not sway, they could be snapped in two by violent wind. The buildings are not pulled out of the ground because they are firmly anchored in strong foundations.

Reinforced concrete can be used to make bearing walls, columns, beams, and flat floor structures called slabs. The simplest kind of concrete structure is made up of columns and flat slabs, without any beams. For buildings with greater distances between columns, or where heavier weights must be supported, beams are used to hold up the slabs. In order to span longer distances, slabs are sometimes made with a ribbed or a waffle-like pattern underneath. These slabs are very strong and stiff without being too heavy or using too much concrete.

There are two ways of making a concrete building. One is called **sitecast construction.** In this method, workers construct wooden molds, or forms, into which steel rods are placed. Then wet concrete is poured, or "cast," into the forms, surrounding the steel reinforcing rods. After a few days the concrete has hardened and the forms are pulled off and re-used for another portion of the building.

The other way of making a concrete building is to cast the concrete in large pieces at a factory. The finished pieces of concrete are brought to the building site on trucks and are assembled in almost the same way as steel beams and columns. This is called **precast concrete construction.**

As soon as the steel or concrete frame of the building is finished, roofers apply a waterproof roof surface to keep out rain and snow. Crews of plumbers, electricians, and sheet metal workers install pipes, wires, air ducts, and elevators. Other workers install the exterior walls, which they bolt to the building frame. These walls are called **curtain walls** because they hang on the building (by means of the bolts), much like a curtain hangs on a wall. Curtain walls can be made of masonry, thin slabs of stone, panels of precast concrete, or light frames of aluminum holding sheets of glass and metal. Thermal insulation materials are put in the walls to make the building easier and more economical to heat and cool.

Once the outside walls are in place, interior partitions, ceilings, and floors can be installed. Interior partitions divide the inside of a building into separate spaces but do not bear any of the building's weight. Painters and a cleanup crew complete the construction.

Some kinds of structures, like basketball arenas, exhibition halls, and auditoriums, need roofs that span very long horizontal distances between the supporting walls or columns. Even steel beams may not be strong enough to safely span such distances. Instead, architects and engineers design other types of

The frame, or skeleton, of a skyscraper is made of sturdy steel columns and beams. The steel is lifted to the top by huge cranes or derricks. Thin "curtain walls" can be hung on the finished frame.

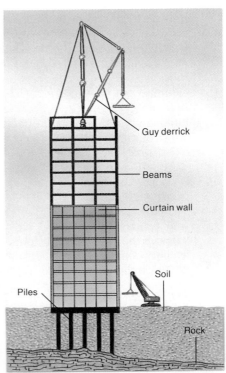

Guy derrick

Beams

Curtain wall

Soil

Piles

Rock

Cloth used in the construction of this airport at Riyadh, Saudi Arabia, makes it look like a huge tent. Air flowing through the waiting area cools people while hot air escapes through openings in the roof.

structural systems that are able to span longer distances. Domes or arches of reinforced concrete or heavy timbers can be designed to span hundreds of feet. Steel can make not only domes and arches, but also trusses and cable-supported roofs. A truss is used like a beam and is made up of slender pieces of steel that are connected together to make a series of open triangles. Cable-supported roofs are held up by strong wire ropes. A new type of long-span roof has been used in recent years on a number of covered stadiums. It is a thin, air-tight fabric reinforced with steel cables and held up by slight air pressure from within the stadium. The air pressure needed to hold the roof up—created by blowers in the heating and air conditioning system—is so slight that most people do not even notice it.

How We Learned to Build

Our earliest ancestors built from whatever materials were easily available. In forested areas tree trunks, branches, and saplings were fashioned into shelters of many kinds. Where stone was abundant, it was gathered and stacked into walls, with mud sometimes used between the stones. In regions with no stone, buildings were made of mud. Mud could be smeared over loosely woven mats of sticks, vines, or reeds to make thin walls. Or it could be mixed with straw and piled up to make very heavy, thick walls. Mud could also be molded into bricks that were dried by the sun. The bricks, joined by wet mud, could then be stacked into walls.

Although materials of construction (mud, stone, and wood) did not change for many thousands of years, people gradually learned how to build better buildings from them. These buildings were warmer, dryer, longer lasting, and more beautiful. People found that by raising the floors of their buildings off the ground, they could stay dry even during wet seasons. They learned to protect wooden building parts from water so they would not rot. They discovered ways to build sloping roofs from shingles or thatch (bundles of grass, reeds, or palm leaves) that would shed water without leaking. In cold climates, they discovered ways to build fires inside their buildings to keep warm in the winter, using holes in the roofs to let out the smoke. In hot, dry climates they learned that thick, heavy walls and roofs of stone or mud keep rooms cool even in the hottest weather. In humid tropical climates, where heavy walls would be damp, people developed light, airy houses on stilts so cooling breezes could pass through the rooms.

As time passed, builders became more skilled at cutting stone from quarries and carving it to the exact shapes they wanted for their buildings. They learned to make their mud bricks hard and durable by heating them to high temperatures in wood-fired kilns. Fireplaces and chimneys were developed to heat buildings better and remove smoke from the rooms. With metal saws and axes, tree trunks were squared into heavy posts and beams and sliced into thin boards for exterior and interior

Prefabricated buildings are those that were partly made in a factory. Large sections are transported to the site and assembled there to make a complete structure.

surfaces. Such metals as bronze, lead, and iron gradually came into use for fastening stones and timbers together and for covering roofs of public buildings.

More than 2,000 years ago the ancient Romans discovered how to make concrete, which they used to construct their enormous temples, baths, markets, and law courts. During the Middle Ages, the knowledge of how to make concrete was lost, but masons continued to develop their skills, building impressive churches, mosques, and public buildings that were covered with soaring domes and vaults (arched ceilings or roofs) made of brick or stone.

The Industrial Revolution began in the 1700's. During that time, people began using iron for columns and beams in buildings, especially factories. In the late 1800's, Gustave Eiffel built his famous iron tower in Paris. The making of concrete was revived, and glassmakers learned how to make larger and clearer sheets of glass for windows. Skyscrapers were built in Chicago and New York City using frames made of iron and steel. The first true skyscraper was the ten-story Home Insurance Building in Chicago, completed in 1885. Architects and engineers began using mathematics to make sure that their building frames were strong enough to stand up safely.

During the 1900's there have been many changes in building construction. Many kinds of machines are used on the construction site to cut, shape, lift, and install building materials. The use of mathematics in building design has increased so much that engineers now use computers to do most of their calculations. Much building construction is now done in factories rather than at the building site. Whole finished pieces of buildings are transported to the site and assembled rapidly in a process called **prefabrication.** Prefabrication saves money and time because it is faster and easier for the work to be done in a factory than out in the open.

Over the last century, ways have been developed to keep buildings well lighted and comfortable year-round. Electric lights, telephones, and computer networks are made possible by copper wiring run through buildings. Buildings are heated and cooled with many machines and devices designed to heat or chill air and control humidity. Sunlight is also better used to heat and light buildings. Modern plumbing systems enable people to wash, bathe, and cook in complete comfort and convenience. Computers are now used to control heating and cooling systems in many buildings. Computers will continue to be used more and more, not only to design buildings but to manage every aspect of their operation as well.

EDWARD ALLEN
Author, *Fundamentals of Building Construction*

See also ARCHITECTURE; BRICKS AND MASONRY; CEMENT AND CONCRETE; IRON AND STEEL.

BULGARIA

Bulgaria is situated on the Balkan Peninsula of southeastern Europe. It is bordered on the north by Romania, on the south by Greece and Turkey, and on the west by Serbia and Montenegro and Macedonia. Its location has played an important role in the nation's turbulent history.

Although it is now a small country, Bulgaria was a great regional power during the Middle Ages. In the late 1300's, however, Bulgaria was conquered by the Ottoman Turks, who then ruled it for nearly 500 years. A self-governing Bulgarian state, greatly reduced in size, was re-established in 1878, and a fully independent kingdom of Bulgaria, with borders similar to the country's present-day borders, was proclaimed in 1908.

In 1946, after World War II had ended, the monarchy was abolished and the Communist Party took control of the government. Communists ruled the country as a dictatorship until 1989, when they yielded to demands for reform and adopted a democratic form of government.

▶ **PEOPLE**

Slavic tribes settled in what is now Bulgaria during the A.D. 500's. In the 600's, the Bulgars, from Asia, conquered the Slavs and established a kingdom. They were later absorbed into the larger Slavic population.

Most of the people today are Bulgarian Slavs. Turks, the largest minority group, make up about 9 percent of the population. Bulgaria also has smaller numbers of Roma (also called Gypsies), Armenians, Greeks, and Russians.

Most Bulgarians are of Slavic descent. Many live in villages nestled in mountain ranges.

Left: Blue jeans are as popular with young Bulgarians as they are with teenagers the world over. *Below:* A bishop of the Bulgarian Orthodox Church blesses a parishioner. Most Bulgarians are orthodox Christians, although people of all religions are free to practice their faiths.

▶ **LAND**

Land Regions. Bulgaria has four major geographic regions: the Balkan Mountains, the Danube Plateau, the Thracian Plain, and the Rhodope Mountains.

The Balkan Mountains run east and west and split Bulgaria in two. North of the mountains the Danube Plateau slopes gradually to the Danube River. The Danube Plateau is an important agricultural area. Between the Balkan Mountains and the Rhodope Mountains lies the Thracian Plain, drained by the Maritsa River, which has an especially fertile valley. The Rhodope Mountains, the highest

Language. Bulgarian, the official language of the country, belongs to the South Slavic group of the Slavic languages. Bulgarian is closely related to Russian. Like Russian, it is written in the Cyrillic alphabet.

Religion. Historically, most Bulgarians have belonged to the Bulgarian Orthodox Church, an independent branch of the Eastern Orthodox Church. The head of the Bulgarian church is the Patriarch. Most of the Turks in Bulgaria are Muslims. Bulgarian-speaking Muslims are called Pomaks. There are also small communities of Jews, Roman Catholics, and Protestants.

Education. Education in Bulgaria is free and compulsory for all children ages 7 to 16. Primary schools follow a four-year program. Secondary schools are divided into two four-year cycles. Sofia University, founded in 1888, is the oldest and largest of Bulgaria's many institutions of higher learning.

FACTS and figures

REPUBLIC OF BULGARIA is the official name of the country.

LOCATION: Balkan Peninsula in southeastern Europe.

AREA: 42,823 sq mi (110,912 km²).

POPULATION: 7,800,000 (estimate).

CAPITAL AND LARGEST CITY: Sofia.

MAJOR LANGUAGE: Bulgarian (official).

MAJOR RELIGIOUS GROUPS: Bulgarian Orthodox, Muslim.

GOVERNMENT: Republic. **Head of state**—president. **Head of government**—prime minister. **Legislature**—National Assembly.

CHIEF PRODUCTS: Agricultural—vegetables, fruits, tobacco, livestock, wine, wheat, barley. **Manufactured**—machinery and other metal products, processed foods, chemicals, construction materials. **Mineral**—lignite (brown coal), iron ore, copper, zinc, lead, petroleum.

MONETARY UNIT: Lev (1 lev = 100 stotinki).

range in the Balkan Peninsula, form the southern boundary with Greece. Bulgaria's highest point, Musala Peak, rises 9,596 feet (2,925 meters) in this region.

Rivers and Coastal Waters. Bulgaria's chief rivers are the Danube, which forms its northern boundary with Romania, and the Maritsa. Other important rivers include the Tundzha, Struma, and Mesta. The Black Sea forms Bulgaria's eastern border.

Climate. The Balkan Mountains act as a divider between two main climatic regions. The northern regions have a continental climate, marked by humid summers and cold winters. The southern valleys have a Mediterranean climate, with mild but rainy winters and dry, hot summers. Annual precipitation averages 25 inches (635 millimeters).

Natural Resources. About one-third of Bulgaria is covered with valuable forests. Some three-quarters of the forests in the mountains are deciduous; the rest are coniferous. Beech trees and evergreen scrub plants are found along the Maritsa River valley and the Turkish border. The country's wild animal life includes bears, wolves, foxes, elk, and wildcats, which roam the mountain forests.

Bulgaria has a variety of limited mineral resources, including lignite (brown coal), iron ore, copper, zinc, and lead. Some petroleum is produced in the Black Sea region, but not enough to meet the country's energy needs.

▶ **ECONOMY**

Services, Bulgaria's largest economic sector, make up about 50 percent of the economy. They include banking, wholesale and retail trade, government services, and services related to the tourism industry.

Manufacturing. At the close of World War II in 1945, Bulgaria was one of the least industrialized countries in Europe. But emphasis by the government on industrialization brought about the rapid development of manufacturing. The primary goods manufactured today are machinery and other metal products, processed foods, chemicals, and construction materials.

Agriculture. About half of Bulgaria's land is suitable for agriculture. The rest is too dry, marshy, or mountainous. Much of the farmland, however, is very fertile. The chief crops include vegetables, fruits, tobacco, wine, wheat, and barley. The famous Valley of Roses, which lies in the heart of the country, is the center of Bulgaria's rose-growing industry. It produces attar of roses, an oil used in making perfumes. Bulgaria has nearly a world monopoly on the production of this oil.

Trade. Bulgaria's primary trade partner, traditionally, has been Russia. During the 1990's, Bulgaria sought expanded trade relations with the United States and countries in Western Europe, notably Germany and Italy. The country's main exports are machinery

Sunshine barely penetrates the winter mist covering Sofia, Bulgaria's capital and largest city. Although settlement dates from ancient times, Sofia first became the national capital after it was freed from Turkish rule in 1878.

and metal products. Its chief imports include fuels, minerals, and other raw materials.

▶ MAJOR CITIES

Sofia is Bulgaria's capital, largest city, and primary center of commerce and culture. More than 1 million people live in the city proper, and nearly a million more live in its greater metropolitan area.

The city has been a site of settlement since ancient times. Its oldest structure, the Church of St. George, was built on the ruins of a public bath dating from Roman times. Russian influences can be seen in the more modern Alexander Nevsky Cathedral, which contains a famous collection of religious icons. The city is also home to the National Art Gallery.

Plovdiv, with a population of about 1.2 million, is Bulgaria's second most populous city. Located on the Maritsa River, it is an important regional center of commerce.

▶ CULTURAL HERITAGE

In the 1800's, an independence movement revived native Bulgarian cultural traditions, which had declined during the five centuries of Ottoman rule. Khristo Botev, a leader of revolution against the Ottoman Turks, is still considered Bulgaria's greatest poet.

Today, Bulgarians are known more for music and art. Opera singers Boris Christoff and Nikolai Ghaiouroff won international acclaim. Bulgaria's most celebrated modern artist, Christo Javacheff, became recognized the world over for wrapping buildings and other large objects with acres of cloth.

In an effort to preserve its ancient cultural heritage, Bulgaria has had several of its historic monuments—such as ancient Thracian tombs of Kazanlŭk—declared World Heritage Sites by UNESCO, an agency of the United Nations.

▶ GOVERNMENT

Bulgaria is a republic governed under a constitution adopted in 1991. It provides for a president as head of state, elected along with a vice president for a 5-year term. The legislative body is the National Assembly, made up of 240 members elected to 4-year terms. The head of government is the prime minister, who is formally the Chairman of the Council of Ministers. The prime minister is chosen by the political party or coalition of parties having the largest number of seats in the National Assembly.

The third branch of government is the judiciary, or court system. The chairman of the supreme court is appointed by the president to a 7-year term. An additional body, the Constitutional Court, is responsible for interpretations of the constitution. It is composed of twelve justices, four each appointed by the president, the National Assembly, and the justices of the supreme courts to 9-year terms.

Below: Bulgaria's Valley of Roses is the world's chief source of attar (oil) of roses, used in making perfume. *Right:* Heavy industry, particularly the manufacture of machines and other metal products, makes up a large segment of Bulgaria's economy.

The First Bulgarian Empire.

The Bulgars arrived in the region from Central Asia in the A.D. 600's and conquered the part of the Balkan Peninsula inhabited by Slavs from the Byzantine Empire. In 681, Byzantium recognized the first Bulgarian empire, which lasted until 1018. Although they ruled the country, the Bulgars adopted the language and most of the customs of the conquered Slavs.

Bulgaria in the Middle Ages was a great military power. It fought many wars against the Byzantine Empire and against other neighbors and invaders. In 865 its ruler, Czar (emperor) Boris I, accepted Christianity. He established the independent Bulgarian church and introduced the Cyrillic alphabet. Boris' son Czar Simeon I (reigned 893–927) was one of Bulgaria's greatest rulers. During his reign, Bulgaria flourished as a center of Slavic culture and learning. Simeon I also conquered many new territories. At his death in 927, Bulgaria stretched from the Black Sea on the east to the Adriatic Sea on the west.

Byzantine Rule and the Second Empire.

Bulgaria declined in importance after Simeon's death. In 1018 the Byzantine emperor Basil II conquered the country and ended the first Bulgarian empire. Bulgaria remained part of the Byzantine Empire until 1186.

In 1186, John Asen I and his brother Peter regained Bulgaria's independence. Their descendant Czar John Asen II (reigned 1218–41) established the second Bulgarian empire, which included most of the Balkan Peninsula. But in 1396, along with the rest of the Balkan states, Bulgaria was conquered by the Ottoman Turks.

Turkish Rule.

Bulgaria remained a part of the Ottoman Empire for nearly 500 years. During that time the Bulgarian nobility disappeared, and Bulgarian farmers were bound to Turkish masters. The Bulgarian church, too, lost its independence and was placed under the control of the Greek Patriarch in Constantinople (now Istanbul).

The Bulgarians almost lost their national identity, for the ability to read and write had declined and few could remember the history of their people. However, a Bulgarian national revival began in the 1800's, and some Bulgarians began a guerrilla campaign against Turkish rule. An independent Bulgarian church was restored in 1870.

The Rila Monastery, built in the A.D. 900's during the first empire, is one of the glories of Bulgaria's past. It was destroyed and rebuilt several times over the centuries.

Independence.

Russia helped Bulgaria win political independence from the Turks in the Russo-Turkish War of 1877–78. But the western European powers feared possible Russian expansion. Therefore, only the northern part of Bulgaria was made independent. In 1885, however, the southern part of the country, called Eastern Rumelia, broke away from Turkey and was reunited with Bulgaria. A foreign monarch, Prince Alexander of Battenburg, was chosen by the European powers to rule the new nation.

Balkan Wars.

In 1908, Prince Ferdinand of Saxe-Coburg-Gotha took the title of czar and claimed the rest of the areas of old Bulgaria, especially Macedonia. A Balkan alliance between Bulgaria, Serbia, Montenegro, and Greece was formed. This alliance fought against the Turks in the First Balkan War, in 1912. In the Second Balkan War, in 1913, Bulgaria was defeated by an alliance of Greece, Serbia, Romania, and Turkey, and was forced to give up its claims to Macedonia.

In 1989, pro-democracy demonstrators in Sofia signaled "V" for victory after Bulgaria's Communist government yielded to demands for political and economic reforms. A democratic constitution was adopted in 1991.

Two World Wars. In World War I (1914–18), Bulgaria, an ally of Germany and Austria-Hungary, found itself on the losing side and was compelled to give up more territory. Ferdinand was forced to abdicate, and the throne was inherited by his son Boris III. In 1934, Czar Boris and the army outlawed political parties and established a dictatorship.

In 1941, during World War II, Bulgaria again allied itself with Germany and declared war on the United States and Britain. However, it never declared war on the Soviet Union. Boris III died in 1943. The following year the Bulgarian government opened peace talks with the Allies.

Communism to Democracy. But the government had moved too slowly. While the talks were under way, the Soviet Union declared war against Bulgaria and the Communists seized power. In 1946 the monarchy was abolished, and the young czar, Simeon II, was sent into exile. The Communists allowed little political or cultural freedom. The economy was brought under government control, and private farms were transformed into large, state-run collective farms.

By the late 1980's, far-reaching political changes swept across the Soviet Union and the other Communist nations of Eastern Europe. In 1989, Todor Zhivkov, who had led the Bulgarian Communist Party since 1954, was removed from power by his fellow Communist leaders. The new leadership allowed the formation of opposition political parties.

The first elections under the new constitution were held in 1991. They were won by the Union of Democratic Forces (UDF), an alliance opposed to the Communists, who promised to maintain political democracy. In 1994, the Bulgarian Socialist Party, made up of former Communists, won a majority in legislative elections. But in 1997, the UDF regained power. In 2000, the government began making economic reforms as a condition of future membership in the European Union (EU).

By 2001, declining living standards and corruption in the top levels of government generated support for a new political group, the National Movement, led by the long-exiled King Simeon II. In the legislative elections held that June, he became the first former monarch in post-Communist eastern Europe to regain control in his native land, although as prime minister, not as king. The following November, Georgi Parvanov, leader of Bulgaria's Socialist Party, was elected president. Bulgaria joined NATO in 2004. In 2005, Sergei Stanishev succeeded Simeon as prime minister.

GEORGE W. HOFFMAN
University of Texas at Austin
Reviewed by JOHN D. BELL
Author, *The Bulgarian Communist Party from Blagoev to Zhivkov*

BULGE, BATTLE OF THE. See WORLD WAR II (Attack on Germany, 1944–45).

BULIMIA. See DISEASES (Descriptions of Some Diseases).

BULLETIN BOARDS

A bulletin board is a board for posting notices and other bits of information. A bulletin board of your own can serve many purposes. Perhaps it can make you smile by reminding you of the wonderful vacation you had last summer. It might make you feel proud by displaying your very best school papers. Maybe it can help keep you organized by providing a place to put important schedules and reminders. However you might use it, a bulletin board is a decorative showcase for your interests and accomplishments.

Ready-made bulletin boards are available at hardware and stationery stores. They come in a variety of sizes, ranging from the very large ones usually used in classrooms to the more usual 60- by 90-centimeter (2- by 3-foot) home size. Most bulletin boards are made out of cork. They can be purchased with a plain wood or metal frame or with no frame at all.

Bulletin boards are easy to make. Cork squares found in a hardware or decorating supply store can be used singly or in groups. A sheet of fiberboard, available at building supply stores, makes a good bulletin board. You can even use layers of cardboard glued together. Cover them with fabric or any of the other materials suggested below, and you have an attractive bulletin board at little or no cost.

Bulletin boards are usually hung like pictures on walls. But there are other places where bulletin boards can be just as effective. Try putting a large one behind your bed as a headboard. Or tack cork to the back of a bookcase or a dresser. In this way you can turn a piece of furniture that has an unfinished back into a free-standing piece that makes an excellent room divider.

Just as a bulletin board does not have to be on the wall, neither does it have to be a rectangle. You can easily cut cork or cardboard to any shape. Perhaps you can pick up a decorative shape, such as a flower or a star, from a fabric in your room. Or you can reflect an interesting hobby in the shape of your bulletin board. A car shape, baseball bat shape, or even the letters of your name or initials, cut out of cork and mounted, can provide a decorative touch to your room.

Background Material. There are many materials that can give a nice texture or design to the background of your bulletin board. Paper is a good choice because it can be changed easily when you change your board display. Try large sheets of poster board, construction paper, wallpaper, gift wrap, adhesive-backed paper, or shelf paper. Effective for certain themes are road maps, newsprint, or even aluminum foil. For a more permanent covering, fabrics are a good choice. Burlap, felt, leather, suede, or even fake fur lend good texture to the surface.

Borders. Borders give a finished look to your bulletin board. Pieces of braided or twisted yarn, crepe paper, ribbon, or paper chains can be used. Try stringing halves of paper plates or paper doilies together. See the diagram on the following page for the technique of making cut-paper borders.

Lettering. If you want to label your bulletin board display, letters can be cut from magazines or made freehand. They can be made from paper or fabric. The diagram on page 449 shows you how to fold and cut paper to make letters.

Fasteners. Use straight pins, map pins, push pins, or double-faced tape to put materials on your bulletin board. Or try gluing magnets to the back of pictures. The magnets will stick to thumbtacks on the board.

On the following two pages, you will find some sample bulletin boards. They should give you some ideas for possible themes and techniques to make your bulletin board exciting and attractive.

ESTHER FINTON
Author, *Bulletin Boards Should Be More Than Something to Look At . . .*

BORDERS

1. Cut large sheets of colored construction paper into strips of 46 X 8 cm (18 X 3 in). Make as many as you need to surround your bulletin board.

2. Fold each strip in half, and in half again.

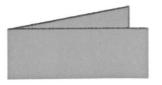

3. Select a pattern from the examples at right. You may want to make a cardboard sample of your pattern to trace onto each of your folded strips. Cut along the pencil lines indicated in your pattern.

4. Use straight pins to place the unfolded strips around your bulletin board.

Sample Borders

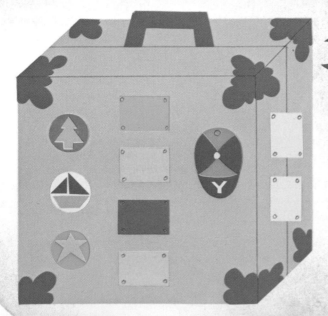

ABOUT THE BULLETIN BOARDS

Left: Reminders of summer camp include badges, a camp hat, and perhaps some photos of friends. The trunk-shaped board makes an appropriate background for any travel display. **Above right:** The food theme board decorated with heart borders is a handy place to keep school lunch menus or recipes. **Above far right:** A board cut into the shape of a fish is as decorative as an aquarium — and the cut paper fish do not have to be fed! **Right:** A semicircle bordered with paper umbrellas serves as a weather reporting station.

dicta

LETTERS

Cut pieces of paper or fabric to the letter size you want. Fold each piece as indicated by the dotted line on the letter you wish to make. Some letters require a vertical fold; others a horizontal; and letters G, J, N, Q, S, and Z require no fold at all. Using the entire paper, cut the shape for your letter, unfold — and enjoy the professional-looking results. You can change the style of your letters by rounding the edges or by changing the shape of the paper.

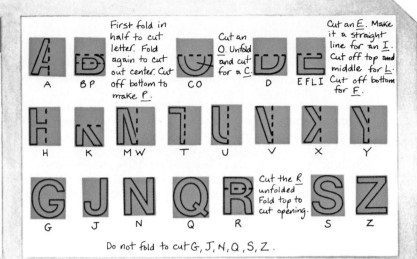

First fold in half to cut letter. Fold again to cut out center. Cut off bottom to make P.

Cut an O. Unfold and cut for a C.

Cut an E. Make it a straight line for an I. Cut off top and middle for L. Cut off bottom for F.

A | B P | C O | D | E F L I

H | K | M W | T | U | V | X | Y

Cut the R unfolded. Fold top to cut opening.

G | J | N | Q | R | S | Z

Do not fold to cut G, J, N, Q, S, Z.

BULLFIGHTING

Bullfighting has been called Spain's favorite sport. But to call it this is wrong for two reasons: first, soccer (called *fútbol* in Spain) is the most popular sport; and second, bullfighting cannot really be called a sport. It should be called, more properly, a spectacle, an exhibition, or a performance, like a ballet. However, this ballet is like dancing on a tightrope, because if the bullfighter makes a mistake, he is likely to be injured or killed.

A bullfight is not really a contest between a man and a bull. Actually it is a contest between a man and himself. The audience goes to the ring to see a man conquer his own fear of the horns and take as many chances with the bull as possible. The men who most gracefully execute the most daring maneuvers become the stars.

Bullfighting is one of the few ways a poor boy can become rich and famous in Spain and Latin America—and many *matadores* have become millionaires. But for every successful *matador,* there are hundreds who have fallen by the wayside and are forgotten. Many do not have the necessary grace and skill. Some are crippled by the bulls, and some are killed.

▶ HOW DID BULLFIGHTING BEGIN?

Bullfighting has existed in one form or another for more than 2,000 years. The ancient Cretans used to perform what they called bull dancing. Both men and women would leap over the bulls' horns in graceful, reckless exhibitions.

One of the reasons that Spain has been the leading place for bullfighting is that the fighting bull first lived there. Bullfighting cannot be done with ordinary animals. It requires the special *toro de lidia,* or *toro bravo,* which is as different from a domestic bull as a cobra is from a gopher snake, or a wolf is from a dog. For centuries, herds of these fierce bulls roamed wild over Spain. The Romans imported them for their savage battles against men and other animals in the Colosseum. The bulls usually won, even when pitted against lions and tigers. The Arabs in Spain helped make bullfighting popular around the early 12th century. In those days the spectacle consisted of a skillful horseman killing a wild bull with a lance while guiding his horse so as to avoid injury both to his mount and to himself. It is said that the famous cavalier El Cid was the first Spaniard to take part in organized bullfighting in an arena.

Bullfighting quickly became very popular, and for centuries rich Moors and Christians, nobles, and even kings practiced it. No feast day was complete without a *corrida de toros.*

The common people used to help the nobles fight the bulls, but they did so on foot. They used capes to distract the bull and keep it from charging at their bodies. Little by little this became the more exciting part of the act, and the ritual developed as we know it today.

Left: *Paseo,* or entrance parade, into the bullring in Madrid. Each *matador* leads his *cuadrilla,* or team of assistants. Right: The *matador* performs a classic *verónica.* The bull charges hard, passing before the *matador,* who swings the cape in front of its nose.

THE ARENA AND THE TOREROS

The first thing a person sees in the *plaza de toros,* or arena, is the gaily dressed and excited crowd. When the band strikes up, *toreros* stride into the arena and parade around it while the *aficionados,* or fans, cheer.

All people who fight bulls are called *toreros.* The *matadores* are the stars of the show, and there are usually three in an afternoon's program. Each one has two *picadores* and three *banderilleros* to help him. It is old-fashioned and incorrect to refer to bullfighters as *toreadores.* (The "toreador" of Bizet's opera *Carmen* is actually a *matador.*)

THE CONTEST

The men stride across the sand of the arena, and then the ring is cleared and the bull charges in. The bull has not been trained or tortured or starved; yet, because of its centuries of breeding, it knows it is supposed to fight. A *banderillero* will run out and swirl his cape a few times in front of the animal to demonstrate to his *matador* how this particular animal charges, since each bull has a different style of fighting.

Now the *matador* goes out. Where the *banderillero* was awkward and stayed safely away from the bull's horns, the *matador,* being the star, must stand very close to the animal. He swings the cape gracefully and lets the horns slice just by his legs. On each pass that the *matador* performs well, the crowd yells and cheers. If the *matador* bends over awkwardly and steps back out of the path of the bull as the *banderillero* did, the crowd boos loudly. The audience would like to see the bullfighters behave exactly opposite from the way they would behave if they had to stand in front of a huge bull with only a cape for protection. The bull goes at the cloth not because it is red, but because the *matador* knows just how to shake the cape to attract the animal and make it go at the lure instead of his body. The cape is yellow on one side and red on the other, but because bulls are color-blind, it makes no difference which side the *matador* presents to the animal.

After the *matador* does several passes, called *verónicas,* a trumpet blows and the *picadores* enter on horseback. They prick the bull with their lances in order to weaken his neck muscles. They do this so that at the end the *matador* will be able to reach over the horns and place the sword blade where it should go—between the bull's shoulder blades. The horses have been safely padded since 1930, so there is less chance that they will be injured by the charging bull.

Next, each of the three *banderilleros* places two *banderillas* ("barbed sticks") in the animal's shoulders. These further weaken the bull's neck muscles.

Finally the *matador* goes out with the sword and a little cape called the *muleta.* This is the most dangerous time of the fight, in spite of the fact that the bull is tired. There have been about 125 great *matadores* since 1700, and 42 of them have been killed, generally during this part of the bullfight. This is because the little cape is so small, the bull has learned so much during the course of the fight, and the man must make his most dangerous passes at this time.

THE KILL

Killing the bull, called "the moment of truth," is the most dangerous maneuver of all. The man must run at the bull at the same time that the bull runs at him, and plunge the sword between the shoulder blades. When this is done correctly, the bull will drop over dead almost instantly.

If the *matador* has done his job well, the crowd applauds, and he is awarded the ear of the bull as a trophy. If he has done a superior job, he is given both ears and the tail. The meat of the bulls is sometimes given to the poor, but usually the animals are butchered in back of the arena and sold for steaks.

Joselito and Manolete, two of the greatest bullfighters of the 20th century, were killed by bulls. Joselito died when he was only 25; Manolete at the age of 30. Many other *matadores,* like the great Antonio Ordóñez and El Cordobés of Spain, have been severely injured in the bullring. The ambition of most bullfighters, who usually come from poor families, is to make enough money to buy a bull ranch and retire at about the age of 30.

The best fights in Spain are held in Madrid, Seville, Valencia, and Málaga during the spring and summer. In Latin America the best fights can be seen in Mexico City or Lima, Peru. In Portugal the only ring of importance is in Lisbon.

BARNABY CONRAD
Author, *La Fiesta Brava, The Death of Manolete*

BUNCHE, RALPH (1904–1971)

Ralph Bunche was the first African American awarded the Nobel Peace Prize. He received this honor in 1950 for his work as a United Nations mediator in the Middle East.

Bunche, the grandson of a slave, was born in Detroit, Michigan, on August 7, 1904. His parents died when he was 13, and he and his sister went to live with their grandmother in California. He received a scholarship to the University of California but still had to take odd jobs to pay for his books, meals, and carfare. Nevertheless he managed to play on three basketball championship teams and to graduate with highest honors. He continued his education at Harvard University, receiving an M.A. degree in 1928.

Bunche began his career teaching political science at Howard University and, soon after, married Ruth Harris, who had been one of his students. The couple had three children. Bunche left Howard for a time to continue his studies at Harvard and received a Ph.D. degree in 1934.

From 1938 to 1940, Bunche worked as the chief assistant to Swedish sociologist Gunnar Myrdal on a survey of race relations in America. The result was an important book titled *An American Dilemma* (1944). He later worked for the U.S. government, eventually becoming the first black to head a division of the U.S. State Department. In 1946 he accepted a permanent post at the United Nations.

In 1948, war broke out between Israel and its Arab neighbors. Count Folke Bernadotte was appointed by the United Nations to help end the dispute. When Bernadotte was assassinated, Bunche took his place. He received the Nobel Peace Prize for his role in persuading the warring countries to stop fighting.

He continued to serve the United Nations in various troubled parts of the world, including the Congo (now Zaïre) and Cyprus as well as the Middle East. From 1967 until his retirement in 1971, he was the undersecretary–general of the United Nations. Bunche died on December 9, 1971.

Reviewed by MARGUERITE CARTWRIGHT
Hunter College, City University of New York

BUNKER HILL, BATTLE OF. See REVOLUTIONARY WAR.
BUOYANCY. See FLOATING AND BUOYANCY.

BURBANK, LUTHER (1849–1926)

Luther Burbank once remarked: "I shall be contented if because of me there shall be better fruits and fairer flowers." In 50 years of work, he more than achieved his goal. He developed 618 new varieties of plants.

Burbank was born on a farm near Lancaster, Massachusetts, on March 7, 1849. In his early years, Luther attended a one-room school. At 15 he entered Lancaster Academy, where he received some instruction in science. But it was in the Lancaster library that Burbank—at the age of 19—discovered the writings of Charles Darwin. From Darwin, Burbank learned how better varieties of plants could be developed. The secret was to select seeds from those plants with the most desirable traits and to breed for those traits.

A few years later, Burbank was able to purchase land near Lunenburg, Massachusetts. There he set about developing his first "new creation," a larger and firmer potato. He planted potato seeds and selected the best potatoes from the resulting crop for replanting.

The variety he developed in this way is still known as the Burbank potato.

In 1875, Burbank sold his farm and moved to Santa Rosa, California. There he set up a small nursery garden, greenhouse, and orchard, where he grew and sold plants to support his research. He continued his selection process and also developed new plants, such as the Shasta daisy, by crossbreeding.

Burbank bought more acres and established a world-famous experimental farm. His yearly catalog, *New Creations*, issued from 1893 to 1901, described his experiments. He used scientific principles and methods, yet Burbank's main interest was in practical results.

Burbank died on April 11, 1926. Although he left behind little documentation of his work, Burbank is considered a significant contributor to the field of science.

JOHN S. BOWMAN
Author and science editor

BURGER, WARREN. See MINNESOTA (Famous People).

BURKINA FASO

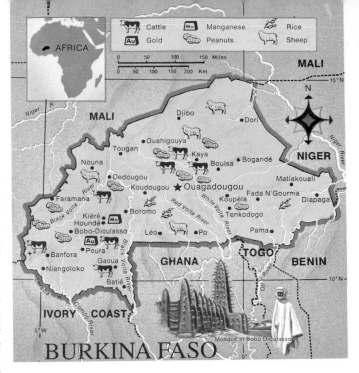

Mosque at Bobo Dioulasso

BURKINA FASO

Burkina Faso is an inland nation of West Africa. For centuries it was the site of a great empire ruled by the Mossi people. The Mossi are still the most numerous people of Burkina Faso. But their empire has long ceased to exist, and Burkina Faso today is one of the poorest nations of Africa.

In 1896, Burkina Faso became a colony of France as part of French West Africa. It gained its independence in 1960. It was called Upper Volta until 1984, when it adopted the name Burkina Faso, which is sometimes translated as "land of the honest [or upright] people." Politically, "Faso" has the approximate meaning of People's Republic.

▶ PEOPLE

Most of Burkina Faso's people live in the central and southwestern parts of the country. The Mossi, who inhabit the central region, make up about one third of the population. Other ethnic groups include the Bobo, Lobi-Dagari, Senufo, Gurunsi, and Mande. The sparsely settled northeast is the home of the Songhai, Fulani, and Tuareg.

Language. French is the official language, but each of Burkina Faso's peoples has its own language or dialect. Moré, the language of the Mossi, is widely spoken in central Burkina Faso.

Religion. The majority of the people practice traditional African religions. About 25 percent are Muslims and some 10 percent Christian.

Way of Life. The Mossi way of life still reflects the discipline enforced by early Mossi rulers. The actions of every individual must conform to a strict code of behavior. The family is the most important unit. Each family lives in a walled compound containing several small, round clay-and-mud huts. Most Mossi are farmers. The family fields surround the compound.

The Bobo, like the Mossi, are family-centered. Their dwellings, however, are larger than those of the Mossi and are built together in compact villages and towns.

The Fulani and Tuareg of the northeast are nomadic herders, who travel with their livestock seeking grazing land.

▶ LAND

Most of Burkina Faso is a vast plateau consisting of savanna, or grassland. The northeast is part of the Sahel, a region of sparse vegetation on the edge of the Sahara desert. The country's three principal rivers are the Red Volta, the Black Volta, and the White Volta.

The soil is generally poor, although crops can be grown where there is adequate rainfall. When the rains are long delayed, however, drought results.

Climate. Burkina Faso has a hot, dry climate, with an average daytime temperature of 82°F (28°C). Rainfall is heaviest in the southwest and scantiest in the northeast. During the hottest season, from about March to May, the harmattan, a dry, searing wind, blows south from the Sahara.

Cities. Ouagadougou, which lies in central Burkina Faso, was once a capital of the Mossi empire. It is now Burkina Faso's capital and largest city, with a population of more than 240,000. Bobo-Dioulasso, the second largest city, is located in the southwest.

▶ ECONOMY

Burkina Faso's economy is based on agriculture and the raising of livestock, particularly cattle, sheep, and goats. The chief food crops include millet, sorghum, peanuts, cassava, and rice. The major exports are livestock and livestock products, gold, and cotton. Severe droughts periodically devastate the economy.

Industry is limited, and young Burkinabe men often seek work in neighboring countries. The country depends heavily on foreign aid.

▶ HISTORY AND GOVERNMENT

The ancestors of the Mossi probably arrived in Burkina Faso in the 1000's. They founded several kingdoms, the most important centered at Ouagadougou.

Europeans first arrived in the region in the late 1800's. France subdued the Mossi kings and became the dominant power. The colony of Upper Volta was created by the French in 1919. It was divided among the other colonies of French West Africa in 1932 but was restored as a separate territory in 1948. Upper Volta gained self-government in 1958 and complete independence in 1960.

Since Independence. The country's history since independence has been stormy. The first president, Maurice Yaméogo, was deposed in 1966 in a military coup led by Lieutenant Colonel Sangoulé Lamizana. Lamizana remained in power until 1980, when economic woes led to his overthrow.

Young radicals led by Captain Thomas Sankara seized power in 1983. The popular Sankara encouraged local efforts to build schools, clinics, and agricultural cooperatives. In 1984 he changed the name of the country to Burkina Faso to end a link to its colonial past.

FACTS and figures

BURKINA FASO is the official name of the country.

LOCATION: West Africa.

AREA: 105,869 sq mi (274,200 km²).

POPULATION: 11,300,000 (estimate).

CAPITAL AND LARGEST CITY: Ouagadougou.

MAJOR LANGUAGES: French (official), Moré, other African languages.

MAJOR RELIGIOUS GROUPS: Traditional African religions, Muslim, Christian.

GOVERNMENT: Republic. **Head of state**—president. **Head of government**—prime minister. **Legislature**—National Assembly.

CHIEF PRODUCTS: Agricultural—livestock (cattle, sheep, goats), cotton, sorghum, millet, peanuts, cassava, rice. **Manufactured**—livestock products, processed foods. **Mineral**—gold.

MONETARY UNIT: African Financial Community (CFA) franc (1 franc = 100 centimes).

In 1987, Sankara was killed by one of his associates, Captain Blaise Compaoré, who then seized power. A multiparty constitution adopted in 1991 reduced the powers of the presidency and allowed for the president and members of the legislature to be elected directly by the people. Compaoré was elected president in 1991 and again in 1998.

H. R. JARRETT
Author, *Physical Geography for West African Schools*

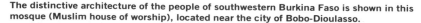

The distinctive architecture of the people of southwestern Burkina Faso is shown in this mosque (Muslim house of worship), located near the city of Bobo-Dioulasso.

BURMA. See MYANMAR.
BURNS. See FIRST AID.

BURNS, ROBERT (1759–1796)

Robert Burns, Scotland's greatest poet, becomes the world's favorite each New Year's Eve with the traditional singing of his "Auld Lang Syne." It is fitting tribute to a poet who loved good company, good song, and simple pleasures.

Burns was born on January 25, 1759, in Ayrshire, Scotland. His father was a poor farmer who valued education and strict morality. Although Robert's help was needed on the farm, his father encouraged him to read and gave him as much schooling as he could.

Robert read everything he could, from collections of songs to Shakespeare and Milton. He carried small volumes in his pocket and studied them while he was in the fields or at the table. He began writing his own verses and collected them in a scrapbook.

When his father died in 1784, Robert and his brother Gilbert tried to make a success of farming but failed. Robert then fell in love with Jean Armour, but her father refused to have him as a son-in-law.

In 1786, Burns published *Poems, Chiefly in the Scottish Dialect*. The poems were a great success, and a second edition appeared the following year. Burns began to collect, adapt, and compose lyrics of folk songs for a publication called *The Scots Musical Museum*. For this and for George Thomson's *Select Collection of Original Scottish Airs* (1793), Burns composed over 300 lyrics. Some of his best-known poems are "Sweet Afton," "To a Mouse," "John Anderson, My Jo," and the patriotic "Scots, Wha Hae."

In 1788, Burns began a new life of farming, at Ellisland, near Dumfries, and finally married Jean Armour. But he failed again at farming. He took a government position as a tax officer and moved to Dumfries in 1791. His outspoken sympathy for the French Revolution damaged his popularity. Illness added to his troubles. He died in Dumfries on July 21, 1796, a broken and bitter man. But his poems found a permanent place in literature.

Reviewed by GEORGIA DUNBAR
Hofstra University

BURNSIDE, AMBROSE EVERETT. See RHODE ISLAND (Famous People).

Robert Burns wrote in both standard English and the dialect of the Scottish farmers and villagers he had known all his life. Some of his poetry was written in a mixed language, using English grammar and Scottish vocabulary. Sometimes he simply spelled English words in the Scots fashion. In the following poem, the Scottish word "gang" means "go," and "weel" means "well."

A Red, Red Rose

O, my luve is like a red, red rose,
That's newly sprung in June
O, my luve is like the melodie,
That's sweetly played in tune.

As fair art thou, my bonie lass,
So deep in luve am I,
And I will luve thee still, my dear,
Till a' the seas gang dry.

Till a' the seas gang dry, my dear,
And the rocks melt wi' the sun!
And I will luve thee still, my dear,
While the sands o' life shall run.

And fare thee weel, my only luve,
And fare thee weel a while!
And I will come again, my luve,
Tho' it were ten thousand mile!

Aaron Burr was a Revolutionary War hero and a leading lawyer and politician whose career was destroyed by poor judgment and uncontrolled ambition.

BURR, AARON (1756–1836)

Aaron Burr was a brilliant lawyer, a hero of the Revolutionary War, and a vice-president of the United States. But most Americans remember Burr only as the man who killed Alexander Hamilton in a duel.

Burr was born in Newark, New Jersey, on February 6, 1756. His father was president of the College of New Jersey (now Princeton University). Aaron was admitted to the college when he was 13 and graduated with honors at 16. Later he studied law.

At the outbreak of the Revolutionary War, Burr joined the Continental Army. He served in the American march on Quebec in 1775. Later he was a staff officer under George Washington. Once, by disobeying orders, he saved an entire brigade from capture by the British. But poor health cut short his military career, and Burr left the army in 1779.

In 1782, Burr married Theodosia Prevost, the widow of a British officer. They had one child, a girl named Theodosia after her mother. Burr carefully educated his daughter since he believed girls should be as well educated as boys. Burr's wife lived only 12 years after their marriage, but she was a steadying influence on her husband.

Burr was a leading figure in the legal, social, and political life of New York. He served in the U.S. Senate and in the New York State Assembly. In his early years in New York, Burr had become friendly with another prominent young lawyer, Alexander Hamilton. But political rivalry soon turned the two men into bitter enemies.

In the presidential election of 1800, Burr and Thomas Jefferson both received the same number of votes. So the election was decided by the House of Representatives. After 36 ballots, Jefferson was elected president, and Burr became vice-president.

Hamilton had led the fight to block Burr's election. The hatred between the two men finally led to a duel near Weehawken, New Jersey, on July 11, 1804. Hamilton fired into the air, but Burr's bullet hit home. Hamilton died the next day, and Burr fled to escape arrest.

After leaving the vice-presidency in 1805, Burr found private life dull. He could not live in New York again because of the duel. He began to plan an expedition against Spain's Mexican possessions. In 1805 and 1806 he traveled down the Mississippi River, but his real reasons for this journey are still a mystery. Some people said that he planned to set up his own empire in the Southwest, with himself as emperor.

In 1807, General James Wilkinson, who was secretly in the pay of the Spanish, denounced Burr to Jefferson. The President ordered Burr's arrest for treason. He was tried at Richmond, Virginia, with Supreme Court Justice John Marshall as judge. Burr was accused of trying to separate the western states from the Union. Marshall ruled that there was no clear proof of treason, and Burr was freed. But his reputation was ruined.

Burr went to Europe and did not return to the United States until 1812. He had hoped to devote his declining years to his daughter and grandson. But both Theodosia and her son died within a year of each other.

Burr spent his last years practicing law. He died, almost forgotten, on Staten Island, New York, on September 14, 1836, and was buried at Princeton, near his father.

Perhaps Thomas Jefferson best summed up the fatal flaw in Burr's character when he wrote: "No man's history proves better the value of honesty. With that, what might he not have been?"

Reviewed by RICHARD B. MORRIS
Columbia University

See also HAMILTON, ALEXANDER.

BURROUGHS, JOHN (1837–1921)

One of America's greatest nature writers was John Burroughs. He delighted in exploring the quiet world of nature and then sharing his appreciation and knowledge with others through his lyrical prose.

Born on April 3, 1837, John Burroughs was one of ten children. His youth was spent on a small family farm near Roxbury, New York. It was there that he began his lifelong study of nature as he tramped along the untamed Rock Creek, observing the flowers and animals around him.

At various times in his life, Burroughs was a teacher, treasury clerk, and bank examiner. But it was as a naturalist and author that he became well known. Burroughs began his publishing career by contributing essays to the *Atlantic Monthly* and other magazines. A biography of his close friend Walt Whitman, *Notes on Walt Whitman as Poet and Person* (1867), was his first book to be published.

Never comfortable with the clamor and noise of city life, Burroughs made his home in the Catskill Mountains. "Where cattle and woodchuck thrive, there thrive I," he once

wrote. For much of the time, he lived in a log house, called Slabsides. As he gained recognition for his work, friends and important men of his day came to visit "the Sage of Slabsides."

During his long life, Burroughs completed 27 books. They include *Wake-Robin* (1871), *Winter Sunshine* (1875), *Fresh Fields* (1884), *Signs and Seasons* (1886), *Ways of Nature* (1905), and *The Breath of Life* (1915). He also received honorary degrees from several universities and was elected a member of the American Academy of Arts and Letters.

John Burroughs died on March 29, 1921. Each year in his honor, the John Burroughs Society presents awards for outstanding nature essays and books for young people and adults.

BARBARA TUFTY
Conservation Editor, Audubon Naturalist Society

BURTON, SIR RICHARD (1821–1890)

Sir Richard Burton was a man of extraordinary and varied gifts. He was one of the preeminent explorers of his time, an unequaled linguist who is said to have mastered 35 languages, and the author of dozens of books on his travels and other subjects. His most famous literary achievement is a 16-volume translation of *The Arabian Nights*.

Richard Francis Burton was born near Elstree, England, on March 19, 1821, and taken abroad by his parents at an early age. Although he received almost no formal education, he everywhere learned the local languages and dialects. He attended Trinity College, Oxford, but was expelled, and at 21 he joined the army of the British East India Company.

In India, Burton added to his knowledge of languages, learning Hindi, Farsi (Persian), and Arabic and living with native peoples. On

his first great journey, in 1853, he made a perilous trip to the Muslim holy cities of Medina and Mecca, disguised as a Muslim pilgrim. The next year he and John Speke explored East Africa, seeking the source of the Nile River. On a second expedition, in 1858, Burton discovered Lake Tanganyika. But, ill with malaria, he did not accompany Speke north and so did not share in the discovery of Lake Victoria, a main source of the Nile.

In 1861, Burton married Isabel Arundell. She was a devoted wife but had little sympathy for many of his chief interests. Burton's remaining years were spent as a British consular official, at posts around the world, exploring and writing. He was knighted in 1885. He died in Trieste (now in Italy) on October 20, 1890.

ARTHUR CAMPBELL TURNER
University of California, Riverside

BURUNDI

Burundi, one of the world's poorest countries, is a small, densely populated nation in the heart of east central Africa. It became an independent kingdom in 1962 and a republic in 1966. Since independence, ethnic violence and civil war have resulted in the deaths of more than 500,000 people.

▶ PEOPLE

Burundi's people belong to three major ethnic groups—the Hutu, the Tutsi (also known as Watusi), and the Twa.

The Hutu, the largest group, have traditionally made their living by farming, raising food for themselves and their families. The Tutsi, who make up about 15 percent of the population, have traditionally raised cattle. The Twa, or Pygmies, are historically hunter-gatherers. They were the region's earliest inhabitants. Today they make up about 1 percent of the population.

Kirundi and French are Burundi's official languages. Some people also speak Swahili. Nearly 70 percent of the people are Christian—mostly Roman Catholic—and about 10 percent are Muslim (followers of Islam). About 25 percent practice traditional African religions.

Primary education, beginning at age 6, is officially required. However, only about half the children attend school because there are

Two young drummers perform for a group of onlookers. Most of Burundi's people belong to three major ethnic groups—the Hutu, the Tutsi, and the Twa.

not enough schools and because many children are needed at home. Even young children herd livestock in the mountain pastures.

Burundi's educational system has expanded and now includes several universities. The oldest is the University of Burundi, which has campuses in and around the capital city of Bujumbura and in Gitega. It is Burundi's only public university.

▶ LAND

Burundi's western border lies along the Great Rift Valley, which includes part of Lake Tanganyika, the world's largest freshwater lake. From there, the land rises to a chain of mountains. This area includes Burundi's highest point, Mount Heha, which has an elevation of 8,760 feet (2,670 meters). The rest of the country consists of high, rolling plateaus that rise to more than 5,000 feet (1,500 meters) above sea level. This high elevation makes the climate pleasant, even though Burundi is near the equator. Rainfall varies, however, and long droughts often cause crop failures. Burundi's natural vegetation is primarily savannah grassland.

▶ ECONOMY

Burundi's economy is based largely on agriculture. Coffee, cotton, and tea are the main agricultural exports, followed by sugar and hides. Important food crops include corn, sorghum, sweet potatoes, banana, and cassava. Many cattle, sheep, and goats are also raised. Mineral resources include nickel, uranium, rare earth oxides (metals), and peat.

Burundi's industry is fairly limited and includes the manufacture of light consumer goods (such as blankets and soap), assembly of imported components, public works construction, and food processing. Services make up about one-third of Burundi's economy.

▶ **MAJOR CITIES**

Bujumbura, the capital, is Burundi's principal city, with a population of about 320,000. Located on Lake Tanganyika, it is the country's chief port. **Gitega**, Burundi's second largest city, has 23,500 residents.

▶ **HISTORY AND GOVERNMENT**

Burundi's original inhabitants were most likely the Twa. The ancestors of the present-day Hutu migrated to the area about A.D. 800. The ancestors of today's Tutsi arrived between 1300 and 1500.

Burundi, one of the last African lands to be colonized, became part of German East Africa in the 1890's. After Germany's defeat in World War I (1914–18), the League of Nations placed Burundi and what is now Rwanda under the administration of Belgium. The area became known as Ruanda-Urundi. Belgium governed the region, as a trust territory of the United Nations, until 1962, when Rwanda and Burundi gained independence as separate nations.

FACTS and figures

REPUBLIC OF BURUNDI is the official name of the country.

LOCATION: East central Africa.

AREA: 10,745 sq mi (27,830 km²).

POPULATION: 6,400,000 (estimate).

CAPITAL AND LARGEST CITY: Bujumbura.

MAJOR LANGUAGE: Kirundi, French (both official).

MAJOR RELIGIOUS GROUPS: Christian, traditional African religions, Muslim.

GOVERNMENT: Republic. **Head of state and government**—president. **Legislature**—National Assembly and Senate.

CHIEF PRODUCTS: Coffee, cotton, tea, sweet potatoes, cassava, corn, sorghum, livestock.

MONETARY UNIT: Burundi franc (1 franc = 100 centimes).

Since Independence. Following its independence, Burundi was a constitutional monarchy ruled by a *mwami* (king). In 1966 the *mwami* was deposed by army captain Michel Micombero, who proclaimed Burundi a republic and himself president. An unsuccessful attempt to overthrow Micombero in 1972 led to the massacre of some 150,000 Hutu by Tutsi soldiers. In 1976, Micombero was ousted by Colonel Jean-Baptiste Bagaza. Bagaza was overthrown by Major Pierre Buyoya in 1987. All three presidents were ethnic Tutsi.

Ethnic hostilities erupted in 1988 and 1991. But in 1992, voters approved a new, democratic constitution. In 1993—in the first open elections in many years—Melchior Ndadaye, a Hutu, became president, but he was soon assassinated by rebels in the Tutsi-dominated army. In 1994, parliament elected another Hutu, Cyprien Ntaryamira, but he was killed when his plane was shot down. His successor, Sylvestre Ntibantunganya, was overthrown in 1996 by the army, which reinstalled Buyoya as president. Meanwhile, new ethnic violence erupted between the government and various rebel groups. Thousands were killed, and many more fled the country.

In 2001, a three-year transitional government was installed to divide power between the Hutu and Tutsi. Accordingly, President Buyoya handed over power in 2003 to Domitien Ndayizeye, who became the first Hutu to lead the country in seven years.

In 2002 and 2003, the government signed cease-fire agreements with the country's largest Hutu rebel group, Forces for the Defense of Democracy (FDD). Despite this agreement and the presence of UN peacekeeping forces, the fighting continued.

In March 2005, voters overwhelmingly approved a new constitution that guaranteed the Hutu and Tutsi would share power, thereby ending the longstanding conflict in which more than 300,000 people had been killed. The constitution called for a president, a council of ministers, and a two-house legislature, consisting of the National Assembly and Senate. In August, parliament elected FDD leader Pierre Nkurunziza president.

PAUL J. KAISER
African Studies Center
University of Pennsylvania

See also RWANDA.

BUSES

Every day, buses carry millions of people to work from their homes in the cities or the suburbs and back again in the evening. Thousands of other passengers take long bus trips for business or pleasure, and millions of children rely on buses to get to school.

The bus is relatively new as a means of travel. Motor buses came into use only when automobile travel began to gain popularity in the early 1900's. But the bus has ancestors much older than the automobile.

In the 1820's, twelve-passenger horse-drawn carriages began carrying people along Broadway in New York City. This marked the start of public transportation in the United States. Similar vehicles, called omnibuses, began to be used in other cities as well. *Omnibus* is a Latin word that means "for all."

Motorized bus lines were operating in some cities as early as 1905. The early buses, built by truck manufacturers, were designed to transport heavy loads rather than to provide for the comfort of passengers. The buses were dirty, bumpy to ride on, and lacked heating systems to keep passengers warm in winter.

In the following years, buses were improved with more comfortable seats, a lower floor for easier boarding, safety features such as shock-absorbing bumpers, and other features for easier maintenance. Today, buses are the most common form of public transportation in the United States and around the world.

▶ BUS SERVICES

There are many kinds of buses, and they are used in many different ways.

Public Transportation. The bus is an important part of the public trans-

portation systems. Hundreds of bus routes may crisscross a single city. Special routes may link city hotels with shopping areas, museums, and other points of interest.

Many cities are able to offer bus service within 1/4 mile (0.4 kilometer) of nearly all their residents. Today's public-transit buses offer improved comfort and convenience. On some buses, a ramp or lift makes boarding easier for elderly riders and people with disabilities. In some areas, door-to-door services called "Dial-a-Ride" use small buses or vans to carry older people or others who may have trouble using the regular system.

Vehicles called articulated buses have been popular in Europe and are now seen in some cities in the United States. These buses are actually two units connected by a hinge mechanism that looks somewhat like a giant accordion. This mechanism makes it easier for the bus to turn corners.

In many areas, public-transit buses are part of special systems that make getting from place to place easier. Express buses for commuters run on special lanes on some major highways so that they can bypass traffic and get into town very quickly. In some downtown areas, automobiles have been banned from certain streets to create transit malls. Buses and pedestrians move freely through these malls.

The long-distance bus that travels the highways today is designed to be comfortable and

A public-transit bus in Portland, Oregon, slows as it comes to one of its designated stops. These buses are an important means of transportation in many cities in the United States and around the world.

convenient. The passengers sit in upholstered chairs that can be tilted back for resting or sleeping. Each seat has its own reading light, so that a passenger can read while the person alongside, who may wish to sleep, is not disturbed. The large windows are tinted to keep out the sun's glare. Most long-distance buses

Above: Riding a school bus is part of the daily routine for millions of children.
Right: With picturesque scenery in the background, a tour bus travels on a quiet highway. These buses, used for long trips, are specially designed for passenger comfort.

have washrooms with hot and cold running water. They also have television screens for video movies. Under the floor is a huge baggage compartment.

Bus companies operate long-distance lines all over the United States and Canada. Their routes extend from coast to coast and from Alaska to Mexico. Some terminals resemble railroad stations, with checkrooms, restaurants, barbershops, and newsstands.

School Buses. The school bus has changed the lives of schoolchildren. Once there were thousands of small one-room schools with one teacher for all the grades. This was because every child who lived on a farm had to be near enough to a school to walk to it. These one-room schoolhouses have been replaced by large central schools that serve a wide territory. School buses pick up children each day at their homes and take them back

when school is over. School buses are usually painted bright yellow or orange so that they can be seen easily. As a further safety measure, most states forbid automobile drivers to pass a school bus that has stopped to pick up children or let them off. In addition, many communities have passed local laws requiring seat belts on school buses because it has been proved that seat belts reduce the risk of injury in traffic accidents.

Specialty Buses. Other types of buses include tour buses, charter buses, and airport buses. On a tour bus, people may take short sight-seeing trips to local historic landmarks or other places of interest. They may also take long bus tours that can last several

weeks and tour one or more countries. On long bus tours, bus companies will usually make all the arrangements for the passengers' daily needs, such as meals and hotel room accommodations.

Charter buses are hired by specific groups of people who wish to travel together. Airport buses are small buses that operate between various airport terminals and hotels.

GAIL E. WILLIAMS
Public Affairs Specialist
Urban Mass Transportation Administration
U.S. Department of Transportation

GEORGE BUSH (1924–   )

41st President of the United States

FACTS ABOUT BUSH

Birthplace: Milton, Massachusetts
Religion: Episcopalian
College Attended: Yale University
Occupation: Businessman, public official
Married: Barbara Pierce
Children: George W., John (Jeb), Neil,
   Marvin, Dorothy (Robin, died 1953)
Political Party: Republican
Office Held Before Becoming President:
   Vice President
President Who Preceded Him:
   Ronald W. Reagan
Age on Becoming President: 64
Years in the Presidency: 1989-1993
Vice President:
   James Danforth (Dan) Quayle
President Who Succeeded Him:
   William (Bill) Clinton

DURING BUSH'S PRESIDENCY

U.S. troops ousted Panama's dictator,
General Manuel Noriega (1989). A
U.S.-led military alliance, authorized
by the United Nations, liberated Kuwait
from Iraqi occupation in the Persian
Gulf War (1991). The Soviet Union
broke apart (1991) into 15 independent
countries. The United States, Canada,
and Mexico signed the North American
Free Trade Agreement (1992). *Left:* U.S.
Marines were sent to Somalia (1992),
to ensure that emergency food supplies
reached Somalis threatened with starva-
tion. *Above:* Bush and Russian president
Boris Yeltsin signed (1993) the second
Strategic Arms Reduction Treaty (Start II).

BUSH, GEORGE. Few presidents in recent years have entered the White House with as much broad experience in government as George Bush. He served as a member of Congress and as U.S. representative to the United Nations. He was one of the first officials to represent the United States in the People's Republic of China. He is a former director of the Central Intelligence Agency (CIA). And he was vice president under President Ronald Reagan for eight years, before winning the presidency himself in 1988. Bush was the first sitting vice president to be elected president since Martin Van Buren won office in 1836.

▶EARLY YEARS

George Herbert Walker Bush was born in Milton, Massachusetts, on June 12, 1924. His parents were Prescott Sheldon Bush and Dorothy Walker Bush. His father was a Wall Street investment banker and later served as a U.S. senator from Connecticut. Four other children, three sons and a daughter, were born to the Bushes. George was named after his maternal grandfather, George Herbert Walker, who established the Walker Cup trophy for American and British amateur golfers.

When George was still an infant, the Bush family moved to Greenwich, Connecticut. There he was raised amid wealth. Three maids tended to the needs of the family. A chauffeur drove young George to the Greenwich Country Day School. The Bushes spent the summers at their vacation home in Kennebunkport, Maine, where George loved to go boating and fishing for mackerel in the waters of the Atlantic Ocean. Bush still maintains a summer home in Kennebunkport.

Bush attended an exclusive prep school, Phillips Academy, in Andover, Massachusetts. He was captain of the basketball and soccer teams, played on the baseball team, and was elected president of his senior class. During his senior year, on December 7, 1941, the Japanese attacked Pearl Harbor, Hawaii, drawing the United States into World War II. Bush was impatient to graduate in 1942 so that he could volunteer for the Navy air service.

▶WAR SERVICE, MARRIAGE, AND COLLEGE

On his 18th birthday, Bush enlisted in the Navy as a seaman second class. Following flight training, he was commissioned as an ensign in 1943 and became a torpedo bomber pilot. At age 19, he was the youngest pilot then serving in the U.S. Navy. During 1943 and 1944, he took part in 58 combat missions in the Pacific. His worst wartime experience occurred in 1944, when his plane was hit by Japanese anti-aircraft fire over Chichi Jima, one of the Bonin Islands. His two crewmen were killed. Bush parachuted to the water. He lay helpless in a rubber raft until he was rescued by a U.S. submarine.

In 1945, while still in uniform, Bush married Barbara Pierce, the daughter of a magazine publisher. The Bushes had five children who lived to maturity, George W., John (known as Jeb), Neil, Marvin, and Dorothy. Another daughter, Robin, died in 1953.

When the war ended in 1945, Bush was discharged from the Navy with the rank of lieutenant, junior grade. He had won the Distinguished Flying Cross and three Air Medals.

Bush resumed his education at Yale University, where he majored in economics. Still interested in sports, he played first base on the Yale baseball team. In 1948, during the home game against Princeton University, Bush got a chance to meet one of his baseball heroes, Babe Ruth. In one of his last public appearances before his death that year, Babe Ruth presented Bush, then the team captain, with the manuscript of his autobiography, which he was donating to Yale.

▶OIL AND POLITICS IN TEXAS

On his graduation from Yale in 1948, Bush was offered a job in his father's investment banking firm. But Bush preferred to make it on his own. With his wife and young son, he headed for Texas. His first job was painting oil rigs. But soon he was selling oil drilling equipment. In 1950 he and a partner formed a company that bought land in hopes of finding oil or natural gas. Three years later, Bush merged the company with the operations of other oil speculators, founding the Zapata Petroleum Corporation. From 1953 to 1966, Bush was the head of the Zapata Off Shore Company, which was a supplier of the drilling equipment used to explore for oil beneath the ocean floor.

A U.S. Navy pilot during World War II, Bush later graduated from Yale University, where he played on the baseball team.

The Bush family gathers at their summer home in Kennebunkport, Maine. The President and Mrs. Bush (in dark sweater) are seated to right of center. The eldest son, George W., is at far right, with his wife and daughter. Seated at left front are sons Neil and Marvin (in white sneakers), with their wives and children. Son John, known as Jeb, is at rear left (in dark shirt). Daughter Dorothy is to John's left, with her husband and children.

Above: Bush (right) served as vice president in Ronald Reagan's administration (1981–89). *Right:* As president, he visited U.S. troops in Saudi Arabia on Thanksgiving Day, 1990, shortly before the Persian Gulf War (1991) began.

Meanwhile, Bush had settled his family in Houston, Texas, and had become active in Republican Party politics. In 1964 he ran for the U.S. Senate but was defeated. Setting his sights elsewhere in government, Bush won election to the U.S. House of Representatives in 1966. He was the first Republican to represent Houston in Congress. He was re-elected in 1968. In 1970, Bush again ran for the Senate and again was defeated.

▶ APPOINTIVE OFFICES

United Nations Representative. In 1971, President Richard M. Nixon appointed Bush U.S. Permanent Representative to the United Nations. It was a crucial time for the world organization. The United States had agreed to allow the admission of the People's Republic of China to the United Nations for the first time since 1949, when the Communists took over the mainland of China. Bush argued forcefully for a so-called two-China policy. Under this compromise, a special seat would have been created for the Republic of China (Taiwan), which had held the China seat since the founding of the United Nations in 1945. But the United Nations rejected the two-China plan and expelled the Taiwan government in favor of the People's Republic.

Party Chairman. In 1973, Bush was named chairman of the Republican National Committee. At this time, President Nixon and the Republican Party were under the cloud of the Watergate scandal. For a long time Bush

defended Nixon. But when the White House tape recordings exposed Nixon's illegal activities, Bush, acting for the Republican Party, asked Nixon to resign. Nixon did so on August 9, 1974.

Envoy to China and CIA Director. The new president, Gerald R. Ford, appointed Bush to what was then the top diplomatic post in the People's Republic of China, chief of the U.S. Liaison Office, in 1974. Bush remained in China until he was called home at Ford's request to become director (1976–77) of the Central Intelligence Agency (CIA).

▶ VICE PRESIDENT

Bush lost the Republican presidential nomination to Ronald Reagan in 1980 but was named as his vice-presidential running mate. The Reagan-Bush ticket won easily in 1980. They were re-elected overwhelmingly in 1984.

Two Presidential Emergencies. On March 30, 1981, President Reagan was shot in an assassination attempt. While Reagan was recovering, Vice President Bush met regularly with the cabinet, White House officials, and congressional leaders. On July 13, 1985, the powers of the presidency were transferred temporarily to Bush while Reagan underwent cancer surgery.

The Iran-Contra Affair. In 1986 it became known that presidential aides had secretly sold arms to Iran in exchange for the release of American hostages in Iran. Some of the arms profits were used, illegally, to help contra guerrillas in their war against the government of Nicaragua. Bush's role in the affair became a point of controversy.

The 1988 Election. In 1988, Bush again sought and won the Republican presidential nomination. He and his vice-presidential running mate, J. Danforth (Dan) Quayle of Indiana, easily defeated the Democratic candidates, Governor Michael Dukakis of Massachusetts and Senator Lloyd Bentsen, Jr., of Texas. The Bush-Quayle ticket won 54 percent of the popular vote and received 426 electoral votes to 111 for the Democrats.

▶ PRESIDENT

Domestic Issues. One of Bush's first measures as president was to propose legislation to bail out the nation's financially troubled savings and loan institutions. Congress passed a $159 million ten-year plan to rescue the ailing industry, but the scope and cost of the problem grew. The large federal budget deficit, inherited from the Reagan years, was a major concern. In 1990, contrary to a campaign pledge, Bush agreed to raise taxes to help pay down the debt. This policy reversal cost him considerable popularity, particularly among conservative Republicans.

Following the resignation of U.S. Supreme Court Justice William J. Brennan in 1990, Bush named David H. Souter to the post. In 1991, after a series of highly controversial Senate hearings, Bush appointed federal judge Clarence Thomas to the court to succeed Thurgood Marshall.

Foreign Affairs. Bush presided during a period of great political change abroad. Between 1989 and 1992, the Communist regimes of Eastern Europe were replaced by representative governments, a divided Germany was reunited, and the Soviet Union broke apart. In 1989, Bush sent U.S. troops to oust Panama's dictator, General Manuel Noriega, who was convicted in the United States on drug trafficking charges. When Iraq invaded Kuwait in 1990, Bush led an international alliance, approved by the United Nations, forcing the Iraqis' withdrawal in 1991. And in 1992, Bush signed the North American Free Trade Agreement with Canada and Mexico. For more information, see the articles PERSIAN GULF WAR and NORTH AMERICAN FREE TRADE AGREEMENT (NAFTA) in the appropriate volumes.

Defeat in 1992: Last Measures. Bush's successes in foreign affairs were offset by an economic recession at home, which became a decisive issue in the 1992 election campaign. Bush's Democratic opponent was Governor William (Bill) Clinton of Arkansas. H. Ross Perot, a Texas businessman, also ran as an independent candidate. Clinton won overwhelmingly, with 370 electoral votes to Bush's 168.

During his last months in office, Bush dispatched U.S. Marines to Somalia, to ensure that relief supplies reached its starving people, caught up in civil war. He signed the second Strategic Arms Reduction Treaty, or START II disarmament treaty, with Russian president Boris Yeltsin. He also authorized new air strikes against Iraq for violating United Nations agreements.

After leaving office, Bush published two books, *A World Transformed* (1998), written with his former national security adviser Brent Scowcroft, and *All the Best, George Bush: My Life in Letters and Other Writings* (1999). In 2000, his eldest son, Texas governor George W. Bush, was elected president. They became the first father and son to occupy the White House since John Adams and John Quincy Adams. In 2005, at the request of President George W. Bush, former Presidents Bush and Clinton led a joint fund-raising effort to relieve the nations devastated by an earthquake and resulting tsunami that struck South Asia on December 26, 2004.

WILLIAM A. DE GREGORIO
Author, *The Complete Book of U.S. Presidents*
Reviewed by JAMES E. CHURCHILL, JR.
Executive Editor, *The Americana Annual*

IMPORTANT DATES IN THE LIFE OF GEORGE BUSH

1924 Born in Milton, Massachusetts, June 12.
1942–45 Served in the U.S. Navy.
1945 Married Barbara Pierce.
1948 Graduated from Yale University.
1953–66 Was president and then chairman of the board of the Zapata Off Shore Company, Texas.
1967–71 Served in the U.S. Congress.
1971–72 U.S. Permanent Representative to the United Nations.
1973–74 Chairman of the Republican National Committee.
1974–75 Chief of the U.S. Liaison Office, China.
1976–77 Director of the Central Intelligence Agency.
1981–89 Vice president of the United States.
1989–93 41st president of the United States.

GEORGE W. BUSH (1946–)

43rd President of the United States

FACTS ABOUT BUSH

Birthplace: New Haven, Connecticut
Religion: Methodist
Colleges Attended: Yale University, Harvard University School of Business Administration
Occupation: Oil executive, Major League Baseball executive, public official
Married: Laura Welch
Children: Barbara and Jenna
Political Party: Republican
Office Held Before Becoming President: Governor of Texas
President Who Preceded Him: William Clinton
Age on Becoming President: 54
Years in the Presidency: 2001–
Vice President: Richard B. Cheney

BUSH, GEORGE W. With his victory in the 2000 election, George W. Bush became the first son of a president to win the White House since John Quincy Adams, son of John Adams, in 1824. On the road to winning the nation's highest office, he benefited not only from the example of his father, George Herbert Walker Bush, the 41st president, but also that of his grandfather, Prescott Bush, a widely respected U.S. senator. And his victory over Democrat Al Gore, vice president to Bill Clinton, who had ousted Bush's father only eight years earlier, gave the new President Bush the opportunity to restore his family's political reputation.

▶ EARLY YEARS

George Walker Bush was born on July 6, 1946, in New Haven, Connecticut, where his father, just returned from World War II, was attending Yale University. Bush's mother, the former Barbara Pierce, later gave birth to three more sons, John (Jeb), Neil, and Marvin, and two daughters, Dorothy and Robin. After George Bush graduated from Yale, he set out for Texas, hoping to make his fortune in the oil business. The Bushes settled in Midland, where young George had a relatively untroubled childhood, apart from the tragic death of his sister Robin from leukemia in 1953.

As he reached high school age, George left Texas to attend the same elite eastern schools as had his father, Phillips Academy and Andover. But his years in the Lone Star State helped shape his life. "I was educated up East, but my heart was always back in Texas," he later told an interviewer. He was not an outstanding student, nor an exceptional athlete. His greatest strength was in getting along with his fellow students.

After high school, George entered Yale University, again following in his father's footsteps. A few months before graduation, he entered the Texas Air National Guard.

George W. Bush, pictured with his parents George and Barbara in 1955, became the first son of a president to win the White House since John Quincy Adams.

In 1970, George worked for his father in another losing bid for the Senate. Seeking to gain focus for his life, he entered Harvard Business School, earning a master's degree in business administration in 1975.

OIL AND BASEBALL
Bush decided to make his start in the business world in the same place his father had begun—the oil fields of Texas, where he founded his own oil company, Arbusto Energy. In 1977 he married Laura Welch, a librarian who four years later gave birth to twin daughters, Jenna and Barbara.

In 1978, Bush embarked on his first political campaign, running for a seat in the U.S. House of Representatives. He won the Republican nomination but lost the election. He returned to the oil business but could not achieve the success his father had gained. He began to drink heavily until he realized "it was interfering with my energy level." On his 40th birthday, in 1986, he stopped drinking. Bush soon sold his oil business and served as an adviser in his father's 1988 presidential campaign. After the elder Bush was elected, his son entered a new field, major league baseball. He headed a group of investors who bought the Texas Rangers baseball team.

GOVERNOR OF TEXAS
In 1993, Bush announced his candidacy for the governorship of Texas. In his campaign, he concentrated on four issues: welfare, education, juvenile crime, and legal reform. In November 1994 he won his first 4-year term as governor. When he ran for re-election in 1998, he captured nearly 70 percent of the vote, becoming the first Texas governor to win two consecutive 4-year terms.

THE 2000 ELECTION CAMPAIGN
Bush's big victory in Texas opened the way to the Republican presidential nomination and helped him raise more money than any other candidate. In the general election against Democratic vice president Al Gore, Bush supported cutting income tax rates and making changes in social security. The race turned out be one of the closest in American history. Nationwide, Gore won 500,000 more popular votes than Bush. But the race in Florida was so close, it took five weeks to certify the state's results. It was finally determined that Bush won Florida by slightly more than 500 votes. In a controversial decision, the U.S. Supreme Court declared Bush the winner. The final electoral vote totals were 271 for Bush and 266 for Gore.

PRESIDENT: FIRST TERM
First Year: 2001. The new president's most important accomplishment was the enact-

On the campaign trail during his unsuccessful run for Congress in 1978, Bush met with oil refinery workers in West Texas.

ment of a sweeping income tax cut expected to cost $1.35 trillion over eleven years. The new law repealed the inheritance tax and cut individual tax rates.

On September 11, 2001, eight months after he took office, Bush's presidency was suddenly transformed by several simultaneous acts of terrorism that stunned the nation. U.S. forces struck back in Afghanistan, the main base for the Al Qaeda terrorist network responsible for the attacks. The United States and its allies defeated the ruling Taliban regime, which had harbored the terrorists. For more information, see the article TERRORISM, WAR ON in Volume T.

Second Year: 2002. The war against terrorism continued to dominate Bush's presidency. In his annual State of the Union address to Congress on January 29, Bush warned of the dangers of new attacks. He singled out three countries—North Korea, Iran, and Iraq—as making up an "axis of evil" and vowed to prevent them from using "the world's most destructive weapons" against the United States. On other foreign policy issues, Bush also tried to improve the prospects of peace. He signed a nuclear arms reduction treaty with Russia and pledged to support the creation of an independent Palestinian state in the Middle East.

In 2002, Republicans won enough seats in Congress to increase their majority in the House and, more important, regain control of the Senate. One of the first acts of the new Congress was to approve Bush's proposal for a new cabinet department, called Homeland Security, to focus federal efforts against terrorism.

Third Year: 2003. Bush devoted most of his State of the Union address to the prospect of war with Iraq. Bush accused Saddam Hussein's government of hiding chemical and biological weapons of mass destruction from United Nations inspectors. He also said the United States had evidence that Hussein was trying to build nuclear weapons and that the Iraqi ruler was aiding Al Qaeda, the terrorist group that had launched the September 11 attacks. In response, he promoted the **Bush Doctrine**, a policy that advocates striking out at a suspected aggressor nation before that nation attacks first.

Despite opposition to war abroad and at home, Bush, with the support of Great Britain, ordered an invasion of Iraq on March 19 (March 20 in Iraq). U.S.-led forces soon seized Baghdad and drove Hussein from power. On May 1, Bush announced the end of major combat operations. But supporters of Hussein and other Iraqis who resented the U.S. occupation continued to wage guerrilla warfare against American troops. The failure to find evidence of weapons of mass destruction led to increasing criticism of the war. For more information, see the article IRAQ WAR in Volume I.

On the domestic front, the president's major accomplishment was approval of another tax cut, this one for $350 billion. He won a big legislative victory when Congress broadly revised the Medicare program to help seniors pay for prescription drugs. The president also signed a controversial law banning "partial-birth" abortions (pregnancies that are terminated after 16 weeks).

Fourth Year: 2004. A national commission investigating the September 11, 2001, terrorist attacks concluded that neither the Clinton nor Bush administrations had done enough to prevent the assaults and charged that the war on Iraq had used resources that could have been used to fight terrorism.

In domestic issues, Bush signed into law the fourth major tax cut of his presidency. He also backed a proposal for a constitutional amendment banning gay marriage, but Congress blocked its approval.

The 2004 Campaign. Early presidential campaign surveys indicated that voters were closely divided between Bush and the Democratic challenger, Massachusetts senator John Kerry. The final decision came down to winning the electoral votes of a single state: Ohio, which Bush finally carried with 51 percent of the popular vote, the same margin he won on the national level. The final electoral college vote totals were 252 for Kerry and 286 for Bush.

▶ **PRESIDENT: SECOND TERM**

First Year: 2005. After the election, Bush made a number of changes in his cabinet. The most significant were the appointments of Condoleezza Rice as secretary of state and Alberto R. Gonzales as attorney general. With terror still a constant threat, Bush signed an intelligence reform bill to help prevent future attacks.

Above: On Thanksgiving Day 2003, President Bush made a surprise visit to the troops in Iraq.
Right: President Bush with his wife Laura and their twin daughters Barbara (far left) and Jenna.

In his State of the Union speech, Bush vowed to keep U.S. troops in Iraq until the country was secure. On the domestic front, he called for a fundamental change in the social security system, which he said would eventually go bankrupt. He proposed allowing Americans under the age of 55 to voluntarily put part of the money they would normally contribute to social security into their own private retirement accounts. Polls showed that voters were skeptical of the proposal.

In July, U.S. Supreme Court justice Sandra Day O'Connor announced her retirement, and Bush nominated federal appeals judge John G. Roberts, Jr. for the position. While Roberts' nomination was still pending, Chief Justice William Rehnquist died, and Bush renominated Roberts for Rehnquist's position. After Roberts was confirmed by the Senate, Bush nominated White House counsel Harriet Miers to replace O'Connor.

In August, Bush took advantage of Congress' recess to bypass the Senate and install John R. Bolton as ambassador to the United Nations. Senate Democrats had blocked Bolton's nomination, stating he had been overly critical of the UN in his previous post as undersecretary of state for disarmament.

Despite these accomplishments, Bush's standing in the polls declined because of public frustration with the war in Iraq. His political fortunes also suffered from a natural calamity, Hurricane Katrina. The storm devastated the Gulf Coast and Mississippi Delta, particularly New Orleans. More than 1,000 were killed and hundreds of thousands made homeless. Bush later acknowledged that the slow response to the crisis was "unacceptable" and took the blame for the federal government's failure to relieve the victims.

Adding to Bush's problems were charges of misconduct against two prominent Republican congressional leaders, House Majority Leader Tom Delay of Texas and Senate Majority Leader Bill Frist of Tennessee. Also, Miers' Supreme Court nomination proved so unpopular with both Republicans and Democrats, she withdrew from the process. Bush then selected federal appeals judge Samuel Alito in her place.

ROBERT SHOGAN
Author, *Constant Conflict: Politics, Culture, and the Struggle for America's Political Future*

IMPORTANT DATES IN THE LIFE OF GEORGE W. BUSH

1946 Born in New Haven, Connecticut, July 6.

1968 Graduated from Yale University.

1975 Graduated from Harvard Business School.

1977 Married Laura Welch.

1977 Started his own oil company, Arbusto Energy

1978 Ran unsuccessfully for Congress.

1987–92 Served as aide to his father, President Bush.

1989–94 Served as managing general partner of Texas Rangers baseball franchise.

1994–2001 Served as governor of Texas.

2001 Inaugurated as 43rd president of the United States.

2004 Won election to a second term as president.

The fortunate individual who owns and operates this business is able to work outdoors, surrounded by the beautiful flowers and colorful balloons he sells.

BUSINESS

How do your parents earn their living? How will you earn your living? Chances are that the answers to both questions will involve a business. Most people earn their livelihood either by working for a business owned by someone else, or by operating their own business.

There are many kinds of businesses, from small shops owned and operated by one person to large companies owned by many people and employing thousands of workers. A factory is a business. A store is a business. Other examples include beauty salons, professional sports, and all kinds of entertainment.

A business is any establishment that produces or distributes goods and services. Goods are tangible items like clothing and food. Services are intangible things like entertainment and the services of doctors and lawyers.

▶ TYPES OF BUSINESS ORGANIZATION

There are three basic types of business organization: (1) the individual proprietorship; (2) the partnership; and (3) the corporation.

The Individual Proprietorship

An individual proprietorship is a business owned and managed by a single individual. This owner, or **proprietor**, makes all business decisions, receives all profits from the business, and is legally responsible for all of the losses and debts of the business. This legal responsibility for losses and debts, known as **unlimited liability**, is a major disadvantage of an individual proprietorship. It means that if debts cannot be paid, the owner can lose the business and also personal assets such as savings, home, and automobile. While an individual proprietorship can be started rather easily, often with little money, it is usually difficult to raise money for expansion or to improve efficiency. For this reason, it is often difficult for a proprietorship to compete successfully with larger businesses. An individual proprietorship also has a limited life. If the proprietor dies or retires, the business may cease to exist.

The Partnership

A partnership is a business owned by two or more individuals who are called partners. These partners make business decisions together and share all business profits and losses. They also share in unlimited liability for the business. As in a proprietorship, this means that all debts are the responsibility of all of the partners. If debts cannot be paid, they could lose the business as well as their own personal assets.

A partnership is relatively easy and inexpensive to establish. Since more than one person is involved, it is also generally easier to

The partners in an accounting firm meet often to discuss how to attract new clients and make decisions that will affect the firm's profitability.

raise money for expansion or other needs. A partnership also provides an opportunity for specialization, allowing one partner to specialize in production, another in finances, still another in sales, and so on. This usually enables a partnership to handle more work than an individual proprietorship. A partnership also has a limited life. If one partner dies, retires, or resigns, the business may be forced to close unless other partners are willing and able to buy out that partner's share of the business.

The Corporation

A corporation is a business that has the legal status of an individual but is owned collectively by many people. Most large businesses that employ hundreds or thousands of workers are corporations.

To establish a corporation, the potential owners must meet various legal requirements of federal, state, and local governments. One basic requirement is a corporate charter, which is a legal document that gives the corporation the authority to operate in a particular state. The charter establishes the corporation as a legal entity that can enter into contracts and make commitments under its own name. This means that the individual owners of the corporation have only a limited liability. No matter what happens to the corporation, the owners can lose no more than their initial investment, and they cannot be held personally liable for corporate debts or losses. This is one of the major advantages of a corporation.

Another advantage of a corporation is its unlimited life. When owners die or choose to leave the business, the corporation continues to operate unchanged because their shares in the company can be sold to other people. A corporation also has the ability to raise large sums of money through the sale of stocks. One disadvantage of a corporation is that because of its size and complexity decision-making may become slow. Sometimes it may not be able to respond as quickly as it should to changing economic conditions.

How a Corporation Works. A corporate charter authorizes the sale of shares of stock in order to raise money for starting a corporation, for expanding its business, or for other needs. The people who buy these shares of stock are called **stockholders**. In return for their investment, stockholders receive **dividends**, or shares of the corporation's profits.

Boards of directors of large corporations establish and review the basic policies their companies will follow and hire the executive officers who will actually manage their businesses.

The stockholders are the actual owners of a corporation and it is their responsibility to vote on major corporate issues. In most cases, stockholders have one vote for each share of stock owned. Stockholders also elect a board of directors, which is responsible for determining basic corporate policies and for hiring executive officers to carry out the decisions of directors and stockholders. These executive officers are responsible for the day-to-day operations of the corporation. To help them do this, they hire managers for specialized departments within the corporation. The number of managers and departments depends on the size of the corporation and the types of goods or services it provides. Most corporations have at least three specialized departments to provide the services of production, finance, and marketing. Corporations may also have personnel, research, and public relations departments.

WONDER QUESTION

What are gross income and net income?

Gross income is the total amount of money a business earns without considering expenses. Net income, also known as profit, is the total amount of money a business earns after expenses and other operating costs have been subtracted.

HOW TO BE AN ENTREPRENEUR

An **entrepreneur** is a person who sees the need for a particular product or service and then creates a business to supply that product or service. There are many opportunities for young people to become entrepreneurs. In some communities there may be a need for services such as babysitting, taking care of pets, or making deliveries. They might produce and sell goods — for example, growing and selling fresh fruits or vegetables or making and selling lemonade. Or they could become involved in woodworking, knitting, quilting, or pottery, and sell their finished products.

Before starting any business, a smart entrepreneur will find out if there is a need or market for a particular good or service, whether or not anyone is already providing it, and the possible costs of running the business. You will probably want to do some research at your local library. Additional information might be available from your town or city hall, chamber of commerce, church hall, or local newspaper. These might also be good places to **advertise** your product or service after your business has been established. Researching such issues is one of an entrepreneur's most important tasks. Now let us look at an example of how to become an entrepreneur.

Suppose your community has many homes with large lawns. You begin to wonder if some homeowners would pay you to mow their lawns. The potential may exist for a lawn-mowing business. You decide to become an entrepreneur.

You begin by asking neighbors if they would like to have their lawns mowed. You might also advertise by posting announcements on bulletin boards in schools, churches, supermarkets, and community centers. After lining up customers, you buy a lawn mower. The money you spend for it is consid-

ered an **investment** in your business. If the money comes from your savings, it is called **capital**. If it is borrowed, it is called a **capital loan**. Of course, if you borrow money you will have to pay it back, perhaps with **interest** — a fee that a lender charges for loaning money.

The income you receive from your business is called **revenue**. Out of this you must pay for fuel and any other costs, called **operating expenses**. If revenue is greater than expenses, your business has made a **profit**. If expenses are greater than revenue, your business has sustained a **loss**.

As your business grows, you decide to buy another lawn mower and hire a friend to help. Now you have become an **employer**, and your friend is your **employee**. The **wages** you pay your employee are part of your operating expenses.

After a few weeks, someone else starts a lawn-mowing service as **competition** to yours. With competition, the price of your service becomes very important. If one person charges less, or **undersells**, the other, the person charging more may begin to lose customers and eventually may be forced out of business. On the other hand, if one person charges too little, the income may not be enough to cover expenses and that business may go **bankrupt**. However, you and your competitor charge similar prices, and there are plenty of customers for both businesses.

As your business grows, you discover that some customers want the grass clippings removed from their lawns. You purchase grass catchers for your lawn mowers and consider paying someone to haul away the clippings. But then you have an idea — grass clippings make good mulch to place around shrubs, flowers, and vegetables. They could, therefore, be considered a product with a potential market. Soon you have found customers who want to buy mulch — you have created a new business and a new source of revenue.

You are a successful entrepreneur and manager of two businesses! The profit you earn is what motivated you to start your businesses, and it is what keeps them in operation. It is the potential for earning a profit that motivates most entrepreneurs.

▶BUSINESS IN A FREE ENTERPRISE SYSTEM

In a free enterprise system, such as the economies of the United States and Canada, businesses produce the goods and services people need and want. While doing this, they also try to make a profit—to have more income than expenses. Profit is essential for a business to remain in operation, and it is one of the most important principles of a free enterprise system.

One of the key factors affecting profit is competition. If a business has competitors—other companies producing and selling similar goods or services—it cannot charge prices that are much higher than those of its competitors without losing customers. However, it cannot charge prices that would result in less income than expenses without jeopardizing the survival of the business. Competition thus helps regulate profits businesses earn and prices consumers pay for goods and services.

Government Regulation of Businesses

Businesses often adjust their operations and their prices in an attempt to increase profits. But in the United States, Canada, and other countries with free enterprise systems, the government often establishes regulations concerning what a business can and cannot do.

The government often enacts laws to promote safe working conditions and ensure safe products. For example, laws limit the number of hours people can work and provide workplace safety standards. Product safety is another concern. For example, if a company develops a new medicine, a government agency requires extensive testing to determine the safety and effectiveness of the medicine before it can be sold to the public.

Government regulates business in other ways as well. Antitrust laws are enacted to help prevent companies from merging, or joining together, in order to control the supply and price of a product or service. These laws

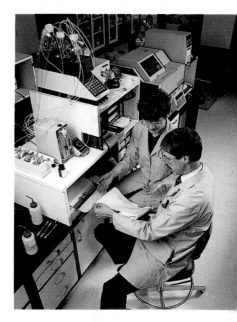

By opening restaurants so close together, these businesses face stiff competition from one another. Each business must offer good food and service at low prices to attract and keep customers. They must also be careful not to let costs exceed earnings or they will lose money and be forced to close.

New drugs and medicines must undergo extensive testing before the federal government allows doctors to prescribe them for their patients.

help maintain competition among businesses. In certain industries, such as public utilities that supply gas, electricity, and water, the government often grants one company the exclusive right of operating in a specific market but then establishes regulations to ensure that the quality of its services is adequate and its prices are not too high.

Aside from regulations to ensure safety, to promote competition, and to protect consumers, businesses in a free enterprise system are generally left alone to operate according to the laws of supply and demand.

ALLEN SMITH
Author, *Understanding Economics*

See also BANKS AND BANKING; ECONOMICS; STOCKS AND BONDS.

BUTTE. See MONTANA (Cities).

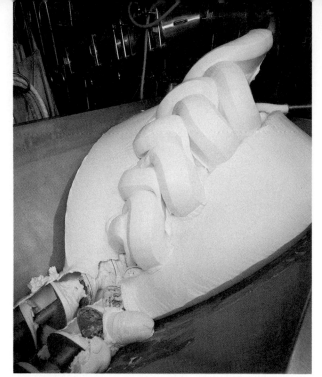

The spiral blades of a continuous churn push braids of freshly kneaded butter into stainless steel tanks. The butter is then pumped to machines for packaging.

BUTTER

Butter is a dairy product made from butterfat, a fat found in milk. It is used chiefly in cooking and baking and as a spread for bread. All of the butter produced in the United States is made from cow's milk, although in many other countries butter is made from the milk of reindeer, sheep, goats, water buffalo, or even horses. About 10 quarts (9.5 liters) of milk are needed to make 1 pound (0.45 kilograms) of butter.

Years ago buttermaking was a long and tiring job. After a batch of cream had been skimmed from milk, it would be left to cool and ripen in an earthernware crock. After several days, the slightly sour, or ripe, cream would be poured into a bell-shaped wooden churn. It would then be beaten with a long plunger until the butterfat separated from the rest of the cream into lumps about the size of peas. After draining off the leftover liquid, or buttermilk, the butter would be washed and kneaded until it was smooth.

In the 1930's automated churns were developed to make the production of butter more efficient, economical, and consistent. Today continuous churns can produce up to 15,000 pounds (6,800 kilograms) of butter an hour.

Most of the butter sold today is made by large creameries that buy milk from many different farmers. The manufacturing process begins by mechanically separating the cream (containing 35 to 40 percent butterfat) from the milk. The cream is then pasteurized (heated to destroy bacteria). Then the pasteurized cream moves into huge rotating cylinders, called churns, where it is beaten until the butterfat separates from the buttermilk. The buttermilk is drained off and dried into a powder to be used in foods, such as baked goods, ice cream, and pancake mixes. The remaining butterfat is washed and kneaded until it has a smooth, firm texture. Salt is usually added to improve the flavor and stop the growth of bacteria. Vegetable coloring, such as annatto, may be added to produce a desirable color.

In 1923 Congress delcared that butter could be made only from milk or cream and that the resulting product must consist of at least 80 percent fat. Today, butter is tested, evaluated, and graded by the U.S. Department of Agriculture according to its flavor, texture, and aroma. Grade AA is the best quality followed by Grades A, B, and C. Inferior butter, graded UG for undergrade, is usually reprocessed for industrial uses.

As a food, butter is a rich source of Vitamin A. It also contains limited amounts of vitamins D and E, calcium, phosphorus, sodium, and potassium. One tablespoon of butter contains approximately 100 calories.

Because butter is relatively high in cholesterol (a natural element found in all animal fats that has been linked to heart disease and hardening of the arteries), consumers who are health conscious have been using less and less butter each year. In the past 20 years, average yearly consumption of butter in the United States has fallen from nearly 8 pounds (3 kilograms) to just under 4 pounds (2 kilograms) per person. Margarine and other spreads made from vegetable oils that have little or no cholesterol in them have risen in popularity as butter substitutes.

The world's leading butter-consuming nations, per capita, are Germany, followed by New Zealand, Ireland, Denmark, and Finland. In the United States, the leading butter-producing states are Wisconsin, California, and Minnesota.

ROBERT L. BRADLEY, JR.
University of Wisconsin

Butterfly at rest (*left*) has fully erect wings. Resting moth (*above*) folds back wings.

BUTTERFLIES AND MOTHS

Anyone who touches the wings of a butterfly or a moth finds that something like dust comes off on the fingers. The dust is actually made up of tiny scales. The scales grow in rows and give the wings their patterns of colors. The scales also account for the scientific name for butterflies and moths. Together they are called Lepidoptera, which means "scaly winged."

There are about 112,000 different kinds of moths and butterflies in the world, and they live in almost every kind of environment. In the United States and Canada there are probably about 11,000 species, or kinds, of butterflies and moths.

As microscope shows, a butterfly's wing has rows of scales that give it color and pattern.

How Can You Tell a Butterfly from a Moth?

Many butterflies and moths look very much alike. Yet it is possible to tell them apart. In general, butterflies are brighter in color than moths. This is not always true—a few moths are as bright and beautiful as any butterfly. Butterflies are active during the day. Most moths are active only at night and are attracted by lights.

Butterflies and moths differ in other ways, too. Moths have thicker, more hairy bodies. Both have two pairs of wings. But a resting moth usually folds its front wings back upon its hind ones. A butterfly at rest leaves its wings full and erect.

A butterfly, like a moth, has two antennae (feelers) on its head. A butterfly's antennae have slightly enlarged tips, while a moth's antennae do not. In some moth species the antennae have featherlike plumes but the tips are never enlarged.

▶LIFE CYCLE

Butterflies and moths are among the insects that pass through four stages of development in their life cycles.

The first stage is the egg. Adult females lay eggs on the kind of plant their young will later need as food.

The eggs hatch into wormlike creatures known as **larvae**. The common name for the larvae of butterflies and moths is caterpillar. Caterpillars are busy and hungry. They may

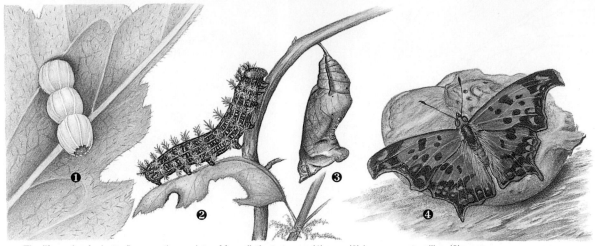

The life cycle of a butterfly or moth consists of four distinct stages: (1) egg, (2) larva, or caterpillar, (3) pupa, and (4) adult. The question mark butterfly is shown here as it goes through this process of development, or metamorphosis. When the egg, which is laid by the female usually near a food source, hatches, the larva emerges. The pupa stage follows as, within a shell-like covering, the larva changes form and becomes an adult.

eat once or twice their own weight in leaves each day. After several days of such constant feeding, caterpillars outgrow their own skins. When this happens they molt, splitting the skin and crawling out of it. Caterpillars may shed their skins four or five times in this second stage of the life cycle.

In the third stage the caterpillar goes into a resting state and is called a **pupa**. Different caterpillars pupate in different ways. For example, many moth caterpillars burrow into the ground; others hide behind loose bark or in hollow logs. Some caterpillars rest in silken cocoons, which they make by spinning thread from their mouths. (Silk cloth is made from the threads in the cocoon of the silkworm moth.) The pupa does nothing except rest. This stage may last two weeks; it may last a whole winter. During this period the caterpillar changes into a full-grown butterfly or moth.

In its new and adult form, the butterfly or moth emerges wet and shaky from the cocoon. As blood flows into the veins of the wings the adult flutters and dries them. In a few hours, when the wings are strong and dry, the butterfly or moth flies off to live out its fourth, or adult, stage.

▶ WHERE THE COLORS COME FROM

The colors that mark an adult may be of several types. Some scales hold pigment, or colored matter; it accounts for the blacks, browns, reds, oranges, yellows, and whites. Other scales catch the sunlight and separate it into different colors. This second effect may be caused by a thin, oily film on the scales or by a scale's fine lines or ridges. (The green of many caterpillars is caused by their diet of plants.)

▶ THE SENSES

Both moths and butterflies have keen senses of sight, smell, and taste. A few moths are able to hear, too. The organs of taste in most butterflies and moths are in the mouth. Most organs of smell are on the antennae. However, the mourning cloak, the red admiral, and some other butterflies smell things through "noses" on their feet.

Sight

The eyes of butterflies are very sensitive to colors. Butterflies are especially attracted to red flowers. Moths, most active at night, are attracted to light-colored flowers. Most night-blooming flowers are white.

Scents and Smell

Many butterflies and moths have odors, or scents, which they use for two purposes. One kind of scent is used to attract the opposite sex. The other kind of scent is used to drive away enemies.

The scents of male butterflies come from scales in pockets on their hind wings. During courtship a male monarch butterfly may scatter these scent scales over the female. The scents of many kinds of male butterflies resemble those of flowers or spices and are often pleasing to humans.

Female butterflies produce their scents in

Adult life of butterfly begins when it emerges from pupal case, as shown in these photos of monarch butterfly. Legs break out, grab case, and pull rest of body free.

Within about 2 minutes, butterfly is free and hangs on empty pupal case. Newly emerged butterfly, still crumpled and wet, has small, fleshy wings and a flat abdomen.

As butterfly hangs there, its abdomen pulsates vigorously. This causes body fluids to circulate. After 10 or 20 minutes, wings will have expanded to full size.

Even after wings are fully expanded, adult butterfly remains clinging to pupal case for several hours, depending on weather, before it tries its first flight.

Monarch butterflies gather in dense, hanging clusters on the branches of trees and bushes.

special glands in their bodies. Most of these female odors are disagreeable to the human nose.

Taste

The taste organs of a butterfly are far more sensitive to sweet things than our tongues are. Their chief food, flower nectar, is a sugar solution, and they are easily able to find it. When a butterfly finds nectar in a flower, it uncoils its proboscis, a long, hollow tongue-like structure, and sucks in the liquid.

Not all butterflies live on nectar. Some are attracted to rotting fruits. A few prefer the flesh of dead animals.

▶ MIGRATING BUTTERFLIES AND MOTHS

People have known for hundreds of years that birds travel over special routes during certain seasons. Such travel is called migration. More recently it has been learned that many butterflies, and some moths, also migrate. For example, the painted-lady butterfly travels from Mexico to California each spring. The same kind of butterfly flies across the Mediterranean Sea in spring, from North Africa to Europe. In butterfly migration thousands, even millions, of insects travel together.

The Monarch Butterfly

The best known of the migrating butterflies is the monarch that winters along the Gulf of Mexico and other southern areas. In spring the young female lays her eggs on the milkweed plants that have begun to grow. The caterpillars that hatch from the eggs feed on the milkweed leaves. When the adult butterflies develop, they fly some distance north. There they mate and lay eggs on the milkweed that has just begun to grow with the advance of spring. Thus, within a few months' time, several generations of monarch butterflies travel farther and farther north in search of milkweed. By late summer, descendants of the original monarchs reach Canada.

With the cooler weather of autumn, surviving monarchs fly back south in great swarms. There are reports of monarchs spread out in a swarm more than 20 miles (30 kilometers) wide. Year after year such masses of butterflies follow the same routes. Every night they settle on trees and bushes, which are often called butterfly trees.

▶ ENEMIES AND DEFENSES

Butterflies and moths have many enemies. There are tiny wasps that lay their eggs inside the eggs of the butterfly. The wasp larvae then feed on the butterfly eggs. Caterpillars also have enemies. Birds and bats eat them. Tiny flies and wasps invade caterpillars and live inside them. Farmers and gardeners also kill the ever-hungry caterpillars in order to protect their plants.

From all the eggs that hatch, only two caterpillars out of every hundred live to become butterflies. If this were not so, caterpillars would be much more serious pests than they are. Caterpillars eat the leaves and fruit of plants and bore into the trunks and roots. The larvae of the clothes moth chew holes in wool and silk and also eat fur.

A few kinds of butterflies and moths have developed defenses against their natural enemies. Some are nearly invisible because they look like twigs or dead leaves. Some caterpillars have stinging hairs or poison spines that drive off enemies. Others release bad odors. The monarch butterfly seems to taste bad to birds, and birds leave the handsome orange and black creature alone.

More kinds of butterflies and moths are shown in the pictures on pages 479–83.

ROSS E. HUTCHINS
Author, *Insects*

See also INSECTS; METAMORPHOSIS.

The kallima butterfly of southern Asia and the Pacific islands, the hawkmoth, and the geometrid moth and its caterpillar (also called looper, measuring worm, or inchworm) are nearly invisible to their enemies. They have a protective coloring or shape that camouflages them and makes them look like plant life. Can you find the butterfly, the moths, and the caterpillar in the pictures on this page?

Kallima butterfly or leaf?

Hawkmoth or tree bark?

Geometrid caterpillar or twig?

Geometrid moth or leaf?

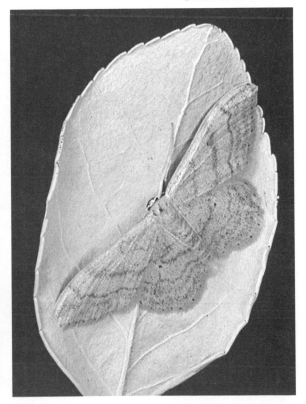

BUTTERFLIES OF THE WORLD

AGRIAS
SARDANAPALUS

EUROPEAN
SWALLOWTAIL
(PAPILIO
MACHAON)

BLUE MOUNTAIN
BUTTERFLY
(PAPILIO ULYSSES)

CHRISTMAS
BUTTERFLY
(PAPILIO
DEMODOCUS)

ORCHARD
SWALLOWTAIL
(PAPILIO AEGEUS)

SILVERSTRIPE
(PANDORIANA
PANDORA)

ANCYLURIS
FORMOSISSIMA

PEACOCK
(NYMPHALIS IO)

PAPILIO
SEMPERI

APOLLO
(PARNASSIUS
APOLLO)

MORPHO
CYPRIS

MESENE
PHARAEUS

BRIMSTONE
(GONEPTERYX
RHAMNI)

TAILED
BIRDWING
(PAPILIO
PARADISEA)

480

BUTTERFLIES OF THE UNITED STATES

**QUESTION MARK
ANGLEWING
(POLYGONIA
INTERROGATIONIS)**

**MORNING CLOAK
(NYMPHALIS
ANTIOPA)**

**WOOD NYMPH
(MINOIS ALOPE)**

**PAINTED LADY
(VANESSA CARDUI)**

**MONARCH
(DANAUS
PLEXIPPUS)**

**DOG FACE
(COLIAS
CESONIA)**

**GREAT PURPLE
HAIRSTREAK
(ALTIDES HALESUS)**

**GIANT SWALLOWTAIL
(PAPILIO CRESPHONTES)**

**LEONARDUS SKIPPER
(HESPERIA LEONARDUS)**

**VARIEGATED FRITILLARY
(EUPTOIETA CLAUDIA)**

**WHITE ADMIRAL
(LIMENITIS
ARTHEMIS)**

**BLACK SWALLOWTAIL
(PAPILIO POLYXENES
ASTERIUS)**

CABBAGE

**CABBAGE LARVA
(PIERIS RAPAE)**

**ZEBRA SWALLOWTAIL
(PAPILIO MARCELLUS)**

481

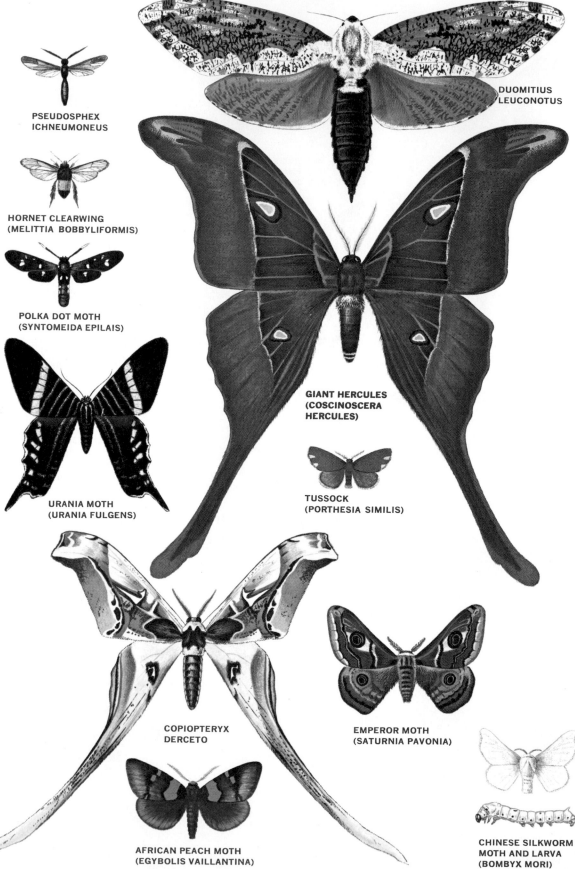

MOTHS OF THE WORLD

PSEUDOSPHEX
ICHNEUMONEUS

HORNET CLEARWING
(MELITTIA BOBBYLIFORMIS)

POLKA DOT MOTH
(SYNTOMEIDA EPILAIS)

URANIA MOTH
(URANIA FULGENS)

DUOMITIUS
LEUCONOTUS

GIANT HERCULES
(COSCINOSCERA
HERCULES)

TUSSOCK
(PORTHESIA SIMILIS)

COPIOPTERYX
DERCETO

AFRICAN PEACH MOTH
(EGYBOLIS VAILLANTINA)

EMPEROR MOTH
(SATURNIA PAVONIA)

CHINESE SILKWORM
MOTH AND LARVA
(BOMBYX MORI)

482

MOTHS OF THE UNITED STATES

STRIPED MORNING SPHINX
(DEILEPHILA LINEATA)

POLYPHEMUS
(ANTHERAEA
POLYPHEMUS)

LUNA
(ACTIAS
LUNA)

IMPERIAL
(EACLES
IMPERIALIS)

GYPSY MOTH
(PORTHETRIA
DISPAR)

HAWK MOTH
(SMERINTHUS
GEMINATUS)

IO
(AUTOMERIS IO)

CLOTHES MOTH
AND LARVA
(TINEOLA
BISSELLIELLA)

GLOVER'S SILKWORM
(SAMIA GLOVERI)

ARMY WORM MOTH
AND LARVA
(CIRPHIS UNIPUNCTA)

AMERICAN TIGER
MOTH AND LARVA
(ISIA ISABELLA)

FOREST TENT—
CATERPILLAR AND MOTH
(MALACOSOMA DISSTRIA)

CECROPIA MOTH AND LARVA
(HYALOPHORA CECROPIA)

483

A glass button (*left*) shows the English countryside, 1770–85. Above is a 19th-century French button of painted enamel.

BUTTONS

Buttons were probably first used to hold clothes together in the 13th century. At that time most people still fastened their clothes with clasps, but the nobility used beautiful buttons of silver and gold, hammered out by craftsmen.

In the next few centuries an almost endless variety of materials and designs were used by button makers. A popular button covering in the 1700's was made of metal threads wound into an intricate pattern. The button maker needed all his skill and patience to weave the threads of different colors into tiny stars or triangles. Miniature scenes were painted on buttons of ivory or glass. Some buttons were covered with beads and pearls. Button makers also cut designs in hard button bases and filled the cuts with silver.

The buttons that took almost the longest time and most painstaking care to make were surprisingly enough made of paper. The pieces of paper were cut with fine paring tools into shapes of tiny houses, people, or various other forms. These were made into scenes and fastened onto strong button bases.

Buttons were made by hand in these elaborate styles until the 19th century. Manufacturers then began to use powered machines to turn out large quantities of buttons cheaply. Brass buttons became very popular because designs could be stamped on them quickly. Many of the brass buttons were made for work clothes and had railroad signs or colorful slogans on them. Children's buttons were often stamped with a tiny Jack Horner or some other nursery hero.

New materials changed button manufacturing, too. Hard-rubber buttons were tried in the 1840's, but they did not wear well. Celluloid, a synthetic compound that looks like ivory, was developed toward the end of the 19th century. Delicate buttons that seemed to be hand painted could be mass-produced in the new material.

Buttons today are made of plastics or natural materials such as wood, leather, metal, pearl, and shell. Shanks, which are the fastening loops on the backs of buttons, can be put on in minutes by machines. Other buttons have holes punched out so that they can be sewn on clothes. Automatic machines cut and shape most buttons, but some buttons are still finished by hand. There are as many different ways of making buttons as there are kinds of buttons. Button making still demands the imagination and skill of the craftsman.

Collecting Buttons

Collecting pretty and unusual buttons is a popular hobby and an easy one to start. To have an interesting collection and not just a lot of buttons rattling around in an old shoe box, it is best to work according to some plan.

You may want to collect buttons made of certain materials such as pewter, brass, enamel, bone, glass, wood, porcelain, silver, or gold. Or you may prefer to collect according to subjects, choosing perhaps fairy tales, animals, flags, ships, or your favorite sport. Perhaps covered buttons will interest you most, or you might want variety.

Whatever you decide on, you will certainly want to display your collection. Buttons should be mounted if they are to be seen to the best advantage. A good way to mount them is on cards. Posterboard is a good weight. Plain cardboard that is faced with colored paper is often used.

The National Button Society has a junior division for boys and girls ages 8 to 18. It publishes the *News-Sheet* and provides adult leadership. For information write to NBS, 2733 Juno Place, Akron, Ohio 44313.

Reviewed by THEODORE ABRAMS
Associated Button Company, Inc.

From left are a shiny glass button with enamel from the late 1800's, a hand-painted Japanese button from about 1900, and a French button showing a hare and a hunting horn, 1850–75.

BYARS, BETSY. See CHILDREN'S LITERATURE (Profiles).

BYRD, RICHARD EVELYN (1888–1957)

Rear Admiral Richard E. Byrd was a daring aviator and America's greatest Antarctic explorer. He was the first man to fly over the South Pole. His five expeditions to Antarctica helped to unlock the mysteries of that vast, frozen continent. He also claimed to have been the first to fly over the North Pole, but recent evidence suggests that he probably fell short of reaching that goal.

Byrd was born on October 25, 1888, in Winchester, Virginia. In 1912 he graduated from the United States Naval Academy. A leg injury forced him to retire from active sea duty in 1916, but he was soon back in the Navy as an aviator.

On May 9, 1926, Byrd and his copilot, Floyd Bennett, took off from Spitzbergen in the Arctic Ocean. According to them, they circled the North Pole and returned almost 16 hours later. For their achievement Byrd and Bennett each won the Congressional Medal of Honor. In 1927, Byrd attempted a nonstop flight from New York to Paris, carrying the first transatlantic airmail. But bad weather forced him to crash land on the coast of France.

In 1928, Byrd led his first expedition to Antarctica. He established his base, Little America, on the Ross Ice Shelf. The camp of more than a dozen huts was equipped with electricity and telephones. Airplanes were used to explore large areas of the continent. On November 28–29, 1929, Byrd and three crewmen, including his pilot Bernt Balchen, made the first flight over the South Pole.

During Byrd's second expedition, from 1933 to 1935, great emphasis was placed on scientific research. While gathering weather information, Byrd lived alone for five months. His tiny cabin was built under the snow, 123 miles (198 kilometers) from Little America. Carbon monoxide fumes from a leaky stove almost poisoned him before he was rescued. He wrote about this experience in his book *Alone* (1938).

Byrd headed a third expedition, which began in 1939. In 1946–47 he was officer-in-charge of the largest Antarctic expedition in history—a U.S. Navy project called Operation High Jump. The purpose was to continue the work of exploring and mapping the South Polar region.

On his last journey, in 1955–56, Byrd helped supervise another project, Operation Deep Freeze, in preparation for the International Geophysical Year, 1957–58. He died in Boston on March 11, 1957.

Reviewed by D. M. COONEY
Rear Admiral, U.S. Navy

See also ANTARCTICA; ARCTIC.

BYRON, GEORGE GORDON, LORD (1788–1824)

George Gordon Byron, English poet, was born in London on January 22, 1788. His mother was Scottish. His father, an aristocrat and a gambler, died in 1791. Byron became the sixth Baron Byron in 1798, when his great-uncle died. He was born with a lame foot, and he tried all his life to disguise it by acts of physical daring.

Byron attended Harrow, a famous boys' school, and in 1805 he entered Trinity College, Cambridge. He had a volume of his poems printed privately in 1806. A year later, his first published work, *Hours of Idleness,* appeared. When it was harshly criticized in the *Edinburgh Review,* he wrote a satire, *English Bards and Scotch Reviewers* (1809), in reply.

In the summer of 1809, Byron and a Cam-bridge friend, John Cam Hobhouse, began two years of travel in Europe and the Middle East. The first two cantos of *Childe Harold's Pilgrimage* record some of his first year's experiences. The poem, published in 1812, made Byron famous, and he was sought after by London society. But scandalous love affairs damaged his reputation. He married Anne Isabella Milbanke in 1815. She left him a year later, shortly after the birth of a daughter. Byron was cast out by society, and in April, 1816, he left England forever.

In Geneva, Switzerland, he joined the poet Percy Bysshe Shelley. Byron finished the third canto of *Childe Harold,* wrote *The Prisoner of Chillon,* and began the poetic drama *Manfred.* In October, 1816, he and Hobhouse moved to Venice, Italy. The fourth canto of *Childe Harold* concerns a visit to Rome in the spring of 1817. *Beppo*, published anonymously in February, 1818, satirizes life in Venice. Byron's greatest work, *Don Juan*, was begun in September, 1818. It continues the satiric style of *Beppo*.

In 1819 he met Countess Teresa Guiccioli, whose love gave him a new steadiness. In their years together he completed *Don Juan* and wrote the satire *The Vision of Judgement*, seven poetic dramas, and many shorter poems.

In 1823 he was elected to a committee helping Greece gain freedom from Turkey. He went to Greece and was warmly welcomed by the Greek leaders. He was eager to lead an attack. But he died, instead, of a fever in the city of Missolonghi on April 19, 1824.

GEORGIA DUNBAR
Hofstra University

CHILDE HAROLD'S PILGRIMAGE
(excerpt from Canto III, describing the eve of the Battle of Waterloo)

There was a sound of revelry by night,
And Belgium's capital had gathered then
Her Beauty and her Chivalry, and bright
The lamps shone o'er fair women and brave men;
A thousand hearts beat happily; and when
Music arose with its voluptuous swell,
Soft eyes looked love to eyes which spake again,
And all went merry as a marriage bell;
But hush! hark! a deep sound strikes like a rising knell!

Did ye not hear it?—No; 'twas but the wind,
Or the car rattling o'er the stony street;
On with the dance! let joy be unconfined;
No sleep till morn, when Youth and Pleasure meet
To chase the glowing Hours with flying feet—

But hark!—that heavy sound breaks in once more,
As if the clouds its echo would repeat;
And nearer, clearer, deadlier than before!
Arm! Arm! it is—it is—the cannon's opening roar!

Within a windowed niche of that high hall
Sat Brunswick's fated chieftain; he did hear
That sound the first amidst the festival,
And caught its tone with Death's prophetic ear;
And when they smiled because he deemed it near,
His heart more truly knew that peal too well
Which stretched his father on a bloody bier,
And roused the vengeance blood alone could quell;
He rushed into the field, and, foremost fighting, fell.

THE PRISONER OF CHILLON
(excerpt; the story of a man imprisoned for trying to free Geneva from a tyrant)

There are seven pillars of Gothic mold,
In Chillon's dungeons deep and old,
There are seven columns, massy and gray,
Dim with a dull imprisoned ray,
A sunbeam which hath lost its way,
And through the crevice and the cleft
Of the thick wall is fallen and left;
Creeping o'er the floor so damp,
Like a marsh's meteor lamp:
And in each pillar there is a ring,
And in each ring there is a chain;
That iron is a cankering thing,
For in these limbs its teeth remain,
With marks that will not wear away,
Till I have done with this new day,
Which now is painful to these eyes,
Which have not seen the sun so rise
For years—I cannot count them o'er,
I lost their long and heavy score,
When my last brother drooped and died,
And I lay living by his side.

They chained us each to a column stone,
And we were three—yet, each alone;
We could not move a single pace,
We could not see each other's face,
But with that pale and livid light
That made us strangers in our sight:
And thus together—yet apart,
Fettered in hand, but joined in heart,
'Twas still some solace, in the dearth
Of the pure elements of earth,
To hearken to each other's speech,
And each turn comforter to each
With some new hope, or legend old,
Or song heroically bold;
But even these at length grew cold.
Our voices took a dreary tone,
An echo of the dungeon stone,
    A grating sound, not full and free,
    As they of yore were wont to be:
    It might be fancy, but to me
They never sounded like our own.

486

BYZANTINE ART
AND ARCHITECTURE

Byzantine art is the art of the Eastern Roman Empire. Constantine, the first Christian emperor of the Roman Empire, moved his capital from Rome to the old Greek city of Byzantium. He renamed the city Constantinople after himself. But the art of the Eastern Roman Empire that he founded is known as Byzantine.

Byzantine art extends from the founding of Constantinople in A.D. 330 until the Turks captured the city in 1453. However, long after the fall of Constantinople, artists in the Greek islands, in the Balkans, and in Russia continued to create works in the Byzantine style.

In the days of its glory, Constantinople was the most magnificent city in the world. Above the gates and towers of the city walls rose the golden domes of the churches and the tall, shining columns set up by the emperors. Some of the most famous statues of ancient Greece had been brought to the city. The huge palace of the emperor blazed with gold and silver, marble and mosaics. There the emperor, covered with jewels, was surrounded by priests in shining robes and by men-at-arms of every barbarian race.

The Byzantine Empire was a religious state. The emperor was not only the ruler of his people but God's representative on earth. The ceremonies of the church and of the court were meant to show the emperor's sacred character. His magnificent jewels, robes, and crown were intended to give him a majestic and saintly appearance.

The purpose of Byzantine art was to glorify the Christian religion and to express its mystery. All of Byzantine art is filled with a kind of spiritual symbolism—things on earth are meant to stand for the order of heaven. Another characteristic of the art of this rich empire is a love of splendor.

Byzantine art is a combination of Eastern and classical Western art. The Byzantine Empire inherited the ideas and forms of art of the classical world of Greece and Rome. However, part of the empire was in Asia and Africa. The shores of Asia could be seen from Constantinople. It was natural that the art of this empire should be greatly influenced by the art of the Near East.

The art of Greece and Rome was naturalistic—artists wanted to show the world about them as it actually looked. Their greatest interest was in the human body. To create an ideal beauty, they showed the body as it would look if it were perfect.

The art of the ancient Near East was more an art of decoration. Artists filled large, flat areas with patterns that were repeated again and again. Instead of copying nature, they made natural forms into flat patterns. They did not have the great interest in the human body that classical artists had, and they did not hesitate to change the shape of the body to fit into their designs. Another characteristic of Eastern art was a use of glowing color.

▶ THE LATE ANTIQUE PERIOD: THE BEGINNING OF THE BYZANTINE STYLE (330–527)

For the first 200 years of the Byzantine Empire, artists worked in the same style as the artists of ancient Greece and Rome. Because the art was still based on that of the old classical world, these years are called the Late Antique period. During these years the new Byzantine style gradually grew out of the decaying art of the classical world.

In this period the Roman Empire lost its lands to the barbarian invaders from the north. Much of the art of this time of violence and disorder shows a loss of skill and craftsmanship. Artists were no longer able to make the human body look like that of a living person. They could no longer achieve the realism or ideal beauty that Greek and Roman artists had. Instead, for representing heads and bodies, they used certain rules that made human figures look unreal—stiff and wooden. This unreality was made-to-order for expressing the spiritual ideals of Christianity.

▶ THE FIRST GOLDEN AGE (527–726)

The earliest true Byzantine style appeared in the First Golden Age. By the 6th century Byzantine artists had broken away from the classical styles. They had created a new style to show the supernatural nature of Christ and the sacredness and grandeur of the emperor.

Justinian

The most important ruler of the First Golden Age was the Emperor Justinian. He is remembered for his code of laws and his

Above: *Theodora and her Court*, a 6th-century mosaic in the church of San Vitale, Ravenna. Below: A mosaic of the Emperor Justinian in the same church.

great building projects in Constantinople and Italy. After recapturing much of Italy from the Goths, Justinian chose the city of Ravenna as the center of Byzantine rule in Italy.

There is a famous mosaic picture of the great emperor in the church of San Vitale at Ravenna. He is shown surrounded by his attendants. His stiff pose and rich robes make him a symbol of majesty. On the opposite wall is a picture of his wife, the Empress Theodora, with her ladies-in-waiting. At the end of the church, in the half dome behind the altar, Christ is shown among the angels. Christ, the All-Ruler, is surrounded by the members of his court in heaven just as Justinian and Theodora are surrounded by a court on earth.

These pictures are done in mosaic. A mosaic picture or design is made of thousands of small glass or marble cubes, called **tesserae**, set in cement. The walls and domes of the great churches of Ravenna and Constantinople were decorated with glass tesserae, brilliantly colored or covered with gold.

A picture made out of many pieces of glass cannot be as freely done or copy nature as exactly as a painting. In the pictures of Justinian and Theodora in San Vitale, the figures are stiff. The bodies are flat, and the magnificent robes do not seem to cover any solid shapes. The feet point downward on the flat ground, giving the illusion that the bodies are floating in air. However, the stiff poses of the rulers, and their long, flat shapes, are not simply the result of the use of mosaic. These are characteristics of the new Byzantine style. The heads of the figures show us that the artist was capable of a much more realistic portrayal. The faces are almost like portraits in the old Roman tradition. However, Byzantine artists were not interested in realism, in showing solid forms in real space. Instead, they developed a formal style, a style in which the body is just another part of a flat design.

Hagia Sophia, the Church of Holy Wisdom

The greatest building of the whole Byzantine world is the church of Hagia Sophia, in Constantinople. Hagia Sophia, known as the Church of Holy Wisdom, was built on the site of an ancient temple to Pallas Athene, the Greek goddess of wisdom. It was dedicated to the Virgin Mary.

The church was designed by the architects Anthemius of Tralles and Isidorus of Miletus. Construction was begun in A.D. 532, and it is believed that the Emperor Justinian himself personally supervised the work. A legend tells that he followed the orders of an angel.

Hagia Sophia is so large that the human eye cannot take in the whole huge shape of the interior. If you stand inside the great church, you must look at it one part at a time. Your eyes are led from the pillars to the vaults, then to the smaller domes, finally to the central dome 180 feet (55 meters) high. This may be what the architects wanted. The eyes of the worshiper finally come to rest on the great mosaic figure of Christ in the dome, looking down as though from heaven itself. The feeling of endless space in Hagia Sophia makes it one of the most impressive buildings in the world. The many marble columns are enormous, but in the huge interior they seem small. At the same time the mounting of domes of increasing sizes up to the great central dome gives a feeling of order.

The splendor of Hagia Sophia also comes from color. The columns, brought from every corner of the empire, are of stone and marble of many different colors—blue, green, and blood-red. Even more brilliant in color is the mosaic decoration. The floor is covered with marble mosaic and the walls glitter with glass mosaics. The mosaics have designs of vines and pomegranates—the fruit of the pomegran-

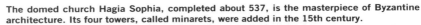

The domed church Hagia Sophia, completed about 537, is the masterpiece of Byzantine architecture. Its four towers, called minarets, were added in the 15th century.

ate was a symbol of life after death—and imaginary beasts. Below the central dome are mosaic pictures of star-eyed angels. On the golden background of the vast, topmost dome is the figure of Christ as judge and ruler of all.

The Dome on Pendentives

Byzantine architects did not invent the plans or building methods that they used; they adapted them from the architecture of the Near East and Rome. However, the architects of Hagia Sophia did solve the problem of placing a round dome on the square plan of the walls that support it. They did this by building up masonry from the corners of the walls in the shape of a triangle. This contruction is called a pendentive. Pendentives not only support the

The throne of Bishop Maximian, Ravenna, is a fine example of Byzantine relief carving. It is made of wood and covered with elaborately carved ivory panels.

dome but join the dome to the walls in one continuous sweep.

The pendentives of Hagia Sophia rest on four massive piers. The stone blocks of these piers are set in lead rather than in mortar. The dome is also made stronger by half domes that carry its outward-pushing weight to huge buttresses, or supports, on the outside. To make it lighter the dome was built out of a special kind of light brick.

Some scholars believe that Byzantine architects learned how to build domes from earlier Roman buildings. Others think that they learned from Near Eastern architecture. However, the meaning of the dome in religious architecture came from Persia. In the ancient Near East, people thought that heaven was like a cup placed upside down over the earth. In Persia from the 3rd to 7th century A.D., architects used the shape of the dome to suggest the architecture of heaven. Since Byzantine architects also used this idea, it seems likely that both the knowledge of how to build a dome and the meaning of this shape came to Byzantium from her eastern neighbors.

Ivory Carving: A Bishop's Throne

The Byzantine Church did not approve of sculpture in the round—sculpture that can be seen from all sides. The Church feared that it would recall the idols of the Greek and Roman religions. However, small carvings in relief (raised from a flat surface), especially in ivory, were allowed as church decoration. One of the most beautiful examples of ivory carving of the First Golden Age is the throne of the Bishop Maximian at Ravenna. He is the priest to the right of Justinian in the mosaic at San Vitale.

The wooden chair is covered with many ivory panels of different sizes. In the center of the long rectangular panel on the front of the throne is the monogram of Christ. On either side are carved peacocks, symbols of paradise or everlasting life, and grapevines, symbols of the wine of Communion. Byzantine designs of birds and animals placed among the curling branches of vines are like the complicated patterns in Oriental rugs. Byzantine artists probably adapted these designs from textiles or carvings made in the Near East.

Four ivory carvings on the front of the throne show Saint John the Baptist and the four Gospel writers. The thinness of the saints and their haggard appearance is typical of Byzantine art. In the early centuries of Christianity, many holy men fasted and tormented themselves. One famous hermit, Saint Simeon Stylites, even spent many years sitting on top of a column. The bodies of such holy men were very different from the healthy bodies of the Greek athletes. Extreme thinness came to be a sign of holiness, and this is one reason that the artist has carved such tall figures. By making the bodies of the saints very tall and fragile, they appear to be more spirit than flesh. The flat pattern of the saints' robes also makes their bodies look weightless, as if the cloth did not fall over any solid shapes.

The entire chair is carved with great precision and delicacy. The patterns of vines, birds, and beasts are wonderful examples of the Byzantine craftsman's creativeness in making a rich and exciting pattern.

▶ THE PERIOD OF ICONOCLASM (726–843)

In the 8th century the mosaics of the churches of Byzantium were covered with whitewash, and the sculpture was destroyed. This was done by the iconoclasts (image-breakers), who did not approve of representations of the saints or the Holy Family. They believed that many people really worshiped the picture or statue instead of the holy figure it represented. During the period when the iconoclasts were in power, no pictures of the Deity were allowed. The iconoclast movement not only interrupted the development of Byzantine art but caused the destruction of nearly all the great treasures of the First Golden Age.

▶ THE SECOND GOLDEN AGE (843–1204)

When the iconoclasts lost power, a new golden age began. Constantinople was still a city of great treasures, shimmering with gold. It was the richest city in the world. The art of this period shows an Eastern fondness for things that are richly ornamented and perfectly made. Everything is on a smaller scale. Artists made small, beautiful things that are delicate rather than impressive. Compared with the grand monuments of the time of Justinian, the churches of this period are tiny. Religious art was made to appeal to the worshiper in much more human terms. Instead of the solemn grandeur that made Christ unapproachable, there was a new emphasis on his sufferings as a man.

The Little Metropole, in Athens, was built during the Second Golden Age. Its small size and square, balanced plan are typical of the churches of this period.

Architecture

The churches of the Second Golden Age are like little jewel boxes in stone. They are most impressive from the outside, where the harmony and logic of the construction can be seen. The plan is square. Within the square is a cross with arms of equal length. A typical example is the Little Metropole in Athens. Three stories high, the church has a blocklike ground floor. The arms of the cross plan project into the second story. On the third level a small dome is placed over the center of the cross. Domes are also built between the arms of the cross plan on the second level, but these cannot be seen from the outside.

Another feature of the buildings of the Second Golden Age is the texture of the walls. In some places the surface is rough, in others smooth. This kind of surface causes an ever-changing activity of light and shade. The walls of the church at Athens are decorated with fragments of ancient Greek carving as well as reliefs of that time.

Saint Mark's. The famous church of Saint Mark's in Venice has nearly the same plan as the Little Metropolitan but is many times larger. Begun in 1063, it was probably copied from a church in Constantinople. The domes, like those in Hagia Sophia, have a ring of windows at their bases to let in light. The sunlight shining on the gold mosaics makes the domes look like golden shells hung in the air. The glow of gold mosaics and the sheen of colored marble make the visitor feel that he is really in a heaven brought to earth. On the outside the round domes are covered by domes of fantastic shape that make Saint Mark's look like an Eastern fairy palace. Marbles and mosaics of many different periods decorate the outside of the church.

The Mosaics at Daphni

The style of the mosaics of the Second Golden Age is like an echo of the great age of Greek art. In Greece, not far from Athens, is the church of Daphni. Inside the church are some of the finest mosaics in the whole history of Byzantine art.

In the dome there is a large picture of Christ. Only his head and shoulders are shown. His hand is raised in blessing, but his bearded face is solemn, even frightening. The large size of this picture, the beard, and the fearful solemnness of the face are like an ancient representation of the Greek god Zeus. The artist wanted to show Christ as the tremendous power that rules over the fate of man. It was natural that he should have turned to the noble beauty of Greek art for inspiration. He may even have been influenced by the bearded head of a statue of a Greek god.

On the pendentives are four scenes from the life of Christ. In the Crucifixion scene there are only three figures: Christ is on the cross, and Mary and Saint John are at the foot of the cross, one on each side. The figures are arranged in the shape of a triangle against the empty golden background. Each figure is separate and yet unified with the other figures.

Begun in the 11th century, Saint Mark's cathedral in Venice took centuries to build. The last details of this colorful church were added in the 1400's.

An 11th-century Italian cross made of enamels and gold.

A 14th-century mosaic in a Constantinople church shows the Holy Family paying taxes.

The balanced arrangement is like that used by Greek sculptors in placing their figures in the pediments of temples. Also, the position of Saint John—bending, with his weight on one leg—is a pose often used by Greek sculptors. The body of Christ is almost like that of a classic athlete. However, unlike Greek sculpture, the anatomy is not true to life. The Byzantine artist changed the body into a pattern of flat shapes. In doing this he tried to show Christ as perfect, unlike any ordinary human being.

The faces of Saint John and the Madonna have the flatness and heavy lines of the Byzantine style, but they express the calm of Greek statues. The emptiness of the background and the nobility of the figures show that this is an event that is not part of the everyday world. The artist has not tried to make a picture of the actual happening or to show what the real scene was actually like. Instead he has made a symbol of the Crucifixion.

Our Lady of Vladimir

Few examples of paintings on wooden panels have survived from the Second Golden Age. One of them is the famous Madonna of Vladimir, one of the first paintings to depict the Madonna and Child as mother and son, showing affection for each other. The picture reveals a new interest in human feeling. The softness of the features and the expression of sadness in the eyes are like the technique and feeling of late Greek painting.

Our Lady of Vladimir was taken to Russia in the 11th or 12th century and became the model there for many later representations of the Madonna. This new, more human idea of divinity also influenced the religious painting of Italy in the 14th century.

Byzantine artists were not supposed to invent new compositions but to repeat as closely as possible the shapes of famous images. The Church wanted the representations of religious figures always to look the same. Artists followed rules written in manuals. In a beautiful ivory carving of the Madonna and Child, we can see that the artist has followed certain of these rules. The Madonna is carved in one of the standard poses—standing, she holds the Christ Child on her left arm. The carver has also used the Byzantine system of proportion for the body. The Madonna's body is extremely long and drawn out—9 or 10 times as long as the head. In ancient Greece artists usually made the bodies of athletes or gods seven times as long as the head.

The ivory carving has features that are typical of the Second Golden Age. The carved Madonna has the same sad, wistful look as the Madonna of Vladimir. Her oval head is delicate, with large, almond-shaped eyes and a tiny mouth. The strange, ghostly face under a heavy hood makes us feel that we are looking at a being from another world.

A delicately carved ivory panel of a Byzantine empress holding her scepter and orb.

A particularly beautiful feature of this ivory is the flattened pattern of the drapery arranged in a fanlike design.

The End of the Second Golden Age

The Second Golden Age came to an end with the capture of Constantinople by the Venetian crusaders in 1204. Like earlier crusades, it had been organized to fight the Turks in the Holy Land. Instead the crusaders attacked the most powerful city in the Christian world. When Constantinople fell into their hands, the invaders plundered the churches and palaces and burned the libraries. Many ancient works that had lasted from Greek and Roman times were lost in the flames. When the Venetians were finally driven out,

the last period of Byzantine civilization, the Third Golden Age, began.

▶THE THIRD GOLDEN AGE (1261–1453)

The architecture typical of the Third Golden Age can be seen in many churches in the Balkans. These buildings differ from earlier churches like the Little Metropolitan because they give the impression of being tall, soaring buildings. Tiny domes are set on tall bases that sprout from the first story. The upward feeling is increased by the number of **pilasters** on the outside of the church. Pilasters are column-like strips built into the side of a wall. These churches do not look massive and solid like the churches of the Second Golden Age.

The Paintings of Kharieh Djami

In the paintings of this period, we seem to be looking at real dramatic happenings. The painters of the wall paintings of the church of Kharieh Djami in Constantinople were interested in storytelling. The figures in the Christian stories are placed in actual settings instead of on an empty golden background. Many of the old rules survive, but there is a new life and movement and a real beauty of color. Byzantine painters finally became interested in experimenting with realism, and in this respect they are the equals of their famous contemporaries in 14th-century Italy.

The End of Byzantium

Hagia Sophia was the spiritual center of the Byzantine Empire for 900 years. There the sacred emperors were crowned; there the priests celebrated the mass until that last dark night in Byzantine history, May 29, 1453. On that night the crowds prayed for the last time in the shadow of the great dome as the armies of the Turkish sultan attacked the city. Gathered inside the church, waiting for a miracle, they must have heard the crumbling of the city's walls. They must have heard the rattle of bridle chains in the streets, the clamor of the Turkish soldiers, the sound of axes hewing down the great doors as the sultan came to still forever the heart of the Byzantine world.

BENJAMIN ROWLAND, JR.
Harvard University

See also ARCHITECTURE; DECORATIVE ARTS; PAINTING; SCULPTURE.

BYZANTINE EMPIRE

A thousand years ago Constantinople was probably the largest and richest city on earth. It was the capital of the great Byzantine Empire. About a million people lived in Constantinople, and visitors marveled at its huge palaces, beautiful churches, and many shops. One visitor wrote that if he described a hundredth part of its wealth, it would seem like a lie and no one would believe it.

In A.D. 330 Constantine, the Roman emperor, had moved the seat of government from Rome to the old Greek city of Byzantium. Constantine named his capital New Rome, but most people called it Constantinople (Constantine's city), or still used the old name, Byzantium.

After Constantine died, the emperors who succeeded him found it difficult to rule the vast Roman Empire. In 395 the empire was officially divided; the lands in the east were ruled from Constantinople and those in the west from Rome. In the 100 years that followed the division, Rome lost most of the lands of the Western Empire (Italy, Spain, France, Britain, northwest Africa). In the east, however, the emperors still ruled. This part of the Roman Empire, ruled by emperors living in Byzantium, is known as the Byzantine Empire. But the rulers of the Byzantine Empire still called themselves Romans, and, for a time, the Byzantine Empire was still called the Eastern Roman Empire. The language of the Eastern Empire was Greek, rather than Latin, the Roman language.

▶ **DEFENDING THE EMPIRE**

The Byzantine Empire lasted for hundreds of years. It had a long life, but not an easy one. Its neighbors tried for centuries to overrun it. The Persians threatened the empire at one time. They had scarcely been defeated in 628 before the Arabs began a conquest of the East. The Byzantines at different times had to stand off attacks by a number of peoples from Asia, such as the Avars, Bulgars, and Turks. Because of the invasions the size of the empire varied from time to time. Generally the Byzantine emperors ruled most of the Balkan Peninsula and Asia Minor.

▶ **THE ARMY**

The Byzantine Empire lasted as long as it did because of its military strength. The armies were usually well organized and equipped. They had medical and ambulance services, signalmen who flashed messages with mirrors, and even marching bands to keep up their spirits. The navy possessed a secret weapon, "Greek fire." This was an inflammable mixture that was thrown on enemy ships in hand grenades or sprayed, flaming, from tubes in the prows of Byzan-

Justinian and His Court, a mosaic in the church of San Vitale, Ravenna, Italy. Justinian, who ruled from A.D. 527 to 565, was one of the great Byzantine emperors.

tine ships. Greek fire was a fearful weapon in the days of wooden ships. It was no wonder that the Byzantines kept the directions for its manufacture a carefully guarded secret.

▶ THE WONDERS OF THE CAPITAL CITY

The Byzantines encouraged foreign rulers and ambassadors to visit their capital. They went to great lengths to impress the visitors with the wealth and power of the emperors. When an ambassador was presented to the emperor, he was ushered into a large, richly decorated hall. Before the throne stood a gilded bronze tree. On its branches were little mechanical golden birds that whistled beautiful songs. On either side of the throne stood lifelike bronze lions that roared and beat their tails. As the awe-struck foreigner bowed to the floor the throne on which the emperor sat rose slowly toward the ceiling. Ambassadors who had never seen such marvelous devices were always impressed by the clever Byzantines. Foreign visitors also gazed in wonder at the gold- and marble-covered walls of the palaces and churches. In particular they noticed the great church of Hagia Sophia, which still stands today. Although Constantinople had many poor people, visitors gave them little attention. They were more impressed with the large number of rich people, who rode fine horses and wore silk garments.

▶ THE TRADE OF THE EMPIRE

Most people within the empire worked on the land, but the wealth of the capital came largely from trade. The city stood at a crossroads. All ships carrying goods between the Mediterranean Sea and the Black Sea had to pass Constantinople. The main road from Europe to the Middle East also passed through the city. The emperors taxed all goods carried in or out of their crossroads capital.

Goods from far-off places filled the markets of Constantinople. There were furs from Russia, spices from Ceylon, rugs from Asia, leather from Morocco, and ivory from East Africa. Skilled craftsmen made the fine cloth, jewelry, and other rich goods sold in the shops. The emperors owned the only workshops permitted to make silk cloth. The shops were grouped together according to their business. The perfume shops were all located near the palace so that their wares would sweeten the air.

▶ SCHOOLS AND BOOKS

Constantinople had schools as well as shops. Since Greek was the language of the Byzantines, they studied the writings of such ancient Greeks as Plato and Aristotle. Many ancient books would have been lost had they not been kept and studied in the Byzantine schools, for scarcely anyone could read Greek in the West at this time. Byzantine authors also wrote new books, especially histories.

▶ THE BYZANTINE CHURCH

The Byzantine Empire was a Christian empire. Its missionaries spread Christianity among the Slavic peoples of eastern Europe, including the Russians. Byzantine Christians disagreed with those of the West about a number of matters. The pope at Rome condemned the Eastern emperor's great powers over the church. Eastern Christians, however, did not recognize the pope's authority. Disagreements between the Eastern and Western churches grew so great that they divided in 1054. Churches that grew from the church of the Byzantines are known as the Orthodox churches—for example, the Greek Orthodox Church and the Russian Orthodox Church.

▶ THE END OF THE EMPIRE

The struggle to rule was often a bitter one. Sometimes an emperor's son inherited his father's place, but often the throne was seized by a strong man. Some men would stop at nothing to be emperor—not even murder.

These struggles weakened the empire. It was during a struggle for the throne that an army of Crusaders from the West captured Constantinople in 1204. The rule of the Westerners lasted only until 1261, but the Byzantine emperors never became powerful again. A Muslim people, the Turks, conquered the Byzantine lands piece by piece until only Constantinople remained, a capital without an empire. Finally, in 1453, a Turkish army took the city. The last piece of the old Roman Empire had finally fallen.

KENNETH S. COOPER
George Peabody College

See also EASTERN ORTHODOX CHURCHES.

Index

picture(s)
flag **F:**227
San Salvador **B:**16
Bahasa Indonesia (language) **I:**206; **S:**329
Bahasa Melayu (Bahasa Malaysia) (language) **M:**54; **S:**329
Bahia (Brazil) *see* Salvador
Bahrain (emirate in the Persian Gulf) **B:**18–19; **P:**115
map(s) **B:**19
picture(s) **B:**18
flag **F:**227
Bahutu (Bantu people) *see* Hutu
Baikal, Lake (Russia) **L:**25, 28; **R:**362
picture(s) **L:**28; **R:**361
Baikal-Amur Mainline Railroad (Russia) **S:**170
Bail (in law) **C:**575; **L:**90
Bail (of a fishing reel) **F:**210
Bailey (of a castle) **C:**131
picture(s) **C:**132
Bailey, Ella Wilkins (American tennis player) **T:**94
Bailey, James A. (American showman) **C:**310
Baird, Bil and Cora (American puppeteers) **P:**548
Baird, John Logie (Scottish inventor) **T:**64–65
Baird's tapirs (hoofed mammals) **H:**217–18
picture(s) **H:**216
Bait (for fishing) **F:**210–11, 213
Bait-casting (fishing) **F:**209, 210, 211–12
Baja California (Mexico) **M:**245
off-road racing **A:**538
Bajans (name for the people of Barbados) **B:**60
Ba Jin (Chinese writer) **C:**279
Bakelite (plastic) **P:**328
Baker, Ellen (American astronaut)
picture(s) **S:**344
Baker, Josephine (American singer and dancer) **M:**378 *profile*
picture(s) **M:**379
Baker, Samuel White (British explorer) **U:**6
Baker Island *see* Howland, Baker, and Jarvis islands
Baker v. *Carr* (1962) **S:**509
Baking and bakery products **B:**385–B:388b; **C:**541 *see also*
Flour and flour milling
agricultural fairs **F:**14
experiments and other science activities **E:**397
flour, kinds of **F:**276–77
table(s)
metric conversions for the kitchen **W:**113
Baking powder **B:**386, 388b
Baking soda **B:**386
Bakke decision *see* Affirmative action
Bakken, Jill (American athlete) **O:**118
Bakken Amusement Park (Copenhagen, Denmark) **P:**78
Bakongo people (of Africa) *see* Kongo people
Bakony Mountains (Hungary) **H:**296
Bakota (a people of Gabon) **G:**2
Bakst, Léon (Russian artist)
picture(s)
costume for *The Firebird* **R:**385
Baku (capital of Azerbaijan) **A:**573
Bakunin, Mikhail (Russian anarchist) **A:**226
Balaguer, Joaquín (Dominican president) **D:**283
Balakirev, Mily Alekseevich (Russian composer) **R:**385
Balaklava, Battle of (1854) **C:**587
Balance (in design) **D:**133–34; **I:**258
Balance, sense of **E:**5–6
Balance beam (use in gymnastics) **G:**432
picture(s) **G:**432
Balance of nature (Homeostasis) **E:**54, 300
ants **A:**324
fungi **F:**500
organisms maintain their internal environment **B:**196
Balance of payments (of trade) **I:**271
Balance of power (among nations) **D:**182; **I:**269
Balance of trade **I:**271
Balance scales (for weighing) **F:**365; **W:**114
Balance sheet (in bookkeeping) **B:**312
Balance wheel (in watches and clocks) **C:**370, 372; **W:**45

Balanchine, George (Russian-American ballet choreographer)
B:30, 33; **D:**26
picture(s)
Allegro Brillante (ballet) **B:**33
Jewels (ballet) **B:**32
Balante (a people of Africa) **G:**407
Balata (gum) **R:**185
Balaton, Lake (Hungary) **H:**296; **L:**28
picture(s) **H:**296
Balbás, Jerónimo (Mexican sculptor) **L:**62
Balboa (Panama) **P:**49
Balboa, Vasco Núñez de (Spanish explorer) **B:**20; **E:**410; **P:**5, 50
picture(s)
Panama City statue **P:**47
Balboa Park (San Diego, California) **S:**29
Balcones Escarpment (Texas) **T:**126
Balcony (second floor of a theater) **T:**157
Balcony, The (painting by Manet)
picture(s) **I:**104
Baldassare Castiglione (painting by Raphael)
picture(s) **W:**264
Bald cypress (tree) *see also* Cypress
picture(s) **L:**315; **T:**302; **W:**145
Bald eagles **A:**276; **B:**229; **E:**2
Great Seal of the United States **G:**329
picture(s) **A:**276; **B:**209, 221, 234; **E:**2; **N:**290; **U:**90
Baldness (loss of hair) **H:**6
Baldr (Norse god) **N:**278, 281
Baldwin, James (American writer) **A:**219; **B:**21; **F:**116; **N:**363
picture(s) **B:**21
Baldwin, Matthias William (American industrialist and
philanthropist) **R:**88 *profile*
Baldwin, Robert (Canadian statesman) **C:**83; **O:**135
Baldwin I (Baldwin of Boulogne) (French crusader and king of
Jerusalem) **C:**600
Baldy Mountain (Manitoba) **M:**80
Balearic Islands (off the east coast of Spain) **I:**362; **S:**373
Baleen (whalebone) **W:**149, 151, 152, 154
picture(s) **W:**151
Baleen whales (Mysticetes) **W:**149, 151–53, 154
Balers (farm machines) **F:**58
picture(s) **F:**59
Balewa, Sir Abubakar Tafawa (prime minister of Nigeria)
N:258
Balfour, Arthur James (British statesman) **B:**21
Balfour Declaration (1917) **B:**21; **J:**107; **P:**41; **Z:**386
Bali (Indonesia) **I:**206, 209, 211
dancing is an ancient art **D:**32
Hinduism **H:**142
picture(s)
dance **D:**31; **I:**206
Bali cattle **O:**286
Balk (in baseball) **B:**83
Balkan Mountains **B:**22, 442, 443
Balkans **B:**22–23
Albania **A:**159–62
architecture: late Byzantine churches **B:**494
Bulgaria **B:**441–46
Crimean War **C:**587
Croatia **C:**588–89
Macedonia **M:**4
New Year customs **N:**209
Romania **R:**296–301
Serbia and Montenegro **S:**123–27
Slovenia **S:**203–4
World War I **W:**285
World War II **W:**299
Yugoslavia **Y:**364–69
Balkan Wars **B:**22–23, 445
Balkhash, Lake (Kazakhstan) **L:**29
Ball (used in sports and games) **B:**23
baseball **B:**78
basketball **B:**95a, 96

Ball (cont.)
  bowling ball   **B:**348–49
  field hockey   **F:**119
  golf   **G:**253
  handball   **H:**18
  Hohokam people played a game like basketball   **I:**169
  jai alai   **J:**12
  paddleball   **R:**35
  paddle tennis   **P:**11
  platform tennis   **R:**37
  racquetball   **R:**36
  soccer   **S:**220
  softball   **S:**233
  squash   **R:**34d
  volleyball   **V:**387
  picture(s)
    tennis ball   **T:**89
Ball, Lucille (American actress and TV producer)   **N:**224
    profile
  picture(s)   **T:**70
Balla, Giacomo (Italian futurist painter)   **M:**391
  picture(s)
    Dog on a Leash (painting)   **M:**390
Ballade (musical form)   **M:**538
Ballad operas   **M:**552
Ballads   **B:**24
  communication, history of   **C:**463
  country music   **C:**572
  folklore   **F:**308–9
  folk music   **F:**324
  narrative poems suitable for singing   **P:**353
  Scandinavian literature   **S:**58h
  Spanish romances   **S:**387
Ball-and-socket joints (in the skeleton)   **S:**184b
Ballard, Martha (American midwife and healer)   **M:**48 *profile*
Ballard, Robert (American underwater explorer)   **U:**20, 26
  picture(s)   **O:**40
Ballast (for railroad roadbeds)   **R:**79
Ballast (weights)   **F:**252, 253
Ballet   **B:**25–33; **D:**25–26, 34
  Canada   **C:**69
  New York City Ballet at Lincoln Center   **L:**248
  Stravinsky's ballet music   **R:**386; **S:**467
  Tallchief, Maria and Marjorie   **O:**95
  picture(s)
    Royal Winnipeg Ballet rehearsal   **C:**68
Ballet at the Paris Opera (drawing by Degas)
  picture(s)   **D:**308
Ballet Russe de Monte Carlo   **B:**32
Ballet skiing   **S:**184d
Ballets Russes (ballet company organized by Diaghilev)
    B:29–30; **D:**26; **F:**447–48
Ballett (musical form)   **E:**292
Ballinger, Richard A. (American politician)   **T:**5
Ballistic missiles   **M:**343, 344, 346, 347, 348–49
  United States Navy submarines   **U:**114
Ballistics (study of motion of projectiles)   **R:**258
Ball lightning   **T:**187; **U:**32
Balloon angioplasty (used to widen channel in blocked artery)
    H:83
Ballooning (of spiders)   **S:**406
Balloons and ballooning   **B:**34–38
  aerodynamics, principles of   **A:**41
  altitude control   **F:**252
  aviation history   **A:**560
  helium used to inflate   **H:**106; **N:**105
  Piccard, Auguste   **P:**244
  transportation, history of   **T:**287
  What makes a balloon rise?   **B:**36
  picture(s)   **C:**428; **F:**252
    weather balloon   **W:**91
Ballot   **B:**23; **E:**131
Ball-peen hammer (tool)   **T:**227
Ballpoint pens   **I:**229; **P:**142–43
Ballroom dancing (social dancing)   **D:**26–28

Ball's Bluff (Virginia, site of Civil War battle)   **C:**338
Ball valves
  diagram(s)   **V:**269
Balmoral Castle (Scotland)   **E:**192
Balsa (tree)
  Ecuador is major producer   **E:**68
  lightest wood in commercial use   **W:**227
  wood used for airplane models   **A:**107; **P:**298
Balsas (reed boats)   **P:**161
  picture(s)   **B:**306
Baltic languages   **E:**353
Baltic Sea   **E:**345; **O:**43
Baltic States
  Estonia   **E:**323–25
  Latvia   **L:**79–81
  Lithuania   **L:**261–63
  World War II   **W:**296
Baltimore (Maryland)   **B:**39; **M:**120, 123, 124, 127, 134
  aquarium   **A:**337
  Harborplace   **M:**128
  War of 1812   **W:**10–11
  picture(s)   **M:**121
    cargo ship in harbor   **M:**126
    Harborplace   **B:**39; **M:**129
    National Aquarium   **M:**125
Baltimore, Lord *see* Calvert, George
Baltimore and Ohio Railroad   **B:**39; **M:**134; **R:**87
  first electric locomotive   **L:**287
  first in United States   **T:**285
  Maryland section   **M:**120
Baltimore Clippers (sailing ships)   **M:**120
Baltimore orioles (birds)
  picture(s)   **B:**246; **M:**121
Baltimore *Sun* (newspaper)   **M:**127
Baltimore-Washington International Airport   **M:**127
Balto-Finnic languages   **E:**323
Balto-Slavic languages   **L:**39
Baluchis (a people of Asia)   **P:**35
  picture(s)   **P:**35
Balustrades (of escalators)   **E:**188
Balzac, Honoré de (French writer)   **B:**40; **F:**441; **N:**360; **R:**114
  picture(s)
    Rodin's *Monument to Balzac*   **M:**387
Bamako (capital of Mali)   **M:**62
Bamana (a people of Africa)
  picture(s)
    headdress   **A:**74
Bambara (a people of central West Africa)   **M:**61
Bambara (language)   **M:**61
Bambara, Toni Cade (American writer)   **A:**219
Bambi (animated cartoon)
  picture(s)   **D:**216
Bamboo (giant grass)   **G:**318–19
  books made from   **B:**320
  houses made from   **A:**76
  jungle growth   **J:**157
  pandas' main food   **P:**52
  picture(s)   **G:**318
Banaba (island in the Pacific Ocean)   **K:**265
Banabans (people of Ocean Island)   **K:**265
Banabhatta (Indian poet)   **I:**141
Banana   **A:**90–91; **B:**40–42; **F:**484
  abaca fiber comes from plant's stalk   **F:**109
  food transport, modern origins of   **F:**334
  Honduras is a leading producer   **H:**206, 207, 209
  plantain   **L:**53
  picture(s)   **E:**68; **F:**334; **H:**207, 209; **M:**303; **N:**300
Banaras (India) *see* Varanasi
Banat (region of Romania)   **R:**297
Bancroft, George (American historian)   **A:**210; **H:**152
Bancroft Library (Berkeley, California)   **C:**24
Banda, Hastings Kamuzu (president of Malawi)   **M:**53
Bandama River (Ivory Coast)   **I:**419
Bandanas (kerchiefs worn by cowboys)   **C:**577

sculpture   **S:**100–101
Spain   **S:**384
picture(s)
   Boulle cabinet   **F:**509
Baroque literature   **F:**437
Baroque music   **B:**69–72; **M:**539–40
German composers   **G:**184–85
opera, development of the aria in   **O:**140–41
sonatas   **C:**350
Barotseland (region, Zambia)   **Z:**377, 378
Barracudas (fish)   **F:**199
Barragán, Luís (Mexican architect)   **M:**244
Barrage balloons (to block enemy aircraft)   **B:**36
Barranquilla (Colombia)   **C:**406
Barre (railing used in ballet practice)
picture(s)   **B:**26
Barre (Vermont)   **V:**312
Barred owls   **O:**284
Barred Plymouth Rock (chicken)   **P:**416
Barred spiral galaxies   **U:**214
picture(s)   **U:**215
Barrel cacti   **C:**5
picture(s)   **P:**316
Barrel racing (rodeo event)   **R:**280
picture(s)   **H:**229
Barrels (of guns)   **G:**415, 421
Barrel vault (in architecture)   **A:**368
picture(s)   **A:**368
Barrett, Stan (American automobile racer)   **A:**538
Barrie, Sir James Matthew (Scottish writer)   **B:**73–74
English literature, place in   **E:**289
Peter Pan   **F:**12
Peter Pan, excerpt from   **B:**73–74
Barrientos Ortuño, René (president of Bolivia)   **B:**310
Barrier beaches   **L:**316; **T:**124
Barrier islands   **I:**360
Barrier reefs   **C:**556
Great Barrier Reef (Australia)   **A:**504
Barringer Crater *see* Meteor Crater
Barrios (Mexican American neighborhoods)   **H:**148
Barron, Robert (English inventor)   **L:**284
Barrow (Alaska)   **A:**144
Barrow, Clyde (American outlaw)   **O:**264 *profile*
picture(s)   **O:**264
Barry, Charles (English architect)   **E:**262
Barry, Rick (American basketball player)   **B:**95i *profile*
picture(s)   **B:**95i
Barrymore, Drew (American actress)   **B:**74
Barrymore, Ethel (American actress)   **B:**74
picture(s)   **B:**74
Barrymore, John (American actor)   **B:**74
picture(s)   **B:**74
Barrymore, Lionel (American actor)   **B:**74
picture(s)   **B:**74
Barrymore family (American actors)   **B:**74
Bars, steel   **I:**336
Barter (system of economics)   **M:**412; **T:**264
Egypt, ancient   **E:**107
Bartered Bride, The (opera by Smetana)   **O:**150–51
Barter Theatre (Abingdon, Virginia)   **V:**351
Barth, Heinrich (German explorer)   **E:**412
Barth, John (American novelist)   **A:**219
Barthelme, Donald (American author)   **A:**219
Bartholdi, Frédéric Auguste (French sculptor)   **L:**169
Bartholomew, Saint (one of the 12 Apostles)   **A:**329
Bartholomew Fair (England)   **F:**18
picture(s)   **F:**18
Bartlesville (Oklahoma)   **O:**82
Bartlett, Josiah (American physician and Revolutionary War patriot)   **N:**162 *profile*
Bartlett pear   **P:**113
Bartlett's Familiar Quotations   **R:**129
Bartók, Béla (Hungarian composer)   **B:**75; **C:**184; **H:**297; **M:**398

Barton, Clara (founder of American Red Cross)   **B:**75; **J:**124; **R:**127
Barton, Otis (American inventor and explorer)   **E:**415–16; **U:**27
picture(s)   **U:**27
Barton, William (co-designer of Great Seal of the United States)   **G:**329
Bartram, William (American naturalist)   **F:**274 *profile*
Barú (mountain, Panama)   **P:**45
Baruch (apocryphal book of the Bible)   **B:**164
Baruch Plan (1946, to control nuclear weapons)   **D:**181
Barye, Antoine Louis (French sculptor)   **S:**102
picture(s)
   statue of a boa and a stag   **S:**102
Baryshnikov, Mikhail Nikolayevich (Russian dancer)   **D:**34
picture(s)
   in *The Sleeping Beauty*   **B:**33
Basal ganglia (structures inside the cerebrum)   **B:**365, 367
Basalt (lava rock)   **R:**267
crust of Earth   **E:**10; **G:**112, 117
moon   **M:**453, 455
Oregon coast   **O:**202
volcanic action   **V:**382
picture(s)   **G:**118; **R:**266
Basant (Hindu fire festival) *see* Holi
Base (in algebra)   **A:**183
Baseball   **B:**76–94 *see also* Little League Baseball; Softball
Aaron, Henry Louis (Hank)   **A:**142
Canada   **C:**53
Dean, Jay Hanna (Dizzy)   **A:**418
Doby, Larry   **S:**310
Gehrig, Lou   **G:**67
Hispanic Americans   **H:**147–48
Japan   **J:**33
Little League Baseball   **L:**264–67
major league records   **B:**85
Maris, Roger   **N:**334
Mexico   **M:**243
modern game began in New York City   **N:**218
National Hall of Fame and Museum   **B:**88, 91, 92; **N:**214
professional game born in Ohio   **O:**68
Reese, Pee Wee   **K:**225
Robinson, Jackie   **R:**252
Russian game *lapta* is similar   **R:**360; **U:**36
Ruth, Babe   **R:**387
salary arbitration   **A:**349
softball   **S:**233
spring training in Florida   **F:**267
Tee Ball, Little League   **L:**266
World Series   **B:**86
picture(s)
   Cleveland Indians game   **O:**68
   game in Chicago's Grant Park   **P:**77
   major-league game   **U:**76
Baseball Writers' Association of America   **B:**88
Basedow, Johann (German educator)   **P:**223
Base-five system   **N:**407–8
Basel (Switzerland)   **S:**544
Baseline (of a radio telescope array)   **R:**68
Basenji (dog)
picture(s)   **D:**250
Base number (of a positional numeration system)   **N:**405, 407
Bases (building blocks of genes)   **E:**376; **G:**77–78
Bases (in chemistry)   **C:**204; **E:**390
Base-sixteen system *see* Hexadecimal number system
Base-sixty system   **N:**405
Base-ten system *see* Decimal system
Base-twelve system *see* Duodecimal system
Base-two system *see* Binary number system
Bashir, Omar Hassan Ahmad al- (Sudanese president)   **S:**480
Basic oxygen process (in steelmaking)   **I:**332–33
Basic research   **C:**197; **R:**181; **S:**67
Basidia (of fungi)   **F:**499

Basie, Count (American bandleader and jazz pianist)   J:61, 62
    picture(s)   **A:**79L; **J:**56
Basil (herb)   **H:**120
    picture(s)   **H:**120
Basil II (Byzantine emperor)   **B:**445
Basilar membrane (of the inner ear)   **E:**4
Basilica (building plan)
    church architecture   **I:**392
    France, architecture of   **F:**422
    Romanesque architecture   **A:**370
    Roman forum   **A:**369
    Spain, architecture of   **S:**382
Basilisk lizards
    picture(s)   **L:**277
Basin and Range Province (United States)   **A:**394; **N:**124, 182; **O:**204; **U:**81
    climate   **U:**88
    rivers draining area   **U:**84
Basins (of lakes)   **L:**24–27
Baskerville (typeface)
    picture(s)   **B:**327
Baskerville, John (English type designer)   **T:**369
Basketball (sport)   **B:95–99**
    Canada   **C:**53
    common terms   **B:**97
    Lithuania   **L:**262
    Olympic Games   **O:**108
    women's basketball   **B:**98, 99
    picture(s)   **G:**137; **I:**149; **M:**141; **N:**311
        Malone, Karl   **U:**248
        Orlando Magic game   **F:**266
        University of Connecticut women   **C:**513
        University of Tennessee women   **T:**79
        women's basketball   **B:**99
Baskets, hanging
    picture(s)   **G:**38
Basketweave bond (in masonry)
    picture(s)   **B:**391
Basketweave stitch (in needlepoint)   **N:**100
Basket weaving
    Africa, art of   **A:**75
    Indian art   **I:**186, 189
    picture(s)   **F:**305
        Hopi basket   **I:**183
Basking sharks   **S:**143
Bas Mitzvah *see* Bat Mitzvah
Basophils (white blood cells)   **B:**260, 261
Basotho (Basuto) (a people of Africa)   **L:**156, 157; **S:**272
Basque language   **L:**40; **S:**370
    possible origin of word "Arizona"   **A:**392
    Pyrenees section of Spain   **S:**370, 386
Basques (a people of Spain and France)   **S:**370
    Idaho, immigrants to   **I:**50–51
    jai alai   **J:**12
    picture(s)   **E:**353; **S:**369
        Nevada sheepherding   **N:**130
Basra (Iraq)   **I:**314
Bas-relief (in sculpture)   **A:**365, 376; **S:**90
    picture(s)
        Assyrian sculpture   **I:**315
Bass (fish)   **F:**213
    picture(s)   **F:**209, 213
        white bass fishing in Missouri   **M:**371
Bass (in music)   **C:**282
    voice training   **V:**377
Bass, George (English explorer and doctor)   **A:**515
Bass clef (F clef) (in musical notation)   **M:**534
Bass drum   **D:**338–39; **M:**551
Bassein (Myanmar)   **M:**560
Bassetaille (enameling technique)   **E:**205
Basseterre (capital of Saint Kitts and Nevis)   **S:**13
Basset hound (dog)   **D:**244
    picture(s)   **D:**246

Bassoon (musical instrument)   **M:**550; **O:**194; **W:**184
    orchestra seating plan   **O:**196
    picture(s)   **M:**549; **W:**184
Basswood (tree)
    picture(s)   **W:**223
Bastarache, Michel (Canadian Supreme Court justice)
    picture(s)   **S:**505
Bastet (Egyptian goddess of the east and of fire)   **E:**108
Bast fibers   **A:**74; **F:**109
Bastille, fall of the (1789)   **F:**415, 468; **P:**74
    picture(s)   **F:**467
Bastille Day (July 14)   **F:**406, 468; **H:**168; **J:**153
Bastille Opera House (Paris, France)
    picture(s)   **P:**75
Basting stitches (in sewing)
    picture(s)   **S:**130
Bastions (of forts)   **F:**379
Bastogne (Belgium)   **W:**314
Basutoland *see* Lesotho
Basuto *see* Basotho
Bat, baseball   **B:**78
Bat, The (operetta) *see* Fledermaus, Die
Bata (Equatorial Guinea)   **E:**309
Bataan (Philippines)   **W:**303, 305
Batavia (former name of Jakarta)   **J:**14
Batavian Republic (in Dutch history)   **N:**121
Batéké people (of Africa) *see* Téké people
Batéké Plateau (Congo)   **C:**505
Bates, Daisy Lee Gatson (American civil rights leader)   **C:**329
    profile
    picture(s)   **C:**329; **N:**25
Bates, Katherine Lee (American professor and author)   **N:**23
Bateson, Gregory (British anthropologist)   **P:**334
Bath (England)   **U:**54
Bath Iron Works (Maine)   **M:**43, 50
    picture(s)   **M:**42
Ba'th Party (in Syria)   **S:**552
Baths and bathing
    Ganges River (India) religious bathing   **G:**25
    Indian ritual   **I:**121
    Japan   **J:**29
    knights of the bath   **K:**277
    picture(s)
        Ganges River   **G:**25
Bathsheba (Biblical character)   **B:**159
Bathurst (The Gambia) *see* Banjul
Bathurst Island (Northwest Territories, Canada)   **G:**437
Bathyl zone (of the ocean)   **O:**23
Bathyscaphe (underwater ship)   **E:**416; **P:**244; **U:**27
Bathysphere (used in underwater research)   **E:**416; **U:**27
    picture(s)   **U:**27
Batik (method of printing textiles)   **D:**72; **I:**207; **M:**58; **T:**143
    picture(s)   **D:**374; **I:**207
Bating (preparation of leather)   **L:**110
Batista y Zaldívar, Fulgencio (Cuban dictator)   **C:**133, 610
Batlle Ibáñez, Jorge (Uruguayan president)   **U:**241
Batlle y Ordóñez, José (Uruguayan statesman and journalist)   **U:**241
Bat Mitzvah (ceremony in Judaism)   **J:**146b
Batoche National Historic Site (Saskatchewan)   **S:**47
Baton Rouge (capital of Louisiana)   **L:**319, 320, 321, 323, 328
    picture(s)   **L:**324
        Louisiana State University   **L:**319
Batoro (a people of Africa)   **U:**4
Bats   **B:100–103**
    cave dwellers   **C:**157
    diet   **M:**73
    echo   **E:**49
    flying mammals   **M:**72
    guano   **C:**158
    hand pattern changed for flying   **F:**84
    hibernation   **H:**126, 127
    Kitti's hog-nosed bat   **M:**66

nectar-feeding bat **A:**282
plant pollination **F:**285
sensory system **B:**366; **S:**265
diagram(s)
wings **F:**84
picture(s) **A:**269; **M:**68
cave dwellers **C:**158
embryo development **E:**374
Battalion (army troop unit) **U:**104
Battambang (Cambodia) **C:**37
Battered children (victims of physical abuse) **C:**222
Batteries (devices that produce electricity) **B:**103a–103c;
E:142–44
automobiles **A:**541, 547–48
bacterial fermentation produces electricity **F:**92
clocks, battery-operated **C:**370, 372
Davy's experiments **E:**138
diodes **T:**275
electric motors **E:**154
electronic watches **W:**45, 46
inventions **I:**282
ionization, principle of **I:**289
lead used in storage batteries **L:**93
oxidation and reduction **O:**287
plastics, uses of **P:**329
solar batteries **S:**240
picture(s) **B:**103a
bacterial fermentation produces electricity **F:**91
Battery (artillery troop unit) **U:**104
Batting average (in baseball) **B:**83
Battle, trial by **D:**349; **J:**163
Battle Creek (Michigan) **M:**262, 269
"Battle Cry of Freedom, The" (song) **N:**23
Battledore and Shuttlecock (game) *see* Badminton
Battlefields, national *see* National battlefields
"Battle Hymn of the Republic, The" (by Howe) **N:**23
Battlement (of a castle) **C:**131
Battle of Constantine, The (painting by Piero della Francesca)
picture(s)
detail **R:**167
Battles (in wars) **B:**103d–103f *see also* names of battles
Battleship Potemkin (motion picture, 1925) **M:**490
Battleships *see* Warships
Batts, Thomas (American explorer) **W:**136
Batumi (Republic of Georgia) **G:**148
Batutsi (a people of Africa) *see* Tutsi
Batwa (a people of Africa) *see* Twa
Baudelaire, Charles (French poet) **F:**441
Baudot, Emile (French inventor) **T:**51
Baudouin (king of the Belgians) **B:**135
Bauer, Georg (German minerologist) *see* Agricola, Georgius
Baugh, Sammy (American football player) **F:**362 *profile*
picture(s) **F:**362
Bauhaus (design school in Germany)
architecture, history of **A:**374
furniture design **F:**516–17
industrial design **I:**214
influence on decorative arts **D:**78
Kandinsky, Wassily **K:**173
Mies van der Rohe, Ludwig **M:**306
twentieth century German art and architecture **G:**173
Baule (Baoulé) (African tribe) **A:**72; **I:**421
Baum, L. Frank (American journalist and author of children's
stories) **N:**276; **S:**326 *profile*
Bauxite (ore of aluminum) **A:**194f
Arkansas leads U.S. production **A:**413
Australia is the world's largest producer **A:**510
France is Western Europe's leading producer **F:**409
Guinea is the world's second largest producer **G:**406a
Guyana is an important producer **G:**428a
Hungary has large reserves **H:**297
Jamaica is a leading producer **J:**17
natural resource **N:**62–63
North American mineral resources **N:**293

Bavaria (Germany)
Czech way of life influenced by **C:**618–19
food specialties **G:**151
Thompson, Benjamin: service in government **T:**180
picture(s)
Neuschwanstein (castle) **G:**149
Bavarian Alps (Austria–Germany) **G:**153–54
Bay (geographic term) **O:**43 *see also* the names of bays, as
Fundy, Bay of
Bayaderka (ballet)
picture(s) **D:**32
Bayamón (Puerto Rico) **P:**530
Bayar, Celal (president of Turkey) **T:**349
Bayberry (shrub) **W:**78
Bayeux tapestry (medieval embroidery) **N:**100
picture(s) **E:**238
Bayezid I (Ottoman sultan) **O:**259
Bay horses **H:**237
picture(s) **H:**238
Baying (of dogs) **D:**247
Bay Islands (Honduras) **H:**205
picture(s) **H:**207
Bayle, Pierre (French philosopher) **E:**296 *profile*
Baylor, Elgin (American basketball player) **B:**95i *profile*
picture(s) **B:**95i
Bay lynxes *see* Bobcats
Bay of Pigs Invasion *see* Pigs, Bay of
Bayous (marshy creeks) **L:**314; **M:**352
picture(s) **L:**315
Bayou State (nickname for Louisiana) **L:**315
Bay Psalm Book **H:**324; **P:**551
Bayreuth (Germany)
Festival of Wagner's operas **M:**555; **W:**2
Bay State (nickname for Massachusetts) **M:**136, 137
Bazán, Emilia Pardo (Spanish writer) *see* Pardo Bazán, Emilia
Bazookas (small rocket launchers) **T:**14
BBC *see* British Broadcasting Corporation
B.C. (abbreviation used with dates) **C:**16
B.C.E. (abbreviation used with dates) **C:**16
B cells (in the immune system) **B:**261, 262; **I:**96–97
BCG (vaccine against tuberculosis) **D:**204
B-complex vitamins **V:**370c–370d
B.E. 2a (early British airplane) **A:**562
Beach, Amy Marcy (American pianist and composer) **N:**162
profile
Beach Blanket Bingo (motion picture, 1965) **M:**495
Beach Boys (American rock group) **R:**262d *profile*
Beaches *see also* Seashores
barrier beaches of Louisiana **L:**316
erosion **E:**319
Maine places of interest **M:**44
picture(s)
Alabama **A:**131
Delaware **D:**89, 92
Florida **F:**261
Hawaiian black sand beach **H:**53
Israel **I:**371
Los Angeles **L:**306
Puerto Rico **P:**528
Rhode Island **R:**213
Virginia Beach **V:**352
Waikiki (Honolulu) **H:**215
Wildwood (New Jersey) **N:**168
Beach plum **P:**108
Beaconsfield, Earl of (English statesman and novelist) *see*
Disraeli, Benjamin
Beaded lizard **L:**276
Bead lightning *see* Chain lightning
Beads (jewelry) **A:**72; **G:**229
picture(s) **I:**180
Beads (of a tire) **T:**211
Beagle, **H.M.S.** (British ship) **D:**40; **E:**375
Beagles (dogs) **D:**250; **H:**300
Beaked whales **W:**151

BATTALION–BEAKED WHALES • 505

Beaks (Bills) (of birds)   **A:**277; **B:**221
  eagles   **E:**2
  parrots   **P:**85
  waterfowl   **D:**345, 347
Beaks (of cephalopods)   **O:**50
Beam bridges   **B:**395
  picture(s)   **B:**396
Beamon, Bob (American track-and-field star)   **T:**259 *profile*, 263
  picture(s)   **T:**259
Beams, steel   **I:**336
Beam trawlers (fishing boats)   **F:**218
Bean, Roy (American judge)   **T:**138 *profile*
Beanies (hats)   **H:**45
Beans   **C:**543; **N:**423; **V:**290, 292 *see also* Soybeans
  picture(s)
    seed   **P:**307
Bear cats *see* Binturongs
Bearded collie (dog)
  picture(s)   **D:**250
Bearded seals (animals)   **S:**107
Beardmore Glacier (Antarctica)   **G:**224
Beards (facial hair)
  Muslim men   **I:**348
  Vandyke beard   **B:**67
Bear Festival (of the Ainu)   **J:**41
Bear Flag Revolt (California)   **C:**30; **T:**109
Bearings (of machinery)   **D:**148; **W:**45
Bearing wall construction (of buildings)   **B:**437
Bear Mountain Bridge (New York)
  picture(s)   **R:**242–43
Bear Paw Battlefield (Montana)   **M:**436
Bears   **B:**104–7
  Alaska's wildlife   **A:**149
  black bears   **M:**73; **W:**129
  cave bears of the Ice Age   **I:**12
  foot bones   **F:**81
  grizzly bears   **M:**70
  hibernation   **H:**126, 127–28; **M:**75
  How dangerous are bears?   **B:**106
  pandas related to   **P:**52
  polar bears   **A:**272
  Yellowstone National Park   **Y:**355
  picture(s)   **K:**255
    black bear   **B:**208
    brown bears   **A:**148; **M:**66; **U:**90
    polar bears   **A:**272; **C:**60; **M:**70; **N:**283
Bears (in stock exchanges)   **S:**459
Beast epics   **F:**4
Beasts of burden   **T:**281
Beat (in music)   **M:**533, 536; **O:**198–99; **S:**262
Beaten barkcloth (Tapa) (kind of felted material)   **T:**142
  picture(s)   **T:**141
Beatification (in Roman Catholic Church)   **S:**18c
Beating (in sailing)   **S:**11
Beatles, The (English rock group)   **B:**108; **R:**262c, 264
  picture(s)   **B:**108; **R:**262c; **W:**274
Beatrice (Dante's ideal and inspiration)   **D:**37; **I:**405–6
Beatrix (queen of the Netherlands)   **N:**120d
  picture(s)   **N:**121
Beats (sections of a city)
  assignments of newspaper reporters   **N:**200
  covered by patrol officers   **P:**363
Beats, The (group of poets)   **A:**217
Beaubourg (art museum, Paris) *see* Pompidou Center
Beauchamp, Charles Pierre (French ballet dancer and choreographer)   **B:**26; **D:**25
Beau de Rochas, Alphonse (French engineer)   **I:**265
Beaufort scale (to estimate wind speed)   **W:**88, 189
Beaufort Sea (part of the Arctic Ocean)   **O:**44
Beaujoyeulx, Balthazar de (Italian-born French choreographer)   **B:**25
Beaumarchais, Pierre Augustin Caron de (French playwright)   **D:**302; **F:**440

Beaumont, William (American frontier surgeon)   **B:**109
  picture(s)   **B:**109
Beauport (Quebec)   **Q:**13
Beauregard, Pierre Gustave Toutant de (Confederate general)   **C:**332, 337, 345 *profile*
  picture(s)   **C:**345
Beauty culture *see* Cosmetics; Perfumes
Beauty quark (subatomic particle) *see* Bottom quark
Beauvoir (Mississippi home of Jefferson Davis)   **M:**358
Beauvoir, Simone de (French writer)   **F:**443; **W:**214 *profile*
Beaux-arts style (in architecture)   **U:**131
Beavers   **B:**110–12
  adaptations for water living   **M:**72
  aplodontia (mountain beaver)   **R:**276
  family life   **M:**68
  Rhode Island   **R:**215
  picture(s)   **C:**60; **M:**67
Beaver Scouts   **B:**360
Beaver State (nickname for Oregon)   **O:**202, 203
Beavertail cactus (plant)
  picture(s)   **N:**286
Bebop (style of modern jazz)   **J:**61–63
Beccaria, Cesare Bonesana, Marchese di (Italian philosopher)   **E:**296 *profile*
Becharof Lake (Alaska)   **A:**146
Bechet, Sidney (jazz musician)   **J:**59
Bechuanaland *see* Botswana
Becker, Boris (German tennis player)
  picture(s)   **T:**89
Becket, Saint Thomas à (English churchman)   **B:**113; **E:**240; **H:**108
Beckett, Samuel (Irish playwright and novelist)   **D:**305; **F:**442; **I:**322, 328; **N:**363
Beckley Exhibition Coal Mine (West Virginia)   **W:**134
  picture(s)   **W:**133
Becknell, William (American pioneer)   **O:**272
Bécquer, Gustavo Adolfo (Spanish poet)   **S:**389
Becquerel, Antoine-César (French physicist)   **P:**196
Becquerel, Antoine Henri (French physicist)   **B:**113; **C:**210–11; **R:**47; **U:**230
Bed (of a platen press)   **P:**474
Bedbugs (insects)   **H:**263
Bede (the Venerable Bede) (English priest, scholar, and historian)   **E:**269; **M:**294 *profile*
"Bed in Summer" (poem by Stevenson)   **S:**451
Bedivere (knight of King Arthur's court)   **A:**438
Bedloe's Island (New York Harbor) *see* Liberty Island
Bedouin (nomadic Arabic tribes)   **A:**344; **D:**128
  Egypt   **E:**99
  Iraq   **I:**311–12
  Jordan   **J:**129
  Kuwait   **K:**308, 309
  Saudi Arabia   **S:**58a
  Syria   **S:**550
  picture(s)   **A:**343; **J:**129; **M:**298
Beds
  camp beds   **C:**45
  crewelwork bed hangings   **N:**97
  furniture of the Middle Ages   **F:**509
Bed warmers
  picture(s)   **C:**410
Beebe, William (American naturalist, explorer, and author)   **E:**415–16; **U:**27
  picture(s)   **U:**27
Bee boles (stone shelters for beehives)   **H:**212
Beecher, Henry Ward (American preacher)   **B:**114; **C:**335; **O:**191
Beecher, Thaddeus (American educator)   **E:**83
Beech Starship (airplane)   **A:**117
  picture(s)   **A:**571
Beech trees
  picture(s)   **T:**304; **W:**223
Bee-eaters (birds)
  picture(s)   **B:**234

Beef (meat of cattle) **C:**151, 152; **M:**196
    inspection and grading of meat **M:**198
    picture(s)
        cuts of beef **M:**197
Beef cattle **C:**151–53; **K:**183
    picture(s) **K:**183
Beefeaters *see* Yeomen of the Guard
Beehive State (nickname for Utah) **U:**242, 243
Bee hummingbird **A:**270
Beekeeping **H:**210–11, 212
    picture(s) **B:**116
Beer, Jakob Liebmann (German opera composer) *see* Meyerbeer,
    Giacomo
Beer and brewing **B:**114–15
    Egypt, ancient **E:**106
    leavened bread, history of **B:**388a
    malt extract from barley **B:**60b; **G:**284–85
    picture(s)
        German festival **G:**150
        Wisconsin brewery **W:**199
Beerbohm, Sir Max (English writer) **E:**288
Bees (insects) **B:**116–21 *see also* Honey
    biological classification **L:**207
    color vision **C:**428
    flower pollination **F:**285; **P:**308
    honey **H:**210–12
    strength of **I:**241
    picture(s)
        eggs in the hive **E:**96
        honeybees **H:**211
        mouthparts **I:**238
        nests **B:**121
Bees (social gatherings to accomplish tasks) **C:**412; **P:**257
Beeswax **B:**118; **W:**78
    candles made of **C:**96
    products made from **H:**212
    storing of honey **H:**210, 211
Beethoven, Ludwig van (German composer) **B:**122; **G:**186
    chamber music **C:**184
    choral music **C:**284
    classical age, compositions of the **C:**349, 351, 352;
      O:196
    Fidelio was his only opera **C:**351; **O:**144, 154
    picture(s) **G:**185; **M:**542
        studio **M:**542
Beetle Bailey (comic strip)
    picture(s) **C:**129
Beetles (insects) **B:**123–27
    boll weevils **C:**568–69, 570
    bombardier beetle **I:**243
    carpet beetles **H:**263
    plant pests **P:**286–87, 289, 290
    strength of **I:**241
    used as biological control for weeds **W:**106
    vectors of disease **V:**282
    picture(s) **I:**248
        boll weevil **C:**568
        scavenger beetle **I:**234
        tiger beetles **I:**230
        wings **I:**240
Beets **V:**286, 290
    sugar beets **S:**482, 483, 484
    picture(s)
        sugar beets **S:**484
Beet sugar **S:**483, 484
B.E.F. *see* British Expeditionary Force
Befana, La (Italian Santa Claus) **C:**300
Beggar's Opera (play by Gay) **E:**277, 292–93; **O:**142–43
    Hogarth, William **H:**159a
    musical theater **M:**552
    picture(s)
        scene painted by William Hogarth **E:**277
Beggar's tick (plant) **P:**313
Begin, Menachem (Israeli political leader) **B:**127a; **I:**376
    picture(s) **U:**202

Behaim, Martin (German merchant and navigator) **M:**98
Behan, Brendan (Irish playwright) **I:**328
Béhanzin (king of Dahomey) **B:**144
Behavior, animal *see* Animal intelligence and behavior
Behavior, human
    autism **A:**526–27
    brain function **B:**365, 366–67
    effect of drugs on **D:**326
    ethics **E:**328–29
    etiquette **E:**337–39
    gene interactions **G:**80
    hypnotism **H:**327–29
    identical twins raised apart **T:**364
    learning **L:**98–106
    lie detection **L:**193
    lies **L:**194
    mental illness **M:**221–26
    mental retardation and adaptive behavior **R:**189
    psychology **P:**499
    sociology, study of **S:**230–31
Behavioral disorders
    ADHD **A:**23
Behavioral objectives (in education) **P:**483
Behavioral sciences
    public health **P:**515
Behaviorism (psychology) **P:**507, 509
Behavior modification (in psychology) **P:**500–501
    ADHD, treatment of **A:**23
Behring, Emil von (German bacteriologist) **B:**127a
Behring, Vitus (Danish explorer) *see* Bering, Vitus
Beiderbecke, Bix (American jazz musician) **J:**61
Beijerinck, Martinus (Dutch scientist) **V:**363
Beijing (Peking) (capital of China) **B:**127b–127d; **C:**259, 265
    Forbidden City **A:**366
    student demonstrations **C:**272–73
    picture(s) **C:**256
        bicycles **C:**259
        Fu dog statue at Forbidden City **C:**257
        "Goddess of Liberty" (statue) **C:**474
        temple **A:**366
        Tiananmen Square demonstrations (1989) **C:**273
Beijing Opera **D:**298; **T:**162
Beira (Mozambique) **M:**509
Beirut (capital of Lebanon) **L:**121, 122–23
    picture(s)
        Syrian troops patrolling **L:**123
Bekaa plain (Lebanon) **L:**120
Bel (pagan god) *see* Baal
Béla III (king of Hungary) **H:**298
Bela IV (king of Hungary) **B:**422b
Belarus **B:**128–29; **U:**34
    Chernobyl fallout **F:**36
    Commonwealth of Independent States **C:**460
    picture(s)
        flag **F:**227
        horse farm **B:**129
        schoolchildren **E:**356
Belau (island nation, Pacific Ocean) *see* Palau
Belaúnde Terry, Fernando (president of Peru) **P:**165
Belcher Islands (in Hudson Bay) **N:**410
Belém (Brazil) **B:**375, 381
    picture(s) **B:**378
Belém (Portugal) **L:**256
Belfast (capital of Northern Ireland) **N:**336; **U:**59
    picture(s) **N:**336
Belgian Congo *see* Congo, Democratic Republic of
Belgian horses **H:**240–41
Belgian sheepdog **D:**241
Belgium **B:**130–35
    Albert (kings) **A:**163
    Congo, Democratic Republic of **C:**502–3
    Flemish and Dutch art **D:**357–70
    homosexuals can legally marry **H:**204
    Industrial Revolution **I:**224

Belgium (cont.)
    medieval fairs **F:**18
    Where and what are the Low Countries? **E:**349
    World War I **W:**278–80, 281, 282
    World War II **W:**296, 297, 298, 310, 312, 313–14
    picture(s)
        Bruges **B:**130
        Brussels **B:**132, 134, 135
        flag **F:**227
        flax being stacked to dry **B:**133
        hikers **B:**131
        people **B:**130
Belgium Luxembourg Economic Union (BLEU) **B:**133
Belgrade (capital of Serbia and Montenegro) **B:**136; **S:**125, 126
    picture(s) **B:**136; **S:**125
Belinsky, Vissarion (Russian writer) **R:**381
Belize (Central America) **B:**137–38; **C:**172, 173, 174
    Latin America **L:**50, 59
    nature preserve for jaguars **C:**150
    picture(s)
        African Creole man **C:**172
        flag **F:**227
        Peace Corps activities **P:**104
Belize City (Belize) **B:**137, 138
Bell, Alexander Graham (Scottish-born American inventor and scientist) **B:139–40; I:**283
    airplane research **A:**562
    Alexander Graham Bell Museum (Nova Scotia) **N:**355–56
    Bell Homestead (Ontario) **O:**133
    invented the Graphophone **O:**58
    telephone **C:**468; **T:**46
    picture(s) **T:**54
Bell, Currer, Ellis, and Acton *see* Brontë, Anne; Brontë, Charlotte; Brontë, Emily
Bell, Gertrude (British archaeologist) **A:**358
    picture(s) **A:**358
Bell, Joseph (English doctor and model for Sherlock Holmes) **D:**291
Bell, Joshua (American violinist) **I:**156 *profile*
    picture(s) **I:**156
Bell, Mabel Hubbard (wife of Alexander Graham Bell) **P:**67
Bella Bella (Indians of North America) **I:**188
Bella Coola (Indians of North America) **I:**188
Belladonna (poisonous plant) **L:**117; **P:**316; **V:**290
Bellange, Jacques (French artist) **F:**426
Bellay, Joachim du (French poet) **F:**435, 437
Belle Isle, Strait of (north of Newfoundland and Labrador) **C:**126; **N:**140
Bellerophon (hero in Greek mythology) **G:**364
Belleville Breviary (illuminated manuscript)
    picture(s) **B:**321; **D:**68
Bellevue (Nebraska) **N:**89
Bellingrath Gardens (Alabama) **A:**138
Bellingshausen, Fabian von (Russian admiral) **A:**295; **E:**414
Bellini, Giovanni (Venetian painter) **B:**140; **I:**398; **P:**21; **R:**169
    Giorgione, influence on **G:**210
    Titian was a pupil of Bellini **T:**212
    picture(s)
        Madonna of the Trees (painting) **B:**140
Bellini, Vincenzo (Italian composer) **I:**412; **O:**145, 159
Bellini family (Italian painters) **B:**140
Bellman, Carl Michael (Swedish poet and singer) **S:**58i
Bello, Andrés (South American educator, statesman, and author) **L:**68
Bello, Joaquín Edwards (Chilean writer) *see* Edwards Bello, Joaquín
Bellow, Saul (American novelist) **A:**219; **B:141; F:**116; **N:**363
Bellows, George Wesley (American artist) **C:**444; **P:**30
    picture(s)
        Cliff Dwellers (painting) **U:**132
Bells **B:141–42**
    Christmas customs **C:**299

    communication, use in **C:**466
    early mechanical clocks **T:**201
    Liberty Bell **L:**170
    orchestra, use in **P:**149
Bell's vireo (bird)
    picture(s) **B:**208
Bell system (telephone system) **P:**523
Bell towers *see* Campaniles
Bell X-1 (airplane) **A:**116
Bell XS-1 (research rocket plane) **A:**567
Bell XV-15 (airplane)
    picture(s) **A:**121
Bell XV-22 (tilt-rotor aircraft) **A:**571
Belmont, Alva Smith Vanderbilt (wife of William Kissam Vanderbilt) **V:**277
Belmont Stakes (horse race) **H:**234
Belmopan (capital of Belize) **B:**138
Belo, Carlos Ximenes (East Timorese bishop) **T:**208
Belo Horizonte (Brazil) **B:**381
Belorussia *see* Belarus
Beloved (novel by Morrison) **M:**462
Belshazzar (Biblical character) **B:**159
Belt (to drive an alternator) **A:**547
Belted-bias tires **T:**211
Belter, John Henry (American furniture maker) **F:**514
Belts (ranking system in martial arts) **J:**150; **K:**195
Beltsville Small White (turkey)
    picture(s) **P:**416
Belugas (White whales) **W:**150
    picture(s) **W:**150
Bely, Andrei (Russian author) **R:**383
Bemba (a people of Africa) **Z:**377
Ben (meaning in names) **N:**5
Benalcázar, Sebastián de (Spanish conquistador) **E:**69
Ben Ali, Zine el-Abidine (Tunisian president) **T:**336
Ben & Jerry's (ice cream company) **V:**318
    picture(s) **V:**312
Benares (India) *see* Varanasi
Benavente, Jacinto (Spanish writer) **S:**391
Ben Bella, Ahmed (premier of Algeria) **A:**188
Bench, Johnny (American baseball player)
    picture(s) **B:**92
Bench plane (tool) **T:**228
Bendjedid, Chadli (Algerian political leader) **A:**188
Bends (knots) **K:**288
Bends, the (caisson disease) **B:**400; **H:**106; **U:**22–23
Benedict X (antipope) **R:**292
Benedict XIII (antipope) **R:**293
Benedict I (pope) **R:**292
Benedict II, Saint (pope) **R:**292
Benedict III, Saint (pope) **R:**292
Benedict IV (pope) **R:**292
Benedict V (pope) **R:**292
Benedict VI (pope) **R:**292
Benedict VII (pope) **R:**292
Benedict VIII (pope) **R:**292
Benedict IX (pope) **R:**292
Benedict XI (pope) **R:**293
Benedict XII (pope) **R:**293
Benedict XIII (pope) **R:**293
Benedict XIV (pope) **R:**293
Benedict XV (pope) **R:**293
Benedictine Cloister Church (Ottobeuren, Germany)
    picture(s) **G:**171
Benedictines (Rule of Saint Benedict) (religious order) **C:**290; **R:**287, 289
Benedict of Nursia, Saint (Italian monk) **C:**290; **R:**287; **S:**18d *profile*
Beneficiation (preparation of coal) **F:**488
Benefits (part of wage agreement) **L:**8
Benefit societies (industrial organizations formed to aid members who could not work) **S:**225
Benefit Street (Providence, Rhode Island) **R:**220
Ben Eliezer, Israel (Jewish teacher) *see* Eliezer, Israel ben

Benelux (economic union of Belgium, the Netherlands, and
    Luxembourg) **N:**121
Benenson, Peter (British attorney) **H:**287
Beneš, Edvard (Czechoslovakian statesman) **C:**623, 624;
    M:135; **S:**201
Beneventum, Battle of (275 B.C.) **P:**559
Bengal, Bay of (arm of the Indian Ocean) **O:**44
Bengali (Bangla) (language) **B:**48, 50
Bengalis (a people of Bangladesh and India) **B:**48, 51
Bengal tigers *see* Indian tigers
Benghazi (Libya) **L:**188, 189
Ben-Gurion, David (first prime minister of Israel) **B:**142; **I:**375
    picture(s) **I:**375; **J:**107; **P:**459
Ben-Haim, Paul (Israeli composer) **I:**373
Benign tumors (of the body) **C:**92; **D:**190
Beni Hasan (Egypt) **E:**113
Benin (kingdom in Africa) **N:**258
    art achievements **N:**257
    sculpture **A:**71
    picture(s)
        ivory bracelet **A:**74
Benin (modern African country) **B:**143–44
    picture(s)
        flag **F:**227
        village **B:**144
Beni River (Bolivia) **B:**307
Benito Bonito of the Bloody Sword (pirate) **P:**264
Benjamin (Biblical character) **J:**133
Benjamin, Judah Philip (British-born American lawyer and
    statesman) **L:**326 *profile*
    picture(s) **L:**326
Bennett, Floyd (American aviator) **B:**485
Bennett, Richard Bedford (Canadian prime minister) **C:**77
    profile
Bennett, William Andrew Cecil (Canadian political leader)
    B:406d
Bennett's cassowaries (flightless birds) **O:**245
Ben Nevis (highest mountain in the United Kingdom)
    S:85–86; **U:**51
Bennington (Vermont)
    picture(s)
        saltbox house **C:**415
Bennington, Battle of (1777) **R:**204; **V:**318
    monument **V:**314
Benny, Jack (American comedian) **I:**74 *profile;* **T:**326
Benoit, Joan (American runner) **O:**113
    picture(s) **O:**113
Benoit, Peter (Belgian musician) **B:**133
Benson, Simon (Norwegian American lumberman) **O:**214
    profile
Bentham, Jeremy (English reformer and philosopher) **E:**296
    profile, 297, 328
Benthic (Bottom) environment (of the ocean) **O:**23, 26
Benthos (organisms living on the ocean bottom) **O:**26
Benton, Thomas Hart (American artist) **B:**144a; **U:**132
    teacher of Jackson Pollock **P:**378
    picture(s)
        Arts of the West **B:**144a
        Independence and the Opening of the West (mural)
            M:372
Benton, Thomas Hart (American statesman) **M:**380
Bentonville, Battle of (1865) **N:**319
Bent Pyramid (Dahshûr, Egypt) **E:**108
Bent's Fort (Colorado) **C:**438
Benue River (west Africa) **N:**255
Benz (automobile)
    picture(s) **A:**541
Benz, Karl (German engineer and automobile manufacturer)
    A:540; **I:**265, 281; **T:**286
Benzene (colorless, highly flammable liquid) **F:**47; **P:**174
Beograd (Yugoslavia) *see* Belgrade
Beowulf (epic poem) **B:**144a–144b; **E:**265, 268; **P:**354
    fairy characteristics **F:**12
    oral poetry later put in writing **F:**309
Be Prepared (Scout motto) **B:**358

Bequia (island, Saint Vincent and the Grenadines) **S:**19
Berber (language) **A:**56
Berbera (Somalia) **S:**255
Berbers (people) **A:**55, 185, 188
    Libya **L:**187
    Morocco **M:**458, 461
    picture(s) **A:**54, 185; **L:**187; **M:**458
Berceo, Gonzalo de (Spanish poet) *see* Gonzalo de Berceo
Berceuse (musical form) **M:**542
Berea College (Berea, Kentucky) **K:**217
Berengar II (king of Italy) **H:**177
Bérenger, Paul (prime minister of Mauritius) **M:**181
Berezhnaya, Elena (Russian athlete) **O:**117
    picture(s) **O:**117
Berg, Alban (Austrian composer) **B:**145; **G:**189
    chamber music **C:**184
    expressionism **M:**544
    modern music **M:**398
    opera **O:**148
    Wozzeck **O:**165
    picture(s) **B:**145
Berg, Patty (American golfer) **G:**258 *profile,* 260
    picture(s) **G:**258
Bergelson, David (Yiddish author) **Y:**361
Bergen (Norway) **N:**347–48
Bergen, Edgar (American ventriloquist) **V:**302
Berger, Hans (German psychiatrist) **B:**369
Bergerac, Cyrano de (French poet and soldier) *see* Cyrano de
    Bergerac, Savinien de
Berger Perdomo, Oscar (president of Guatemala) **G:**398
Bergman, Ingmar (Swedish film director) **M:**493 *profile,* 494
Bergman, Ingrid (Swedish actress) **M:**486 *profile*
Bergy bits (melted-down icebergs) **I:**18
Beriberi (disease) **N:**429; **V:**370c
Bering, Vitus (Danish explorer) **A:**156; **B:**145; **D:**112; **E:**414
    picture(s) **A:**156
Beringia (Ice Age plain connecting Alaska and Siberia) **I:**164
Bering Sea **A:**381; **O:**44
Bering Strait (Asia–North America) **B:**145; **O:**44; **P:**2
    divides Asia from North America **A:**438d
Berisha, Sali (Albanian president) **A:**162
Berkeley, Lord John (English colonial proprietor) **N:**176
Berkeley, Sir William (English colonial governor) **I:**202;
    W:136
Berkeley Springs (West Virginia) **W:**134
    picture(s) **W:**134
Berkelium (element) **E:**171
Berkshire Hills (Massachusetts) **M:**138
Berkshire Music Festival (at Tanglewood in Lenox,
    Massachusetts) **M:**555
    picture(s) **M:**555
Berkshire Valley (Massachusetts) **M:**138
Berle, Milton (American comedian) **T:**69
Berlin (Germany) **B:**146–49; **G:**154, 156
    "Cold War" between East and West **G:**164
    Kennedy administration **K:**208–9
    Olympic Games (1936) **O:**111
    World War II **W:**316
    picture(s)
        American sector border sign **G:**166
        children play in rubble **G:**164
        war memorial **B:**147
        World War II **W:**316
Berlin (New Hampshire) **N:**159
Berlin, Irving (American songwriter) **B:**150; **M:**554; **U:**208–9
    Christmas songs **C:**118
    patriotic songs **N:**23
    ragtime **J:**58
Berlin Airlift **B:**149; **C:**401; **G:**164; **T:**327; **U:**197
    picture(s) **B:**148
Berlin Blockade **C:**400–401
Berliner, Emile (German-American inventor) **P:**195; **R:**122
Berliner Ensemble (theater, Berlin) **T:**161
Berlin Philharmonic Orchestra **O:**197

Berlin Wall (separating East and West Berlin) B:146, 149;
    C:401; G:166; H:210
    picture(s) W:275
Berlioz, Hector (French composer) B:150; F:446
    band music B:43
    choral music C:284
    harp, use of H:36
    La Damnation de Faust F:73
    opera O:147
    orchestra conducting O:197
    romantic orchestral music R:304
    picture(s)
        handwritten orchestral score O:197
Berlusconi, Silvio (premier of Italy) I:390
Bermuda (British crown colony of islands in the Atlantic Ocean)
    B:151–52
    What is the Bermuda Triangle? B:152
Bermuda grass G:317
Bermuda onions O:123
Bermuda Triangle B:152
Bermúdez, Juan de (Spanish navigator) B:152
Bern (capital of Switzerland) S:544
Bernadette of Lourdes, Saint S:18d *profile*
Bernadotte, Count Folke (Swedish diplomat) S:529
Bernadotte, Jean Baptiste *see* Charles XIV (Charles XIV John)
    (king of Sweden)
Bernal Jiménez, Miguel (Mexican composer) L:73
Berne Convention (1886) C:555
Berners-Lee, Tim (British network designer) I:286
Bernese Alps (Switzerland) A:194d
Bernhardt, Sarah (French actress) T:160 *profile*
    picture(s) T:160
Bernice P. Bishop Museum (Honolulu, Hawaii) H:55
Bernini, Giovanni Lorenzo (Italian sculptor, painter, and
    architect) B:152; I:400
    baroque architecture A:372; B:65
    fountains F:394
    high altar in Saint Peter's Basilica V:280
    place in the history of sculpture S:100–101
    picture(s)
        Apollo and Daphne (sculpture) I:400
        David (statue) B:65; S:100
        equestrian statue of Louis XIV B:152
        high altar in Saint Peter's Basilica V:281
        Throne of Saint Peter I:400
Bernoulli, Christoph (Swiss naturalist) B:153
Bernoulli, Daniel (Swiss scientist and mathematician)
    A:37–38; B:153; M:167–68
Bernoulli, Jakob (I) (Swiss mathematician; 1654–1705)
    B:153; M:167–68
Bernoulli, Jakob (II) (Swiss mathematician; 1759–1789)
    B:153
Bernoulli, Johann (I) (Swiss mathematician; 1667–1748)
    B:153; M:167–68
Bernoulli, Johann (II) (Swiss mathematician; 1710–1790)
    B:153
Bernoulli, Johann (III) (Swiss scientist; 1746–1807) B:153
Bernoulli, Nikolaus (II) (Swiss mathematician; 1687–1759)
    B:153
Bernoulli, Nikolaus (III) (Swiss mathematician; 1695–1726)
    B:153
Bernoulli family (Swiss mathematicians) B:153
Bernoulli's principle (law in physics) A:38, 109; B:153;
    M:168
Bernstein, Carl (American investigative reporter) W:061
Bernstein, Leonard (American conductor, pianist, and
    composer) O:199 *profile*
    musical theater M:554
    picture(s) O:198; U:210
Berra, Lawrence Peter (Yogi) (American baseball player)
    M:378 *profile*
Berries (fruit) C:542; G:51, 298–301
Berruguete, Alonso (Spanish artist) S:383

Berry, Charles Edward Anderson (Chuck) (American rock music
    performer) R:262c, 262d *profile*
    picture(s) R:262d
Berry, Halle (American actress) A:79c
Berry, Raymond (American football player) F:362 *profile*
    picture(s) F:362
Berryman, John (American poet) A:218
Berry's World (cartoon) C:129
Bertha (Berthrada) (mother of Charlemagne)
    believed to be original Mother Goose N:415
Berthold Missal (illuminated manuscript)
    picture(s) G:167
Bertin, Rose (French seamstress) C:381
Beryl (gem mineral) G:70, 71, 73
    picture(s) M:314
    table(s) M:315
Beryllium (element) E:171; M:318
Berzelius, Jöns Jakob (Swedish chemist) C:209, 210
Berzins, Andris (prime minister of Latvia) L:81
Beslan (Russia) R:373
Bessarabia (Moldova–Ukraine) M:403; R:300
Bessel, Friedrich Wilhelm (German astronomer) A:472, 474
    profile
Bessemer, Sir Henry (English inventor of Bessemer steel
    process) B:154; I:333
Bessemer process (for producing steel) B:154; I:333, 338
Best, Charles H. (Canadian physiologist) B:59
"Best Friend of Charleston" (locomotive) L:287; R:88–89
    picture(s) L:287
Best in Show (dog show award) D:248
Best of Breed (dog show award) D:248
Beta-blockers (drugs) O:116
Beta brass (alloy) B:410
Beta-carotene (a source of vitamin A) B:214
Betancourt, Rómulo (Venezuelan statesman) V:299
Beta particles (of radioactive atoms) R:46, 65
    diagram(s) R:64
Beta Pictoris (star)
    picture(s) S:249
Beta rays (streams of beta particles of radioactive elements)
    R:65
Beta video cassette system V:332e
Betelgeuse (star) S:430
Bethlehem (Jordan) C:300; J:86
Bethlehem (Pennsylvania) M:556; P:135
    picture(s) C:413
Bethune, Mary McLeod (American educator) A:79k; B:154;
    F:274 *profile*
Betrothed, The (novel) *see Promessi sposi, I*
Betsy Ross House (Philadelphia, Pennsylvania) P:180
Bettas (fish) F:196, 204
Better Business Bureaus C:534
Bevel gauges (tools) T:230
Bevel gears G:66
    picture(s) G:66
Beverages
    beer B:114–15
    coffee C:396–97
    grain products G:284–85
    recycling containers from R:125
    tea T:34–36
    whiskey and other distilled beverages W:161
    wine W:190–90a
Beverly Hills Hotel (Los Angeles, California)
    picture(s) L:307
Bewick, Thomas (English engraver) C:232
Beyle, Marie Henri (French writer) *see* Stendhal
Beyond the Horizon (play by O'Neill) O:122
Bhagavad Gita (Hindu sacred poem) H:139; I:140; P:354,
    431
Bhagavat (name for Buddha) B:422b
Bhakti (Hindu religious movement) H:140, 141–42; I:141
Bharal (kind of wild sheep) S:147
Bharat *see* India
Bhaskara (Indian mathematician) M:164

Big Sioux Falls (South Dakota)
  picture(s) S:315
Big Sky Country (name given to Montana) M:428, 429
Big South Fork National River and Recreation Area
  (Kentucky–Tennessee) T:82
Big stick (foreign policy of Theodore Roosevelt) R:331
Big Sur (California)
  picture(s) C:20
Big Thicket National Preserve (Texas) T:132
Big top (circus tent) C:307
Bihar (state, India) I:126
Biharis (a people of Bangladesh and India) B:48
Bihzad, Kamal ad-Din (Persian painter) I:357
Bikini (coral atoll in the west central Pacific) M:113
Bilateral treaties (between two nations) T:296–97
Bilbao (Spain) A:377
  picture(s) A:377
Bile (secretion of the liver) B:281; D:163, 164–65; G:227;
  L:267, 268, 269
Bile ducts (that carry bile to the gallbladder) L:268
Bilingual education E:86; H:149
Bilingual Education Act (United States, 1968) H:149
Bilirubin (bile pigment) L:269
Billboards (used for outdoor advertising) A:31–32
  Ogden Nash poem against H:291
Billets (steel ingots) I:334
Bill Haley and the Comets (rock music group) R:262c
Billiard balls P:327
Billiards B:179–80
Billings (Montana) M:434, 435, 437
  picture(s) M:435
Billings, William (American hymn composer) H:324
Billings Farm and Museum (Woodstock, Vermont) V:314
  picture(s) V:314
Bill of Rights, American B:181–84 *see also* Civil rights; United
    States, Constitution of the
  American Civil Liberties Union A:199
  civil rights, historical origins of C:326
  The Federalist, position of F:78
  First Amendment freedoms F:163
  jury, trial by J:163
  Madison was the principal author M:12
  National Archives N:24
  ten original amendments to the Constitution U:147,
    155–56
Bill of Rights, Canadian *see* Charter of Rights and Freedoms
Bill of Rights, English B:184; E:246
  civil rights, historical origins of C:326
  human rights H:285
  jury trial, right to J:163
  taxation T:25
Bill of Rights, French *see* Declaration of the Rights of Man and
    of the Citizen
Bill of Rights, Universal *see* Universal Declaration of Human
    Rights
Bill of Rights Day B:181
Bills (of birds) *see* Beaks
Bills (suggested laws) G:276; U:142–44, 166–67, 168
  how laws are made L:86
Billy goats G:244
Billy the Kid (American outlaw) N:192 *profile*
Bilonog, Yuriy (Ukrainian athlete) O:120
Biloxi (Mississippi) M:354, 357, 359
  picture(s) M:357
Biltmore House and Gardens (Asheville, North Carolina) N:314
Bimetallic strips (in thermometers) T:163–64
Bimini Islands (Bahamas) B:17
  Ponce de León's search for the Fountain of Youth P:382
Binary fission (of bacteria) B:11
  picture(s) B:11
Binary form (basic design used in writing music) M:533
Binary number system N:409
  digital sound recording S:267a
  electronics E:160
  fiber optic telephone transmission T:54

Binary stars A:472; S:430, 432, 433
  black holes B:253
  relativity, theory of R:144
  picture(s)
    artist's impression of X-ray system B:252
Binchois, Gilles (Flemish composer) D:371; F:444; R:172
Binder's board (for book covers) B:333
Binding energy (in physics) S:491
Binding knots K:288
Binding of books *see* Bookbinding
Bindweed W:104
Binet, Alfred (French psychologist) I:253, 254; P:508
Binge drinking (consuming many drinks in a row) A:173
Bingeing (eating excessively large amounts of food) M:223
Bingen, Hildegard von (German composer) *see* Hildegard von
    Bingen
Bingham, George Caleb (American artist)
  picture(s)
    Raftsmen Playing Cards M:380
    Traders Descending the Missouri O:268
Bingham, Hiram (American missionary in Hawaii) H:61 *profile*
Bingham Canyon copper mine (Utah) U:248–49
Bin Laden, Osama (international terrorist) A:45; N:234;
    T:115, 116
  Kenyan terrorism linked to K:233
  Qaeda, Al Q:2
  picture(s) T:116
Binnie, W. Ian (Canadian Supreme Court justice)
  picture(s) S:505
Binnig, Gerd (German scientist) E:164; M:285
Binoculars O:181
  prism binoculars L:147
  picture(s) O:180
Binocular vision *see* Stereoscopic vision
Binomial nomenclature (method of naming living things)
    K:254; T:29
Binomial theorem (mathematical formula worked out by
    Newton) N:206
Binturongs (Bear cats) (mammals related to mongooses)
    M:419
Bío-Bío River (Chile) C:251
Biochemistry (study of the composition of living things)
    B:185–90; C:205, 210; S:66 *see also* Body
    chemistry; Genetics; Photosynthesis
  body chemistry B:295–99
  careers in biology B:199
  chemistry, history of C:211
  life L:198–200
  Pasteur, Louis P:97
  sulfur S:486
Bioclip (process to harvest wool without shearing) W:234
Biodegradable materials W:062
  detergents and soap D:141
  plastics P:327
Biodiversity (variety of species in an environment) B:214;
    C:525; E:53–54, 55
Bioengineering B:214
Biofeedback (method to control body processes)
  picture(s) D:239
Biofield therapy (type of alternative therapy) A:194e
Biogeography (study of geography of plants and animals)
    G:100–101
Biographical novel B:192
Biography (author's account of a person's life) B:191–92
  Boswell's *Life of Samuel Johnson* E:279; J:124
  children's literature C:246–47
  English literature E:288
  library arrangement L:183
  literature, types of L:258
  Pulitzer Prizes P:535–36
Bioko (formerly **Fernando Po**) (province of Equatorial Guinea)
    E:309
Biological anthropology A:301, 305

Biological clock   B:193–94; L:203–4 *see also* Rhythm (in plant and animal life)
  clock-compass in birds and bees   B:237, 239
  migration, timing of   H:200
  millipedes   C:169
Biological computers   C:494
Biological control (of pests)   F:57, 482; I:249–50; P:290
  ants used in ancient China   A:321
  mosquitoes   M:471
  vegetable growing   V:288
Biologically based therapies (category of alternative therapy)   A:194e
Biological oceanography *see* Marine biology
Biological psychology   P:504
Biological rhythm *see* Rhythm (in plant and animal life)
Biological sciences *see* Life sciences
Biological warfare (warfare in which living organisms are used to transmit disease to an enemy)   D:182
  smallpox could be used as a weapon   M:205
Biology   B:195–204 *see also* Biotechnology; Botany; Evolution; Microbiology; Zoology
  biochemistry   B:185–90
  biological clock   L:203–4
  biological oceanography   O:35, 40
  cells   C:159–62
  crime, theories on causes of   C:585
  experiments and other science activities   E:395–96, 397
  extinction   E:425–26
  genetics   G:77–91
  kingdoms of living things   K:253–59
  Mendel created a new experiment combining biology and statistics   M:218
  science, milestones in   S:70–71, 72, 74
  science, modern   S:72–73
  taxonomy   T:27–29
  picture(s)
    biologists at work   B:196–97
Bioluminescence (light emitted by living organisms)   B:205
  centipedes and millipedes   C:169
  deep-sea fish   F:183; U:22
  ocean life   O:24, 27
  vampire squids   O:51
Biomarkers (in genetic engineering)   G:82
Biomedical engineering   E:225; M:208g–208h
Biomedical sciences (life sciences used in medicine)   S:66
Biomes (communities of plants and animals)   B:206–12; G:100
  plants   P:318, 319
  specific regions of the biosphere   L:203
  tundra   T:331
  map(s)
    major biomes of the world   P:318
  picture(s)
    plants   P:320–21
Biondi, Matt (American swimmer)   S:537 *profile*
  picture(s)   S:537
Biophysics   S:66
Biopsy (examination of living tissue)   C:93
Bioremediation methods (of cleaning up hazardous wastes)   H:73
Biorhythm *see* Rhythm (in plant and animal life)
Biosatellite (satellite that carries living matter into space)   S:340d
Biosphere   B:198, 206–12; L:201–6
Biostatistics   P:515
Biota (organisms in an environment)   G:100
Biotechnology   B:213–14; G:83–86; S:73
  control of plant pests   P:291
  dairy farming   D:11
  drugs   D:334
  food supply   F:351
  hormones   H:228
  inventions   I:286
  Japanese industry   J:39

United States agriculture   U:93
  vegetable growing   V:292
  What is golden rice?   B:214
Bioterrorism (the purposeful spreading of disease)   H:182; P:402; T:115
Biotin (B-complex vitamin)   V:370d
  table(s)   V:372
Bipedalism (ability to walk on two feet)   H:281
Bipolar disorder (mental illness)   M:221
Bipolar transistors   T:276
Bipropellant (rocket fuel)   R:259
Biratnagar (Nepal)   N:109
Birch trees
  picture(s)   M:328; N:151; T:304; W:223
Bird, Larry (American basketball player)   B:95i *profile*
  picture(s)   B:95i
Birdbanding   A:491
"Bird Came Down the Walk, A" (poem by Dickinson)   D:155
Bird Day *see* Arbor Day
Bird in Space (sculpture by Brancusi)   B:370
  picture(s)   S:105
Bird of paradise   A:270–71
Birds   A:266; B:215–48
  acid rain's effects   A:10
  animal communication   A:284
  Audubon's paintings   A:491
  beaks (bills)   A:277; B:221
  biological clocks and compasses   B:193
  caring for their young   B:236
  cassowaries   O:245
  descended from dinosaurs   D:170; E:374
  doves and pigeons   D:289–90
  ducks, geese, and swans   D:345–48
  eagles   E:2
  Earth, history of   E:28
  eggs and embryos   E:96
  eggs and incubation   B:230–31
  emus   O:245
  experiments and other science activities   E:396
  extinct and endangered species   B:247–48
  falcons   F:32–33
  feeding their young   B:233, 236
  feet   A:276; F:84
  flightless birds   O:242–45
  fossil birds   B:247
  habitats   B:248
  hawks   H:64
  herons, bitterns, and egrets   H:124
  hibernation   H:127
  history and evolution of   B:247
  hummingbirds   H:288–89
  imprinting   B:232
  kiwis   O:245
  largest   A:271
  life cycle   B:228–29
  life spans   A:83
  magnetism helps migration   M:32
  Malheur National Wildlife Refuge   O:210
  mating   B:228
  migration   B:237–39; H:198, 200; M:139
  navigation   H:202
  nest building   B:228–30
  New Zealand birdlife   N:238
  oil spills' effect on   W:065–066
  ornithologists study birds   B:198
  ostriches   O:243
  owls   O:284–85
  parrots   P:85–86
  pelicans   P:119–20
  penguins   P:120b–124
  pets *see* Birds as pets
  pollination of flowers   F:286
  pollution in the food chain   B:248
  poultry   P:414–17

Birds (cont.)
    prehistoric animals **P:**433
    protective coloration **B:**218
    provincial *see* individual Canadian province articles
    quail **Q:**4a
    reproduction **R:**178
    rheas **O:**243–45
    seed dispersal **P:**313
    smallest **A:**270
    songs and other sounds **B:**227
    South America thought to have more species than any other continent **S:**283
    state **U:**80 *see also* individual state articles for pictures
    turkeys **T:**350
    vultures **V:**394
    West Nile virus, primary hosts for **V:**283
    wetlands **W:**146, 148
    What is the most precious fossil in the world? **F:**388
    winter inactivity of non-hibernators **H:**128
    diagram(s)
        wings **F:**84
    picture(s)
        orders of **B:**234–35
Birds as pets **B:**249–50a; **P:**178–79
Birdseye, Clarence (American inventor) **F:**341
Bird's nest ferns **F:**94
Birds of prey **A:**276, 280–81
    eagles **E:**2
    falcons **F:**32–33
    hawks **H:**64
Birdsongs **B:**227
Birdwatching **B:**225
Bird Woman *see* Sacagawea
Birendra (king of Nepal) **N:**110
Birettas (hats) **H:**46
Birkirkara (Malta) **M:**64
Birmingham (Alabama) **A:**130, 135, 137, 142, 143
    African American history **A:**79n
    picture(s) **A:**131
        Civil Rights Memorial **C:**325
        sculpture **A:**138
Birmingham (England) **U:**49, 59
Birney, Alice McLellan (American educator) **P:**67
Birney, James G. (American abolitionist) **A:**6b; **P:**376
Biro, Laszlo (Hungarian inventor) **P:**142–43
Birr Castle (Ireland)
    picture(s) **G:**32
Birth ceremonies (in Judaism) **J:**146b
Birth certificates **G:**76b
Birth control **B:**250a–251; **F:**41
    Roman Catholic Church **P:**102
    Sanger, Margaret **W:**215
    Supreme Court decisions **W:**213
Birth control pills *see* Pill
Birthday cards **G:**375
Birthday parties **P:**87–91
    Why do we put lighted candles on a birthday cake and then blow them out? **C:**96
Birthdays (of famous people)
    arranged by the month *see* individual month articles
    holidays honoring **H:**164–65
Birthday stones *see* Birthstones
Birth defects *see* Congenital disabilities and diseases
Birthing rooms (in hospitals) **H:**247
"Birthmark, The" (story by Hawthorne) **S:**162
Birth of a Nation, The (motion picture, 1915) **M:**488
Birth of Venus, The (painting by Botticelli) **U:**3
    picture(s) **I:**386
Birth rate (number of births per 1,000 people) **P:**385
    countries with highest and lowest birth rates, list of **P:**386
Birthstones **G:**74 *see also* the names of stones and articles on individual months
Bisexuality (sexual attraction to both sexes) **H:**204
Bishkek (capital of Kyrgyzstan) **K:**313

Bishop, Bernice Pauahi (American educator) **H:**55, 61 *profile*
Bishop, Charles Reed (American banker in Hawaii) **H:**55, 61
Bishop, Elizabeth (American poet) **A:**217
Bishop, Maurice (prime minister of Grenada) **G:**379
Bishops (of a church)
    cathedral is a church containing the bishop's throne **C:**133
    Christianity, history of **C:**289; **R:**285, 286, 287, 288
    Roman Catholic Church, government of the **R:**283
Bishops' Bible (early English version) **B:**158
Bishops' schools *see* Cathedral schools
Bishop's University (Lennoxville, Quebec) **Q:**11
Bislama (language) **V:**279
Bismarck (capital of North Dakota) **N:**329
    picture(s) **N:**330
Bismarck, Otto von (German statesman) **B:**251–52; **F:**452; **G:**161; **W:**277, 278
    picture(s) **B:**251; **P:**459
        William II dismissing Bismarck, cartoon of **G:**162
Bismarck Archipelago (Pacific island group) **P:**8, 58d
    New Britain **P:**9
    New Ireland **P:**10
Bismarck Sea **O:**44
Bismuth (element) **E:**171
Bisnaga (kind of cactus) **C:**5
Bison (hoofed mammals) **B:**430; **H:**219
    Bialowieza Forest (Poland) **P:**358
    dung as fuel source **P:**253
    Ice Age **I:**12
    Kansas **K:**179
    National Bison Range (Montana) **M:**431, 436
    South Dakota **S:**316, 320
    Wood Buffalo National Park (Alberta) **C:**60–61
    picture(s) **B:**430; **I:**181; **N:**323; **S:**316; **W:**335
        Montana **M:**436
        prehistoric carving **A:**428
        Yellowstone National Park **Y:**355
Bisque dolls **D:**267–68
Bissau (capital of Guinea-Bissau) **G:**408
Bissell, Emily Perkins (American social welfare worker) **D:**100 *profile*
Bisymmetrical balance (in design) **D:**133
Bit (mouthpiece for a horse) **H:**230
Bite (in dentistry) **O:**232
Bites (of animals)
    animal bites, first aid for **F:**161
    insect bites, first aid for **F:**161
    mosquitoes **M:**471
Bitonality (in music) **M:**398
Bits (Binary digits) (of information) **C:**481, 491; **T:**49
Bitter (sense of taste) **B:**290
Bitterns (wading birds) **H:**124
Bitterroot (flower)
    picture(s) **M:**429
Bitumen (hydrocarbon) **P:**175
Bituminous coal (soft coal) **C:**388; **F:**488–89
Bivalves (mollusks with two shells) **M:**406; **O:**290–91; **S:**150
Biwa, Lake (Japan) **J:**35
Biya, Paul (Cameroon president) **C:**41
Bizerte (Tunisia) **T:**336
    picture(s) **T:**334
Bizet, Georges (French composer) **O:**152
Bjoerndalen, Ole Einar (Norwegian athlete) **O:**118
Bjørnson, Bjørnstjerne (Norwegian writer) **N:**348; **S:**58h, 58i
Blab schools **L:**241
Black (color) **C:**425
    Christian funeral custom **F:**493
    symbolism of **C:**372, 429
Black, Hugo La Fayette (American jurist) **A:**142 *profile*
Black, Joseph (Scottish scientist) **M:**27; **S:**71
Black, Shirley Temple (American actress and public official) *see* Temple, Shirley
Black American literature *see* African American literature
Black Americans *see* African Americans

Black-and-tan coonhound (dog)   D:250
Black-and-white negative film (in photography)   P:204, 207
Black Arts Movement   A:218
Blackball (to vote against)   B:23
Black Bart (British pirate)   P:262 profile
Blackbeard (British pirate)   P:262 profile, 264
    picture(s)   P:262
Black bears   B:104, 105–6, 107; M:73; W:129
    picture(s)   B:107
Black Belt (area of Alabama)   A:132
Black belt (expert rank in martial arts)   J:150; K:195
Blackberries   G:298, 301
Black blizzards (dust storms)   D:355
Black Boy (book by Wright)   W:327
Blackbuck (antelope)   A:297
Black Cabinet (of Franklin Roosevelt's administration)   A:79k
Black Canyon of the Gunnison National Park (Colorado)   C:438
Black-capped chickadees (birds)
    picture(s)   B:220; N:138
Black Caribs (people of Guatemala) see Garífuna
Black cats   S:504
Black Codes (laws passed by Southern states just after Civil
        War)   A:79f; J:117; R:117; U:186
Black-crowned night herons (wading birds)   H:124
    picture(s)   B:235
Black Death see Bubonic plague
Black-eyed Susans (flowers)
    picture(s)   M:121
Black-figure pottery (of ancient Greece)   G:347; P:411
    picture(s)   G:347; P:411
Blackfish (Shawnee Indian leader)   B:334
Blackfoot (Indians of North America)   I:180
Black Forest (Germany)   G:153
    picture(s)
        acid rain effects   E:304
Blackfriars (London theater)   S:134
Black Hawk (Native American chief)   I:74–75, 204–5, 303
    Black Hawk Historic Site (Rock Island, Illinois)   I:70
    Iowa nicknamed Hawkeye State in his honor   I:290
Black Hawk War (1865–1868)   I:74–75; U:254; W:205
Black-headed snakes   S:212
Blackheads (clogged skin pores)   D:187
Black Hills (South Dakota–Wyoming)   S:312, 315, 325;
        W:334
    gold rush   G:252
    mineral resources   S:317
Black Hills National Forest (South Dakota–Wyoming)   S:316
Black Hills spruce trees
    picture(s)   S:313
Black History Month   A:80
Black holes (in astronomy)   A:474; B:252–53; S:433;
        U:212–13, 215
    galactic nucleus   M:309
    gravitation   G:325
    Hawking, Stephen William   H:63
    quasars   Q:9; U:217
    radio galaxies   R:71
    space telescopes   S:368
    picture(s)
        artist's impression   B:252
Black homelands (South Africa) see Tribal homelands
Black Iris (painting by O'Keeffe)
    picture(s)   U:132
Black Kettle (Cheyenne Indian chief)   I:180 profile
Black light see Ultraviolet radiation
Blacklisting (not permitting people to work)   U:13
Black lung (disease that comes from breathing coal dust)
        C:391
Black Madonna (Polish religious symbol)   P:358
    picture(s)   P:358
Black mambas (snakes)   S:217
Black Mansion (Ellsworth, Maine)   M:44
Black market (market in violation of government regulations)
        P:485

Black Mask (magazine)
    picture(s)   M:567
Black Mass (supposed activity of witches)   W:208–9
Black Mesa (highest point in Oklahoma)   O:84
Black Mountain (highest point in Kentucky)   K:212, 213
Blackmun, Harry Andrew (American jurist)   I:74 profile
Black Muslims (Nation of Islam)   A:79c, 79o, 79p; M:59
Black olives   O:101
Black Panther Party   A:79o
Black Peter (Saint Nicholas' helper) see Swarte Piet
Black plague (disease) see Bubonic plague
Blackpoll warblers (birds)   H:198
    picture(s)
        migration route   H:201
Black powder (early gunpowder)   E:420, 421; G:415
"Black Power" (slogan of the civil rights movement)   A:79o
Black Reflections (painting by Kline)
    picture(s)   M:396a
Black Renaissance see Harlem Renaissance
Black rhinoceroses (mammals)   H:217; R:211
Blacks see also African Americans; the names of African
        countries, black leaders, and organizations
    Africa   A:55
    Africa, art of   A:70–76
    Africa, early kingdoms of   A:65–66
    Africa, literature of   A:76a–76d
    African Americans   A:79a–80
    Caribbean dance   D:30
    Costa Rica, people of   C:564
    Haiti   H:9, 11
    Jamaica   J:15, 18
    Latin America   L:49, 50, 58
    music   A:77–79; L:72
    sickle-cell anemia   D:201
    slavery   S:193–97
    Suriname   S:516
Black Sea   M:211; O:44
Blackshirts (fascist parties)   F:63, 64; M:556
Black Sox Scandal (in baseball)   B:91
Blackstone, Sir William (English jurist)   L:85
    picture(s)   L:85
Black Stone of Mecca see Ka'ba
Blackstone River (Massachusetts–Rhode Island)   R:214
Blackstrap molasses   H:79; S:482
Black-tailed deer   H:218
Black tea   T:34–35
Black-thighed falconets (birds)   F:32–33
Blackton, J. Stuart (American illustrator)   A:290
Blacktop (asphalt for roads)   R:250
Black vultures   V:394
Black walnuts   N:435, 436
Black Warrior River (Alabama)   A:132, 133
Blackwater River (Ireland)   I:319
Blackwell, Elizabeth (English-American physician)   B:253
    picture(s)   B:253
Blackwell, Rosa (American slave)   S:195
Black widow spiders
    picture(s)   F:161
Bladder   B:286
Bladensburg, Battle of (1814)   W:10
Blades (of broad leaves)   L:112; P:306
Blaese, Michael (American scientist)   G:91
Blaine, James Gillespie (American statesman)   G:54; M:48
        profile
Blair, Bonnie (American speed skater)   I:44 profile
    picture(s)   I:42
Blair, Eric (English writer) see Orwell, George
Blair, Tony (British prime minister)   B:254; E:255
    picture(s)   B:254; E:255; U:170
Blair House (Washington, D.C.)   W:166
Blais, Marie-Claire (Canadian writer)   C:87
Blaize, Herbert A. (prime minister of Grenada)   G:379
Blake, Nicholas (English poet) see Day Lewis, C.

Blake, William (English poet and artist)   **B:**254; **E:**278
  book illustration   **E:**261
  children's literature   **C:**237
  illustration of books   **I:**80
  romanticism   **R:**302
  picture(s)
      engraving from *Songs of Experience*   **E:**278
      Jacob's Ladder (painting)   **R:**302
      romanticism   **R:**303
Blalock, Alfred (American surgeon)   **T:**24
Blanc, Mont (mountain, France–Italy)   **A:**194d; **F:**408; **M:**504
  picture(s)   **A:**194d; **E:**340; **F:**408
  table(s)
      first ascent   **M:**500
Blanchard, Jean-Pierre François (French balloonist)   **B:**35
Blanchard, Madeline-Sophie (French balloonist)   **B:**35
Blanco, Salvador Jorge (president of Dominican Republic)
      D:283
Bland-Allison Bill (1877)   **H:**71
Blanes, Juan Manuel (Uruguayan artist)   **L:**63
Blankers-Koen, Fanny (Dutch track star)   **O:**113; **T:**263
Blanket toss (Inuit custom)
  picture(s)   **I:**272
Blank verse (unrhymed verse)   **S:**135–39
Blantyre (executive and judicial capital of Malawi)   **M:**53
Blasco Ibáñez, Vicente (Spanish author)   **S:**390
Blast (of a nuclear explosion)   **N:**376
Blast furnaces   **F:**489; **I:**330–32
  picture(s)   **O:**217
Blasting (in quarrying)   **Q:**6
Blasting agents (explosives)   **E:**421
Blasting caps   **E:**420–21
Blasting mats (used in construction)   **E:**423
Blastula (stage in cell division)   **E:**97
Blatch, Harriot Stanton (American reformer)   **W:**212a–212b
Blaue Reiter, Die (German art group) *see* Blue Rider, The
Blazoning (describing arms in heraldry)   **H:**116, 118
  picture(s)   **H:**117
Bleaching
  hair   **H:**8
  oxidation and reduction   **O:**287
  paper making   **P:**55
Bleaching, coral *see* Coral bleaching
Bleak House (novel by Dickens)   **D:**151; **M:**566
Blechynden, Richard (English tea merchant)   **T:**36
Bleeding
  first aid   **F:**158–59, 160, 161
  hemophilia   **D:**193
Bleeding Kansas   **A:**6b; **K:**176, 188, 191
Blended families   **F:**37–38
Blenheim, Battle of (1704)   **S:**377
Blennerhassett Island (West Virginia)   **W:**134
Bleriot, Louis (French engineer)   **A:**562
Blessed Virgin Mary *see* Mary, Virgin
Bless Me, Ultima (book by Anaya)   **A:**219
Bligh, William (British naval officer)   **B:**255; **P:**295
Blimps *see* Airships
Blindfish   **C:**158
Blindman's Buff (painting by Goya)
  picture(s)   **G:**277
"Blind Men and the Elephant, The" (fable by Saxe)   **F:**7
Blindness   **B:**255–58
  cave-dwelling animals   **C:**158
  computer assistance   **C:**485
  disabilities, people with   **D:**178, 179, 180
  dreams and eye movements   **D:**319–20
  echoes used by   **E:**49
  Keller, Helen   **K:**203
  library service   **L:**176
  night blindness   **V:**370b
  public assistance   **W:**120
  seeing-eye dogs   **D:**242
  syphilis may cause   **S:**202
  typewriters for the blind   **T:**374
  what to do when you see a blind person   **B:**256

Blindness of Tobit, The (etching by Rembrandt)   **G:**304
Blind rivets   **N:**3
Blind snakes   **S:**209, 212, 213, 217
Blind spot (in the eye)   **E:**431
Blips (spots on a radar indicator)   **R:**39
Bliss, Mary Elizabeth Taylor (acting first lady in Taylor's
      administration)   **F:**170
  picture(s)   **T:**32
Blister beetles
  picture(s)   **B:**124, 126
Blithedale Romance, The (novel by Hawthorne)   **A:**210; **H:**65
Blitz (bombing of England, 1940)   **L:**298; **W:**299
Blitzkrieg (sudden military attack)   **R:**320
Blixen, Baroness Karen (Danish novelist) *see* Dinesen, Isak
Block, Adriaen (Dutch explorer)   **R:**224
Blockade (to prevent supplies from reaching the enemy)
  Berlin airlift   **B:**149
  castles, attacks on   **F:**379
  Cuban missile crisis   **C:**611
Blockhouse (used in spacecraft launchings)   **S:**340d
Blockhouses (forts)   **F:**379
Blocking (giving stage directions in a play)   **P:**336, 337–38
Blocking (in football)   **F:**353
  picture(s)   **F:**354
Block Island (Rhode Island)   **R:**212, 214, 220
  picture(s)   **R:**215
      nautical chart   **N:**72
Block lava   **V:**383
Block plane (tool)   **T:**228–29
  picture(s)   **T:**228
Block printing   **C:**464; **P:**472; **W:**229
Block rubber   **R:**345
Blocks (rock fragments)   **V:**383
Bloc Québécois (Canadian political party)   **C:**75
Bloemfontein (judicial capital of South Africa)   **S:**271
Blok, Aleksandr (Russian writer)   **B:**383
Blondie (American rock group)   **R:**264
Blondie (comic strip)
  picture(s)   **C:**129
Blondy, Alpha (Ivorian reggae singer)   **I:**421
Blood   **B:**259–62
  AIDS transmitted by exchange of blood   **A:**100b
  anemia   **D:**188
  calcium needed for clotting   **V:**371
  cells are produced in bone marrow   **S:**184a
  circulation, studies of   **B:**201; **M:**208b
  circulatory system of human body   **B:**283–85; **C:**304–6
  Drew, Charles, and blood storage   **D:**325
  Harvey's contribution to studies of circulation   **H:**44
  heart   **H:**80–85
  hemophilia   **D:**184
  insect's blood system   **I:**239
  kidneys filter blood   **K:**242, 243
  leukemia   **D:**195–96
  liver, functions of the   **L:**267–69
  muscles receive fuel from   **M:**521
  Red Cross blood service programs   **R:**126, 127
  stain removal   **L:**82
  transfusion *see* Transfusion, blood
  vitamin K aids clotting   **V:**370d
  picture(s)
      nurse monitoring blood donors   **N:**419
Blood banks   **T:**273
Blood clots   **D:**189
Blood groups (blood types)   **B:**261; **R:**30–31; **T:**273
Bloodhound (dog)   **D:**241–42, 244, 250
Blood pressure   **D:**194; **H:**85; **K:**244
Blood tests   **D:**145, 207
Blood transfusion *see* Transfusion, blood
Blood vessels   **B:**283, 285; **C:**304, 305, 306
  blushing   **B:**300
  heart, function of   **H:**80–81
  iodine used in taking X-rays of   **X:**350
  picture(s)
      in human head   **B:**284

Bloodworms W:321
Bloody Mary see Mary I (queen of England and Ireland)
Bloody Sunday (Northern Ireland massacre, 1972)
   picture(s)
      anniversary N:337
Bloomington (Minnesota) M:335
Blooms (rapid growth of algae) P:284
Blooms (steel ingots) I:334
Blount, William (American political figure) T:86
Blow, Taylor and H. T. (American abolitionists) D:323
Blow drying (of hair) H:8
Blowholes (of whales) D:275; W:149, 150, 151
Blow molding (plastics manufacturing process) P:326
Blowouts (from oil wells) P:175
Blowpipes (glassmaking) B:346; G:229, 233
Blubber (fatty tissue) W:149, 154, 155
   manatees M:77
   seals S:107
   walruses W:6
Blucher (steam engine) R:87
Blue (color) A:482; C:425; G:4
Blue and Green Music (painting by O'Keeffe)
   picture(s) D:135
Blue babies (children born with defective hearts) H:85; T:24
Blue-Backed Speller (by Webster) W:99
Blue bears see Glacier bears
Blueberries G:301
   picture(s) G:299; N:166
Bluebirds
   picture(s) I:47; M:367; N:123, 211
Blue Boat, The (painting by Homer)
   picture(s) U:130
Bluebonnet (flower)
   picture(s) T:125, 126
Bluebottle flies
   picture(s) I:244, 245
Blue Boy, The (painting by Gainsborough) G:4
   picture(s) G:4
Blue cheeses D:10
Blue chip stocks S:455
Blue crabs (crustaceans) C:581
Blue Dancers (drawing by Degas)
   picture(s) F:430
Bluefin (fish) F:217
Blue-footed booby
   picture(s) B:220
Bluegill (fish) F:213
   picture(s) F:209
Blue goose (bird) D:348
Bluegrass Basin (of Kentucky) K:214
Bluegrass music C:571; K:225; W:132
   picture(s) F:322; K:217; W:197
Bluegrass State (nickname for Kentucky) K:212, 213
Blue-green algae see Cyanobacteria
Blue Grotto (Capri, Italy) C:156; I:363
Blueground (Kimberlite) (diamond-bearing rock) G:70–71
Blue hen chicken
   picture(s) D:89
Blue jays (birds) B:246
   picture(s) B:221, 234; P:460
Blue Lake (New Mexico) N:194
Blue laws (legislation on matters of individual conscience or
   conduct) L:88
Blue Licks, Battle of (1782) K:220, 225
Blue-light lasers L:46d
Blue Man Group (performers) D:307
   picture(s) D:297
Blue Mosque (Istanbul, Turkey) see Sultan Ahmed Mosque
Blue Mountains (Jamaica) J:16, 17
Blue Mountains (Oregon–Washington) O:204; W:16
Blue Nile River (Africa) E:331; L:33; N:260; S:478
Blue notes (in jazz) J:57, 58
Blueprint (photographic reproduction method) B:263
   picture(s) B:263
Blue Riband (award for the fastest Atlantic crossing) O:31

Blue Rider, The (modern art group in Germany) E:424; G:172;
   K:173, 271; M:391–92
Blue Ridge (mountain range, eastern United States) N:285
   Maryland M:122
   North Carolina N:308
   Pennsylvania P:128
   South Carolina S:298, 299
   Tennessee T:74
   Virginia V:348
   West Virginia W:128
   picture(s) G:133; N:104
      Maryland M:121
      North Carolina N:307
      Virginia V:348
Blue Ridge Parkway N:314; V:354
Blue-ringed octopuses (mollusks) O:51
Blues (in printing) B:330–31
Blues, the (music) H:325; J:58; T:74, 86; U:208
Blue shift (change in galaxy spectrum) L:226
Blue spruce trees
   picture(s) C:431; U:243
Blue supergiant stars S:429
Blue whales M:66; P:284; W:152–53, 155
   picture(s) W:152
Blue-winged teal (duck) D:345
Bluff (New Zealand) N:239
Bluford, Guion S., Jr. (American astronaut) A:79c; S:348
   profile
   picture(s) S:348
Blum, Léon (French statesman) F:418
Blume, Judy (American writer) B:263
   picture(s) B:263
Blunderbuss (smooth-bore gun)
   picture(s) G:417
Blushing (body action) B:300
Bly, Nellie (American newspaper reporter) B:264
B lymphocytes see B cells
BMX (Bicycle motocross) bicycles B:175, 177
   picture(s) B:176
B'nai B'rith International (Jewish organization) C:326
Boadicea (British queen)
   picture(s) W:261
Board games G:12–15; V:332c
Boarding pass (permission to board an airplane) A:126, 127
Boarding schools P:443
Boardsailing (sport) B:264–65
   picture(s) O:203
Boards of directors (of corporations) B:471; E:128
Boars (male pigs) H:219; P:248
"Boar's Head, The" (English carol) C:118
Boas (snakes) S:210, 217, 218
Boas, Franz (German-American anthropologist) A:304; B:265;
   F:312
Boatbuilding W:231–32
Boat racing B:269; R:340–41
Boats and boating B:266–69 see also Canoeing; Rowing;
      Sailing; Water sports
   ancient water craft S:155–57
   boatbuilding W:231–32
   canal boats E:315
   canoeing C:99–101
   early transportation T:281
   floating and buoyancy F:253
   houseboats H:189
   hydrofoils H:315
   iceboating I:19–20
   kayaking C:101; K:199
   reed boats on Lake Titicaca P:161
   rowing R:340–41
   safety measures S:5
   sailing S:8–12
   snag boats L:323
   picture(s)
      Bangladesh B:48

Boer War (1899–1902)   **B:**302; **E:**251; **K:**270; **S:**273
    picture(s)   **S:**272
Bogart, Humphrey (American actor)   **M:**486 *profile*
    picture(s)   **M:**486
Bogazköy (ancient city in Turkey)   **A:**236
Bogdan (Moldavian prince)   **M:**403
Boggarts (mischievous fairies)   **F:**9
Bogie wheels (of tanks)   **T:**14
Bogosian, Eric (American playwright)   **D:**307
Bogotá (capital of Colombia)   **B:**303; **C:**404, 406, 408; **S:**289
    picture(s)   **B:**303; **C:**407; **S:**288
Bogs   **M:**513; **N:**63; **W:**145, 146–47
    picture(s)   **G:**300
Bog turtles   **T:**355
Bogue Sound (North Carolina)   **N:**308
Bohème, La (opera by Puccini)   **O:**151
Bohemia (historical region in central Europe)   **C:**619, 622;
    H:2, 306; **T:**179
Böhl de Faber, Cecilia (Spanish writer) *see* Caballero, Fernán
Bohr, Niels (Danish atomic physicist)   **B:**304; **C:**211;
        D:112; **P:**231
    physics, history of   **P:**237–38
    quantum theory   **L:**223, 224–25
    picture(s)   **B:**304; **P:**237
Bohrium (element)   **E:**171
Boiardo, Matteo Maria (Italian poet)   **I:**406
Boileau-Despréaux, Nicolas (French poet)   **F:**438
Boilers   **H:**96, 97; **S:**445
Boiling (method of cooking)   **C:**542
Boiling point   **H:**90–91
    different boiling points make distillation possible
        D:218–19
    geysers   **G:**193
    liquids, properties of   **L:**254
    liquids boil at lower temperatures in a vacuum   **V:**262
    water   **W:**48
    picture(s)   **H:**90
Boils (skin infections)   **D:**195
Bois de Boulogne (park, Paris)   **P:**70, 72
Boise (capital of Idaho)   **I:**51, 55
    picture(s)   **I:**55
Boitano, Brian (American figure skater)   **I:**44 *profile*
Bojaxhiu, Agnes Gonxha (Roman Catholic nun) *see* Teresa,
    Mother
Bokassa, General Jean-Bedel (emperor of the Central African
    Empire)   **C:**171
Bokher, Eli (Yiddish author)   **Y:**360
Bolaños Geyer, Enrique (president of Nicaragua)   **N:**248
Bolas (hunting devices)   **I:**108, 199
Bolden, Charles F., Jr. (American astronaut)
    picture(s)   **S:**341
Bold New City (nickname for Jacksonville)   **J:**10
Bolero (kind of jacket)   **C:**377
Boleyn, Anne (2nd queen of Henry VIII of England)   **C:**292;
    E:242; **H:**114
Bolger, Jim (prime minister of New Zealand)   **N:**242
Bolingbroke *see* Henry IV (king of England)
Bolívar, Pico (highest point in Venezuela)   **V:**296
Bolívar, Simón (South American liberator and patriot)   **B:**305,
    310
    Colombia's independence   **C:**408
    San Martín, José, meeting with   **S:**36
    Simón Bolívar's birthday holiday   **H:**165
    Venezuela, history of   **V:**298–99
    picture(s)   **S:**294; **V:**299; **W:**270
Bolivia   **B:**306–10; **L:**48, 49, 50, 55
    Indians, American   **I:**196
    lakes   **L:**33–34
    languages   **S:**285, 288
    Tiwanaku civilization   **I:**170
    map(s)   **B:**307
    picture(s)
        Andes   **B:**308
        Catavi tin mine   **T:**209

corn being dried   **S:**291
flag   **F:**227
La Paz   **B:**309
llamas   **B:**306
people   **B:**306
tin mine   **B:**309
Titicaca, Lake   **B:**306; **S:**280
Bolkiah, Sultan Sir Muda Hassanal *see* Hassanal Bolkiah, Sultan
    Sir Muda
Böll, Heinrich (German writer)   **G:**182
Bolling, Richard Walker (American politician)   **U:**142 *profile*
Boll weevils   **B:**127; **C:**568–69, 570
    picture(s)   **B:**126; **C:**568; **I:**234; **P:**288
Bologna, University of   **E:**356; **I:**382; **U:**219
Bolshevik Party (in Russian history)   **C:**473; **L:**140; **R:**371;
        U:33, 40, 41
    Nicholas II executed by   **N:**249
    Stalin's Great Purge   **R:**372; **U:**42
    Stalin was an organizer for   **S:**419
    picture(s)
        1917 coup   **R:**371
Bolshoi Ballet
    picture(s)   **B:**30
Bolt-action (of guns and rifles)   **G:**420–21, 422
Bolts (fasteners)   **N:**3
Boltwood, Bertram (American chemist)   **G:**111
Bolus (chewed food)   **S:**460
Bolyai, János (Hungarian mathematician)   **G:**128; **M:**168
Bombardier, Joseph-Armand (Canadian inventor of the
    snowmobile)   **S:**218a
Bombardier beetle   **B:**125; **I:**243
    picture(s)   **B:**124
Bombay (Mumbai) (India)   **B:**310a–310b; **I:**129–30
    picture(s)   **B:**310a, 310b
Bombay Hook National Wildlife Refuge (Delaware)   **D:**92, 96
    picture(s)   **D:**91
Bombers (airplanes)   **U:**109; **W:**318
    picture(s)   **W:**306, 316
Bombings (terrorism)   **T:**114–15
    Atlanta (Georgia)   **O:**113
    Bali (Indonesia)   **I:**212
    Birmingham (Alabama)   **A:**79n
    Cole, USS   **U:**117; **Y:**359
    Madrid (2004)   **Q:**2; **S:**379
    Oklahoma City (1995)   **F:**77; **O:**96, 97
    Russia   **R:**373
    Uffizi Gallery (Florence, Italy)   **U:**3
    U.S. embassy in Kenya   **C:**368–69; **K:**233
    U.S. embassy in Tanzania   **C:**368–69; **T:**19
    World Trade Center (New York City, 1993)   **N:**234
Bombs *see* Atomic weapons; Bombings; Hydrogen bombs;
    Neutron bomb; Nuclear weapons
Bomb shelters
    picture(s)   **C:**401
Bomb squads (in police departments)   **P:**365
Bomoseen, Lake (Vermont)   **V:**309
Bonaire (island in the Caribbean Sea)   **C:**114
Bonanza farms (in North Dakota)   **N:**335
Bonaparte, Jérôme (king of Westphalia)   **N:**13
Bonaparte, Joseph (king of Spain)   **N:**13; **S:**378
Bonaparte, Louis (king of Holland)   **N:**13, 121
Bonaparte, Louis Napoleon *see* Napoleon III
Bonaparte, Napoleon *see* Napoleon I
Bonavista (Newfoundland and Labrador)   **N:**146
Bond, James (fictional character)   **M:**564
Bonding (of adhesives)   **G:**242
Bondone, Giotto di (Italian painter) *see* Giotto di Bondone
Bonds (certificates of loans)   **S:**454–55; **T:**294
Bonds, chemical   **A:**487; **C:**201, 204; **M:**151–52
Bone china (kind of porcelain)   **P:**413
Bone marrow *see* Marrow
Bones (of animals and humans)
    anthropological studies   **A:**301
    babies have more bones than adults   **S:**184a

Bones (cont.)
  birds **B:**222
  body, human **B:**278
  broken bones, prevention of **S:**3
  feet **F:**80–82
  first aid for broken bones **F:**160
  hands **F:**83–84
  periodontal disease causes deterioration of bones that
     support the teeth **D:**197–98
  running strengthens the bones **J:**111
  skeletal system **S:**183–84b
  strength training for strong bones **P:**224
  X-rays, medical uses of **X:**350
Bongo (antelope) **A:**297; **I:**420
Bongo, Omar (Gabonese president) **G:**4
Bongo drums **D:**340
  picture(s) **D:**339
Bonhomme Richard (ship commanded by John Paul Jones)
     J:127–28; **R:**205–6
  picture(s) **U:**116
Boniface, Saint (English missionary) **R:**287–88; **S:**18d *profile*
Boniface VII (antipope) **R:**292
Boniface I, Saint (pope) **R:**292
Boniface II (pope) **R:**292
Boniface III (pope) **R:**292
Boniface IV, Saint (pope) **R:**292
Boniface V (pope) **R:**292
Boniface VI (pope) **R:**292
Boniface VIII (pope) **P:**182; **R:**293
Boniface IX (pope) **R:**293
Bonin (Ogasawara) **Islands** (Pacific Ocean) **J:**35; **P:**8
Bonism (kind of nature worship) **B:**155a
Bon Marché (early department store in Paris) **D:**118
Bonn (Germany) **B:**146; **G:**157
Bonnefoy, Yves (French poet) **F:**442
Bonnet Carré Spillway (Louisiana) **L:**316
Bonnets, feathered (worn by Native Americans) **H:**46
Bonneville, Benjamin L. E. de (French-born American explorer)
     O:276
Bonneville, Lake (ancient lake, Utah) **L:**25, 31
Bonneville Dam (Oregon–Washington) **D:**19; **O:**216; **W:**27
Bonneville Power Administration **E:**218
Bonneville Salt Flats (Utah) **A:**538
Bonney, William H. (American outlaw) *see* Billy the Kid
Bonnie and Clyde (American outlaws) *see* Barrow, Clyde
Bonnin, Gertrude Simmons (American civil rights activist and
     author) **S:**326 *profile*
Bonny, Anne (British pirate) **P:**262–63 *profile*
  picture(s) **P:**262
Bonobos (Pygmy chimpanzees) **A:**325, 326, 327
Bonspiel (curling tournament) **C:**615
Boobies (seabirds)
  picture(s) **B:**220, 236
Book, Shrine of the (Jerusalem) *see* Shrine of the Book
Book awards *see* Awards, literary
Bookbinding **B:**332–33; **P:**471
Book clubs **P:**524
Book design **B:**321, 327, 329; **E:**206; **T:**369–70
Book fairs (exhibitions of books) **P:**525
Bookkeeping **B:**57, 311–12, 313
Bookkeeping machines **O:**60
Booklist (periodical) **L:**181
Book of Common Prayer *see* Prayer, Book of Common
Book of Kells *see* Kells, Book of
Book of Mormon **M:**457; **S:**205
Book of the Duchess, The (poem by Chaucer) **C:**191
Book paper **P:**56
Book reports **B:**314–17
Book reviews **B:**314, 333
Books **B:**318–33 *see also* Illuminated manuscripts; Libraries
  from author to reader **B:**323–33
  Aztec books had no words **A:**577
  back matter **B:**329
  bibliographic form **R:**183

binding *see* Bookbinding
blind, books for the **B:**257
bookmaking **B:**323–33
care of **L:**181–82
children's literature **C:**228–48
collecting autographed books **A:**528
commercial art **C:**457–58
communication, history of **C:**464
copyright protection **C:**555
design *see* Book design
education, history of **E:**79
encyclopedias **E:**206–7
etiquette books **E:**337
Frankfurt Book Fair **P:**525
front matter **B:**329
history of bookmaking **B:**318–22
illuminated *see* Illuminated manuscripts
illustration and illustrators **I:**79–84
indexes *see* Indexes and indexing
Islamic illustrations **I:**357–58
layout **B:**329
manuscript books **C:**463–64
mass communication tool **C:**471
Newbery, John **N:**137
novels **N:**358–63
paper **P:**53
paperback books **P:**58a, 524
prayer books **P:**431
printing **P:**468–79
publishing **P:**523–25
reference materials **R:**129
reports and reviews **B:**314–17
on storytelling **S:**464
What is a talking book? **B:**258
word origins **W:**241
writing as a career **W:**332
Boole, George (English mathematician) **A:**184; **L:**290; **M:**169
Boolean logic (used by computers) **C:**487
Boom (of a sailboat) **B:**264; **S:**8
Boomerang (throwing stick) **A:**7
Boom operators (for motion pictures) **M:**485
  picture(s) **M:**483
Boomslangs (snakes) **S:**214
Boone, Daniel (American pioneer) **B:334**
  Horn in the West (outdoor drama, Boone, North Carolina)
     N:312
  settlement of Kentucky **K:**225
  West Virginia **W:**135
  westward movement **W:**143
  Wilderness Road **O:**270–71
  picture(s) **K:**224; **W:**142
Boone's Trace (pioneer road) **P:**260
Boorstin, Daniel Joseph (American historian) **O:**94 *profile*
Booster shots (of vaccines) **V:**261
Booster stage (of multistage rockets) **R:**261, 262
Boot camps (for recruits) **U:**120
  picture(s) **J:**169; **U:**123
Boot Dance (of South Africa) **F:**302
Boötes (constellation) **C:**531
Booth, Edwin Thomas (American actor) **T:**160 *profile*
Booth, John Wilkes (assassin of Lincoln) **B:335; C:**347;
     G:418; **L:**247
  picture(s)
     wanted poster **L:**247
Booth, William (English evangelist) **S:**25
Boothe, Clare (American writer and political leader) *see* Luce,
     Clare Boothe
Boot Heel (area of Missouri) **M:**366, 368, 369, 374
Boot Heel Museum (Dodge City, Kansas) **K:**184
Booths, Feast of the (Jewish holiday) *see* Sukkoth
Bootlace worms *see* Ribbon worms
Bootleggers (providers of illegal goods) **C:**547; **O:**224, 225;
     P:485
Boots and shoes *see* Shoes
Bor (Norse god) **N:**279

Bora (wind of Adriatic region)   **A:**161; **M:**212; **W:**187
Borah, William Edgar (American lawyer and political leader)
      I:58 *profile,* 59
Borah Peak (highest point in Idaho)   **I:**48
Borazon (artificial abrasive)   **G:**392
Bordaberry, Juan M. (Uruguayan president)   **U:**241
Bordeaux (France)   **F:**410
Borden (Prince Edward Island)   **P:**460, 462
Borden, Sir Robert Laird (Canadian prime minister)   **C:**76
         profile, 84–85
         picture(s)   **C:**77
Border states (in the American Civil War)   **C:**495
Borduas, Paul-Emile (Canadian artist)   **C:**73
Boreal forests   **B:**210; **C:**60; **F:**375, 376
Bores (of guns)   **G:**415
Bores (tidal waves)   **N:**138; **T:**196–97
Borg, Bjorn (Swedish tennis player)   **T:**96 *profile,* 99
         picture(s)   **T:**91, 96
Borges, Jorge Luis (Argentine author and university professor)
         A:386a; **L:**70
         picture(s)   **L:**70
Borgia, Alfonso de (pope) *see* Calixtus III (pope)
Borgia, Cesare (Italian soldier)   **R:**160
Borgia, Lucrezia (Italian duchess)   **R:**160
Borgia, Rodrigo (pope) *see* Alexander VI (pope)
Borgia family (in Renaissance Italy)   **R:**160 *profile*
Borglum, Gutzon (American sculptor)   **I:**58 *profile*
         picture(s)
            Mount Rushmore National Memorial   **S:**320
Boring *see* Drilling and boring
Boriquén (name for Puerto Rico)   **P:**532
Boris I (czar of Bulgaria)   **B:**445
Boris III (king of Bulgaria)   **B:**446
Boris Godunov (opera by Mussorgsky)   **O:**151
Boris Godunov (play by Pushkin)   **D:**302; **R:**381
Borlaug, Norman Ernest (American agricultural scientist)
         I:302 *profile;* **W:**158
Borman, Frank (American astronaut)   **S:**347 *profile*
Bormann, Martin Ludwig (German Nazi leader)   **N:**80 *profile*
Born, Max (German physicist)   **P:**238
Borneo   **B:**336–37; **I:**206, 208, 209, 210 *see also* Malaysia
         Brunei   **B:**415
         picture(s)
            houses on stilts   **B:**337
            rain forest   **S:**331
            wildfire   **W:**83
Bornholm (island, Denmark)   **D:**110
Born to Kill (organized crime group)   **O:**223
Borodin, Alexander (Russian scientist and composer)   **O:**146;
         R:385
Borodino, Battle of (1812)   **N:**13
Boron (element)   **E:**171
         California   **C:**26
         magnetic qualities   **M:**32
         nuclear reactor safety   **N:**372
         p-type semiconductors   **T:**275, 278
Boron, Robert de (French author)   **H:**175
Bororo (Native American language)   **I:**197
Borstal Boy (book by Behan)   **I:**328
Borzoi (dog)   **D:**245, 246
Börzsöny Mountains (Hungary)   **H:**296
Bosch, Hieronymus (Flemish painter)   **D:**360; **P:**23
         picture(s)
            Temptation of Saint Anthony (painting)   **D:**363
Bosch, Juan (Dominican president)   **D:**283
Bosc pear   **P:**113
Bosnia and Herzegovina   **B:**22, 23, **338**
         "ethnic cleansing"   **G:**96, 97
         Yugoslavia, history of   **Y:**365, 367, 369
         map(s)   **B:**338
         picture(s)
            civilians in wartime   **U:**68
            flag   **F:**227
Bosniaks (a people of Europe)   **B:**338
Bosons (subatomic particles)   **A:**489; **F:**366b

Bosporus (strait, Turkey)   **I:**377; **T:**345, 347
Bosses, political   **E:**131
Bossier City (Louisiana)   **L:**323
Boston (capital of Massachusetts)   **B:**339–42; **M:**136, 142,
         143, 149, 150
         aquarium   **A:**337
         Boston Metropolitan Area   **M:**145
         colonial sites you can visit today   **C:**422
         fire fighting, history of   **F:**145
         first high school (1820)   **E:**84
         lighthouse   **L:**229
         museums and libraries   **M:**141
         police strike (1919), Coolidge's stand on   **C:**546–47
         Quincy Market   **A:**376
         map(s)   **B:**341
         picture(s)   **B:**339; **M:**137, 143
            Faneuil Hall   **M:**137
            Old North Church   **C:**423
            outdoor market   **M:**141
            Quincy Market   **B:**340
            State House   **M:**145
Boston Brahmins (wealthy Boston families)   **M:**150
Boston Celtics (basketball team)   **B:**99
         picture(s)   **M:**141
Boston Gazette (early newspaper)
         picture(s)   **N:**204
Boston Latin Academy   **B:**340; **C:**418
Boston Marathon   **B:**341; **M:**141
Boston Massacre (1770)   **A:**12; **D:**58; **R:**196; **U:**176
Boston Mountains (Arkansas)   **A:**408
Boston News-Letter (newspaper)   **J:**140
Boston Pops Orchestra   **O:**200
Boston Port Bill (1774)   **R:**197, 198
Boston Public Library   **L:**175
Boston Symphony Orchestra   **M:**555
Boston Tea Party (1773)   **D:**58–59; **R:**197; **U:**176
         Adams, Samuel, organizes   **A:**20
         Hutchinson, Thomas   **H:**308
         legends, historical   **L:**130
         Revere, Paul, participates in   **R:**192–93
         picture(s)   **M:**148
Boston terrier (dog)   **D:**244, 245
Boswell, James (Scottish biographer)   **D:**148; **E:**279; **J:**124
Bosworth Field, Battle of (1485)   **H:**110
Botanical gardens   **B:**342–43; **M:**523
         picture(s)
            Royal Botanical Gardens (Hamilton, Ontario)   **B:**343
Botany (study of plants)   **B:**198, **343**; **S:**66 *see also* Plants
         archaeological studies   **A:**353, 355
         botanical gardens   **B:**342–43
         Carver's agricultural research   **C:**130
         cell structure   **C:**159–62
         fossils   **F:**380–89
         genetics   **G:**77–91
         leaves   **L:**112–18
         Linnaeus invented classification system   **L:**250
         Mendel's experiments   **G:**90; **M:**218
         photosynthesis   **P:**219–21
         reproduction   **R:**175–76
         taxonomy   **T:**27–29
Botany Bay (Australia)   **A:**515
Botero, Fernando (Colombian artist)   **L:**65
         picture(s)
            sculpture   **L:**64
Botev, Khristo (Bulgarian revolutionary leader and poet)
         B:444
Botha, Pieter Willem (South African political leader)   **S:**273
Bothnia, Gulf of (arm of the Baltic Sea)   **O:**43
Bothwell, James Hepburn, 4th earl of (husband of Mary, Queen
         of Scots)   **M:**118
Botocudo (Native American language)   **I:**197
Botrange (mountain, Belgium)   **B:**131
Botswana   **B:**344
         picture(s)
            flag   **F:**228

Böttger, Johann Friedrich (German alchemist)   P:413
Botticelli, Sandro (Italian painter)   B:345; I:396; R:161, 166
   Florentine painting   P:20
   Primavera (painting)   B:345
   Uffizi Gallery   U:3
   picture(s)
      The Adoration of the Magi (painting)   N:37
      The Birth of Venus (painting)   I:386
Bottle bills (laws to promote recycling of beverage containers)
   R:125
Bottlenose dolphins   D:274, 275, 277
Bottlenose whales *see* Beaked whales
Bottles and bottling   B:346–47
   plastics   P:324, 327, 328
   recycling plastic soda bottles   F:112
   vacuum (thermos) bottles   V:263–64
   picture(s)
      millk bottling plant   D:8
      modern baby bottle design   I:213
Bottomfish *see* Groundfish
Bottom quark (subatomic particle)   A:488
Botulism (type of food poisoning)   F:339; H:212; L:203;
   V:264
Bouchard, Lucien (Canadian political leader)   Q:17
Boucher, Anthony (American editor)   S:82
Boucher, François (French painter)   D:318; F:428; P:24
Boucicault, Dion (British-American dramatist)   D:306
Bouffant (shape in fashion design)   F:65
Bougainville (island in southwestern Pacific)   P:8, 59
   picture(s)
      open-pit copper mine   P:4
Bouillon, Godfrey of (French crusader) *see* Godfrey of Bouillon
Boulanger, Nadia (French composer)   F:448; M:399
   picture(s)   M:397
Boulder caves   C:157
Boulder clay (soil deposited by glaciers)   S:238
Boulder Dam *see* Hoover Dam
Boulez, Pierre (French composer)   F:448
Boulle, André (French cabinetmaker)   D:77
   picture(s)
      cabinet   F:509
Boulton, Matthew (English businessman)   I:221
Boumédiene, Houari (Algerian political leader)   A:188
   picture(s)   A:188
Boundaries
   defined by rivers   R:239
   modern African countries do not correspond to tribal
      boundaries   A:61
   territorial expansion of the United States   T:103–13
Boundary Peak (Nevada)   N:124
Bounties (for military service)   D:292
Bounty, Mutiny on the   B:255; P:295
Bouquet garni (used to flavor soups and stews)   H:119
Bourassa, Henri (Canadian journalist)   Q:15
Bourbon, House of (French royal family)   F:414, 417
   Louis XIII   L:310–11
   Louis XIV   L:312–13
   Louis XV–Louis XVIII   L:311
   Spain, history of   S:377–78
Bourgeoisie (social class)   F:467
Bourguiba, Habib (president of Tunisia)   T:336
Bourke-White, Margaret (American photographer)   P:211
   profile
   picture(s)   P:211
Bournemouth (England)   U:55
Bournonville, Auguste (father of Danish ballet)   B:31–32
Bourque, Ray (Canadian hockey player)   I:32
Bourse (money exchange)   S:455
Bouteflika, Abdelaziz (Algerian president)   A:188
Boutet de Monvel, Bernard (French illustrator)   I:82
Bouto dolphins
   picture(s)   D:275
Boutros-Ghali, Boutros (secretary-general of the United Nations)
   U:70 *profile*

Bouts, Dierik (Dutch painter)   D:359
   picture(s)
      The Last Supper (painting)   D:362
Bovidae (family of mammals)   H:219
   antelopes   A:297–98
   cattle   C:151
   oxen   O:286
Bovines (cattlelike hoofed mammals)   H:219
Bovine somatroptin (hormone) *see* BST
Bovine spongiform encephalopathy *see* Mad cow disease
Bow and arrow *see* Bows and arrows
Bowdoin College (Brunswick, Maine)   M:41
   picture(s)   M:41
Bow drill (tool)   T:233
Bowe, Riddick (American boxer)   B:351, 353
Bowed kites   K:266b, 267
   picture(s)   K:268
Bowed stringed instruments   M:547–48
Bowell, Sir Mackenzie (Canadian prime minister)   C:76
   profile; O:135
Bowel movements *see* Feces
Bowen, Elizabeth (English writer)   E:290
Bowersox, Kenneth D. (American astronaut)
   picture(s)   S:343
Bowhead whales   W:151–52, 154
Bowhunting (hunting with bows and arrows)   A:362
Bowie, James (American soldier and frontiersman)   B:347
Bowie knife   B:347
Bowker, R. R., Company *see* R. R. Bowker Company
Bow knots   K:287
Bowler hats   H:45
Bowl games (in football)   F:360–61
Bowlines (knots)
   picture(s)   K:286
Bowling (game)   B:348–50a
   picture(s)   B:348
Bowling (pitching in cricket)   C:583
Bowling Green (Kentucky)   K:218
Bowl riding (skateboarding)   S:182
Bowls (lawn bowling)   B:350a
Bowman's capsules (in the kidneys)   K:243
Bowring, Sam (geologist)   R:268
Bow River (Alberta)
   picture(s)   B:46
Bows and arrows   A:360–62; H:300
   picture(s)   A:360
Bowsprit (on a sailing ship)   S:157
Bow-steerers (iceboats)   I:19, 20
Bow Street Runners (early London police)   P:368
Box and whisker graphs   G:312
Boxboard (a type of paperboard)   P:57
Boxcars (of railroads)   R:82
   picture(s)   R:82
Boxer (dog)   D:245
Boxer, Barbara (American political figure)
   picture(s)   W:214
Boxer Rebellion (uprising against foreigners in China)   C:270;
   M:194
Boxing   A:143; B:350b–354; F:85
   Ali, Muhammad   A:189
   picture(s)   B:350b, 354
Boxing Day   H:169
Box jellyfish *see* Sea wasps
Box kites   K:266b, 270
   picture(s)   K:267, 268
Box turtles   P:179; T:356–57
   picture(s)   T:355
Box wrenches (tools)   T:229
Boyce, William D. (American publisher, organized Boy Scouts
   of America)   B:360
Boycotts
   Martin Luther King's bus boycott   A:143; K:251
   Olympic Games   O:111–12
   struggle for African American civil rights   A:79m, 79n
Boyd, Belle (American Civil War spy)   S:408 *profile*

Boyden, Seth (American inventor and manufacturer) **N:**178
   profile
Boye, Madior (prime minister of Senegal) **S:**118
Boyer, Herbert (American scientist) **G:**91; **I:**286
"Boy in the bubble" disease *see* Severe combined
   immunodeficiency
Boy Jesus (Bible story) **B:**173–74
Boyle, Richard (English architect) **A:**372
Boyle, Robert (English scientist) **B:**354; **C:**207–8; **P:**234
   gases **G:**57
   medicine, history of **M:**208a
   vacuum experiments **V:**265
Boyle, Willard (Canadian-American scientist) **P:**218
Boyle's law **B:**354; **C:**207; **G:**57
Boyne, Battle of the (1690) **I:**323
Boyne River (Ireland) **I:**319
Boy Prisoners in the Tower (legend)
   What happened to the Princes in the Tower? **E:**241
Boys, Charles Vernon (British scientist) **F:**105
Boys & Girls Clubs of America **B:**355
Boys' camps *see* Camping, organized
Boy Scouts **B:**356–60
   picture(s)
      camping **B:**356
      Canadian scouts **B:**360
      merit badges **B:**358–59
      uniforms, insignia, and badges **B:**357
Boysenberries **G:**301
Boy's Life (magazine) **M:**17
Boys Town (Nebraska) **N:**95
Bozeman (Montana) **M:**433, 435
Bozeman Trail (frontier trail) **O:**282; **W:**344
   map(s) **O:**273
Bozizé, François (president of Central African Republic)
   C:171
Bracchae (trousers worn in the Middle Ages) **C:**375
Brace (tool used to make holes) **T:**229, 235
Bracelets (jewelry) **J:**95
   picture(s) **J:**100
      carved ivory bracelet **A:**74
Braces (tools of the orthodontist) **O:**232–33
Brachiopods (ancient animals) **F:**385, 387
   picture(s) **E:**26
Brachiosaurus (dinosaur) **D:**173
   picture(s) **D:**167
Brackenridge, Hugh Henry (American novelist) **A:**208
Brackish water (mixture of fresh and salt water) **W:**148
Bracts (modified leaves of plants) **L:**117
Bradbury, Ray (American author) **S:**80 *profile*
   picture(s) **S:**80
Bradbury, Steven (Australian athlete) **O:**118
Braddock, General Edward (British soldier) **F:**464; **O:**270;
   W:38
Braddock, James J. (American boxer) **B:**351
Bradford, Andrew (American printer and magazine publisher)
   M:19
Bradford, William (American printer) **P:**58
Bradford, William (governor of Plymouth Colony) **A:**203;
   M:148 *profile;* **P:**347; **T:**172
   picture(s) **T:**171
Bradley, Omar Nelson (American army officer) **M:**379 *profile*
Bradley, Thomas (Tom) (American political figure) **L:**308
   profile
Brads (small nails) **N:**2
Bradstreet, Anne (American poet) **A:**203; **P:**551
Brady, Mathew B. (American photographer) **N:**224 *profile*
Bradycardia (abnormally slow heartbeat) **H:**83–84
Brady Law (United States, 1993) **G:**426
Braga (Portugal) **P:**393
Bragg, Braxton (Confederate general) **C:**342, 345 *profile;*
   M:239b
Brahe, Tycho (Danish astronomer) **A:**470; **B:**361; **D:**112
   picture(s) **R:**162
Brahmagupta (Indian mathematician) **M:**164

Brahman (Atman) (Hindu spiritual principle) **H:**139–40;
   R:149
Brahman (breed of beef cattle) **C:**151
   picture(s) **C:**152
Brahmaputra River (Asia) **B:**49; **G:**25; **I:**124; **R:**240
Brahmins (caste in Hindu society) **E:**77
Brahmo Samaj (Hindu movement) **H:**142
Brahms, Johannes (German composer) **B:**361; **C:**285; **G:**187;
   O:199–200
   picture(s) **B:**361
   score for *German Requiem* **M:**543
Braid, James (English doctor) **H:**329
Braided rug **R:**356
Braille (alphabet of the blind) **B:**257, 258
   picture(s) **B:**322
Braille, Louis (French teacher and musician) **B:**257
Brain **B:**362–69
   ADHD **A:**23
   aging process **A:**83–84, 85
   Alzheimer's disease **A:**196; **D:**188
   balance, sense of **E:**5–6
   biological research **B:**203
   body's senses **B:**291
   central nervous system **N:**118
   cerebral palsy is caused by brain damage **D:**190
   child development **C:**225
   damage caused by alcoholism **A:**173
   damage caused by a stroke **D:**202
   disabilities, people with **D:**178–79
   Do we use only 10 percent of our brains? **B:**367
   dreaming **D:**317–18
   drugs' effect on **D:**330, 331
   emotions **E:**203
   energy use of brain cells **B:**297
   epilepsy **D:**192
   gray matter **N:**117
   How does sleep affect learning? **L:**104
   how we hear **E:**5
   human beings **H:**281
   learning **L:**100–101
   learning disorders **L:**107, 108
   mammals **M:**66
   mental illness **M:**221–26
   nervous system **B:**288–89; **N:**115, 116
   primates **P:**456
   psychology **P:**499–511
   Reye's syndrome affects **D:**200
   Variant Creutzfeldt-Jakob disease **D:**205
   diagram(s) **B:**365
   picture(s)
      colored image of brain structures **B:**364
      computerized image **D:**206
      magnetic resonance imaging **B:**362, 369
      nerve cell **C:**159
      of person with obsessive-compulsive disorder **M:**224
Braine, John (English novelist) **E:**290
Brain stem **B:**288, 365, 368; **N:**116
Brakemen (on trains) **R:**84, 86
Brakes
   air brakes **H:**314; **R:**89
   automobiles **A:**543–44, 546, 550–51
   dynamic braking **L:**287
   hydraulic brakes **H:**313
   railroads **R:**84
   trucks **T:**319
   Westinghouse, George, and air brakes **W:**125
   diagram(s)
      hydraulic brakes **H:**313
Bramante, Donato (Italian architect) **A:**372; **I:**397; **R:**167
   picture(s)
      Tempietto of San Pietro Church (Rome) **I:**397
Bran (of grain)
   flour and flour milling **F:**276, 277
   rice **R:**228
   wheat **G:**281; **W:**156

Bran (cont.)
picture(s)
wheat **W:**157
Branca, Giovanni (Italian architect) **E:**229; **T:**342
Branches (of department stores) **D:**118
Branching coral
picture(s) **J:**76
Brancusi, Constantin (Romanian-French sculptor) **B:**370;
F:432; **S:**103
picture(s)
Bird in Space (sculpture) **S:**105
Mademoiselle Pogany (sculpture) **B:**370
Princesse X (sculpture) **A:**427
Brand, Mount (highest point in Namibia) **N:**8
Brandeis, Louis Dembitz (Supreme Court justice) **K:**224
profile
Brandenburg (former state, Germany) **F:**461
Brandenburg Gate (Berlin, Germany) **B:**147
Brandenburg v. Ohio (1969) **F:**163
Branding (of cattle) **C:**578; **R:**105
picture(s) **R:**104
Brand names *see* Trademarks
Brando, Marlon (American actor) **M:**486 *profile*
picture(s) **M:**495
Brandon (Manitoba) **M:**82, 83, 85
Brandt, Willy (German political leader) **G:**165; **S:**59
Brandy (distilled beverage) **W:**161
Brandywine, Battle of (1777) **P:**139
Brandywine Creek (Delaware)
picture(s) **D:**90
Branle (dance) **D:**29
Branley, Franklyn M. (American science writer) **C:**240
Bransfield, Edward (British naval officer) **A:**295
Branson (Missouri) **M:**366
picture(s) **M:**370
Brant, Joseph (Thayendanegea) (Mohawk Indian) **B:**370–71;
I:176 *profile,* 204; **R:**205
picture(s) **I:**176
Brants (geese) **D:**347
Braque, Georges (French painter) **B:**371; **F:**432; **P:**30
collage **C:**402
cubism **C:**612
modern art **M:**390
Picasso and Braque **P:**243
picture(s)
Guéridon, Le (painting) **B:**371
The Portuguese (painting) **F:**431
Bras d'Or Lakes (Nova Scotia) **N:**351
Brasília (capital of Brazil) **B:**372, 375, 380–81, 382; **L:**65
picture(s) **B:**380; **L:**65
Brass **B:**410
alloys **A:**192, 193
antiques **A:**316b
buttons **B:**484
Waterbury (Connecticut) **C:**517
zinc **Z:**385
Brass band **B:**42
Brass instruments **M:**549–50
orchestra **O:**194
orchestra seating plan **O:**196
wind instruments **W:**184–85
picture(s) **W:**185
orchestra **O:**194
Brass rubbings **R:**348b
Brasstown Bald Mountain (Georgia) **G:**134
Bratislava (capital of Slovakia) **S:**200–201
Brattain, Walter (American inventor) **I:**285
Braun, Carol Moseley (United States senator) **A:**79c; **C:**221
profile
Braun, Wernher von (German-American rocket engineer) *see*
Von Braun, Wernher
Brave New World (novel by Huxley) **E:**289; **H:**309; **S:**81–82
Bray, Thomas (English clergyman) **S:**301
Brazauskas, Algirdas (Lithuanian political leader) **L:**263

Brazil **B:**372–84
Amazon River **A:**197–98
art and architecture **L:**62, 63, 65
Carnival **H:**163
coffee **C:**397
coffee, world's largest exporter of **S:**290
diamonds **D:**146–47
food **F:**333
government, history of **L:**58
history **S:**293, 294
landforms of South America **S:**276
Latin America **L:**49, 50, 51, 55, 56, 57
literature **L:**68
Marajoara civilization **I:**170
origin of name **D:**375
Portugal, history of **P:**395
Rio de Janeiro **R:**232–33
rubber trees **R:**344, 348a
São Paulo **S:**38–39
World War II **W:**303
picture(s)
Amazon River **B:**378; **R:**237
automobile industry **S:**291
Brasília **B:**380; **L:**65
Cabral taking possession of Brazil **L:**58
candomblé ceremony **B:**373
Carnival **B:**374; **H:**163
Carnival costumes **S:**284
coffee beans being sifted **S:**275
factory workers sorting cashews **B:**379
farmer **B:**377
flag **F:**228
gauchos driving cattle **B:**377
iron mine **B:**379
Itaipu power plant **P:**64, 422
Manaus **B:**382
people **B:**372; **S:**284
Rio de Janeiro **B:**381; **C:**320; **R:**233; **S:**285, 289
Rio de Janeiro soccer fans **B:**375; **S:**284
São Paulo **B:**380; **S:**38, 288, 289
wheatfields **G:**98
workers unloading fruit from boats **B:**378
Brazil Current (of Atlantic Ocean) **A:**479
Brazilein (dye) **D:**375
Brazilero (language) **U:**237
Brazil nuts **N:**432–33
Brazilwood (tree) **B:**372; **D:**375
Brazing **W:**118
Brazos River (Texas) **T:**127
Brazza, Count Pierre Paul François Camille Savorgnan de (French
explorer) **C:**506
Brazzaville (capital of the Congo) **C:**504, 505, 506
Breach of contract (in law) **L:**90
Bread **B:**385–88b *see also* Flour and flour milling
automated bread makers **A:**532
black or rye bread **R:**390
chemical preservatives **F:**342
Egyptians were the first to make leavened bread **C:**540
flour from different kinds of wheat **F:**276
how to grow bread molds **A:**307
mold **F:**497, 499
unleavened and leavened compared **F:**89
wheat **W:**156, 158
picture(s)
Russian industry **R:**363
Bread-and-butter notes **L:**160
Bread and Butter State (nickname for Minnesota) **M:**326, 327
Breadbasket of America (nickname for Kansas) **K:**177
Breadfruit (tropical fruit) **F:**126; **T:**317
picture(s) **E:**411; **T:**317
Bread machines **B:**388a
Bread mold **A:**307; **F:**497, 499
Bread wheats **W:**158
Breakers (giant waves) **S:**511
Breakers (hard-coal preparation plants) **C:**390

Bridges, Robert (English poet) E:287
Bridget of Sweden, Saint S:18d profile
Bridge to Terabithia (book by Paterson)
  picture(s)
    Donna Diamond illustration C:238
Bridgetown (capital of Barbados) B:60
Brigade (army troop unit) U:104
Brigade system (for fur trading) F:524
Briggs, Henry (British mathematician) M:165
Brigham Young University (Provo, Utah) U:247
Brighella (clown) C:386
Brightfield microscopes see Compound light microscopes
Brightness (of stars) see Magnitude
Brighton (England) U:55
Bright's disease see Nephritis
Brilliance (of pigment colors) C:425
Brilliancy (of gems) G:69
Brimstone see Sulfur
Brindle coats (of dogs) D:245
Brine (salt and water solution) S:22–23
    food preservation F:344
    leather process for preserving hides L:109–10
    processing of fish F:220–21
    refrigerated warehouses, use in R:135
    water desalting W:56
Brine shrimps (crustaceans) C:601
Bringing Up Baby (motion picture, 1938) M:492
Brisbane (capital of Queensland, Australia) A:512, 514
    picture(s) A:512
Bristlecone pine trees T:300
Bristle worms (Polychaetes) W:319, 321
Bristol (Rhode Island) R:217, 220
Bristow, George F. (American composer) U:206
Britain (ancient name of England, Scotland, Wales) C:163;
    E:235–38, 400
Britain, Battle of (1940) W:298–99
Britannia metal K:285
British Broadcasting Corporation (BBC) R:54; U:58
British Columbia (Canada) B:402–7
    Expo '86 (Vancouver) F:17
    forestry C:61
    gold discoveries G:252
    Indians, American I:188–90
    Pacific Ranges and Lowlands C:55–56
    Vancouver V:275
    map(s) B:406
    picture(s)
        baling hay B:404
        Butchart Gardens B:406b
        dam on Kootenay River C:61
        Mount Assiniboine B:403
        pulp mill B:405
        rain forest C:58
        Vancouver B:406a; C:66; V:275
        Victoria B:406d
        vineyards B:404
British Columbia, University of B:406a, 406b
British Commonwealth of Nations see Commonwealth of Nations
British East India Company see East India Company
British Empire E:249, 251; U:62; W:270 see also
    Commonwealth of Nations
    extent of (1939) E:252
    United Kingdom U:58
British Expeditionary Force (B.E.F.) W:281, 283, 287, 298
British Guiana see Guyana
British Honduras see Belize
British Isles (group that includes Great Britain, Ireland, and
    many smaller islands) U:58
British Library (national library of Britain) L:179
British Mountains (Yukon Territory) Y:370
British Museum (London) G:350; L:179; M:525, 528
British Nationality Act (Britain, 1983) I:94
British North America Act (now Constitution Act) (Britain, 1867)
    C:75, 83; M:2
British Open (golf tournament) G:260

British Patent Office P:99
British shorthair cat C:138
British Somaliland (now Somalia) S:255
British South Africa Company Z:378, 383
British thermal units (BTUs) (measure of heat) H:88
British Togoland (United Nations trust territory, west Africa)
    G:194, 198; T:217
British Virgin Islands see Virgin Islands, British
Brit Milah (Covenant of Circumcision) (in Judaism) J:146b
Britons (early people of England) E:235–37
Brittany (region of France) F:404
    picture(s) W:066
Brittany spaniel (dog) D:249
Britten, Benjamin (English composer) E:293; O:148, 161
Brittlebush (plant)
    picture(s) N:286
Brittlewood (poisonous plant) L:117
Briullov, Karl (Russian painter) R:377
    picture(s)
        The Rider (painting) R:377
Brno (Czech Republic) C:621
Broadax (tool) T:235
Broadbent, Donald (English psychologist) P:507
Broad-Breasted Bronze (turkey) P:417
Broad-Breasted Large White (turkey) P:417
Broadcasting (of seed) A:98
Broadcasting (radio and television) T:67–68
    advertising A:31
    Canadian-content ruling C:67
    communication, history of C:469
    hate propaganda G:96
    journalism J:135
    radio R:50, 53–54, 56–57, 58–60
    television programs T:69–71
Broad jump see Long jump
Broadsides (newssheets) B:24; N:22
Broad-spectrum antibiotics A:308, 311
Broadway Boogie-Woogie (painting by Mondrian)
    picture(s) M:410
Broadway theater district (New York City) N:230; T:159
Broadwood, John (English piano builder) P:242
Broca, Paul (French surgeon) B:368
Broccoli (vegetable) V:288, 290
Broch, Hermann (German writer) G:182
Brock, Sir Isaac (British soldier) O:135
Brock, Lou (American baseball player)
    picture(s) B:94
Brockton (Massachusetts) M:145
Broilers (chickens) P:415
Broiling (method of cooking) C:541
Brokaw, Irving (American ice-skating promoter) I:45
Brokaw, Tom (American television journalist) S:326 profile
Broken Arrow (Oklahoma) O:91
Broken-color technique (in painting) I:104
Brokers (Agents) (negotiators of sales and purchases) R:113;
    S:457–58
Bromeliads (plants) B:212
Bromine (element) E:171; O:28
Bronchial tubes (of the respiratory system) B:283; L:343
    picture(s) L:344
Bronchioles (small tubes in the respiratory system) L:343,
    345
Bronchitis (inflammation of the bronchial tubes) A:10;
    D:189–90, 192
Bronck, Jonas (early Dutch settler in New York) N:228
Broncos (untamed horses) C:578; R:279 see also Mustangs
Brong-Ahafo (a people of Africa) G:194
Brontë, Anne (English novelist) B:408; E:286
Brontë, Branwell (English painter and writer) B:408
Brontë, Charlotte (English novelist) B:408; E:286; N:359
Brontë, Emily (English novelist) B:408; E:286; N:359
Brontosaurus (dinosaur) see Apatosaurus
Brontotherium (prehistoric mammal)
    picture(s) P:434

Bronx (New York City)   N:226, 228
  picture(s)
    apartment buildings   N:230
Bronx-Whitestone Bridge (New York City)   N:233
Bronx Zoo (New York City)   Z:390, 393
Bronze   B:409–10
  alloys   A:192
  armor   A:423
  battles with early bronze armor and weapons   B:103d
  bell casting   B:141
  chemistry, history of   C:206
  Chinese decorative arts   C:276
  decorative arts   D:70, 72, 74, 75, 76
  Greek sculpture   G:349
  Japanese gilt bronze sculptures   J:48
  metallurgy, history of   I:279; M:236
  prehistoric people   P:442
  picture(s)
    African sculpture   N:257
    decorative arts   D:71
    door   L:122
    Islamic candlestick   I:358
    Persian sculpture   P:156
Bronze Age   B:409
  Greece, art and architecture of   G:345
  metallurgy   M:236
  prehistoric people   P:442
  time of the Trojan War   T:316
  tool use   T:233–34
  picture(s)
    tools   T:233
Bronze catfish   F:204
Bronze Star (American award)
  picture(s)   D:70
Brooches (jewelry)   J:95
  picture(s)
    gold brooch designed by Leonor Fini   D:69
Brood chamber (in a beehive)   H:210–11
Brooding (of birds)   P:86
Brood parasites (birds that use others' nests)   B:231–32
Brood patch (in birds)   B:231
Brood pouch (of a crustacean)   C:602
Brooke, Edward William (United States senator)   A:79c;
    M:148 *profile*
Brooke, Sir James (British ruler, White Rajah) of Sarawak
    M:58
Brooke, Rupert (English poet)   E:287
Brook Farm (utopian community, Massachusetts)   A:210;
    H:65
Brookgreen Gardens (South Carolina)   S:304
Brookings (South Dakota)   S:318, 319
Brooklyn (New York City)   A:337; N:226, 227
Brooklyn-Battery Tunnel (New York City)   N:233
Brooklyn Bridge (New York City)   B:398; N:233
  picture(s)   I:329
Brooklyn Children's Museum (New York)   M:526
Brooklyn Dodgers (baseball team)   B:92
Brooks, Gwendolyn (American poet)   A:79c, 218
Brooks, Phillips (American Episcopal bishop)   C:118
Brooks Range (Alaska)   A:146
"Brooms" (poem by Aldis)   F:124
Brossard, Nicole (Canadian writer)   C:87
Brossa Valley (Australia)   A:509
Brosse, Salomon de (French architect)   F:425
Brotherhood of Locomotive Engineers (BLE)   R:86
Brotherhood of Sleeping Car Porters (labor union)   A:79k
Brothers Karamazov (novel by Dostoevski)   D:287; F:115
Brotulids (deep-sea fish)   F:182
Broughton, Jack (English boxer)   B:351
Broughton, William R. (English explorer)   O:215
Brow-antlered deer   D:82
Brown, "Aunt" Clara (American benefactor)   C:442 *profile*
Brown, Charles Brockden (American novelist)   A:208
Brown, David (American astronaut)   S:352

Brown, Denise Scott (African-born American architect) *see*
    Scott Brown, Denise
Brown, Ford Madox (English artist)   E:263
Brown, George (Canadian statesman)   B:411; M:2
Brown, Jim (American football player)   F:362 *profile*
  picture(s)   F:362
Brown, John (American abolitionist)   A:6b; B:411; S:196;
    V:360
  events leading to Civil War   C:335
  John Brown's Body (song)   N:23
  West Virginia   W:138
  picture(s)   A:6a; C:335; W:138
Brown, John (American Revolutionary leader)   R:224 *profile*
Brown, Joseph (American manufacturer and architect)   R:224
    profile
Brown, Karen (American ballerina)
  picture(s)   B:33
Brown, Kootenai (Canadian conservationist)   G:220
Brown, Marcia (American author and artist)   C:230 *profile*
Brown, Margaret Wise (American author and editor)   C:230
    profile
  picture(s)
    illustration by Clement Hurd for *Goodnight Moon*
    C:241
Brown, Moses (American merchant)   R:225 *profile*
Brown, Nicholas (American merchant)   R:224 *profile*
Brown, Robert (Scottish physicist)   A:483–84
  picture(s)   A:484
Brown, William Hill (American novelist)   A:208
Brown, William Wells (American reformer, historian, and writer)
    A:79c
Brown algae   A:180
Brown Angels (book by Walter Dean Myers)
  picture(s)   C:248
Brown bears   B:104, 106
  picture(s)   B:104; M:66; U:90
"Brown Bess" (musket)
  picture(s)   G:416
Brown coal *see* Lignite
Browne, Frances (Irish writer)   F:21
Browne, Sir Thomas (English author)   E:274
Brown family (American manufacturers and philanthropists)
    R:224–25 *profile*
Brown fat (tissue which metabolizes fat to produce heat)
    H:126
Brown hyenas (animals)   H:319
Brownian motion (in science)   A:484
Brownie Girl Scouts   G:215, 217
  picture(s)   G:215
Brownies (fairies)   F:9
Browning, Elizabeth Barrett (English poet)   B:412; E:284–85
  "How do I love thee?"   B:412
Browning, John Moses (American inventor of firearms)   G:423;
    U:254 *profile*
Browning, Kurt (Canadian figure skater)   I:44 *profile*
Browning, Robert (English poet)   B:412–13; E:284
  "The Pied Piper of Hamelin," excerpt from   B:413
  quotation from *Pippa Passes*   Q:21
Brownlee, Don (American astronomer)   C:452
Brownlee particles (dust from asteroids and comets)   C:452
Brown lung (respiratory disease)   O:13
Brown rats *see* Norway rats
Brown recluse spiders   S:406
Brown rice   G:282; R:228
Brownshirts (Nazi storm troopers)   F:64; N:79, 80
Brown sugar   S:482
Brown Swiss (breed of cattle)   C:154
  picture(s)   C:153; D:5
Brown thrashers (birds)
  picture(s)   G:133
Brown University (Providence, Rhode Island)   R:217
Brown v. Board of Education of Topeka, Kansas (1954)   A:79m;
    C:328; S:114, 509
  Jim Crow laws, elimination of   J:109
  NAACP   N:26

Browsers, web (computer programs) *see* Web browsers
Broz, Josip *see* Tito
Bruce, Ailsa Mellon (American philanthropist)   N:37–38
Bruce, Blanche Kelso (American political figure)   M:362
   profile
Bruce, James (Scottish explorer)   A:66; E:412
Bruce, Robert *see* Robert I (The Bruce) (king of Scotland)
Bruce, Thomas (British diplomat) *see* Elgin, Lord
Brucellosis (Undulant fever) (disease)   D:212
Brücke, Die (German art group)   E:424; G:172; M:391
Bruckner, Anton (Austrian composer and organist)   C:284–85;
   G:188
Bruegel (Brueghel), Jan (Flemish painter)   B:414
Bruegel, Pieter, The Elder (Flemish painter)   B:414; D:360
   picture(s)
      Children's Games (painting)   D:362
      The Harvesters (painting)   R:170
      Hunters in The Snow (painting)   B:414
      Peasant Wedding Feast (painting)   W:264
Bruegel, Pieter, The Younger (Flemish painter)   B:414
Bruges (Belgium)
   picture(s)   B:130
Bruises (injuries)   F:160
Brûlé, Étienne (French explorer)   G:327, 328; M:269; P:138;
   T:243
Brumbies (Australian wild horses)   A:506; H:242
Brumidi, Constantino (Italian-American painter)   C:104
Brunei (sultanate on the island of Borneo)   B:336, 337, **415**
   Bandar Seri Begawan   S:333
   economy   S:332, 333
   picture(s)
      flag   F:228
      Muslims   S:329
Brunel, Isambard Kingdom (British engineer)   T:339
Brunel, Marc (French-English inventor)   T:339
Brunelleschi, Filippo (Italian architect)   A:371; D:313; I:395;
   R:164
   picture(s)
      Foundling Hospital (Florence)   R:165
Bruner, Jerome (American psychologist)   L:100
Brunhoff, Jean de (French author and illustrator)   C:230
   profile
Brünnhilde (in Norse mythology)   O:162–63
Brunswick (Maine)   M:41
Brushes (for painting)   P:34; W:054
Brushes (of electric generators and motors)   E:134, 153
Brusilov, Aleksei Alekseyevich (Russian general)   W:282
   profile, 288
   picture(s)   W:282
Brussels (capital of Belgium)   B:130, 132, 134, 135
   rug-weaving   R:353
   picture(s)
      European Union headquarters   B:134
      guildhalls on Grand'Place   B:135
      seafood market   B:132
Brussels sprouts (vegetable related to cabbage)   V:290
Brussels Universal and International Exhibition (1958)   F:17
Brutus, Dennis (South African poet)   A:76d
Brutus, Lucius Junius (Roman hero)   R:310
Brutus, Marcus Junius (Roman statesman)   A:317; R:316
Bryan, John Neely (first settler in Dallas, Texas)   D:14
Bryan, William Jennings (American politician and orator)
   B:416; D:38; M:192; O:191; S:84
   picture(s)   N:95
Bryant, Charles Gyude (president of Liberia)   L:168
Bryant, Paul ("Bear") (American football coach)   A:142–43
   profile
Bryant, William Cullen (American poet and editor)   A:209;
   B:416
Bryce, Lord James (British ambassador to United States)
   N:56
Bryce Canyon National Park (Utah)   U:250
   picture(s)   E:16; U:243
Bryde's whales   W:153
Brynhild (in Norse mythology) *see* Brünnhilde

Bryophytes (plants)   M:472–73; P:301, 302
BST (Bovine somatroptin) (hormone)   D:11
Bt corn   P:291
BTUs *see* British thermal units
Bubastis (Egypt)   M:512
Bubble chamber (in physics)   A:195; C:563
   picture(s)
      tracks of atoms   A:483
Bubi (a people of Africa)   E:309
Bubka, Sergei (Ukrainian pole vaulter)   T:259 *profile*
   picture(s)   T:259
Bubonic plague (disease)
   Christianity, effect on   C:291
   Florence (Italy)   F:259
   medieval England   E:240
   Middle Ages   M:295
   Norway   N:349
   Roman Catholic Church damaged by   R:290
   vector-borne disease   V:284
   picture(s)   W:263
Buccaneers (pirates of the Spanish Main)   P:264
   picture(s)   P:263
Buchanan, James (15th president of the United States)
   B:417–20
   picture(s)   P:447
      1856 campaign poster   P:370
Bucharest (capital of Romania)   B:421; R:297, 298
   picture(s)   B:421; R:299, 300
Büchner, Georg (German dramatist)   G:179
Buck, Pearl (American author)   B:422
   The Good Earth, excerpt from   B:422
   picture(s)   K:208
Buck dancing   F:302
Bucket brigades (for fire fighting)   F:145
Bucket dredge *see* Ladder bucket dredge
Bucket masks *see* Helmet masks
Buckeye (tree)
   picture(s)   O:63
Buckeye State (nickname for Ohio)   O:62, 63
Bucking (in logging)   L:339, 341
Buckingham Palace (of Britain's royal family)   E:192; L:293
Buckland-Wright, John (English artist)
   picture(s)
      Nymphe Surprise II (engraving)   E:294
Buckley, William F., Jr. (American writer and editor)   N:232
   profile
Buckminsterfullerene (form of carbon)   C:106
Bucks (male deer)   D:80
Buckskin horses   H:237
   picture(s)   H:238
Buck teeth (orthodontic problem)   O:232
Buckwheat (grain)   G:284; H:211
   picture(s)   G:283
Buckyballs (form of carbon) *see* Buckminsterfullerene
Bucrania (sculptured ornament)   D:74
Buda (section of Budapest)   B:422a, 422b
Budapest (capital of Hungary)   B:422a–422b; H:297; W:315
   picture(s)   B:422a; E:287; H:298; R:241
Buddha (founder of Buddhism)   B:422b–423
   Buddhism   B:423, 426; R:149
   picture(s)
      Buddha Amida (statue by Jocho)   J:48
      Great Buddha of Kamakura (Japan)   A:438d; J:27;
      S:90
      sculpture   I:135; R:150
Buddhism (religion founded by Buddha)   B:423–27; R:146,
   149–50
   angels, beings similar to   A:258
   Asian architecture   A:366
   Asian religions   A:448
   Buddha   B:422b–423
   China   C:278
   Dalai Lama   D:12
   dance combines with religion   D:31

Bulgaria
picture(s) (cont.)
people **B:**441
pro-democracy demonstration **B:**446
Rila Monastery **B:**445
Sofia **B:**443
teenagers in denim **B:**442
Valley of Roses **B:**444
Bulgarian Orthodox Church **B:**442, 445
picture(s)
bishop **B:**442
Bulgars (people) **B:**441, 445
Bulge, Battle of the (1944–1945) **B:**135; **E:**124; **W:**313–14
picture(s) **W:**314
Bulimia (eating disorder) **D:**190; **M:**223
Bulkers (ships) *see* Dry bulk carriers
Bulk food sales **F:**348; **S:**498
Bull (constellation) *see* Taurus
Bull, John (English composer) **N:**20
Bull, Olaf (Norwegian poet) **S:**58i
Bull, Ole (Norwegian violinist) **G:**381; **I:**2
Bull dancing (of ancient Crete) **B:**450
Bulldog **D:**244–45, 251
Bulldozers **E:**30; **F:**53–54; **R:**249; **T:**15
Bulletin boards (for posting information) **B:**447–49
computer bulletin boards **C:**493; **L:**160b
Bulletproof and bullet-resistant clothing **A:**425; **B:**214; **F:**111; **P:**329
Bullets (ammunition for guns) **G:**414, 418–19, 420; **L:**93
Bullet trains *see* Turbo trains
Bullfighting **B:**450–51
How did bullfighting begin? **B:**450
Mexico **M:**243
Portugal **P:**391
Spain **S:**371
picture(s) **B:**450; **M:**244; **S:**371
Bullfrogs **F:**477
picture(s) **A:**222
Bullheads (fish) **F:**213
Bullion (gold bars) **G:**247
Bull Moose Party *see* Progressive Party
Bullocks *see* Steers
Bull of Minos (in Greek mythology) **G:**366
Bullpen (in baseball) **B:**83
Bull Run, Battles of (1861, 1862, Civil War) **C:**337, 339; **J:**9
Bulls **C:**151
dairy cattle **D:**4
elephants **E:**180, 182
rodeo riding **R:**279
picture(s)
Minoan art **A:**236
Bulls (in stock exchanges) **S:**459
Bull sharks **S:**143
picture(s) **S:**144
Bull snakes **S:**212
Bumblebees **B:**121
Bumi (a people of Africa)
picture(s)
traditional hairstyle **H:**6
Bumppo, Natty (hero of Cooper's *Leatherstocking Tales*) **A:**208; **C:**549
Bunche, Ralph (American educator and United Nations mediator) **A:**79c; **B:**452
Bunching onions (without bulbs) **O:**123
Bund, The (street, Shanghai, China) **S:**140
picture(s) **S:**141
Bundesrat (German parliament, upper house) **G:**157
Bundestag (German parliament, lower house) **G:**157
Bunin, Ivan (Russian author) **R:**383
Bunker Hill, Battle of (1775) **R:**200
early railroad carried granite for monument **R:**87
picture(s) **R:**200
Bunkers (fortifications) **F:**378
Bunny suits (overalls worn by forensic investigators) **F:**372

Bunraku (Japanese puppet play) **J:**32–33, 53; **P:**545; **T:**162
picture(s) **P:**548
Bunt (in baseball) **B:**83
Buñuel, Luis (Spanish motion picture director) **D:**13; **M:**244, 494
Bunyan, John (English writer and preacher) **C:**229; **E:**276
Bunyan, Paul (American folk hero) **C:**237; **G:**202; **M:**334
Bunyoro (former kingdom, Uganda) **U:**6
Buonaparte (Corsican family) *see* Bonaparte
Buonarroti, Michelangelo *see* Michelangelo
Buoninsegna, Duccio di *see* Duccio di Buoninsegna
Buoyancy (upward push on a floating object) **A:**363; **F:**250–53; **O:**17
Buoys (floats) **N:**73
Buran (Soviet space shuttle) **S:**365
Burbage, Richard (English actor) **S:**133
Burbank, Luther (American horticulturalist) **B:**452
Burchell's zebras *see* Plains zebras
Burckhardt, Johann (Swiss explorer) **E:**413
Burdock (weed)
picture(s) **W:**105
Bureaucracy **E:**108; **G:**276 *see also* Civil service
Bureaus (of the United States government) *see* individual names
Burgan oil field (Kuwait) **K:**309
Burger, Warren Earl (American jurist) **M:**338 *profile*
picture(s) **C:**322
Burgess, Anthony (English novelist) **E:**290; **N:**363
Burgess, Gelett (American humorist)
"I Wish That My Room Had a Floor" **N:**276
Burghers of Calais (statues by Rodin)
picture(s) **S:**102
Burghley, Lord (English statesman) *see* Cecil, William
Burglar alarms **P:**197
Burglary (crime) **J:**167
Burgos (Spain) **S:**382
Burgoyne, John (English military commander) **R:**203–4, 208 *profile;* **W:**40
Burgundian period (in Dutch and Flemish music) **D:**371
Burgundy, Dukes of (in European history) **N:**120d
Buri (Norse god) **N:**279
Burial customs *see* Funeral customs
Burial mounds (at archaeological sites) *see* Mounds
Buried treasure **P:**264
Burins (tools used in engraving) **D:**76; **E:**294; **G:**303; **W:**229
Burjanadze, Nino (acting president of the Republic of Georgia) **G:**148
Burke, Edmund (English statesman) **O:**191
Burke, Robert O'Hara (British explorer) **E:**411
Burkert, Nancy Ekholm (American illustrator)
picture(s)
illustration for Lear's *Scroobious Pip* **C:**237
Burkina Faso **B:**453–54
picture(s)
Bobo-Dioulasso **B:**454
flag **F:**228
Burlesque (form of humor) **H:**291
Burlington (Vermont) **V:**310, 312, 315
picture(s) **V:**315
Burma *see* Myanmar
Burma Road **W:**315
Burmese (a people of Myanmar) **M:**557
Burne-Jones, Sir Edward Coley (English painter) **E:**263
picture(s)
Praising Angels (tapestry) **T:**21
Burners (DVD recording drives) **V:**332f
Burnett, Peter H. (American pioneer) **O:**277
Burnett, William Riley (American author) **M:**564
Burnham, Forbes (political leader of Guyana) **G:**428a
Burning *see* Combustion
Burns, Lucy (American reformer) **W:**212b
Burns, Robert (Scottish poet) **B:**455; **E:**278
festival **U:**50
figures of speech **F:**122; **P:**351

miniature 1786 edition of his *Poems* **D:**262
quotation from "To a Louse" **Q:**22
"A Red, Red Rose" **B:**455
picture(s) **B:**455
Burns, Tommy (Canadian boxer) **B:**351
Burns and scalds **F:**148, 161; **S:**4–5
Burnside, Ambrose Everett (American soldier and statesman)
  C:340; **R:**225 *profile*
Burping (body action) **B:**301
Burr, Aaron (American lawyer and politician) **B:**456
  close U.S. presidential elections **E:**132
  duels and dueling **D:**350
  Hamilton and Burr **H:**16
  Jefferson and Burr **J:**69, 71
  vice presidency **V:**325 *profile*
  picture(s)
    duel with Hamilton **D:**349; **J:**70
    as vice president **V:**325
Burritt, Elihu (American advocate of peace) **P:**105
Burros (donkeys) **H:**235
Burroughs, John (American naturalist and writer) **B:**457
  picture(s) **B:**457
Burrowing bees **B:**121
Burrowing owls **B:**243; **O:**285
Burrowing snakes **S:**217
Burrows (of animals) **R:**276
Burr puzzles **P:**553–54
Bursae (fluid sacs in the joints of the skeleton) **S:**184b
Bursters (office machines) **O:**60
Burton, James Henry (American gunsmith) **G:**418–19
Burton, Sir Richard (British explorer) **A:**66; **B:**457; **E:**412
  picture(s) **A:**66; **B:**457
Burton, Robert (English author) **E:**274
Burundi **B:**135, **458–59**
  map(s) **B:**458
  picture(s)
    drummers **B:**458
    flag **F:**228
    traditional drum music **F:**327
Bus and truck tours (of theater groups) **T:**159
Busch Gardens (amusement park, Florida) **F:**270; **P:**79
  picture(s) **F:**270
Buses **B:**460–61; **T:**288
  airport shuttle buses **A:**126, 128
  bus segregation case **S:**115
  double deckers in London **L:**297
  Federal Motor Carrier Safety Administration **T:**293
  New York City **N:**233
  United States **U:**95
  picture(s) **B:**460, 461
    school bus **E:**75
Bush, Barbara (daughter of George W. Bush)
  picture(s) **B:**469
Bush, Barbara Pierce (wife of George Bush) **B:**463, 466;
  F:180a–180b
  picture(s) **B:**467; **F:**180b
Bush, George (41st president of the United States) **B:462–65,**
  466, 467; **R:**112b; **U:**204–5
  Cold War **C:**401
  Iran-Contra Affair pardons **I:**310
  vice presidency **V:**331 *profile*
  picture(s) **P:**453; **U:**204
    with family (1955) **B:**467
    political cartoon **H:**291
    with Ronald Reagan **B:**464
    visiting troops in Saudi Arabia **B:**464
Bush, George W. (43rd president of the United States)
  B:466–69; **U:**205
  Dalai Lama, meeting with (2001) **T:**191
  election of 2000 **E:**129, 132
  Hickok, Wild Bill, distantly related to **H:**129
  Iraq War **I:**316a, 316b
  signature reproduced **A:**528
  stem cell research, restrictions on **M:**208h–209

terrorism, war on **A:**45; **T:**116
  picture(s) **B:**466, 467, 469; **P:**453; **U:**170
Bush, Jenna (daughter of George W. Bush)
  picture(s) **B:**469
Bush, Laura Welch (wife of George W. Bush) **B:**467; **F:**180b
  picture(s) **B:**469; **F:**180b
Bush balladists (Australian poets) **A:**500
Bushmen (a people of Africa) *see* San
Bushnell, David (American inventor) **S:**473
Bush people (of Suriname) **S:**516
Bushpigs (wild pigs) **P:**248
Bush pilots (of airplanes) **A:**152
Bushwhackers (proslavery men of pre-Civil War days) **C:**335
Business **B:**470–73
  advertising **A:**29–35
  agribusiness **A:**95
  automation **A:**532
  bookkeeping and accounting **B:**311–13
  commercial art created for a business purpose **C:**456–58
  commercial officers in foreign service **F:**371
  computer graphics, uses of **C:**484
  computers used in **C:**483
  credit cards **C:**582
  depressions and recessions **D:**121, 122
  electronics **E:**162
  fairs and expositions **F:**13–18
  farming as a business **F:**60–61
  how to be an entrepreneur **B:**472
  international trade **I:**270–71
  magazines **M:**16
  mail order **M:**34–35
  mathematics in careers **M:**160
  newspapers' business operations **N:**203
  office machines **O:**55–60
  percents, uses of **P:**146
  public relations **P:**517–18
  ranching **R:**102, 103–6
  sales and marketing **S:**20–21
  special libraries **L:**179
  stocks and bonds **S:**454–59
  tariff influences buyers **T:**23
  trademarks **T:**266–67
  trade shows **F:**15–16
  unemployment **U:**28–29
  What are gross income and net income? **B:**471
  white-collar crime **C:**585
Business cycles (recurring series of good times and bad)
  depressions and recessions **D:**121–22
  inflation and deflation **I:**227–28
  unemployment **U:**28
Business letters **L:**160b–161
Business machines *see* Office machines
Busing (of students) **D:**93; **S:**115
Busnois, Antoine (French musician) **D:**371
Butadiene (gas) **R:**346
Butane (gas) **F:**488
Butchart Gardens (British Columbia) **B:**406b
  picture(s) **B:**406b
Butcher, Susan (American sled dog racer) **A:**156 *profile*
  picture(s) **A:**157
Butchering *see* Meat and meat packing
Buteos (soaring hawks) **H:**64
Butkus, Dick (American football player) **F:**362 *profile*
  picture(s) **F:**362
Butler, Frank E. (American marksman) **O:**2
Butler, John (American Loyalist) **R:**205
Butler, Nicholas Murray (American educator) **P:**106
Butler, Octavia (American author) **S:**80–81 *profile*
  picture(s) **S:**80
Butler, Samuel (English satirist) **E:**286
Buto (ancient Egyptian kingdom) **A:**234
Butte (Montana) **M:**433, 435, 437
  picture(s) **M:**429

PHOTO CREDITS

The following list credits the sources of photos used in THE NEW BOOK OF KNOWLEDGE. Credits are listed, by page, photo by photo—left to right, top to bottom. Wherever appropriate, the name of the photographer has been listed with the source, the two being separated by a dash. When two or more photos by different photographers appear on one page, their credits are separated by semicolons.

Gregory K. Scott.
236 © Jeff Foott; © Jeff Foott; © Clarence Postmus—Root Resources; © Doug Allan—Animals Animals.
237 The Granger Collection
238 © Jeff Foott
247 © Alix—Sipa Press
249 © Erika Stone—Photo Researchers
250 © H. V. Lacey—Annan
250a © Tom McHugh—Photo Researchers
250b © Tonya A. Evatt; © John Kaprielian—Photo Researchers; © Tonya A. Evatt; © SIU—Photo Researchers.
251 Mansell/TimePix
252 © Seth Shostak—Photo Researchers
253 Hulton/Archive by Getty Images
254 © Thierry Monasse—AP/Wide World Photos
255 The Granger Collection
256 © Martin R. Jones—Unicorn Stock Photos
257 Sally Di Martini—American Foundation for the Blind, Inc.; American Foundation for the Blind, Inc.
258 © James D. Wilson—Woodfin Camp & Associates
259 © Microworks—CNRI/Phototake; © Andrew Syred—Science Photo Library—Photo Researchers; © NIBSC—Science Photo Library—Photo Researchers.
260 © Lennart Nilsson—BonnierAlba (all photos on page).
261 © Lennart Nilsson—BonnierAlba
262 © Walter Reinhart—CNRI/Phototake; The Granger Collection.
263 © Avery Architectural and Fine Arts Library—Columbia University in the City of New York; Courtesy of Penguin USA.
264 The Granger Collection
266 © Charles Moore—Black Star
270 © Myles Adler
271 UPI/Bettmann Newsphotos
272 © Stone
273 © Anthony Edgeworth—The Stock Market; © Jerry Wachter—Photo Researchers.
274 © Gerald Schatten—Science Photo Library—Photo Researchers
275 © Lennart Nilsson—Behold Man, Little Brown and Company; © Lennart Nilsson—Behold Man, Little Brown and Company; © Michael Kevin Daly—The Stock Market; © Lennart Nilsson—Behold Man, Little Brown and Company; © Lennart Nilsson—Behold Man, Little Brown and Company.
276 © Janet Gill—Stone
277 © W. Metsen—H. Armstrong Roberts, Inc.; © Erika Stone—Peter Arnold, Inc.; © H. Armstrong Roberts, Inc.
279 © Michael Abbey—Photo Researchers; © Dwight R. Kuhn; © Biophoto Associates/Science Source/Photo Researchers.
280 © Alon Reininger—Contact Press Images/Woodfin Camp & Associates
281 © Lennart Nilsson—Behold Man, Little Brown and Company; © David Scharf—Peter Arnold, Inc.
282 © CNRI/Science Photo Library/Photo Researchers
284 © Manfred Kage—Science Photo Library—Photo Researchers
285 © Lennart Nilsson—The Incredible Machine, National Geographic Society
286 © Francis Leroy—Biocosmos Science Photo Library—Photo Researchers; © Omikron/Photo Researchers.
287 © Petit Format/Nestle/Science Source/Photo Researchers; © Benser/Z.E.F.A./H. Armstrong Roberts, Inc.
288 © M. Raichle—Peter Arnold, Inc.
289 © Will McIntyre—Photo Researchers; © Jose Azel—Contact Press Images/Woodfin Camp & Associates; © Lennart Nilsson—Behold Man, Little Brown and Company.
290 © Lennart Nilsson—Behold Man, Little Brown and Company
291 © NASA/Science Source—Photo Researchers
292 © Melissa Grimes-Guy—Photo Researchers
293 © R. Mackson/FPG
294 Courtesy of Joe Weider, Photo Library; © Jean-Pierre Laffont—Corbis-Sygma.
303 © Rafael Macia—Photo Researchers
304 © I. Fat—Black Star
305 The Bettmann Archive
306 © Lineair/Peter Arnold, Inc.; © Kevin Schafer—Peter Arnold, Inc.; © Sergio Ballivian—Network Aspen.
308 © Sergio Ballivian—Network Aspen
309 © Miréille Vautier—Woodfin Camp & Associates; © Robert Frerck—Woodfin Camp &

Associates.
310a © Catherine Karnow—Corbis; © Porterfield-Chickering/Photo Researchers.
310b © Alain Evrard—Liaison Agency
318 The Granger Collection (all photos on page).
319 The National Archeological Museum of Naples
320 New York Public Library, Spencer Collection; New York Public Library, Spencer Collection.
321 Bibliothèque Nationale
322 © Tonya A. Evatt; © Blair Seitz—Photo Researchers.
323 © Jennifer Whitfield—Photo Researchers
324 Grolier photograph by John Kane—Silver Sun Studio
326 © H. Mark Weidman
327 © H. Mark Weidman
331 © H. Mark Weidman
332 © K. B. Kaplan Photography; © H. Mark Weidman.
333 © H. Mark Weidman
334 Washington University Gallery of Art, St. Louis
335 The Granger Collection
337 © Robert Knight—Leo de Wys
339 © Brian Smith—Getty Images
340 © Ellis Herwig—The Picture Cube
343 © W. Griebeling—Miller Services
345 Uffizi Gallery, Florence
346 © Cameramann International Ltd.
347 The Alamo Museum, San Antonio, Texas
348 © Michael Newman—PhotoEdit
350 © Al Bello—Allsport
352 AP/Wide World Photos
353 © Al Bello—Allsport
354 © Al Bello—Allsport
355 Courtesy, Boys & Girls Clubs of America
356 © Dick Luria—FPG International
357 © Boy Scouts of America (all photos on page).
358 © Boy Scouts of America
359 © Boy Scouts of America
360 © Boy Scouts of Canada
361 © Corbis
362 Image created by Dr. Leigh Nystrom, Ph.D., in collaboration with Dr. Jonathan D. Cohen, Princeton University and the University of Pittsburgh.
363 © Phototake/PNI
364 Stone
366 © Lori Adamski Peek—Stone
368 Stone; © Jim Sugar—Rainbow/PNI.
369 © Hank Morgan—Rainbow/PNI
370 Philadelphia Museum of Art: Louise and Walter Arensberg Collection
371 © Hubert Josse—Art Resource
372 © Harvey Lloyd—The Stock Market; © Vince DeWitt—DDB Stock Photo; © Mauricio Simonetti—DDB Stock Photo; © Jonathan Kirn—Liaison Agency; © Erling Soderstrom—Liaison Agency; © Stephanie Maze—Woodfin Camp & Associates.
373 © Stephanie Maze—Woodfin Camp & Associates; © Claus Meyer—Black Star.
374 © Stephanie Maze—Woodfin Camp & Associates; © Robert Fried.
375 © Peter Read Miller—Sports Illustrated
377 © Viviane Moos—The Stock Market; © Dmitri Kessel—The Stock Market.
378 © Jacques Jangoux—Stone; © Will & Deni McIntyre—Stone.
379 © Paula Lerner—Woodfin Camp & Associates; © Juca Martins—DDB Stock Photo.
380 © Siegfried Tauquer—Leo de Wys; © Charles Bowman—Leo de Wys.
381 © Will & Deni McIntyre—Photo Researchers
382 © Claus Meyer—Black Star
383 © Diane Walker—Liaison Agency
385 © Steven L. Raymer—NGS Image Collection
388 © Mark Scott—FPG International/Getty Images
388a © Justin Pumfrey—FPG International/Getty Images
389 © Daniel Simon—Liaison Agency
390 © Art Resource
391 © Bob Burch—SuperStock
392 © Henry J. Ritzer—SuperStock
394 © Bruce Coleman Inc.
395 © Tom Bell
396 © Glen Thomas Brown—Stock Solution; © Bob Daemmrich—The Image Works.
397 © Bill Bachman—Photo Researchers; © Pierre Berger—Photo Researchers.
398 © Tony Freeman—PhotoEdit
399 Courtesy, Figg and Muller Engineers Inc.; © MacDonald Photo—Envision.
403 © Kennan Ward—Bruce Coleman Inc.; © Pat Bates—Stone.
404 © Thomas Kitchin—Tom Stack & Associates (all photos on page).

405 © Thomas Kitchin—Tom Stack & Associates
406a © Jim Corwin—Photo Researchers
406b © Chuck O'Rear—Woodfin Camp & Associates; © Lee Rentz—Bruce Coleman Inc.
406d © Sandra Baker—Liaison Agency
408 National Portrait Gallery, London
409 Olin Mathieson Chemical Corp.
413 © Frederick Warne and Co., Ltd., London and New York
414 Vienna Kunsthistorisches Museum
415 The Detroit Institute of Arts
417 The White House Collection, © copyright White House Historical Association
418 Mercersberg Academy; The James Buchanan Foundation for the Preservation of Wheatland, Lancaster, Pa.
419 The Bettmann Archive
420 The Bettmann Archive
421 © Jeremy S. Hibbert—Stone
422a © Grandadam—Louvet—Photo Researchers
423 © Dennis Budd Gray—Stock, Boston
424 © Paul Chesley—Stone/Getty Images
425 © Dinodia Picture Agency, Bombay, India/Bodhgaya, Bihar, India/The Bridgeman Art Library
426 © SuperStock
429 © Chad Ehlers—Stone/Getty Images
430 © Ted Kerasote—Photo Researchers; © Don W. Fawcett—Photo Researchers.
431 Montana Historical Society, Helena
432 © Mark Segal—Stone/Getty Images
433– © John Kane (all photos on page).
436
437 © Eric Carle—SuperStock
438 © Cameramann International Ltd.
439 © Image Source Inc.
440 © Wendell Metzen—Bruce Coleman Inc.; © Don Fountaine—Duo-Fast Corp.
441 © Steve Benbow—Woodfin Camp & Associates; © Margot Granitsas—The Image Works.
442 © Filip Horvat—SABA; © Alfred Yaghobzadeh—Sipa Press.
443 © Patrick Forestier—Corbis-Sygma
444 © John Launois—Black Star; © Shepard Sherbell—SABA.
445 © Jill Ergenbright—Ric Ergenbright Photography
446 © Christian Vioujard—Liaison Agency
450 © Vincent Jean Kehoe
454 © Halperin—Monkmeyer
455 © H. Armstrong Roberts, Inc.
456 © E. R. Degginger—H. Armstrong Roberts, Inc.
458 © Giacomo Pirozzi—Panos Pictures
460 © Jeffrey Aaronson; © Raymond Piat—Liaison Agency.
461 The Granger Collection
462 The New York Historical Society
463 Brown Brothers; Corbis-Bettmann.
464 George Bush Presidential Library; © J. Scott Applewhite—AP/Wide World Photos.
465 © Kay Honkanen—Ostman; © Diafrica (Belgium).
466 © Greg Vaughn—Tom Stack & Associates
467 © Roy Gumpel—Liaison Agency; © Tom Campbell—Photo Network.
468 Office of the Vice President; © Les Stone—Corbis-Sygma; © Vlastimir Shone—Liaison Agency.
469 © Anja Niedringhaus—Pool/EPA/AP/Wide World Photos; © Jim Bourg—Reuters/Landov.
470 Office of the Vice President; © Gilles Bassignac—Liaison Agency.
472 Courtesy, Governor George W. Bush's Office; © Khue Bui—Reuters Newsmedia Inc./Corbis; Courtesy, Governor George W. Bush's Office; © Darren McCollester—Newsmakers/Liaison Agency.
473 © George W. Bush Presidential Library/AP/Wide World Photos; Corbis-Sygma.
474 © Rick Wilking—Liaison Agency
475 © David Woo—Corbis-Sygma
476 © Allen Russell—ProFiles West/Index Stock; © Karen Holsinger Mullen—Photo Network.
477 © Chuck Keeler—Stone
479 © Terry Farmer—Stone; © Ed Wheeler—The Stock Market.
480 © Cameramann International Ltd.
481 © Annan; © Hugh Spencer; © Lynwood M. Chace.
483 © T. Shaw—Annan
484 © Tom McHugh—Photo Researchers
485 © Visage—Jacana; © Karl Maslowski—Photo Researchers; © Roman Vishniac; © Jacques Six.
490 Mrs. Tony Frith—The Button Queen, London, photo by R. Harrigan
494 Scala/Art Resource; © SuperStock.

For Jack

All rights reserved. Published in the United States by Doubleday, an imprint of
Random House Children's Books, a division of Penguin Random House LLC, New York.
First published in the United Kingdom by words & pictures,
an imprint of Quarto Publishing Plc, London, in 2015.

Doubleday and the colophon are registered trademarks of Penguin Random House LLC.

Visit us on the Web! randomhousekids.com

Educators and librarians, for a variety of teaching tools,
visit us at RHTeachersLibrarians.com

Library of Congress Cataloging-in-Publication Data is available upon request.
ISBN 978-0-553-53856-4 (trade) — ISBN 978-0-553-53857-1 (ebook)

MANUFACTURED IN CHINA
10 9 8 7 6 5 4 3 2 1
First American Edition

Mr. Hare's BIG Secret

Hannah Dale

DOUBLEDAY BOOKS FOR YOUNG READERS

In the wild, wild wood there stood a big, tall tree.
And under that tree lived a very hungry hare.

Now, as everyone knows, hares are very
clever. And Mr. Hare was especially clever,
because he knew a big, fat, juicy secret.

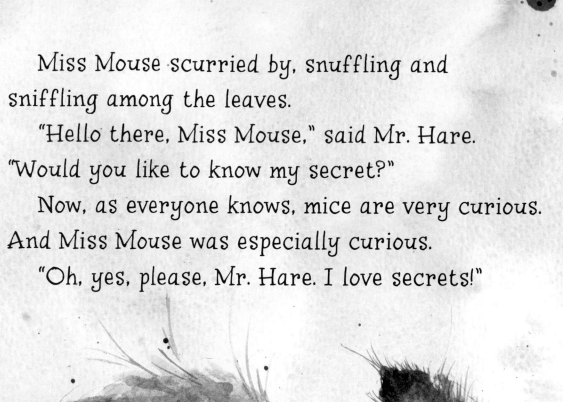

Miss Mouse scurried by, snuffling and sniffling among the leaves.

"Hello there, Miss Mouse," said Mr. Hare. "Would you like to know my secret?"

Now, as everyone knows, mice are very curious. And Miss Mouse was especially curious.

"Oh, yes, please, Mr. Hare. I love secrets!"

"Well, if you *really* want to know my secret, then you must dance with me first, right here underneath this tree."

In the wild, wild wood there
stood a big, tall tree.
And under that tree, Mr. Hare
hopped and Miss Mouse jiggled.

When Mr. Fox ran by, he stopped to stare.
What a sight!
A jiggling mouse and a hopping hare!

"Yoo-hoo, Mr. Fox!" called Miss Mouse.
"Do you want to know Mr. Hare's secret?"
    Now, as everyone knows, foxes are very nosy.
And Mr. Fox was especially nosy.
    "Oh, yes, please, Mr. Hare. I love secrets!"

"Well, if you *really* want to know my secret, then you must dance with us first, right here underneath this tree."

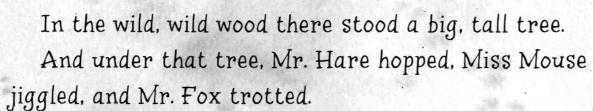

In the wild, wild wood there stood a big, tall tree.
And under that tree, Mr. Hare hopped, Miss Mouse
jiggled, and Mr. Fox trotted.

When busy Mrs. Duck waddled by, she stopped to stare.
What a sight!
A trotting fox, a jiggling mouse, and a hopping hare!

"Oh, busy Mrs. Duck!" cried Mr. Fox. "Do you want to know Mr. Hare's secret?"

Now, as everyone knows, ducks are very forgetful. And Mrs. Duck was especially forgetful. She had completely forgotten why she was so busy!

"Oh, yes, please, Mr. Hare. I love secrets!"

"Well, if you *really* want to know my secret, then you must dance with us first, right here underneath this tree."

In the wild, wild wood there stood a big, tall tree.
And under that tree, Mr. Hare hopped,
Miss Mouse jiggled,
Mr. Fox trotted,
and Mrs. Duck wiggled.

When Mr. Frog leaped by, he stopped to stare.
What a sight!
A wiggling duck, a trotting fox, a jiggling mouse, and a hopping hare!

"Oh, Mr. Frog!" called Mrs. Duck. "Do you want to know Mr. Hare's secret?"

Now, as everyone knows, frogs can be very grumpy. And Mr. Frog was especially grumpy because Mr. Hare knew a secret that he didn't.

"Hmph!" said grumpy Mr. Frog. "Yes, I really would like to know the secret."

"Well, if you *really* want to know my secret, then you must dance with us first, right here underneath this tree."

In the wild, wild wood
there stood a big, tall tree.
And under that tree, Mr. Hare hopped,
Miss Mouse jiggled, Mr. Fox trotted,
Mrs. Duck wiggled, and Mr. Frog leaped.

When Mr. Owl flew by, he stopped to stare.
What a sight!
A leaping frog, a wiggling duck, a trotting fox,
a jiggling mouse, and a hopping hare!

Now, as everyone knows, owls are very wise.
And Mr. Owl was especially wise.
So, soon Mr. Owl guessed Mr. Hare's secret,
because all that hopping, jiggling, trotting . . .

...wiggling, and leaping made his branch **shiver** and **shake**.

Then, with a **plip** and a **plop** ...

... the ground under the big,
tall tree was covered in
big,
fat,
juicy cherries.
And all the friends
had a great feast.

As the moon rose over the wild, wild wood,
a very tired Mr. Hare stretched out with a
big, round, and very full tummy . . .

...and he wasn't hungry anymore.